Infancy

This book is dedicated to our six children, Alison, Carter, Diego, Tessa, Edwin, and Charlie, who inspired all of the stories in this book and who continue to inspire us every day.

Infancy

The Development of the Whole Child

Lisa M. Oakes

University of California, Davis

Vanessa LoBue

Rutgers University

Marianella Casasola

Cornell University

 Sage

FOR INFORMATION:

2455 Teller Road
Thousand Oaks, California 91320
E-mail: order@sagepub.com

1 Oliver's Yard
55 City Road
London EC1Y 1SP
United Kingdom

Unit No 323-333, Third Floor, F-Block
International Trade Tower Nehru Place
New Delhi – 110 019
India

18 Cross Street #10–10/11/12
China Square Central
Singapore 048423

Printed in the United States of America

Library of Congress Control Number: 2023945543

ISBN: 978-1-0718-3098-7

Acquisitions Editor: Adeline Grout

Editorial Assistant: Izumi Sunada

Production Editor: Aparajita Srivastava

Copy Editor: Colleen Brennan

Typesetter: diacriTech

Cover Designer: Candice Harman

Marketing Manager: Victoria Velasquez

BRIEF CONTENTS

DETAILED CONTENTS

PREFACE

This book reflects how we think about and teach infant development. For all three of us, our teaching and research about infancy were shaped by our experiences as mothers of infants. We have learned so much about what infancy really looks like by watching our children grow and change, and we bring this to our teaching. One of our primary aims in writing this book was to provide students and instructors with an engaging textbook to explore the science of the study of infant development. As we embarked on this journey, we had three broad goals.

First and foremost, we wanted the book to be interesting, engaging, and enjoyable to read. Our approach was to tell stories—stories about our own children, stories about development, and stories about research. When we teach the topics covered in this book, our lectures are sprinkled with examples from our own children's infancies—it's how we bring the topic to life for our students. So we thought what better way to bring a textbook to life than to include those same stories. We also adopted a more casual writing style than is often found in textbooks. Telling stories about our infants provided a good foundation for this approach, and we have attempted to describe scientific concepts and research details in an approachable, engaging way as well. The feedback we got from undergraduate students who saw early drafts of some of the chapters suggested that we were successful. Not only did they fall in love with our six infants, but they also enjoyed reading the other parts of the text.

A second goal in writing this textbook was to move away from the focus in developmental science on research with mostly White infants from middle-class families—often living in college towns in the United States—as the norm in development. Although the six infants in this book grew up in different households, in different parts of the United States, at slightly different points in U.S. history, as a group they represent only a small slice of the world's infants, that is, those infants born to developmental psychologist mothers who are married to professionals and who live U.S. middle-class lives. Although some of our children have Latine heritage and even learned both Spanish and English as infants, all of our children share a European heritage. Thus, while the examples help to show how the concepts discussed reveal themselves in the real development of real children, they do not show the wide diversity of the contexts in which infants around the world develop, grow, and thrive.

Increasingly, scientists have realized that it is problematic to draw conclusions about the development of all infants from the convenience samples that are used in many studies of infant development. The challenge for us as we wrote this book was to figure out how to describe development in a way that recognizes that children around the globe develop, and they do so whether they live with two parents or in a multigenerational household, learn one language or

many, grow up in high- or low-income families (and communities), or live in an industrialized or technologically advanced society or in an agricultural society.

Addressing this challenge was difficult for several reasons. First, as mentioned earlier, most research on infant development has been done with convenience samples by researchers who are primarily from North America and Western Europe. Thus, much of what we know about infant development may not be true for many infants in the world. Second, it was not common to report details about participant populations until relatively recently. For a large number of research findings, it is impossible to know the race, ethnicity, SES, or other information about the infants and families. Indeed, it is sometimes difficult to even determine what country the infants lived in.

In the book, we have tackled this problem in two ways. First, we scoured the literature and, whenever possible, discussed findings from infants who are not typically represented in published studies of infant development. Second, throughout the book we described who was studied, whenever possible. We decided that it was critically important to make it explicit that most of the research has been conducted with samples of infants who come from similar backgrounds. Although we can't change what work has already been done, we hope that by highlighting this aspect of the work, we will allow instructors and students to engage in conversations about whether findings are generalizable to other infants, how the environment and context may be important for aspects of development, and how the field can (and should) broaden representation.

Our third goal in writing this book was to focus on the development of the whole child. As is typical in a book like this, there are separate chapters for different areas of development, which may seem antithetical to considering the development of the whole child. However, within the chapters, we made efforts to make connections across domains of development, pointing the reader to sections in other chapters that may be relevant. We illustrate how motor development is related to perceptual and emotional development. We describe connections between memory development and social development, discussing some of the same research on infant imitation in both sections. We show how language and social interactions develop together. We hope that explicitly making these connections will help the reader to recognize that nothing develops in isolation.

As part of our focus on the whole child, we also describe development in context. This is the main focus of the final chapter in the text, but it is a theme throughout the book. That is, we not only include research findings from underrepresented groups of infants, but we also examine how contextual and cultural factors interact with development. This ranges from exploring how cultural expectations for face-to-face interactions might influence language and social development, to how much freedom children around the world have to move independently contributes to the emergence of motor milestones. Our goal was to move away from describing infant development as a set of universal milestones, to help our readers and instructors consider how the timing and specifics of developmental achievements in infancy reflect broader factors.

Finally, we need to explain some of the conventions we adopted in describing different groups of people in this book. We have adopted an identity-first approach to describing certain populations. For example, throughout the book we describe autistic children and deaf children, rather than children with autism or children who are deaf. Although there is disagreement about whether identity-first or person-first language is most appropriate, our decision was based on work by autistic advocates, such as Jim Sinclair, and researchers of autism, such as Morton Ann Gernsbacher, arguing that person-first language may accentuate stigma and does not accurately represent how integral autism or deafness is to the individual.

In addition, because this book focuses on development from conception to age 3, we have adopted the term *sex* in favor of *gender*. We recognize that this is not a perfect substitution, but because the vast majority of children described in this book are too young to have a well-defined and articulated understanding of their gender, we use the word *sex* when it is relevant to divide children along this dimension. We do not mean to imply that the distinctions we make based on sex are purely biological and do not reflect environmental input. We also do not mean that what we refer to as "sex" will perfectly map onto the individual's gender later in life. However, given that gender refers to a socially constructed identity, which includes the way a person presents themselves, feels, and behaves and is influenced by biological, cognitive, and social factors, it is not an appropriate term for most of the infants described in this book.

Finally, we have decided to capitalize all racial and ethnic labels we use in this book. Thus, when referring to racial groups, we will use *White* and *Black*, rather than *white* and *Black*. We recognize that this is controversial and that even prominent Black scholars disagree about the capitalization of White. As with gender, we recognize that these categories are complex social constructions and how they are depicted is important. We therefore follow the lead of Black scholars such as Kwame Anthony Appiah, Eve L. Ewing, Ibram X. Kendi, and Nell Irvin Painter and recommendations of organizations such as the National Association of Black Journalists and capitalize all groups. One of the main themes of this book is that no one group of children is the standard or the default or "normal." Because so much of the research on infancy has been conducted with White infants, we believe adopting this approach will help to highlight the fact that this research was done with one group of infants, and we need to think carefully about how the work extends to infants from other groups.

INTENDED COURSES AND READERS

We wrote this book with college students in mind, particularly those studying psychology or human development. However, we hope that it may be useful for students in any discipline who are interested in infant development, including early childhood education and nursing. Although our approach (and expertise) is on basic research, we believe that students whose education is more focused on applied areas will also benefit from an understanding of the basic research. Where possible, we have included examples of how an understanding of infant development is relevant to policy, parenting, and being consumers of information about development.

ORGANIZATION, FEATURES, AND PEDAGOGY

We adopted a topical approach to this book, including chapters covering broad domains of development. Textbooks on development can be organized either chronologically or topically. We elected to use a topical approach for several reasons. First, given that the book focuses only on the period from conception to the third birthday, much of what is included would be covered in the "infancy" or "early childhood" section of a chronological text. Second, in our own teaching, we have found the chronological approach to be somewhat awkward and redundant, with some topics being revisited several times throughout the term. Therefore, this book reflects how we teach these topics. Finally, by organizing the book by topic, it allows individual instructors to more easily select the content they want to cover in their course. Although there are connections made across chapters, each chapter can stand alone, and instructors should be able to include only the content and topics that are relevant for their courses.

Broadly, the chapters in this book can be divided into three categories. The first chapters review foundational topics. In Chapter 1, we review theory and methods as an introduction to the field. We examine the biological factors that contribute to development, prenatal development, perceptual and motor development, in Chapter 2 through 5. Chapters 6 through 9 are devoted to topics related to cognitive development, early symbolic understanding, and language development. Finally, Chapter 10 through 12 explore topics related to emotional and social development and the broader context of infant development.

Despite this division, however, we have focused in each chapter on the development of the whole child, often referring to achievements in multiple domains, even as we focus on the development of a specific domain. In this way, throughout the book, we emphasize how none of the areas we discuss develop in isolation. In several cases, the same studies are used to describe development in multiple chapters. For example, research on imitation is discussed in Chapter 6 in the context of memory development and again in Chapter 11 in the context of how children learn from social interactions. Other topics, including joint engagement, parenting style, and caregiver–infant interaction are relevant to many different aspects of development and are mentioned in multiple chapters.

In addition, we focus on the cascading effects of development in each domain on development in other areas. For example, during infancy, motor achievements, such as the ability to sit independently, crawl, and walk, have significant effects on infants' developing perceptual, cognitive, linguistic, emotional, and social systems. Throughout the text we highlight these connections.

One approach we have taken to address our overarching goals is to include one to three boxes in each chapter focused on "infancy in real life," "infancy research," or "the whole infant." The goal of the first type of box is to connect the content in the text to infants' everyday experiences. Some examples are the effects of head shape from the back-to-sleep campaign, a discussion of the learning benefits of educational toys, and the controversy surrounding cochlear implants with young deaf infants. The goal of the second type of box is to provide a deeper understanding into research with infants. These boxes include a discussion of who is actually tested in research in infant development (and why it matters), the violation of expectation procedure, and the challenges for assessing infants' expressive language. Finally, the goal of the whole infant boxes is to highlight connections across domains. For example, these boxes include a discussion of connections between attention and emotional development, and between motor development and the development of spatial skills.

Finally, we have adopted best practices to enhance students' learning throughout each chapter. Concepts and research findings are often tied to relevant real-world examples. In addition, in each chapter we have included many stories from the early lives of our own children. Although these children represent only a small slice of the world's infants, and reflect, in many ways, the biases that exist in the literature, using real-life examples to illustrate concepts aids in students' understanding of those concepts. The students who previewed this text became attached to our six infants. As we had hoped, the use of these examples brought the content to life for students, and they were more invested in learning the material as a result. In addition, consistent themes are used throughout the text, and explicit connections are made between chapters, helping students to recognize the connections across chapters. Our explicit discussion of those connections, and the development of the whole child, provides students with a framework for understanding the individual topics covered.

Each chapter begins with a set of learning objectives, review questions appear throughout the chapter, and review and critical thinking questions can be found at the end of each chapter. These features encourage students to reflect as they read.

TEACHING RESOURCES

This text includes an array of instructor teaching materials designed to save you time and to help you keep students engaged. To learn more, visit sagepub.com or contact your Sage representative at sagepub.com/findmyrep.

ACKNOWLEDGMENTS

This book was made possible only because of the support of many people. First, we need to thank Alison Luck, Carter Luck, Charlie Reeb, Diego Danner-Casasola, Edwin Reeb, and Tesalia Danner-Casasola for teaching us so much about infancy and for graciously allowing us to share their stories here. Alison Luck also provided comments on several of the chapters, giving us valuable feedback from the perspective of a college student. We also thank the students enrolled in Psychology 143, Infant Development, at UC Davis in the Winter of 2022. These students workshopped many of the chapters, providing extensive comments and suggestions for how to improve the text. A special thanks to Patrick Dwyer, an autistic scholar studying autism, who helped us to understand the nuances of describing neurodivergent and disabled populations.

Throughout the process we received incredible support from SAGE. Lara Parra was with us from the beginning, teaching us about the process and providing encouragement and support. Liz Cruz, Ivey Mellem, and Audra Bacon helped with permissions, scheduling meetings, and helping us to understand the process. Our editors Jessica Miller and Adeline Grout tirelessly answered our questions, procured and interpreted reviews, and helped to keep us on track.

We learned so much from the review process, and the book benefited from significant work by a large number of anonymous reviewers. These reviewers carefully reviewed and commented on early versions of the chapters, pointing out both strengths and weaknesses. We found their input to be very useful as we revised the chapters. As a result of their work, the chapters are more consistent in tone and level. In addition, we appreciated the reviewers noting gaps in the content that needed to be filled.

We would also like to thank our mentors and colleagues who have shaped our understanding of development during infancy. In particular, we would like to thank Les Cohen and Judy DeLoache for the excellent training we got as graduate students in their labs. This book also reflects what we have learned from others in the field, and although there are far too many to mention here, we have described many of their important contributions in the pages of this book.

We thank Garin Danner, Steve Luck, and Nick Reeb not only for their outstanding co-parenting but also for the support they give as we embark on projects like this one. We are extremely lucky to have excellent partners who share our excitement for our work and appreciate how meaningful this work is to us. And finally, we thank our parents, who not only provided us with a model for how to parent but also made sure we survived our own infancies so that we could write this book.

Charlie, Age 1

By studying infants, we can gain insight into the developmental *process*. That is, as developmental scientists we do not only want to know *what* happens *when*, but we also want to know *how* development happens. Uncovering developmental processes is very difficult. We can easily see *changes* in infants—6-month-old infants don't talk yet, 18-month-old children have a handful of words, and 30-month-old children can carry on a conversation. But how can we see the *processes* that allow these changes to happen? This is a harder question to answer, and it is something that developmental scientists and scholars have argued over for quite some time. However, many researchers do agree that we can begin to understand developmental processes by studying infants (Table 1.1).

ACKNOWLEDGMENTS

This book was made possible only because of the support of many people. First, we need to thank Alison Luck, Carter Luck, Charlie Reeb, Diego Danner-Casasola, Edwin Reeb, and Tesalia Danner-Casasola for teaching us so much about infancy and for graciously allowing us to share their stories here. Alison Luck also provided comments on several of the chapters, giving us valuable feedback from the perspective of a college student. We also thank the students enrolled in Psychology 143, Infant Development, at UC Davis in the Winter of 2022. These students workshopped many of the chapters, providing extensive comments and suggestions for how to improve the text. A special thanks to Patrick Dwyer, an autistic scholar studying autism, who helped us to understand the nuances of describing neurodivergent and disabled populations.

Throughout the process we received incredible support from SAGE. Lara Parra was with us from the beginning, teaching us about the process and providing encouragement and support. Liz Cruz, Ivey Mellem, and Audra Bacon helped with permissions, scheduling meetings, and helping us to understand the process. Our editors Jessica Miller and Adeline Grout tirelessly answered our questions, procured and interpreted reviews, and helped to keep us on track.

We learned so much from the review process, and the book benefited from significant work by a large number of anonymous reviewers. These reviewers carefully reviewed and commented on early versions of the chapters, pointing out both strengths and weaknesses. We found their input to be very useful as we revised the chapters. As a result of their work, the chapters are more consistent in tone and level. In addition, we appreciated the reviewers noting gaps in the content that needed to be filled.

We would also like to thank our mentors and colleagues who have shaped our understanding of development during infancy. In particular, we would like to thank Les Cohen and Judy DeLoache for the excellent training we got as graduate students in their labs. This book also reflects what we have learned from others in the field, and although there are far too many to mention here, we have described many of their important contributions in the pages of this book.

We thank Garin Danner, Steve Luck, and Nick Reeb not only for their outstanding co-parenting but also for the support they give as we embark on projects like this one. We are extremely lucky to have excellent partners who share our excitement for our work and appreciate how meaningful this work is to us. And finally, we thank our parents, who not only provided us with a model for how to parent but also made sure we survived our own infancies so that we could write this book.

Reviewers of the First Edition

Kathleen Bryan, University of Cincinnati

Allison E. Constable, Community College of Philadelphia

Ilse DeKoeyer, University of Utah

Jessica Stoltzfus Grady, University of the Pacific

Elaine Liberato Jenkins, The University of North Carolina at Charlotte

Manuela Jimenez, Assistant Research Professor, Arizona State University

Nancy Aaron Jones, Ph.D., Florida Atlantic University

Danielle L. Mead, San Jose State University

Kristen Pickering, Ivy Tech Community College Terre Haute

Pamela L. Shue, Appalachian State University

Joan E. Test, Associate Professor, Childhood Education & Family Studies, Missouri State University

Kari Visconti, Arizona State University

Kristen Votava, University of North Dakota

1 WHY AND HOW WE STUDY INFANT DEVELOPMENT

As we begin this journey of understanding development in infancy, we want to introduce you to six infants: Alison, Carter, Diego, Tesalia, Edwin, and Charlie. These are our own six babies, so we know them well. Throughout this book we will tell you stories about these children and how they developed. These six infants were different in many ways. Alison and Carter were born into a household where only English was spoken, whereas the other infants heard some combination of English and Spanish in their homes (to different degrees). Carter, Diego, and Edwin were quiet and cautious, whereas Charlie and Tesalia were rambunctious and fearless. Diego was always highly social with peers but quiet with adults. Edwin was highly social with adults but more reserved with peers. Tesalia and Charlie were outgoing with everyone but often preferred solitary play to social interactions. Alison always preferred to be with people—whether children or adults—than to be alone. As we discuss different aspects of development, we will describe some of the events from these six children's infancies to illustrate the many different ways in which typical development unfolds.

Despite the many differences among them, these six infants also have quite a lot in common, and they can provide insight into the many variations of culture, context, and experience that infants have around the world. All six of these infants were born to educated parents, their mothers were all developmental psychologists (who happened to study infancy), they were all exposed to music from an early age, and their infancy was full of the "stuff" of middle-class North American families (lots of books in the home, adults and other children with which to play, outings, multiple strollers, toys, etc.). Thus, they represent a fairly narrow slice of the world's infants. Many infants across the globe grow and develop in very different contexts (The movie *Babies* by Thomas Balmès shows how infants grow and thrive in very different environments.) We will use our own infants to illustrate development, but we recognize that they can't illustrate every context or environment of development. Our goal is to show not only what is common across infant development but also how infants thrive in many different environments, in different kinds of families, and with very different resources. Thus, as we discuss development, we will describe what we know of the development of infants from all around the world.

After reading this chapter you will be able to:

1. *Describe* several reasons why scientists are interested in *infancy*, and how the study of infancy addresses important scientific questions.

2. *Compare* methodological designs used to study development, and *identify* the contexts in which each is appropriate.

3. *Examine* infant development in context, and *consider* factors that influence or contribute to development.

WHY INFANCY?

This book focuses only on development during **infancy**. The first question we need to answer is why focus just on *infant* development? You've probably taken courses—or at least heard of courses—that cover child development or even development over the entire lifespan. In this book we will cover many of the same topics that are covered in those other books and courses, but we will focus on the development that happens just in the first couple of years of life. In this first chapter, we will help you see why focusing on development during infancy is both important and exciting. We believe, and we hope you will agree, that studying how development unfolds in infants provides an important framework for appreciating development in older children and adults.

First, though, we need to be clear on what we mean by infancy. The term *infancy* comes from the Latin word *infans*, which means "unable to speak." Thus, many people have defined human infancy as the period before language. (We will talk about what is meant by language and how to distinguish it from communication in Chapter 9.) Obviously, this doesn't work well for other species that have periods of infancy but that never learn to speak. As you will learn in Chapter 9, this definition is a problem even for human infants, as researchers continue to discover that infants have some awareness and understanding of language at earlier and earlier ages. The journal *Infancy*, which is focused on reporting psychological research on infant development, defines infancy as the first 2 years. However, when describing infancy, researchers and scholars often include development during the prenatal period (see Chapter 3), and many researchers include the period between 2 and 3 years of age as well. For this book, infancy will include the period from conception through age 3, but our primary focus will be on birth to age 2.

So why focus on just this period of development? No doubt you already know that babies are cute, and that might be part of why you are interested in infant development. In fact, many people who study infants (including us) do so, in part, because babies are so darn cute. But we also focus on development in infancy to address important scientific questions and to understand how to care for infants and young children.

Studying Infants to Address Important Scientific Questions

Many questions important to scientists and scholars can be answered by studying the infancy period. For example, focusing on infancy can help us to understand *development,* or the process of change, itself. During infancy, development happens very quickly—more quickly than most other periods of the lifespan. Look at the pictures of Charlie as a newborn and as a 1-year-old. You can see that he changed a lot during that short 12 months! As a newborn, Charlie, like all infants, was pretty helpless and unable to control his body. Newborn infants depend on reflexes (see Chapter 3) to be able to eat. They cry when distressed, but they don't know why they're distressed or how to make themselves feel better (see Chapter 10). They are completely dependent on caregivers to meet their physiological needs, move them from one place to the other, and keep them safe from danger. However, within a few weeks and months after birth, infants become able to control their bodies, they recognize their own needs and desires, they can move from one place to another on their own, and their ability to understand the world around them develops. As you can see in second photo, by their first birthday, infants are engaging in social interactions, communicating, and moving themselves around. The fact that so many abilities change in such a short time gives researchers the ability to study development in a way that is more difficult when children are older and developmental change is more subtle and may happen over longer periods of time.

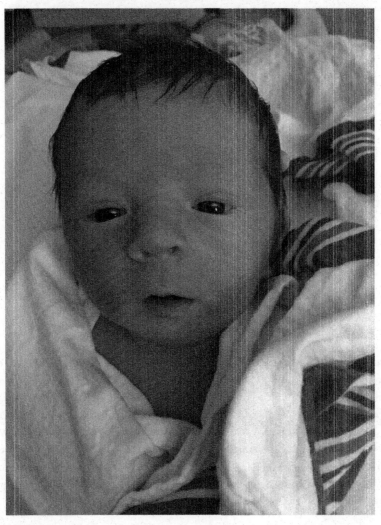

Newborn Charlie

Charlie, Age 1

By studying infants, we can gain insight into the developmental *process*. That is, as developmental scientists we do not only want to know *what* happens *when*, but we also want to know *how* development happens. Uncovering developmental processes is very difficult. We can easily see *changes* in infants—6-month-old infants don't talk yet, 18-month-old children have a handful of words, and 30-month-old children can carry on a conversation. But how can we see the *processes* that allow these changes to happen? This is a harder question to answer, and it is something that developmental scientists and scholars have argued over for quite some time. However, many researchers do agree that we can begin to understand developmental processes by studying infants (Table 1.1).

TABLE 1.1 ■ Scientific Questions Addressed by Studying Infancy	
Scientific Question	**Why Studying Infants Addresses This Question**
Qualitative vs. quantitative change in development	Development in infancy is characterized both by dramatic qualitative change and by dramatic quantitative change.
The role of nature and nurture in development	Many experiences occur for the first time in infancy, allowing researchers to examine developmental change both in the absence of experience and after some experience has occurred.

Qualitative Versus Quantitative Change

One aspect of the developmental process is whether development is a series of gradual, continuous changes or big abrupt, discontinuous changes—in other words, whether development is best characterized as **qualitative change** or **quantitative change**. Qualitative change, or changes that are discontinuous, refers to changes in *kind*. With development, new features emerge and old ones disappear, or the features themselves actually change. For example, during the lifecycle of a butterfly the individual is both a caterpillar and a butterfly, which are two very different kinds of beings (i.e., they have different body parts, and they navigate in different ways). Many aspects of development across infancy seem qualitative. Consider again the comparison of newborn Charlie and 1-year-old Charlie. Although you might see similarities in some of his features, newborn Charlie is not just a smaller version of toddler Charlie. Newborn infants look physically different than older infants. At birth we have different body proportions, and our hair and eyes may be a different color than they will be later. Even our features, such as the shape of our nose and chin, are different. Notice that when Charlie was born he had dark brown hair and dark blue eyes. But at age 1, he had light blonde hair and dark brown eyes! It was not just that he had more hair or bigger eyes; the features of his hair and eyes changed *qualitatively* over the first year. There are lots of these qualitative changes in infancy. Remember, the term *infancy* itself refers to having no language. The development from being *prelinguistic* (or having no language) to being *linguistic* (or having some language) is a qualitative change. It is not a bigger, better version of what the child was; rather, the emergence of language seems to create an individual who has qualities and features that were not there before. When we were new parents, each of us felt disbelief that our helpless, uncommunicative newborn infant would become an articulate adult who can play basketball, read books, and create virtual worlds.

Of course, development during infancy also involves quantitative, or continuous, change. *Quantitative* changes are not changes in kind but rather changes in amount. Development during the first 2 years is not only a series of abrupt changes in features and skills; some things simply gradually increase over this period. One of the important measurements pediatricians take is the infants' weight. Although gaining weight might not seem that important, it is a good proxy for development. Healthy infants grow, and it is relatively easy to accurately measure weight. At the same time Charlie's eye and hair color were changing, he was steadily gaining weight, increasing his weight by a few pounds every month. His parents kept a chart of his growth and they watched as his weight increased from 7 ½ pounds at birth to just over 20 pounds on his first birthday. During infancy, these kinds of quantitative changes are seen only as children gain weight and grow inches, but also once they begin to crawl and walk, they develop from moving slowly for short distances to moving faster and going longer distances. During early language development, toddlers learn more and more new words. Clearly, some aspects of development are changes in *quantity*.

This distinction between qualitative and quantitative changes is important for our understanding of developmental processes. When scientists and scholars think about these different kinds of changes, they also consider different mechanisms of change, or the precise reason why a change occurs. For example, changes in how fast information is processed or how quickly children can form a memory—quantitative changes—might be attributed to increased number of neurons or more myelination (see Chapter 2). The emergence of a new ability—qualitative changes, such as the emergence of language or the ability to walk—might be attributed to a reorganization within the brain or newly formed connections between different brain regions. Moreover, you may have noticed that development is not qualitative *or* quantitative, but it is both. The shift from having no language to having some language may be qualitative, but the gradual increase in vocabulary size is quantitative. Throughout the book, you will see discussions of both kinds of changes and how researchers have used those changes to speculate about developmental processes.

Nature and Nurture

The nature versus nurture debate is as old as history itself. As far back as the fourth century BCE, Ancient Chinese philosophers have discussed the relative contributions of innate qualities and external influences on human development (Chan, 2019). In Western thought, these ideas can be traced back to Plato, who argued in 300-400 BC that people have some concepts or ideas about the world from birth as a result of their souls having encountered these ideas in heaven before they are born. In contrast, Aristotle believed that experience is important in learning concepts. Western philosophers have debated these issues for centuries. Philosopher John Locke (1632–1704) argued that we are not born with any innate ideas or knowledge, but rather the human mind starts out as a *tabula rasa*, or a "blank slate." Locke believed that all of our ideas and knowledge are a product of experience. René Descartes (1596–1650), in contrast, argued that although some ideas (thoughts, knowledge) come from experience, or senses, some knowledge is inborn and unlearned.

These philosophical debates have had a significant influence on how psychologists have thought about the roles of nature and nurture in development. John B. Watson (1878–1958), the father of American behaviorism, believed that development was primarily (if not solely) determined by experience, or nurture. In his 1924 book *Behaviorism*, Watson wrote:

> *Give me a dozen healthy infants, well-formed, and my own specified world to bring them up in and I'll guarantee to take any one at random and train him to become any type of specialist I might select—doctor, lawyer, artist, merchant-chief and, yes, even beggar-man and thief, regardless of his talents, penchants, tendencies, abilities, vocations and the race of his ancestors.* (Watson, 1924, p. 104)

Arnold Gesell (1880–1961), who was a contemporary of Watson, argued instead that development reflected biology or *nature*. Influenced by Charles Darwin's theory of evolution and work in embryology, Gesell developed a *maturation* view of human development. He believed that the traits and individual differences that distinguish people are present from birth, and development is the result of factors internal to the child and, in particular, the genes. He did not discount the contribution of the environment, but his emphasis was on biological factors (see Chapter 5 for more on Gesell).

Contemporary theories take an intermediate position, recognizing that development must reflect *both* nature and nurture. Although theorists differ in how they balance these two influences, we know now that both nature and nurture are critically important for development. **Nature** refers to something inherent in the individual. Often, this is described as something that is innate. Researchers don't always agree about what it means for something to be **innate**, but in general when we use this term we are talking about something that is based in biology and it is not learned or gained from experience. When we conclude that development comes from nature, we mean that it is due to our genes or biology. **Nurture**, in contrast, refers to our treatment or experience. When we conclude that development comes from nurture, we mean that it is due to something in our experience.

Researchers have assumed that we can better understand how experience shapes development by studying infants. The logic is that if we observe that some ability, characteristic, or mental process is present early in infancy, it must be determined by nature because infants have had few experiences. If some ability, characteristic, or mental process emerges slowly over time, and varies in children in different countries, language communities, household configurations, etc., then it must be a function of nurture. You will see throughout this book how this classic nature versus nurture debate is a central theme in the study of infant development. If development is due to *nature*, and therefore there are innate, or inborn, abilities, knowledge, or characteristics, then we should be able to see those abilities, knowledge, or characteristics in very young infants—maybe even at birth. For example, some research has shown that minutes after birth, infants prefer to look at images that resemble human faces—infants will look longer at face-like images than other images, such as black and white stripes or random patterns (Goren et al., 1975). Because this happens at birth, before infants have much experience with human faces, it suggests that infants have some kind of biological predisposition that attracts them to human faces. Other studies have shown that at birth infants already have different temperaments, and infants' temperaments are consistent throughout infancy (Matheny et al., 1985). That is, infants who are highly active at birth also tend to be more active later. This kind of research is aimed at uncovering the effects of nature in development.

Other researchers have asked how experience shapes development by comparing infants who do and do not yet have specific experiences. For example, Joseph Campos and his colleagues studied the effects of crawling experience on how infants perceive depth (Campos et al., 1992). They used a classic "visual cliff" apparatus (see photo of visual cliff), which was designed to help researchers study infants' depth perception.

As you can see, the visual cliff is a tabletop with a red and white checkerboard pattern covered with a glass surface. On the "shallow" side of the table, the glass is right on the surface, but for the "deep" side, the pattern is several feet below the surface, giving the appearance of a large

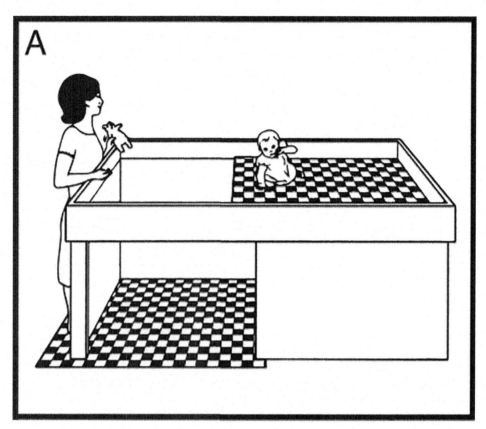

Visual Cliff
Reprinted with permission from LoBue and Adolph (2019).

drop-off. Campos and his colleagues measured infants' heart rate as an experimenter placed them on the deep side of the cliff. Changes in heart rate can tell us something about how infants are perceiving the drop-off. They found that infants who had crawling experience showed a different pattern of heart rate changes than did infants who did not have crawling experience, suggesting that the experience of crawling changed their depth perception.

Most modern developmental psychologists ask how development is shaped by both nature and nurture. It is easy to think about how the two might have an *additive* effect on development. For example, a child inherits genes from his mother and father for height; a child with genes for being tall will be taller than a child with genes for being short. However, nutrition and exercise can add to the equation. If you are well fed and get adequate amounts of exercise, you will be more likely to reach, or even exceed, your genetic potential.

Consider the story of one of our grandmothers. This grandmother, Martha, was born in the 1920s and was raised by a single mother during the Great Depression. They were not extremely poor, but they did struggle, and this young mother was raising three children on her own during a very difficult time in U.S. history. As a result, Martha was not well nourished during her childhood. At age 17 she was about 5 feet 6 inches tall, a perfectly respectable height (and even a bit above average) for a woman. The same year, Martha went through a significant change in her life—she got married. Martha's new husband was well established and expected proper meals with meat, vegetables, and more. They were not wealthy, but for the first time, Martha began to eat regular, healthy meals. Over the first few years of her marriage, Martha grew a couple of inches. On their wedding day, Martha and her husband were about the same height; by their third anniversary, Martha was several inches taller than him. The point of this story is to show you how nutrition (and other factors) seem to *add* to genes in determining height, or conversely, how a lack of nutrition can stifle one's genetic potential. Martha had genes for being tall, but her ultimate height was influenced first by her poor nutrition and later by better nutrition.

But in most cases this isn't really how nature and nurture work together to determine development. Instead, the two factors usually *interact*. We now understand that these interactions really reflect how your genes (nature) make you susceptible or vulnerable to specific aspects of the environment (nurture). This will be discussed in more detail in Chapter 2, but let's consider a brief example here. Phenylketonuria (PKU) is a genetic condition. Individuals with PKU are unable to break down a protein (phenylalanine) that is found in many common foods, including meat and dairy. If a person with PKU eats these foods, a chemical builds up in the blood and will cause permanent damage to the nervous system.

Importantly, the effects of PKU show a *gene by environment (G X E) interaction*. The genetic condition makes the individual susceptible to protein in food. If PKU goes undetected, the individual will consume those foods and cause damage to the nervous system, which will eventually result in severe developmental delays. However, just having the genes for PKU is not sufficient for the damage to occur; if an infant is born with the genes for PKU and is exposed to a phenylalanine-free diet, that infant will develop normally, with no nervous system damage. Having the genes sets the stage for the damage but only if the environment is not well controlled. Newborn infants are routinely screened for PKU at birth, so parents know if they should avoid these foods.

These examples—Martha's ultimate height and the nervous system damage associated with PKU—are somewhat simpler than most of the questions asked by developmental psychologists. These are important examples to show how nature and nurture work together, but they are much easier to explain than examples such as why some children are shier than others or why some children develop motor abilities, such as sitting and walking, earlier than others. We'll get to those in later chapters.

In addition, the nature and nurture question becomes more complicated when we consider how children develop in the different cultures of the world. To show that development reflects nature, researchers have looked for commonalities across cultures. All children around the world learn to walk and talk and they all develop relationships with others, regardless of cultural practices and values. Does this mean those aspects of development reflect nature? The answer is not a clear yes, as children develop these abilities differently and at slightly different times in different cultures, probably because of different parenting practices and experiences in infancy. As you will see throughout the book, this complicated interaction of nature and nurture is discussed in many aspects of infant development.

We Study Infants Because Understanding Infancy Is Important for Caring for Children

There is an African proverb that says, "It takes a village to raise a child." This is especially true for infants who are unable to take care of even the most basic needs (like getting food or moving out of the way of danger). But, if the "village," or society, is going to be able to raise a child, it is important that we know *how*. And to do that, we need to know about development. As adult members of a society, we are involved in making decisions that directly affect the welfare of children, even if we don't realize it. We elect leaders and vote for laws that determine things like caregiver-to-child ratios in daycare centers, who should receive free food and medical care, and how children who are separated from their parents should be treated. By understanding and studying development, we as a society can make policy decisions about families and young children that support and nourish rather than harm development.

Consider an example. You may have heard of the WIC program, or the USDA Food and Nutrition Service's "Women, Infants, and Children" program. This is a program for pregnant women, new mothers (especially those who are breastfeeding), and infants and young children who are at nutritional risk (e.g., underweight or have a poor diet) to give them access to healthy food. Programs like these are informed by our understanding of the importance of development during the prenatal period and early childhood for brain development and for establishing strong physical and mental systems that will support the child throughout life.

People are not only concerned about this in the United States, but they are also concerned that children around the world are well fed and well cared for in the first 1,000 days, that is, the period from conception to about the second birthday. The focus on this period reflects the fact that we know from research that there are **critical periods** during this time. Critical periods are windows of time when development is most vulnerable or susceptible to variations in experience or conditions. (We will talk about critical periods for brain development in Chapter 2 and for language in Chapter 9.) With respect to brain development and nutrition, research has shown that these first 1,000 days are critically important for brain development. This is when the brain is "built." If the child experiences poor nutrition during this critical period, a smaller brain may result; if too severe, a smaller-than-normal brain (called microcephaly) can result in seizures, developmental delays, and motor problems. The first 1,000 days are when all the neurons are created and most of the connections between neurons are formed (more about this in Chapter 2). Good nutrition is needed for these processes. If the child experiences poor nutrition during this critical window—and, as a result, there are fewer neurons and connections between neurons at age 2 than is optimal—better nutrition later in life cannot correct those problems. That is why it is called a critical period; this is a time that is particularly important for the development of brain tissue. Programs like WIC are designed to help children during this critical period. Importantly, designers of such programs and policy makers who determine that these are important programs to fund rely on findings from research with infants; they only know that they should focus their efforts on this short period of time because of the kinds of research we will discuss in this book.

Another example relates to decisions made by leaders about whether children can grow and thrive in the absence of caregivers. As is clear from the discussions of immigration policies in the United States in 2016 through 2020, this is something that is important even in modern times. We know from extreme examples that infants do not thrive when they are separated from caregivers. In the 1980s, state infant centers—or institutions—in Romania became overcrowded. Many children in these centers were left there by parents who had the intention of returning to pick them up; other children were orphans and did not have parents. In 1989, the world became aware of the dire conditions of the children in these institutions. Images were released showing children crying in cribs, and it became known that these children were not well cared for. When children were adopted internationally, they were developmentally behind their non-adopted peers in those new countries. Although these institutionalized children improved considerably when they had consistent caregivers, better nutrition, and a stimulating environment, many of them never fully caught up in either physical size or mental ability.

In 2000, Charles Nelson, Nathan Fox, and Charles Zeanah launched the Bucharest Early Intervention Project (BEIP; Ghera et al., 2009; Nelson et al., 2009) to examine whether putting Romanian children in foster care, rather than having them raised in an institution, would result in fewer long-term problems. They found that infants raised in foster care did not experience as many developmental delays as their peers who stayed in institutions. In fact, the effects were so dramatic that although there remain institutions in Romania, there are now more foster parents, and fewer children are institutionalized.

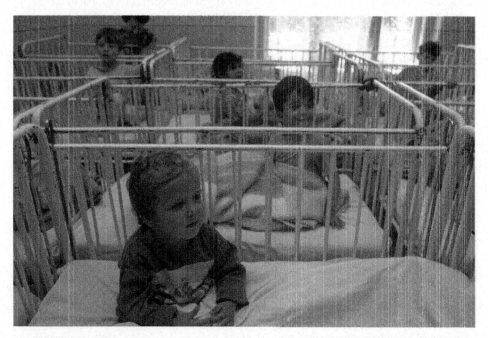

Children in Romanian Orphanage
BSIP/Contributor/Getty

BOX 1.1—INFANCY IN REAL LIFE: HOW HAVE THE RESULTS OF RESEARCH SHAPED CHILDREN'S LIVES?

Parents and policy makers do not typically peruse the scientific literature to decide how to parent, vote on legislation, or put policies in place. When parents are trying to make research-based decisions, they often ask their pediatrician or read a parenting magazine. Parents trust that their pediatrician will be up on the latest research findings, and articles in parenting magazines are written in ways that are meant to help parents stay informed. Policy makers and parents also read articles in newspapers and on blogs and websites. Parents may find information on social media such as Twitter, Instagram, and Facebook.

However, the articles that are found in newspapers, magazines, and media may not always be accurate and might actually mislead parents and policy makers. Consider the Mozart effect. In the 1990s, parents learned, mostly from the media, that listening to Mozart could make their infants smarter. This idea came from a 1993 study by Frances Rauscher, Gordon Shaw, and Catherine Ky (1993). These researchers found that undergraduate students' performance on a spatial IQ test was improved when they listened to Mozart compared to when they listened to a relaxation tape or listened to silence. This idea that Mozart, in particular, made people smarter was consistent with ideas promoted by French scientist Alfred Thomatis that listening to music helped the brain to heal and develop. These ideas were popularized first in an article in the *New York Times* in 1994 arguing that the study by Rauscher and colleagues showed the superiority of Mozart over Beethoven, and by a book in 1997 by Don Campbell in which he recommended playing Mozart to infants to help their mental development (Campbell, 1997). Although none of the actual research was done with infants, baby toys and materials were developed to promote brain development based on these theories, and the governor of Georgia even proposed that the state should provide every newborn with recordings of classical music (Sack, 1998)!

The problem is that the Mozart effect is not real. Not only was the original finding with adults and not infants, other researchers have not been able to replicate the results. To be clear, this was not necessarily a case of research creating real problems for infants and parents; the worst this did was make people spend money on classical music they might not have otherwise spent. But, it does show how research findings can be taken the wrong way and be popularized in a way that is not helpful.

There are other examples showing how the results of research have had an important positive effect on infants' lives. A good example of this is the Back to Sleep campaign (now called the Safe to Sleep campaign), which also happened in the 1990s. This campaign resulted from the observation that in some cultures, infants were routinely put on their backs to sleep and sudden infant death syndrome (SIDS) was relatively rare. By the early 1990s, pediatricians in Europe and the United States began to encourage parents to position their infants on their back or sides when being put down to sleep. Later this recommendation was revised to be positioning infants only on their backs. The results were remarkable. As can be seen in Figure 1.1, as the percentage of infants positioned on their back increased (the diamonds), the number of infants who died from SIDS decreased dramatically (the light blue and gray bars). The Back to Sleep Campaign involved providing health care professionals and parents with materials and information about putting infants to sleep on their backs. Although we don't know exactly why putting infants on their backs seems to lower their risks for SIDS, this is an example of popularizing the results of research that likely saved many children's lives.

FIGURE 1.1   ■   SIDS Rates and Back Sleeping (1988–2006)

Rates of sudden infant death syndrome (SIDS) in the United States over time as a function of the percentage of how many parents put their infants to sleep on their backs.

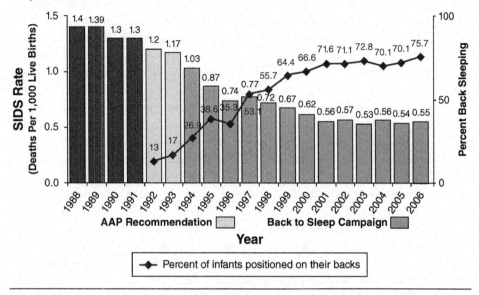

AAP Recommendation □   **Back to Sleep Campaign** ▨

Year

━◆━ Percent of infants positioned on their backs

Source: From the National Institute of Child Health and Human Development.

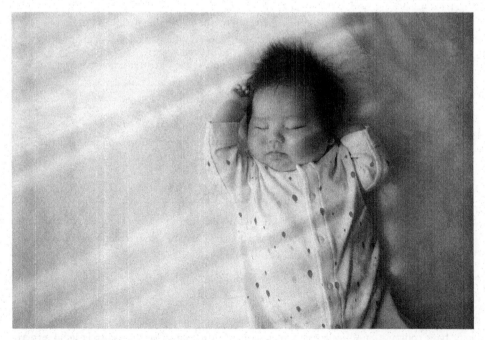

Infant Sleeping on Her Back

iStock/Yagi-Studio

It is not always easy to translate research findings into good policies to help children. A dramatic example of this was the popularization of the finding that vaccines caused autism. In 1998, Andrew Wakefield and his colleagues published a study that they claimed showed that the measles, mumps, and rubella vaccine (MMR) was linked to the development of autism. The original study was published in a medical journal and claimed to show in a very small sample of children ($n = 12$) that the onset of autism corresponded to when the MMR vaccination was given. The study was later shown to be false—and in fact, Wakefield was discredited and lost his ability to practice medicine or do research (Flaherty, 2011). However, the damage was already done. When the study was published, there was a lot of publicity about the finding, particularly by celebrities who believed that their own children's autism was caused by the MMR vaccination. This has been a tragedy for children around the world, as parents began to resist life-saving vaccinations based on the unfounded fear that their child may become autistic. Diseases such as measles that were essentially nonexistent in many parts of the world began to show up in unvaccinated children. The controversy about vaccinations is tragic because the fear of vaccinations is based on this one flawed study, with results that the scientific community agrees are false. Many studies have shown that vaccines are safe, that the rates of autism are not greater in vaccinated than unvaccinated children, and that the health risks of being unvaccinated are much greater than the side effects of the vaccines (DeStefano & Shimabukuro, 2019). The point of this example is that although we do research in order to help infants, it is very important that the results of research are appropriately and accurately reported to the public so that decisions about policies and parenting are not based on misinformation that may end up doing more harm than good.

Check Your Learning

1. Give an example of a qualitative change in infant development and an example of a quantitative change in infant development. How do these two types of changes differ?

2. How would you define nature? How would you define nurture? Explain how nature and nurture can have an *additive* effect on development and how it can have an *interactive* effect on development.

3. How would you describe a critical period in development? Why is knowing about critical periods in development important for parents, educators, and policy makers?

HOW DO WE STUDY INFANT DEVELOPMENT?

Now that we have established why we study infants, we need to consider *how* we study infants. There are two major things we need to think about: (1) research designs for studying development, and (2) what can we actually measure in infants.

Research Designs

You probably already know something about different types of research designs, but we will review some basic concepts. Specifically, here we describe the differences between **correlational**, **experimental**, and **quasi-experimental** designs (Table 1.2). The differences between these designs are

TABLE 1.2 ■ Research Designs				
	Defining Features	**Benefits**	**Limitations**	**Appropriate Verbs**
Correlation	Values on multiple variables are observed and relations between those variables is assessed	Can evaluate relations between variables that are impossible or unethical to manipulate	Difficult to draw cause and effect conclusions	Is linked to Is associated with Is correlated with Prefer May predict Are more/less likely to Is tied to Goes with
Experiment	Participants are randomly assigned to conditions or groups	Can assess the effect of one variable on another (e.g., cause and effect)	Some variables cannot be manipulated (e.g., age)	Causes Affects Changes Promotes Increases/decreases Results in
Quasi-experiment	"Natural" variables (e.g., age, sex, SES) are treated as groups	Can treat variables that are not manipulated (e.g., age) as grouping variables	At their core, these are correlational designs that do not allow causal conclusions	Is linked to Is associated with Is correlated with Prefers May predict Is more/less likely to Is tied to Goes with

important for understanding what studies using each kind of design actually tell us about development. You likely already know that correlational designs are when a researcher simply measures two (or more) features or characteristics, or variables, of a group of people and looks at how those characteristics are related. Remember the children raised in Romanian institutions? As part of this research, children's growth and development was measured when they were adopted into European households. The researchers also recorded how much time the children had spent in the Romanian institutions. This study showed that there was a correlation between how much time children spent in Romanian orphanages and their growth and development scores. Children who had spent more time in the orphanages were more delayed compared to children who spent less time in the orphanages. That is, time spent in orphanages was correlated with the amount of developmental delay.

What can we conclude from this finding? Because the researchers simply measured two variables (growth and time in the orphanage) and observed the relation between them, we can't draw any causal conclusions about that relation. It is tempting to think that these differences in children's development were *caused* by being raised in an institution. Indeed, this was part of the worldwide outrage that was expressed when the images emerged from Romania. People concluded that children's development was being harmed by being raised in an institution.

However, we can't actually know for sure if this is true based on this observation. Specifically, there may be other reasons why these two variables were related. The correlation between the amount of time children were in institutions and their growth and development might be due to the institutions not providing a context to support these children's development. It is also possible that parents were more likely to abandon children who were small and sick. In this case, living in the institution may have made it harder for them to thrive without *causing* their growth and developmental delays.

BOX 1.2—INFANCY IN REAL LIFE: CORRELATIONAL STUDIES AND ADVICE TO PARENTS

In 1999 Graham Quinn and his colleagues published a study that led to the conclusion, especially in the media, that exposure to light at night interfered with visual development during a critical period in infancy (Quinn et al., 1999). They asked parents of 437 children between the ages of 2 and 16 years about the child's light exposure across the lifespan. Children who were exposed to more light at night (e.g., with a night light or the room light on) before the age of 2 were found to have more significant vision problems (see Figure 1.2; emmetropia

FIGURE 1.2 ■ Myopia and Ambient Lighting at Night

The percentage of children with different levels of vision problems as a function of whether they slept in darkness, with a night light, or with the room light on.

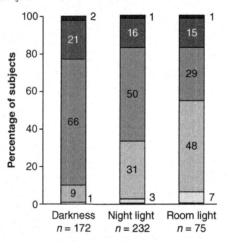

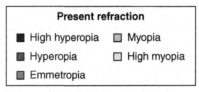

is "normal" vision). Note that most of the children who slept in darkness had normal vision (66%), but only half of the children who had a night light and about one third of the children who slept with the room light on had normal vision. From this observation, researchers and the media concluded that exposure to light during the night caused the children to develop vision problems.

Several news outlets jumped on this conclusion, and articles appeared with headlines like "Night Lights Linked to Babies' Nearsightedness" (Maugh, 1999) and "Night Lights Linked to Vision Problems" (Associated Press, 1999). The problem is, of course, that these are causal conclusions drawn from correlational findings. From the original study, we know that night light use and poor vision are *associated*, but we don't actually know whether the night light use *caused* differences in infants' visual development. The two variables might be linked for a different reason. Karla Zadnik and her colleagues did a follow-up study and found that children who slept with night lights or room lights on were not more likely to have vision problems than were children who slept in the dark; that is, there was no cor-relation between vision problems and night light use (Zadnik et al., 2000). Zadnik and col-leagues also measured the parents' vision problems. They found that parents with poor vision were more likely to use night lights in their children's rooms than were parents with normal vision; that is, there was a correlation between parental vision problems and night light use. Because many of the causes of vision problems are genetic, and parents can pass those problems to their children, Zadnik's study suggested that the correlation observed in Quinn's original study might be due to a third variable. Specifically, parents with poor vision used night lights and their children were genetically predisposed to poor vision. This is still a correlation, but it shows that the conclusions from Quinn's original study should not have been described to parents as night lights causing vision problems.

Unlike correlational designs, in experimental designs, study participants are *randomly assigned* to different groups to determine the levels of one or more variables. In an experiment, the variable we manipulate is the *independent variable*, and the variable we measure is the *dependent variable*. Because we randomly assign participants to different levels of the indepen-dent variable, we can conclude that differences in the dependent variable are *caused* by that assignment.

Even though we can't know from the original observation if time in the Romanian orphan-age caused children's developmental delays, Charles Nelson and his colleagues in the BEIP study conducted an experiment that does answer this question. At the time of this study, foster care was virtually nonexistent in Romania. So Nelson and his colleagues created one. They found foster care families and randomly assigned children to be raised either in an orphanage or in a family household (i.e., foster care). In this case, the rearing environment is the independent variable and developmental outcomes—size, scores on cognitive tests, etc.—are the dependent variables. Because Nelson and his colleagues randomly assigned children to one of two rearing conditions, we know that the groups of children did not differ in some important way *before* they were assigned to one rearing condition or the other. Nelson and his colleagues observed that the children who were assigned to a foster family had better outcomes than children who remained in the institutions. This study allows us to conclude that children develop better when they are in a family context than when they are in an institution.

Given that experiments are the only way we can draw causal conclusions, why don't we always use this approach? This remarkable study was only possible because prior to this study Romania did not have a large foster system. Charles Nelson and his colleagues could randomly assign children to foster care because the foster care system in Romania was essentially nonexistent. However, it is not ethical to randomly assign children to grow up with their parents or in an institution. Further, some have argued that even Nelson's study was not ethical because even without the study it was clear that the treatment in these orphanages was not good for children. Unfortunately, at the time of the study, there wasn't widespread agreement in Romania that this was true (Zeanah et al., 2012), and improving the treatment of children *required* this kind of causal study. The issue is whether it is ethical to give only some children a "better" treatment and leave other children in the "standard treatment," especially if we have a strong belief that this standard treatment is harmful. This is a complex and difficult question. Although prior to the study, the Romanian government did not recognize that foster care was better, the American investigators surely did. But by conducting this experiment, the BEIP study encouraged the Romanian government to create a system that was better for all orphans. Now Romania does have a foster care system. In 2018, over 36,000 children in Romania were being raised in a family home and fewer than 7,000 children were being raised in institutions, and many of those children were children with disabilities placed in institutions that cared specifically for children with disabilities.

In other cases, random assignment simply is not possible. For example, we could test whether exposure to night lights affects visual development by randomly assigning some infants to sleep with a night light and other infants to sleep in the dark, and then measure their vision later on. This experiment not only poses an ethical problem (if we believe that sleeping with a night light will cause vision problems), but it is likely that the random assignment won't work. Some children can't sleep with a night light on and other children won't sleep without one. Therefore, even if you did randomly assign children to night light or no night light conditions, your study might fail because children in each group would be unable to sleep, and parents might end up doing what they wanted to anyway. Indeed, this is one benefit of correlational studies: They allow us to examine the relation between two variables that are impossible or unethical to manipulate.

In many studies, researchers treat existing group differences (e.g., whether or not an infant sleeps with a night light, sex or gender, age) as independent variables. This design is called a quasi-experiment because we have variables that look like conditions in an experiment, but we didn't randomly assign people to those conditions. In the original observation of children raised in Romanian orphanages to children raised in homes with their biological parents, the conditions that were being compared were not randomly assigned, but rather children were "assigned" to an orphanage or a home based on aspects of their life circumstances (i.e., where they were born). This design is sometimes referred to as a natural experiment, because the conditions reflect people's "natural" state. In the night light study described in Box 1.2, children were grouped into "darkness," "night light," or "ambient light." But, they weren't randomly assigned to those groups; these are their groupings based on their experience. So, it *looks* like an experiment—because we have groups—but it is really a correlation.

This is the design we are using whenever we compare groups of children of different ages. Consider, for example, a researcher interested in comparing perception from 4 months to 8 months. It is impossible to randomly assign some children to be 4 months and others to be 8 months. Instead, we find infants who are 4 months old and we find other infants who are 8 months old, and we compare them. We will talk about designs for comparing different ages of children later, but for now it is important to remember that whenever we compare children of different ages, we are doing a quasi-experiment.

Designs for Studying Infant Development

Because we are interested in development, we need to design studies that look at change. The main way we do this is by comparing children at different ages. This allows us to draw conclusions about how children of different ages respond on those tests. The two main designs for studying development are **cross-sectional** and **longitudinal** designs. These two designs differ in whether the *same* children are tested at different ages (longitudinal designs), or whether *different* children are tested at each age (cross-sectional designs).

Imagine you want to know at what age infants first start sitting on their own—that is, when can you put them on the floor and let go and they will be able to sit without falling down? Perhaps we think this develops between 5 and 8 months of age. We could study this using a cross-sectional design by asking parents of infants who are 5 months, 6 months, 7 months, *or* 8 months to our lab for testing. We might have 15 infants at each age come to the lab and we would record them sitting. Maybe we find that 1 of the infants at 5 months could sit, 3 of the infants at 6 months could sit, 9 of the infants at 7 months could sit, and all of the infants at 8 months could sit. We might conclude that 7 months is when infants learn to sit on average and that infants can sit by the time they are 8 months old.

This study would give us important insight into when we can expect that children in general will be able to sit. But this study doesn't really tell us anything about when the infants we tested first learned to sit. For example, we don't know *when* the nine 7-month-old infants who could sit actually acquired that ability. They may have started sitting when they were 5 months old, or they may not have started sitting until the week before they came to the lab. So, although this cross-sectional study allows us to determine when children can sit on average, it does not tell us much about how individual infants learn to sit.

To answer this question, we would need to test the *same* infants over time. Instead of having different groups of 5-, 6-, 7-, and 8-month-old infants visit the lab once, we would ask parents to bring their infants into the lab 4 times—once each month between 5 and 8 months. Now we would be able to determine when each infant learned to sit.

How do researchers decide which kind of design to use? Each has benefits and each has limitations (Table 1.3). As we just saw, longitudinal studies allow us to look at the development of individuals. But, it might be hard to get parents to agree to come to the lab every month for testing, so a longitudinal study might be harder to conduct. In addition, a longitudinal study will take *longer* to conduct. In our example, it would take us 4 months to test our subjects. If we were interested in bigger age differences—for example, some difference between 1-year-old and 2-year-old children—it would take even longer. If you conduct a cross-sectional study, however,

TABLE 1.3 ■ Designs for Studying Development				
Type of Design	**Defining Features**	**Benefits**	**Limitations**	**Type of Conclusion**
Cross-sectional	Different children are examined at each age	Relatively quick and requires less of a commitment from families	Age differences are confounded with group differences	Age-related differences
Longitudinal	The same children are examined across time	Allows the evaluation of how the same children develop, and allows the study of the individual differences	Takes longer and requires a bigger commitment from families; differences across repeated testing may reflect differences in age or the effect of repeated testing	Developmental change, continuity and stability
Cohort-sequential	Groups of children are examined multiple times, at overlapping ages	Can explore development longitudinally over a relatively long time span in less time; less of a commitment from each family	Different cohorts of children may be different in ways other than age	Both age-related and developmental change, continuity and stability within a cohort
Microgenetic	The same children are examined multiple times at short intervals, usually at a time of developmental transition	Can actually observe development in real time; can help us understand how development unfolds	Requires commitment from families to several sessions; effects of multiple testing sessions	Developmental trajectories
Age-held-constant	All children are the same age but differ in some other characteristic or experience	Allows the evaluation of the role of some experience or milestone without the effect of age	Only tests children at one time	How behavior is different in children with and without specific experience

you can test all the ages at the same time. In the case of our sitting example, you could test the 5-, 6-, 7-, and 8-month-old infants at the same time, perhaps completing the testing in less time than it would take you to follow a single infant from 5 to 8 months. The benefit is even clearer when we consider comparing 1-year-old and 2-year-old children; in this case, you can test children of both ages in the same weeks or months (rather than waiting a year for your children to reach the next age), thus keeping the time to finish the study much shorter.

Another potential problem with longitudinal studies is that age and number of visits is confounded. A *confound* is an extra variable that might influence your results in unintended ways.

In this example, when children are older, they necessarily have participated in more visits. If you find that children in your longitudinal study are better or faster when they are older compared to when they were younger, it might be because they are older *or* it might be because they are more familiar with the study setting or materials. That is, we need to be careful to design our study so that children don't improve simply because of repeated testing. When we test children cross-sectionally, this isn't a problem. In a cross-sectional study, the oldest children are tested on their first visit, just like the youngest children. Thus, the fact that they are better or faster can't be because they are more familiar with the setting. For this reason, researchers may use a **cohort-sequential** design, which combines elements of both cross-sectional and longitudinal designs. As in a longitudinal design, all children in a cohort-sequential design are evaluated at multiple time points. However, different groups, or cohorts, of children are tested, each starting the study at different ages. This has the advantage of being able to compare the same children at different time points, while at the same time testing different groups of children reducing both the effects of repeated testing and the time required to complete the entire study.

These are practical reasons for why you might choose one approach or the other, but the most important difference between the two kinds of designs is what conclusions can be drawn from differences between older and younger children. In cross-sectional studies, you can draw conclusions about *age-related differences*. In the sitting example, you could conclude that the number of infants who could sit increased at each age. You can't draw conclusions about *development*, however. Because you see each child only one time, it is impossible to know anything about a child's skills or abilities before they visited the lab or how those skills and abilities changed after their lab visits. In cross-sectional studies, we can only make conclusions about how groups of children are similar or different *on average*.

Longitudinal studies, in contrast, do allow for conclusions about development. Because we observe the same child at different time points, we can learn about when particular children achieve a skill or ability, how some skills or abilities develop into different skills or abilities, and importantly, how different children show different patterns of development.

In fact, it is this last feature of longitudinal designs that is particularly important. The only way we can know about the development of individual children is by doing longitudinal studies. This gives us insight into *individual differences*, or differences between individual children, and whether those differences are stable. Both Edwin and Carter were somewhat cautious as infants, whereas Charlie and Tesalia were practically fearless. If we only evaluated how they were at 12 months of age, for example, we would only know that some infants are cautious and others are not. However, Carter and Edwin remained cautious throughout infancy and were a bit shy as preschoolers. Tesalia and Charlie remained fearless as toddlers, and both became social butterflies once they entered school. So, if we followed these children from 12 months to 3 years, we would see that these differences between them remained pretty stable.

Given how important longitudinal designs are for understanding development and individual differences, it might seem odd that people do cross-sectional studies at all. However, even if we might ultimately be interested in development and individual differences, sometimes the main question is simply whether older and younger children differ. We might know more if we studied this longitudinally, but the cost and time and potential problems with a longitudinal study just aren't worth it given what our primary questions are. Many studies have shown that older and younger infants differ in motor development, perceptual abilities, emotional responses, and much more. These studies provide an important foundation for our understanding of development in infancy. And they provide a good starting point for designing a more costly and time-intensive longitudinal study later on.

A variation of a longitudinal design is to study children frequently separated by a short time interval. In these **microgenetic** studies, children are observed daily or weekly. Typically, these studies do not follow children for months or years, as in a traditional longitudinal study. Rather, children are observed repeatedly after short intervals but only for a relatively short time period. As an example, consider a study conducted by Manuela Lavelli and Alan Fogel (2013). The goal of this study was to understand how mother–infant face-to-face communication changed over the first 3 months after birth. The researchers observed mother–infant pairs every week as they interacted face-to-face. The first observation was when the infants were 1 week old and the last was when the infants were 14 weeks old. By observing these interactions every week, Lavelli and Fogel were able to identify *developmental trajectories*—that is, how mothers and infants' behaviors changed over time. If they had observed the pairs less frequently—for example, just in the first and last session—they would have observed developmental changes, but they would not have seen how those behaviors changed gradually over time.

Microgenetic studies are especially useful for understanding how change happens during times of transition. In traditional longitudinal studies involving more spread-out repeated assessments, researchers can link behaviors across time. Microgenetic studies can show how behavior changes from day to day or week to week. Such studies can be important for learning how development unfolds.

Sometimes development can be best understood by conducting a study in which all participants are the same age. This is particularly true when the researcher is interested in the role of a specific kind of experience on development. In these **age-held-constant** designs all children tested are the same age, but they vary in some other way that we believe influences or contributes to development. In these studies, researchers compare children who are the same age—and thus who have experienced the same amount of time developing—but who have different experiences. For example, researchers might compare infants who were exposed to one language with infants who were exposed to multiple languages (Brito & Barr, 2012), or infants who are crawlers with infants of the same age who do not yet crawl (Campos et al., 1992).

Measuring Infant Development

As we will discuss throughout this book, infants have limited abilities. Unlike older children and adults, infants can't talk, follow directions, fill out questionnaires, or press keys on a computer keyboard. It is hard to get them to point or hand you an object that you ask them for, even once they have those abilities. On top of that, they get bored easily and cry or fuss if they are tired or hungry. How in the world can we measure their development?

What Can We Measure in Infants?

There are some things that infants can do, and all of those things can be potential variables—either variables to correlate or dependent variables in an experiment (Table 1.4). For example,

TABLE 1.4 ■ Measurements of Infant Development			
What Measured	**How Measured**	**Benefits**	**Limitations**
Behavior (sitting, crawling, walking)	Observation Parental report	Naturally occurring	If infants haven't yet developed a behavior (e.g., crawling), it can't be used to measure other aspects of development
Looking	Observation Eye tracking	Easy to observe Present from birth	Researchers don't always know why infants look at a stimulus
Physiological responses (heart rate, EEG)	Electrodes record the physiological response	Automatic response	Requires special equipment; researchers don't always know why infants show a physiological response

BABY CRAWLING TO MOM: An example of an infant crawling to a caregiver, or engaging in proximity seeking.

iStock/fotostorm

infants can move, and thus, infants' motor behavior is something we can measure. Many researchers are interested in how infants perceive the world and what they think and feel. We could measure infants' motor behavior to help us understand these aspects of development. For example, researchers who use the visual cliff apparatus (depicted earlier) are mostly interested in studying depth perception, reasoning that infants won't cross the visual cliff if they can perceive depth. Similarly, in Mary Ainsworth's strange situation (see Chapter 11), infants' relationship to their caregiver is measured, in part, by how much they "seek proximity," or work to remain close to that caregiver. Both are useful ways of measuring infant development, and we have learned a lot by measuring infants' behavior.

But, measuring motor behavior isn't always possible, and in some cases, can be problematic. If an infant does not yet have the ability to crawl, we won't know if they "refuse" to crawl on the deep side of the visual cliff because they don't perceive depth or because they don't yet have the ability to crawl. Similarly, we might be able to measure proximity seeking in terms of how much the infant looks at his mother, or reaches for her, but it will be harder to judge whether or not a non-crawling infant is (or is not) seeking proximity than a crawling infant. In each of these cases, our interpretation of the infant's behavior is influenced both by the behavior we are interested in measuring and in whether or not infants have developed the ability required to produce that behavioral response. In fact, this was one of the biggest criticisms of Piaget, who is considered the father of the study of cognitive development. As you will see in Chapter 7, many people believed that Piaget underestimated infants' cognitive abilities because he relied on their motor behaviors to uncover those abilities. For example, a classic Piagetian task involves hiding one object (such as a toy) under a cloth or a cup. Piaget concluded that infants have *object permanence*, or recognize that the object continues to exist even when it is out of sight, if they remove the cover and retrieve the object. However, researchers have argued that infants could fail this test of object permanence because they have forgotten that the object existed *or* because they have difficulty reaching for and removing the object covering the hidden object.

So when specific motor behaviors fail us, what other things can we measure in infants? One of the most common behaviors that researchers measure is infant looking behavior. In the 1950s, a developmental psychologist named Robert Fantz first discovered that we can measure infants' looking behavior. Before his studies, people believed that very young infants were essentially blind and that looking was learned, just as all behaviors are learned. Fantz made an amazing discovery. He found that when he presented infants different images, infants looked longer—or preferred—some images to others. For example, in one study Fantz (1963) found that infants who were just a few days old looked longer at patterned images (e.g., black and white stripes, a face-like image) than at unpatterned images (e.g., a solid red image). By simply recording how long infants looked at images, Fantz could conclude that newborn infants can see. As you will see in later chapters, where infants look has become one of the most common dependent variables in infancy research.

Technological advances have made measuring where infants look even easier. Researchers can now use automatic eye trackers, which involve infrared light sources and special cameras, to precisely record infants' looking behaviors. Look at the next photo. This infant is being tested in an experiment using an eye tracker. The infant is seated in an undecorated room on the father's lap. They are in front of a computer screen and there are interesting images on the screen. As you can see here, it is not too hard to tell that the infant is looking at the images.

So far we have focused on which *behaviors* we can measure in infants. In addition to these behaviors, we can measure *physiological responses*. Physiological responses are automatic physical responses triggered by the presentation of a stimulus. For example, when someone says "boo"

An Infant's Looking at an Experimental Stimulus

loudly behind you, your heart rate increases. When you are about to take a test, your palms sweat. We can measure these kinds of responses in infants to gain insight into their development. The most common physiological responses are *heart rate*, or echocardiogram (ECG), and *brain activity*, or electroencephalogram (EEG). These two physiological responses can be measured simply by attaching electrodes to the infants' chest (for ECG) or scalp. These electrodes will painlessly record the infants' heart rate or brain activity as they are exposed to stimuli. For example, Joseph Campos and his colleagues (in the visual cliff study described earlier) measured changes in heart rate as infants were placed on the deep side of the cliff. Campos could test infants who did not yet crawl by measuring heart rate and placing infants on the cliff, rather than evaluating whether or not infants would crawl across the cliff. Similarly, researchers can measure brain activity from electrodes attached to the head. These electrodes record the electrical activity that is produced when different regions of the brain are active. For example, Martha Ann Bell and Nathan Fox (1992) found that infants who could solve Piaget's object permanence tasks (described earlier) had different EEG patterns than did children who could not yet solve those tasks.

We will talk more about these physiological measures in other chapters, but there are several things to keep in mind. Unlike motor behaviors and looking, physiological measures are *automatic*. Changes in heart rate or brain activity happen—and can be recorded—regardless of whether or not the infant wants to look more at one stimulus than another or crawl across a

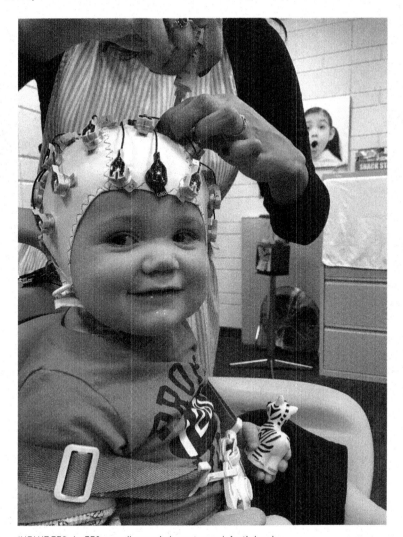

INFANT EEG. An EEG recording cap being put on an infant's head.

visual cliff. For this reason, these measures have advantages over the other behaviors we might measure. But to accurately record physiological responses, you need special equipment and training. It may be harder to get infants to cooperate with the procedures needed to get good physiological measures. So, although they are widely used to study infant development, they have both advantages and disadvantages over other measures.

What Can We Conclude From the Things We Can Measure in Infants?

Even when you can accurately measure behaviors in infants, it isn't always obvious what you can (and can't) conclude from those behaviors. When Alison was just over 6 months old, she started to crawl. She was an enthusiastic crawler. There was a coffee table in the living room with a lip that hung down. Little Alison would crawl under the coffee table and bang her head into that lip. Despite the fact that it clearly hurt every time, she did it over and over again. What can we conclude from this behavior? Well, we can certainly conclude that Alison could crawl. But it's harder to know what we can conclude from the fact that she crawled right into the coffee table over and over again. Did she have a vision problem and she couldn't see that part of the coffee table? Did she not understand her body size in relation to the coffee table? Did she not understand that the coffee table was made of solid wood and could not be crawled "through"? Was she so determined to get under the table that she ignored all obstacles in her way?

This story shows how difficult it is to understand *why* infants behave in the way they do. When we study older children and adults, we give them instructions. They may not follow those instructions, but we hope that by giving them a goal, they will engage in specific kinds of behaviors. If we tell subjects that they will need to remember items for a test later, they will (hopefully) engage in memory processes. If we ask subjects to judge a set of pictures for who they'd like to play with, we assume that their judgments will reflect something about their appraisal of the people in the pictures. We can't give infants such instructions.

This is an important point because in studies of infant development there are often multiple explanations for the behavior we observe. That is, we measure a behavior (e.g., infant looking), but we draw conclusions about an underlying **psychological construct,** the concept we wish to measure (e.g., infant preference). The psychological construct is the underlying *process*, for example, the infants' preference or perception or memory. The difficulty is knowing whether the behavior we record is a **valid measure** of that construct (see Table 1.5). In other words, are we recording something that accurately reflects the process we are interested in measuring? In the Fantz study described earlier, newborn infants looked longer at patterned images than at unpatterned images. Fantz concluded that newborn infants could see patterned images. This is a valid conclusion from this study—if infants couldn't *see* the images, they would not have had a preference. Thus, measuring whether or not infants prefer a patterned image over an unpatterned image accurately reflects whether or not infants can

TABLE 1.5 ■ Comparing Constructs and Observable Behaviors	
Construct	**Behavior or Response**
Fetal learning (see Chapter 3)	Changes in fetal heart rate
Preferences (see Chapter 4)	Looking time
Memory for an action (see Chapter 6)	Imitating a modeled action
Object permanence (knowing that an object exists even when out of sight, see Chapter 7)	Searching for a hidden object
Understanding the meaning of a word (see Chapter 8)	Looking at a labeled object
Emotion (see Chapter 9)	Facial expression, heart rate change
Attachment security to caregiver (see Chapter 10)	Seeking closeness to caregiver, looking at caregiver

see the pattern. But others might want to draw other kinds of conclusions. For example, a researcher might observe the same pattern Fantz did and conclude that infants *liked* the patterned images better. That is, infants looked longer at the patterned images not only because they could see them but also because those images caused them to have some sort of pleasant feeling. Another researcher might conclude that infants found the unpatterned images boring and infants prefer excitement. A third researcher might conclude that infants prefer stimuli that offer information for them to learn, and they couldn't learn anything from the unpatterned images. We don't know if any of these conclusions are correct, and we can't know simply from the fact that infants prefer to look at patterned images than at unpatterned images. In other words, we don't know whether infants' preference is a valid measurement of what they liked, their drive for excitement, or their interest in learning new information. All we really know is that they looked longer at the patterned images.

This example illustrates a real problem in interpreting how infants respond in many research studies. Often researchers are most interested in these more difficult-to-measure constructs, things like infants' emotional reactions, their reasoning, or their surprise. However, given the limitations of infants' abilities, it is not always clear whether measures we use to assess those abilities are valid. In some areas, such as emotional responding, this issue has led some to argue that we need to look at multiple measures (LoBue et al., 2020).

There is another problem with what we conclude about infants' behavior. Not only does the process or ability we are studying develop, but so does the behavior itself. You might be surprised to know that even infants' looking behavior develops. We will talk about this in Chapter 4, but it turns out that infants' ability to look away develops in the first months. As a result, a 3-month-old infant may look for a very long time at an image not because she prefers it, finds it interesting, or is surprised, but because she is "stuck" and doesn't yet have a well-developed ability to look away from an image when she is no longer interested in it. What this means is that a long look by a 3-month-old infant might mean something completely different than a long look by a 6-month-old infant. The same behavior—looking at an image for a long time—in the young infant might reflect the inability to "let go" of the look, and in the older infants it might reflect how the infant is learning or thinking about the image.

Another important thing to remember about interpreting infants' behavior is that most infant research focuses on averaging behaviors of groups of infants. For example, going back to the example of Joseph Campos's visual cliff study, he found that *on average,* infants' heart rate *increased* as they were placed on the deep side of the visual cliff. The researchers came to this result by measuring the heart rate change of several infants and calculating an average of those heart rate changes. This tells us something about how most infants tend to respond to a drop-off. However, it is almost always the case that the individual infants in studies respond somewhat differently. In Campos's study, for example, most infants' heart rates went up when lowered onto the visual cliff, but there were likely at least some infants whose heart rates didn't change at all when being lowered onto the drop-off, or whose heart rates actually went *down*. Because most infants showed the same response—an increase in heart rate—the average was an increase.

But, studies that report only group averages don't tell us anything about individual differences among the infants or why some infants were different from the rest of the group. On one hand, it could be that some infants just weren't paying attention when being lowered onto the drop-off and that differences in their behavior when compared to the group just reflected the fact that their mind was wandering. On the other hand, it's also possible that any infant who showed an increase in heart rate had more crawling experience than the few infants who didn't show a heart rate increase. These "nonresponding" infants might have been more like the non-crawlers in this study, and infants might need some experience crawling to respond physiologically to the drop-off.

This example is relevant to our discussion of the different kinds of experimental designs and what conclusions can be drawn from them. Campos and his colleagues studied the relation between crawling and heart rate changes in response to the visual cliff by comparing groups of different infants (all the same age), some who had crawling experience and some who did not. This age-held-constant design is similar to a cross-sectional design, except that the groups of infants differed in experience rather than age. But, as in a cross-sectional study, all we can conclude is whether the groups of infants were the same or different. We can only understand whether infants show the same or different patterns across development by studying infants longitudinally, in this case measuring their heart rate changes to the visual cliff both before and after they began crawling.

BOX 1.3—INFANCY RESEARCH: WHO IS TESTED IN INFANT RESEARCH?

In this chapter, we have discussed several issues with respect to conducting research to understand infant development. We have described designs for conducting research and how we measure infant development. What we have not tackled is *who* is studied in infancy research. Throughout this book, you will see descriptions of findings from studies that we (like others in the field) will use to draw conclusions about how infants develop. It is important to point out, however, that not all infants are studied in psychological research and that what we know about infant development is based on research with specific populations. In particular, because research with infants is conducted primarily on college and university campuses, the families who participate are often families who live near those campuses. In addition, participating in research takes time and requires (usually) that families visit labs, often in the middle of a weekday. Further, most researchers studying infant development are in North America or western Europe. Thus, in general, subject populations in infant research are likely to be White, have educated parents, and be from middle-class families. Infants who have a stay-at-home parent are also more likely to be able to participate in studies. These *convenience samples* are the families who are easiest for researchers to identify, contact, and recruit for their studies, and these are the families who have the time and resources to volunteer to participate in research.

For decades, the use of convenience samples was not thought to be a problem. If we are studying basic processes like visual abilities, memory, or mother–infant

Infants From Different Racial, Ethnic, and Cultural Backgrounds

iStock/Rawpixel

bonding, it shouldn't matter who our subjects are, right? It was believed that relying on convenience samples was scientifically acceptable because our findings should apply broadly to children raised in different circumstances. There were some researchers who explicitly asked how differences in culture contributed to differences in development. However, these **cross-cultural approaches** to development often focused on differences between our convenience samples and other samples from different cultural, economic, or regional contexts and were not considered central to our understanding of development.

As you will see throughout this book, however, cross-cultural comparisons have revealed important differences in development—differences that make it clear that we should not assume that the patterns observed when testing convenience samples are universal. Instead, infants' environments and their experiences shape development in important ways, and differences in families, culture, practices, environments, and so on, all likely impact development. Thus, an important factor to keep in mind is how those variables have contributed to the development of whatever behavior we are studying.

Unfortunately, the field has only relatively recently understood the importance of considering who is studied. Thus, there are decades of published research that does not report important details about the infants, like their race or ethnicity, the education level of their parents, if they are raised in an urban or rural environment, what languages are spoken in the home, and whether the parents are wealthy or live in poverty. In fact, sometimes it is not even clear what country the children lived in when a study was conducted! Although it is now a requirement in most journals to publish this kind of information, there is a large body of research that does not include this kind of potentially important information about the subject population.

We will not be able to describe the subject population for every study we include here. However, in an effort to be as clear as possible who was studied, we will include information about the infants who were included in a study or what the general population is of the body of work when we can. But it's important to keep in mind when thinking about this research that developmental psychology, like all areas of psychology, still has a long way to go in making sure our samples are representative and sufficiently diverse.

Check Your Learning

1. Describe the difference between a correlational study and an experiment. What are the advantages and disadvantages of using correlations versus experiments to study infant development?

2. What is the difference between a "true" experiment and a quasi-experiment? How do these differences influence the ability to draw causal conclusions?

3. What is the difference between a longitudinal and cross-sectional study?

4. How are behavioral and physiological measures different? What are the advantages and disadvantages of each?

5. Give an example of a psychological construct, and explain why it is important that a measure be valid.

DEVELOPMENT DOES NOT HAPPEN IN A VACUUM

One of the important themes in this book is that infant development does not happen in a vacuum. You will see that studies often focus on only a single ability or development. Researchers might ask questions about how infants' color vision develops or how they come to recognize emotions in others. Such studies provide an important starting point for understanding infant development, but they are not the whole picture. In the real everyday lives of actual infants, color vision emerges as other aspects of vision are developing and as the infant becomes better able to direct where his head is pointed. In addition, during this same period, infants' emotional responses are becoming refined and differentiated, they are gaining control over their bodies, and their ability to form memories of the sights they encounter is undergoing change. Connections between brain regions are emerging and the infant is growing. Although we may understand something about how the infant sees the world by studying only their color vision, it is clear that changes in color vision are happening at the same time as many other changes across the infants' whole body, brain, and mind. Thus, although this very textbook is parsed into isolated topics like perceptual, cognitive, and emotional development, it is important to keep in mind that all of these systems interact over the course of development and that development is happening in the **whole child**, and not just in a single isolated system. Throughout this text, we will point you to connections across the chapters.

In addition, the child is developing in a family, cultural, and societal context. Variations in family composition, cultural values with respect to infancy, and societal expectations for parenting all provide the context for infant development. Often research assumes that such factors are unimportant in determining development, unless the development in question is directly related to those factors. But, as we will see, just as individual systems do not develop in isolation, individual infants develop in a context and their development reflects the people and practices of that context. In this final section we will introduce how such factors might influence infant development.

Families With Infants

iStock/Rawpixel

Emphasis on the Whole Child

Many modern theories of development acknowledge that development occurs in the whole child. According to such theories, it is difficult to really understand development of a system if it is studied completely in isolation, without considering how the development of that system reflects and is influenced by other systems in the child. Two approaches that make this connection explicit are the **dynamic systems theory** of development (Thelen & Smith, 1994) and the idea of **developmental cascades** (Oakes & Rakison, 2019). Each of these approaches acknowledges how the development of systems are dependent on one another.

In dynamic systems views, behaviors, such as walking or reaching for a hidden object, emerge as the result of multiple, independent systems. In the case of walking, for example, Esther Thelen (e.g., Thelen & Ulrich, 1991) argued that the emergence of independent walking depends on the development of several abilities, including to balance on one leg, monitor and perceive the environment, and anticipate and plan for changes in the terrain (e.g., obstacles, change in surface), to name just a few. The ability to *walk* is assembled from these other developing abilities and emerges when they all have developed enough so that walking is possible when used together. The point is that no single system or behavior is responsible for walking; walking reflects the co-development and coordination of many systems.

In a developmental cascade, achievements that occur at one point in development have effects at a later point, even in a different area of development. For example, once infants are able to crawl, their whole interaction with the world changes. Infants can now move across a room to seek out a favorite toy. They can approach a parent or caregiver and begin an interaction. And, for the first time, they have the ability to reach objects that might be dangerous, which could change the emotional environment when their mothers tell them not to do things they might very much want to do, like stick their fingers in sockets or play with knives.

Thus, changes in one area (the ability to crawl) influence how infants interact with and learn from the world. For example, advances in walking are linked to advances in language development (Karasik et al., 2014). You might scratch your head at this association—why would the development of walking and talking be related? They presumably involve different brain systems and different parts of the body. Language and walking also have different functions in the infant's life. But, once infants develop the ability to walk, they can carry objects much more easily than an infant who is crawling. This means that infants who can walk are better able to include objects in their interactions with others, providing more opportunities for object naming. And in this case, Lana Karasik and colleagues found that mothers of walking infants talk to their infants more than mothers of crawling infants, providing specific directions on what objects or things to bring to them. The point is that two infants who are the same age may have very different experiences because of their difference in motor skills. An infant who can crawl but not yet walk will be able to initiate interactions with caregivers, but those interactions will be less likely to include objects than if the infant can walk. So, advances in one domain, such as the transition from crawling to walking, may create opportunities to gain more input, such as caregiver speech, which in turn, can benefit an infant's acquisition of language.

Both the dynamic systems theory and the developmental cascades approach recognize that development happens across the whole child. Although we will again discuss many developmental achievements in this book that have been studied in isolation, when possible we will try to focus on how systems work together and influence each other.

Family and Social Context

Just as development involves the whole child, the child develops in the context of a broader system, and aspects of that system play an important role in how children develop. Urie Bronfenbrenner's (1979) **ecological systems theory** of development is often used to understand how different aspects of the social and cultural context influence development. The theory is depicted in Figure 1.3. The child is at the center of the figure, and characteristics such as the child's personality, age, and health will determine, to some extent, the child's development. This is the nature part of the model.

The other rings show different kinds of environmental influences—or the nurture influences on development. What is important is that the rings that are closer to the individual are presumed to play a larger role. Notice that the innermost ring includes family, peers, and other daily influences on development. For infants, family is likely the most important of these. Infants are born into families with one or two (or more) parents and with no siblings, one sibling, or multiple siblings. Infants may live in a house, an apartment, or a yurt. Families may live in isolation, far from grandparents, aunts, uncles, and cousins. Or they may live close to relatives and larger family groups. The infant may be in a culture where multiple caregivers typically care for the child or one in which there is a single caregiver. Infants may be part of a society in which

FIGURE 1.3 ■ **Bronfenbrenner's Ecological Theory of Development**

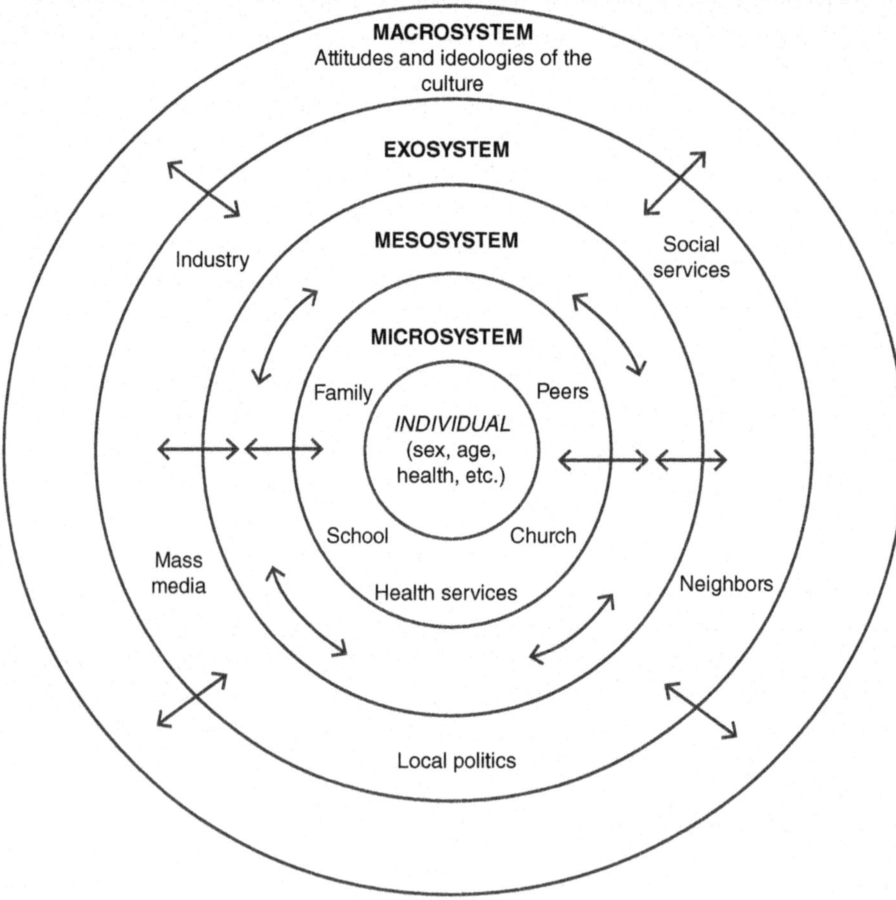

caregivers are given time away to be with their infant, whereas in other societies caregivers must return to work soon after the birth of the infant.

Considering the larger family and social context of an infant allows us to understand how government, communities, and family structure can impact aspects of early development. A new parent who has the resources to be with their newborn will have greater opportunities to bond than a parent who needs to begin work soon after the birth of their child. One of us remembers meeting an expectant mother in a childbirth class. This mother worked at a gas station convenience store and was thinking she could take at most 2 weeks off when she gave birth before returning to work. The mother was saying that breastfeeding would be impossible with her schedule. As professors, we recognize that we all had the privilege of good maternity leave, time to bond with our newborns, and the ability to breastfeed as long as we wished. These differences in the resources available to new mothers influence development. Mothers who are better supported feel less stress during this early period. Maternal stress can affect prenatal infant development (see Chapter 3). Although this example is about differences in the experiences of mothers in the United States, there are even bigger differences across cultures. For example, in Canada, most employed mothers can have up to a year of maternity and parental leave after the birth of a child. In France, mothers are *required* to take 8 weeks of leave following the birth of a child and may take up to 16 weeks of leave. India has a generous maternity leave policy, allowing 26 weeks of leave for new mothers; however, only a small fraction of working mothers are eligible.

Infants are also raised in families that differ in many ways. They may have a single parent, two parents, or parents plus other caregivers, such as grandparents. Importantly, parents are not all the same. Not only do parents differ in their level of support and stress, they vary in their personalities, their experience with children, their expectations, and their confidence in their parenting. All of these factors will influence how they interact with their children. In addition, children may or may not be born into a family that already has other children. Older siblings influence development, especially aspects of social and emotional development. For example, having a sibling is related to demonstrating more prosocial emotions like sympathy (Harper et al., 2016). Importantly, it is not that children with older siblings develop *better* than children without older siblings; simply the context of development is different, which can influence aspects of the developmental trajectory.

The overall social context plays a role in development as well. The outer rings in the ecological theory are about factors such as politics, neighborhood, and cultural attitudes and practices. We discussed earlier in this chapter how politics and social policy can influence development. Local politics may determine how much funding is spent on schooling and early childhood education versus policing. Neighbors vary in terms of how much social support they provide one another. These issues became quite clear during the global pandemic of 2020. During the winter and spring of that year, COVID-19 infections rose across the world. The experience young children had in this situation varied as a function of local politics, neighborhood, and region of the world. While Spain did not allow children outside for months, U.S. states allowed outdoor activities. Within countries, children's experiences varied as a function of poverty, race, and neighborhood. Privileged educated families who could easily work from home arranged "pods" where they could share childcare and provide support for each other. Poorer families who depended on delivery or factory jobs for their livelihood, struggled with school closing and the lack of dependable childcare. Not only did these differences yield differences in how stressful the pandemic was for families, but they also created differences in terms of how much children were exposed to illness, how much schooling children experienced, and other factors that no doubt influenced their development. What was striking was how different political and cultural systems created different environments for child development.

The outermost ring is the most distal influence, but it is nevertheless very important. This influence refers to cultural attitudes and ideals. Most of what we know about infant development derives from work on infants from Western cultures, specifically with only a subset of infants in those cultures (see Box 1.3). When work has been done comparing development across cultures, the differences sometimes have been striking. For example, researchers examined infant–parent relationships in the United States and Japan, using a tool that was developed in the United

States. This work suggested that Japanese infants were not as secure in their relationships with parents as were U.S. infants (Rothbaum et al., 2000). This conclusion is problematic, however, because the tool used emphasizes the infants' autonomy, independence, and exploration. These are Western values for children. Japanese culture has different goals for infants; secure infants are those who are connected to others. They value interdependence rather than independence. As a result of these different cultural values, the expectations for infants' behaviors are different and what looks like a "good" mother–child relationship is not the same. The point is that cultures vary in their expectations for infants and their goals for the period of infancy. We see these differences in parenting practices and how those parenting practices are related to when and how infants develop particular skills.

The major point is that understanding infant development should not be an attempt to identify when all infants reach milestones at the same time, at the same age, and in exactly the same way. Despite the fact that much of the research we discuss focuses on general patterns of behavior across groups of infants, all infants (and children) are unique in their development. One infant may crawl at the average age, another may crawl several weeks later, another may "crawl" within the typical milestone window but have a unique form to their crawling (always extending one leg and dragging it along). There is no one pattern of development that fits all infants, and many, many factors play a role in determining developmental trajectories. Throughout this book we will describe these differences when such work exists. Importantly, this is not a discussion of how some infants differ from some standard or "normal" developmental trajectory, but rather to understand how development is influenced by the different environmental systems in which children live. We will revisit these ideas again in the final chapter.

Check Your Learning

1. What does it mean to focus on the *whole child* when thinking about development?

2. Name two ways that cultural differences might influence infant development.

3. What is the ecological systems theory?

SUMMARY

This chapter presented an introduction to this textbook, previewing many of the important themes and ideas that will reemerge throughout the book. As you read the chapters, think about qualitative and quantitative change. Consider whether researchers are emphasizing nature or nurture in their explanations. Carefully examine the research designs used and what conclusions researchers draw from those designs. As you read about studies, think about the measures used and the valid conclusions from those measures. Finally, consider development in the context of the whole child, recognizing who was studied in the research discussed; what role culture, politics, and society might have in that development; and what changes might need to be made for research findings in this area to be more broadly applicable to infants around the world.

KEY TERMS

age-held-constant design

cohort-sequential design

correlational design

critical periods

cross-cultural approach

cross-sectional design

developmental cascades

dynamic systems theory

ecological systems theory

experimental design

infancy

innate

longitudinal design

microgenetic design

nature

nurture

psychological construct

qualitative change

quantitative change

quasi-experimental design

valid measure

whole child

REVIEW QUESTIONS

1. What are the issues that studying development in infancy gives insights into?

2. How can studying infant development help policy makers argue for programs for supporting families with children under 5 years? What are some examples of infant development informing policies?

3. Describe the designs used to study development. What are the advantages and disadvantages of each? What are the factors that researchers must consider when deciding which design to use to study development?

4. What infant behaviors and physiological responses are used to study infant development? Why are these behaviors and responses used, and how are they limited?

5. What are the different levels of context that are acting on infant development?

CRITICAL THINKING QUESTIONS

1. Your friend is about to have a baby and wants her baby to love food the way she and her partner do. She has heard that food preferences might be genetic but also that what babies eat is important. Given what you know about how nature and nurture can shape development, what do you tell her? Do you think food preferences might reflect an interactive or additive influence of nature and nurture? Why?

2. Why is it important for policy makers and parents to know about infant development when making decisions about how infants should be treated? Can you think of examples of recent decisions made by policy makers or politicians that were (or should have been) informed by research with infants?

3. You want to study how infants learn new words during the first 2 years. Which methodological design would you choose to study this aspect of development, and why? What would be its advantages? And what would be its disadvantages?

4. Consider the BEIP study done with Romanian orphans. What aspects of this study were a *correlation*? What aspects were an *experiment*?

5. Why are studies of development often *quasi-experiments*?

6. What is the difference between a *measure* and a *construct*? Choose one example from Table 1.5 to illustrate this difference.

7. Use experiences from your own life to explain how development doesn't happen in a vacuum. Consider a specific developmental milestone (e.g., learning to read, learning to talk, learning to walk). What aspects of the context shaped this development?

2 BIOLOGICAL AND BRAIN DEVELOPMENT

When Tesalia was born full-term, at nearly 40 weeks, she weighed only 5 pounds (lbs.), 15 ½ ounces (oz.), and her head circumference was only 33 cm. She was in the 10th percentile of all infants. Doctors and parents worry when a baby has a small head like Tesalia did because it might mean that there could be problems with brain development. However, over her infancy and early childhood, Tesalia's head continued to grow, alleviating any concern that she had suffered a problem with the development of her brain before birth.

In fact, as she got older, Tesalia stayed small compared to her peers—she was petite throughout infancy and childhood. Why was she relatively small? Recall when we discussed Martha in Chapter 1, we talked about the interaction between *genes* and *environment* in determining Martha's height. Just as Martha had genes to be tall, Tesalia has genes to be on the petite side. Both of her grandmothers are 5'3" or shorter, and even her mother is average height at 5'4." Thus, we think that Tesalia is relatively small because, at least in part, she has the genes for being relatively small.

This chapter is about these aspects of development—the biological foundations of development in infancy and the early development of the nervous system. We will review the topics of genetics and outline the types of cells in the brain, their function, and how they give rise to the hemispheres. These topics are crucial for understanding the biological foundations of development in infancy. And they are also topics that parents and pediatricians care a lot about.

After reading this chapter, you will be able to:

1. *Define* heredity, genotype, phenotype, genes, DNA, chromosomes, alleles, and autosomes, and explain how each of these relates to the others.

2. *Distinguish* among gene–environment correlations, gene–environment interactions, and epigenetics.

3. *Label* the function and parts of a neuron and *explain* the difference between experience-expectant and experience-dependent plasticity using an example of each to highlight the difference.

THE "NATURE" IN THE NATURE–NURTURE QUESTION

Of the six infants we are following, there are three pairs of siblings: Alison and Carter, Diego and Tesalia, and Edwin and Charlie. Each sibling pair shares a family resemblance, and they are more similar in appearance to each other than to the other four children, to whom they are unrelated.

For example, Diego and Tesalia both have curly hair that coils into ringlets, whereas the other four have fairly straight hair. Diego and Tesalia's complexions also hint at their Central American heritage, whereas Alison and Carter's complexions hint at their northern European heritage. At the same time, there are striking differences within the sibling pairs. Diego's midnight hair is so black, it shines, a contrast to Tesalia's chestnut brown hair, which reflects hues of red. Charlie is blonde while his brother Edwin has brown hair. Alison and Carter have greater similarity in their hair color, but as newborns, Carter came into the world with red hair and Alison with dark brown, and by their first birthdays shifted to strawberry blonde for Carter and blonde for Alison. Edwin and Charlie both have brown eyes, but the other sibling pairs differ in eye color; Alison and Diego have brown eyes, but each of their siblings, Carter and Tesalia, has blue-gray eyes.

The sibling pairs also share family resemblances in their *behavior*. Alison and Carter have similar senses of humor, and both can be a bit cautious. Both Edwin and Charlie love to dance. Tesalia and Diego are musical. But the sibling pairs also differ. Alison is more social, and Carter would definitely prefer to be alone. Charlie and Tesalia are highly energetic and adventurous (sometimes to the point of seeming reckless), whereas their siblings Edwin and Diego are calm and cautious. It took Diego and Edwin weeks and weeks of experience in a swimming pool to dip their faces in the water. At 11 months, Tesalia and Charlie dove right in, literally. As infants, Charlie, Diego, and Alison were quick with smiles toward *everyone*, even strangers, whereas their siblings, Edwin, Tesalia, and Carter reserved their most radiant smiles for their caregivers (much to their parents' delight).

What accounts for the physical and behavioral differences (and similarities) of our six infants? Our goal in this section is to provide a basic understanding of **heredity**, or the transmission of genetic information across generations, and how that genetic information translates to differences in physical characteristics and behavior.

How Genes Influence Development

You may already know that **genotype** refers to the unique genetic makeup of an individual (i.e., their individual collection of genes). **Phenotype** refers to the observable characteristics, or traits, of an individual, and includes any characteristic from physical ones (e.g., freckles, dimples, height) to psychological ones (e.g., personality, intelligence). Our phenotype is the expression of our genotype. We inherit our genotype, but our phenotype reflects both our particular combination of genes *and* our environment (Table 2.1). The interplay between genes and environments differs not only across genes but also across environments, adding many layers of

TABLE 2.1 ■ Genotype vs. Phenotype		
	Definition	**How It Is Determined**
Genotype	All of a person's genes	The genes inherited from the biological parents
Phenotype	A person's traits, or observable characteristics	The particular combination of the genes, as influenced by the environment

complexity to the story of how genes and environments contribute to development. Before we tackle this complex interaction, we will first review basic information about genes, their structure, and their expression.

What Are Our Genetics?

Although this is not a biology or a genetics textbook, it is important to review some key points about the biology of genetics to appreciate how genes and environments interact. As a starting point, we need to understand the relation between **DNA**, **chromosomes**, and **genes**. Our bodies contain trillions of cells, which vary in structure and function. Within the nucleus of each cell is an impressively long molecule, known as deoxyribonucleic acid (DNA). DNA is tightly coiled around proteins, and this is what makes up our chromosomes. Our genes are segments of DNA, and each gene has a unique address on a chromosome (Figure 2.1).

The autosomes are 22 pairs of chromosomes. For these pairs, a gene on one chromosome in a pair will have the same gene on the other chromosome in that pair (Figure 2.2). The final pair of chromosomes are the sex chromosomes, the X and Y in humans. The sex chromosomes differ from each other in size (the X chromosome is much larger than the Y) *and* in the number and

---

FIGURE 2.1 ■ Chromosome

The relationship between a cell, a cell nucleus, chromosomes, DNA, and a gene.

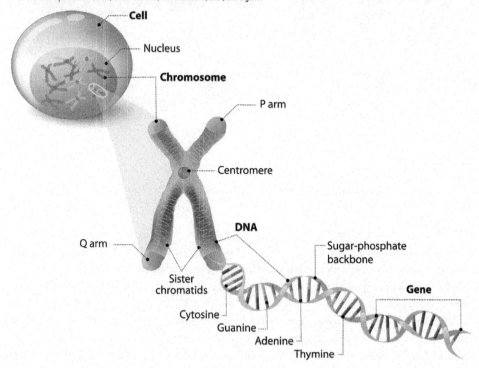

Source: iStock/ttsz

FIGURE 2.2 ■ Karyotype

This is a karyotype, an illustration of chromosomes, arranged in their pairs and by chromosome number.

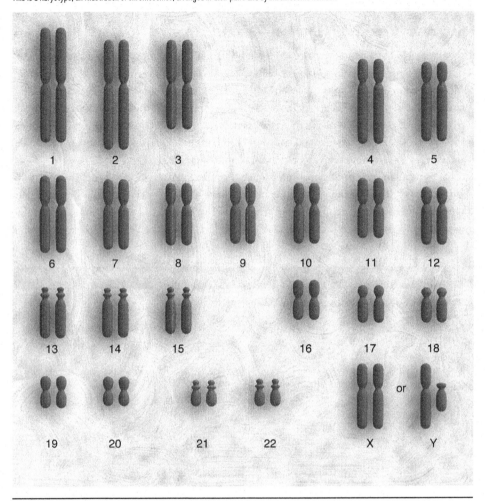

Source: iStock/somersault18:24

type of genes that each carries. So, unlike the other pairs of genes, each gene in the X chromosome does not necessarily have a pair on the Y chromosome. As we will see in Chapter 3, this fact about the sex chromosomes means that some traits are inherited differently for individuals with two X chromosomes (genetically female) versus individuals with an X and a Y chromosome (genetically male).

You may wonder where these 23 pairs of chromosomes come from. Most cells in our bodies have 23 pairs of chromosomes, summing to a total of 46 chromosomes. However, the sex cells in our bodies, known as the gametes (the egg in females and the sperm in males), have only one chromosome from each of the 23 pairs (one chromosome from pair 1, one from pair 2, and so on). Thus, these cells have half the number of chromosomes that other cells have. Importantly, what these cells contain is one chromosome of each *pair*. So, instead of having two chromosomes at location 1, two at location 2 and so on, these cells have just one chromosome at each location. When the egg and sperm combine at conception (see Chapter 3), the chromosomes at each location become a pair. The result is a *zygote,* a single cell that divides and develops into a new human, with 23 pairs of chromosomes. Each pair contains one chromosome from the egg (i.e., the female parent) and one chromosome from the sperm (i.e., the male parent). Thus, each of our cells has chromosomes from each parent.

Patterns of Inheritance

This combining of the chromosomes (and genes) of the two parents is what determines the individual's genetic *inheritance.* You may have noticed that some children look more like one parent than the other (although family resemblance can shift as children age). For example, Edwin is nearly a miniature version of his mother (see photo). Other children are a blend of both

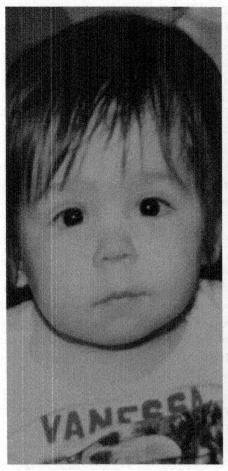 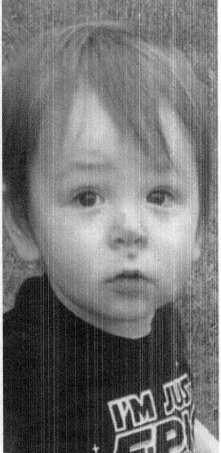

Edwin's mother, age 1 and Edwin, age 1.

parents. For example, Carter has blonde hair and blue-gray eyes, like his father, but his eye and face shape are more like his mother. What determines how a parent transmits their traits (e.g., extroversion, love of math, hair or eye color) to a child? Amazingly, most humans share the same DNA, with individuals differing by only about 0.1%! How can such a tiny amount of DNA explain the uniqueness of an individual?

Children's characteristics reflect, in part, the fact that although the two genes in each pair relate to the same characteristic (e.g., eye color, shyness), they may be different *forms* of those genes, or different **alleles**. The types of alleles that make up the pair of genes determines the patterns of inheritance and the traits expressed in an individual's phenotype. When both parents contribute the same allele of a particular gene, then the child is **homozygous** for that gene and will express the trait associated with that allele. For example, one of the authors and her spouse (and you would know which one immediately from our photos) both have curly hair. Each of their children inherited the same allele from each parent for hair shape, and as a result, both children have curly hair. With homozygous genes, it doesn't matter if the allele of the gene inherited from each parent is dominant or recessive (a pattern of inheritance that we describe in the next paragraph); either way, the child will express that allele.

However, when each parent contributes a different allele for a particular gene, the child is **heterozygous** for the gene. In this case, how the alleles interact to express a trait in the phenotype can follow several distinct patterns of inheritance (Table 2.2). Specifically, when a child is heterozygous for a trait, how the trait is expressed depends on the *dominance* of the allele. When a child has two different alleles for a gene, and only one of the two alleles is expressed in their phenotype, the expressed allele is considered **dominant** and the non-expressed allele is considered **recessive**. Note that when an individual has a dominant trait in their phenotype, they could have one allele that is dominant and one that is recessive, or they could have two dominant alleles (i.e., is homozygous for the dominant allele). The point is that two individuals may display the same phenotype even though they have different genotypes. If an individual has a recessive trait in their phenotype, they must have two copies of the recessive allele (one from each parent).

Several traits follow the dominant–recessive pattern of inheritance. Dimples, freckles, cleft chin, widow's peak, dark hair color, and brown eyes reflect alleles of genes that are dominant. To express these traits requires inheriting the allele from just one parent. To express the alternate trait (i.e., no dimples, no freckles, no cleft chin, blonde hair, and blue-gray eyes) requires inheriting the recessive allele from both parents. Interestingly, individuals who show a dominant trait in their phenotype could be (a) homozygous with two copies of the dominant allele, and therefore can only pass on the dominant allele to their offspring, or (b) heterozygous with one dominant and one recessive trait. In this second case, the individual is said to be a carrier of the recessive allele and can pass it to their offspring.

We can see this pattern of inheritance in our own children. For example, all three authors of this book have brown eyes, but among us only one spouse also has brown eyes. When the parents with brown eyes had their first child, it was no surprise that their son also had brown eyes. After all, the alleles that contribute to brown eye color are dominant. What *was* surprising was that their second child had blue-gray eyes. This could only happen because both parents were heterozygous and carriers of the recessive alleles that code for blue eye color. Both Alison

TABLE 2.2 ■ Patterns of Inheritance			
Inheritance Pattern	**Description**	**Notes**	**Example(s)**
Autosomal Dominant	One allele is seen in the phenotype, the other is silent. The "seen" allele is dominant.	Only one allele is needed to express the trait in the phenotype. A child who is homozygous (i.e., has two dominant alleles) will have the same phenotype as a child who is heterozygous (i.e., has only one copy of the dominant allele).	Huntington's disease Widow's peak Freckles Right handedness Dimples
Autosomal Recessive	Two "silent" alleles are needed to express this phenotype.	Both parents must pass the recessive allele to their child to express the trait. Parents who are heterozygous are carriers of the recessive allele.	Sickle-cell anemia Cystic fibrosis Left handedness Attached earlobes
Codominance	Two distinct dominant alleles are expressed.	Phenotype of child differs from either parent.	Blood type AB Blood cell shape
Incomplete Dominance	A blend of two alleles is expressed.	Phenotype of child differs from either parent.	Hair color or shape

and Carter have freckles, as do both of their parents. Because freckles are the dominant trait, we don't know if the parents have one or two alleles for freckles. Alison and Carter may have one or two dominant alleles. The point is that when a dominant trait is expressed, we can't know if the recessive gene is "hidden" in the genotype.

The story is made more complicated by the fact that there are other types of inheritance patterns. When there is codominance between the alleles, one dominant allele cannot silence the expression of the other allele. As a result, the phenotype expresses *both* alleles. This can happen when both alleles are dominant. One example is AB blood type. The alleles for the A and B blood types are both dominant. So, for example, if a child inherits the recessive allele for blood type O from one parent and a dominant allele for blood type A or B from the other parent, the offspring's blood type will be A or B, respectively. But, if the infant inherits the allele for the A blood type from one parent and the allele for the B blood type from the other parent, the infant's phenotype will express both alleles, displaying AB blood type.

In another inheritance pattern, called incomplete dominance, we don't see a single dominant trait (suppressing the recessive trait), but the phenotype is a *blend* of the alleles. For example, Edwin's brown hair is a blend of his father's blonde hair and his mother's dark hair. Hair shape can also display incomplete dominance. An infant can have wavy hair because they express a blend of the straight hair of one parent and the curly hair of the other parent. In both codominant and incomplete dominance patterns, the phenotype of the infant is different than the phenotype of either parent, just like the AB blood type is distinct from type A or type B blood, and wavy hair is a distinct hair shape than either curly or straight hair. In summary, how two distinct versions of an allele are expressed in a phenotype varies with the relation between the alleles of a gene.

Regardless of the particular pattern of inheritance observed, we can see how the alleles from each parent work *together* to determine the phenotype. This is nicely illustrated by single-gene traits—or traits that are determined by only one gene (or pair of genes). Free-hanging versus attached earlobes, the presence or absence of a widow's peak in the hairline, having or lacking freckles, blood type, as well as genetic disorders, like Huntington's disease, sickle-cell anemia, and Tay-Sachs disease are traits determined by a single gene. (We will talk more about these genetic disorders in Chapter 3.)

The story is much more complicated because the vast majority of human traits, including height, weight, skin and hair pigmentation, are polygenic, or influenced by many genes. As you may now guess, eye color is a polygenic trait, believed to be influenced by as many as 16 distinct genes, although there are 2 main genes associated with eye color in humans (located on chromosome 15, in case you were wondering). Behavioral traits, such as intelligence or aggression, and those linked to diseases, such as type 2 diabetes, are also polygenic. The involvement of many genes to express a trait makes it much harder to see the effects of heterozygous and homozygous pairs of alleles; you may have the dominant allele for one gene contributing to a trait, but two recessive alleles for a second gene contributing to that trait at the same time. As you can see, the story of how genes interact with each other can be complicated.

Check Your Learning

1. Define DNA, genes, alleles, and chromosomes. What is the relation among each of these?

2. What is the difference between genotype and phenotype?

3. List the patterns of inheritance for single-trait genes on autosomal chromosomes. Describe the difference among these inheritance patterns.

UNDERSTANDING HOW GENES INFLUENCE DEVELOPMENT

As we discussed in Chapter 1, understanding the relative roles of nature and nurture in human characteristics has been debated for centuries. How can we tell how much of who we are is due to our genes and how much is due to our environment? We can't just look at everyone's genes and link their genes to specific characteristics. The human genome project took many years just to describe human genes. There are methods, such as genome-wide association studies (GWAS), used to identify the parts of genes associated with a trait. In GWAS, researchers scan the genomes of individuals within a population to identify specific single-nucleotide polymorphisms (SNPs), or a single change in a DNA base, that is associated with a particular trait. The goal is to link variations in SNPs with particular phenotypes, with a focus on linking SNPs to the occurrence of particular diseases. However, it will take decades of additional research to know how certain genes map onto particular traits, and we will probably never know the whole story. In this section we will discuss how researchers understand the role of genes in development using other methods.

Behavioral Genetics and the Study of the Heritability of Traits

The branch of science called **behavioral genetics** is the study of how an individual's genetic makeup and environment affect behavior. Instead of trying to map specific genes to specific features, behavioral geneticists compare individuals who share different genes and/or environments and observe the ways in which those individuals are similar and different. This is particularly challenging with humans because most of our traits are polygenic and because our environments are complex and difficult to control or quantify. To deal with these issues, many behavioral geneticists study laboratory mice. Mice are ideal research subjects because they can be bred to be genetically identical to each other and then scientists can randomly assign them to be raised in highly controlled environments. Of course, this same approach isn't feasible, or ethical, in humans. We can't clone humans and then randomly assign them to distinct environments to study genetic and environmental contributions in the expression of a trait. Instead, to understand the influence of genes on human behavior, the field of behavioral genetics has used twin and adoption studies to evaluate the relative contributions of genetics and environments in the expression of a specific trait (Table 2.3). Both methods are examples of quasi-experiments, a type of natural experiment in which researchers take advantage of naturally occurring conditions. As we discussed in Chapter 1, in these experiments the "manipulation" is not under the experimenter's control; experimenters can't decide who will be an identical twin or randomly select some children to be adopted. This also means that we can't draw causal conclusions (because the studies are essentially correlational). But, these methods have been important for understanding the relative roles of genes and environment in the development of traits and behaviors.

Twin Studies

Scientists interested in the effects of genes and environment have studied the similarity of traits in pairs of monozygotic and dizygotic twins. Monozygotic twins, or identical twins, result when a single zygote (i.e., a fertilized human egg) divides in two separate zygotes during the first days of a pregnancy. The spontaneous division results in two infants who have all the same genes. Because the identical twins originated from a single fertilized egg, each twin has the same 23 pairs of chromosomes. Dizygotic twins, or fraternal twins, are the result of two eggs released at ovulation and each egg fertilized by a different sperm. Each egg and each sperm will have a unique set of chromosomes because of the random assortment of chromosomes into a particular egg or sperm. Thus, these two fertilized eggs will have distinct genetic information from each parent and, on average, share about half of their genes (just as any set of siblings with the same parents).

TABLE 2.3 ■ Methods for Studying Heritability		
Method	**Description**	**Logic**
Twin studies	Compare the similarities of phenotypes within pairs of monozygotic and dizygotic twins	If traits (phenotypes) are highly heritable, monozygotic twins will be more similar on that trait than will dizygotic twins.
Adoption studies	Compare the similarities of phenotypes between children and their biological parents and between children and their adoptive parents.	If traits (phenotypes) are highly heritable, children will be more similar to their biological parents than to their adoptive parents.
Twin-adoption studies	Compare the similarities of phenotypes between twins who were adopted into different households.	If traits (phenotypes) are highly heritable, identical twins will be very similar even if they have been raised in different households.

Behavioral geneticists reason that if monozygotic twins are more similar to each other on a trait than dizygotic twins, this greater similarity is the result of their greater overlap in genes. These conclusions are drawn from studies in which the children are *reared together*. They live with both their biological parents and their twin (as well as any other siblings they have in common). Thus, it is assumed that the two children in a twin set share the same environment. Both monozygotic and dizygotic twins share a womb, are born into a family at the same time, and are more likely to experience major life events (moving, birth of a sibling, poverty) at the same age. As a result, the fact that identical twins are more similar to each other (e.g., they are more likely to have the same eye color, hair color, and build) than fraternal twins is thought to reflect the fact that they share more genes.

Of course, even though dizygotic twins' environments are more similar than the environments of siblings born at different times, monozygotic twins have even more similar environments. Dizygotic twins never share a placenta, whereas monozygotic twins may or may not share a placenta. Dizygotic twins can be the same sex or different sexes, whereas monozygotic twins are always the same sex. And the fact that identical twins are physically identical might mean they are treated more similarly than fraternal twins. Thus, the similarities between identical twins may reflect both similarities in their genes and their environments.

Consider two sets of famous twins, Ashley and Mary-Kate Olsen, who are fraternal twins, and Cole and Dylan Sprouse, who are identical twins (see photos). Despite being fraternal twins, as infants, Ashley and Mary-Kate shared the role of a single character, Michelle Tanner, on the TV sitcom *Full House*. As is clear from the next photo, they looked very similar, despite being dizygotic twins. Cole and Dylan Sprouse, on the other hand, are identical twins, who began to differ in appearance as adolescents. Cole Sprouse is taller and leaner than his brother, who is stockier and has a fuller face. The brothers also have different beauty marks. Cole has

IDENTICAL TWINS: Monozygotic or identical twins share all of their genes and are always the same sex.

iStock/kali9

FRATERNAL TWINS: Dizygotic or fraternal twins share on average of only about half of their genes and can be the same sex or different sexes.

iStock/kate_sept2004

THE OLSEN TWINS: Dizygotic twins, Ashley and Mary-Kate Olsen.

David Shankbone/Flickr

one on his chin while his brother sports his beauty mark over his lip. Even though these brothers share 100% of their genes, their appearance is not "identical."

These two examples show that the same genes can vary in how they are expressed. No one trait is dictated 100% by genes—the differences between Cole and Dylan show that some amount of environmental influence must have influenced their physical appearance traits. The similarities between Ashley and Mary-Kate Olsen further suggest that similar environments might make individuals more similar to each other.

Adoption Studies

Adoption studies are a second type of study used to understand the influence of genes and environment on the developing child. These studies compare infants adopted at birth into a biologically unrelated family to their biological and adoptive relatives. When an adopted infant is more similar to their biological than to their adoptive relatives, it points to a stronger influence of genes than environment. The adopted infant shares a genetic, but not an environmental, link to their biological relatives. When adoptive children are more similar to their adoptive than their biological relatives, the expression of the trait is argued to reflect stronger environmental than genetic influence because these children share their environments but not their genes with their adoptive families.

THE SPROUSE TWINS: Monozygotic twins, Cole and Dylan Sprouse.

Piper's Picks® TV, CC BY 2.5 <https://creativecommons.org/licenses/by/2.5>, via Wikimedia Commons

However, children only share 50% of their genes with each biological parent. So, we don't expect them to be exactly the same as their parents. An even stronger test is to compare individuals who have the same genes but are raised in different environments. In a variant of the adoption method, researchers study monozygotic twins who were separated at birth and adopted into distinct families. A clear advantage of this design is the ability to assess the expression of a trait across two genetically identical individuals (i.e., the monozygotic twins) raised in distinct environments (i.e., different adoptive families). There are some famous examples, such as the triplets in the movie *Three Identical Strangers*. Often these comparisons reveal eerie similarities, like twins who prefer the same brand of cigarettes or who married women with the same first name. A challenge with these studies, however, is that adoption agencies often place infants with families that are similar to the birth family in many ways, and so identical twins adopted into different families may actually have similar environments despite being raised with different families. The practice of adopting identical twins into distinct homes has declined in favor of raising the twins together in the same family.

What Have Twin and Adoption Studies Told Us?

Twin and adoption studies have been used for decades to provide insight into how much of the variation in traits and abilities is due to genes. Both types of studies have identified a genetic link to many physical and psychological traits, including psychological disorders and medical conditions (Plomin et al., 2016). Recently, researchers have used this approach to study very specific behaviors. John Constantino and colleagues (2017), for example, compared monozygotic and dizygotic twin infants' looking at the eyes and mouths of human faces (an indicator of social engagement). They observed that monozygotic twins were more similar to each other in their interest in these features than were dizygotic twins. Thus, this early aspect of social engagement seems to be influenced by genes.

Camille Cioffi and her colleagues (2020) studied a large cohort of infants adopted at birth in open adoptions. The families were from across the United States and, unlike many studies, the group of children was racially and ethnically diverse. Cioffi and colleagues measured children's ability to voluntarily regulate their attention, a skill known as inhibitory control. They also measured inhibitory control in their biological parents. Infants whose biological parents were low on inhibitory control were at risk for also being low on inhibitory control. From this, you might conclude that inhibitory control is determined by one's genes. But it turned out that the environment also mattered. Infants who were biologically at high risk for low inhibitory control had better inhibitory control in childhood if they had warm adoptive mothers. Thus, this adoption study shows how one trait, inhibitory control, is influenced by *both* genes and the environment.

BOX 2.1—INFANCY IN REAL LIFE: THE HANSEL AND BIJANI TWINS

There is no better example of the impact of genes and the environment on development than to look at a very special type of twins called conjoined twins. Conjoined twins start out just like typical monozygotic twins, where a single fertilized human egg begins to divide in two during the first days of a pregnancy. However, conjoined twins develop when the egg doesn't fully separate into two individuals, and the two remain physically connected, most often at the chest, abdomen, or pelvis; sometimes they even share one or more internal organs. Like monozygotic twins, because the conjoined twins originated from a single fertilized egg, each twin has the same 23 pairs of chromosomes. But in this case, they also share certain parts of their bodies, or in essence, their physical and social environments.

Conjoined twins are rare, and sadly, many don't survive pregnancy or die shortly after birth. However, advances in medical technology have improved their survival rates, and sometimes surgical interventions are possible to separate the twins physically so that they can live independent lives. The ability to separate conjoined twins depends on whether they share organs and which organs they share.

Perhaps the best known pair of conjoined twins in the mainstream media are Abby and Brittney Hensel. Abby and Brittney were born in 1990, and each has a separate head, heart, lungs, spine, stomach, and spinal cord, but they share two arms, legs, large intestine, bladder, and reproductive organs. Given that they share a body, and most importantly, a single pair of arms and legs, they have to coordinate everything they do. In fact, each twin manages only one side of their body, making all movements an amazing feat of team work. In fact, they can walk, run, swim, play basketball, and even drive a car.

What is most interesting about the Hensel twins is not that they share their genes but that they literally share an environment—they share a family, a home, and a *body*. But, even with a shared "environment," Brittney and Abby are different. They have a seamstress to make clothes for their unique body, each outfit containing separate necklines to emphasize their individuality. One twin would prefer to live in a city, while the other would opt for the calmness of a suburb. Although they both majored in education in college, they each had a different focus. And while they sometimes share meals out of pure convenience, they like different foods (despite sharing a means by which to digest those foods), and often prepare themselves different meals of foods that they each like.

These differences are not unique to this set of conjoined twins. Ladan and Laleh Bijani were conjoined twin sisters who opted for surgical separation despite the high risk of the procedure. The sisters wished to pursue different careers. Ladan wanted to be a lawyer, but Laleh wished to pursue journalism. The sisters also differed in their preference for where to live and had distinct hobbies. One preferred to play computer games, while her sister preferred computer programming. Similar to Brittany and Abby, one sister, Ladan, described herself as more outgoing and talkative while her sister, Laleh, claimed to be quieter and more introverted. Thus, although twins can share genes and are often assumed to share an environment, even twins that literally share a body experience the world in different ways, and as a result, develop differently. The two examples of conjoined twins highlight that genes are not destiny, but instead, that experiences shape each individual, making them unique.

Heritability

Heritability is a statistical measure, referred to as h^2. It is an estimate of the proportion of the differences in the expression of a trait *in a population or group* that is due to genetic differences among those individuals. It tells you the heritability of a trait given the variability in the environment of that population or group. Heritability is a ratio (i.e., fraction), whose value ranges from 0 to 1. It is calculated by dividing the variability in the genotypes of the individuals in a population by the variability in the phenotype (i.e., the trait). Heritability estimates closer to one mean that most of the differences in the phenotype in the population come from genetic differences. Heritability estimates closer to zero mean that the environment accounts for most of the differences in the phenotype of a population.

No known trait has a heritability estimate of 1 (i.e., all the variability that trait is due to genes) or 0 (i.e., all the variability in that trait is due to the environment). Rather, human traits tend to have heritability estimates of .30 to .60, indicating that genes account for only some of the variance in those traits. In other words, 30% to 60% of the variations of a trait within a population are genetic. The rest of the variation is due to environment and can be determined by subtracting the heritability estimate from 1. So, if most human behaviors have a heritability estimate of .30 to .60, then 70% to 40% of the differences in phenotype are attributed to the environment.

What isn't obvious is how heritability estimates are influenced by variation in both the genes and the environment. Basically, if there isn't much variability in one factor, the other factor will have a bigger influence on differences between people. Consider again Cole and Dylan Sprouse. Clearly, the similarity between them is the result of their genes. But, as they got older, they became more different from one another. This presumably reflects the fact that the environment and their experiences shaped their development. If traits were completely determined by genes, they would remain identical throughout their lives.

An extreme example is illustrated by the case of the mixed up brothers of Bogotá (Dominus, 2015). This is the remarkable story of four young men who were raised as two sets of fraternal twins. However, at birth, they were two sets of identical twins. As the result of a series of hospital mix-ups, two families went home with one twin from each set, and assumed that their twins were fraternal, not identical. The four young men are pictured in following photo. It is not hard to tell which brothers are actually identical twins. Despite being raised in different families, in different environments (urban vs. rural), and with different opportunities, the men who share 100% of their genes look quite a lot alike. However, the two men in each set of identical twins look different from each other. They differ in face shapes, overall size, and other aspects of their physical appearance that we assume are due to genes. Because they share 100% of their genes, these differences are 100% due to differences in experience or environment (nutrition, physical activity, disease, and so on).

Heritability estimates refer to the contribution of genes to the expression of a trait within a particular population of individuals living in a particular environment at a particular time. The heritability estimate of a trait is an average for that population given the amount of variation in the environment of that population. The more similar the environment is, the more that variation in traits will be due to genes. As illustrated by the brothers of Bogotá, when there is little variation in genes, differences in traits will be due to variation in the environment; the two men with the same genes were different from each other because of differences in their environment. When a heritability estimate is calculated, it is based on a specific population (with a particular amount of environmental variation). Therefore, the heritability estimate for *that same trait* will differ for a different population, especially if the population has greater variability in the phenotype or environment. For this reason, when interpreting a heritability estimate, consider who is in that population, how similar the individuals in the population are to each other, and the similarity of their environments. If the individuals live in a fairly uniform environment, then heritability estimates will tend to be higher. If instead the individuals come from highly varied or challenging environments, heritability estimates will be lower.

We can see this better by considering some examples. Take height. Physical height is highly heritable, with a heritability estimate as high as .90 in some studies (Macgregor et al., 2006; Perola et al., 2007). This isn't surprising. Tall parents tend to have tall children and shorter parents tend to have shorter children. Remember Tesalia? Once we considered the size of her grandmothers, her petite stature didn't seem so surprising. But the environment influences the expression of height (Dubois et al., 2012; Jelenkovic et al., 2016). Heritability of height is higher in highly resourced countries, where access to food is fairly uniform across the population, than it is for populations in other parts of the world, particularly developing countries in which access to food is not as uniform across the population (Hur et al., 2008; Jelenkovic et al., 2016).

Just like for physical traits, heritability estimates for behavioral traits also differ in different groups of people. For example, heritability estimates for intelligence differ drastically across distinct populations (Gottschling et al., 2019; Nisbett et al., 2012; Scarr-Salapatek, 1971). Intelligence reflects both our genes and our environment, so it is no surprise that its heritability estimate shifts with the environment of a population. For a population that is affluent, with access to resources and enriched environments, the heritability estimate of intelligence is on the higher end, around .72. For such populations the environment supports and facilitates

BROTHERS OF BOGOTÁ: William Cañas Velasco, Wilber Cañas Velasco, Jorge Enrique Bernal Castro, Carlos Alberto Bernal Castro, identical twins who were double switched at birth.

Courtesy of Dr. Nancy L. Segal

intellectual development, and differences between individuals reflect genes. In contrast, for populations raised in impoverished environments, such as children living in poverty, heritability estimates for intelligence are close to zero (Turkheimer et al., 2003). In those environments, differences in access to food, exposure to stress, the quality of schooling, and so on, mean that children are raised in environments that differentially support their intellectual development. In other words, in challenging environments, environmental and not genetic differences account for differences in intelligence among the individuals in the population.

How Do Genes and the Environment Interact?

In the previous section we described how traits can reflect both nature and nurture, but we haven't talked much about how genes and the environment actually interact to shape development. In this section, we will talk about several different ways that genes and the environment work together to shape development.

Gene–Environment Correlations

One way genes and the environment can together shape development is how they are *correlated* (Table 2.4). At first **gene–environment correlations** might seem hard to understand—genes are part of your biology and the environment is your home, your culture, and your society. How can they be correlated? However, the environment is not wholly independent of your genes. The people who gave you your genes, your parents, are also the people who decide your environment, particularly at young ages. If you have a genetic predisposition to dislike spicy and bitter foods, your parents likely share that dislike, and so they are not going to offer you spicy and bitter foods. Alison and Carter's mother loves tomatoes, but their father does not. During their childhood, fresh tomatoes rarely were served, and Alison and Carter dislike tomatoes. They likely inherited something from their father that caused them to dislike tomatoes, but because they were rarely offered tomatoes, they did not have the opportunity to develop a liking for tomatoes. The point is that some aspects of your environment are not completely random with respect to your genes. Rather, genes and environment can be correlated with each other. Genes not only create differences in individuals but also may be responsible for different environments, as in the case of disliking tomatoes and being raised in a tomato-reduced environment. This is an example of a *passive gene–environment correlation*. In such cases, the parents transmit both the genes and the environment, and as a result, the environment may be well suited to promote the expression of a particular trait. Another

TABLE 2.4 ■ Gene-Environment Correlations

	Description	Mechanism	Examples
Passive gene–environment correlations	Characteristics of the parent and child are similar; as a result, the parent's preferences support the child's genetic traits.	The (biological) parent provides both the genes that the child inherits and the home environment.	Children who are high on effortful control, a type of self-regulation, have parents who also are high on effortful control. At the same time, these parents provide structured home environments that are low on chaos and conducive to building effortful control (Lemery-Chalfant et al., 2013).
Evocative gene–environment correlations	Characteristics of the child elicit, or evoke, environments that support genetic traits.	Genetically determined traits are reinforced by how others respond to the child.	Children at genetic risk for aggressive behaviors are more likely to have peers respond aggressively to them, even when the peers are unfamiliar and randomly paired (DiLalla, 2002).
Active gene–environment correlations	The child seeks out environments or experiences that support genetic traits, a process called "niche picking."	As children become older, they select environments that match their traits.	Children who are extroverted seek out different social environments than those who are shy and withdrawn (Jaffee & Price, 2008)

example is parents who love to read. The parents not only give their child these bibliophile genes but also expose their children to experiences that foster an enjoyment of books and reading. Thus, the child's genotype is reinforced, supported, and enhanced by the environment created by the parents who almost certainly share this same genotype.

Other gene–environment correlations are *evocative*. In these cases, a child's trait elicits a nonrandom response or environment. Imagine seeing an infant who breaks into a smile when your eyes happen to meet. Try not smiling back! It is hard to resist breaking into your own smile when confronted with such a happy face. A child who is genetically predisposed to smile more—perhaps a temperamentally easy child (who we'll talk more about in Chapter 10)—will evoke more positive interactions from a parent and other people than a child who is less prone to smile. In contrast, a child who is aggressive with a sibling or peer will elicit a very different response, one likely to include directives to cease the unwanted behavior (e.g., "no yelling"). In *evocative gene–environment correlations*, the child's genetic characteristics shape the responses of others, which influences the child's experiences.

Finally, *active gene–environment correlations* are those that result from the individual actively seeking particular experiences. A child who enjoys sports may seek activities that allow them to be active; a child who loves music may participate in the school musical or play in the marching band. When he was 3 years old, Itzhak Perlman heard a violin playing on the radio and begged his parents for a violin. Eventually, his parents relented and Itzhak began learning the instrument at age 4. Itzhak persisted in his passion for learning the violin and now is one of the best known classical violinists. His story is an example of genetic propensities that inspire an individual to seek particular experiences, even when those may not be present in their home environments.

Gene–Environment Interactions (G×E)

In many cases, the genes and the environment interact to determine development. One way to think about these **gene–environment interactions** (G×E) is that one's genes make one especially susceptible, vulnerable, or sensitive to specific environmental influences. For example, genetic differences cause some children to be more vulnerable to the effects of stress. Children with a higher genetic susceptibility to environmental experiences, sometimes called *orchid children*, thrive only when the conditions are optimal. They have difficulty adapting to stressful events (e.g., poverty, family discord, an illness), and their development is negatively shaped by those experiences. However, when the environment is supportive and reduces stress, these children thrive. Other children thrive regardless of stressors or traumas that they may experience; these children are sometimes called *dandelion children*. The botanical references allude to the distinction between nurturing an orchid so that it not only survives but blooms (a gardening feat that many novice plant lovers never achieve) and the dandelion, which is a weed that will sprout and duplicate at an alarming rate with no care and minimal growing conditions (and despite intense efforts to eradicate it). Akin to these plants, environmentally sensitive children are disproportionately more impacted by their contexts, whether positive or negative, than children who are less sensitive to their environment (Lionetti et al., 2018, 2019).

We can see how these G×E interactions shape development in a study by Grayzna Kochanska and her colleagues (2011). These researchers compared children who differed in their genotype for a particular gene, the serotonin transporter linked polymorphic region, or in the parlance of geneticists, *5-HTTLPR*. Individuals with the short allele of this gene are more likely to develop depression, anxiety, aggression, risk taking, and alcohol abuse than are individuals with the long allele of the gene (Carhart-Harris & Nutt, 2017; Caspi et al., 2003; Martínez et al., 2020).

Kochanska and her colleagues asked whether variation in these genotypes made children more or less susceptible to maternal responsiveness (mother's attunement and engagement with their child). In other words, are children who have the short allele more susceptible to their environments (i.e., are more orchid-like) than children who have the long allele? To find out, they followed children from 1 to 5 years of age and they measured maternal responsiveness, social competence, and rule following (or moral internalization). They found that children with the long form of the allele were dandelion children; their development was minimally related to maternal responsiveness. Regardless of the level of maternal responsiveness they experienced, these children became socially competent and followed the rules. Children who had the short form of the allele, in contrast, were orchid children; their social competence and moral development depended on whether their mother was high or low in responsiveness. When maternal responsiveness was very low, these children were low on social competence and moral internalization. As maternal responsiveness increased, children's moral competence and moral internalization increased. In fact, these orchid children actually developed *better* moral internalization than did children with long alleles if they had highly responsive mothers. The main point is that unlike children with long alleles, development in children with short alleles depends on their environment. Children with a short allele developed optimally if their mother was responsive but not if their mother was unresponsive.

Epigenetics

Epigenetics is another way the *expression* of genes is influenced by experience (Alegría-Torres et al., 2011; John & Rougeulle, 2018). Epigenetics involves changes in how the genes are expressed, *without changes in the DNA itself*. Many factors can cause epigenetic changes, such as diet, physical activity, working habits, smoking and alcohol consumption, psychological stress, or environmental pollutants. Epigenetic changes can alter gene expression through several processes, but the most commonly studied is a chemical process called *methylation*, in which a methyl group is added to the DNA. This changes how cells read the DNA instructions. Importantly, these changes are passed on as cells divide (creating new genes) and can even be passed onto the offspring of the individual.

Epigenetics is often discussed in terms of how specific experiences negatively alter how genes are expressed. For example, there was significant discussion about the effects of the Dutch famine of 1944–1945 on the genes of the people who experienced it. During this period of World War II, the Nazis blocked all food supplies to the Netherlands, and everyone in the country experienced famine. To understand the effect of malnourishment during prenatal development, researchers followed the individuals whose mothers were pregnant during this time. What was fascinating was that it was during adulthood that these individuals began to look different from their peers whose mothers did not experience famine during pregnancy. Individuals that had been in utero during the Dutch famine were as adults more likely to be obese, have higher cholesterol, and develop diabetes. This seems like a mystery—how can something that happened during prenatal development show effects in adulthood? The answer is epigenetics. Because the pregnant mothers were starving, a methyl group was added to some of the fetuses' genes as an adaptation to their mother's undernourishment, silencing those genes. This change may have aided the fetus in surviving, but once the famine had ended, this change in the functioning of the genes created health problems later in adulthood. They entered life with methylated DNA sequences that would be interpreted differently by cells throughout life.

One definition of epigenetic changes is that they can be inherited. This is clearly seen when cells divide and create new cells that contain the altered functioning of DNA. But, epigenetic changes in germ cells can be transmitted to the next generation. In fact, the epigenetic effects on pregnancies during the WWII Dutch famine continued to future generations. Adults whose paternal grandmothers were pregnant with their fathers during the famine are heavier and more obese than adults whose fathers had not experienced undernourishment during their prenatal development (Veenendaal et al., 2013). Thus, the epigenetic changes in the father as a fetus were passed on to his own offspring.

It's important to point out that epigenetics is a part of normal development. Not all epigenetic effects are negative. Physical exercise can create epigenetic modifications that yield health benefits, such as promoting the expression of genes that suppress tumors. Similarly, diet has been shown to reduce or increase the risk of particular cancers (Nystrom & Mutanen, 2009).

BOX 2.2—INFANCY IN REAL LIFE: NICU STRESS, PARENTAL SENSITIVITY, AND EPIGENETICS

One way we can see the effect of epigenetics in infant development is by carefully studying children who spend the first weeks or months after birth in the neonatal intensive care unit (NICU). The NICU is a very stressful place for an infant to be. Infants in the NICU frequently experience painful procedures (e.g., heel sticks to draw blood), they do not have the physical

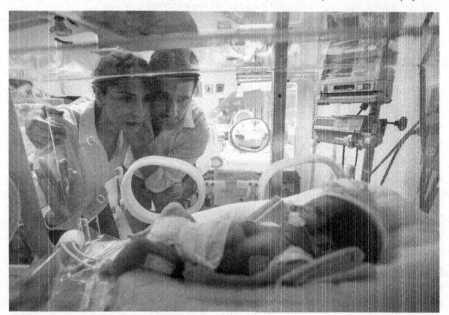

BABY IN NICU: A newborn in the neonatal intensive care unit.

iStock/andresr

contact with a caregiver that is optimal for development, and they are in the NICU because they are sick and fragile.

Rosario Montirosso and her colleagues conducted work to understand exactly *how* the NICU experiences alter development. This work focused on the epigenetic effects of pain-related stress in the NICU. Specifically, in one study they observed that preterm infants who experienced more pain-inducing procedures (e.g., blood draws) had more methylation of genes in the serotonin transport system—a system in the brain that is involved in stress regulation (Provenzi et al., 2015). As we have discussed, this methylation can silence the gene. Thus, we may expect that methylation of these genes would create problems for how children cope with stress in the future.

In fact, Montirosso and her colleagues followed these children over time and found that the methylation that occurred as a result of their pain-induced stress while in the NICU was related to later emotion and stress regulation. They observed that infants' temperament (see Chapter 10) at 3 months was related to methylation of these genes (Montirosso et al., 2016), and methylation in premature newborns was related to expressions of anger at 4 years (Provenzi et al., 2020). This shows how epigenetic changes as a result of stress very early in life can have a long-lasting effect on emotion and stress regulation.

But, across development children do not have experiences at just one time that determine outcomes. Development is a *cascade*. The early experiences influence gene expression, which in turn both determine future experience and how children will respond to future experience. In another study, Provenzi and Montirossso (Provenzi et al., 2017) found that the level of methylation at birth and maternal sensitivity together contributed to how full-term 3-month-old infants responded to the stress of a face-to-face interaction with their mothers in which their mother maintained a still face (see Chapter 10). Specifically, when mothers were less sensitive in general, infants with more methylation had a more negative response to the still face. This is important because it shows that experience, in this case interactions with the mother, continue to shape the way genes are expressed.

Check Your Learning

1. What is behavior genetics?

2. List the methods researchers use to study the heritability of traits.

3. Why do researchers compare monozygotic and dizygotic twins to understand the role of genes in the expression of traits?

4. What is a heritability estimate?

5. What are the three types of gene–environment correlations?

6. Describe how genes and environments can mutually influence each other.

BRAIN AND NERVOUS SYSTEM DEVELOPMENT

Besides genetics, one of the most remarkable things about human biology is how our brains work. You may have heard that humans are born too early because of their big brains (see Chapter 3). And, in Chapter 1, we talked about how programs like WIC focus on the first 1,000 days of development because that is a time that is critically important for brain development. In this section of this chapter, we will discuss the remarkable development that happens during those first 1,000 days.

Development at the Cellular Level

As we will see, the structure of the brain is a product of development. As you will learn in more detail in Chapter 3, during the prenatal period, the development of all body systems, including the nervous system, emerge from a single cell. Thus, the brain and nervous system develop as a function of development that happens at the cellular level.

You likely have learned in other classes that there are two types of cells in the nervous system, **neurons** and **glia**. These cells have different functions within the nervous system. The neurons are the basic units of the nervous system. They create networks that allow information to be passed throughout the brain. The glia play important support roles, making it possible for neurons to survive, make networks, and send information efficiently.

Look at the picture of the neuron in Figure 2.3. It has several parts, each of which is important for the transmission of information. As is true of any cell, neurons have a cell body with a nucleus. In addition, neurons have dendrites that branch from the cell body. The dendrites pick up information in the form of chemical signals from other neurons. This is the main way that the neuron receives messages. Each neuron also has an axon extending from the cell body toward a set of axon terminals. This is the main way neurons send messages. Once a signal is

---

FIGURE 2.3 ■ Neuron

This shows the parts of a neuron, including its cell body, nucleus, axon (which includes the myelin sheath) and axon terminal. Extending from the cell body are the dendrites.

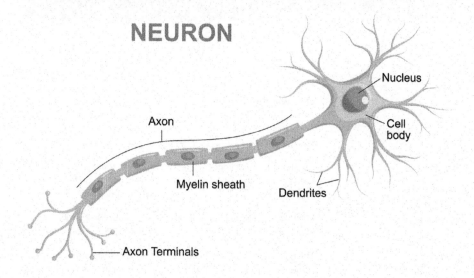

Source: iStock/Vitalii Dumma

detected by the dendrites, the message is passed down through the axon in the form of an electrical signal. The information is then passed on through the axon terminals in the form of chemical messages (neurotransmitters), to be picked up by another neuron. In Figure 2.3 you can also see that the axon has myelin sheaths. These are areas of a fatty insulation layer surrounding the axon, which allows the electrical signal to move more quickly along the axons. Although some axons are as short as one millimeter—and thus information will travel pretty quickly over that short distance—other axons are as long as one meter! Myelin helps to make sure that electrical signals are transmitted rapidly even over these very long distances.

The other cells of the nervous system—the glia—are more numerous than neurons. The glia do not transmit information. Instead, the many different types of glial cells hold neurons in place, supply oxygen and nutrients to neurons, provide the myelin, and remove debris. The glial cells also play an important role in the migration of neurons. Thus, the glia are critical for normal development of the nervous system.

The neurons and glial cells are created through neurogenesis and gliogenesis (Table 2.5). Another process that contributes to the development of the nervous system is neuronal death; even during the period of neurogenesis, both neurons and glia die. Although it may seem silly to create neurons and then have them die, cell death is an important part of the developmental process. It is so important to the development of the nervous system that a lack of cell death is thought to play a role in developmental disorders (Kolb, 1989). Even though some neurons die even before birth, human newborn infants have about 100 billion neurons, whereas as adults they will have about 85 billion. Interestingly, unlike other cells in the body, neurons themselves don't divide and replicate. This means that nearly all the neurons that an individual will ever have are created during the early period of prenatal development.

TABLE 2.5 ■ Process of Brain Development

Process	Definition	Timing
Neurogenesis	Creation of new neurons from stem cells	Mostly between 3rd and 15th week of prenatal development but occurs to a limited level even into adulthood
Cell migration	Migration of newly formed neurons from the ventricular or subventricular zone to their final home	About 4 weeks after conception to about 6 months after conception
Synaptogenesis	Creation of connections between neurons	Begins at about 20 weeks after conception and continues into early adulthood
Synaptic pruning	The loss of synapses due to lack of use or cell death	From about age 2 until adolescence
Myelination	The formation of a fatty sheath on neuronal axons to facilitation conduction of electrical signals	From about 5 months postconception into adulthood

When neurons are first created, they are not fully formed with dendrites and axons; they start out as a cell body. As you will learn in Chapter 3, the nervous system develops from the creation of the neural tube. Once the neural tube is complete, its cells begin to proliferate, or to create new cells. These new cells are special stem cells; some of those stem cells become neurons and some become glial cells. The region where these cells are created is called the ventricular zone. This is a temporary layer of tissue that is involved in neurogenesis, or the creation of new neurons, and gliogenesis, the creation of new glia. As the neuronal stem cells that make up this ventricular zone are depleted (from the creation of new neurons and glia), this region disappears. Thus, neurogenesis happens in the ventricular zone only prenatally.

Neurogenesis also occurs in the subventricular zone (SVZ), and this region persists into adulthood. Although it was once believed that neurogenesis occurred only prenatally, we now know that in some animals neurogenesis can occur in the SVZ as well as the hippocampus in adulthood, although neurogenesis is not as prolific beyond the prenatal period. Neurogenesis is mostly complete by 4 months postconception. During this period of prenatal development, there is an overproduction of neurons; that is, the system creates more neurons than it will need.

While all neurons are created in the ventricular or subventricular zone, the mature brain has neurons in many regions. How does the structure of the brain emerge from cells that are all created in only a couple of locations? The answer is that the brain develops from the inside out. Neurons and glial cells are created in the ventricular zone and then **migrate** to other regions of the brain. That is, they move toward different regions of the brain that will become their final location. This is accomplished, in part, by the glial cells acting as guides for the migration. The glial cells create a radial pattern from the ventricular zone to the outer layers of the developing brain. The newly formed neurons travel along these paths to form those outer layers. The guides are temporary, however, and after migration the glial cells that provided these pathways either degenerate or become part of other supporting structures in the brain. This system helps to create the laminar structure of the cortex, or the fact that it contains six layers of cells. As each new set of cells migrates, the glial guides help them migrate *past* the previously migrated cells. Thus, the older cells remain in the inner layers, and the newer cells migrate to create the outer layers. This active migration shows how this layered pattern of the cortex is a product of development.

Although this is the main way that cells migrate, it is not the only kind of migration that happens in brain development. Some cells do not use the glial pathways and instead migrate perpendicular to them. Some regions of the brain are the product of both kinds of migration. These other forms of migration yield different organization and structures than the more common form of migration.

Once neurons have clustered in a region, they begin to form **synapses**, or connections between them. To do this, the dendrites and axons begin to grow, as synapses typically involve the dendrites of one neuron connecting with the axon of another neuron (although synapses can form between axons of two neurons or between dendrites of two neurons). During this phase of **synaptogenesis**, or creation of synapses, neurons make synapses in every direction, apparently preparing for any contingency. During this process, neurons grow, and their axons extend toward other neurons, apparently randomly. Unlike the other processes of neuronal development discussed so far, this begins prenatally (after migration), but it continues for many years. The number of synapses increases exponentially, reaching a peak between 1 and 4 years, depending on the area of the brain. As was true for the creation of neurons, there is an overproduction of synapses during this period; that is, more synapses are created than are needed, or than will be used. During this period of development, the focus is on creating as many connections between neurons as possible.

Thus, these early processes of neurogenesis and synaptogenesis result in a large number of neurons making a large number of connections. You would think that this was good—big, connected brains should make us really smart. But, it turns out that having many neurons and connections does not allow the brain to operate *efficiently*. Because information travels through too many connections, processing is slow, and it is difficult for the resources available to maintain the neurons to support the system. Thus, development also includes **pruning** of synapses, or eliminating some.

Some pruning results from neuronal death that occurs as a normal part of brain development. Other pruning results from the loss of synapses (axons and dendrites) as the networks are used. Although it might seem like this is a waste of energy (to create connections that will be lost), this system creates more robust processing networks than if development involved creating fewer, more efficient networks from fewer synapses right from the start. As connections are stimulated, those that are used are maintained and become more stable, and those that are redundant or not used as often are eliminated. In this way, the brain adapts to experience, keeping the connections that are useful and efficient given the kinds of experience and input that the infant has.

Finally, the process of **myelination**, or the formation of the myelin sheaths on the axons of neurons, occurs. Myelination begins prenatally but continues for many years, with this process happening in some brain regions into the 20s! Myelination occurs as a particular kind of glial cells, oligodendrocytes, develop and create the fatty substance that is wrapped around neuronal axons. Once myelinated, the electrical signal travels more quickly down the axon, allowing for more efficient communication in the nervous system. For example, before the neurons of the motor system are myelinated, infants have jerky and uncoordinated movements. Myelination in these brain regions allow for smoother, more controlled movement. The importance of myelin can be seen in the effect of demyelinating disorders, such as multiple sclerosis (MS). In these disorders, the existing myelin is destroyed. For example, in MS, the immune system attacks myelin. As these diseases progress, patients experience muscle weakness, visual and speech impairments, and motor problems. Although many people live with MS for many years, experiencing periods where their symptoms are worse and then better, for some people the symptoms are severe and can lead to confinement to a wheelchair.

Brain Structures as Developmental Products

The previous section was about how the cells of the nervous system are created and develop. But what about the *structure* of the brain? The brain is not a single, uniform thing; it is made up of different regions (Figure 2.4). You likely know that the brain is made up of two hemispheres, each with different functions. In fact, you may have heard people talking about being "left-brained" or "right-brained," which usually means that they are saying that they are more or less creative. This is a fun way of thinking about the two hemispheres, but in reality we are

FIGURE 2.4 ■ Brain Organization

The structures of a mature human brain.

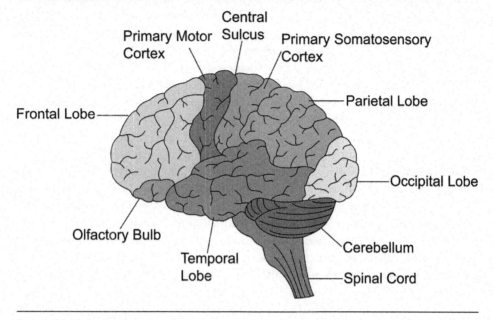

Source: iStock/mrhighsky

all "whole-brained" and everyone uses both halves of the brain. However, it is the case that the two hemispheres are specialized for different skills and functions. For example, in most adults, language is mostly represented in the left hemisphere, and emotions are mostly represented in the right hemisphere (which supports the left-brain/right-brain distinction). But the regions of the brain are even more specialized. For example, the occipital lobe, which is located in the back of the brain, is where vision is represented and controlled. The frontal lobe, which is at the front of the brain, is the region involved in planning, inhibitory control, and other high-level functions. The question is how does this structure develop? These structures and their specialization are well established in children and adults. When do they become established?

The structure emerges, in part, from precisely the processes described in the previous section. Brain structure is a product of the creation and migration of cells, synaptogenesis, and pruning. Recall that from the start there is structure in the nervous system. The nervous system emerges from the formation of the neural tube (see Chapter 3). This neural tube already shows specialization, with the proliferation of neurons occurring on one side of the tube and the spinal cord developing from the other side of the tube. Remember also that the ventricular zone, where the neurons are created, is *transient*—it disappears when the neuronal stem cells that make up this region are depleted (because they have all become neurons). The prenatal development of the brain involves other temporary structural changes. At the same time that there are the transient ventricular and subventricular zones, there are other transient zones, such as a transient cortical plate, which is the future cortex. The cortical plate is densely packed with post-migra-tion neurons. This temporary structure develops rapidly during the fetal period, growing in size and eventually creating the folds (gyri) and indentations (sulci) that characterize the adult brain. So even early in development the brain has structure, and the different structures serve different functions. But, some of the structures present during development disappear, and many structures present in the adult brain are not present during the early phases of brain devel-opment. Thus, the structure of the brain is a *product* of development.

So how do brain structures develop and become specialized, as they are in adults? When does the left hemisphere become specialized for language and the right temporal lobe become specialized to process faces? This is a very complicated question with no easy answers. Consider how we know about brain specialization in older children and adults. To determine which brain regions are involved in a particular task or type of processing, researchers use functional mag-netic resonance imaging (fMRI). In an MRI, a part of the body is scanned using a magnetic field and radio waves. When you are in the scanner, the magnetic field causes the water mol-ecules in your body to realign, and the radio waves are used to create a faint signal from this realignment. This is used to create an image of the structures of the brain.

In fMRI, scans are taken when a person is doing a task. For example, a researcher might present a person with pictures of faces and houses while that person is being scanned. This pro-cedure would show that different parts of the right temporal lobe of the brain were active when the person was looking at the faces and the houses; in adults, studies like this have shown that there is a part of the brain specialized for processing images of faces and a different part of the brain specialized for processing images of places (Cohen Kadosh & Johnson, 2007).

Clearly, this procedure cannot be used easily with preverbal infants. It is difficult to imagine how you would do fMRI with infants and examine differences in brain activity in response to different tasks. Some people have done it, though. For example, Ghislaine Dehane-Lambertz and her colleagues (2002) conducted MRI scans of 3-month-old French infants as they lis-tened to 20 seconds of speech played forward and 20 seconds of speech played backward. The infants' "task" was to recognize that forward speech, but not backward speech, was language. Like adults, the left (or language) regions of these 3-month-old infants' brains showed more activation during forward speech. This shows that some of the structure in the brain related to how speech and language is processed is specialized by the time infants are 3 months old. Other studies have shown that there is some specialization of brain structures related to language pro-cessing even in newborns (May et al., 2011). As you will see in Chapters 3 and 9, however, the fact that newborns already have brain areas specialized for speech processing likely shows how their prenatal experience shapes their language and brain development.

Mark Johnson (2011) has suggested that specialization develops across infancy and is the result of the initial connections formed in the brain and of experience. As the brain develops, different regions are connected. For example, the occipital lobe gets input from the optic nerve, which is connected to the retina in the eye. The temporal lobe gets input from the cochlea in the ear. These connections mean that when the retina or cochlea detect information, the signal is sent to different parts of the brain. However, according to Johnson, specialization for particular types of inputs comes from experience. So, as infants look at and process faces, input about faces connects to the future "face region" because of how the brain is initially connected. With experience looking at faces, this face region becomes specialized for processing faces.

Plasticity

An important consequence of the way the nervous system develops is that it is characterized by **plasticity**. That is, development is not fixed by some biological program; rather, it adapts in response to variations in the environment and experience. Children have different experiences: Some children hear only one language and other children hear more than one language, some children are exposed to music from early on, some children are read to, some children spend many hours outdoors with different types of plants and animals. These differences in experience shape how the brain develops. Remember, synapses are formed based on experience, and synapses are pruned based on experience.

Classic work revealed that laboratory rats raised in environmentally complex environments (e.g., with other rats, with toys and other experiences) developed bigger brains than laboratory rats raised in a typical environment (e.g., individual cages without extra toys or experiences) (Greenough et al., 1987). This work suggested that the number of synapses that were formed and maintained depended on experience. In other words, the development described earlier is not fixed but rather is plastic and depends on experience.

What about human children? We obviously can't manipulate children's experiences, but we can compare the brains of children with very different experiences.

Let's return to the Romanian orphans we discussed in Chapter 1. Compared to their counterparts who were not raised in institutions, children from Romanian orphanages showed abnormal brain activity (Chugani et al., 2001). These differences likely reflect the effect of neglect and impoverished early experience on brain development. But these comparisons, and those described earlier, reflect correlational findings. Because it is not ethical to randomly assign children to be in institutions or to experience neglect, these studies can't tell us that the brain differences were *caused* by experience.

But, the Bucharest Early Intervention Project (BEIP) discussed in Chapter 1 did randomly assign children to remain in institutions or to be put in foster care. This study then provided an opportunity to ask how different experiences cause differences in brain development. In general, this research showed that children who were randomly assigned to foster care had better brain development than did the children who remained in the institutions (Bick et al., 2015). In addition, the earlier children were put in foster care, the better their outcomes (Nelson et al., 2009). Although we would never want to have the opportunity to do this study again, there are important things we can learn from this work about plasticity and brain development. Specifically, brain development *adapts* to the kinds of experiences the child has. If the child is well nourished, stimulated, and provided with many different experiences, brain development is optimal. If the child is neglected and raised in an impoverished environment, brain development is not optimal.

These examples are extremes. It does not mean that children in poverty always experience poor brain development. Children who are fed, nurtured, and given interesting experiences, whether with expensive toys or sticks and cardboard boxes, will have the opportunity to adapt to those experiences and develop. It is when children are neglected and the environment is severely impoverished that damage occurs. Even when there is adequate nutrition, social and emotional support, and stimulation, the brain adapts to differences in experience. The brains of infants exposed to two languages develop differently than the brains of infants exposed to only one language. The brains of children who learn to read using vision will differ from the brains of children who learn to read by touch using Braille. The brains of infants who spend a lot of time building with blocks and puzzles will develop differently than the brains of infants who never engage in spatial play. The point is that plasticity is a part of *normal* brain development, and our brains, even during infancy, reflect differences in our experiences.

Remember, however, that we said that there is similarity in how individual people's brains are structured. Most adults have language in the left hemisphere and have an area of the right temporal lobe specialized for processing faces. How can brains both be so similar and reflect this adaptive process?

Greenough and his colleagues (1987) described two types of plasticity, experience-expectant and experience-dependent, that help to explain how the brain adapts to experience and yet we see similarities across different brains (Table 2.6). Specifically, **experience-expectant plasticity** is a way of describing the commonalities across people in how the brain is organized and specialized. In this case, plasticity reflects the brain adapting to experiences that are common to virtually all members of a species. For example, virtually all human infants see with two eyes, are exposed to a caregiver, and hear (or see) human language. Because those experiences are common to all members of the species, it isn't immediately obvious how brain development reflects that experience— our experiences are all the same and our brain structures (that reflect that experience) are all the

TABLE 2.6 ■ Experience-Expectant and Experience Dependent Plasticity

Type of Plasticity	Definition	Characteristics	Examples
Experience-expectant	The brain adapts to the presence or absence of an experience that is typical of human experience	— Experience occurs during a *critical period* in development. — Experience is typical of virtually all members of the species.	— Binocular vision depends on coordinated input from two eyes. — A region in the right temporal lobe specific for face processing depends on early visual experience.
Experience-dependent	Individual differences in brain organization and structure develop from idiosyncratic differences in experience.	— Can occur throughout development. — Reflects individual differences in experience.	— Formation and maintenance of synapses in networks that are stimulated by experience.

same. But, when we find people who didn't have this typical experience, we see that their brains adapted in a different way, giving us insight into how the common structure and specialization of the brain across individuals is related to common experience. Specifically, we can see the effect of this experience by looking at the brains of individuals whose two eyes don't work together, as in amblyopia or strabismus; or who do not have a caregiver, as in the Romanian orphans; or who are not exposed to any language, such as deaf infants whose parents don't sign.

Consider the case of strabismus. For decades, children with crossed-eyes (strabismus) or a lazy eye (amblyopia) would have their eyes surgically corrected in early childhood. The thought was that it was best to have the surgery when children were a bit older, and that the main reason for the surgery was cosmetic. However, normal vision requires good vision in both eyes and alignment between the two eyes. The normal or expected visual experience is coordinated, good visual information from both eyes. When a child has or develops a lazy eye or crossed-eyes, the brain does not receive coordinated, good visual information from both eyes. For example, it is often the case in amblyopia that the brain receives clearer visual input from one eye than the other. In addition, because the child can't easily keep the two eyes in alignment, the brain can't reconcile the differences between the input from the two eyes. Without any treatment, the brain will rely more heavily on the clearer input from the "good" eye and will suppress the less clear input from the other eye. The brain will "see" by relying on the information from just one eye, and it will be as if the individual is blind in the other eye. Importantly, as we will see in Chapter 4, depth perception depends on binocular vision, or the ability to coordinate the input from the two eyes. If strabismus is left uncorrected, normal binocular vision and depth perception will not develop. Now doctors carefully examine how infants use their eyes together. Each of us remembers our pediatrician carefully examining how our infants moved their eyes and telling us what to look for so we could spot the emergence of a lazy eye early on. We now know that this experience is so important for vision development that it is not unusual to see an infant with glasses or an eye patch, which is the way doctors treat these early vision problems.

This is an example of experience-expectant plasticity because it shows how the brain develops "normally" when it receives the ubiquitous experience in human experience. Virtually all children have two functioning eyes that work together; only about 4% of children have some form of strabismus. We only see evidence of plasticity—or the brain adapting to differences in experience—in the rare cases when the typical experience is not present. And we see plasticity in how the infant brain responds to treatment. When strabismus and amblyopia are treated in infancy, by strengthening a weak eye or surgically adjusting how tight the muscles are around the eye, the effects of these conditions are minor. But, if these conditions are not "fixed" until the child is several years old, the visual parts of the brain will never be like those of a child with "normal" visual experience. This is why Greenough et al. called this experience-expectant; normal brain development occurs when the individual has the expected experience. When the individual does not have that experience, atypical or abnormal brain development occurs, for example, resulting in the inability to use the two eyes together to perceive depth.

Another characteristic of experience-expectant plasticity is that it occurs early in development and requires that the experience happens during a specific critical period. In the case of strabismus, the infant brain develops rapidly as visual input is detected, perceived, and processed. With each day, the parts of the brain dedicated to processing and representing visual information become organized in response to visual experience. The longer the system experiences uncoordinated input and a weak signal from one eye, the longer the brain will suppress the input from that weak eye and the brain organization will be focused only on the input from the good eye. At some point in development, the organization of those brain areas will stabilize, and it will be impossible to undo that organization. However, if the strabismus is treated early in infancy—either by patching the good eye (forcing the brain to use the information from the weak eye) or by surgically correcting the problem—and children become able to use the two eyes together, binocular depth perception can develop. The point is that the experience of using the two eyes together must occur at a specific point in development for the brain to be able to effectively use the coordinated information to perceive depth.

The other kind of plasticity, **experience-dependent plasticity**, refers to how brain development adapts to idiosyncratic experiences. In this case, there is no "normal" or expected experience. Some children are first born, and others are born with older siblings. Some infants are raised in a noisy city, and other infants are raised in the quiet countryside. Some children live in small communities and see hundreds of people and other children live in big cities of millions. None of these experiences are common to virtually all members of the species, and yet they all have the potential to influence brain development.

Consider the effect of your hometown size on your ability to process faces. Ben Balas and Alyson Saville (2015) measured face memory in two groups of adults. One group was raised in small hometowns (fewer than 1,000 people). The other group was raised in towns of at least 30,000 people. Although these subjects were adults (between 18 and 24 years of age), they had spent their whole lives (until college) in either a very small or medium sized hometown. Balas and Saville wondered if the parts of their brain that are involved in face processing would be shaped by this difference in experience.

The results were striking. First, the adults who were raised around few people had poorer memory for faces than did the adults who were raised in larger towns. But, Balas and Saville also measured brain responses to faces in these adults. Many studies have shown that adults have a very specific brain response, or ERP (event-related potential), to faces. The ERP is a measure of the electrical activity that can be recorded on the scalp. By linking the electrical activity that is recorded to the presentation of specific images, researchers can get insight into how those images are processed. Specifically, in adults, the ERPs to face stimuli are different from the ERPs to other stimuli, such as chairs. Balas and Saville found that their adults who were raised in larger towns showed the pattern that has been observed in many studies, whereas adults who were raised in small towns did not show this effect. The way in which the brains responded to faces was different between these groups, presumably because of their different early life experience with faces. This is an example of experience-expectant plasticity because both groups of adults had experience with faces. But, the kind of experience they had was different. In addition, all of the people in the study could see and remember faces; it's just that their ability to do so differed as a function of their experience with faces during the time when their brain's ability to process faces was developing.

What both of these kinds of plasticity show is how brain development is adaptive and that brain structure and organization are a product of development. We have similarities in our brains because of the similarities in our experiences. The differences we observe reflect differences in our experiences. The overproduction of neurons and synapses and the processes of cell death and synaptic pruning allow this adaptability.

BOX 2.3—INFANCY IN REAL LIFE: SES AND BRAIN DEVELOPMENT

One way we see plasticity in brain development is in the relationship between socioeconomic status (SES) and brain development. SES refers to one's position in society, and it has implications for many aspects of development. Children from low SES households—households with fewer financial resources, lower levels of parental education, and that are in less affluent neighborhoods—likely experience poorer nutrition, more stress, and less time dedicated to parent–child interactions than do children from higher SES households. Thus, differences in SES are not a single thing, but rather SES is a proxy for a number of different variables that may contribute to brain development.

Many studies have revealed differences in high and low SES infants in their cognitive and language abilities (e.g., Clearfield & Niman, 2012; Fernald et al., 2013). Indeed, in a large study of mostly White midwestern U.S. children, Kimberly Noble and her colleagues (2015) found effects of SES on memory and language scores in toddlers. The question is whether we can see differences in the brain itself. One MRI study of African American 5-week-old female infants in Philadelphia from poor and middle-class families revealed that lower SES infants had smaller brain structures than their higher SES peers (Betancourt et al., 2016). Another study of 6- to 10-month-old infants in London (mostly White) showed that the electrical signal recorded from the scalp (EEG) differed as a function of SES (Tomalski et al., 2013). Because other work has shown that across childhood cortical thickness is related to SES (higher SES children have thicker cortices), and that cortical thickness is related to language and other cognitive abilities (Brito et al., 2017), it seems likely that the observed cognitive differences in high and low SES infants reflect brain differences. Thus, there is increasing evidence that across studies conducted in different regions of the world with children from different racial and ethnic backgrounds, SES is associated with brain development.

The question is *why* and *how* these relations exist. We have already pointed out that SES is not one thing. Because effects are often observed for low SES, it is likely that some of these effects reflect the kind of epigenetic changes on gene expression we discussed earlier. Poor children are more likely to experience food insecurity or undernutrition; family stress, such as from the loss of a job, is likely higher; and other environmental factors associated with poorer neighborhoods might contribute to how genes are expressed (Hackman et al., 2010; Hackman & Farah, 2009). There are some more direct effects too. Poor children are less likely to have access to good medical care, so it is possible that some of the effects reflect poorer health.

In fact, the differences in care are evident even before birth. Low SES women have more pregnancy-related complications, including premature birth, stress, and poor nutrition (Hackman et al., 2010). Given how much brain development happens during prenatal development, these factors likely have an impact on brain development. But as we have seen, the brain continues to develop after birth. Low SES parents are more likely to experience stress after the birth of their child, which may affect their parenting and sensitivity to their infant.

Low SES households also tend to have lower levels of cognitive stimulation, for example, fewer books, fewer trips, and fewer words spoken to the infants. These are all correlational, however, making it difficult to know how each of these factors *causes* differences in brain growth and development. Some understanding can be found in studies with animals, for example, by raising some animals in a more stressful environment than other animals. We also can see from the work with the Romanian orphans who were randomly assigned to foster care that rearing conditions can cause differences in brain development. Of course, we don't know what it was exactly about the foster care that caused the effect, but this work suggests that we should be designing interventions to help children from lower SES households.

In fact, in 2014, pediatricians recommended that all parents read to their babies, which led to a campaign to encourage parents, especially parents with low SES, to read more to even the youngest infants. This was accompanied by the observation that there existed a "word gap"; children from low SES families simply hear fewer words each day than do children from higher SES families (Rowe, 2008, 2012). This led to campaigns to encourage families to talk to their babies. In 2013, the Clinton Foundation partnered with Next Generation, a California nonprofit organization, to create "Too Small to Fail" (http://toosmall.org/). The initial mission of this organization was to promote brain and language development by giving parents and caregivers information and tools to talk, sing, and read to children from birth. This is a great example of how research translates to action that is taken in the service of helping all children develop.

MOM READING WITH BABY: Mom reading to her infant. This may be one way that mothers with more education provide enriched experience to their infants from an early age.

iStock/fizkes

Check Your Learning

1. What are the main processes of cellular brain development? Define each one.

2. What do we know about how brain specialization develops in infancy?

3. What are the primary differences between experience-expectant and experience-dependent plasticity?

SUMMARY

This chapter provided an overview of the biological foundations of development in infancy and the early development of the nervous system. Our biology and the environment come together in various (and sometimes complicated) ways to produce our physical and behavioral characteristics. Individuals' genetic makeup and their environments dynamically influence each other throughout infancy. This chapter also highlighted the various ways we can study the relative contributions of genetics and the environment in the lab, and how twin and adoption studies can be particularly useful in helping scientists quantify the relative contributions of genes and the environment on behavior. Finally, we discussed the types of cells that are found in the brain, their genesis, and their function, which all set the stage for infant development across the various domains we will explore in the coming chapters.

KEY TERMS

alleles	heredity
behavioral genetics	heterozygous
chromosomes	homozygous
DNA	migration
dominant	myelination
epigenetics	neuron
experience-dependent plasticity	phenotype
experience-expectant plasticity	plasticity
gene–environment correlations	pruning
gene–environment interactions	recessive
genes	synapse
genotype	synaptogenesis
glia	

REVIEW QUESTIONS

1. Define the basic structures that determine our genetics. How do these structures determine the traits that are observed in people?

2. What is heritability? How do we study heritability?

3. What are gene–environment correlations? Give an example of each of the three types.

4. What are gene–environment interactions?

5. Describe an example of epigenetics in development.

6. What are the parts of the neuron? What is the function of each of these parts?

7. Give examples of experience-expectant and experience-dependent plasticity in development.

CRITICAL THINKING QUESTIONS

1. The study of genetics in development is often thought of as the study of "nature" in development. How is genetics the study of nature? In what ways is the study of genetics actually the study of the relative roles of nature and nurture in development?

2. Why do adoption studies focus on studying infants adopted at birth rather than those adopted at older ages?

3. In the text, we described an example in which every member of a family had a dominant trait (freckles). Why is it impossible to know the underlying genotypes of these individuals? How would it be different if every member of the family had a recessive trait (e.g., light colored eyes)?

4. Why are twin and adoption studies *quasi-experimental*?

5. Heritability estimates are typically used to describe the level to which a trait is genetic. How are heritability estimates influenced by the environment? What does this mean for estimating how much a trait is due to genes?

6. The case of the "mixed up brothers of Bogotá" has fascinated psychologists as the "perfect experiment." How is this case similar to and different from other twin studies, and why are those similarities and differences important for the conclusions we can draw from this case?

7. How are passive, evocative, and active gene–environment correlations different? What does each mean for the way genes and the environment together influence development?

8. One characteristic of development of the nervous system is that neurons and connections between neurons (synapses) are overproduced, and as a result young children have more neurons and more synapses than they will ever have. Why is this characteristic of the development of the nervous system important?

9. Explain how experience-expectant and experience-dependent plasticity are each examples of how the brain adapts to differences in experience across development.

3

PRENATAL, SENSORY DEVELOPMENT, AND THE NEWBORN

When she was pregnant, Diego's mom took cello lessons. Throughout her pregnancy—and Diego's prenatal development—she would practice the cello with the instrument resting right on her belly. She noticed that as a fetus, Diego often moved in response to the vibrations of her playing. This movement suggested that he felt the vibrations or heard the sounds, both indications of his developing sensory systems. After he was born, Diego also showed signs that he recognized the sounds of the cello; he would sit still and listen whenever he heard cello music fill the room and clearly preferred the songs he had heard during the last months of pregnancy to the other songs his mom would play. Like all newborns, Diego had difficulty regulating his emotional state, often becoming fussy or upset as he transitioned from sleep to wakefulness. Hearing the familiar cello sounds helped him with these transitions and calmed him when he was fussy.

In this chapter you will learn about development during the prenatal period—the time when Diego as a fetus responded to and learned about the sounds of the cello. You will also learn about fetal development and how the sensory systems develop. As you can see from this example, many aspects of sensory system development develop before birth. Finally, you will learn about birth and the newborn.

After reading this chapter, you will be able to:

1. *List* the stages of prenatal development, from conception to birth, and explain how they differ from the trimesters of pregnancy.

2. *Understand* the development of the sensory systems, and how development of these systems gives rise to prenatal learning.

3. *Describe* the stages of labor and delivery and the major states of a newborn.

PRENATAL DEVELOPMENT

In this section, you will learn about prenatal development from conception to birth, about the stages that a fetus undergoes during typical development, and about a variety of things (both good and bad) that can impact the fetal environment. As the prenatal period progresses, you will notice that the fetus will come to behave more and more like a newborn. Although we think of birth as a major transition in an infant's life (and it certainly is), there are aspects of development that are continuous, even across this major change in scenery. In fact, the newborn period is often referred to as the fourth trimester of pregnancy.

As we discuss prenatal development, there are a few basic principles to keep in mind. The first is that prenatal development tends to happen in **cephalocaudal direction**, or from head to foot. This means that when you're thinking about the timing of prenatal development, things like the fetus's hands will develop before things like the fetus's feet. Second, prenatal development tends to go from basic to more specialized. For example, a fetus will develop small hand buds that look rather round before some of the buds' cells slowly die off to give shape to the fetus's fingers and toes. Finally, prenatal development generally goes in order of importance, with more important organs that help keep the fetus alive, like the heart, developing at earlier stages than things that are less critical for survival (even though they are important), such as the nose or ears.

Stages of Prenatal Development

Prenatal development lasts about 38 weeks, starting at *conception* and ending at *birth*. You are probably used to thinking about pregnancy as 40 weeks long. How can pregnancy be 40 weeks if prenatal development only lasts 38 weeks? This is because generally women give birth about 40 weeks after their last menstrual period (LMP). We use this as an indicator of pregnancy even though conception usually happens about 2 weeks after a woman's last period. But, it is easier to tell when a woman last had her menstrual period than to tell when conception happened, so when talking about pregnancy we usually refer to the 40 weeks between the woman's LMP and birth. When talking about prenatal development, we focus on the 38 weeks that starts with conception.

Conception begins with the joining of a single sperm and a single egg. During a woman's menstrual cycle, one of her **ovaries**—a pair of female glands where eggs form and hormones like estrogen and progesterone are made—typically releases a single egg into the **fallopian tube**, which connects the ovaries to the woman's uterus. This happens during *ovulation*, which is usually about 2 weeks after the woman's menstrual period. When sperm enter a woman's body, they must travel through the uterus and navigate up the fallopian tube and to the egg. This isn't an easy journey, and only sperm with a good head shape and tail motion make it all the way up the fallopian tube, a journey that can take hours. Even then, only one sperm can penetrate the egg. Once the contents of a single sperm make it inside the egg, the egg will shut down so that no additional sperm can enter. The newly joined sperm and egg form a zygote, a process that we have come to know as conception.

After the sperm and egg join, the cells inside the newly formed zygote begin to divide, at first slowly and then more quickly as it floats down the fallopian tube toward the uterus. Once the zygote reaches the uterus, it implants and burrows beneath the uterine wall. This first stage of prenatal development, which takes about 1 to 2 weeks from conception to implantation, is called the **zygotic stage**. This stage is characterized by cell duplication, which allows the formation of the structures that will become all of the systems that will support the embryo and fetus until birth. Notice that this first stage of prenatal development happens in the first month of pregnancy, before the woman even knows she is pregnant.

The next stage, called the **embryonic stage**, lasts from about 2 to 8 weeks following conception, and it is when the support structures that allow the fetus to grow first develop. These include the **amniotic sac,** which is a thinned walled sac filled with liquid (called amniotic fluid) that will hold the fetus and protect it from getting injured during pregnancy. The **placenta** is a small organ that filters the exchange of materials between the mother and the fetus, allowing some things (like food and antibodies) in and carrying other things (like waste) out. The **umbilical cord** connects the fetus to the placenta (Figure 3.1).

Besides the support structures, there is also a great deal of anatomical and structural development that happens during the embryonic stage. First, the cells that were dividing during the zygotic stage begin to move from where they started; this is a process called cell migration, which we talked about in Chapter 2. These cells, which are initially all the same with no fixed function or fate, begin to differentiate or become specialized for different structures and functions. Some of these cells, for example, will migrate upward and become part of the heart. Some will become part of the kidneys, or liver, or lungs. Some of these cells become a three-layered

FIGURE 3.1 ■ Fetus and Support Structures

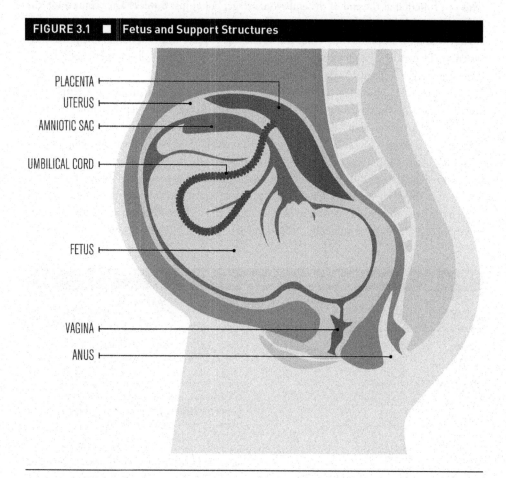

PLACENTA

UTERUS

AMNIOTIC SAC

UMBILICAL CORD

FETUS

VAGINA

ANUS

Source: istock/Lalocracio

structure that forms a **neural plate**, which folds into itself forming the **neural tube**. One side of the neural tube will become the spinal cord, and on the other side is the region that produces neurons and glia for the development of the nervous system and the brain (see Chapter 2). Around 22 days after conception, the neural tube will "zip" itself up and close. Failure for the neutral tube to close completely (likely due to an inadequate amount of folic acid or vitamin B) can result in a condition called spina bifida, where parts of the spine might actually be exposed.

As cell migration is taking place, sheets of cells will come together over an open cavity that will make up the nose and mouth to form the fetus's face. In fact, if you touch the part of your face between your nose and mouth, you will feel a groove, called the philtrum. This is where those sheets of cells came together between 5 and 7 weeks after you were conceived. Around 8 weeks, cells between the hand and leg buds begin to die to form the fetus's feet, hands, fingers, and toes, a process called programmed cell death.

Importantly, the embryonic stage is characterized by *organogenesis*. This refers to the fact that all of the organ systems' foundations are established during this stage. None of those systems can function at the end of the embryonic stage, but at just 8 weeks after conception the embryo has the beginnings of a heart, lungs, kidney, limbs, and all the other major systems that are essential for life outside the womb. It will take many more weeks of development for those systems to be mature enough for the fetus to be able to survive outside the mother's body, but all those systems get their start in these first few weeks.

After cell migration takes place, and most of the structures that make up a fetus's vital organs are laid down, the fetus enters the third prenatal stage, appropriately named the **fetal stage**, which lasts from about 8 to 38 weeks after conception, or from about the 10th week of pregnancy until birth (Table 3.1). During the fetal stage, there is significant development of the fetus's brain, lungs, and sensory systems (which we will discuss in the next section), and the fetus will gain a significant amount of weight. At 8 weeks, at the start of the fetal stage, the fetus is only about a half an inch long but has a beating heart, which is disproportionately large to keep the fetus alive; it even has its own blood type. In fact, a mother can't even feel the fetus move at this point; it isn't until around 16 weeks that the fetus will be big enough for her to feel.

TABLE 3.1 ■ Stages of Prenatal Development			
Prenatal Stage	**Duration**	**Pregnancy Trimester**	**Major Development**
Zygotic	1–2 weeks	First	Conception followed by cell duplication and implantation in the uterine wall.
Embryonic	2–8 weeks	First	Support systems develop, including the placenta, amniotic sac, and umbilical cord. Neural tube forms and closes. Organogenesis, in which internal organs begin to form.
Fetal	8–38 weeks	Second and Third	Significant development of the fetus's brain, lungs, and sensory systems. The fetus grows in size and weight.

Even at 16 weeks, fetal movement might feel like a flutter, and the mother may not be certain what it was she felt. The exact time when a mother can feel her fetus's movements varies based on the size and activity level of the fetus. Tesalia's mother, for example, felt her move as early as 14 weeks because Tesalia was so active in the womb, even at that early stage of development. As the fetus gets bigger and stronger, their movements get more and more pronounced. In fact, in their third trimester, Edwin and Charlie's mom could see elbows and even a head move the skin on her belly back and forth as her soon-to-be infants repositioned themselves in a uterus that felt smaller and smaller for their growing bodies. Alison's mom even could see a tiny foot move back and forth across her belly in the last weeks before Alison was born.

Sex and Gender

When the sperm and the egg first join in the fallopian tube, the genetic contents of each parent also join together to contribute chromosomal material to the developing zygote. As you learned in Chapter 2, a mother contributes 23 chromosomes to the developing fetus, and the father contributes the other 23. The 23rd chromosome is made up of either two X chromosomes, or an X and a Y chromosome (Figure 3.2). Fetuses always get one X chromosome from the egg, and the sperm can either carry another X or a Y. When they come together, XX chromosomes will

---

FIGURE 3.2 ■ Sex Chromosomes

The X is much larger than the Y and carries significantly more genes.

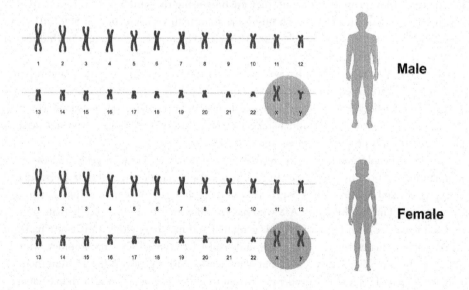

Source: iStock/olando_o

typically guide the development of female sex organs, while XY chromosomes typically guide the development of male sex organs. Most people have exactly two chromosomes on the 23rd pair, but there are rare cases in which people have 3 chromosomes on this pair (a trisomy) or only one X chromosome (Turner syndrome).

The development of the sex organs begins 11 weeks after conception. Around that time, if present, the Y chromosome causes the fetus to begin to produce a hormone called androgen. All fetuses produce some androgen, but the Y chromosome causes the fetus to produce enough androgen to stimulate the development of testes and, as a result, to begin producing testosterone. If low levels of androgen are present, the fetus will go down the path to developing female sex organs. There is a rare condition, androgen insensitivity syndrome (AIS), in which an individual has a Y chromosome and yet their developing tissue is not sensitive to androgen. Thus, individuals with AIS do not develop male genitalia and do not develop male secondary sex characteristics (e.g., facial hair, Adam's apple) at puberty. These individuals are often raised as girls and identify as such. The opposite can also occur—where a fetus with two X chromosomes overproduces androgen and begins to develop male genitals—a condition called congenital adrenal hyperplasia (CAH).

This brings us to a very important distinction between sex and gender. *Sex* is related to the type of sex chromosomes an individual has. Although it is complicated and our understanding is changing every day, the most common way that people think about sex is that it is an individual's genotype, or what is written into our genetic code. Because a person's genitals at birth usually reflect their sex chromosomes, doctors, parents, and others assign the infant a sex based on their genitalia. For most people, their *sex assigned at birth* corresponds to their genotype or whether they have an XX or XY pair of sex chromosomes. When people assign a sex to a fetus based on information gained through a genetic test, such as amniocentesis or genetic tests from the mother's blood, they are only using this chromosomal information to assign sex. It is estimated that sex chromosome abnormalities occur in 1 in 500 births. For these people, as well as some people with AIS or CAH, their sex assigned at birth does not reflect their genotype in the same way.

In contrast to sex, *gender* is what is expressed—the way a person looks, feels, and behaves. Gender can be influenced by several factors. For many people, it is a phenotype that is directly related to their genotype. For cisgender people, for example, their gender expression is the same as their sex assigned at birth. This may reflect a strong influence of the genotype on a person's phenotype, the way people are treated, and other socializing factors.

For other people, gender may be related to the interaction between genes and the environment in a more complicated way. In AIS, for example, female physical characteristics will be expressed, and a child with AIS may later identify as a girl or woman despite having a Y chromosome. Thus, a child with AIS who has chromosomes that are typically male may be assigned female at birth (because of their genitalia) and may have either a male or female (or other) gender. Finally, there are people who do not have atypical sex chromosomes, who do not have conditions like AIS or CAH, but who identify with a gender different from their sex assigned at birth. People whose gender is different from their sex assigned at birth may identify as transgender, or they may not identify with either male or female genders and instead identify as nonbinary. The point is that *gender* is what is ultimately expressed, and it is not relevant to preverbal infants who do not yet have a gender identity. Gender identity first begins to develop by the age of 2 or 3, and recent research suggests that both cisgender and transgender children are capable of identifying their gender reliably by age 5 (Olson et al., 2015). When a family holds a "gender reveal" party during pregnancy, they are actually revealing the sex of the fetus; it will be some time before the child's gender is known. For the purposes of this textbook, when we refer to infants, we will be referring to their sex assigned at birth, and not their gender.

The sex chromosomes are not just involved in the development of the sex organs themselves; they also can lead to sex-linked traits. Recall from Chapter 2 that autosomal chromosomes come in homologous pairs. For the purposes of this discussion, we will refer to individuals with XY sex chromosomes as males and individuals with XX sex chromosomes as female, using those terms to refer to the individual's chromosomal sex (not their gender or their sex assigned at birth).

Males and females are equally likely to express the trait of an autosomal allele. But in the case of sex chromosomes, males and females differ in their expression of sex-linked traits because the X and Y sex chromosomes each carry distinct genes. In fact, the X chromosome is significantly larger than the Y; whereas the X has about 900 genes, the Y chromosome has only about 55 genes. These differences in the sex chromosomes create a pattern of inheritance that is distinct from the ones we described for the autosomal chromosomes in the last chapter. Specifically, when sex-linked traits have genes on the X chromosome, these traits are more likely to be expressed in males (i.e., individuals with XY sex chromosomes). This may seem counterintuitive because females have two X chromosomes. However, because they have two X chromosomes, genetic females will have two alleles for any trait on the X chromosome. If they have one dominant and one recessive allele, the recessive trait will not be expressed. But genetic males who inherit a recessive allele for a trait on their one X chromosome may not have a corresponding allele (recessive or dominant) on the Y chromosome. Thus, recessive traits on the X chromosome will be more likely to be expressed in males than in females.

One example of a sex-linked trait is hemophilia, a disorder that impedes the body's ability to clot blood, which can result in bleeding to death. Hemophilia is caused by a mutation in a gene on the X chromosome that instructs the body to create a protein important for blood clotting. Genetic males, or individuals with XY sex chromosomes, can inherit the mutated X-linked gene from their mothers (their fathers are contributing the Y chromosome). In addition, genetic males who inherit only one X chromosome with the affected allele will express the disorder. Genetic females (individuals with XX sex chromosomes), in contrast, will only express the disorder if they have the mutation on both of their X chromosomes (i.e., they would have inherited it from both their mother and father). For this reason, the prevalence of hemophilia is lower in females than males.

Another example of a sex-linked inheritance pattern is fragile X syndrome, a condition that leads to cognitive impairment. The allele is also X-linked. A father who carries the X-linked chromosome will only pass the chromosomes to their genetically female offspring (children with XX sex chromosomes) but not their genetically male offspring (children with XY sex chromosomes). In contrast, mothers who carry the allele for fragile X can pass on this allele to both their genetically male and genetically female offspring. Just as with hemophilia, therefore, the prevalence of this disorder is higher in genetic males. Importantly, these sex-linked traits are single-gene traits. Y-linked traits can only be passed from father to son (as only males have a Y chromosome). For this reason, we do not describe a Y-linked trait as dominant or recessive. If a father has a Y-linked trait, their male child will inherit this trait.

BOX 3.1—INFANCY IN REAL LIFE: SEX, GENDER, SEA TURTLES, AND GLOBAL WARMING

Although people often use the terms *sex* and *gender* interchangeably, as we learned earlier, these terms have very different meanings. Again, *sex* is related to our chromosomes and is assigned at birth. *Gender* is what actually gets expressed in our feelings, cognitions, and behaviors. We don't completely understand all the factors that determine a person's gender, but we do know that for cisgender people, their sex chromosomes, physical characteristics, sex assigned at birth, and expression of gender all align. Transgender individuals, in contrast, have a gender identity that contrasts with their sex assigned at birth. A trans woman might have an XY chromosome and was thus assigned a male sex at birth, but she identifies as a woman. Likewise, individuals who identify as nonbinary might have been assigned a male or female sex at birth, but they identify as neither gender. For these individuals (and for many others), gender exists on a spectrum.

We can see how complicated this issue is by considering biological sex in nonhuman animals. For many animals, biological sex is related to chromosomes, just like in humans. But some species of nonhuman animals don't have sex chromosomes at all. For these animals sex is determined entirely by conditions in the environment. Consider coral reef fish. Coral reef fish generally swim in schools with a single male and many females; the male releases testosterone in its urine, which inhibits the females from becoming male. If the dominant male in the school has an unfortunate encounter with a larger (hungrier) fish, there is nothing in the environment to prevent the most dominant female in the school from becoming male, which she does, and then begins releasing testosterone, keeping the rest of the school female.

Similarly, the sex of turtles, crocodiles, alligators, and some lizards is not determined by sex chromosomes; instead, for these animals, sex is determined by the temperature of the surrounding environment while their eggs are being incubated. For example, sea turtle eggs incubated at high temperatures hatch as females, and eggs incubated at low temperatures hatch as males. In fact, researchers have recently reported that because of rising temperatures due to global warming, female sea turtles are being born at a rate of 100 to 1 compared to males (Jensen et al., 2018). Moreover, there are species of rodents that only have X chromosomes, no Ys; researchers still don't know exactly what determines whether they become male versus female, but recent research suggests that their stem cells are sufficiently flexible to develop into either ovaries or testes (Honda et al., 2017) (see Chapter 2).

The point is that although we have talked about biological sex as reflecting a person's chromosomes, it is clear that this is too simplistic to explain biological sex *in general*. Across animal species, sex refers to a role in reproduction and may involve chromosomes, hormones, and physical structures. This is clearly not the same thing as gender, which is a human construct and determined by multiple factors, including biological, environmental, and social factors. In fact, as we just learned, the prenatal environment plays a role in whether or not a fetus develops male versus female sex organs. For example, for someone with androgen insensitivity syndrome (AIS), despite having a male genotype, the prenatal environment did not support the development of male sex organs, which most often leads to the development of female sex organs and a female gender identity. Furthermore, for someone with congenital adrenal hyperplasia (CAH), despite having a female genotype, the prenatal environment supported the development of male sex organs, potentially leading to a male gender identity. So despite having XX or XY chromosomes, the prenatal environment and the fetus's biology work together to determine the development of the sex organs. Similarly, the child's gender identity will develop over time, reflecting the interaction of biological, social, and environmental factors.

Teratogens

The prenatal environment can impact the developing fetus in a number of ways. As we saw earlier, the functioning of the prenatal hormonal environment even guides the development of the fetus's sex organs. And as we learned in Chapter 2, good health and nutrition can impact development in positive ways. However, this also means that negative environmental events can impact prenatal development in not so positive ways, possibly causing birth defects or developmental abnormalities. Any factor that causes malformation in prenatal development is called a **teratogen**. It can be prescription drugs, environmental factors, a disease, malnutrition or metabolic conditions (e.g., diabetes) in the pregnant mother, or something toxic in food. In this section, we will talk about the impact of common teratogens on the developing fetus and how the timing of exposure can sometimes be vital to determining the severity of a teratogen's impact on development.

Common Teratogens

When a woman finds out that she is pregnant, she will quickly learn that there are a lot of substances she can no longer consume. Doctors in the United States commonly suggest that pregnant women avoid uncooked meats, unpasteurized cheeses, raw fish, processed foods, and even unwashed produce. This is generally because bacteria from some of these foods can potentially make the mother sick and, as a result, have negative consequences for the fetus. On top of that, expecting mothers are often told that many over-the-counter (OTC) drugs are now off limits. The Food and Drug Administration (FDA) has even come up with a rating system to help parents navigate which OTC medications are safe to take during pregnancy, and which ones are not. Decisions are based on experiments with animals and with pregnant mothers, examining the birth defects that follow from exposure to a drug. In these studies, pregnant mothers are assigned to either receive the drug or a placebo (usually a sugar pill). Then when the infants are born, the researchers look at what kinds of birth defects—and how many—are found in each group. If the two groups have similar rates of birth defects, the drug is determined to be safe during pregnancy. Researchers also look at the effects that occur when the drug is taken during each trimester—or each equal third of pregnancy. Unlike prenatal development, which is divided into three stages of different lengths, we often divide pregnancy into three equal lengths. As we discussed earlier in the chapter, different things are developing at different prenatal stages. The first trimester includes the first two prenatal stages (the zygotic and embryonic), and the fetal stage is divided into two trimesters. Given that development is different during each of these stages, it is not surprising that the effects of teratogens can differ depending on when exposure occurs.

Deciding whether a pregnant woman should take a particular drug is not as simple as looking at the effects on the developing embryo or fetus. It is also important to consider the effect on the mother. Sometimes a drug—like antidepressants—may be so beneficial to the mother that it may be used even if it increases the risk to the developing fetus. For example, when Carter's mom was pregnant with him, she had a series of ear and sinus infections, which are not uncommon when you have a toddler at home. Her doctor gave her antibiotics, which can be harmful during pregnancy. However, the risks of being sick are also harmful, and Carter's mom and her doctor considered the importance of dealing with the infection and the low risk given her stage of pregnancy. But for the most part, only drugs that have been shown to be safe in humans get recommended by doctors (Table 3.2).

Based on the FDA's system, pain medications like Tylenol (i.e., acetaminophen), for example, have received a B/B/B rating from the FDA, suggesting that human studies have shown no adverse effects on the fetus in any trimester (each trimester gets its own rating). However, aspirin gets a D/D/D rating, suggesting that it is not safe for the fetus in any trimester in most circumstances, and ibuprofen (i.e., Advil, Motrin) and naproxen (i.e., Aleve) each have a B/B/D rating suggesting

TABLE 3.2 ■ FDA Classification System for OTC Drugs	
Category A	Controlled studies in women fail to demonstrate a risk to the fetus in the first trimester (and there is no evidence of risk in later trimesters), and the possibility of fetal harm appears remote.
Category B	Either animal reproduction studies have not demonstrated a fetal risk but there are no controlled studies in pregnant women, or animal reproduction studies have shown an adverse effect (other than a decrease in fertility) that was not confirmed in controlled studies in women in the first trimester (and there is no evidence of risk in later trimesters).
Category C	Either studies in animals have revealed adverse effects on the fetus (teratogenic or embryocidal or other) and there are no controlled studies in women, or studies in women and animals are not available. Drugs should be given only if the potential benefit justifies the potential risk to the fetus.
Category D	There is positive evidence of human fetal risk, but the benefits from use in pregnant women may be acceptable despite the risk (e.g., if the drug is needed in a life-threatening situation or for a serious disease in which safer drugs cannot be used or are ineffective).
Category X	Studies in animals or human beings have demonstrated fetal abnormalities or there is evidence of fetal risk based on human experience, and the risk of the use of the drug in pregnant women clearly outweighs any possible benefit. The drug is contraindicated in women who are or may become pregnant.

Source: Reproduced from Briggs, Freeman, & Yaffe (2008).

that while they might be safe in the first and second trimesters, evidence suggests that they could have adverse effects on the fetus if taken in the third trimester (Black & Hill, 2003). For this reason, most U.S. doctors recommend that pregnant women stick with Tylenol unless otherwise directed.

There are other substances that may act as teratogens. For example, alcohol can have a serious effect on fetal development. As you can imagine, it is difficult to study the effects of alcohol in controlled experiments. You can't exactly randomly assign mothers to either drink during pregnancy or abstain; it wouldn't be ethical. The effects of alcohol on fetal development was discovered in the 1970s, when doctors started to notice a set of features that seemed to occur together. Infants were born with specific facial features, heart defects, and were developmentally delayed. These early observations were followed up with animal studies showing that alcohol does negatively affect prenatal development. Since that time, a number of correlational studies with human infants suggest that heavy drinking during pregnancy can lead to a condition called fetal alcohol syndrome (FAS). Infants with FAS are generally born smaller than infants without FAS. In addition, they have a smaller head circumference and may have facial abnormalities that include widely spaced small eyes and a thin upper lip. They are also more likely to have cleft palate, or a condition where the sheets of cells that come together to form the face fail to merge completely, causing a split in the upper lip where the philtrum should be. Besides physical abnormalities, infants with FAS can also experience cognitive deficits and attentional problems later in development (Thackray & Tifft, 2001).

Importantly, many studies of FAS involve mothers who drink frequently during pregnancy, perhaps even binge drinking. There is far less research on moderate or occasional drinking during pregnancy and its effects on the fetus, again because doing this research experimentally with random assignment would not be ethical. And even correlational studies aren't always incredibly informative because mothers who tend to drink frequently during pregnancy (and are willing to report it to researchers) also tend to engage in other activities that could hurt the fetus, such as illegal drug use, and they may have poor nutrition and less access to prenatal care. However, we do know that FAS is the most extreme outcome of drinking during pregnancy. A wide spectrum of effects can result from alcohol consumption while pregnant; these effects, referred to as fetal alcohol spectrum disorders (FASDs), range from milder physical and cognitive deficits to the more extreme outcomes. What we do know for sure is that when consumed, alcohol passes from the mother's blood into the fetus's blood and can damage or kill developing cells in the fetus, particularly in earlier stages of pregnancy. The severity of fetal alcohol effects will depend on how much alcohol is consumed, how often it is consumed, and at what stage of the pregnancy.

Smoking is another common teratogen. Smoking generally reduces oxygen flow to the fetus and exposes the fetus to dangerous chemicals like nicotine and carbon monoxide. Smoking during pregnancy most commonly results in infants being born too early, or what we call premature, or the fetus being born too small. Recall that pregnancy typically lasts 40 weeks from the mothers' last menstrual period (LMP), or 38 weeks from conception. Infants born before 37 weeks of pregnancy (i.e., before 35 weeks after conception) are considered to be premature. Fetuses who are born early did not have time to fully develop and their body may not be ready to survive out in the world. In addition, infants who are born before 37 weeks of pregnancy are at risk for being born too small, or weighing less than 5 lbs. 8 oz. at birth. Some infants are born on time or at term and still weigh less than 5 lbs. 8 oz.; these infants are called small for gestational age. Infants born this small, whether preterm or full-term, often have underdeveloped lungs and have difficulty breathing and eating on their own. These infants may need to be in the neonatal intensive care unit (NICU) at the hospital in an incubator until they gain weight and can breathe and eat without intervention. Importantly, because the fetus develops over a full 38 weeks, the earlier infants are born, the more systems are underdeveloped and the worse their potential outcomes. Infants born after 24 weeks of gestation are considered viable; that is, they have greater than a 50% chance of surviving. However, infants born this early are very small, will need significant medical intervention because their organs are underdeveloped, and may have long-term health problems, such as respiratory illnesses. Further, prematurity is associated with greater risk of sudden infant death syndrome (SIDS), which is the sudden and unexplained death of a newborn. Smoking during pregnancy increases all of these risks, as does frequent exposure to second-hand smoke.

Thus far, we have talked about the dangers of OTC drugs, smoking, and alcohol use, mostly because they are some of the most common teratogens and they can be the easiest to acquire and misuse. They are not the only teratogens, however, and many things that act as teratogens are out of the mother's control, such as the level of a toxin in the environment or whether she contracts a particular disease. Efforts are made to help women avoid teratogens that are within their control. You probably have seen warnings that drinking alcohol or smoking cigarettes can cause birth defects. Some researchers have examined how women can avoid such teratogens even further with treatment. In one study, researchers studied three groups

PREMATURE BABY: Premature newborn baby girl in the hospital incubator after C-section in week 33 of pregnancy.
iStock/Ondrooo

of women—one who never drank during pregnancy, one who drank during pregnancy but quit drinking after receiving counseling, and one group who continued to drink throughout pregnancy (despite receiving counseling). When their infants were born, infants of mothers who continued to drink throughout pregnancy had the smallest head circumferences and the lowest birth weights when compared to the infants in the other two groups. Further, while all alcohol-exposed infants performed worse than infants who were never exposed in pre-math and reading skills as children, the infants who were exposed to alcohol throughout pregnancy had the most persistent problems (Coles et al., 1991). This suggests that although alcohol exposure of any kind can have lasting effects on infant development, interventions that help mothers stop drinking can significantly reduce the impact of alcohol exposure on the fetus.

Again, although alcohol and smoking might be the most commonly used teratogens, there are many, many others. Marijuana and illegal drugs are also teratogens, along with prescription drugs and opioids. The important thing to remember is that a mother's body determines the prenatal environment for the fetus, so anything that can affect her body can also affect the developing fetus, for better or, in the case of teratogens, for worse.

Timing of Development (The Case of Thalidomide)

Importantly, the effect that teratogens have on the fetus depends on the *timing* of exposure (among other things). A teratogen may have a serious effect at one point in development and little or no effect at a different point. This difference in the effect of teratogens on development helps to illustrate critical periods in development. As mentioned in Chapters 1 and 2, a critical period is a time when the development of a system or function is most susceptible to or influenced by environmental factors, including teratogens. The timing of exposure to a teratogen can be incredibly important for assessing its impact on fetal development. The big question is: When does a teratogen cause the most damage? The answer might become clearer if you take a look at Figure 3.3. The darker bars in mark "very important" periods of development for parts of the body like the central nervous system, eyes, and heart, while the lighter bars mark less important periods. What you might notice right away is that the dark orange bars tend to be arranged to the left—corresponding to earlier stages of prenatal development—and they tend to shift to yellow as we move to the right, or to later stages of prenatal development. You can think about those orange regions as the critical periods for those systems; it is during that time that the development of those systems is most influenced by environmental factors.

As we learned earlier in this chapter, one of the principles of prenatal development is that systems develop in order of importance. This means that a lot of our most vital organs are developing in the first and second trimesters. As a result, teratogens have the potential of making the most devastating impacts when exposure occurs early in fetal development. For example, the neural tube (which will make up the spine and parts of the brain) closes around 22 days after conception, and failure for this to happen could result in spina bifida. Note that once the neural tube has closed, spina bifida will not develop. Thus, the critical period for this development is before the neural tube closes, and it is before that point that teratogens can alter the course of development. However, at 22 days after conception, a mother might not even know that she is pregnant, yet teratogens are already capable of exerting devastating effects on the developing fetus.

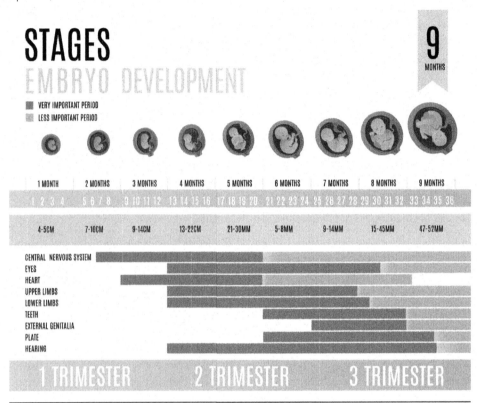

FIGURE 3.3 ■ Stages of Fetal Development

Stages of embryonic and fetal development, marked by importance of the developmental period. The embryonic stage is from 2 to 8 weeks and the fetal stage is from 8 to 38 weeks after conception. (Recall that these two stages follow the zygotic stage, which is 1 to 2 weeks and is from conception to implantation.)

Source: iStock/sabelskaya

Let's also consider the effect of thalidomide on prenatal development. Thalidomide was an OTC medication commonly prescribed in the 1950s and 1960s in Europe, Japan, and Australia for morning sickness, or nausea associated with pregnancy, especially in the first trimester. (Thalidomide was not approved by the FDA and therefore was not used widely by pregnant mothers in the United States, although there were some cases of birth defects due to thalidomide in the United States.) The drug had been tested safely in animals, showing no negative side effects and was being given to pregnant women without any human testing. The effects on affected fetuses were devastating; many mothers who took thalidomide in the first trimester gave birth to infants with no arms, no legs, or no limbs at all. Not all infants were born with abnormalities, and one factor that determined the abnormalities was exactly when the drug was taken. Taking the drug between 34 and 38 days of pregnancy could result in infants born with no ears, between 38 and 46 days could result in infants with malformed arms, and between 40 and 46 days could result in infants with malformed legs. However, taking the drug after 50 days of pregnancy results in *no side effects at all*, likely because the affected sites (mostly the arms and legs) had already developed, even in this short window of time (Franks et al., 2004). From this example, we can see how the effect of the teratogen differs depending on when exposure happens. (This was only one factor; some women who took thalidomide during these time periods had infants who had no apparent abnormalities.) We also can see different critical periods, as the effects of thalidomide varied depending on whether it was taken during the critical period for the development of ears, arms, or legs.

This example, although extreme, shows us how teratogens can cause their most devastating effects in earlier parts of prenatal development, when structures are first forming and are thus most vulnerable to disruption. Further, the specific timing of exposure can have very specific consequences for the fetus. Indeed, the thalidomide example (which is obviously no longer used to treat morning sickness) demonstrates how small the critical windows can be for early structural development in the prenatal period.

Maternal Stress, Anxiety, and Depression

Teratogens are not only substances that mothers can breathe or ingest. There are many chemical changes in the mother's body that can affect the development of a fetus, and often those chemical changes occur without the mothers' knowledge or control. For example, mothers who have clinical anxiety while they are pregnant are more likely to give birth to children who have later emotional problems (O'Connor et al., 2002; Van den Bergh et al., 2004). Likewise, infants of mothers who are clinically depressed during pregnancy demonstrate different stress responses and brain activity when they are born (Field et al., 2004; Jones et al., 1996). How does this happen? Researchers believe that the mothers' mood may cause physiological changes in the prenatal environment that impact the biology of the developing fetus (Kaplan et al., 2008).

As you can imagine, mothers who are anxious or depressed before pregnancy are likely to continue to be anxious or depressed after pregnancy, especially with a newborn to care for. In fact, postpartum depression is experienced by 1 in 7 new moms, and a milder form of postpartum depression, often called the postpartum "blues," is experienced by *most* new mothers. Thus, a challenge for researchers is how to separate the unique effects of stress during pregnancy from the impact of maternal depression and anxiety after the infant is born. Recently, new advances in neuroscience have allowed some researchers to scan the brains of fetuses *while they are still in the womb* to determine whether maternal stress experienced before the infant is born impacts fetal development. Using prenatal fMRI, Moriah Thomason and colleagues (2021) have shown that maternal stress during pregnancy is associated with differences in fetal brain connectivity, with better connectivity in fetuses of mothers who experienced less stress and better social support. In fact, several studies done in the past 10 years have suggested that maternal stress while pregnant is associated with myriad problems for the developing fetus both early and later in development, including problems with attention, impulsivity, cognitive control, and, as Thomason found, functional brain connectivity (Van den Bergh et al., 2020). So emotional support for mothers during and after pregnancy is important for healthy infant development. Sometimes prescribing a medication to help with a mother's depression or anxiety may provide a better outcome for the fetus, even with the risks of that medication.

Prenatal Genetics Screening

Besides teratogens, other things can go wrong with fetal development, such as genetic abnormalities, many of which parents have little control over. Some of these issues can be screened for with prenatal genetics testing. This usually involves getting a saliva or blood sample from the mom and from the dad before they even conceive. These samples are then sent to a lab to determine whether one of the parents carries a recessive gene that could cause a specific genetic disorder in the fetus. Most genetic disorders require a recessive allele from both parents. As we learned in Chapter 2, for an infant to carry the genotype for these genetic disorders, both parents need to carry at least one recessive allele. Individuals with cystic fibrosis, sickle cell anemia, and Tay-Sachs disease, for example, inherited a recessive allele from each parent. These are serious conditions that may be managed but that may cause the individual to be more prone to infections or have a shorter life expectancy than healthy individuals in the case of cystic fibrosis, anemia in the case of sickle cell anemia, or even death during childhood in the case of Tay-Sachs. Parents who are aware of a family history of an inherited disorder will seek genetic counseling to understand the probability of passing on the disorder to a child. If they find they are at significant risk for a serious genetic disorder, they may decide it is too risky to conceive with their own genetic material (e.g., the mother's egg and father's sperm) and consider other ways to have a child, including donor sperm or eggs or adoption.

The examples just discussed are *recessive* traits, and the individual has to inherit the recessive allele from both parents to have the condition. There are also examples of inherited disorders that are linked to the dominant allele of a gene mutation. Recall, when the allele for a trait is dominant, inheriting only one of these alleles suffices to express the disorder, which means that if a parent has a dominant allele, there is a 50% chance of transmitting that condition to their children. Examples of autosomal dominant traits are Huntington's disease, neurofibromatosis type 1, and Marfan syndrome. Although neurofibromatosis type 1 and Marfan syndrome are dominant traits, severity of symptoms vary widely across affected individuals, but typically, individuals have a normal life expectancy. In contrast, Huntington's disease is a progressive brain disorder that affects motor control, diminishes thinking and reasoning abilities, and leads to changes in personality. The disease is fatal. How can a fatal disorder that is genetically dominant persist in the population? Symptoms of Huntington's disease (also known as Huntington's chorea) do not emerge until adulthood, typically when an individual is in their 30s or 40s, typically after the person has already had children. The symptoms become progressively worse over the next 10 to 15 years. Because the onset of symptoms is relatively late, most people are not aware they have the disorder when they have children and can pass on the dominant allele to an offspring.

The well-known American folk singer and songwriter, Woody Guthrie, who wrote the song "This Land Is Your Land" (among many others), died at age 55 of Huntington's disease. Woody Guthrie had eight children; two of which inherited the fatal disorder. With a 50% probability of inheriting the dominant Huntington's allele from their father, why were only two of Guthrie's eight children afflicted? The probability of inheritance refers to the transmission of the allele for Huntington's disease to a specific child. It is not an average across all children. Each of Woody Guthrie's eight children had the same 50% probability of inheriting the disease. The fact that only 25% of his children inherited the disorder highlights the randomness by which the alleles of a gene are sorted into gametes (the sperm in this case) and which of those will then be fertilized and grow into a human.

Besides testing for both dominant and recessive alleles in the parents, genetics screening can also test for genetic abnormalities in the fetus itself. For decades, these genetic tests were conducted on samples of the amniotic fluid taken by inserting a needle in the mother's abdomen, or amniocentesis, or by inserting a thin hollow tube in the mother's cervix, called chorionic villus sampling (CVS). Recently, procedures have been developed that allow doctors to examine fragments of the fetus's DNA that can be found in the mother's blood. This new type of genetic testing simply involves a routine blood draw from the mother.

These genetic tests reveal whether there are abnormalities in the fetus's genes. Trisomy 21—more commonly known as Down syndrome—for example, is caused by extra copies of chromosome 21 in each cell of the body. It is likely caused by a problem with the zygote's cells dividing after conception, and it is most closely linked to maternal age. For example, in women who get pregnant before the age of 30, having a child with Down syndrome is rare, with a risk of less than 1 in 1,000. However, if a woman is over 40 when she conceives, the risk is more like 1 in 100, and it's 1 in 30 if she is 45 or older (Yoon et al., 1996). Individuals with Down syndrome have a distinct set of physical, cognitive, and emotional characteristics. Physically, individuals with Down syndrome tend to have almond-shaped eyes that turn slightly up, a short neck, and small ears, hands, and feet. Cognitively, they have mild to moderately low IQ, and possibly some speech delays. Emotionally, individuals with Down syndrome tend to demonstrate more positive affect and smiling when compared to other children (see Chapter 10).

One thing that is important to point out here is that these genetic disorders are the result of a single gene or gene mutation. Genetics screenings do not test for other developmental problems (e.g., schizophrenia) that are the result of an interaction of many, many genes. In fact, most of the time, developmental problems are the product of an interaction between many genes and environmental factors, so genetics screening can only go so far to predict a fetus's outcomes. Furthermore, other problems can occur when the zygote's cells are dividing after conception, or when the fetus's support structures or first systems are developing, possibly resulting in miscarriage. Miscarriage is the spontaneous loss of a pregnancy before 20 weeks gestation. You may not hear about it too often, but miscarriage, especially at this early stage in pregnancy, is quite common, affecting 10% to 15% of early pregnancies. In fact, the first pregnancy of one of the authors ended in a miscarriage very early in the pregnancy. Although the miscarriage was surprising and sad for her family, her later pregnancies were healthy and without complication.

Check Your Learning

1. Name three principles of prenatal development.

2. What is the difference between sex and gender?

3. Name two common teratogens and describe their potential effects on a developing fetus.

4. During which trimester can teratogens exert the most damage and why?

THE DEVELOPMENT OF SENSORY SYSTEMS

An important part of prenatal development is the development of the sensory systems. The sensory systems are vital for how we experience input from the environment—through taste, smell, touch, sight, and sound. Although it seems like these sensations are only relevant after birth, these systems develop prenatally, and prenatal exposure to different sensations is key to guiding their development. Recall Diego as a fetus sensing the vibrations and sounds of his mother's cello playing. Similarly, during prenatal development, the fetus hears and learns the sounds of its mother's voice and the sounds and smells of the food she eats. In this section, we will talk about the development of each of our sensory systems, what sensory experiences are available to the fetus, and what the fetus can learn from those experiences.

Taste and Smell

We all experience taste differently, and we prefer different foods and flavors. Some of us have a strong sweet tooth, whereas others prefer salty snacks. Some of us would jump at the chance to order sautéed Brussels sprouts or kale, whereas others can't even comprehend how anyone would want to eat those foods. Some of the differences we see in our flavor preferences are cultural, and while some cultures emphasize sweet flavors and milder spice levels, others emphasize umami (savory flavors, like meat or mushrooms) or spicier flavors.

Even infants have these preferences. When Carter was about 5 months old, his mom and dad wanted to transition him from only breastmilk to mostly breastmilk and one bottle of formula a day. Carter's mom had read that the way to get a breastfed baby to accept formula is to give the baby bottles that are a combination of breastmilk and formula. The logic is that if babies are used to breastmilk, and they have a preference for that flavor, it will be too shocking to simply give the baby a bottle of formula. So, you add the novel flavor (the formula) to the familiar flavor (the breast milk) to help the baby learn the new flavor.

Carter was a champ at taking a bottle, as long as it contained his familiar breastmilk. But once his mom combined breastmilk with formula, Carter would have none of it. He would spit out the nipple and turn his head away. He didn't get especially upset; he just wouldn't eat. This was very stressful for Carter's parents. Finally, one day, Carter's mom gave him a bottle of 100% formula, and Carter sucked it right down. The problem wasn't that Carter didn't like the formula; the problem was that Carter didn't like that funny-tasting breast milk. From that point on, he got breastmilk *or* formula, but never a combination. This was an early indication that Carter had strong flavor preferences, and he just would not eat things that didn't taste the way he wanted them to taste. How do we come to develop our taste preferences, and where do these differences in taste preferences come from?

How we experience flavors is a function of both taste, or gustation, and smell, or olfaction. Both of these sensory systems develop prenatally, and prenatal experience is important for their development. On top of that, the ability to distinguish between different tastes and smells and having preferences for some tastes and smells over others are important for survival. For example, preferring sweet tastes over bitter ones may help individuals select foods that are high in calories and avoid poison, which might be pretty important if you don't know anything else about a substance except how it tastes.

Both gustation and olfaction develop early during the prenatal period. You probably know that our experience of taste is determined by our **taste buds** (Figure 3.4). On average, humans have between 3,000 and 10,000 taste buds. These are the gustatory receptors that detect different chemicals in our food (and other things that we encounter) and that we experience as salty, sour, sweet, bitter, and umami. The taste buds are in the **papillae**, which are mostly on our tongue but are also found in the cheek, epiglottis, soft palate, and the esophagus. This means that we experience taste with more than just our tongues. We experience taste when parts of

FIGURE 3.4 ■ Taste Receptors

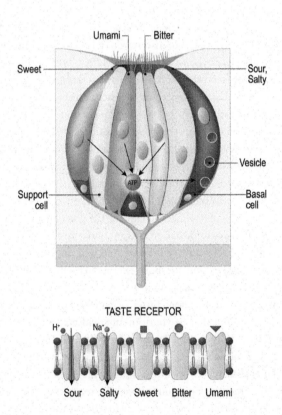

Source: iStock/ttsz

food dissolve in saliva and go into the taste pore, where they come into contact with taste receptors. These taste receptor cells send information to the brain. The papillae have receptors for different tastes. Many people have the misconception that different taste receptors are located on different parts of the tongue. In fact, the papillae all over the tongue have receptors for different types of taste, so you can taste sweet, salty, bitter, sour, or umami on any part of your tongue.

The taste buds start forming at about 8 weeks postconception (Bradley & Stern, 1967) and probably start their gustatory function (i.e., transmitting information about taste to the brain) by 14 weeks postconception (Witt & Reutter, 1996). This means well before birth, the fetus has the opportunity to experience, and learn from, taste. Indeed, during the prenatal period, the fetus swallows and tastes the amniotic fluid. Because the taste of the amniotic fluid depends on food in the mother's diet, the fetus can learn about flavors by "tasting" the amniotic fluid. Interestingly, there is little change in the number of taste buds from birth at least until middle adulthood (Cowart, 1981). This might surprise you, since children are notoriously picky eaters, at least in some cultures. This pickiness is not because infants have more taste buds than adults.

Like taste, olfaction undergoes significant development during the prenatal period. We experience odors (i.e., the sense of smell) when airborne molecules travel to our nasal passages and connect with receptors. As is illustrated in Figure 3.5, these chemicals can come from the nose (nasal passages), but they also can come from the mouth, through the throat. Our experience of *flavors* involves not only taste but also retronasal olfaction, a process by which small molecules from the mouth make their way to the olfactory system through the throat. The stimulated olfactory receptors send signals to the olfactory bulb, at least in the fully developed system. From there, the information is passed on to other parts of the brain.

Olfactory receptors start forming by 9 weeks postconception (Doty, 1986). These receptors are exposed to chemicals when the fetus breathes amniotic fluid. Thus, just like the developing gustatory system, the early developing olfactory system is stimulated by the chemical components in the amniotic fluid. Of course, just because olfactory receptors are present and exposed to input early in prenatal development, this doesn't mean that fetuses *smell*. There is much that we still don't know about how the olfactory systems of the brain develop in human infants, but we do know that the olfactory bulb is functional during the prenatal period and that other parts of the brain that process olfactory information are functional at least shortly after birth.

Although the gustatory and olfactory systems function during the prenatal period, this doesn't tell us about how fetuses and newborn infants actually experience taste and smell. Clearly, newborn infants can't say "that's yummy" or "ick." Instead, researchers study how infants behave when exposed to different tastes or smells. For example, Diana Rosenstein and Harriett Oster (1988) found that newborn infants had recognizable facial expressions in response to different flavored substances. In this study, Rosenstein and Oster video recorded newborn infants from the United States as they were presented with substances that were sweet, salty, bitter, or sour. Then observers (who did not know which substance infants were tasting or were *unaware* of the experimental condition) viewed the recordings and described changes in the infants' eyes, mouth, and so on. It was pretty easy to tell how the infants felt about the different substances; when given substances that were sweet, infants opened their mouths and licked their lips, much like we do when we taste something we like. When given substances that were sour, they were more likely to purse their lips or stick out their tongue. Overall this shows that at

FIGURE 3.5 ■ Olfaction System

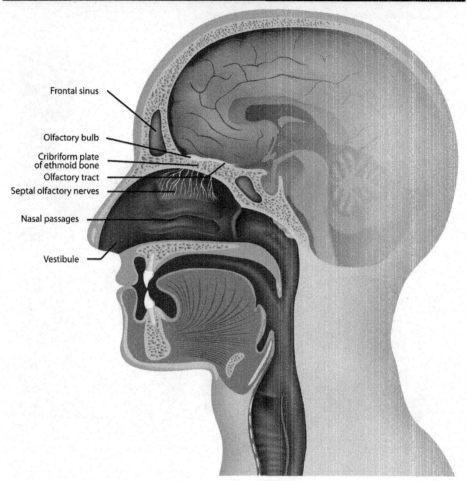

Frontal sinus

Olfactory bulb

Cribriform plate
of ethmoid bone

Olfactory tract

Septal olfactory nerves

Nasal passages

Vestibule

Source: iStock/medicalstocks

birth, infants can taste the differences in the foods they eat, and they react in similar ways that adults do.

Schaal and his colleagues (Schaal et al., 2000) used this approach to study what fetuses learn about the tastes and smells they were exposed to. The researchers asked one group of European pregnant mothers to routinely eat and drink anise-flavored juices and foods and a second group of pregnant mothers to not consume any anise during pregnancy. If you don't know what anise is, it's quite potent and has the strong taste and smell of black licorice. When the infants were 1 day old, the researchers recorded their facial expression as they were presented with cotton swabs that smelled like anise or had a more neutral odor (Figure 3.6). Perhaps not surprisingly, infants whose mothers did not consume anise-flavored foods and drinks during pregnancy responded more negatively to the anise odor than the infants of mothers who consumed anise,

FIGURE 3.6 ■ Newborn Infants' Olfaction

The facial reactions of newborn infants when they are presented with an anise odor.

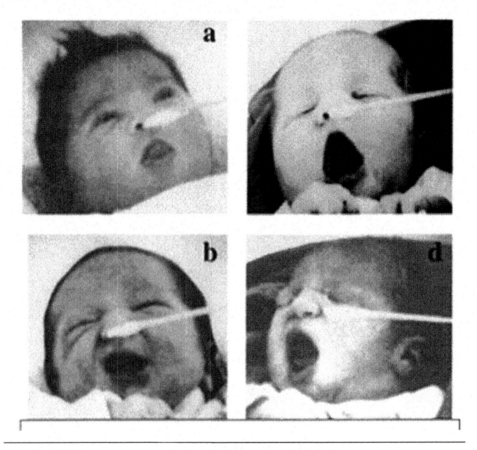

Source: Reproduced with permission from Schaal, Marlier, & Soussignan (2000).

showing that infants whose mothers consumed anise during pregnancy learned about that odor during their prenatal development.

Newborn infants don't just make different faces when they experience different flavors. Infants also *consume* different amounts of differently flavored substances. Just like adults, who are likely to eat more of something that tastes good and less of something that doesn't taste good, newborn infants sucked more when they received sugar water than when they received plain water (Nowlis & Kessen, 1976). In fact, at birth, infants around the globe prefer sweet tastes, suggesting that this preference is not learned during childhood. This is certainly a function of evolution, and as we mentioned earlier, sweet taste signals that foods are high in calories. It also suggests that at birth, infants already experience differences in tastes. How does the experience of taste during prenatal development influence the development of this system?

To find out, a group of researchers from the United States famously asked whether the flavors that fetuses are exposed to prenatally affect their taste preferences as infants. They studied two groups of pregnant mothers. One group of mothers was asked to drink carrot juice 4 days a week for 3 consecutive weeks in the last trimester of pregnancy. The second group of mothers drank water instead of carrot juice. Six or 7 months later, when the infants were 5 months of age and their mothers were starting to feed them baby cereal, the researchers gave the infants cereal prepared with carrot juice and cereal prepared with water, and measured their responses. The infants whose mothers drank carrot juice during pregnancy were willing to eat more carrot flavored cereal than were the infants of mothers who just drank water during the last trimester, and they made fewer negative facial expressions in response to the carrot flavored cereal (Mennella et al., 2001). This study has three important implications. First, it suggests that fetuses can taste the flavors from the foods that mothers consume in their amniotic fluid. Second, it suggests that infants learn these familiar tastes, even prenatally. Third, it suggests that these flavors might shape infants' taste preferences to some extent, up to 5 months after they're born. It is not clear how long-lasting prenatal taste preferences are, but they could form the basis for taste preferences in the long term.

These taste preferences at birth are just one part of the cascade of taste perception development. Even before infants are given "real" food, such as pureed vegetables or bits of food from the family table, what they eat shapes their preferences. We saw this with Carter's preference for breastmilk. Julie Mennella with her colleagues systematically studied how formula-fed infants' preferences are shaped by the *particular* formula they were fed (Mennella et al., 2009). They compared the preferences of infants who were fed cow's milk formula (the kind most infants eat) and partially hydrolyzed formulas (PHF) (formulas made with milk protein that has already been broken down into small pieces; typically infants who have difficulty digesting formulas made with cow's milk are given PHF to eliminate gas and the fussiness and crying that often go along with a grumpy, gassy baby). Cow's milk formula and PHF formulas taste quite different: Cow's milk formulas are savory, whereas PHF are more bitter and sour. Mennella and colleagues found that when infants were weaned and introduced to a wider variety of foods, infants who were fed PHF preferred sour- and bitter-tasting food compared to infants who were fed cow's milk formulas. The experience tasting a particular formula day after day shaped the kinds of foods infants preferred to eat.

But that's not all. Mennella and colleagues found that it wasn't only being fed a particular formula day after day that mattered. It turned out that infants' flavor preferences were shaped by *when* and *how long* they had experience with specific flavors (Mennella et al., 2011). They conducted a study with a group of racially diverse U.S. 7-month-old infants. Infants who had only been fed cow's milk formula rejected a bottle with the unfamiliar (and somewhat bitter) PHF formula—just like Carter when he was given the formula/breastmilk mix. Infants who had been fed only PHF enjoyed a bottle of the familiar PHF. Thus, the PHF was an "acquired" taste; infants who had been eating it all their lives seemed to enjoy it. But infants who had primarily been fed cow's milk formula did accept the PHF if they had been fed PHF for a short time when they were very young, that is, between the ages of 1.5 and 2.5 months. Interestingly, infants who had been given PHF for a short time when they were a little older (between 3.5 and 4.5 months) did not like the PHF when they got it at 7 months. Thus, being exposed to the flavor early was important for acceptance. In addition, infants who were fed PHF for the whole 7 months were most accepting of the formula, suggesting that they preferred the flavor when they had been exposed to it for a long time.

Of course, once infants are introduced to real food, there are more opportunities for their experience to shape their flavor preferences and perception. When solid foods are introduced, infants who are given a variety of foods are more accepting of new foods than infants who are given fewer foods to try (Gerrish & Mennella, 2001), and they are still more accepting of new foods when they are 6 years old (Maier-Nöth et al., 2016). Although very little is known about differences in flavor preference development in different cultures, it seems likely that differences in how new flavors are exposed to infants contribute to the difference preferences in adults from different cultures. For example, mothers in Alen, Germany, breastfeed their children longer and expose their children to less variety of vegetables after weaning compared to mothers in Dijon, France (Maier et al., 2007). A review of the first foods given to infants in cultures from around the world showed a wide range of variation in what infants are given from the first weeks after birth to when solid foods are introduced (Pak-Gorstein et al., 2009).

Clearly, therefore, flavor preferences reflect a cascade of events, starting from the early weeks of prenatal development. Biological factors determine how the taste and olfactory receptors develop, and they also contribute to the initial preferences infants have. But experience with substances both prenatally and during infancy shape the preferences infants develop for the particular flavors they prefer.

BOX 3.2—INFANCY IN REAL LIFE: PICKY EATING BEHAVIOR

A lot of parents know what it's like to have a picky eater at home. Most of our children had all the promise of champion eaters when they started eating solid foods, devouring prunes and string bean purées with the same enthusiasm as they gulped down mashed bananas and avocados. This all seemed to change around the age of 2. This is when all of a sudden Edwin decided he no longer liked half of the foods that he happily ate before, Charlie started to refuse some of his regular favorites, like mashed potatoes and peas, Carter refused to eat any eggs, and Tesalia turned up her nose at deli meats and chicken nuggets. Diego insisted on only his absolute favorite foods, a total of exactly three items: pasta, oatmeal, and raisins; he even refused to eat pizza. Why the sudden change in behavior?

Picky eating—or what researchers define as fussy, or choosy eating—typically starts around the age 2 and peaks between the ages of 2 and 6. Picky eating behavior is also quite common; anywhere from 8% to 50% of parents report that their kids are picky eaters, depending on how strictly you define the word *picky* (Taylor et al., 2015). Picky eating is also observed around the world. One study showed that whereas 6- to 11-month-old infants in China were not particularly picky, about one third of 2- to 3-year-old children were picky eaters—very similar to the proportion of children who are picky eaters in other countries (Li et al., 2017). Importantly, picky eating doesn't typically have long-term negative consequences for health. However, despite the fact that it's not unusual to have a toddler who will regularly refuse to eat the food you put on the table, picky eating can drive parents crazy, and despite the general lack of long-term consequences, picky eaters do tend to get less variation in their diets, with less exposure to fruits, vegetables, and fiber, when compared to infants and children who are less picky.

Of course, not all children are picky eaters, and some children are pickier than others. Why? We don't really know, but research has provided some hints. Breastfeeding seems to be an important factor. One study of children in Illinois suggested that infants who are breastfed exclusively for 6 months are less picky than infants who are not exclusively breastfed for 6 months (Shim et al., 2011). This could be because infants are exposed to a variety of flavors and tastes through breastmilk. Picky eating can also be influenced by how parents introduce new foods to their infants and how they respond when their child rejects a new food. But, picky eating is a function of both *nature* and *nurture* (Patel et al., 2020). There are biological differences in taste preferences that make some children have strong food dislikes. Whereas Diego never cared for cheese but was willing to eat lamb kabobs and vegetables such as broccoli at 18 months, Tesalia loved all cheese and fruit but rejected meat and green vegetables. So, becoming a picky eater, like many aspects of early development, is influenced by several factors.

Fortunately for parents, most children grow out of the picky eater stage, and many solutions for helping children accept more foods are simple. Parents can model good eating habits. When children observe their parents demonstrating picky eating habits, they are more likely to engage in picky eating behaviors themselves (Hafstad et al., 2013). Relatedly, the types of foods that are available regularly in the home are related to the types of foods that children most like to eat (Ventura & Worobey, 2013). So parents can help children by eating and buying the foods that they want their own children to eat too.

Most importantly, children cannot be forced to accept new food. The best approach is to be patient and not push young children too hard toward foods they initially reject. Research has shown that for children to accept a new food, they often have to try it between 10 or even 20 times before they decide they like it, so lots and lots of exposure to new foods is important. Also, rejections may not necessarily be related to disgust responses; children are happy to eat some pretty disgusting things. For toddlers and even older children, eating can instead be a power struggle, or a place where children are looking to assert some control over their own behavior, and importantly, their own bodies. Forcing them to eat teaches them that eating isn't fun. As a result, mealtimes can become a place for anxiety and frustration for both the infant and the parent. Further, research suggests that forcing infants and children to eat something that they reject can actually lead to *more* picky eating and can even teach children not to use their own hunger signals to adjust their portion size, which could lead to overeating and even obesity (Birch & Fisher, 1998).

Picky eating is challenging for parents. When their infant refuses to eat or their child says "I don't like that," parents can feel discouraged and worried. But, it's important to keep in mind that infants and young children have very small stomachs and it's not unusual for them to eat small amounts at one time. Picky eating is also something that decreases over the course of development, and most children begin to accept more new foods as they get older.

Touch

Touch is defined as stimulation of the skin by one of many types of stimuli. It might be a change in temperature, a change in pressure, a chemical reaction, or an electrical stimulation. Like taste and smell, the ability to experience touch develops in utero. As fetuses move their bodies and bump against the uterine wall, the stimulation of the skin is detected and registered by the developing brain. In fact, these tactile sensations may be the fetuses' first sensory experiences, occurring between 4 and 7 weeks gestation. However, we don't know very much about the development of touch and tactile sensory processes. Despite the fact that touch occupies more of our bodies than all the other senses combined—think about how much skin we have compared to our eyes, nose, ears, and mouth—it has not gotten as much attention by researchers as the other senses. In part this is because even though we have sensors all over our body, we actually don't get as much information from touch as we do from our other senses.

We do know that some aspects of the sensation of touch have developed by birth. To test this, researchers took advantage of a reflex newborns have: They reflexively grasp things that are placed in their hands (see Chapter 5). Once newborn infants automatically grasp things, they hold onto them for different amounts of time before they let go. For example, Maria Hernandez-Reif and Bahrick (Hernandez-Reif & Bahrick, 2001) found that when a group of racially diverse infants from lower middle-class U.S. families who were less than 2 days old were repeatedly given a light object (a cotton-filled vial) to hold, the infants held it for shorter and shorter amounts of time. This decrease in response to a repeated stimulus is called *habituation*. When the newborn infants were then given a heavy object (a vial filled with pellets) to hold, they held it for a relatively long time, suggesting they detected a difference between the heavy and light objects. Hernandez-Reif and her colleagues also showed the same pattern when infants were given warm and cold objects to hold (Hernandez-Reif et al., 2003). Thus, newborn infants do experience tactile sensations and can discriminate between different tactile stimuli, suggesting that the sensation of touch developed during the prenatal period.

One of the touch sensations that has been of particular interest to researchers (and parents) is pain. For decades it was believed that newborn infants do not experience pain. Crying responses when infants experienced painful procedures, such as heel sticks to draw blood, were interpreted as reflexes and not as a reaction to pain. It is now recognized that newborn infants do experience pain, and when they do, they cry, change their facial expression, and make bodily movements. But, not all infants, especially preterm infants, cry when they experience painful procedures. In addition, they cry for lots of other reasons too, like when they are hungry, tired, gassy, or wet. Indeed, as we will discuss in Chapter 10 infants' expressions of negative emotions are hard to distinguish. Thus, it may not always be clear that infants are crying because they are experiencing pain.

Interestingly, while touch can cause infants pain, touch can also be the remedy for pain in young infants. Skin-to-skin contact and massage have been shown to help newborns deal with pain. For example, a study conducted with premature infants in a Hong Kong neonatal intensive care unit (NICU) showed that massage after a blood draw reduced infants' pain response (Chik et al., 2017). Studies like these show that even newborns experience touch sensations and that they can experience pain and relief through touch. We will talk more about the benefits of touch for reducing infants' negative emotions in Chapter 10.

Hearing

Hearing, or audition, also undergoes significant change during prenatal development. There are receptors in our ear—hair cells—that detect information and transmit that to our brain as sound. These hair cells are stimulated by vibrations that are caused by a complex interaction of the tympanic membrane (the eardrum), a chain of three bones connecting the tympanic membrane to the cochlea, and fluid in the cochlea. These structures begin to develop in the first 20 weeks of a pregnancy, but it is not until 25 weeks of gestation that the system begins to connect to the brain in a way that allows it to become functional.

Sound is measured in terms of two features. One is *intensity,* or *volume,* or how loud a sound is, and it is measured in decibels (dB). The other is *frequency,* or *pitch,* or how high (like a soprano) or low (like a baritone) a sound is, and it is measured in hertz (Hz). Importantly, humans can only hear a specific range of each of these features. In terms of volume, 0 dB is the quietest sound a human ear can detect; a whisper is at about 15 dB and a normal conversation at 60dB. In terms of frequency, adults can hear sounds in the frequency range of 20 to 20,000 Hz. Infants can hear sounds at slightly higher frequency than adults, but as we age, we lose this ability, which begins to decline starting at 8 years of age.

In the fetus, hair cells for lower frequency sounds are tuned first. The uterine environment protects the fetus's hearing to hear the internal and external sounds that are meaningful, such as the mother's heartbeat or voice. At this point, low frequency sounds, such as dog barks, can pass through the placenta and reach the newly functional auditory system. If there is a loud noise, the developing fetus will respond to it. Further development of auditory perception requires exposure to meaningful sounds, such as speech and music. Starting at 25 weeks gestation, the hair cells of the cochlea, the auditory nerve, and the neurons in the auditory cortex become tuned to the specific sounds (speech or music) (Hall, 2000). This process continues for several months after birth (Graven & Browne, 2008).

But not all sounds are good or meaningful. During development, exposure to intense noise (79–80 dB) will interfere with the hair cell's tuning, even though these levels are not harmful to adults. For a developing auditory system, background noise levels that are low frequency and loud (> 50 dB), such as television or loud music, can limit access to the meaningful sounds, such as mother's voice. Too much exposure to such background noise will inhibit the tuning of the hair cells and can block infants' access to meaningful sounds. Fetuses that are exposed to this kind of noise may not have the neural circuitry as newborns to recognize phonemes, speech patterns, and pitch. For preterm infants, medical interventions can create noise levels beyond the recommended levels while also providing limited exposure to language (Best et al., 2018; Pineda et al., 2017). These challenges may contribute to why preterm infants, particularly those born very preterm, often display language deficits of up to about 2 months (Barre et al., 2011). As such, it is important to avoid exposure to loud noises for prolonged periods for both fetuses and preterm infants in the NICU. Voices and music around middle C frequency are ideal.

Fetuses don't only *hear* sounds, they also *learn* from them. One of the most important sounds fetuses and infants learn to perceive is human speech. In utero, infants gain experience with their mother's voice, and they use this input to tune their hair cells to the frequency of her speech. In fact, there is evidence that fetuses prefer their mother's voice, as measured by changes in their heart rate (Kisilevsky et al., 2009). Of course, fetuses also attend to their father's voice, but they demonstrate a preference for mom (Lee & Kisilevsky, 2014).

This early learning is thought to be particularly important for infants' language development. Indeed, infants begin to acquire language even before birth (May et al., 2011). Newborn infants prefer to listen to human speech over other types of sounds, such as monkey vocalizations (Vouloumanos et al., 2010). Moreover, the brain regions in the left hemisphere that are involved in speech processing specialize prenatally in their responses to language (May et al., 2018). Newborn infants' brains also show neural responses that are specific to language, whether it is for their native language or a foreign language (i.e., an unfamiliar language). Thus, young infants already discriminate between human speech and human non-language sounds.

At birth, infants also discriminate between their native language (i.e., the language that was heard during prenatal development) and a foreign language (i.e., a language not heard during prenatal development). One study showed Japanese newborn infants differentiated between familiar Japanese and unfamiliar English (Sato et al., 2012). There is also evidence that fetuses exposed to English prefer their native language (English) to an unfamiliar language (Mandarin) even before birth (Kisilevsky et al., 2009). They even prefer familiar sequences of language at birth that they heard in utero. In one classic study, researchers asked mothers to read a rhythmic story like *The Cat in the Hat* aloud (to their bellies) twice a day for most of the last trimester. At birth, infants who heard the story showed a preference for the familiar story, by modifying their sucking on a pacifier at a rate that produced the familiar story over a novel one (DeCasper & Spence, 1986). The fetuses in this study weren't learning *The Cat in the Hat* per se; instead, they likely learned to recognize the familiar rhythm and changes in pitch rather than specific sounds or words. Such preferences for familiar rhythms and changes in pitch preferences predict later language skills (Sorcinelli et al., 2019), documenting the role of early exposure to language for infants' acquisition of language.

Eino Partanen and colleagues further showed the connection between early sound preferences and later language skills in a clever experiment in which they "taught" fetuses a new nonsense word. They recruited pregnant mothers in Finland. One group of fetuses were repeatedly exposed to three-syllable nonsense word "tatata" from 29 weeks gestation until birth (Partanen et al., 2013). Another group of fetuses did not receive this exposure to the nonsense word. Using EEG to measure brain responses to the nonsense word, Partanen and colleagues found that as newborns, the infants who heard the word before birth showed different brain responses than the infants who had not heard the word before birth. This suggests that prenatal experiences with language actually shape the development of speech perception.

BOX 3.3—INFANCY IN REAL LIFE: NEWBORN AUDITORY TESTING

One theme of this chapter on prenatal development is that early experience matters, even for the fetus. In terms of auditory perception, early experience with hearing is important for language development and for social interactions with others. Approximately 1 or 2 infants in every 1,000 live births in the United States have permanent hearing loss; the numbers are similar in other parts of the world. This is a significant concern for several reasons. If a hearing loss is not identified early, children may not be exposed to language during early infancy. As a result, these children can experience delays in speech, language, and cognitive development and have long-lasting problems with learning and school. In addition, the lack of auditory input means that infants do not have experience *hearing*; in other words, the auditory regions of the brain do not get stimulated. Thus, identification of hearing loss at birth provides the opportunity for intervention. For example, the use of devices to augment hearing, such as hearing aids or cochlear implants, will facilitate both speech and language development and also the development of auditory pathways in the brain. Other language interventions, such as exposure to sign language, can facilitate language development whether or not other interventions are used. For these reasons early identification of hearing loss has been a priority for many policy makers and organizations concerned with children's health and welfare.

Marion Downs was an audiologist who in the 1960s developed a way to screen infant hearing in the hospital. These early tests involved measuring infants' behavioral reactions, for example, their eye blinks or startle reactions, when they were presented with auditory stimuli. These early screening tests were not always accurate, and many audiologists were concerned that they were unnecessarily stressful for parents. However, screening was still used with infants who were at risk for hearing loss. Over the following 15 years, technological advances increased the accuracy of screening tests.

Now over 95% of newborns in the United States and England are screened by being presented with sounds directly into their ears while their brain responses are recorded through the use of electrodes placed on their scalp. This procedure reveals whether or not the brain responds to auditory signals. Based on this procedure, children are divided into one of two groups: those more likely to have permanent congenital hearing loss and those less likely to have permanent congenital hearing loss. The children in the first group are followed up for further testing and intervention if needed.

Not all countries screen such a high proportion of newborn infants. In countries where most births are in a hospital setting, such as the United States, it is relatively easy to include neonatal hearing screening as part of routine newborn care. However, in some countries half or more of births occur at home, often without trained medical professionals. The minimal contact between newborns, mothers, and trained professionals is a challenge for routine newborn hearing screening. In low-resource countries, or resource-constrained countries, the rate of screening in hospitals may be low. For example, fewer than 50% of medical colleges in India have newborn hearing screening (Das et al., 2020).

Universal newborn hearing screening still is debated. Although modern procedures are more accurate than the tests Marion Downs developed, there still are a significant number of false positives; that is, there are a number of newborns identified as having hearing impairments when in reality their hearing is fine. The accuracy of the test depends on how it is administered and the training of the person giving the test. For example, false positives can be reduced by testing infants when they are asleep and in a quiet room. In some settings training is so poor that the tests are very unreliable. It is very stressful for parents to be told their child has a hearing loss, and thus some have argued that universal testing should not be done. But in general, policy makers have agreed that the benefits of universal hearing screening for newborns outweigh the negatives.

Vision

Unlike the other senses we have talked about, infants get very little visual experience before birth. This is at least partly why the visual system is less well developed at birth than the other senses: Unlike taste, smell, audition, and touch, the fetus has little visual experience to stimulate the development of the visual system. This doesn't mean that the visual system does not develop prenatally. In fact, as with all of the systems described here, a lot of development happens before birth. The kind of tuning we just described for the auditory system can't really happen for the visual system before birth, as there is little visual input inside the uterus. But the developmental events that occur during the prenatal period set the stage for infants to take advantage of the visual input they encounter after birth.

Like audition, vision is extremely complex and includes many different systems. Obviously, vision involves our eyes. We get our eyes checked and we get glasses or contacts if we need them. But the eyes are only part of the system. Of course, you already know that in order to see, you must have your eyes open and directed at the thing you want to see. This means that the muscles we use to turn our head, open our eyes, and move our eyes are all important. You also likely know that light enters the eye through the pupil, or the hole in the iris, which is covered by the cornea. The pupil constricts when conditions are bright and there is a lot of light, and the pupil dilates when it is dark. This is how the pupil controls how much light falls onto the *retina*, the light-sensitive layer of tissue at the back of the eye (Figure 3.7). From your own everyday experience, you know how hard it is to see when too little light falls on the retina, for example, when you walk into a dark room at night or try to read a menu in a dim restaurant. You also know how hard it is to see when too much light falls on the retina, for example, when you first walk outside on a bright sunny day. The pupil opening up (dilating) and getting smaller (constricting) is how the visual system adjusts to make sure that you have the optimal amount of light on the retina to see well.

FIGURE 3.7 ■ How the Eye Works

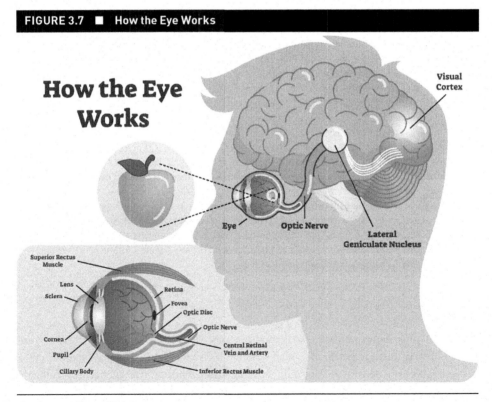

Source: iStock/VectorMine

The retina is light sensitive because it contains **photoreceptors**. These are neurons that absorb light and send information via the **optic nerve** to the brain. You remember from Chapter 2 that neurons are the cells of the nervous system that transmit information. This means that the retina—which is in the eye—is actually part of the nervous system. The retina contains two types of photoreceptors, **rods** and **cones**, which play different roles in vision. There are approximately 120 million rods and only 6 to 7 million cones. The more numerous rods are more sensitive to all stimuli except for color. This means that rods are very important for how we see in the dark. (Have you ever noticed that you can't really see color in low light?)

The cones are less sensitive, so they are most responsive in bright light, and they are responsible for our color vision. Although cones are found throughout the retina, they are most densely packed at the **fovea**; this is the part of the retina that has the sharpest, clearest vision. In fact, the fovea only contains cones. As a result, we see most clearly when we continually move our eye to focus the light from the object of interest falling on the fovea. The **lens** in the eyeball helps to make sure that light is focused on the retina. The lens changes shape, or accommodates, to focus light at different distances; this is how we can see things clearly that are far away and close up.

But seeing doesn't end at the eye. The information detected by the retina is transmitted to the **visual cortex**, or the part of the brain that processes, represents, and interprets information transmitted from the retinas, by way of the optic nerve. The visual cortex is a complex network of brain areas that respond to and represent colors, shapes, orientations, movement, as well as more complex features of the visual world like faces and places, and that develops considerably after birth based on the visual input it receives.

Although there are significant and substantial developmental changes after birth, this system does develop prenatally. In general, the physical structures of the eye, including the retina, develop prenatally. For example, the retina begins to develop in the second month after conception, and it has a complete set of cells by about 5 months gestation. Of course, as we will see, the retina is not fully developed at this point, but it does appear that the basic structure of the retina, including an area that will become the fovea, develops prenatally. In addition, the eyeball and muscles that control the movement of the eyeball develop prenatally.

Similar to the other sensory systems we have discussed, although visual structures develop early, they do not function as they will later. For example, the pupils of infants who are born at less than 32 weeks gestation do not constrict in response to light. This means that very preterm infants have difficulty controlling how much light hits the retina, and premature infants need to be protected from light. Although newborns have some ability to control their eye movements, this ability develops over the first months after birth. Components allowing input from the eye to be communicated to the brain develop late in the prenatal period and well into infancy. Experience is an essential part of the development of the visual system, including even some prenatal experiences. Specifically, the visual pathways in the brain engage in spontaneous activity during prenatal development, apparently "practicing" the kinds of activity that will be used later in response to light. The cells of the retina fire together during prenatal development, even before there is exposure to light.

Despite these prenatal developments, infants' vision at birth is quite poor. As a result, infants will often spend a lot of time looking at things that to us seem uninteresting. One of us has a niece who spent hours looking at the stripes on her couch. Her parents called them her "friends." Young infants' poor vision reflects the fact that several aspects of vision are underdeveloped. First, although infants have a fovea, it is not well developed. As adults, we see clearly because our fovea has densely packed cones. At birth, however, the cones are more sparsely packed in the fovea. Figure 3.8 shows the fovea of the human retina at 5 days, 11 months, 4 years, and 13 years of age. The cones (indicated by the letter *c* in each figure) are more spread out (and have a lot more distance between them) at 5 days (panel a) than at 13 years (panel d). One change over development

---

FIGURE 3.8 ■ The Eye

Fovea of the human retina at (a) 5 days, (b) 11 months, (c), 4 years, and (d) 13 years..

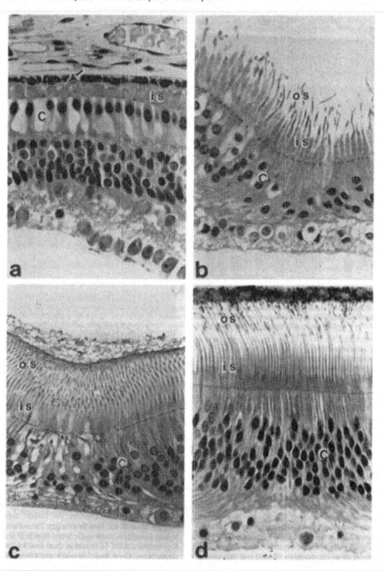

is that the cones become more densely packed, which will mean that vision becomes sharper in the fovea. Thus, although the retinal cells are formed during prenatal development, they undergo significant changes in the period after birth, and those changes affect how well the individual can see.

A second reason that vision improves is because the photoreceptors themselves develop. You may also notice from Figure 3.8 that the photoreceptors become longer and skinnier across age (which is why more of them can fit in the fovea). This means that with development, the photoreceptors actually change in shape. At 5 days and 1 month, the cones are "stubby"—short and fat. With increasing age, the cones get longer and narrower. This is why more of the cones can get packed together, resulting in sharper vision with age.

Other changes are related to how visual information is processed by the brain. For example, information from the retina is transferred to the visual cortex via the *optic nerve* (see Figure 3.7). Although myelination of the optic nerve begins during the prenatal period and during the last weeks of prenatal development the myelin sheaths on the optic nerve become thicker and more numerous, the optic nerve is not completely myelinated at birth. Nearly all the fibers of the optic nerve are myelinated by 7 months, and the myelin sheaths continue to get thicker over the first 2 years (Magoon & Robb, 1981). This means that in addition to the photoreceptors themselves becoming more effective at detecting information, the optic nerve becomes better at transmitting information over infancy.

There are even more significant changes in areas of the visual cortex involved in controlling where we look; perceiving movement, shape, and color; recognizing familiar faces; and detecting the difference between natural objects (e.g., trees) and human-made objects. The development of this system is complex and occurs over many years. For example, although infants can detect motion at birth, the parts of the brain that allow them to discriminate between different directions of motion are not developed until 2 months of age. An important function of the visual cortex is to coordinate the information from the two eyes. This ability develops by 4 months of age, as experience and maturation allow the brain areas responsible for this integration to develop. The developmental changes we will discuss later—for color perception, depth perception, object perception, and face perception—all reflect changes in the visual cortex.

Check Your Learning

1. How do we know that some taste preferences develop prenatally?

2. How can loud noises potentially impede the development of audition prenatally, and even postnatally?

3. Describe how language learning might begin before birth.

4. How does prenatal experience affect the development of the visual system?

BIRTH AND THE NEWBORN

There are a lot of different ways to bring an infant into this world. Some moms give birth in a hospital with a doctor, while others have their infants at home with a doula. Some moms labor for days with no pain relief, while others labor for hours, choose pain medications, or even schedule a C-section. Indeed, no two births are quite alike, not even the births of our three pairs of siblings.

When Alison was born, her mom never went into labor. Instead, her water broke, she went to the hospital, and the doctors started her on a drug called Pitocin that induces labor. After having an epidural to numb the pain, Alison was born at 2 a.m. after 14 hours of labor, with a doctor using forceps to pull her out. Alison's brother Carter was also induced. It was a much shorter labor—only 5 hours—but this time, his mom didn't have an epidural, and so she felt every single contraction (ouch). Edwin's mom's water broke as well, but she went into labor only 30 minutes later. Edwin was born reluctantly as the sun rose over Central Park on New Year's Day, after 7 hours of labor and a whole 2 hours of pushing. Like Carter, Charlie was induced shortly before his due date, and after about 10 hours of Pitocin and an epidural, he came right out after only 5 pushes. Diego's mom had a natural birth with no pain medication and with the help of a doula. Her water never broke and labor started very gently, as she was practicing cello. Her labor was quite bearable for the first 8 hours. After a whopping 17 and a half hours of labor, including 2 hours of pushing, Diego was born in a hospital soaking tub. When his sister Tesalia was born almost 2 years later, the labor was much shorter—only about an hour. Like Diego, Tesalia was also born in a bathtub. But unlike Diego, with Tesalia, there was no need to push. Tesalia was so petite that she just quietly made her entrance into the world, just as the doula was arriving. Since their mom didn't have enough time to make it to the hospital, Tesalia was born in the tub at home, which happened to be the faculty-in-residence apartment of a university dorm.

No one knows exactly what causes labor to begin. All we know for sure is that typical gestation is about 38 weeks from conception, or 40 weeks of pregnancy. An infant born anytime between 3 weeks before or 2 weeks after their due date is considered to be on time, or at term. As you can see from our six infants, no two births are exactly the same—even births in the United States to moms with good health care. There are even more variations as we consider how women around the world give birth. Here we will talk about the process of labor and birth, with a few details about how birthing traditions might vary from place to place. We will also discuss the newborn and newborn states, especially the two most salient—crying and sleeping.

Labor and Birth

The traditional view of birth was that it is a traumatic and scary process for the newborn. In the 1920s, Austrian psychoanalyst Otto Rank published a book called *The Trauma of Birth* (1929), where he described how traumatic the birth experience is for an infant, an experience that takes the child years and years to recover from. Likewise, in 1975, French doctor Frederick Leyboyer pitched a similar story in his book *Birth Without Violence*. In this book, Leyboyer proposed that to eliminate potential trauma of birth, women should give birth in a pool of warm water, mimicking the conditions of the uterus, where the fetus is surrounded by warm amniotic fluid.

Contrary to these old-fashioned beliefs, we know now that birth is not necessarily painful or traumatic for the infant. During the birthing process, the newborn mostly feels pressure on the head. If you try to put as much pressure as possible on your head right now, you'll see that even intense pressure isn't necessarily painful. And mothers, like Tesalia and Diego's mother, still choose to give birth in warm baths, but mostly for their own comfort and pain relief.

In contrast to these older perspectives, recent research suggests that the birthing process may be incredibly beneficial for the infant. For example, some researchers have suggested that infants are exposed to specific kinds of bacteria in the vagina that can help them with the development of their digestive systems and might even help them fight disease (Dominguez-Bello et al., 2010). Indeed, studies conducted in the United States show infants born vaginally are less likely to develop various allergies (Renz-Polster et al., 2005), asthma (Neu & Rushing, 2011), and even experience childhood obesity (Huh et al., 2012) when compared to infants born via C-section (which we will discuss more later).

But unfortunately, whereas birth is not painful for the newborn, it is painful for the mother. Labor and birth happen in three stages (Figure 3.9). The first is called *dilation*. During this stage, the mother's cervix opens up (**dilation**) and it grows thinner (**effacement**). During the first stage

FIGURE 3.9 ■ Stages of Labor and Birth

Stages of Childbirth

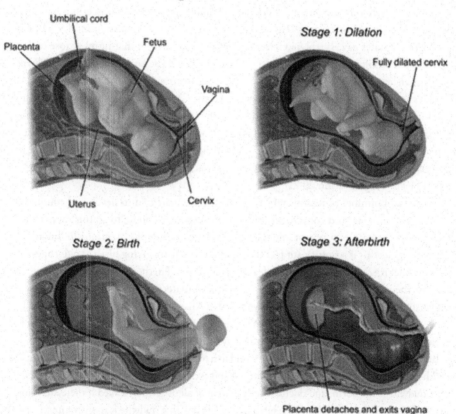

Source: BruceBlaus, CC BY-SA 4.0 <https://creativecommons.org/licenses/by-sa/4.0>, via Wikimedia Commons

of labor, the muscles around the uterus contract to help the cervix to open up so that the fetus can move down. These muscle contractions are what you typically think of when you think of labor, and this stage of labor is the longest. What doctors call "active labor" usually lasts between 4 and 8 hours, but by the time a mom is in active labor her contractions are regularly spaced, and the cervix has already dilated to 6 centimeters (starting from zero). Once the cervix has opened to about 10 centimeters, labor typically proceeds to the next stage, which is called *transition*. This is the stage you usually see in movies where a mother is in the delivery room, pushing the infant out and yelling profanities at her partner or the doctors. During this stage, the newborn moves from the uterus past the cervix, and into and out of the vagina as the mother uses her muscles to actively push the newborn out. This stage can be less than an hour but can last up to 2 hours. The third and final stage of labor, called *afterbirth*, is the shortest; this is when the mother pushes the placenta and all remaining support structures out after the newborn is born.

These three stages are typically shared by women who have a natural birth. However, there is a lot of variation in how this process happens, who delivers the newborn, and where the newborn is delivered. For example, in cases where a vaginal birth can put the newborn or the mother in danger, mothers may have a cesarean section (C-section), which is a surgery that involves making an incision on the mother's abdomen to remove the newborn. C-sections have been on the rise in the United States in recent years. For example in 1965, only about 4.5% of women in the United States gave birth via C-section (Taffel et al., 1987); that number rose to 33% by 2010–2011 (Hamilton et al., 2013). Most startling is that in the United States over 25% of low-risk pregnancies end in C-section. The rates of C-section are similar in other Western industrial countries and are even higher in Latin America and the Caribbean, where rates can be over 40% of all births. Interestingly, the rates are lowest in the least developed countries, accounting for only 5% of births in sub-Saharan Africa. This dramatic difference probably indicates that there are many fewer medically unnecessary C-sections in the least developed countries, but it also means that women in these countries may not have access to C-sections when they need them (World Health Organization, 2021).

There are a number of reasons why C-sections have increased in developed countries. For one, a C-section is fast and convenient, so some mothers may choose to go this route instead of experiencing the pain of a potentially long labor. The number of C-sections in low-risk pregnancies suggests this is a significant factor. Second, women are giving birth at older ages, which heightens the risk of complications that lead to a C-section. Further, in cases where the newborn goes past their due date, or the mother is of advanced maternal age, doctors may induce pregnancy using a drug called Pitocin, which was used in Alison, Carter, and Charlie's births. This is done to avoid potential complications, like those associated with delivering a very large or heavy newborn. But induced labors are also more likely to end in C-section.

But it is not common everywhere in the world to have a C-section, or to even give birth in a hospital with a doctor. In many countries and cultures, and even in parts of the United States, giving birth with a midwife is the norm, and doctors aren't present at all or are only called if there are complications. In Germany, for example, giving birth in a hospital with a midwife is most common. In other countries, giving birth at home is more of the norm. In fact, in the early part of the 20th century, giving birth at home was also the norm in the United States. And while home births in the United States are on the rise, less than 1% of women in the United States gave birth at home in 2012. This is low for even

Western industrialized countries; indeed, in countries like the Netherlands, about 20% of women choose to give birth at home (Zielinski et al., 2015). Some women don't have access to a hospital or birthing center and home birth is their only choice. Others choose home births because they fear that a hospital birth is more likely to lead to unnecessary interventions or C-section. Others, like Tesalia and Diego's mom, choose a middle of the road route and give birth in the hospital with the help of a midwife or with the support of a doula. Others still choose to give birth in a hospital with a doctor in order to avoid any risk of complications. There are also differences in who is present at birth. In hospital births in the United States and around the globe, a woman probably will give birth in the presence of her partner and a midwife, a doctor, and many nurses. In Bangladesh, in contrast, a woman will give birth at home surrounded by her female relatives and friends. In Nigeria, women give birth at home alone; a birth attendant comes only after the child is born to cut the cord and bury the placenta. Again, there are many ways to give birth, but the goal of all birth methods is to deliver a healthy newborn.

Newborn States

The newborn period is considered to encompass the first 4 weeks of life, when the newborn is establishing patterns of eating, sleeping, and waking. In many ways, newborns' life is not that different from their life before birth: They spend their time drifting from an awake to a drowsy or alert state, they take in nutrients and expel wastes, and they practice moving their bodies. Of course, unlike before birth, once born, infants have to eat and breathe air, and they can hear better and they can see. But, during the first weeks after birth, newborn infants are focused on adjusting to the world outside the womb. They spend most of their time sleeping or drowsy. They spend the rest of their time awake, either alert, or fussing/crying. This varies from infant to infant and changes each month as infants get older.

Newborn Sleep

Newborns spend most of their first few months of life sleeping, a pattern of behavior that begins prenatally. Starting in the third trimester, fetuses sleep a lot. In fact, during one particularly memorable prenatal visit, Edwin was sleeping warmly in his mom's uterus during a routine exam. The doctor needed to check whether Edwin's organs were developing normally, but his position made it impossible to see. The doctor poked at his mom's abdomen to get Edwin to wake up. After that didn't work, the doctor made Edwin's mom drink sugary juice and literally do jumping jacks in the exam room. It worked, and Edwin woke up with a yawn (which was amazingly captured in the ultrasound).

Not only do fetuses and newborns sleep a lot, but they also engage in a lot of **REM sleep**. REM sleep, or rapid eye movement sleep, is a deep cycle of sleep where the brain is very active. On average, newborns spend about 16 hours a day sleeping, and half of that sleep time (50%) is composed of REM sleep. As we get older, we not only spend less time sleeping, but we also spend less time in REM sleep. In fact, an adult in their 20s generally spends 6 to 8 hours a day sleeping, 22% of which involves REM, and an adult in their 60s spends 6 to 7 hours a day sleeping, 13% of which involves REM (Pandi-Perumal et al., 2002).

Why do fetuses and newborns need so much REM sleep? Recall when we were talking about the development of the visual system, we talked about how the visual pathways in the brain engage in spontaneous activity during prenatal development, apparently "practicing" the kinds of activity that will be used later in response to light. Researchers also believe that the brain activity involved in REM sleep functions to stimulate the developing visual system in the absence of exposure to visual stimuli. To test this hypothesis, in one classic study, James Boismier exposed newborns, while they were awake in their cribs, to either an interesting checkerboard image or a less interesting gray square. Then he measured how much they slept. His theory was, if REM sleep functions to engage the underdeveloped visual system, then newborns who get lots of visual stimulation (i.e., with the checkerboard) will need less REM sleep than newborns who don't get as much visual stimulation (i.e., with the gray square). As he predicted, Boismier found that the newborns who looked at the checkerboard engaged in less REM sleep and were more alert when they were awake than the infants who looked at the gray square (Boismier, 1977). This suggests that sleep serves a number of functions, and REM sleep is particularly important for newborns, as it can help create important connections in the brain.

Crying and Colic

Unfortunately for new parents, newborns cry. They don't cry that much—on average, for about 2 hours a day—but those 2 hours can feel like a lifetime for a new parent. Newborns cry for a variety of reasons, and it isn't always clear which of those reasons is the source at any particular time. Newborns cry when they are hungry, tired, overwhelmed, in pain, wet, gassy, or uncomfortable. There is a lot of variability in how much newborns cry. When she was 24 hours old, Alison's dad started to be concerned that she hadn't cried much yet. He was waiting for

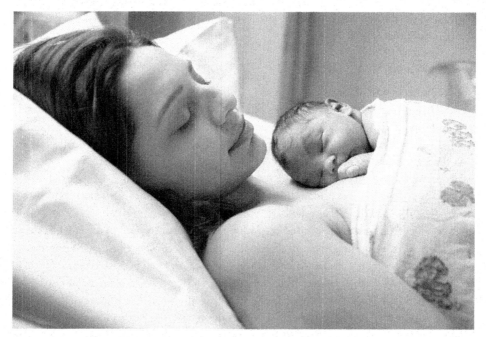

Newborn (and mom) sleep

iStock/SelectStock

the floodgates to open, for her to cry for hours. It turned out that as a newborn Alison didn't cry much. Excessive crying, inconsolable crying for more than 3 hours a day, is called **colic**. Although like Alison, Tesalia didn't cry a lot at first, when she was 3 weeks old, she developed colic. Every day, at about 7 p.m., she would begin an endless stream of high-pitched cries that were so loud, her mother would have to leave the house and walk her (in a stroller), and the family dog, outside for 2 hours. Unlike other times of day, Tesalia could not be soothed during this time and her mother simply accepted that she would get some fresh air and exercise during these shriek-filled hours. Tesalia's crying lasted until about 9 p.m. and then she would settle down for the night, sleeping like a champ. She would awake a happy baby, until about 7 p.m. the next night, when she again transformed into an inconsolable screaming infant. Then, at about the time Tesalia turned 3 months, the evening crying was not so bad and by 4 months, it was gone. In fact, one night, it simply didn't happen. As quickly as it started, her colic disappeared. Only the family dog, Rica, was disappointed that the 2-hour nightly walks with a screaming infant had stopped. No one knows for sure what causes colic, but it is generally thought to be caused by some digestive or gastrointestinal issue, like acid reflux, in most infants.

Although a crying newborn can be distressing, there is little evidence that crying or even colic will hurt the infant. However, colic can be incredibly stressful for *parents*. Shaken baby syndrome (SBS), which is head or brain injury caused to an infant from excessive shaking, is related to how much infants cry (Barr et al., 2006). Further, colic is also related to the incidence of postpartum depression in mothers (Akman et al., 2006). These studies are only correlational, so we can't say for sure that the crying *causes* parents to feel depressed, or that crying *causes* parents to shake their infants (likely out of frustration or anger), but the link is suggestive that the best intervention for excessive crying might be for the parents instead of the infants.

Check Your Learning

1. What are the three stages of labor and birth?

2. What are the potential benefits of a vaginal birth?

3. What is the function of REM sleep for a newborn?

SUMMARY

In this chapter, we discussed prenatal development and introduced you to the world of the newborn infant. Although you might have thought that prenatal development is driven mostly by biological processes, we discussed how the prenatal environment can play an important role in fetal development and how teratogens, in particular, can cause damage to that environment, especially at the earliest stages of prenatal development. When discussing the sensory systems, we saw how early experience with the senses can shape prenatal development, and that in the third trimester, the fetus can even acquire preferences for familiar tastes, smells, and sounds that are evident after birth. This suggests that as prenatal development comes to an end, the fetus begins to function more and more like a newborn who is capable of experiencing and learning from the world around them.

KEY TERMS

amniotic sac

cephalocaudal direction

colic

cones

dilation

effacement

embryonic stage

fallopian tube

fetal stage

fovea

lens

neural plate

neural tube

optic nerve

ovaries

papillae

photoreceptors

lacenta

REM sleep

rods

taste buds

teratogen

umbilical cord

visual cortex

zygotic stage

REVIEW QUESTIONS

1. What are the three stages of prenatal development?

2. When is the fetus most susceptible to teratogens and why?

3. What is the difference between sex and gender?

4. Name one common teratogen, and describe its potential effect on the developing fetus.

5. Discuss how the development of one sensory system gives rise to prenatal learning.

6. What are the three stages of labor and birth?

7. What potential function does REM sleep serve for both the fetus and the newborn?

CRITICAL THINKING QUESTIONS

1. If you were a high school teacher, what examples could you use to describe each of the three principles of prenatal development?

2. If you were a nutritionist advising a woman planning to become pregnant, what foods would you recommend they incorporate into their diet and when? What foods would you advise the woman to avoid during each trimester of her pregnancy?

3. Can a father who carries the chromosome for fragile X pass the allele to his son? Explain.

4. Suppose you have trained to become a genetics counselor. When you meet with a family expecting twins, one male and one female, concerned about a family history of hemophilia, what information can you share about the likelihood of each twin expressing

hemophilia? Is there a difference in likelihood for the male versus female twin, and why? How would your counseling change if Huntington's disease was present in the family history?

5. You are traveling with a family member who is expecting. She develops a terrible headache and asks you for some pain relief. What medication could you safely give? How might this change depending on the trimester of pregnancy?

6. Using what you know about prenatal development of the sensory systems, provide an example of how development is continuous from the prenatal to newborn period.

7. A friend of yours has a baby with colic. What advice would you give her about what to do for her baby and for herself?

4 PERCEPTUAL DEVELOPMENT

When Edwin was only a few months old, every day he would stare at a wooden shelf that was above his changing table and "talk" to it while his mom changed his diaper and got him dressed for the day. The shelf was just a plain wooden plank that held his toys and books and was several feet away from his little newborn face. Despite the fact that this shelf was not particularly special to anyone else, it was absolutely fascinating to Edwin. Without fail, he would greet the shelf with a smile every morning and babble to it without pause until he was whisked away for the day. In fact, this became such a regular occurrence that his mom and dad would often comment

Edwin Talking to Shelf

Shelf

that Edwin started his day "just talkin' to Shelf." After weeks of this, curiosity finally got the better of his mom, and she got underneath Shelf to look at it from Edwin's point of view. What she saw explained a lot: Shelf had a series of wooden knots on the bottom, right in line with Edwin's head, that made the shape of a face. From Edwin's perspective—given his ability to see and his experience in the world—this visual scene was as interesting as it gets.

Infants' ability to see is pretty limited in the first weeks and months after birth, and this example shows that what infants find interesting to look at can be pretty different from what we, as adults, find interesting to look at. In fact, very young infants' experience of the world is pretty different from ours. As we saw in Chapter 3, newborns' vision is not very well developed, but they can hear, smell, taste, and even recognize sounds and tastes they experienced frequently as fetuses. The first year of life is a period when infants' understanding of the information they get from their senses changes rapidly.

One reason this development is important is because infants' sensory experience and perception determines the *input* they receive to learn about the world. The abilities and developments we describe in later chapters of this book—memory and attention in Chapter 6, cognition in Chapter 7, language in Chapter 9, emotion in Chapter 10, and social interactions in Chapter

11—all depend on what information infants take in from their sensory experiences and how they interpret, remember, and make sense of those sensory experiences. As we saw in Chapter 3, although sensory systems develop prenatally, there is still a lot of development that needs to happen after birth. Because infants get their information about the world from what they see, hear, smell, touch, and taste, the development of these sensory systems is very important for what they learn. In fact, a small change in a sensory or perceptual experience may be responsible for a significant cascade of changes over time. In this chapter we will describe the development of four aspects of perception in infancy: **visual perception**, **auditory perception**, **haptic perception**, and **intermodal perception**. We will discuss what factors determine these changes, as well as how development in these systems change the information infants can learn.

After reading this chapter you will be able to:

1. *Describe* the important theoretical issues in perception and the methods used to study their development in infants.

2. *Compare* the development of different basic visual abilities.

3. *Describe* the developmental changes in infants' object perception.

4. *Identify* the changes in auditory perception from birth to childhood, especially changes in speech perception.

5. *Describe* how infants can use touch to learn about objects.

6. *Explain* how infants connect information across modalities.

THEORETICAL ISSUES IN THE STUDY OF PERCEPTION

Defining Perception

Why is the story of Edwin's reaction to Shelf so fascinating? Looking at the photo of the shelf, we get a sense of what Edwin could see—round blobs on the bottom of Shelf. We discussed the development of sensory systems in Chapter 3, and we know that Edwin's visual system was not very well developed at birth. So, although we know what he was looking at, we don't really know what Edwin *saw*. Moving from understanding the development of the sensory systems, in this case the retina, optic nerve, and so on, to understanding how infants *interpret* what they see is broadly what we mean by **perception**. In this chapter, we will talk about perception as it relates to the sensory development introduced in Chapter 3.

In this chapter, we will go beyond discussing whether infants can *detect* particular sensory information and discuss what we know about how infants *make sense* of that sensory information. So, when we look at a human face, the processes and developmental changes we discussed in Chapter 3 help us understand when infants can detect patterns of light. Throughout this chapter, we will uncover how infants' brains process that information and how infants consider previous experience and knowledge about the world to see a *face*. Although the particular processes are different for the different sensory modalities, we usually focus on questions such as whether infants can *discriminate*, or tell the difference between sensory experiences, whether they have preferences for some sensations over others (and why), and whether they recognize a sensory experience as similar to other experiences. In asking these questions, we also probe how developmental changes in these processes reflect infants' experience, or the roles of nature and nurture in perceptual development.

We can ask questions about perception as it relates to any sensory modality—gustation, audition, vision, and so on. In this chapter we focus on visual, auditory, and haptic (touch) perception and how infants combine information from different modalities. This will give you an introduction to the study of perception and illustrate the kinds of questions and solutions researchers put forth when trying to understand perceptual development in infancy.

The Nature and Nurture of Perceptual Development

As in many areas of development, researchers have long asked how *nature* and *nurture* influence perceptual development. For many years, developmental researchers who studied sensation and perception in infancy had views that derived from a famous quote by William James (1890): "The baby, assailed by eyes, ears, nose, skin, and entrails at once, feels it all as one great blooming, buzzing confusion" (p. 94).

This quote has been taken to mean that very young infants experience lots of sights, sounds, smells, and so on, but have no way of understanding them. Thus, at first, the infant's experience of the world is chaotic. This view is similar to the classic idea of philosopher John Locke that the mind begins a *tabula rasa*, or blank slate, that is written on by sensory experience (see Chapter 1). For these views, perception changes with experience. At first, sensory experience is simply random and meaningless information from the different senses. With experience, the mind begins to be able to interpret and make sense of that information. This might be through forming *associations*. For example, an infant may come to associate the sight of her mother's face with being fed, comforted, and held. Through the infant's experience with seeing her mother's face while being fed, the infant learns to recognize that face and it takes on the meaning of *mother*. When thinking about Edwin's fascination with Shelf, we might consider that because he had looked at so many faces, he learned the association between two round shapes (eyes) above an upturned curve (mouth). In this way, Edwin's interest in Shelf may reflect his past experiences—minimal as they might be—with faces.

Other researchers have been inspired by Jean Piaget, a psychologist who studied early cognitive development. Piaget argued that infants' perception develops from their experience through a constructive process; they learn about how to visually perceive objects through exploring and acting on them. This has been referred to as **constructivism**. We will talk much more about Piaget's influential theory in Chapters 7 and 8. What is important for understanding perceptual development is that infants are thought to *construct* or *build* their perception from their experiences. Although in this view experiences are important, development is not simply about forming associations; instead, infants are actively involved in creating their understanding from those experiences. In this case, Edwin's perception of Shelf as face-like would not simply come from him associating different shapes but from building information about faces based on first-hand experiences interacting with the faces around him.

However, other researchers have argued that it would be impossible for infants to learn everything they need to know from their experiences, and thus some aspects of perception must be inborn or *innate*. As we reviewed in Chapter 1, this view derives from ideas like that of Descartes, who argued that some knowledge is inborn. Researchers who adopt this view have attempted to show that infants are very sophisticated in their perception from a very early age. For example, one might argue that Edwin was prepared to see patterns as faces when he was born, and his fascination with Shelf came from some innate understanding of what faces look like or some natural attraction to faces.

Most researchers now understand that infants' sensory and perceptual development is not all nature or all nurture. Like most things, it is a combination. Infants' genetic code causes them to develop specific kinds of bodies. They are born with two eyes that are sensitive to light, and those eyes are positioned to point forward in the front of their head, unlike birds and fish with two eyes pointing to either side of their head. This difference in where the eyes are positioned determines the kind of visual input that goes to the infant's brain. For example, having two eyes close together on the front of the head allows human infants to coordinate the input from the two eyes and "see" a single view of the world. This is called a cyclopean image, as if the perceiver were like the Cyclops from Greek mythology and seeing a single image from a single eye. Clearly, because the structure of the face (i.e., how the two eyes are positioned) is a part of human biology, this aspect of infants' visual sensory and perceptual experience is innate.

However, the specific input infants get comes from their experience. Although all typically developing infants have two eyes positioned approximately in the same location in their head, their everyday experience varies. And while some input is likely to be experienced by all or most human infants, other kinds of input vary. All infants around the world see human faces, but not all infants around the world see the same faces or even the same type of faces. For example, the faces infants see vary in terms of race. In addition, depending on where infants live, they will see different kinds of trees and plants, different types of buildings, and different animals. These differences in experience likely influence how infants' vision develops. The point is that although some aspects of sensory and perceptual development must be innate, that development is also influenced by experience and learning.

Studying Perceptual Development

Before we describe what we know about perceptual development, we need to talk about how we study it. This will be a theme throughout this book. In Chapter 3, we described methods we can use to measure infants' preferences for one stimulus over another, for example, by measuring whether infants turn their head toward one stimulus or another. Likewise, we can use infants' **visual preference** to measure their visual perception. In the 1950s, Robert Fantz showed that newborn infants who were shown a patterned stimulus and a blank stimulus at the same time looked longer at the patterned stimulus (Fantz, 1958). Many studies use visual preferences to understand how infants' visual perception develops.

Perception is also commonly studied using *habituation*. Habituation refers to the fact that infants' response to a stimulus decreases when that stimulus is repeated. In other words, infants prefer relatively new things and lose interest as things become familiar. Researchers take advantage of this by familiarizing infants with one stimulus and then testing how interested they are in a new stimulus. In **visual habituation**, we present infants with a visual stimulus, such as a picture of a face, pattern, or object, and measure how long they look when the stimulus is presented. Infants are shown the same stimulus on several successive presentations; initially they find it intriguing and look at it for a long time. But, as infants see the *same* image or object over and over again, they get bored and look at it for shorter and shorter amounts of time. We will talk about why this might be in Chapter 6, but for now it is important to know that as infants learn or form a memory of a stimulus, their looking time decreases, or *habituates*.

Once infants have shown this decrease in looking time, researchers test their reaction to a new image or object. If infants can discriminate, or tell the difference between the old familiar stimulus and this new stimulus, they will look for a long time at the new stimulus, or *dishabituate*. If they are unable to discriminate between the old and new stimuli, then the novel stimulus will not look any different from the familiar stimulus (and it won't be novel), infants will not find it interesting, and their looking time will not increase.

Often, researchers use a variation of the habituation procedure called the **visual paired-comparison** task. This procedure is like the habituation procedure in many ways. Just as in habituation procedures, infants are first familiarized with a stimulus, and then the researchers measure how long they look at the familiar and novel stimuli. Unlike the habituation procedure, however, infants are usually given the familiar stimulus on only one trial (instead of until they habituate). Then, during the test, the now-familiar stimulus is presented side by side with a novel stimulus. The researcher measures infants' visual preference for the novel stimulus during this test.

Importantly, looking is not the only behavior that habituates. We can use habituation to study infants' perception of visual stimuli, as well as many other infant behaviors. In the section on haptic perception, we will see how researchers can study infants' recognition of objects by measuring the habituation of how long infants touch or hold a familiar object. Likewise, we will discuss how researchers can use the habituation of infants' sucking to study speech perception.

Check Your Learning

1. How have theorists argued that experience, or *nurture*, influences the development of perception?

2. Historically, why did some researchers argue that perceptual abilities must be innate?

3. How have researchers used infants' preference for novelty to study perceptual development?

BASIC VISUAL ABILITIES

If you have ever interacted with a newborn infant, you might have wondered if they could see, and if so, *what* they could see. Although at birth infants are alert and have their eyes open, it is difficult to tell what they are focusing on. In the first weeks or months after birth, infants appear to be looking at nothing in particular, making it unclear what they actually see. But, they do *look*. They look in the direction of sounds. They look at things that are held in front of them (if those things are close enough). But, it is clear that what they see when they look is different from what we see when we look. In this section we will talk about the development of infants' basic visual abilities.

The Development of Visual Acuity

Visual acuity refers to the amount of detail you can see. In adults, we can measure this with a Snellen eye chart (Figure 4.1). You almost certainly have seen a chart like this when you've been to the eye doctor. The bottom line in Figure 4.1 corresponds to 20/20 vision. When you

FIGURE 4.1 ■ Snellen Eye Chart

A Snellen eye chart used to assess visual acuity in older children and adults.

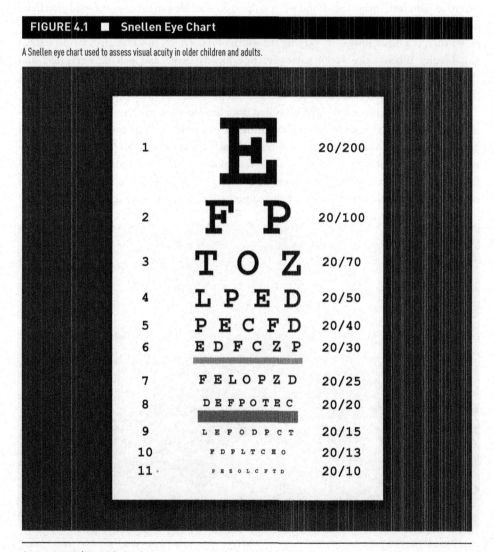

Source: istock/Alexey Bezrodny

stand 20 feet away from the chart, you should be able to see the details of the characters on this bottom line and be able to tell the difference between the D, E, and F. The lowest line that you can see clearly when standing 20 feet away from the chart tells us what your visual acuity is. For example, if you can read line 2, but can't tell the difference between any of the characters in line 3, we say you have 20/100 vision. You can see clearly at 20 feet what someone with 20/20 vision can see clearly at 100 feet.

How can we measure infants' acuity? Obviously we can't ask infants to read letters in order to examine their visual acuity. But, we can take advantage of their preferences to look at some visual stimuli over others to get an estimate of their visual acuity. In a procedure developed by Davida Teller (Dobson et al., 1978; Teller, 1979; Teller et al., 1974), infants are shown a card that has a patterned image (black and white stripes) on one side and no image (a solid gray field) on the other side (see photo). This procedure relies on infants' preference to look at a pattern rather than at a blank image. By varying the width of the stripes, this task gives an estimate of visual acuity. When acuity is poor, narrower stripes blend together and look like a gray field, and the two halves of the card look the same. Teller's task estimates the infants' acuity by identifying the smallest stripes that infants prefer.

Infants' visual acuity can also be measured from their involuntary responses to visual stimuli. Optokinetic nystagmus (OKN) takes advantage of a reflexive response that infants—and adults—make when viewing a moving stimulus. **Visual evoked potentials (VEPs)**, are the electrical activity generated by the brain as the infant looks at a visual stimulus and are recorded from electrodes placed on the infants' scalp. For both of these procedures, researchers or clinicians present different stimuli to the infant and note when the response is observed.

Child Being Tested With Teller Acuity Test

An examiner using teller acuity cards to measure an infant's visual acuity.

These different procedures give different estimates of infants' visual acuity; generally VEP reveals better acuity than the other measures. This may be because infants' brains detect visual information, and so it is recorded in the VEP, but that information does not flow through the brain to influence behavior. That is, to show a visual preference or an OKN response, the system must detect the visual stimulus, the information must then be transmitted to the part of the brain that processes visual information, then the information must be communicated from that region to the part of the brain that controls eye movements and preferential looking. This fascinating issue raises the question of what it means to *see*. Is it enough that the brain registers a stimulus, or does seeing require that information about that stimulus is communicated to other parts of the brain so that it can control behavior?

Regardless of how it is measured, at birth, infants' visual acuity is extremely poor, estimated to be between 20/200 and 20/400 (Table 4.1). This means that when something is 20 feet away, newborn infants can make out the level of detail that an adult with normal 20/20 vision could see if that image was 200 or 400 feet away. On the Snellen chart in Figure 4.1, the big E is what someone with 20/400 acuity can see at 20 feet. Imagine what this means for the newborn infants' visual abilities. They can see very few details of the objects, people, and scenes around them, which has significant implications for what information they can learn about the world.

Fortunately, infants' visual acuity increases rapidly over the first weeks and months after birth, giving them access to more visual details of the world around them. By 4 months, infants' acuity is estimated to be 20/200, at 8 months acuity is estimated to be 20/100, and by 10 months acuity is estimated to be 20/50. This is still poor vision; 20/50 corresponds to the fourth line down on the Snellen chart. But it is clear that infants' visual acuity improves dramatically in the first year. Visual acuity continues to develop beyond infancy, and adult 20/20 vision is achieved when children are about 6 years old.

These rapid changes in acuity certainly reflect, at least in part, the changes in the photoreceptors, fovea, lens, and visual cortex that we discussed in Chapter 3. But experience *seeing*

TABLE 4.1 ■ Methods for Assessing Visual Acuity in Infants			
Method	**Description**	**How Acuity Is Estimated**	**Estimate of Newborn Acuity**
Preference/Teller acuity cards	Measure infants' looking behavior to simultaneously presented pattern (e.g., stripes) and solid gray field	Identify the finest detail (e.g., smallest stripes) that infants show a preference for	20/400
Optokinetic nystagmus (OKN)	Measure reflexive eye movement to moving pattern (e.g., stripes)	Identify the finest detail (e.g., smallest stripes) that elicits the reflexive eye movement	20/400
Visual evoked potential (VEP)	Measure (from the scalp) electrical activity produced by the brain when presented with patterned stimuli (e.g., stripes, checkerboards)	Identify the finest detail (e.g., smallest stripes or checks) that elicits a brain response	20/200

matters too. For decades, Daphne Maurer and Terri Lewis (2018) have studied children who are born with dense central cataracts. Children who have these cataracts are essentially blind at birth and are unable to see any patterned light. Their vision can be restored by fitting them (surgically) with clear lenses. This means we can test visual development in a group of children who did not see from birth but who became able to see only after they had corrective surgery, which in the infants studied by Maurer and Lewis happened between the ages of 1 and 9 months. Not surprisingly, the infants' visual acuity was initially very poor, but just 1 hour after surgery their visual acuity had improved as much as is typically seen between birth and 1 month of age in infants with intact vision. Just 1 hour of clear vision caused a large change in what infants could see, demonstrating how experience *looking* and *seeing* is important for the development of visual acuity. However, development continues to happen even in the absence of experience, and infants have slightly better vision if the surgery is done earlier (Hartmann et al., 2014). Presumably, the longer children have the dense cataracts, and the longer they develop without visual experience, the more difficult it is for acuity to change in response to visual experience. (Remember our discussion of plasticity and critical periods in Chapter 2.) But this cataract surgery also places children at risk for other visual problems, so there are many factors to consider regarding the age that parents and doctors decide when to correct these congenital cataracts.

Color Vision

When people find out that we study infants, we are often asked if infants can see color at birth. This is not such a silly question. Learning how to label colors is really hard for young children. Whenever 20-month-old Charlie was asked, "What color is this?" he would proudly say, "Ye-woah" (yellow), regardless of the actual color of the object being pointed to. You might conclude that he didn't see differences in colors because he answered the question with the same color name every time. (His mom was certainly worried about that for a time.) But we also know that in adults, color perception can be influenced by various factors, including the language spoken (Özgen, 2003). For example, compared to English, some African languages have fewer color names. English has several names for colors near the blue-green boundary (teal, jade), whereas some African languages have only one name for those colors. Adults who speak these languages perceive these colors differently. This raises the question of whether and how infants *see* color before they have words to label colors.

Infants do see some color from birth, but their color perception is not the same as it in adults, or even as the same as it is for 20-month-old Charlie. (His saying everything was yellow turned out not to reflect an inability to see color but rather how hard it is for children to learn color names.) How does this color perception develop? First it is important to understand a little bit about how our visual system perceives color. All light falls on a continuum of wavelengths, and we perceive light of different wavelengths as being different in color. Figure 4.2 shows the spectrum of colors in terms of wavelengths, which are measured in nanometers (abbreviated nm). The *visible spectrum* of light—those wavelengths humans can actually see—range from relatively long wavelengths (i.e., those with a high nm value), which we see as red, to relatively short wavelengths (i.e., those with a short nm value), which we see as blue. We can't see light

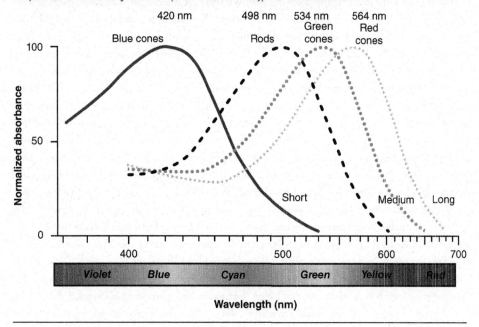

Source: Francois~frwiki, CC BY-SA 4.0 <https://creativecommons.org/licenses/by-sa/4.0>, via Wikimedia Commons. Originally adapted from Bowmaker & Dartnall (1980).

with wavelengths longer than about 700 nm, which is *infrared light*, or light with wavelengths shorter than about 400 nm, which is *ultraviolet light*.

As we learned in Chapter 3, the photoreceptors on our retina that are responsible for detecting color are the *cones*. Newborn infants' cones are short and stubby, less densely packed in the fovea, and inefficient at detecting light. It would therefore not be surprising if newborns' color vision was different from adults. Humans have three types of cones, and each type of cone is sensitive to a different range of wavelengths of light, short wavelengths (our short or blue cones), medium wavelengths (our medium or green cones), or long wavelengths (our long or red cones). As adults, humans are **trichromatic**, which means we see color by comparing how these three types of cones respond to light. For example, when seeing light of 500 nm, the human visual system perceives a blue-green color by comparing the responses of these different types of cones. When an individual is missing one of the three cone types, or if all three cone types are present but one (or more) cone type does not respond as strongly as in a typical human eye, it results in *color vision deficiency*, or what is commonly called *color blindness*. Studies measuring VEPs to different wavelengths of light or infants' visual preferences for different colors have revealed that young infants are only sensitive to bright colors and that objects or patches of color need to be big for infants to see them (Allen et al., 1993; Skelton et al., 2022; Volbrecht & Werner, 1987).

Thus, although baby decorations and nurseries are often pastel colors, young infants probably can't see those colors well.

But we don't just detect differences in color. We also perceive *categories* of color, judging some pairings of wavelengths as more similar than others. For example, adults judge two different wavelengths they would label *blue* as more similar than two different wavelengths they would give different labels to (e.g., blue and violet). In the 1970s, Marc Bornstein and his colleagues used habituation to examine when infants also categorize colors in this way (Bornstein, 1976; Bornstein et al., 1976). Specifically, they asked if infants, like adults, would treat two wavelengths of light that are in the same color category (e.g., that adults would call blue) as more similar than two wavelengths of light that are in different color categories (e.g., one that adults would call blue and another that adults would call green). They tested this question using habituation. Young infants were presented with a single wavelength of light on several successive presentations. They then were shown new wavelengths of light. For example, 4-month-old infants were habituated to a wavelength that adults would call *blue* (480 nm), and then they were tested with a new wavelength that adults would also call *blue* (450 nm) or a new wavelength that adults would call *green* (510 nm). Note that both new colors were exactly 30 nm different from the habituation stimulus. Thus, if all infants do is respond to a change in wavelength, both of these two new colors will be novel. Bornstein and colleagues found that after habituation to the blue color, 4-month-old infants looked for a long time at the wavelength that adults call green but were not interested in the new wavelength that adults also call blue. Bornstein and his colleagues argued that by the time they are 4 months of age, infants perceive colors in the same way as do adults, treating two different blue colors as more similar to one another than a blue color and a green color.

In general, therefore, we would conclude that infants perceive color, and they do so from birth. Very young infants are not as sensitive to color as adults are, but by 4 months they do seem to perceive colors the same way adults do. It is important to remember that these studies have involved testing infants (mostly White infants) from Western cultures, and primarily English-speaking cultures. So we know that infants from these cultures develop color perception that maps onto the color categories of the English-speaking adults in their environment. It seems unlikely that there are cultural differences in the development of color perception in the first few months. However, until studies are conducted with infants from other cultures and other language environments, we can't know for sure that all infants develop color perception in this way.

Although it is likely that maturation of the photoreceptors and other aspects of the visual system are responsible for the development of color vision, just as we saw with acuity, experience looking and seeing also likely plays a role. Specifically, *seeing* color may be important for the development of color perception. In one natural experiment, Bruno Laeng and colleagues (Laeng et al., 2007) found that the color sensitivity of Norwegians differed depending on whether they were born above or below the Arctic Circle. In addition, even for those born above the Arctic Circle, people born during the autumn, and thus are infants during the winter when there is little light, were less sensitive to color than people born during the summer and who were infants when there is little darkness. These results suggest that light exposure during infancy shapes color vision. A study by Sugita (2004) with monkeys confirms this conclusion. In this study, infant monkeys were raised for *the first year* (rather than a few months as was the case for Norwegian infants born above the Arctic Circle) in monochromatic light. They could see—and all their cone types were stimulated—but they spent the first year of their life in an environment that did not have full wavelengths of light. Thus, these monkeys did not have experience seeing all of those wavelengths. As adults, these monkeys could see color, but they did not group colors in the way humans and monkeys raised in typical light do. Specifically, just like humans, monkeys raised in typical light cluster colors into "reddish," "greenish," and "bluish." Monkeys who were deprived of colored light in the first year, in contrast, did not cluster colors in this way. Instead, these monkeys raised in monochromatic light apparently perceived the colors as belonging to more, smaller clusters. Thus, exposure to a wide range of wavelengths of light seems to be necessary for the development of the kind of color perception observed in adults.

Depth Perception

Finally, humans do not see the world as flat, like a two-dimensional photograph, but as three-dimensional, characterized by objects arranged in depth. This perception of depth is critical for the ability to navigate our bodies through the world. If we were unable to perceive depth, we would be consistently walking into things and other people and falling off of curbs and stairs. Infants' perception of depth is one of the earliest aspects of visual perception that has been studied. In Chapter 1 we talked about the visual cliff. Eleanor Gibson (Gibson & Walk, 1960) created this task to see if *crawling* infants could see depth. You might have heard stories of infants crawling off the couch or a bed. These stories led people to question whether infants who could crawl actually perceive depth. In Chapter 1 we described how when Alison first began to crawl at about 6 months, she crawled right into the edge of the coffee table, and she did this many times. This error might mean that Alison did not yet have accurate *depth perception*, or the ability to perceive how the objects in view are arranged in depth. Perhaps she crawled into the coffee table because she did not perceive that it was as close to her as it was.

Gibson created the visual cliff to provide crawling infants with the *illusion* that they were crawling over a deep cliff. The apparatus has a transparent surface that shows a patterned floor several feet below. When the lighting is just right, it looks like you will fall if you step (or crawl) over the edge. We learned in Chapter 1 how infants' experience crawling seems to be important in determining whether or not they will crawl over the edge of the cliff. (We will revisit this in Chapter 5.) Infants with more experience crawling are more reluctant to cross the deep side of the cliff than infants who have just learned to crawl. One conclusion from this might be that infants *learn* to perceive depth from their experience. The problem is that we can't test infants' depth perception in this procedure *until they can crawl*. So infants who can't yet crawl don't cross the cliff, not because they can't perceive depth but because they can't crawl.

In fact, studies using other procedures have revealed that depth perception likely emerges early and that it changes over time. Whereas the visual cliff procedure asks how infants respond to an apparent cliff, other studies have asked how infants use different kinds of information to perceive depth (Table 4.2). For example, if the infant in the previous photo crawled toward you, the infant would get bigger. You could use this **kinematic** (or movement) information to perceive how things are arranged in depth. José Náñez and Albert Yonas (1994) found that when infants as young as 4 weeks were shown an image that appeared to get closer to them (i.e., it got

TABLE 4.2 ■ Types of Depth Cues

Type of Cue	When It Is First Evident	Examples	Description
Kinematic cues	In the first month after birth	Increase and decrease in size	As objects move closer they get bigger; as they move farther away they get smaller
Binocular cues	Approximately 4 months	Each eye has a slightly different view of the world	The brain fuses the separate images from the two eyes
Monocular depth cues	Approximately 7 months	Size	Objects that are closer are bigger
		Occlusion	Objects that are closer may occlude, or partially hide, objects that are farther away
		Texture	The texture and detail are clearer for objects that are closer

increasingly bigger), they blinked and moved their head back. Apparently, they could use the kinematic information to perceive that the looming object was getting closer in depth.

Although very young infants are sensitive to kinematic cues, they are not sensitive to **binocular depth cues**, or information about depth that is available to us by combining the information from both of our eyes, until about 4 months of age. Because our eyes are separated, the brain gets two slightly different views of the object even when that object is perfectly focused on both retinas. The brain fuses those two images, and our experience is that we only see one object, but in 3-D. Using the difference between the two images to see the 3-D structure (and depth) is called **stereopsis**. When infants are about 2 months of age, they become able to move their eyes so the same object is focused on both retinas. This ability gives the brain the input it needs to develop stereopsis and binocular depth. Infants' perception of depth from coordinating the two eyes together emerges by about 4 months, after about 2 months of coordinated information from the two eyes.

BOX 4.1—INFANCY IN REAL LIFE: STRABISMUS AND DEPTH PERCEPTION

Some infants never fully develop the ability to use their eyes together. Strabismus and amblyopia refer to a set of conditions in which the eyes are misaligned, and includes lazy eyes, crossed-eyes or wandering eyes. The ability to align the eyes develops in the first months, and many infants have intermittent strabismus in the first 3 months. However, about 4% of children under the age of 6 in the United States are diagnosed with some form of non-intermittent strabismus (worldwide the incidence is about 2%). These individuals are

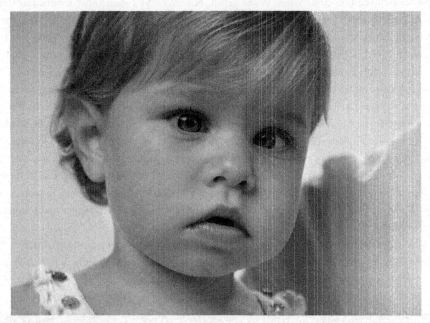

Infant With Strabimus

iStock/teap

unable to adjust their eyes to focus on the same object. As a result, the brain gets information from the two eyes that is difficult or impossible to coordinate. Typically, they will have the impression of two objects, one that is clear and one that is blurred. If the condition remains untreated, the child will not develop the ability to perceive depth from coordinating the information from the two eyes. In untreated strabismus, the brain is unable to resolve the two images and it will suppress the input from the eye that produces the blurred input. The brain will process only the information from the stronger eye, and the individual will never have binocular vision or be able to use binocular depth cues.

Fortunately, strabismus can be successfully treated. Sometimes this simply means patching the strong eye, forcing the infant (and the infant's brain) to rely on information from the eye with poorer vision. Other times, treatment requires surgery to reposition the muscles that control eye movements. You will probably not be surprised to find out that children who had surgery between 6 months and 2 years had better vision than children who had the surgery after age 2 (Simonsz et al., 2005), illustrating the importance of the first years as a *critical period* for visual development. Recall that during infancy the brain is organizing; synapses are forming and being pruned. Thus, the kind of input that is received during these months determines the development of the brain. After this period, the brain does not adapt as easily to changes in the information it receives, so the best outcomes are seen when strabismus is corrected when the brain is still adaptable. Even though it is important to correct the condition early, it is not clear that surgery should always be done when the condition is first detected, often between 4 and 6 months. Many practitioners prefer to wait and see how the child's eyes develop, and do surgery late in the first year. This may reduce the number of unnecessary surgeries, although it may also reduce the ultimate effectiveness of the surgery.

We don't need binocular vision to see depth, however. We can also use **monocular depth cues**, or cues to depth that are available even when we can only use one eye. We can't always perceive depth by coordinating the images from the two eyes. For example, when you look at a picture, you see depth but you can't use movement or binocular cues. Because a photo or image is two-dimensional, the objects are not actually different distances from us, and binocular information isn't available. Your eyes can't adjust differently to focus on objects that are located at different distances because all the objects are the same distance from you. But you clearly see that the mother is farther away than the baby and that the keys are in front of the baby. This is accomplished by monocular depth cues, which are sometimes called *pictorial cues* because they are the kinds of cues we can use to perceive depth in pictures. These are cues such as the size of objects, the texture, and whether or not objects occlude other objects. In the two previous photos, the baby is bigger than the mother, and occludes, or hides, part of the mother's body. We know that the rattle is closer to us than the block because it is bigger and we can see more detail about the rattle.

Albert Yonas and his colleagues have studied infants' sensitivity to monocular depth cues by measuring infants' reaching to the objects in displays like that in Figure 4.3. In this display, real toy frogs were attached to a background (the "floor"). In reality, all of the frogs are the same

FIGURE 4.3 ■ Apparatus Used by Yonas, Elieff & Arterberry

The apparatus used by Yonas, Elieff, and Arterberry to study infants' use of monocular depth cues. Although the four frogs are equally distant from the infant, the single frog on the bottom appears closer, especially when the display is viewed using only one eye.

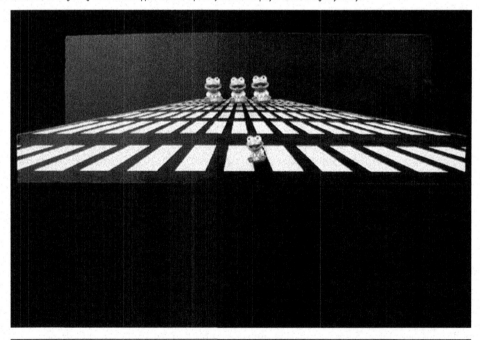

Source: Reprinted with permission from Yonas, Elieff, & Arterberry (2002).

distance from the infant. But several monocular depth cues in the background make it seem like the single frog on the bottom is closer than the other frogs. Notice that the pattern elements are bigger in the bottom row than in the back rows—this is a cue that they are closer in depth. Also notice that you see more of the details of the pattern in the front row than in the back rows—we can see more details of objects that are closer to us.

Yonas, Chryle Elieff, and Martha Arterberry (2002) showed 5- to 7-month-old infants these displays and recorded which frogs they reached for. The reasoning is that infants will reach for objects that they see as closer in depth. When 5-month-old infants had both eyes open, and binocular cues could be used, they reached for the top row of three frogs, probably because they could tell that all the frogs were the same distance and there were more frogs on the top row. However, when one of the infants' eyes was covered with an eyepatch, binocular cues were not available and they had to use monocular cues of texture and size of the pattern elements to see the bottom frog as closer. Under these conditions, it was not until 7 months of age that infants reached more for the single frog at the bottom than at the other frogs. This suggests that infants become sensitive to monocular depth cues between 5 and 7 months.

Thus, over the first year of life, infants become sensitive to different kinds of cues to depth. So asking simply "Do infants perceive depth?" is not the right question. Instead, we have seen that infants see depth differently across the first year. Early on, they can use movement cues to see some aspects of depth. By 4 months, experience using the two eyes together allows infants to use binocular cues to depth. Finally, by 7 months infants are sensitive to monocular depth cues.

Check Your Learning

1. How does visual acuity develop in infancy?

2. When do infants seem to perceive colors as do adults? How do we know?

3. What is the evidence that experience is important for the development of color perception?

4. What are the three different types of cues to depth? What is the difference between them?

5. How can we use infants' reaching behavior to test their depth perception?

VISUAL PERCEPTION OF OBJECTS

Perceiving Objects

When we look at the visual world, we don't just see patterns of light, we see *objects*. When you look at the following photo, you see a mom, a baby, toy keys, a rattle, and many other *objects*. How do we perceive the pattern of light in an image like this as objects? First, we perceive objects as having *boundaries*, and our visual system looks for clues that there is a boundary between two objects. For example, you can parse this photo into a mother, a carpet, a baby, a couch, and many toys, by noticing changes in color or texture; we perceive those as boundaries between objects.

VISUAL PERCEPTION CONCEPTS: This photo illustrates how we can see the objects in the visual world arranged in depth.

iStock/Drazen_

As adults, we expect that parts of an object will have similar features and that abrupt changes in features signal object boundaries. Amy Needham (1998) asked whether infants recognized this type of featural change as an object boundary. She showed infants a display in which a bright yellow, bent hose was adjacent to a blue and white box. In one type of event, a hand reached in and pulled on the hose, and the hose moved away from the box (and the box remained stationary), as if the two objects were distinct. This is what you would expect to see if you perceived the change in color and texture from the hose to the box as the boundary between the two objects. In another type of event, when the hand pulled on the hose, the blue object moved *with* the hose, as if the hose and box were two connected parts of one object. This outcome is not expected from an adult perspective. Needham found that 7.5-month-old infants looked longer when the box moved *with* the hose than when the box moved alone. She concluded that these infants did not expect the two differently colored parts to be connected and hence looked longer when the box and hose moved together as if they were connected.

There are other clues about object boundaries as well. For example, parts of connected objects undergo *common* or *relative motion*; that is, they move together as a unit. In a classic study, Philip Kellman and Elizabeth Spelke (1983) asked if young infants could use common motion to identify object boundaries, using displays like those in Figure 4.4. The habituation displays involved a rod that moved behind a box. On the display on the left, the two parts of the

FIGURE 4.4   ■   Stimuli Used in Kellman & Spelke (1983)

Infants were habituated to either the rod movement or baseline displays. Once they habituated, they were shown two test displays. The display on the left was a solid moving rod, and the display on the right was a broken moving rod.

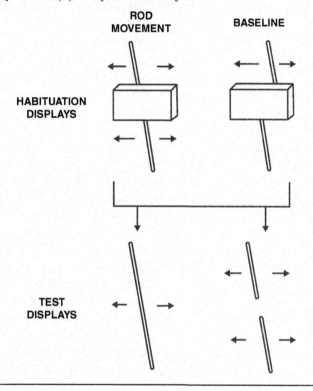

Source: Reprinted with permission from Kellman & Spelke (1983).

rod moved together behind the box, showing common motion. It was as if a solid rod moved back and forth behind the box, which occluded the center part of the rod. On the display on the right, only the top part of the rod moved, so the two parts did not show common motion. Adults would perceive this display on the left as two separate rod pieces.

Kellman and Spelke used habituation to test how infants viewed these events. Infants were habituated to either the common motion event (the display on the left) or to an event in which the parts did not move together (the display on the right). All infants were then shown the solid rod on the bottom left of Figure 4.4 and the broken rod on the bottom right of Figure 4.4. Kellman and Spelke reasoned that if infants perceived the common motion of the rod pieces as indicating that the two pieces were connected, then the solid rod on the left should seem familiar and the broken rod on the right would be more novel. Four-month-old infants who were habituated to the common motion display looked longer at the broken rod display. They seemed to perceive the two rod pieces undergoing common motion as a single, connected object with a clear boundary between the rod in the back and the box in the front. Infants who were habituated to the baseline display—in which only half of the rod moved—looked equally to the broken and connected rod. When only the top part of the rod moved, infants did not perceive the two visible parts of the rod as connected.

Another aspect of our object perception is that we do not see objects as just flat surfaces, but as having three dimensions, with parts and surfaces we can't immediately see. Kasey Soska and Scott Johnson (2008) used habituation to examine whether infants perceive objects in three dimensions as well. They habituated 4- and 6-month-old infants a partial view of a 3D object, as shown in Figure 4.5. In the top row are pictures of what infants saw (but they saw a real 3D object, so they could use binocular vision). The object rotated, but infants could only see the front and side. The question was about what infants perceive about the *back* of this object—the part they could not see during habituation.

To test this, Soska and Johnson then showed the infants new views of the object that revealed its backside. In these test events, the object rotated farther than it had during habituation, so the infant could see the previously unseen side. In one test event (row B of Figure 4.5), this rotation showed a *complete* object. In these displays, the object rotated to show a complete three-dimensional form. The other test event (row C of Figure 4.5) showed an *incomplete* version of the object. In this test stimulus, the object rotated to show that the other side of the object was hollow, as if it was made up of just two 2-dimensional sides, like a folded piece of paper. Soska and Johnson reasoned that if infants see the object as three-dimensional, they would look longer at the incomplete test display (because it was novel or unexpected). In fact, this is just what 6-month-old infants did: These infants looked longer at the incomplete object than at the complete object, preferring the view that adults would say was unexpected. However, 4-month-old infants did not look longer at the hollow display. This suggests that between 4 and 6 months, something seems to change in how infants perceive objects as three-dimensional. We will come back to this study in Chapter 5, when we discuss how changes in infants' motor abilities might influence their visual perception of objects.

FIGURE 4.5 ■ Displays From Soska and Johnson (2008)

Infants were habituated to two sides of a three-dimensional (3D) object. Once they habituated, they were shown two test events. (B) The complete test display showed the same 3D object from different angles. (C) The incomplete test display showed the object with a hollow backside.

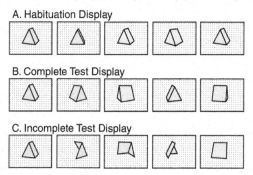

A. Habituation Display

B. Complete Test Display

C. Incomplete Test Display

Source: Reprinted with permission from Soska & Johnson (2008).

Face Perception

Human faces are probably the most important visual objects infants perceive. As we discussed in Chapter 3, newborn infants are relatively helpless and rely on other people to get their basic needs met. As we will see in Chapter 10, human faces are an important source of emotional information. Infants learn language from interacting with human faces (see Chapter 9), and many of their social interactions involve looking at and engaging with faces (see Chapter 11). Faces are also the most common object infants see. Imagine that you're a newborn infant, lying in your crib or rocker. What do you see? Nicole Sugden, Marwan Mohamed-Ali, and Margaret Moulson (2014) asked parents of 1-month-old and 3-month-old infants to have their infants wear a headband with a small camera embedded in. The camera was positioned to capture everything that came into the infants' view. Infants wore the headband whenever they were awake every day for 2 weeks. Human faces were visible to infants 25% of the time. That might not seem like a lot, but it was much more than any other single thing that the infants saw.

In fact, right from birth, newborns prefer to look at stimuli that resemble faces more than they like to look at most other stimuli. Mark Johnson and his colleagues (1991) tested newborn infants' preferences for images that were more or less like faces, specifically the stimuli in Figure 4.6. Although none of these stimuli were realistic, one had the features of a human face, two eyes, eyebrows, a nose, and a mouth, arranged like a face; another had those same features but scrambled up so that it no longer resembled a face; and the third was completely blank. The researchers tested newborns' preferences by presenting each of these three "faces" one at a time while the infants were on their backs. The stimuli were held in front of the infant's face and slowly moved side to side. The researchers measured how far the infants would turn their eyes and head to follow each stimulus. Mimicking Edwin's affinity for Shelf, these newborns turned their eyes and head to follow the face-like stimulus more than they turned their eyes and head to follow the other two stimuli.

FIGURE 4.6 ■ Stimuli used by Johnson et al. (1991)

Newborn infants' preferences for faces are examined in this exercise.

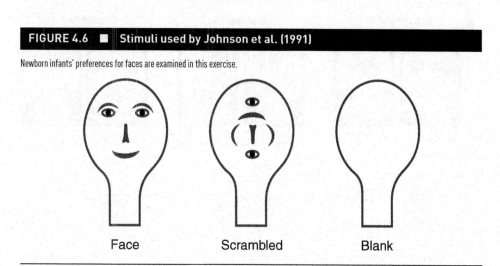

Face   Scrambled   Blank

Source: Reprinted with permission from Johnson, Dziurawiec, Ellis, & Morton, (1991).

These findings suggest that newborn infants are born ready to look at faces. In fact, other baby animals also prefer faces. Baby chicks prefer human faces to non-face stimuli (Rosa Salva et al., 2011). Monkeys who are raised without seeing any faces prefer human and monkey faces to non-faces, but they don't prefer monkey faces over human faces (Sugita, 2008). The question is whether human infants (and chicks and monkeys) prefer *faces*, or is there something about faces that make them attractive?

It turns out that infants' preference for faces aren't super specific to faces after all, at least not at birth. Viola Macchi Cassia, Chiara Turati, and Francesca Simion used a *visual preference task* to ask what kinds of *patterns* newborn infants preferred. They created the faces in Figure 4.7. The "faces" for Experiments 1 and 2 differed from each other in terms of whether or not they were *top-heavy*. In each case, the image on the left was more top-heavy—there was more "stuff" in the upper half than the lower half of the image. When presented with these pairs of images, newborn infants preferred top-heavy images; they looked longer at the image on the left than at the image on the right in both experiments. In Experiment 3, they presented a group of newborn infants with the pair of images to the far right. In this case, both images were top-heavy, but the image on the left was more face-like (i.e., had the normal arrangement of face features). Newborn infants looked about the same amount of time to these two images. When a typical face was paired with a top-heavy pattern, newborn infants did not prefer one image over the other. Thus, infants may not prefer *faces* per se, they instead prefer *top-heavy patterns*. Because human faces happen to be top heavy, these general preferences may be why newborn infants' attention is drawn to faces.

Regardless of what draws infants' attention to faces, the fact that newborn infants prefer face-like images helps them to rapidly learn about the faces around them. Within hours after

FIGURE 4.7 ■ Stimuli Used by Macchi Cassia et al. (2004)

For each pair, the item on the left is top-heavy and the item on the right is bottom-heavy.

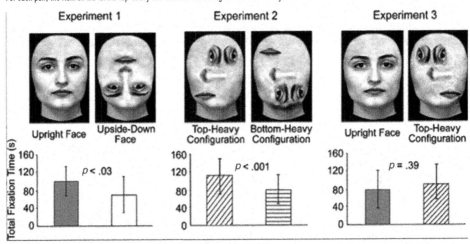

Source: Reprinted with permission from Macchi Cassia, Turati, & Simion (2004).

birth, infants already can tell the difference between their mother's face and a stranger's face (Bushnell et al., 1989). In those first few hours, infants spend time looking at their mother's face and quickly learn it well enough to tell the difference between that face and other faces. It is important to remember that newborn infants' vision is poor, but their gustation and olfaction are better developed. At birth, the infant has already learned about smells and tastes associated with mom, and those familiar smells and tastes likely help them to rapidly learn about what mom's face looks like.

How infants look at faces also changes across development. Daphne Maurer and Philip Salapatek (1976) used special cameras and recorded the position of 1- and 2-month-old infants' eyes as they looked at images of faces. This allowed them to note what features the infants looked at when they looked at the faces. One-month-old infants looked at the outer edges of the faces, where the hairline is. This is the area that has the most contrast, or the biggest difference in color, so it's not surprising that this is the place where infants spent most of their time—it was probably what they could see the clearest. The 2-month-old infants, in contrast, spent most of their time looking at the faces' inner features, especially the eyes. Thus, there was a shift between 1 and 2 months in how infants scanned the faces, and what parts of the faces infants actually looked at. Recall that visual acuity is developing rapidly during these early weeks, so it is possible that this shift reflects a change in what infants can actually see. But visual acuity at 2 months still isn't very good, so the difference probably also reflects the infants' experience with looking at faces between 1 and 2 months. This additional experience contributes to infants' becoming more focused on the faces' most important features.

But infants' face scanning isn't fully developed at 2 months. In one study, a racially diverse sample of 4- to 6-month-old infants mostly scanned the eyes of a set of racially diverse faces (Oakes & Ellis, 2013), just like Maurer and Salapatek's 2-month-old infants. But, infants who were 8 months or older scanned both the eyes and the mouth of faces, at least when they were upright (Oakes & Ellis, 2013). Why did they start looking at the mouths? It might be that mouths become especially important when infants start to learn language (at least hearing infants learning a spoken language) (Pons et al., 2015). Clearly, as infants' visual abilities develop and as they have increased experience with faces, the way they look at faces changes. These shifts in where infants look at faces also determines what infants learn about those faces. If infants are looking primarily at the hairline, they will learn about hairlines. If they are looking at eyes, they will learn about eyes. The point is that across development infants look at faces differently, which also means they probably learn different things about faces.

But with development, infants don't just get better at processing faces *in general*. They also become experts at how they look at and learn about the specific kinds of faces they see every day. That is, weeks and months of looking at some faces (human faces, White faces, adult faces) seems to shape how infants perceive faces. Olivier Pascalis, Michelle de Haan, and Charles Nelson (2002) found that with age, infants become better at perceiving human faces and worse at perceiving nonhuman faces. They used the pairs of faces in Figure 4.8 and a *visual paired-comparison procedure* to test infants' memory for different kinds of faces. Following familiarization with one face, 6-month-old infants looked longer at the novel face than at the familiar face.

FIGURE 4.8   ■   Faces from Pascalis et al. (2002)

Source: Reprinted with permission from Pascalis, De Haan, & Nelson (2002).

It didn't matter if the faces were human faces or monkey faces. At this age, infants apparently learned and remembered the initial face and recognized the differences between the familiar and the novel faces, regardless of whether they were human or monkey faces.

The story was different for 9-month-old infants (and adults). These slightly older infants had no difficulty remembering and distinguishing between the human faces, but they were unable to distinguish between the familiar and novel monkey face. They probably did form a memory of the familiar monkey face, but it did not include the details they needed in order to tell the difference between the old monkey face and the new monkey face. This suggests that between 6 and 9 months, infants appear to have become experts in human face processing, losing the ability to process nonhuman faces well.

This developmental pattern—where perception in younger infants is less specialized and in older infants is more specialized—is called **perceptual narrowing**. It refers to the observation that young infants are broad in their perception, noticing differences between things that are familiar (like human faces) *and* between things that are unfamiliar (like monkey faces), but older infants are narrower in their perception, noticing only differences between things that are familiar. When infants are born, their ability to perceptually discriminate between lots of different kinds of faces is quite flexible. This flexibility prepares them to learn about any faces they encounter in their environment. But as infants gain experience with specific types of faces, like human faces, their brains get better at processing those faces and they lose the ability to distinguish between faces that don't look like the ones they're used to seeing. In other words, with development, infants become experts at perceiving relatively familiar faces.

Perceptual narrowing also happens for the specific kinds of human faces infants see. For example, newborn infants do not have preferences for faces of one race over another (Kelly et al., 2005). If newborn infants are shown two faces side by side, one that is a face of a familiar race and the other that is a face of a novel race, infants will look equally at the two faces. By 3 to 4 months, however, infants prefer faces of their own, familiar race (Kelly et al., 2005; Kelly, Liu, et al., 2007; Liu et al., 2015). When shown two faces side by side, 3- to 4-month-old White infants (Kelly et al., 2005) and Chinese infants (Kelly et al., 2005; Kelly, Liu, et al., 2007; Liu et al., 2015) will look longer at the face that is the familiar race, that is, the one that matches the race of the infants' parents and the people in the community around them. Between 3 and 6 months both White infants (Kelly, Quinn, et al., 2007) and Chinese infants (Kelly et al., 2009) can discriminate between faces within their own familiar race as well as between faces from an unfamiliar race, just like they can discriminate between both human and monkey faces. However, between 6 and 9 months, infants' perception of faces narrows and they only discriminate between faces of their own familiar race and not between faces of an unfamiliar race (Kelly et al., 2009; Kelly, Quinn, et al., 2007). In other words, infants lose the ability to distinguish between faces that they're not used to seeing.

This development is flexible, however, and depends on the environment. In the studies just described, the White infants were tested in a part of England that is overwhelmingly White, and the Chinese infants were tested in China and had little exposure to non-Chinese faces. Yair Bar-Haim and colleagues (2006) found that 3-month-old infants' preference for their own race was dependent on their living conditions. White Israeli infants living in predominantly White parts of Israel and Ethiopian infants living in Israel with only other Ethiopian families showed own-race preferences. However, 3-month-old Ethiopian infants living in a multiracial part of Israel did not show such preferences. Other work has shown that infants' looking at own (familiar) and other (novel) race faces varies as a function of the racial diversity in their community (Ellis et al., 2017; Singarajah et al., 2017), and infants who have more diverse race experience look at faces differently than do infants with less diverse race experience (Oakes, 2021). Furthermore, the effect of perceptual narrowing can be *reversed* if you expose infants to photographs of other-race faces after the 6-month mark (Anzures et al., 2012).

Altogether, this work suggests that although infants have basic preferences for face-like shapes at birth, this preference, and their general ability to differentiate between all different kinds of faces, becomes more specific as infants gain experience with specific types of faces. This process is not specific to face perception, and we will revisit the concept of perceptual narrowing in the next section.

BOX 4.2—INFANCY IN REAL LIFE: FACE PROCESSING AND AUTISM

In 2002, Kevin Pelphrey and his colleagues observed that a group of autistic male adults visually scanned images of human faces differently than did a group of non-autistic male adults[1] (Pelphrey et al., 2002). This finding was of considerable interest because autism is prevalent. In 2020, approximately 1 out of every 50 children in the United States was diagnosed with autism (often referred to as autism spectrum disorder [ASD]; because the use of the term *disorder* is as of this writing controversial, we will simply use the term *autism*). Although there is controversy about how rates are determined, it has been reported that the rates of autism are higher in Hong Kong and South Korea and lower in Finland. In addition, autism is associated with challenges in social functioning and until very recently was not easily identified in children until they were nearly school aged. Although many autistic individuals function well in society, having successful careers and relationships, some individuals experience serious difficulties. For example, almost a third of autistic children have intellectual disabilities, and many are nonverbal. Importantly, early intervention can make a big difference in how autistic individuals function in the larger world and with neurotypical individuals. Many autistic individuals who function well have difficulty making eye contact during interactions with others and may be unable to interpret social signals from others. All else being equal, children who are identified early, and who receive interventions, have an easier time functioning with neurotypical people, especially in terms of social functioning.

For all these reasons, the finding that autistic individuals scan faces differently than non-autistic individuals generated a lot of excitement. Researchers were hopeful that there may be differences even in infancy that would help identify who would and who would not go on to be diagnosed as autistic, as well as identify who might benefit from early intervention. Since the publication of this study by Pelphrey and his colleagues with autistic adults, several labs have asked whether or not there are differences in infants' face processing that predict a later autism diagnosis.

This is not an easy question to answer. Although 1 in 50 children in the United States will be diagnosed as autistic, it would be hard to test enough infants (and follow them over time) who eventually will be diagnosed as autistic. It turns out that autism runs in families. So, researchers began to ask this question by testing infants who have an autistic older brother or sister. A group of researchers across North America as well as in the United Kingdom and Israel have worked together to study younger siblings of autistic children. This Autism Baby Siblings Research Consortium has found that approximately 20% of the younger siblings of an autistic child will themselves eventually be diagnosed as autistic. This fact has made it easier for researchers to study infants who are at higher likelihood to be later diagnosed as autistic and to determine whether their behaviors, such as the way they scan faces, predicts their later autism diagnosis.

For example, Warren Jones and Ami Klin (2013) measured how long infants who were at higher likelihood for being later diagnosed as autistic (because they had an autistic older sibling) looked at the eyes of faces. They followed the infants over time, and found that although all infants looked at the eyes for similar amounts of time at 2 months, by 6 months the infants who later were diagnosed as autistic looked less at the eyes than infants who were not later diagnosed as autistic. Interestingly, this suggests that initially there are no differences between children who are and are not later diagnosed as autistic. Instead, face processing develops differently in children who will go on to receive an autism diagnosis and children who will not. In fact, a number of studies have shown that differences in face processing in 9-month-old infants are related to whether or not those children are later diagnosed as autistic (Wagner et al., 2016, 2020).

In general, research in this area demonstrates how understanding of a neurodivergent population such as autism is gained by studying adults, infants who have a lower likelihood of a later autistic diagnosis, and infants who are at higher likelihood of a later autistic diagnosis. Research focused on identifying the processes and trajectories of face perception in typically developing infants has helped to provide the foundation for understanding this aspect of development in this population of children. In addition, such work may be important for early identification of autism, as well as starting interventions with children at a very young age.

[1.] *There is some disagreement about whether to refer to autistic individuals as autistic or people with autism. Most, but not all, autistic individuals prefer the identity-first label (autistic individuals) over person-first (individuals with autism). We will use the identity-first term because as of this writing it is preferred by most autistic individuals, but we recognize that some autistic individuals prefer to be referred to as individuals with autism.*

Check Your Learning

1. How do infants see the boundaries of objects?

2. How do we use visual habituation to study infants' three-dimensional completion of objects?

3. What preferences do newborns have for faces?

4. What is *perceptual narrowing*, and how is it related to infants' face perception?

AUDITORY PERCEPTION

Basic Auditory Perception

The auditory system is more developed than the visual system at birth. In Chapter 3 we described how fetuses can hear, and how they even learn from their hearing experiences in utero. One reason for the auditory system's head start over the visual system is that while fetuses don't see much within the womb, getting very little visual stimulation, they can hear sounds from the mother's body and from the outside world in the third trimester—sounds that the auditory system depends on for development. However, hearing sound is not enough for infants to make sense of the sounds they hear. They must develop their auditory perception to detect and discriminate between sounds that differ in intensity (i.e., loud or quiet), pitch (i.e., low vs. high), and duration. Auditory perception also makes it possible for infants to localize sound, perceive music, and interpret speech.

How can we tell what and how infants hear sounds? One way is to simply measure if infants turn toward the source of a sound (e.g., Alegria & Noirot, 1978). Researchers also can measure infants' neural responses to auditory stimuli using EEG or fMRI methods (e.g., Trinder et al., 1990). When describing visual perception, we discussed procedures that involved recording how long infants look at stimuli. How can we record how long infants listen? Peter Eimas and his colleagues (1971) used the habituation of very young infants' sucking behavior to study their auditory perception. In this procedure, infants sucking on a pacifier causes a sound to play. When the sound is new, infants suck for a long time, but as the sound becomes familiar over repeated presentations infants suck for shorter amounts of time; that is, they habituate. Infants' preferences for some sounds over others can be measured by recording how long they suck to hear the sounds.

Janet Werker and her colleagues (Werker, 1989; Werker et al., 1981) used a different (and very clever) procedure that takes advantage of infants' ability to learn how two events are connected. As they sat on a caregiver's lap, infants heard a string of sounds repeatedly, such as /la/, /la/, /la/. When the sound changed, or when the /la/'s suddenly changed to /da/'s, a set of fun toys positioned to the infants' right side lit up, making noises to attract the infants' attention. Eventually, infants learned that a change in the sound meant that the toy display would light up. Once they learned this, they began to turn their heads when the sound changed *in anticipation* of the toys lighting up; that is, they turned their heads after they heard the new sound but before the toys lit up. This allows researchers to observe how infants respond to new changes.

Using these methods, research has shown that although the auditory system is more developed at birth than the visual system, it is still not fully developed. Newborn infants are less sensitive to sounds than adults. To detect a change in the intensity of a sound (or loudness), the change in loudness has to be relatively large for newborn infants, and it has to be a much larger change compared to the difference in intensity that adults can detect (Tarquinio et al., 1990). By the time children are about 3 years old, they appear to have adult-like sensitivity to differences in loudness (Berg & Boswell, 2000). Newborn infants also detect changes in the pitch (or frequency) of a pure tone (e.g., imagine hearing a middle C, which vibrates at 256 Hz vs. the A above middle C, which vibrates at 440 Hz). Just like intensity, infants' perception of pitch develops over the first months after birth (He et al., 2009). Moreover, even at 6 months, infants require a larger difference in the frequency of sound to discriminate between two sounds, particularly at low frequencies. Infants are best able to detect changes in frequencies that are higher compared to adults (Sinnott et al., 1983). Newborn infants also detect changes in the duration of a sound (Kushnerenko et al., 2001), but this aspect of their auditory perception continues to improve until about 10 years of age (Elfenbein et al., 1993)

Some aspects of auditory perception require processing more complex auditory information. These include sound localization, perceiving music, and interpreting speech. Sound localization allows infants to know the direction of a sound. Newborn infants will turn their heads to the side on which they hear a sound, such as when a rattle is shaken to their left (Field et al., 1980). This early ability reaches adult accuracy by about 6 years of age (Kühnle et al., 2013). Infants' auditory perception also makes it possible for them to discriminate features of music. Infants between 5 and 10 months rapidly learn a short melody and recognize when the melody has changed (Trehub & Hannon, 2006). They also discriminate changes in musical rhythm, detecting the difference in the pattern of notes over time (Hannon et al., 2011).

Speech Perception

The most important sounds infants need to perceive are the sounds of speech. Languages differ in the sounds, or phonemes, that they use, and researchers have been very interested in the development of **speech perception**, or the ability of listeners to discriminate the sounds in a language. Interestingly, phonemes are categorized, much as wavelengths of light are categorized into colors. Just as wavelengths of light fall along a continuum, human speech sounds also fall along continua of things like the timing of when the speaker opens their mouth and where the tongue is located in the mouth when the sound is made. Speakers (and listeners) of different languages hear sounds as falling into the categories that are used in their native language. For example, English speakers have a category for the sound /r/ and hear all instances of this sound as similar. For English speakers, these sounds are distinct from the sound category of /l/, and speakers hear all the instances of that sound as similar to each other but different from instances of /r/. In Japanese, however, all of the instances that English speakers hear as /r/ or /l/ are combined into a single category. As a result, Japanese speakers do not categorize the sounds as two distinct kinds of sound; rather, they hear all instances of /r/ and /l/ as similar to each other. One of us was at a picnic with a new Japanese acquaintance and several others. Two of the attendees were sisters "Kelly" and "Kerry." After a while, our new Japanese friend asked carefully, "Why did your parents give you the same name?" Only then did we realize that this Japanese acquaintance could not hear the difference between these two names because they differ only in the critical /r/ and /l/ sounds. There are many examples of different languages dividing up speech sounds into different categories, as well as examples of people who speak one language not hearing the categories used in a different language. For example, Hindi has categories of distinct sounds that are treated as a single sound in English.

The question is, do infants categorize speech sounds? Peter Eimas and his colleagues (1971) conducted one of the very first studies to examine young infants' categorization of speech sounds using the habituation of sucking procedure described earlier. Eimas and colleagues habituated infants to one speech sound, /b/, and then tested their response to a new speech sound, /p/. They found that 1- and 4-month-old infants who were raised in English-speaking households discriminated between these two sounds. If they habituated infants to /p/, infants increased their sucking rate, or dishabituated, when tested with a /b/. In addition, these young infants also *categorized* the speech sounds. When habituated to a /p/, the infants did not increase their sucking when tested with a new /p/. Thus, by 1 month of age infants treated sounds from the same category as the same and sounds from different categories as different.

This first study was very important and raised many questions about the origins and early development of speech perception. By 1 month have English-exposed infants already learned the categories of English? Do all infants hear the speech sounds of English, regardless of what language they are hearing? Or do infants hear the speech sounds of *any* language? It turns out that at birth, infants can perceive speech categories in a wide range of languages, whether they have heard those languages or not (Chládková & Paillereau, 2020). For example, 6-month-old infants raised in a Japanese language environment can hear the distinction between /r/ and /l/, even though adult Japanese speakers cannot. Because of infants' remarkable sensitivity to a wide variety of speech categories, they are known as universal speech processors. In other words, infants are prepared to parse the speech sounds of any language, without first requiring experience with the language to do so.

However, over the course of the first year, as infants gain more and more experience with a particular language, their speech perception begins to change and becomes more specific to the language (or languages) they are most accustomed to hearing. Like infants' face perception, infants' speech perception goes through the developmental process of *perceptual narrowing*. Their experience with a specific experience shapes their speech perception.

Using the head-turning procedure described earlier, Werker and her colleagues found that English-learning 7-month-old infants could easily discriminate between both English and Hindi phonemes. Recall in this procedure infants learn that a change in sound is associated with a rewarding stimulus, such as toys that light up and make noise. English-learning 7-month-old infants in Werker's studies turned their heads in anticipation of toys lighting up every time they heard the sound change, whether or the sounds were from English or Hindi. Importantly, adult English speakers could not differentiate the same Hindi speech sounds that the 7-month-old infants easily differentiated, confirming that infants are universal speech processors. However, by 10 to 12 months, English-learning infants did not respond to a change in the sounds when the Hindi phonemes were used (Werker & Tees, 1984). As infants gain experience with one (or more) specific languages, they lose sensitivity to the speech sounds that are not used in their native language, or whatever languages are most often spoken at home. Infants learning two languages maintain the ability to hear the sounds in both languages spoken in the home (Albareda-Castellot et al., 2011). Just as with infants' face perception, speech perception starts out flexible and broad and then becomes more specific, and narrow, with experience.

Check Your Learning

1. When is exposure to sound critical for the healthy development of auditory perception?

2. Describe the changes in auditory perception from early development to adulthood.

3. Describe how infants' perception of speech changes from the first months to their first birthday.

HAPTIC PERCEPTION

In Chapter 3, we saw how the sensory experience of touch emerges in the prenatal period and the effects that touch may have in soothing pain or emotions in newborn infants. However, touch can also be the source of new information, especially about things like texture, object weight, and hardness. Infants can explore and learn about their environment through touching things with their hands, mouths, or even their feet. This exploration helps infants discover new properties of objects, and it can help them recognize objects. Think about reaching into your backpack—you can recognize pens, your sunglasses, and your phone, all by touch. This is haptic perception. In the following sections we will talk about how infants can explore haptically and what they seem to learn about objects from touch.

An Infant Haptically Exploring Toys With His Hands

iStock/Tatiana Dyuvbanova

Infants' Exploration Using Touch

Across the first 2 years, there are dramatic differences in how infants can manually explore and investigate objects. Even with their limited motor abilities, infants explore the world through touch from an early age. In the 1980s and 1990s, Holly Ruff examined the characteristics of infants' manual exploration. She found that the amount of time infants engage in manual activity, such as exploring with their fingers, increases between 6 and 12 months (Ruff, 1984). In addition, the way infants manipulated objects varied with the features of those objects. Infants fingered textured objects (e.g., objects with bumps or indentations) more than they fingered non-textured objects (e.g., objects with smooth surfaces). Infants mouthed smooth objects more than textured objects. Other studies have shown that whether or not infants use one or two hands to explore an object depends on the object size (Rochat, 1989) and that infants scratch hard surfaces more than smooth surfaces (Bourgeois et al., 2005). The point is that infants' manual investigation of objects is adaptive and changes depending on the information that is available in the object being explored.

Infants' manual activity is not only a function of the object properties, however. Kasey Soska and Karen Adolph (2014) found that how infants between 5 and 7 months manipulated objects varied in different positions, whether sitting, lying on their back, or lying on their stomach. For example, they rotated objects more when in a sitting position than when on their backs or stomachs. Such results show that infants' manual exploration is dependent on other aspects of development. Indeed, how infants manually explore objects changes with age. For example, the amount of time infants explore with their mouths peaks at 6 or 7 months and then declines (Palmer, 1989; Ruff, 1984). Actions like scratching and rotating increase over the first year (Palmer, 1989; Rochat, 1989; Ruff, 1984). These changes likely reflect development of motor abilities, but they also likely reflect changes in the kinds of information infants are most interested in as they explore objects.

As we have mentioned before, we need to be careful about drawing conclusions from studies like these to all children. The infants in the studies just described were mostly White children living in North America from middle-class families. Melissa Clearfield and her colleagues have compared manual exploration in infants from U.S. families of high and low socioeconomic status (SES) (Clearfield et al., 2014; Tacke et al., 2015). In these studies, SES was defined in terms of maternal education; generally, in high SES families the mothers were college educated and in low SES families the mothers were not college educated. In general, compared to infants from high SES families, infants from low SES families exhibited fewer rotations of objects (Clearfield et al., 2014) and adapted their touching behavior to the properties of objects less (Tacke et al., 2015). This means that although the findings from research done with infants from middle-class families does tell us about how children's touching and haptic exploration of objects develops, we also know that there are differences in that development in children who have different lived experiences. We don't know precisely why children from high and low SES manually explore objects differently. Perhaps high SES children have more opportunities for exploration, because of increased playtime and less play interactions with parents. Because infants likely learn about *how* to explore haptically from their experience exploring haptically, these differences in exploration by low and high SES infants may reflect differences in their opportunities to explore and learn through touch. Of course, it is also possible that differences in nutrition, stress levels, or other unknown factors, also contribute to the differences in how infants manually explore objects.

Perception of Object Properties Through Touch

What do infants *perceive* as they explore with their hands (and mouths and feet)? As we have seen, as infants explore haptically, they adapt their exploration to the properties of objects. Can infants, like adults, recognize and remember object identities from their manual exploration? Researchers have studied this question using the habituation of *holding time*. That is, infants are given an object to hold and touch with their hands for a period of time, and the duration of their holding of the object (i.e., before dropping it or putting it down) is measured. Just as we saw for looking time, infants' holding time habituates: When the same object is placed in the infant's hand several times in succession, it becomes familiar and their holding time decreases, or *habituates*. Once infants are no longer interested in the original object, they are given a new object to hold. Just as infants look longer at a new image, infants will hold a new object for longer if they recognize the difference between the familiar and new object.

Arlette Streri, Myriam Lhote, and Sophie Dutilleul (2000) placed an object in the hands of 2-day-old infants, out of their sight (so they could hold the objects but not see them), and the researchers recorded how long infants held the object before letting go. At first infants held the object for about 30 seconds. But, after the same object was placed in their hand several times in a row, the infants only held it for about 5 seconds before dropping it. At that point, the researchers gave the infants a differently shaped object—but one that weighed about the same as the first object. These newborn infants held the new object for about 20 seconds, much longer than they were holding the familiar object by the end of the habituation phase. Thus, newborn infants could feel the difference in shape and recognized that the new object was different from the familiar object. This general procedure has been used in several studies and has shown that infants from 2 to 12 months not only notice differences in the shape of objects (Rose et al., 1981; Streri, 1987), they also notice differences in hardness, temperature, and weight (Striano & Bushnell, 2005).

Haptic perception almost certainly develops with motor development. Infants' motor control over their hands and fingers undergoes significant change over the first months. Piaget (1952) described how his 2-month-old son Laurent stroked and grasped a sheet, which became tactile exploration of fabric. Piaget used this example to show how accidental actions become exploratory. In this case, Laurent scratched his mother's skin during nursing. This action shifted and changed to become exploratory grasping of fabric (sheets, handkerchiefs). At 2 months, Laurent did not have the motor coordination to intentionally reach out and manipulate interesting fabric. But, he could touch, scratch, and grasp fabric that his hand happened to land on. In this way he could haptically explore the fabric and perhaps perceive some of its properties.

As infants' motor skills develop, they become able to accurately reach for and grasp objects that are being viewed (i.e., visually directed reaching). They develop fine motor skills that allow them more control over movements of fingers. As a result, infants' exploration of objects—and their discovery of the features of objects through manual manipulation—will change. As infants become better able to grasp and pick up objects, they will gain more access to object weight and learn how to predict which objects are heavier or lighter. As infants gain control over their fingers, their ability to touch and explore textures, small features, and manipulate parts of objects will increase, providing access to new information about objects and their functions.

Check Your Learning

1. How does infants' manual exploration of objects change over the course of development?

2. How do researchers use habituation to study haptic perception?

3. What features of objects can infants' perceive through touch alone?

CONNECTING SENSORY AND PERCEPTUAL INFORMATION ACROSS MODALITIES

In this chapter we've talked about separate perceptual experiences, specifically, how infants hear *or* feel *or* see. But, in fact, we experience things in multiple sensory modalities all at the same time. We see our mother's face and hear her voice. We smell our wet dog, see her wet fur, and feel the water on her body. We see the gooey cheese on the pizza and we taste the warm, salty flavor. Objects (and events) can make information simultaneously available to more than one sense: Objects or events can be seen, heard, and touched, all at once. Moreover, we don't experience these as *separate*, but rather we link this information from different sensory modalities together to perceive *unitary* objects. That is, we do not perceive that the sight of a dog and the sound of a dog are two separate objects, but rather we experience those two perceptions as perceiving the same object.

Thus, in some ways the ability to perceive the connection between or link information in different modalities is the most important aspect of our perceptual experience. Interestingly the connection between perceptual information is not as well studied as the development of separate perceptual experiences. Thus, we know more about how infants *see* objects in the world than we know about how they coordinate what objects look like and how they sound. In this section we will describe what is known about infants' developing abilities to connect information in separate perceptual modalities. This kind of information is characterized by several important features. First, the information from the different modalities is *spatially collocated*. This means it is located in the same physical space. It is also *temporally coordinated*, or occurs at the same time. In addition, sometimes the information in the two modalities is *redundant*. For example, the rhythm of a person's mouth movements during speech is the same rhythm in the speech itself. The questions asked by researchers is whether infants are sensitive to such information and use it to bind or link different perceptual experiences.

The ability to link different perceptual experiences has been referred to as **intermodal or multimodal perception**. Both of these terms refer to infants' recognition that sensory information in two (or more) modalities corresponds in some way and can be linked. Researchers have asked a number of questions about how infants perceive the information that is available in different modalities. This research can be organized around two issues. First, researchers have asked whether infants are sensitive to **amodal information**, or information that is the same in different modalities (like the rhythm of the mouth movements and the speech sound when a person is talking). Sensitivity to amodal information is thought to facilitate perception and learning. Second, researchers have asked whether infants perceive the *correspondence* between the information in different modalities. In this case, researchers have asked whether infants match information that is experienced in different modalities. Researchers have also asked whether infants recognize objects across different modalities. For example, when infants can only feel an object, do they later recognize that object when they see it?

Infant Sensitivity to Amodal Sensory Information

Many researchers who study infants' intermodal perception are focused on how sensitive infants are to invariant features that cut across different sensory modalities. Thus, when a viewer sees, hears, or feels an event, there are amodal features—or features that are not specific to any one modality—that can be perceived. These are features such as tempo and rhythm. When you experience someone beating a drum, you can *see* the rhythm in the movements of their hands, you can *hear* the rhythm in the pattern of the drum beats, and you may *feel* the rhythm in the vibrations in the floor. If you see two drummers side by side, you can match the sound and sight of a particular drummer by matching the rhythm and tempo of the sound and sight. These features are not detected by a specific set of sensory receptors.

Are infants sensitive to these amodal features of events? Elizabeth Spelke (1979) conducted a simple, now classic, study with 4-month-old infants to answer this question. Infants were shown two movies of toy animals bouncing, but each animal hit the ground at different times. As the two movies played side by side, infants heard a sound track that corresponded to one of the two movies—a sound was heard when the toy in that movie hit the ground. The sound was unrelated to when the toy in the other movie hit the ground. Infants looked longer at the synchronized movie (i.e., when the sight and sound of the bouncing happened at the same time) than at the movie that was out of sync. Thus, infants' appeared to be able to match the rhythm, tempo, and timing features of these two events, suggesting they might have been sensitive to those amodal properties.

In fact, Lorraine Bahrick, Robert Lickliter, and Ross Flom (2004) argued that this sensitivity to amodal features is an important feature that allows infants to learn about their world. When the same amodal information is specified in more than one sensory modality, it is called **intersensory redundancy.** This simply means that the same information is in more than one modality. This is the case when you see the tempo and rhythm in the drummer's arm movements and hear the tempo and rhythm in the sound of the drumbeats. Tempo and rhythm, in this example, are *redundantly* specified in two modalities. Infants are sensitive to the tempo and rhythm in many types of events. For example, Elena Nava and her colleagues found that 3- to 4-month-old infants linked a rising pitch with a visual image of a rotating barber pole with the stripes moving up (Nava et al., 2017).

Bahrick and her colleagues suggest that infants' sensitivity to these amodal, redundant properties helps them to focus on what is important and ignore information that is less important. As an example, Bahrick and Lickliter (2000) found that 5-month-old infants more easily learned a rhythm when they both saw and heard it. Infants who were habituated to a bright red hammer hit a surface and heard the banging learned the rhythm better than other infants who just saw the hammer or who just heard the banging. Bahrick and Lickliter argued that experiencing the rhythm in both visual and auditory modalities helped infants focus on the *rhythm* instead of irrelevant information such as the color of the hammer. In another study, Bahrick and her colleagues (2019) showed that 4-month-old infants learned the prosody or rhythm of a woman's speech when they could both see and hear the woman but not when they could only see or only hear her. This suggests that the redundancy of the information in multiple modalities helps to constrain what infants learn by focusing them on that redundant information.

Cross-Modal Matching and Recognition

A related question is whether infants match information experienced in different modalities. Consider reaching into your backpack to find your keys. You can identify them by feel, and through haptic perception you can tell they are not your pens, your sunglasses, or your phone. And, later when the contents of your bag are spilled out on the table, you visually recognize them as the object you felt in your bag. You matched your impressions of the keys across modalities. It has been argued that the ability to transfer experience from one modality indicates that you can convey information that is acquired in one modality to another modality (Gottfried et al., 1977).

Andrew Meltzoff and Richard Borton (1979) asked if cross-modal matching was possible even by newborn infants. They asked if newborn infants could recognize the correspondence between what an object *felt* like and what it *looked* like. First, they gave infants a smooth or bumpy pacifier to suck on, and then they showed them a pair of objects, one smooth and the other bumpy (Figure 4.9). Infants preferred the visual stimulus that matched what they had just sucked: If they had been sucking on a bumpy pacifier, they preferred to look at the bumpy object, suggesting they matched their experiences in the haptic and visual modalities.

Many studies have examined cross-modal transfer in infancy. In the first 6 months, infants can link how objects feel with their hands to what they look like (Hernandez-Reif & Bahrick, 2001). However, very young infants seem to be better able to visually recognize objects they have previously only touched than to haptically recognize objects they have previously only seen (Streri, 1987). And this ability to transfer information from touch to vision seems to develop, with 12-month-old infants requiring less experience of familiarization to recognize the correspondence between the two modalities than 6-month-old infants (Gottfried et al., 1977; Rose et al., 1981).

Recognizing the correspondence between modalities may be especially important in learning a spoken language. As hearing people know, it is much harder to understand language when you only hear it; being able to see mouth movements while hearing sounds facilitates speech perception. Even young infants notice the correspondence between audio and visual speech information. In a classic study, Patricia Kuhl and Andrew Meltzoff (1984) found that when 3.5-month-old English-learning infants heard a woman producing vowel sounds, they

---

FIGURE 4.9 ■ Stimuli Used by Meltzoff and Borton (1979)

Schematic depiction of the stimuli newborns explored orally in the study by Meltzoff and Borton (1979).

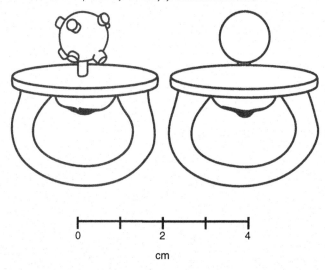

Source: Reprinted with permission from Meltzoff and Borton (1979).

preferentially looked at a video of a woman making that same vowel sound. That is, they matched the shape of the mouth and lips with the appropriate sound. English-learning infants as young as 2 months have been shown to make this type of match and can do so whether the speaker is male or female (Patterson & Werker, 2003).

Ryoko Mugitani, Tessei Kobayashi, and Kazu Hiraki (2008) found that Japanese-learning 8-month-old infants recognized the correspondence between the facial expressions seen and sounds heard for a whistle versus making a "brrrr" sound. Katharina Dorn, Sabine Weinert, and Terje Flack-Ytter (2018) observed that German- and Swedish-learning 4.5-month-old infants recognized audiovisual correspondences for both German and Swedish spoken sentences. Thus, the ability to match facial movements to vocalizations has been observed at different ages, by infants in different parts of the world, and by infants exposed to different languages.

Check Your Learning

1. How might multisensory redundancy facilitate infants' learning of perceptual features?

2. What evidence is there that infants are sensitive to amodal properties of events?

3. What is known about how infants match what an object feels like to what it looks like?

SUMMARY

Infants' ability to make sense of their sensory experiences develops significantly over the first months and years. In Chapter 3 we learned that these sensory experiences begin prenatally, and prenatal experience shapes their development. In this chapter we examined how infants continue to develop their ability to make sense of the tastes, sights, sounds, and touches they experience. In each domain, the particular preferences infants have and their ability to discriminate between different sensory experiences reflect exposure and learning.

KEY TERMS

amodal information

auditory perception

binocular depth cues

constructivism

haptic perception

intermodal or multimodal perception

intersensory redundancy

monocular depth cues

perception

perceptual narrowing

speech perception

stereopsis

trichromatic

visual acuity

visual evoked potentials (VEPs)

visual habituation

visual paired-comparison

visual perception

visual preference

REVIEW QUESTIONS

1. Summarize the major theoretical issues and methods used in the study of perceptual development in infancy.

2. Outline the perceptual abilities of a newborn for vision, audition, and touch. Which is the least developed at birth and why?

3. Compare the role of experience on the development of visual acuity and color perception.

4. How is infants' perception of objects, including faces, shaped by their experiences?

5. What is known about the information infants can learn from simply holding and touching objects?

6. How might attention to amodal features and intermodal redundancy facilitate learning?

CRITICAL THINKING QUESTIONS

1. What is the difference between sensation and perception? Give an example that demonstrates this difference.

2. Habituation and other tasks take advantage of infants' preferences for novel stimuli over familiar stimuli. How have researchers used this preference to study different aspects of perceptual development?

3. In what ways does the role of experience differ for visual and auditory perceptual development? Explain.

4. Why is it incorrect to ask, "Do infants perceive depth?" What is a more appropriate question and why?

5. Researchers often study monkeys to understand the role of experience on perceptual development. What advantage does studying monkeys offer in understanding the connection between experience and perceptual development?

6. What is the difference between detecting color differences and categorizing colors? What do we know about the development of each ability?

7. Cross-modal matching is an important aspect of perceptual development. Describe how to design a study to test infants' ability to match information across perceptual modalities.

5 PHYSICAL AND MOTOR DEVELOPMENT

Every first-time parent waits with bated breath for their infant to reach those all-important developmental milestones. That very first time a baby rolls over, sits by himself, and pulls himself up are all incredibly exciting moments—moments that remind parents that their babies are on the track of typical development. One of the most exciting "firsts" for parents is when a baby crawls. Charlie first began to crawl when he was 8 months old—right on time according to most of the motor milestones charts his parents saw plastered on the walls of the pediatrician's office.

But after the excitement of those first independent strides across the living room floor, the reality of having a mobile baby hit his parents like a ton of bricks. First, Charlie happily crawled across the room and ate the dog's dinner. The next day, he knocked over a potted plant that broke into a million tiny pieces when it came crashing down to the floor. Finally, at the end of the week, he hit his head (hard) on the coffee table. After only a week of independent mobility, Charlie's parents found themselves yelling, "Charlie, NOOO" practically all day long. Over the course of the next month as Charlie got into more and more trouble, his parents proceeded to baby-proof every inch of the house that was within 3 feet of the ground, putting outlet covers in every wall socket, removing breakable items from the floor, locking cabinets, and gating stairwells. Despite the fact that Charlie seemed fearless, absorbing every new adventure with excitement, Charlie's newfound independence instilled a new sense of anxiety in his parents. Suddenly, there seemed to be something hazardous around every corner. This meant that for the first time, there were rules in the house—things you could touch and things that were off limits; rules that could be followed, or broken. As Charlie learned more about his body and the world around him, his parents learned that Charlie was fond of breaking the rules.

If you haven't given much thought or wonder to infants' motor development before this moment, you're not alone. Indeed, many infants crawl, and all typically developing infants eventually learn to walk. Although these are exciting milestones in the baby's (and parents') lives, they don't seem like such noteworthy accomplishments. But these motor achievements are amazing; they rely on a large number of other developmental changes, including growth, changes in strength, and many, many more. Likewise, as infants get bigger and stronger, changes in their motor abilities allow them to interact with the world in new ways, setting the stage for gains in other areas. With every motor development, infants literally gain a new perspective on the world, and a freedom that cascades into exciting new discoveries across a variety of developmental domains.

After reading this chapter, you will be able to:

1. *List* the physical development of the infant over the first year of life and the factors that contribute to it.

2. *Describe* various infant reflexes, why they are present at birth, and why they disappear shortly thereafter.

3. *Discuss* how the idea of motor milestones developed and the problems with using developmental milestones to describe infant behavior.

4. *Explain* how motor abilities cascade into other domains, such as the development of infant perception, language, and social relationships.

PHYSICAL DEVELOPMENT

One of the first questions relatives often ask after a new baby is born is how much did the baby weigh. Some even place bets on the baby's birth date and its poundage, cooing at how petite the little ones are and marveling at the mother's sheer will to birth the chubby 9 or 10 pounders. Our six infants differed widely in their birth weights. The lightest of the bunch was Tesalia, born at 39 weeks and weighing in at just under 6 lbs. Born at 37 weeks, Edwin was also smaller than average, weighing 6 lbs. 9 oz. Charlie and Diego were almost perfectly average, with Charlie at 7 lbs. 6 oz. and Diego at 7 lbs. 5 oz. And finally, Carter and Alison take the heavy weight baby belt, with Carter at 8 lbs. 5 oz. and Alison at a chunky 8 lbs. 11 oz.

If you were to ask your parents about your birth weight and length, they would likely be able to tell you from memory, and if they can't, it is probably recorded somewhere in a baby book. Right after a baby is born, doctors will often place the newborn on mom's chest while they finish delivering the placenta. But as soon as they're sure that mom is okay, they will whisk the newborn away to take some basic measurements. In the United States, in addition to weight, they will record the newborn's length (or height) and head circumference (although the focus on head circumference is not universal). Although this might seem a bit arbitrary, these measurements are indicators of the infant's health. If these measurements reveal that the infant or the infant's head is too small or too large given their gestational age (see Chapter 3), it may mean that there is a problem with the child's health and development.

Growth Charts

For over a century, doctors and parents have compared the weight and height (or length) of newborns (and children) to **growth charts**. Growth charts document norms or averages for healthy infants receiving an appropriate amount of nutrition over time on a number of measurements, including weight, height, and head circumference. In the United States, the average weight for a newborn baby is around 7 pounds, and average length is between 19 and 20 inches, with a head circumference of about 13 to 14 inches. The average 6-month-old baby girl in the United States weighs about 16 pounds and is about 26 inches long, and the average 6-month-old boy weighs about 18 pounds, and is between 26 and 27 inches long.

Based on norms like these, pediatricians can compare how an individual infant is growing based on national averages. If a newborn's weight is exactly average, the newborn will be at the 50th percentile. That means that out of 100 typically developing newborns, half will be bigger and half will be smaller than a newborn whose weight is at the 50th percentile. Similarly, if a newborn is in the 75th percentile, that means that out of 100 typically developing newborns, this particular newborn is bigger than 75 and smaller than 25. In 1978, the Centers for Disease Control and Prevention (the CDC) started publishing growth charts with percentiles that could be used as a common standard in the United States. Based on charts like these, compared to other infants born in the United States, Tesalia was in the 8th percentile for weight as a newborn, and Edwin was at about the 30th percentile. Diego and Charlie were about the 50th percentile and Carter was at the 75th. Alison was at the 95th percentile, meaning that only about 5 out of 100 newborn girls in the United States weighed more than she did, at least in the years around when she was born.

Importantly, an individual child's percentiles can change quickly over time. For example, although Charlie was perfectly average at birth, by 1 month of age, he had ballooned to the 98th percentile in weight and was still there at age 2 and a half. In contrast, Carter stayed at about the 75th percentile until he started solid foods at 6 months. Then, although he continued to grow, his percentile started to drop—60th percentile at 6 months, 40th percentile at 9 months, and by 18 months he was about 12th percentile. His parents and doctors were worried until his pediatricians realized that he had just moved to what was probably the "correct" curve for his body. Infants' percentiles can change over time for a variety of reasons, such as eating patterns or fluctuations due to being sick with a series of colds or ear infections.

One of the major goals of these growth charts is to make it possible to identify infants who are significantly underweight. Infants in this category might be in danger of what doctors call **failure to thrive**, or when their height, weight, and/or head circumference don't match one of these standard growth charts (typically when they are below the 3rd percentile). Failure to thrive is not a disease; it is just a phrase used to describe children who are not growing as expected. When children are classified with failure to thrive, doctors begin to look for why the child's growth pattern has changed. Some children show this pattern because of underlying conditions or diseases, such as heart problems or infections. Other children may be suffering from emotional problems and reacting to stress in the environment. Or, the lack of growth may be the result of poor eating habits. Regardless, when children meet the criteria of failure to thrive, it likely means they aren't getting enough nutrition. This puts them at risk for other problems, such as a delay in other developmental milestones, like rolling over. Of course, some children are just small, and it can be very difficult to tell whether a child is at the bottom of the curve because of some problem that needs to be solved or if they are just petite. When Carter began to fall in his percentile on the growth chart, the doctors were concerned he might be exhibiting a failure to thrive. Carter's mom had to bring him into the doctor to be weighed nearly every month between the time he was 18 months and 2 years old to make sure he was staying between the 10th and 15th percentile. Because he stabilized at that point, his doctor concluded that he was not showing a failure to thrive. Indeed, he continued to grow, and he stayed at a low percentile throughout his childhood.

Even though growth charts are supposed to be a standard, there are differences even in standard growth charts depending on where you are and when the child is being evaluated. For all of our infants, the growth charts used were produced by the CDC, and were based on averages of children in the United States. But, because our children were born in different decades, they were evaluated using *different* CDC charts. Over time, the averages in the United States for infants' size have changed. Specifically, children in the United States have gotten bigger. The original CDC growth charts were revised in 2000 and again in 2006 to reflect changes in how children in the United States grow. For example, although Alison was at the 95th percentile according to the growth chart available when she was born, 8 lbs. and 11 oz. is only at about the 90th percentile for a baby girl born in 2020. Since Alison was born, the growth charts have changed because the average weight at birth has increased in the United States. This is an example of a **secular trend**. A secular trend is any trend that occurs over a long period of time. In addition to U.S. infants getting bigger over time, other examples are the fact that people in the United States live longer, girls are beginning to menstruate at younger ages, and children are growing up to be taller than their parents. There are many reasons why children are getting bigger, including both positive factors like better nutrition, and negative factors like more sugar in their diets. Regardless of why children's average sizes are getting bigger, keeping these growth charts accurate is important because in the United States, the CDC's growth charts are what is typically used when giving parents information on where their child falls at each doctor's visit.

Whereas the CDC publish their growth charts based on information they gather from infants born in the United States, the World Health Organization (WHO) publishes their own growth charts based on information they gather from infants born all over the world. This is important because children in different parts of the world grow differently. The CDC tells us about averages for children in the United States, with the kind of prenatal care, nutrition, access to clean water and health care, and attitudes about how and what to feed infants that is typical of children in the United States. What is average growth in these conditions may not be average growth when resources or cultural attitudes are different. Thus, the CDC and WHO created different growth charts, which allows us to compare a child's growth to other children who have access to similar resources. These growth charts were developed in different ways. For example, the CDC includes only children in the United States, whereas the WHO includes children from around the globe, selecting from diverse locations such as Brazil, Ghana, India, Norway, Oman, and the United States.

Why do these differences matter? Take a look at Figure 5.1, where you can see growth charts generated by the CDC and the WHO. The first thing you'll notice from the graph on the top is that each organization's data yields different growth charts. For example, Diego weighed 18 lbs. at 12 months, which is the 50th percentile according to the CDC but is the 75th percentile according to the WHO. The bottom part of the figure shows how many infants in the United States were low weight or height for age according to each of the growth charts. The graph on the left shows that the two growth charts identified about the same number of infants who were low length for age (i.e., the gray and blue bars are about the same). The graph in the middle,

FIGURE 5.1   ■   WHO Versus CDC Growth Charts for Weight (Left, Boys; Right, Girls)

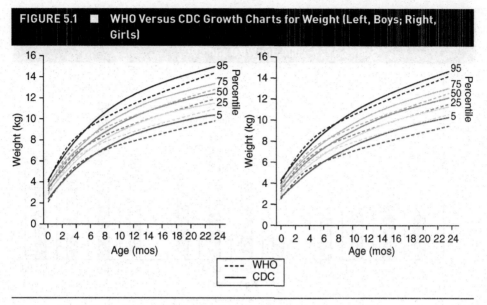

Source: Centers for Disease Control and Prevention, https://www.cdc.gov/mmwr/preview/mmwrhtml/rr5909a1.htm

however, shows that many more infants in the United States were classified as low weight for age when using the CDC growth charts than when using the WHO growth charts (the blue bars are taller than the gray bars). The graph on the right shows that especially for young infants, the CDC growth charts classified more infants as high weight for length than does the WHO growth chart. What this means is that compared to other infants in the United States, infants may be small for their age, but they are not necessarily smaller than infants from around the world who are less likely to have good nutrition and health care, access to clean water, and other health resources that are typically available in Western, industrialized countries.

Thus, while it is appropriate to compare infants born in the United States to growth charts published by the CDC, it isn't necessarily appropriate to compare infants born in other countries to CDC growth charts, as the data included in these growth charts are based on a sample of infants born in the United States, an environment that differs significantly from other environments where infants develop around the world. In fact, there are many, many growth charts available to parents that are specific to infants born in different regions of the world, including Europe, Asia, and South America, and even growth charts that are specific to infants who are born premature (Figure 5.2).

One last thing that is important to note is that these curves represent averages across many, many infants. On these charts, growth looks smooth and continuous, with children gaining a few inches or pounds each month or year. However, growth in infancy doesn't actually look like that. Instead, infant growth happens in spurts (Lampl, 1993, 2020). Instead of growing a little bit each day, infants grow as much as 1.2 cm in length on a single day, followed by days or even weeks of no growth at all. So when a family member tells a child, "It looks like you grew up overnight," sometimes, they're right.

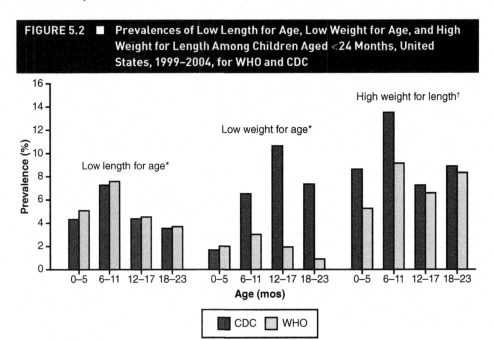

FIGURE 5.2 ■ Prevalences of Low Length for Age, Low Weight for Age, and High Weight for Length Among Children Aged <24 Months, United States, 1999–2004, for WHO and CDC

Source: Centers for Disease Control and Prevention, https://www.cdc.gov/mmwr/preview/mmwrhtml/rr5909a1.htm

Factors That Influence Growth

The Role of Nutrition

What determines an individual's height and weight? As we saw in Chapter 1 with the example of Martha, one contributing factor is genetics (Czerwinski et al., 2007; Dubois et al., 2012), but the environment can also contribute significantly to physical growth. One important environmental factor is the infant's nutrition. Again, as we saw in Chapter 1, Martha did not reach her full adult height until she was eating regular meals. Indeed, **malnutrition**, or lack of proper nutrition, can cause devastating problems for infant development. Malnutrition can be the result of children not getting enough food. It can also result from children not being able to absorb nutrients from the food they eat, because of diseases or parasites. Infants who are malnourished are more at risk for developing severe illnesses and infections, and even death. In fact, over half of the deaths of infants under the age of 5 are associated in some way with malnutrition (Guerrant et al., 2008). Further, malnutrition is associated with long-term physical problems, such as lack of fitness and an inability to absorb medications that can help fight off some of the infections that are commonly associated with malnutrition. Malnutrition is also associated with cognitive problems, including deficits in verbal fluency and executive function (Guerrant et al., 2008).

Infants can be afflicted by malnutrition in a few ways. First, maternal nutrition and health during pregnancy can have long-lasting effects on infants' height and weight at birth, as well as their trajectory of growth and development, including brain development. Maternal malnutrition during pregnancy, particularly during critical periods of fetal development, can also have a negative impact on the fetus's structure, function, weight, and metabolism. Likewise, there are long-lasting impacts of maternal obesity on fetal metabolism, particularly when the fetus is exposed to high-caloric or high-fat maternal diets, possibly affecting a fetus's insulin sensitivity, appetite, and food preferences (Shankar et al., 2018). In Chapter 2, we discussed the Dutch famine of 1944–1945, when the Nazis blocked food supplies to the Netherlands. Because pregnant mothers were malnourished during this time, their developing fetuses did not get the fuel they needed to develop. Infants born to mothers who were pregnant during the famine had low birth weights and were not as long at birth as infants born before or after the famine. However, maternal malnourishment also had epigenetic effects on fetal development, causing those genes to be turned off, increasing the metabolic problems those individuals had later in life.

Second, malnutrition after birth can also have a significant impact on infant growth over the first year of life. Infants who don't receive the needed nutrients show a much slower rate of growth. One group at a particularly high risk to be underweight are preterm infants, who struggle relative to full-term infants to receive adequate nutrient intake (Embleton et al., 2001). Preterm infants have difficulty getting enough food for a number of reasons. Recall from Chapter 3 that during prenatal development, the fetus gets nutrition through the placenta and umbilical cord—there is no need to suck, swallow, digest, or metabolize nutrients. In other words, the mother's body processes nutrients, which are then delivered directly to the fetus. When infants are born prematurely, they are required to receive and process food in a way that their body is not yet developed to do. If infants are very premature, they may have an immature or weak sucking reflex, limiting their ability to suck and swallow on their own (more on this in the next section). Their digestive systems may also not be fully developed, which means they might have difficulty absorbing the nutrients they need to grow. On top of that, premature infants don't always cry when they're hungry, making it harder for parents to know when to feed them. All in all, premature infants not only face a challenge because they were born before their bodies are fully developed but also have more difficulty getting the nutrition they need to support their development.

Given all of the negative repercussions of malnutrition both prenatally and postnatally, making sure that infants are well-nourished is incredibly important for parents, pediatricians, and international health organizations like the WHO. One way that health practitioners promote newborn health and nutrition is by advocating for **breastfeeding**. Why breastfeed? Breastfeeding, or supplying newborns with human milk, is often seen as the standard for infant nutrition. In fact, the American Academy of Pediatrics (AAP) recommends exclusively breastfeeding infants until about 6 months and maintaining breastfeeding as an important source of nutrients until 12 months of age. This recommendation comes from research suggesting that breastfeeding exclusively for at least 6 months is associated with a variety of health benefits for both the infant, in terms of fighting off illness, and for mothers, in terms of a faster recovery time from giving birth and for reducing the risk of various types of cancers (Section on Breastfeeding, 2012). For example, an infant's risk of a respiratory tract infection that would require hospitalization in their first year is reduced by more than 70% when the infants are breastfed exclusively during the first 4 months of life. The incidence of ear infections decreases by 23% with *any* breastfeeding when compared to infants who are exclusively fed with commercial infant formula. When mothers breastfeed exclusively for the first 3 months, the incidence of ear infections drops by 50%. On top of that, infants fed exclusively with breast milk have a 63% lower incidence of serious colds, lower rates of obesity, diabetes, and a lower incidence of clinical asthma, even when there is a family history of this respiratory ailment (Section on Breastfeeding, 2012).

It's important to note that these studies are all *correlational*. As we discussed in Chapter 1, we can't conclude that breastfeeding *causes* these health benefits. It is possible that mothers who breastfeed their infants do other things differently from mothers who don't breastfeed, and those other things lead to all of these positive health outcomes. For example, mothers who breastfeed longer tend to be older and more educated than mothers who breastfeed for shorter durations (Taylor et al., 2006). These mothers might also have better access to health care and other resources that contribute to their infants' better health. This is an example of the kind of question that is difficult, if not impossible, to study in a way that allows us to establish causation. We simply can't randomly assign mothers to breastfeed or use formula; it would be neither possible nor ethical. But a number of studies have shown that breastfeeding has benefits on infants' health and growth even in populations of low education and poverty, suggesting that the differences in mothers' access to health care and resources are not the only reason that breastfeeding seems to be good for infants. What's undeniably true about breast milk is that it is cheaper than expensive formulas. So, if a mother is capable of breastfeeding, it is certainly the most natural and cost-effective option to feed an infant.

Although the AAP recommends exclusively breastfeeding infants until about 6 months and maintaining breastfeeding as an important source of nutrients until 12 months of age, not all moms breastfeed. Some infants simply can't drink breast milk. They may have an allergy that makes it impossible for them to get the nutrition they need from breastmilk. Or they may have difficulty latching onto their mothers' nipples, which is particularly a problem for infants born prematurely. A good latch is important not only for the infant to get milk but also for stimulating the mother's breasts to produce milk. Some infants have other medical conditions that make breastfeeding impossible.

Likewise, some mothers can't breastfeed. Although not common, some moms don't produce enough breastmilk to feed their infants. There are medical conditions, like a previous cancer diagnosis, HIV, and other serious illnesses or infections that make it medically impossible or potentially dangerous for a mother to breastfeed. There are other cases where mothers need certain medications or are addicted to substances like nicotine or alcohol that make breastfeeding unsafe for the infant. Finally, parents who adopt infants can't breastfeed, except under very extreme circumstances. Fortunately, there are high-quality formulas available that provide infants with the nutrients found in breastmilk that we know are important for growth and development. Because what is most important is that infants are fed, there is an organization called Fed Is Best (https://fedisbest.org/) that supports parents feeding their infants in the best way they can.

BOX 5.1—INFANCY IN REAL LIFE: WHY WOMEN CHOOSE THE BOTTLE OVER THE BREAST

Some mothers who could breastfeed choose not to. One big reason for this is that breast-feeding can be difficult. In fact, according to a survey of over 500 new mothers, almost all of them (92%) reported having problems with nursing. Perhaps not surprisingly then, the more problems they experienced, the more likely they were to give up and choose to feed their infant with formula. In fact, up to 87% of mothers in the United States give up breast-feeding before reaching the 6-month milestone that the AAP recommends (Wagner et al., 2013). Importantly, not all mothers around the world can give up on breastfeeding so easily. In some countries, breastfeeding is the *only* option, because of cultural norms or because formula either isn't available or isn't affordable.

National Public Radio recently profiled a group of women in Namibia called the Himba that exclusively breastfeed their infants for long periods of time. What's most interesting about these women is that they report having trouble at first too, just like women in the United States. What's different about the Himba, however, is that breastfeeding is the norm, and it's perfectly acceptable for women to do it pretty much anywhere: in private, in public, standing up, sitting down, while at home, and even while they're working. In addition to breastfeeding being the norm, it is also the norm for Himba women to get support from other women, and expecting mothers usually have their own mothers move in with them shortly after giving birth, providing them with around-the-clock support (Doucleff, 2017). This is less likely to be the case in industrialized countries that have a set amount of paren-tal leave, and then many mothers are expected to go back to work. In fact, according to a recent report by UNICEF, in high-income countries, more than 1 out of every 5 infants is never breastfed; this number is 1 in 25 in medium- to-low income countries (UNICEF, 2018).

The point here is that although breastfeeding is natural, it doesn't mean it's easy. Most mothers tend to find it difficult, at least at first, and might need more support than they expect to keep going. In another survey of new mothers' breastfeeding experiences, many reported that being given strict rules about breastfeeding exclusively for any prescribed amount of time was not very helpful and undermined their confidence as new mothers. Instead, having immediate help from a lactation expert or experienced mother, and addi-tional support through the transition to feeding the infant solid foods, is what they needed most to keep going (Hoddinott et al., 2012).

Hospital practices in the United States can also play a big role in how many mothers are successful at breastfeeding. For example, the WHO developed a baby-friendly hospital initiative that included "Ten steps to successful breastfeeding" (Bass et al., 2019). The initia-tive provided guidance to hospitals, including having newborns room with their mothers, having staff trained in breastfeeding available to new mothers, and having resources for mothers even after discharge from the hospital. Studies have shown that U.S. hospitals that adopted previous versions of these policies reported increased breastfeeding rates (Munn et al., 2016).

So, although not everyone has a village to help them transition to motherhood, per-haps a bit more support for new mothers would help them be more successful when they try to choose the breast over the bottle, at least until the infant is old enough to ask for a juicebox.

The Influence of Toxins on Growth

Another factor that can influence infants' rate of growth are the many teratogens we discussed in Chapter 3. As we already pointed out, mothers' alcohol and drug use, psychopathology, and stress can all have an enduring impact on infants' physical growth as well as their neurological development, especially prenatally. One extreme example is exposure to the Zika virus. Indeed, due to the widespread Zika epidemic in 2015, infants who were exposed to the virus prenatally were more likely than other infants to have microcephaly, which is distinguished by a smaller than usual brain (Mlakar et al., 2016). Another is the water crisis in Flint, Michigan, starting in 2014, where residents, including children, began testing positive for lead poisoning because of dangerously high levels of lead and other bacteria present in the local drinking water. Indeed, according to the CDC, lead exposure can be detrimental to infants when exposed both before and after birth, leading to a variety of problems that include damage to the brain and nervous system, stunted physical growth, learning and behavior problems, and even hearing and speech problems. Infants can be especially susceptible to lead poisoning, even if lead wasn't in the drinking water, as they are much more likely than adults to sample paint chips or swallow dirt that is high in lead content. As a result, infants' lead levels are often checked by pediatricians via blood test throughout the first several years of life.

Check Your Learning

1. What are growth charts, and how are they used to assess infants' physical growth in the first year of life?

2. How does nutrition play a role in infants' growth over time?

3. What is breastfeeding, and what are some of the benefits associated with breastfeeding for infants?

4. List some of the factors that can influence growth prenatally.

INFANT REFLEXES

Besides checking a newborn's weight, height, and head circumference, another important thing that doctors check at birth is the presence of various **newborn reflexes**. A reflex is an automatic behavioral response to a stimulus. In other words, reflexes are our body's natural responses to certain kinds of stimulation; they happen without our conscious control. Have you ever been to the doctor's office to get a physical examination, and the doctor taps your knee to see if it jerks up? The doctor is checking your reflexes, which is a basic indication of whether your brain and central nervous system are in good working condition. Doctors will check for various newborn reflexes at birth for the same reason—to make sure that when an infant is born, his or her brain and central nervous system are functioning normally.

But reflexes are not just important as a diagnostic of how an infant's nervous system is developing. Newborn reflexes also provide a means for newborns to interact with the world, which is how they get important input to help them develop. In the final section of this chapter, we will talk about motor development, and you will see that it takes many months before an infant can move their body across the room, reach out and grab an object, or feed themselves. Even though newborn infants can't voluntarily control their bodies, they do need to interact with the world and to get information from the world around them. One way they can do this is through their reflexes.

The Appearance of Infant Reflexes

Several newborn reflexes are present at birth (Table 5.1). The **grasping reflex** is one that most parents know well: When the infant's palm is touched or stroked, the infant will close its fingers tightly and grasp. You can test this out yourself by simply putting your finger inside of a newborn's hand; before you know it, the infant will be holding onto your finger tightly. Sometimes the grasping reflex is so strong that the grasp can hold the newborn's entire body weight! If you stroke the bottom of the infant's foot, you will see the infant's big toe turn upward and the other toes fan out. This is called the **Babinski reflex** (named after French neurologist Joseph Babinski, who first discovered it). If instead of stroking the infant's foot, you place the infants' feet on a solid surface (while the infant is in a standing position), the infant will move its legs back and forth, mimicking the motion of walking. This has been appropriately dubbed the **stepping reflex**. If the infant experiences a sudden movement or sound, the infant might throw its head back, extend its arms out and quickly pull them back in, almost as if trying to find a place to grab onto for support. This is called the **moro** or **startle reflex**. Moving away from limbs and up to the head, when you stroke the infant's cheek or the corner of the infant's mouth, you will

TABLE 5.1 ■ Description of Newborn Reflexes, Including Their Common Elicitors, and the Infant's Response		
Reflex	**Elicitor**	**Response**
Babinski	Infant's foot is stroked	Infant's big toe turns upward and other toes fan out
Grasping	Infant's palm is stroked	Infant's hand closes and grasps
Moro/startle	Infant experiences a loud sound or sudden movement	Infant throws head back, extends arms out and then pulls them back in
Rooting	Corner of infant's mouth or cheek is stroked	Infant turns head and opens mouth in direction of stroking
Stepping	Infant's feet touch a solid surface	Infant's legs shift back and forth, in a walking motion
Sucking	Roof of infant's mouth is touched	Infant begins to suck
Tonic neck	Infant's head turns to one side	Infant's arm on the side of the turned head stretches out, opposite arm bends up at the elbow

elicit the **rooting reflex**, and the infant will turn its head toward you and open its mouth. If you instead touch the roof of an infant's mouth, the infant will suck; this is called the **sucking reflex**. Finally, perhaps the weirdest reflex of all is called the **tonic neck reflex**; anytime an infant turns its head to one side, the infant's arm on the same side will stretch out, while the opposite arm will bend at the elbow, almost as if the infant is preparing to do some baby archery.

All of these reflexes are present at birth in typically developing, healthy infants, and they develop prenatally. In fact, some parents get lucky enough to catch a glimpse of their fetuses sucking their thumbs (most often the right thumb) in a prenatal ultrasound, giving visual evidence that the sucking reflex is fully intact before birth. Like the presence of adult reflexes, newborn reflexes are generally seen as a sign of central nervous system development, and their presence at birth suggests that everything is functioning normally. The absence of these reflexes at birth, however, is typically a sign that there could be some neurological damage to the newborn's brain, and further testing is needed.

Why do infants have these reflexes? No one knows for sure, although some researchers have suggested that the behaviors themselves have adaptive significance, helping the infant to survive despite having little control over its body. If you were to put your hand on a hot stove, you'd likely pull it away before you even register the feeling of pain. This reflex is adaptive: It keeps you from getting hurt. Likewise, the rooting and sucking reflexes have clear adaptive value. When the mother's nipple touches the side of the newborn's cheek, the rooting reflex enables the infant to turn its head toward the nipple and open its mouth, getting ready to nurse. Once the nipple touches the roof of the infant's mouth, the sucking reflex will help with feeding. The stepping reflex could also be said to have adaptive value, potentially helping the infant practice the motion needed for later walking. And the moro and grasping reflexes might arguably help the infant reach out and grab onto mom when falling.

However, the explanation that newborn reflexes exist because they have adaptive value falls apart when we try to explain the presence of other reflexes. What is adaptive about flexing your leg when your knee is touched? Likewise, it's hard to use this theory to explain the Babinski and tonic neck reflexes: what adaptive purpose does fanning your feet serve, or stretching out one arm while bending the other? The answer is still unknown, but these reflexes are universal, nonetheless, and present in every typically developing infant at birth.

The Disappearance of Infant Reflexes

Perhaps you're thinking at this point that reflexes are quite mysterious, and although everyone has them, it's not clear why. What's perhaps more mysterious about reflexes than their appearance is their *disappearance*. Indeed, all newborn reflexes disappear within months following birth: moro and stepping around 2 or 3 months, rooting around 4 months, tonic neck around 5 to 7 months. Why do they disappear? The traditional explanation is that just as the appearance of these reflexes are a sign of brain health, their disappearance at some point in development is a sign of the infant's brain *growth* or maturation. In other words, as infants' brains are maturing, the parts that are growing begin to inhibit or shut down the more primitive parts of the brain that are responsible for newborn reflexes. More recent research, however, has suggested that the real answer might be a bit more complicated.

Esther Thelen was one of the most famous researchers to question the traditional explanation for the disappearance of newborn reflexes. In her early work, she took a microgenetic approach (see Chapter 1) to study how very young infants come to move their limbs in stereotyped or rhythmic patterns. She recorded infants while lying on their backs and tracked the exact coordinates of each of the infants' legs, focusing on the joints (e.g., ankle, knee, and hip), on each frame of the recording so that she could map the infants' movements over time. She found that although it can often look like infants are just flailing their legs randomly, they actually move their legs in very organized patterns, and those patterns look like walking! When infants were kicking slowly, it resembled the pattern of stepping, like the movements you see in the stepping reflex. When infants kicked faster, the pattern looked just like running. She also found that infants kicked in this stereotyped pattern well after the disappearance of the stepping reflex. This led Thelen to wonder whether the muscles involved in stepping and kicking were related, or even the same. To find out, next she carefully compared infants' movements when stepping and kicking, tracking the actual movements themselves and the muscles required for infants to make those movements. She found that they were exactly the same. The only difference between the stepping reflex and infant kicking is that stepping is done upright and kicking is done vertically.

This work made Thelen wonder—what part of the brain would inhibit stepping when an infant is held upright but not inhibit the very same motion (kicking) when the infant is on its back? And that wasn't all. She also noticed that in heavier infants, the stepping reflex tended to disappear sooner than in lighter infants. These observations led to a new hypothesis: Perhaps brain maturation wasn't responsible for inhibiting the stepping reflex at all; instead, maybe infants just gained weight before they gained muscle and didn't have the strength to lift their increasingly chubby legs when held upright. Gravity doesn't fight against you when you're on your back, making kicking easier than stepping. Could this explain why the stepping reflex disappeared, but infants' ability to kick remained intact? Could it explain why heavier infants tend to lose their stepping reflex sooner than infants who weigh less?

Thelen tested her hypothesis in the logical way: She devised a plan to make skinny infants heavier and chubbier infants lighter. First, she submerged heavy infants whose stepping reflex had already disappeared in a small pool of water, thereby making it easier for them to lift their chubby legs. She found that when heavier infants were in the pool, they stepped. To make lighter infants' legs heavy, she attached small weights to their legs to see if they would still show a stepping reflex when their legs were heavier and gravity posed a bigger challenge. She found that with extra weight added to their legs, lighter infants—who showed the stepping reflex when their legs were not weighted—no longer demonstrated the stepping pattern when held upright (Thelen, 1996).

Based on this work, Thelen concluded that newborn reflexes don't necessarily disappear because of brain maturation. Instead, Thelen believed that infants stopped showing these reflexes because of a combination of factors that include the infants' dynamically changing body size, weight, and ability to control their own movements. She called this perspective the dynamic systems theory, which we introduced in Chapter 1. According to this perspective, behaviors like stepping emerge (or disappear) as the result of multiple, independent systems that develop on their own time course. Stepping depends on the development of several abilities all at the same time, including reflexive responses, the ability to move increasingly heavy limbs against gravity, the motor control to alternate the legs, and many more. Stepping later morphs into the ability to *walk*, which is assembled from these other developing abilities and emerges when they all have developed enough so that walking is possible when used together. Again, just like all other behaviors, no single system is responsible for stepping; stepping reflects the co-development and coordination of many systems all at the same time. Although the other newborn reflexes are not as well-studied as stepping, it is likely that several factors contribute to their appearance and disappearance over the course of development as well. Eventually, infants don't just suck anything that's touching the roof of their mouth; they learn to suck things that taste or feel good. They may suck and later bite objects that feel good on their gums when they're teething, and they might learn that certain toys (like toys made of fabric) don't taste so good and do not afford sucking. All of these factors influence infants' behaviors and change dynamically over time as the infant develops. This will be a consistent theme throughout this chapter and throughout this book.

Check Your Learning

1. What is a reflex, and what are some of the different reflexes that infants have at birth?

2. What is the traditional perspective on why newborn reflexes appear at birth?

3. What is the stepping reflex, and what are the factors that influence its disappearance shortly after birth?

MOTOR MILESTONES

When a parent in North America walks into a pediatrician's office, they might see a series of charts pinned to the walls, illustrating different milestones that their infants are expected to reach in the first 2 years of life. Those milestones represent several aspects of development, including social and emotional, cognitive, and language. However, the chart that is likely the most salient to parents (because the different behaviors are so easy to observe) early in an infant's life lists important **motor milestones,** or physical achievements that the infant is expected to reach in the first year and a half, starting with pushing up and rolling over, and ending with the ultimate feat of walking. As parents we all noted these milestones. Alison walked at 11 months and Edwin at 12 months, Carter crawled at 8 months and Charlie at 9, Diego sat at 6 months and Tesalia rolled over at 3 months. These charts provide parents with the average age that parents should expect their infants to acquire such milestones. But where do these averages come from? What does it mean if an infant doesn't reach them on time, or worse, skips one altogether? In this section, we will discuss theories about motor milestones and their origins, and how reaching these milestones can vary based on a number of factors.

The Origin of Motor Milestones

Believe it or not, the motor milestones that pediatricians use to gauge whether infants are on the right track are based on data that are nearly 100 years old. Psychologist Arnold Gesell first proposed these milestones in the early 1900s after collecting a large longitudinal sample of data of White infants from middle-class families. By recording infants' precise movements over time, he was then able to calculate the average age that this sample of infants typically demonstrated various physical achievements. The most commonly cited ones are presented in Table 5.2. Based on his data, Gesell theorized that *all* infants—regardless of where in the world they are born or what experiences they have—should reach these milestones in the very same sequence, at approximately the same age. He called these milestones **maturational states**. According to Gesell's theory, maturational states are governed by the development of the central nervous system, and any minor differences in when infants reach these states can be attributed to genetic factors (Gesell, 1946). In other words, Gesell emphasized the role of *nature* in the development of motor milestones, leaving little room for the role of experience.

For decades, these milestones were the standards used by scientists and pediatricians to evaluate infant motor development (Figure 5.3). Because they were thought to be a function of how the central nervous system was developing, it was not considered problematic that the group of infants Gesell observed were similar in terms of their background (i.e., all White infants from middle-class families). Gesell's maturational theory was based on the notion that factors such as parenting practices, culture, race/ethnicity, and socioeconomic status were not relevant for understanding or identifying norms for motor development. Thus, the motor milestones that have become the gold standard by which all infants are judged were based on data from a very narrow sample of White, middle-class, American families during a particular time in U.S. history. As a result, any infant, anywhere around the world who surpasses these milestones and dares to walk early is called "precocious," and infants that take their sweet time and happen to sit or walk later than these milestones dictate are called "delayed" (Karasik et al., 2015).

TABLE 5.2 ■ Classic Motor Milestones With Their Approximate Onset Ages	
Milestone	**Approximate Age**
Prone, lifts head	1–2 months
Prone, chest up; uses arms for support	2 months
Rolls over	4–5 months
Sits without support	6 months
Crawls	7 months
Stands with support	7 months
Pulls to stand	9 months
Cruising	10 months
Stands alone	11–12 months
Walks alone	12–13 months

FIGURE 5.3 ■ Motor Milestones Chart

Infant motor milestone chart showing progression of postural and locomotor skills and age norms. Horizontal bars represent the normative range of skill onset; vertical lines show average age of first occurrence. As is typical in such depictions, skills are ordered by chronological age, implying a maturational sequence.

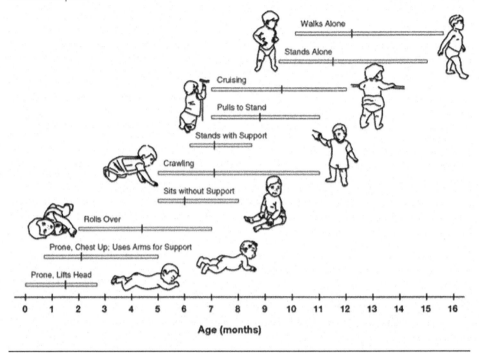

Walks Alone

Stands Alone

Cruising

Pulls to Stand

Stands with Support

Crawling

Sits without Support

Rolls Over

Prone, Chest Up; Uses Arms for Support

Prone, Lifts Head

Age (months)

0 1 2 3 4 5 6 7 8 9 10 11 12 13 14 15 16

Source: Data from Bayley, N. (2006). Bayley Scales of Infant and Toddler Development (3rd ed.). The Psychological Corporation; Frankenburg, W. K., Dodds, J. B., Archer, P., Shapiro, H., Bresnick, B. (1992). The Denver II: A major revision and restandardization of the Denver Developmental Screening Test. Pediatrics, 89, 91–97; Adolph, K.E., Karasik, L.B., Tamis-LeMonda, C.S. (2010). Motor skills. In M. H. Bornstein (Eds.), Handbook of cultural development science: Vol. 1. Domains of development across cultures (pp. 61–88). Taylor & Francis. Copyright © 2010, Taylor and Francis, reprinted with permission.

Although Gesell's important work set the foundation for the study of motor development, many modern researchers and theorists have criticized this work. First, the idea of milestones is problematic. Calling these achievements *milestones* assumes that there is a date of onset for each one. In other words, if walking is a "milestone," infants should just get up and walk one day and walk every day thereafter. In this view, motor development can be best characterized by discontinuous change. This can certainly be true in some cases. In fact, Carter, who stood up on his own at 13.5 months, did not take any additional "steps" toward independent walking for weeks. One day, when Carter was 15 months old, his mom put him on the floor at his daycare center and he just stood up and walked across the room. This is exactly what you'd expect to happen based on the milestones charts: One day, infants aren't walking, and the next day they are. But it turns out, Carter's experience is the exception rather than the rule, and for most infants—including Alison, Charlie, Diego, Edwin, and Tesalia—the ability to walk across a whole room develops continuously, over a long period of time.

Karen Adolph and her colleagues studied the transition to walking across a room in a group of 32 infants (Adolph et al., 2008). The researchers observed these infants every day and found that almost all of the infants had some days when a skill seemed to be present followed by days when the skill seemed to disappear, before they fully mastered the skill. In other words, most infants took a few steps one day, then did not take any for a few days, and then took a few more steps a few days later, and so on. It might take a month of gradually taking a few steps here and there to develop the strength and balance to walk across an entire room. And in between that time, they might not walk exclusively or at all, and instead, revert back to other forms of locomotion, like crawling, that are more efficient. Alison's progression looked more like this. Starting at 10 months, she could stand up independently without holding on to anyone or anything. She gradually moved to taking one step, which she did for several days. Then she started taking two steps before sitting down. Finally, nearly 2 months later, she could walk across an entire room and chose to walk more than she chose to crawl. The transition to being a full-time pro walker was finally complete.

But this is not the end of the development of walking. Even once infants have achieved the "milestone" of walking, their walking continues to develop and improve. Take a look at Figure 5.4, which shows the footprints of two 14-month-old infants as they walked over a special carpet that measured the pressure of each one of their steps. The infant whose footprints you see on the top had been walking for 2 weeks, and the infant whose footprints you see on the bottom had been walking for 2 months. Their walking clearly looks different. The infant who had just begun to walk (the top set of footprints) has small, uneven steps, representing the jerky movements that are typical of a new walker. New walkers have trouble keeping balance, and their steps are usually short, with their legs spread wide apart. The experienced walker (the bottom set of footprints), in contrast, has stable, smooth steps, reflecting the fact that this infant has acquired enough strength and balance to put one foot in front of the other (Adolph & Robinson, 2013). It is clear that Gesell's strategy of pinpointing an exact onset day for any motor milestone is a bit misleading, because for most infants, there isn't a specific day when they successfully "achieve" any new motor ability. For most, the development of any motor achievement is a continuous process, made up of a series of gradual changes.

A second problem with Gesell's theory is that it assumes that certain milestones are important and that all infants must reach them. However, Gesell's list of milestones doesn't include some important behaviors, such as reaching for objects, which, as you will see in the next section, is an important motor ability that leads to a cascade of changes in other developmental domains. In addition, some of Gesell's milestones are not universal. Crawling is on every motor milestones chart. However, a large percentage of infants across the globe never crawl at all. Anthropologist David Tracer observed 113 mother–child pairs of Au hunter-gatherers from Papua New Guinea (Merali, 2009). In this society, infants are typically carried in a sling for up to 86% of the day and parents only put infants on the ground when it is time for them to learn to walk. As a result, most infants in this culture never learn to crawl (before they walk). And this

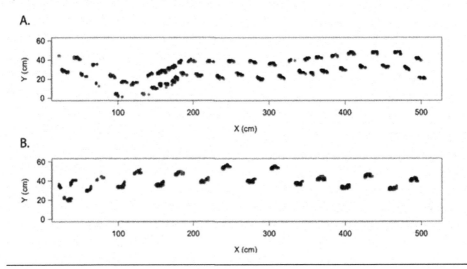

Source: Adolph & Robinson (2013).

isn't unique to Papua New Guinea; Tracer found that mothers in Paraguay, Mali, and Indonesia have similar traditions, and infants in those cultures don't crawl either. What does it mean for Gesell's theory if there are groups of infants who do not learn to crawl at all before they learn to walk? Clearly, it means that at least this behavior is not a universal milestone that is acquired when the nervous system has reached a certain level of development.

The *form* of infants' motor movements is not universal either. For example, not only do some infants never crawl at all before walking, but even infants who do crawl also don't always crawl in the way Gesell said they should, on their hands and knees with their bellies off the ground, as shown in the following photo.

In fact, in studies of North American children, children locomote in many ways. Before they crawl, they may roll or pivot. Once they start to crawl, they may crawl with their bellies on the ground, which sort of looks like army crawling. Others crawl on their hands and one knee, dragging their other leg behind. Some "bear crawl," or literally crawl on all fours, on their hands and feet. Some even scoot or "bum shuffle" from one place to another in a sitting position. Although these different methods of crawling may look funny or "weird" compared to the traditional hand-and-knees crawling that appears on the motor milestones charts, they function the same way—they get the infant from point A to point B. This raises the question of what does it mean to crawl? If an infant discovers that a nontraditional method of crawling works for them—it gets them from one place to the next—why learn another way? Eventually, all typically developing infants will toss whatever crawling method they prefer aside in favor of walking, and there is no evidence that any of these alternative forms of crawling are problematic.

Traditional Crawling

iStock/oksun70

This example also illustrates the final criticism of Gesell's theory. Recall that Gesell's theory is based on the notion that motor milestones are universal and unrelated to parenting, culture, and other factors. As we have just discussed, however, comparisons of children who are raised in different contexts show that this is not true. Depending on the cultural practices surrounding how infants are treated and handled, how and when infants reach the milestones described by Gesell vary. This is an important lesson on why we should pay attention to not only *what* is studied but *who* is studied, and recognize that development may not look the same when other groups are examined.

BOX 5.2—INFANCY IN REAL LIFE: THE SILLY MISTAKES THAT BABIES MAKE

"Weird" crawling isn't the only weird thing that infants do when they are learning to move. When Edwin was a toddler, he regularly got his hand stuck in the door of his Little People school bus, and he often tried to get his whole body *into* the bus so that he could drive it around. He also constantly tried to stick his arms (and toys) between the rails of the family staircase and got his entire body stuck underneath the dining room table several times a week. Similarly, as we discussed in Chapter 1, when Alison was just starting to crawl, she crawled under the coffee table and banged her head on it over and over and over again.

Getting your hand stuck in a toy and banging your head repeatedly are clearly unpleasant. It makes you wonder, why do infants keep making these silly mistakes?

It turns out that when infants start navigating the world on their own, they make a lot of mistakes, especially with their bodies. Judy DeLoache and her colleagues have tried to document these mistakes and figure out why they happen. In one series of studies, DeLoache, with her colleagues David Uttal and Karl Rosengren (2004), documented a phenomenon that they called "scale errors." A scale error is when an infant acts on a small replica object (e.g., a doll-sized bed) as if it were the bigger real-life object (e.g., tries to lie down in it). It sounds silly, but young children make these scale errors quite often. To investigate their occurrence, the researchers had 1½- to 3-year-old children come into a playroom with three large objects that they could physically interact with: a toy slide that they could climb on and slide down, a toy car that they could get into and drive, and a toy chair that they could sit in. After a few minutes, the children took a walk down the hall with their moms while a sneaky researcher switched the big toys with tiny doll-sized replicas. When the children came back, the researcher acted like nothing happened and encouraged the child to play with the toys in the room. To everyone's surprise, the children acted like nothing happened as well: Many of them tried to sit in the tiny chair, slide down the 2-inch slide, and wedge their feet inside the tiny toy car.

You might be thinking, this is crazy, and infants can't possibly be this dumb. But these aren't the only mistakes they make with their bodies. John Franchak and Karen Adolph (2012) found that 1½-year-old toddlers—around the same age infants begin making scale errors—would try to squeeze their heads, bodies, and hands through impossibly small doorways and openings. Infants seemed unaware that the openings were way too small for them, and they got stuck in the process, much like Edwin did with his Little People school bus.

Why do young children make these silly mistakes? We don't know for sure, but there are a few possible reasons. First, it takes a long time for infants to learn about what kinds of actions are possible and impossible. These decisions involve planning their actions based on size information of both their own bodies and objects in the environment. Since infants start making errors with their bodies right after they start walking for the first time, it's possible that they just haven't learned enough about the world yet to know what they can and can't do.

Another possibility is that infants can guess that many of the actions they attempt might not work, but they explore these actions anyway as part of the process of learning. In the case of scale errors, infants can clearly see that the small replica objects are in fact very small, and they scale their fine-motor behaviors accordingly even when making an error. For example, when trying to sit in a tiny doll-sized chair, children meticulously place the chair down on the floor, carefully line up their bodies right above it, and then proceed to sit down. In fact, they still make scale errors even when researchers explicitly point out that the objects are very small (DeLoache et al., 2013). Similarly, the same infants who wedge themselves into impossibly small doorways don't make these errors in judgment when the penalty is falling (e.g., when one side of the opening is a ledge) instead of getting stuck, suggesting that infants might be able to guess when openings are too small but that they don't really think that getting stuck is that bad of an outcome if they happen to guess wrong.

Whether infants know that their actions are likely to be impossible or not, making mistakes is just a part of learning about what their bodies can do. Moving around on their own for the first time opens up a brand new world of possibilities—a world that takes time to explore. Soon they'll be walking up and down stairs, and, as they get better at navigating the obstacles that stand in their way, parents will build up the confidence they need to take down those baby gates. But until then, it's probably best to keep them up; infants make some really silly mistakes.

SCALE ERROR: Edwin, at 17 months, making a scale error (trying to get in and drive a car that is way too small).

Handling Practices

Gesell based his milestones on a very narrow sample: The families were middle-class, two-parent households in New Haven, Connecticut. As we saw with the example of the Au hunter-gatherers of Papua New Guinea, differences in how infants are handled, such as whether or not they are carried all day long, can have a major impact on the development of infants' motor abilities. If an infant is carried all day long, for example, they aren't getting the experience lifting their bodies up against gravity so that they can lift their bodies off the floor. In contrast to Gesell's classic theory, motor development does seem to be influenced by experience.

We can see these effects not just in very different cultures but also at different times in the same culture. Tesalia started walking young at 9 months, as did Alison at 11 months; Edwin and Charlie were right on time at around 12 to 13 months; Diego was a little later at 14 months; and Carter didn't walk till 15 months. Motor abilities are constrained by changes in the infants' bodies (which could be why Tesalia, who was a very small infant, walked first) and by environmental factors, like carrying and sleep practices that vary by culture (Adolph & Robinson, 2013). We also see cohort differences based on when in history an infant was born. Prior to the 1990s, infants in the United States were put to sleep on their bellies, and they tended to crawl and walk sooner than infants born in the 1990s after the Back to Sleep Campaign began recommending that parents put babies to sleep on their backs (Adolph & Robinson, 2013). Infants who sleep on their bellies have more opportunities to use their arms to lift up their torsos when compared to infants who are left on their backs. Those "baby push-ups" can help infants build the strength they need to move their bodies across the room in a crawling posture. But, even though it might "slow down" some aspects of motor development, putting infants on their backs to sleep is the best practice to avoid SIDS; parents in the United States have adjusted when they expect their infants to crawl and walk in response to using safer sleep positions.

There also are several cultural practices that can play a major impact on the timing of motor milestones. One is **swaddling**, or wrapping an infant tightly in some type of cloth. When newborns are taken to the nursery in the hospital after they are born, they are often swaddled tightly in blankets to keep them warm and to keep that pesky startle reflex from

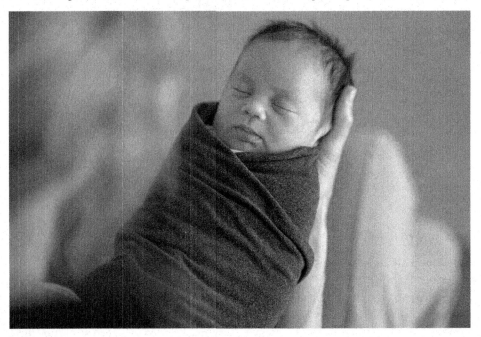

Swaddled Baby
iStock/FatCamera

waking them up from that important newborn slumber. As we learned in Chapter 3, being compressed with blankets might be comforting to newborns, as it mimics the tight compression that they become accustomed to in the womb in the last trimester of pregnancy. Although infants in the United States are typically only swaddled until they can roll over (based on pediatricians' recommendations), infants in other countries are swaddled for much longer and not just during sleep.

In Tajikistan and other areas of Central Asia, for example, it is common practice to use the "gahvora" cradle. The **gahvora cradle** is a crib where infants are wrapped tightly in swaddles, with their entire bodies restricted so that they can't move their arms and legs or move their heads from side to side. Infants spend up to 20 hours a day in the gahvora cradle and aren't even removed for feeding or changing. Moms lean over the cradle to breastfeed, and infants pee through a catheter and poop out of a hole in the bottom of the cradle. Many psychologists and pediatricians would say that restricting infants' movement so dramatically could have negative downstream effects on motor development, since cradled infants aren't getting the opportunity to practice motor movements that are so important for reaching their milestones. However, until recently, there was very little research examining motor development in countries that employ the gahvora method.

Researchers Lana Karasik, Catherine Tamis-LeMonda, Ori Ossmy, and Karen Adolph (2018) studied motor development in a community that used the gahvora method. They recorded the cradling behaviors of 146 mothers in Tajikistan. The researchers discovered that mothers were pretty consistent in their own cradling practices from day to day, but they differed a lot from each other. Some mothers cradled their infants for only 30 minutes a day while other mothers cradled their infants for up to 23 hours! Some mothers only cradled at night, whereas others cradled all day long. As infants got older, they were cradled less, but even 20% of 12- to 24-month-old infants were cradled for significant portions of the day.

Importantly, although many infants spent a significant amount of time in the cradle, they weren't ignored—mothers were very responsive to their infants' needs. In addition, there were often other family members, including grandmothers, aunts, neighbors, and older siblings also present and attentive to the infants. The infants themselves showed little evidence that they didn't like being in the cradle. They rarely protested at being placed in the cradle, and many mothers claimed that their infants actually *enjoyed* it. Most surprisingly, there was little evidence of long-term motor delays compared to U.S. standards. During infancy, cradled infants achieved some motor milestones later than U.S. averages, but eventually, by early childhood, most Tajik children's motor skills were comparable to U.S. norms (Karasik et al., 2023).

So, despite Gesell's claims that motor milestones should occur in a specific order and at a specific time, handling practices can cause the timing of these milestones to shift, perhaps even resulting in a skipped milestone, as in the case of carrying and crawling. Second, although some handling practices that limit infants' mobility might delay the achievement of some motor milestones relative to cultures with different handling practices, by early childhood children across cultures have achieved most of the same skills, and all typically developing infants eventually learn to walk.

A

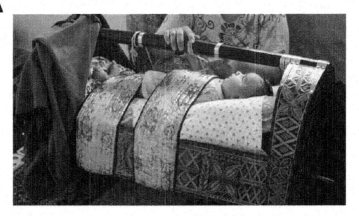

B

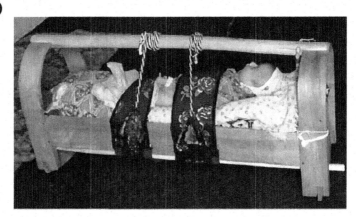

CRADLED BABY: (A) Gahvora with intricately carved details, fancy bindings, and coverings. (B) Plain-looking gahvora from a less affluent household.

Karasik, L. B., Tamis-LeMonda, C. S., Ossmy, O., & Adolph, K. E. (2018). The ties that bind: Cradling in Tajikistan. *PLOS ONE, 13*(10), e0204428.

Experience and Practice Effects

Handling practices might not only result in motor achievements being attained later than U.S. norms; they can also result in those achievements being attained earlier. Brian Hopkins and Tamme Westra (1988) studied groups of mothers in Jamaica who routinely give their infants a little extra boost in motor development. These mothers believe that infants need help to meet their motor milestones and that practice makes perfect. Consistent with this belief, typically during their daily bathing routine, many of these mothers massage their infants and stretch their infants' arms and legs, often suspending infants from their limbs, all to prepare their bodies for when it comes time to learn to walk. The exercises are shown in Figure 5.5;

FIGURE 5.5 ■ Baby Exercise

Samples of exercise routines from Jamaican mothers that include holding the baby up by (1) his or her arms, (2) a single arm, (3) legs, and (4) head, and stretching the baby's (5) legs and (6) arms.

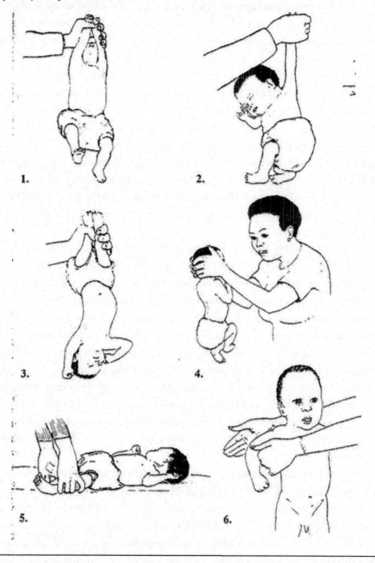

Source: Hopkins & Westra (1988). Reprinted with permission of the author.

they might seem strange, and even dangerous to people in cultures that do not engage in this practice. But, children whose mothers regularly use these stretching exercises do attain motor skills at a younger age.

To demonstrate this, Hopkins and Westra compared the infants of Jamaican moms who moved to Great Britain and maintained their tradition of daily infant stretching, Jamaican moms who moved to Great Britain and did not carry on the tradition of stretching their infants, and British moms who likely never even heard of these Jamaican stretching routines and certainly never practiced them. After 1 month, the infants of the Jamaican mothers who used the stretching routine had better head control when compared to infants of moms in the two other groups. Most importantly, after 6 months, the infants in the stretching group were better sitters than infants in the other groups, suggesting that these exercises do indeed help with the development of motor milestones.

Of course, because the Hopkins and Westra study was correlational, it is impossible to know if the stretching exercises actually caused the differences in motor development. Michele Lobo and James Galloway (Lobo & Galloway, 2012) recruited a sample of mostly White mothers in Delaware and randomly assigned them to two groups. One group was trained on how to do these exercises with their infants, and the other group was instructed to play with their infants but were not trained on the exercises. Lobo and Galloway found that the infants who got the exercises achieved motor milestones before the infants who did not have the exercise experience. Because they randomly assigned mothers and infants to the two conditions, this study helps to confirm that the early exercise actually causes changes in the development of motor milestones.

There is a wide range of experiences that shape children's motor development. For example, Lana Karasik, Catherine Tamis-LeMonda, Karen Adolph, and Marc Bornstein (2015) compared differences in the sitting abilities of 5-month-old infants from six different countries: Argentina, Cameroon, Italy, Kenya, South Korea, and the United States. Specifically, in countries such as Kenya and Cameroon, where mothers often placed their infants on the floor or in adult furniture, many 5-month-old infants already sat independently. In fact, some of these infants could sit for long periods of time (more than 20 minutes!) by themselves without falling over. In these two countries, infants were given practice sitting in contexts that required that they manage the challenges of gravity to stay upright. In most of the other countries, infants were most often positioned with support (e.g., in a mom's arms, in a baby chair). In these countries, few infants could sit independently by 5 months. This difference in experience and practice sitting seems to have translated to differences in when infants developed the strength and ability to sit alone.

Although these results suggest that practice and experience shape the timing of motor development, this work, like the original Hopkins and Westra study, is correlational. There are some studies that examined the effects of experience using random assignment, like the Lobo and Gallaway study described earlier. For example, Myrtle McGraw (1935) randomly assigned a pair of identical twins named Jimmy and Johnny to two conditions: Johnny received lots and lots of exercise and experience with various motor challenges, including swimming and even riding a bike, whereas poor Jimmy received very little. She found that although the extra exercise did not give Johnny a long-term advantage over Jimmy in the basic motor achievements you'd find on milestones charts, Johnny did excel at things like swimming, diving, and even ascending and descending slopes in the ground (which we will talk more about in the next section). This work suggests that extra experience can help infants not only accelerate the development of certain motor skills, but to also become quite proficient at things like swimming and roller skating.

Similarly, Philip Zelazo, Nancy Zelazo, and Sarah Kolb (1972) randomly assigned typically developing 1-month-old infants to an "active exercise" condition, in which the parents were taught to place their infant in an upright position on a surface so that they could practice the stepping reflex, or a "passive exercise" condition, in which parents were instructed to place the infant on their backs while parents moved the infants' legs back and forth for them. After doing these exercises 3 minutes a day for 6 weeks, Zelazo and his colleagues found that the infants in the "active exercise" group continued to show the stepping reflex, whereas infants in the "passive exercise" group stopped showing the stepping reflex at about the time most typical infants do. On top of that, infants in the "active exercise" group also eventually walked sooner. Because the parents were randomly assigned to the two groups, this study tells us that something about the active exercise promoted both the maintenance of the stepping reflex and the early onset of independent walking.

One important caveat is that because different kinds of experiences can speed up or slow down the achievement of various motor milestones, minor delays are not uncommon or something to be alarmed about in otherwise *neurotypical infants*. Motor delays that are extreme, for example, an infant who shows no signs of reaching for objects by 12 months or no signs of walking by 24 months, might signal some kind of developmental or neurological disability.

BOX 5.3—INFANCY IN REAL LIFE: BACK TO SLEEP, PLAGIOCEPHALY, AND TUMMY TIME

When Edwin went to the pediatrician for his 3-month check-up, everything looked completely normal. He was gaining weight (85th percentile in fact), and he was meeting all of his milestones. All seemed well; that is, all except for one thing. The doctor said that he was showing signs of a condition called plagiocephaly, which literally means "flat head."

Plagiocephaly is a relatively new diagnosis and first became popular after the 1990s when the National Institutes of Health launched the "Back to Sleep" campaign. Before this movement, the common wisdom was to place infants to sleep on their stomachs (at the time, doctors thought that while on their backs, infants could spit up in their sleep and possibly choke). However, research began to suggest that infants who slept on their backs were at a markedly lower risk for dying of SIDS (see Chapters 1 and 3). Although no one knows exactly what causes SIDS, researchers believe that infants who sleep on their stomachs might have trouble rousing themselves if they need more oxygen, whereas infants that sleep on their backs can simply turn their heads to get more air. Consistent with this theory, proponents of the Back to Sleep Campaign (and any doctor or nurse you talk to today) urge parents to put their infants to sleep on their backs instead of on their stomachs. Their recommendations turned out to be really good ones, and there has been a dramatic drop in the rate of SIDS in the United States ever since.

Although putting babies to sleep on their backs has had a remarkable and important impact on SIDS deaths, there have also been some unintended consequences. First, infants began developing flatter heads from spending so much time on their backs, and hence plagiocephaly became a popular diagnosis. Although this diagnosis may sound scary to a parent, it does not necessarily mean there is anything wrong with the developing brain or that it is a condition that needs to be "fixed" (Lampl, 2020). However, in the United States, medical professionals began to prescribe cranial orthotics (helmets) to help make infant heads rounder.

Second, as mentioned earlier, infants started experiencing delayed motor milestones, such as later crawling and walking. The idea of anything being "delayed" can sound scary to a parent. But as you now know from what you've read in this chapter, motor "milestones" are quite malleable based on specific cultural and generational differences. So, infants are only delayed relative to a set of standards or averages that are based on how infants in one sample at one point in history developed.

To reduce the problem with "flat head" and with the potential delay in crawling and walking, pediatricians now recommend keeping infants off their backs while they're awake, and doing daily "tummy time"—or putting infants on their stomachs to play. Daily tummy time keeps infants off their heads during the day and helps them practice holding up their heads and pushing up their torsos, giving them the upper body strength they need to start moving around on their own. Indeed, a review of 16 published articles on over 4,000 infants suggests that tummy time is effective in promoting motor development and, specifically, independent mobility (Hewitt et al., 2020). As soon as infants can turn themselves over, they probably won't want to spend much time on their backs anymore, and soon after, parents will have a whole new problem on their hands—a crawling baby.

Check Your Learning

1. What is a motor milestone, according to Gesell's perspective?

2. Name three problems with describing motor achievements as "milestones."

3. Name one example about how everyday practices can slow down the achievements of motor milestones.

4. Name one example of how extra practice might speed up the achievement of motor milestones.

MULTIPLE DOMAINS OF MOTOR DEVELOPMENT

The onset or emergence of any motor skill sets off a cascade of developments in other domains. For example, the development of self-produced locomotion is associated with more flexible memory (Herbert et al., 2007), and there's even evidence that it changes the organization of certain parts of the brain (Bell & Fox, 1996). If you think about it, every motor achievement—sitting, crawling, and walking—literally changes an infant's point of view, which in turn, changes the visual input the infant receives (Oakes, 2017). The youngest infants are completely dependent on adults to move their bodies around for them (Franchak, 2019), so they spend most of their time looking at the faces of their mothers and fathers or at objects that their parents put right in front of them. Once infants can sit on their own, they can for the first time choose which objects they want to bring into view by holding them, turning them around, and placing them on the ground (or for some infants, throwing them across the room). Once they can crawl, infants can choose where to go for the first time, but because of the limits of the crawling position itself, they mostly have to look at the floor when they are moving and can't really carry anything from one place to another. When they finally walk, infants can navigate the room with their hands free to carry objects and with a full view of the brave new world in front of them. As you will see in this section, all of these changes in motor achievements cause changes in what infants perceive and in the social context around them.

Motor Development and Perception

Every motor achievement literally changes an infant's point of view, which in turn, changes what they see. Thus, there is a clear link between motor development and infant perception. As infants gain more independence, they also gain more control over the visual information that they are seeing. When they sit, they are able to choose which objects or toys to investigate, as long as those toys are within reach. Later, as they begin to crawl and walk, they can obtain objects and toys that are out of reach. And all the while as they are learning to navigate their environments, they will also rely more on perceptual information to tell them which objects are safe to touch and which obstacles are safe to navigate.

Object Perception

Infants' active manual exploration seems to be related to infants' object perception, suggesting that the development of infants' ability to explore manually is related to changes in their perception of objects. One catalyst for the development of visual perception is an infant's ability to sit independently. As infants become able to sit on their own, they have a different view of the world, and they have better control over that view than before they could sit independently. Not surprisingly then, the ability to sit independently has been linked to changes in visual perception. For example, infants who can sit seem to be better able to separate figures from the background in visual scenes (Ross-Sheehy et al., 2016). Sitting ability has also been related to infants' face perception (Cashon et al., 2013). Studies like these suggest that infants' visual perception changes as they see the world in new ways and as they develop the ability to control those views.

Another reason that sitting might influence infants' object perception is that infants' ability to sit affects their ability to reach for and pick up objects. Although infants begin to reach and manipulate objects before they can sit on their own, it isn't easy. Indeed, when they are on their backs, gravity can cause any toy to come crashing down onto the infant's face, making it hard to do much playing. Thus, once infants can sit independently, their hands are more free to play with objects. Kasey Soska and Scott Johnson (2008) asked how the experience of sitting and manipulating objects changes the way infants see those objects. Before they can sit, infants mostly look at objects presented right in front of them by their caregivers, without seeing the objects from all angles. When they are sitting and playing with objects for the first time, they can turn the objects around and investigate their three-dimensional (3D) properties.

In Chapter 4, we described a study that Soska and Johnson conducted in which they found that 6-month-old infants, but not 4-month-old infants, seemed to perceive objects as 3D. In another study, Soska and Johnson asked whether infants' ability to manipulate and visually explore objects was related to this ability. They found that the more experience infants had with sitting, the more they explored the toys, and the more likely they were to visualize objects in three dimensions. This suggests that infants' experience sitting and their subsequent experience manipulating objects facilitates 3D object perception (Soska et al., 2010).

Once again, however, this work is *correlational*. Soska et al. compared infants who already could sit or who already were able to pick up and explore objects with infants who could not. How can we test whether the motor experience *caused* development in visual perception? Amy Needham, Tracy Barrett, and Karen Peterman (2002) came up with a clever way to do this. They created "sticky mittens" for pre-reaching infants. These were baby mittens that had Velcro sewn on them. When infants were wearing these mittens, they were given a set of toys, also with Velcro on them, so that infants who had not yet developed the ability to reach and pick up objects could pick them up just by swiping them. Needham and her colleagues found that experience with these mittens caused infants to be more visually engaged with objects. This suggests that infants do indeed look more at objects when they can hold and manipulate them. The ability to hold and manipulate objects also seems to cause other changes in infants' perception of objects. Experience with sticky mittens also enhances young infants' perception that one object causes another to move (Rakison & Krogh, 2012) and young infants' ability to recognize objects from different viewpoints (Slone et al., 2018).

Perception and Action

To summarize what we've learned so far, as infants learn to sit on their own, they gain more experience manipulating objects in space and, as a result, become better able to perceive the dimensions of those objects. What happens, then, when infants learn to crawl and walk for the first time and gain experience manipulating their own *bodies* in space? Obviously, to move in the environment, infants need to perceive which objects in that space are near to them and which objects are far away, or use their depth perception. They also need to perceive the movement that is created as they travel around the room, or what we call **optic flow**. Most adults unconsciously—and seemingly effortlessly—coordinate their movements with what they see, hear, and feel. As a result, adults don't (often) fall down, bump into another person, knock over a small child, or step on a dog. Although you make these calculations automatically, or without much conscious awareness, this ability only developed when you started to move on your own for the first time. And if you try really hard, you can still confuse this otherwise automatic system.

Have you ever been sitting on a train next to another train, both of which were parked at their stations? Picture yourself sitting there, ready for your journey, and peering out your window into the window of the unmoving train next to you. What happens when the train next to you starts moving slowly, but your train stays put? For a second, it probably feels like you're moving too, since perceptually, your brain is sensing movement from your visual system. However, this sensation only lasts for a second; your brain will quickly combine the information you are getting from the position and movement of your body, or what we call **proprioception**, with the information you're getting from your visual system. This reinterpretation of the visual information lets you know that your train hasn't yet left the station.

You can't help but feel the weird sensation that you're moving when the train next to you starts moving, even though you're completely stationary. It's so natural that you might even suppose that this feeling is innate. It turns out that it's not. Researchers found out for sure by using a clever paradigm called the **moving room**. The moving room is essentially a large, human-sized box with three walls and a ceiling (Figure 5.6). The catch is, the back wall moves forward and backward. Here's how it works: A person stands at the open end of the moving room looking at the back wall, and at some point the back wall starts moving toward the person. What do you think you would do if you were in this study? If you thought to yourself "I'd step back" or "I'd fall down," you'd do what most people do in the moving room. The moving room presents the same momentary dissociation between visual and proprioceptive information as the train scenario: Your visual system tells you that you're moving even though your body is perfectly still. So in the moving room, you'd get the same sensation you'd feel in the train example, and if you happen to be standing up, you'd probably feel the urge to readjust your posture, by stepping back or even falling down in some cases.

What you're doing in the moving room is making use of information from optic flow, or the movement of the objects around you in relation to your own body. The big question is, do infants also make use of information from optic flow, even if they don't yet walk or crawl and don't quite need this information to navigate through space? Carol Higgens, Joseph Campos, and Rosanne Kermoian (1996) investigated this question by seating infants in a high chair at the end of the moving room while the walls shifted toward them and back again. To test whether locomotor experience had an impact on infants' responses to the moving walls, the researchers used an age-held-constant design. In this case, all the infants they tested were 8

FIGURE 5.6 ■ Moving Room

It is an apparatus with three walls and a ceiling. The far wall can move back and forth.

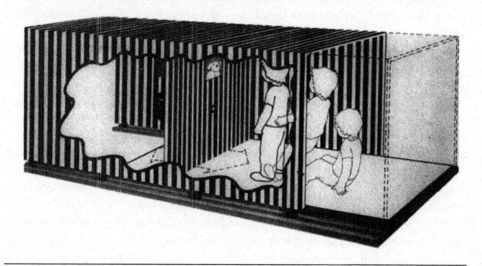

Source: Reprinted with permission from Bertenthal & Bai (1989).

months old, but they varied in terms of their locomotor experience. One group of 8-month-old infants had some experience with hands-and-knees crawling. Another group of 8-month-old infants had no locomotor experience. A third group of infants did not yet crawl, but they had experience moving their bodies around in an infant walker, or a device that allows infants to move around while supported. Only infants who had locomotor experience, either through crawling or with the walker, readjusted their posture as the wall of the moving room came toward them. This doesn't mean that the pre-locomotor infants didn't *see* the walls moving; instead, it just means that they didn't use the information from optic flow to control their posture. And since the researchers tested infants who were all the same age, differences in infants' responses couldn't be attributed to age, or maturation. Instead, infants' responses were most likely a product of experience with self-produced locomotion. The researchers propose that experience moving one's body independently in space requires infants to respond to information from optic flow for the very first time. Thus, over time and with practice moving one's body through space, information from optic flow becomes meaningful, and infants learn to adjust their posture appropriately when their bodies move.

Self-produced locomotion also plays a role in infants' ability to use information about depth. Remember the visual cliff from Chapters 1 and 4? To refresh your memory, the visual cliff is a tabletop with a red and white checkerboard pattern covered with a glass surface. On the "shallow" side of the table, the glass is right on the surface, but for the "deep" side, the pattern is several feet below the surface, giving the appearance of a large drop-off. As described in Chapter 1, Joseph Campos and his colleagues studied the effects of crawling experience on how infants perceive depth (Campos et al., 1992). The researchers measured infants' heart rate as an experimenter placed them on the deep side of the cliff. They found that infants who had crawling experience showed a different pattern of heart rate changes than did infants who did not have crawling experience, suggesting that the experience of crawling changed their depth perception. However, this study was only correlational, which means that we can't conclude for sure that crawling experience, or experience with self-produced locomotion, caused these differences in heart rate.

To address this issue, Campos and colleagues did another study that was experimental, where they gave pre-locomotor infants experience with self-produced locomotion. How do you give infants who can't crawl locomotor experience? They used a walker, as in the experiment described earlier. However, instead of just finding children who had used a walker, in this study Campos and his colleagues randomly assigned half of the infants to get walkers and use them for several hours a day. The researchers found that pre-locomotor infants who were given experience with the walker showed the same pattern of heart rate changes as infants who had crawling experience. Because this was an experiment, where the researchers manipulated how much locomotor experience the infants had, we can conclude for sure that experience with self-produced locomotion (in this case, using the walker) caused differences in infants' heart rates.

What does it mean that infants' heart rate changes when they see the visual cliff? Campos and colleagues also found that whether or not infants actually *crawled* across the deep side of the cliff depended on their locomotor experience. In this study, all the infants could crawl, but some had just begun to crawl and therefore had limited crawling experience. More than half of these infants crawled over the deep side of the cliff, suggesting they did not use the information about depth. In contrast, most of the infants who had been crawling for more than 40 days avoided the deep side. Again, these findings don't necessarily suggest that the pre-locomotor infants didn't *see* the drop-off or can't perceive depth. Instead, these findings suggest that, like with the moving room, it is only after infants have experienced moving their bodies independently that information about depth becomes meaningful, and infants use this information to guide their actions safely.

Perceiving Affordances for Action

After infants learn to crawl or walk, they begin to readjust their bodies in the moving room and avoid crossing the deep side of the visual cliff. Clearly self-produced locomotion teaches infants something important about how to navigate their environments, but what exactly? The traditional explanation for what infants learn is fear of heights. The reasoning is that experience falling while learning to crawl and walk elicits a newfound fear of heights in infants, which is why they avoid the deep side of the visual cliff. However, there are several reasons to think this is not the case. For one, Karen Adolph and colleagues found that infants between the ages of 12 and 19 months take an average of over 2,000 steps in a single hour of walking and fall about 17 times during that same time period (Adolph et al., 2012). That's a lot of falling, and importantly, a lot of getting back up and trying again. In fact, it wouldn't be particularly adaptive to learn to be afraid of heights right when you're learning to navigate the world on your own for the very first time.

But what's even more telling is that infants don't seem to transfer what they learn from one posture to another. Kari Kretch and Karen Adolph (2013) designed a real, adjustable cliff, to examine infants' behaviors on the edge of a real drop-off during the transition from crawling to walking. The real cliff was like the visual cliff but with no safety glass. Instead of observing whether infants crawl over a cliff covered with glass, Kretch and Adolph had infants approach this real drop-off and trained experimenters to catch the infants if they tried to step or crawl in a way that would result in a fall. On top of that, the cliff was adjustable, and the drop-off could vary between 0 centimeters (essentially no drop-off) and 90 centimeters, which is similar to the traditional visual cliff. Using the adjustable cliff, Kretch and Adolph found that experienced 12-month-old crawlers not only refused to crawl over risky drop-offs, but they were also able to judge almost exactly—to the centimeter—which drop-offs they could descend safely in the crawling posture and which ones were too high.

The researchers then tested a second group of 12-month-old infants who were the same age but had just begun to walk. These infants were tested on whether or not they would *step* off the cliff. Unlike the expert crawlers, these new walkers repeatedly stepped off unsafe drop-offs. Even though infants of the same age recognized which drop-offs were safe when tested on their expert crawling, these infants seemed unaware that some drop-offs were unsafe when tested on their new skill of walking. If experience crawling taught these infants to fear depth, these 12-month-old walkers, who all had previously crawled, should have been reluctant to step off of deep cliffs. Importantly, experienced 18-month-old walkers behaved just like the experienced 12-month-old crawlers and refused to walk down drop-offs that were too risky.

These findings suggest two important things. First, what infants are learning from self-produced locomotion isn't a fear of heights. Indeed, if they learned to be afraid of heights once they learned to crawl, this fear should have carried over to walking. Conversely, Adolph and colleagues argued that instead of fear, infants are actually learning to perceive affordances for action (Adolph et al., 2014). An **affordance** is the relation between an infant's real abilities and the properties of the environment. According to this account, what infants are learning through self-produced locomotion is to judge their own abilities relative to the properties of the obstacle, or in the case of a cliff, to the height of the drop-off. Affordances differ based on what posture you're in, since your ability to cross a 10-centimeter bridge, for example, might be different if you're crawling over it or walking over it and different based on how good you are at crawling or walking. In fact, Adolph and colleagues have found this pattern using a number of obstacles, including gaps in the floor, slopes in the ground, bridges of varying widths, and doorways of varying sizes (Figure 5.7). With each obstacle, the story is the same: Infants who have experience in a specific posture can accurately decide what size gaps they can reach over, what size

FIGURE 5.7 ■ Adolph Apparatuses

Various apparatuses used to test infants' reactions to heights. (A) Standard visual cliff, where the entire apparatus is covered in safety glass so that there is not an actual drop off. (B) Actual cliff, where height adjusts from 0 to 90 cm. (C) Adjustable slow apparatus, where the slant adjusts from 0 to 90 degrees. (D) Bridge apparatus, where bridge width adjusts from 2 to 60 cm. (E) Adjustable ledge apparatus, where width adjusts from 0 to 70 cm. (F) Adjustable gap apparatus, where gap width adjusts from 0 to 90 cm.

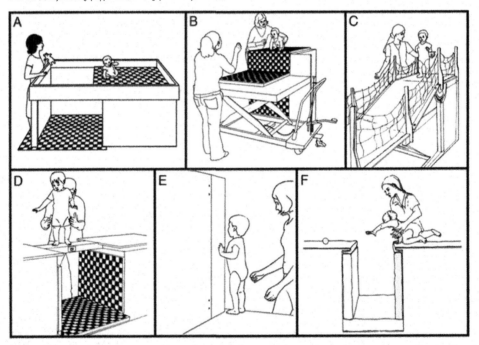

Source: Reprinted with permission from LoBue & Adolph (2019).

slopes they can descend, what size doorways they can fit through, and what size bridges they can cross without falling off. However, once they become novices in a new posture, they have to start over. In fact, if you put an experienced crawler in a crawling posture, they can accurately decide what kinds of slopes in the ground are too steep to descend and which ones are safe, but if you pick up the very same infant from a crawling posture and put him in a walking posture where he has far less experience, he will willingly tumble down the same slope he just refused to descend in a crawling posture (Adolph, 1997). Infants get better and better at making these judgments as they gain more experience in a specific posture. So when presented with a new physical feat, infants explore and try to figure out what actions are possible or impossible based on their ability and the properties of the obstacle itself. In other words, what locomotor experience is teaching infants is to make use of an increasing number of cues—information from optic flow, depth, and other features of the environment—to guide their actions adaptively.

Motor Development and Social Context

Besides changes in perceptual input, motor development can also change the social context in which infants are receiving that input. As we described in the opening of this chapter, when Charlie started to walk, the whole social environment changed around him. All of a sudden there were rules that could be followed, or broken, and as a result, Charlie's parents found themselves interacting with him in new and different ways. Consistent with Charlie's story, Campos and colleagues (2000) hypothesized that once infants start walking or crawling on their own, they are likely to start seeing more negative emotional responses from their caregivers, as infants become free for the first time to navigate a potentially dangerous environment. Parents might also start talking more to their infants and giving them more direct instructions about what to do and what not to do.

This is some evidence from research to support these ideas. For example, Karasik, Tamis-LeMonda, and Adolph (2011) videotaped 50 infants in their homes for 1 hour at two time points—at 11 months and 13 months—to study the social context that accompanies an infant's transition from crawling to walking. They found that once infants started walking, they would travel longer distances to retrieve toys, since they had their hands free to carry objects for the first time. What did they do with those toys? They often brought them to their caregivers to engage with them in play. And in response to infants' bids to share toys, mothers responded with more action directives, telling infants what to do with the toys or how to play with them (Karasik et al., 2014). This suggests that infants' ability to walk, and thus carry objects for the first time, affects their ability to share objects with their mothers, which then in turn shapes the mothers' social behavior as well. In fact, another group of researchers found that infants' pointing and following parents' gaze—what we call joint attention—also increases as a function of infants' experience walking (Walle, 2016) and is even related to infants' own language development (Walle & Campos, 2014).

Although this is a fairly new area of research, it suggests that while crawling and walking open up a brand new world of discovery for infants, it also opens up a brand new world for caregivers' interactions with their infants, changing the social environment.

Check Your Learning

1. What is the relation between independent sitting and an infant's three-dimensional object perception?

2. What is the moving room, and what do the moving room studies tell us about the relation between perception and action?

3. How does infants' ability to use depth perception change with self-produced locomotion?

4. How does self-produced locomotion change the infant's social environment?

SUMMARY

Traditional perspectives on motor development assume that motor achievements, or "motor milestones," unfold as the result of central nervous system development. This means that important motor developments like sitting, crawling, and walking are dependent on brain maturation and should develop around the same time in every infant. However, research suggests that motor achievements—even our most basic reflexes—rely on a large number of other developmental changes, including growth, strength, and experience moving your body in space. So, differences in the way we traditionally handle our infants, differences in where or how they sleep, and differences in the amount of practice we give them can shift the development of any motor achievement significantly. Importantly, changes in infants' motor abilities allow infants to interact with the world in new and exciting ways, setting the stage for gains in other areas, such as changes in object perception, social and emotional development, and the ability to make use of an increasing number of contextual cues to safely navigate their environments. In the end, each motor achievement gives infants a brand new perspective on their environments, opening up a world of new possibilities and new developments in other important domains.

KEY TERMS

affordance
Babinski reflex
breastfeeding
failure to thrive
gahvora cradle
grasping reflex
growth charts
malnutrition
maturational states
moro/startle reflex
motor milestones

moving room
newborn reflexes
optic flow
proprioception
rooting reflex
secular trend
stepping reflex
sucking reflex
swaddling
tonic neck reflex

REVIEW QUESTIONS

1. List several factors that contribute to physical development over the first year of life.

2. What is the stepping reflex? Explain why it is present at birth and why it disappears shortly thereafter.

3. What is a motor milestone, and why might it be a problematic way to describe infant behavior?

4. Describe two ways that everyday experience (or lack thereof) shapes motor development.

5. How does motor ability affect the development of three-dimensional object perception?

CRITICAL THINKING QUESTIONS

1. Compare and contrast traditional maturational perspectives on motor development with the dynamic systems theory.

2. What correlational evidence was presented to show links between distinct experiences and motor development? What experimental evidence was presented to connect experience and motor milestones?

3. Is there a critical period in the first year for reaching motor milestones? What evidence supports your answer?

4. Provide one example of how motor ability shapes visual perception, understanding of objects, or social interactions.

5. A friend is worried that her infant is not crawling even though other infants of the same age are all crawling. What information from this chapter would you share to help her out?

6. An infant is labeled as "failure to thrive." Does this mean that the infant is developing atypically? Why or why not?

7. An infant is at the 25th percentile with the CDC growth chart but a lower percentile with the WHO growth chart. Which percentile is "right"? What information about the infant would you want to know if you had to pick which growth chart to use?

8. Will a 2-month-old who is at the 75% percentile for weight and height stay at this percentile at 6 months of age? Why or why not?

6 THE DEVELOPMENT OF COGNITIVE SKILLS

As a 16-month-old toddler, one of Alison's favorite things to do was to put her "babies" to bed. First, she would take all of her dolls and stuffed animals from her room, bring them into the living room, and line them up face down across the floor. She would then carefully cover each one with a washcloth and pat them on the back saying "nigh-nigh." This amazing ritual reveals quite a lot about Alison's cognitive skills at this age. It showed that she had a *memory* of the bedtime ritual. It also showed that she was able to *categorize* her toys into the ones that should be put to bed (e.g., dolls and stuffed animals) and those that would not be part of a bedtime routine (e.g., trucks, blocks).

These cognitive skills—memory and categorization—were developing over the previous 16 months as Alison played with toys, interacted with others, heard songs, was read to, went on walks, and otherwise engaged with the environment around her. This chapter is about the development of the cognitive skills infants use to gather information about the world and to store and organize that information. In the next chapter we will continue to talk about cognitive development and focus on the infants' models of the world. In short, this chapter is about the *processes* infants use to learn about and represent the world, and the next chapter is about infants' *understanding* of the world. In Chapter 8 we will review the emergence of children's *symbolic understanding*.

In this chapter, we will discover how cognitive skills develop during the course of infancy. It all begins with **attention**, or infants' focus on the objects, people, and events in the world around them. As an infant, Alison was very attentive. She would sit up tall in her stroller, lean forward slightly, and look around to make sure she didn't miss anything. Carter would sit in his bouncy chair and watch, as his older sister flitted by. Attention, especially to particular people, places, and objects, helps infants form memories of those most familiar to them. Learning about the world involves **memory** of the people, places, and objects that infants have encountered. As infants, Tesalia and Diego always greeted the people they knew best with big smiles and coos. As we will see, when infants can remember the things they attend to, they learn to recognize the commonalities between items from the same category. That is, they organize what they have learned by **categorizing** their experiences. As Edwin and Charlie learned more about their dog Charlotte, they were able to recognize that other dogs on the street also liked to be petted under the chin. In this chapter, we will learn about how each of these skills—attention, memory, and categorization—develop during the first years.

After reading this chapter you will be able to:

1. *Define* the three aspects of attention, provide an example of each, and explain how each develops.

2. *Describe* the different types of memory in infancy, and *outline* changes in the memory abilities of infants across the first year into early childhood.

3. *Compare* the different ways to measure infants' categorization, and *summarize* the development of infants' categorization skill.

THE DEVELOPMENT OF ATTENTION

What Is Attention?

At some point in our lives, we have all heard a parent or teacher tell a child to "pay attention!" You've also likely had the experience of trying to read a book or watch a show on television when someone's conversation in the next room draws your attention away from whatever you were doing. Broadly speaking, attention is the act of focusing on something. This is often something that's happening around you—your teacher, your textbook, the pot of water heating on the stove—but you can also pay attention to things that are happening internally, like your own thoughts or what's going on with your body, like when you can't concentrate because you can't stop thinking about how much your head hurts or how hungry you are. As William James (1890) famously put it:

> Everyone knows what attention is. It is taking possession of the mind, in clear and vivid form, of one out of what seems several simultaneously possible objects or trains of thought. (pp. 403–404)

For psychologists, attention is how we deal with the fact that at every moment, we are bombarded with more information than we can deal with. When we are awake, all of our senses are stimulated simultaneously, and we have thoughts, goals, and memories that may be active. Attention is the process of selecting some subset of those things to focus on, while putting other less important things out of focus. Thus, attention makes processing information manageable, but it's also why we miss some things that happen around us. If we don't attend to something, we don't process it. This is why we think that infants' attention—and especially visual attention—is an important mechanism of information gathering.

Importantly, attention is not just one thing, and different aspects of attention develop at different times (Table 6.1). Even though we use "attention" to refer to a single thing in our casual language, it is actually a collection of different skills that must be coordinated and work together for the infant to effectively learn about the world around them. Attention involves **orienting**, or directing attention to specific objects or locations. Even newborns orient their attention, for example, by turning their head toward a source of stimulation (Muir & Field, 1979). Because there is more information available than we can process, once attention has been oriented, we

TABLE 6.1 ■ Aspects of Attention		
Aspect of Attention	**Definition**	**Example**
Orienting	Directing attention or gaze to an object or location	An infant turning her gaze to her mother's face
Selecting	Choosing some information to attend to or process and filtering or ignoring other available information	An infant looking at the shape of her mother's eyes, ignoring her mouth and nose
Maintaining	Continuing to attend to some information, resisting the pull of other information	An infant continuing to look at her mother's face, even as her older sibling is singing and dancing nearby

must **select** some items or information to focus on; in other words, we filter the information available in order to focus on just some of it. Although young infants can select some items and ignore others, selective attention develops during infancy (Kwon et al., 2016). Once information has been selected, it must be *processed*, which requires that the infant **maintains attention** on the information of interest, resisting the pull of other information that might be present and distracting. The ability to maintain attention and ignore distraction develops considerably during infancy and beyond. In the following sections we will talk about the development of these aspects of attention.

Photo of Baby Looking at His Dad

iStock/mihailomilovanovic

As in many areas of infant development, most of the studies on infant attention have been conducted in North America or Europe with infants of middle-class families. Most of the infants in these studies are White. For decades, researchers were not concerned with the fact that the studies were conducted with a narrow slice of the worlds' infants because it was assumed that these attentional abilities were so basic (like breathing or blinking) that they would not vary for infants of different ethnic groups or from families of different socioeconomic status. Some recent studies have been conducted with different groups of infants, and sometimes the results are just the same as when the infants tested are from Western, middle-class families. But sometimes the results are different. So, when drawing conclusions from the research we present here, it is important to understand who has been studied and be careful about assuming that any result is universal to all infants.

How Do We Measure Attention?

The infant in the previous photo is clearly *looking* at his dad. We also would probably say that he is *attending* to his dad. Although we know that adults can attend to an object or location without looking at it, it is extremely difficult to tell whether infants are attending to something unless they look at it. Attending to something without looking at it is called **covert attention**, and it is how you monitor your visual environment without moving your eyes. Covert attention is thought to be important for how your brain decides whether or not to shift your gaze to a new object or location. Although we can study covert attention in adults by telling them to look in one location (e.g., at a fixation cross in the middle of a computer monitor) and then asking them to shift their attention (but not their eyes!) to other items that show up in the periphery, it is difficult to study in infants. Researchers have studied covert attention in infants using EEG (electroencephalogram) or other measures, but we typically study infants' attention by noting where they direct their eyes and assuming that shifts in their gaze reflect shifts in their attention.

In Chapter 1, we described the classic work of Robert Fantz showing that when newborn infants are presented with two images side by side, they look longer at some images over others. For a decade or more, the primary use of this procedure was to understand infants' visual attention. One question was simply, what do infants attend to? Studies showed, for example, that newborn infants look more at patterns than at plain images, demonstrating that they can actually see the patterns. As we saw in Chapter 4, this finding was important in the development of procedures that researchers use to study infants' visual perception.

Several aspects of looking behavior tell us about infants' attention. Therefore, measures of infant attention involve where they look, how quickly they look, and how long they keep looking. Researchers have found that with increasing age, infants look for shorter durations at the same stimulus (e.g., Brennan et al., 1966). As they get older, infants process—or learn about—visual information more quickly, requiring less time to look at a stimulus to learn about it. Leslie Cohen (1972) asked about what kinds of things infants moved their eyes to versus what kinds of things infants continued to look at. He found that infants directed their gaze toward bigger visual objects, but they kept looking at more complex visual objects for longer periods of time. This led him to conclude that different stimulus properties controlled infants' *attention-getting* and their *attention-holding*, what we now call *orienting* and *maintaining* attention.

Orienting and Disengagement

Orienting, or the process of directing one's attention to a stimulus, might seem simple. Orienting just involves directing your head, eyes, and attention to something. However, it turns out that orienting can be hard. Look at the world around you. There are lots of things you could direct your attention to. To orient to any one thing, you need to ignore many other things. In addition, if you are currently attending to something, orienting to something new requires **disengaging** from the current focus of your attention. Think about when someone calls your name while you are focused intently on a sporting event on TV. It may take some time for you to pull your eyes away from the game on the screen to look at the person trying to get your attention.

Although very young infants can orient and disengage their attention, it is remarkably hard for them; orienting and disengagement develop over the first months after birth. Bruce Hood and Janette Atkinson (1993) studied the development of these aspects of attention in young infants. They presented infants in Cambridge, England, with simple displays of an engaging stimulus in the center and distracting stimuli to the sides (Figure 6.1). They made the center

FIGURE 6.1 ■ Stimuli Used by Hood & Atkinson (1993)

The sequence of stimulus events used by Hood and Atkinson (1993) to test young infants' attentional disengagement.

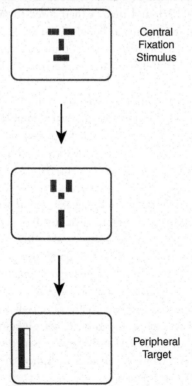

Central Fixation Stimulus

Peripheral Target

Source: Reprinted with permission from Hood & Atkinson (1993).

stimulus really interesting by having the elements in the image alternate between two shapes, in this case, alternating between a face-like stimulus with a surprised expression and a face-like stimulus with a neutral expression. A peripheral target—a simple shape that alternated between a black-and-white pattern—appeared to either the left or right side. Sometimes, the peripheral target was presented after the face-like stimulus had disappeared, as in Figure 6.1. In this case, the infant did not need to disengage from the center face-like stimulus to orient to the peripheral stimulus because they were not attending to it when the peripheral stimulus appeared. Under these conditions, 1-month-old infants looked at the peripheral target, showing that they could orient, but they were slower than were 3- or 6-month-old infants, showing that orienting to a stimulus improves in the first months of infancy.

Hood and Atkisnon also asked whether infants would disengage from the central face-like stimulus to orient to the peripheral flashing pattern when the center and peripheral stimuli were presented *at the same time*. In this case, orienting to the peripheral stimulus required infants to disengage from the central stimulus. At all ages, infants took longer to look at the peripheral target in this condition—in fact, even adults are slower in this situation. Other studies have also shown this difference in infants tested in Japan (Nakagawa & Sukigara, 2019), the Netherlands (Cousijn et al., 2017), and Sweden (Siqueiros Sanchez et al., 2021). Thus, infants across the globe have more difficulty orienting to a new stimulus when they have to disengage from a different stimulus at the same time. However, Siqueiros Sanchez and colleagues (2021) found that in their Swedish sample, disengagement was related to socioeconomic status. Thus, although there are some aspects of the development of orienting and disengagement that are common across children raised in different environments, some aspects of infants' lived experience influences the development of attention.

The amount of time it takes infants to disengage from the center stimulus to look at the peripheral stimulus also depends on what the stimuli are. Some stimuli are harder for infants to disengage from than others. In one study, infants in Finland, Malawi, and South Africa were shown displays like those used by Hood and Atkinson, except that sometimes the central stimulus was a face and sometimes it was not a face (Pyykkö et al., 2019). All three groups of infants disengaged more quickly when the central stimulus was not a face than when it was a face. And some faces seem to be harder to disengage from than others. One study showed that 7-month-old infants in Finland had more difficulty disengaging from *fearful* faces than from *happy* faces (Peltola, Leppänen, Vogel-Farley, et al., 2009).

Clearly, orienting to a new stimulus and disengaging from an attended stimulus are skills that develop. Across the first year, infants become faster to orient and disengage. In addition, infants have more difficulty disengaging when the currently attended stimulus is more meaningful or significant. Thus, orienting and disengaging are not all-or-none phenomena, in which infants either have or don't have each ability. Instead, what infants orient to and how quickly they orient to it depend on their age and what they must disengage from in order to shift their attention to the new stimulus. Infants' experiences with their environments also shape these aspects of attention (see the Whole Infant box).

BOX 6.1—THE WHOLE INFANT: NOT ALL ATTENTION IS CREATED EQUAL—BIASED ATTENTION TO THREAT IN INFANCY

Infants don't allocate their attention evenly. Indeed, they look longer at novel things than at familiar things, longer at faces than at non-faces, longer at things that move than at things that don't move, and longer at a black-and-white striped image than at a gray square. Infants also are faster to attend to—and attend longer to—stimuli that indicate some sort of threat.

As we will discuss in Chapter 10, infants can tell the difference between various emotional expressions in the first few months of life. But, young infants treat different emotions the same way early in infancy. At first, they show equal interest in happy and fearful facial expressions. When infants are about 7 months old, however, they start to respond differently to different types of emotions. At this age, infants tested both in the United States and Finland showed a *bias* for fearful faces—infants looked longer at fearful faces than at happy or neutral expressions (Leppänen et al., 2007; Nelson & De Haan, 1996; Peltola, Leppänen, Mäki, et al., 2009).

One reason that infants may be biased to look at fearful faces is that those faces suggest the presence of imminent threat. Researchers also found that infants had distinct event-related potential (ERP) responses, or the brain activity recorded from the infants' scalp in response to specific stimuli, to fearful faces, suggesting they had heightened attention to those fearful faces (Leppänen et al., 2007; Nelson & De Haan, 1996; Peltola, Leppänen, Mäki, et al., 2009). At this age, infants also show evidence of difficulty disengaging from fearful faces. That is, when infants tested in Finland were presented with an image of an emotional facial expression in the center of a screen, they had more difficulty looking away from the face to a peripheral stimulus if it is a fearful face than if it was a happy or neutral face (Peltola et al., 2008; Peltola, Leppänen, Vogel-Farley, et al., 2009). This suggests that by 7 months, infants are already beginning to notice that emotional faces can carry different kinds of information, and although they aren't necessarily afraid of threatening stimuli at this age, infants notice that threatening information might be something that deserves a bit more attention.

Infants are also faster to *orient* to threatening than to nonthreatening stimuli. In one study, Vanessa LoBue and Judy DeLoache (2010) presented 8- to 14-month-old U.S. infants with two images side by side on a large screen. On one side, the image was threatening, either a snake or an angry face. On the other side, the image was nonthreatening, a flower or happy face. Infants turned their heads faster to look at the snakes and angry faces than to look at the flowers and happy faces. In another study, an ethnically and socioeconomically diverse sample of U.S. infants from 4 to 24 months oriented more quickly to a snake when it was presented with a frog. Thus, threatening stimuli like snakes and angry faces quickly capture infants' attention (LoBue et al., 2017).

Where does this bias come from? One clue comes from comparisons of infants with different kinds of experience with emotional input. Specifically, infants who see more positive emotional expressions (i.e., their moms smile more and have happy expressions more of the time) have a larger bias for looking at fearful faces over happy faces than do infants who see less positive emotional expressions (i.e., their mothers are depressed or who have negative expressions more of the time). For example, one study found that a sample of UK

7-month-old infants with highly positive mothers showed a larger bias for looking at fearful over happy faces compared to infants with mothers who were generally less positive (de Haan et al., 2004). Other studies have shown that U.S. infants whose mothers are depressed or who generally demonstrate more negative affect show less of a bias for negative or threatening faces than infants of nondepressed mothers (Cohn et al., 1986; Field, 1992). Thus, at least in these Western samples, infants' bias to look at negative faces might be stronger in infants who have more experience with seeing positive expressions. This suggests that while attention biases for threat develop early, specific experiences with threat (e.g., seeing your mom show negative expressions) might change these biases or even cause new ones to develop, theoretically functioning to alert the infant to the presence of something potentially harmful.

Selecting

Another important aspect of attention is selection. One of the most vital functions of attention is to whittle down the nearly infinite number of things we can attend to and help us direct our attention to just a small subset of things to focus on. This is probably even more important for infants than for adults because so much of what infants see is brand new, which could make the world an overwhelming place. This raises the question of whether infants can use attention to select some stimuli to focus on, while at the same time ignoring others.

We already saw in Chapter 4 that at birth, infants prefer human faces to other stimuli. However, the studies that measure how long newborns look at faces presented one face at a time, which does not require selective attention. **Selective attention** is needed when the visual world is cluttered and there are many things that you could look at, for example, when looking at a living room filled with toys, people, and furniture. To study selection, researchers show infants relatively simple visual scenes with more than one object and then record what the infants look at. For example, studies conducted in the United States and Europe have shown that when infants are presented with a pair of items and one item is a face and the other is a different type of object or a pattern, infants prefer the face (DeNicola et al., 2013; Turati et al., 2005). In other words, when infants are presented with two things to attend to at one time and one of them is a face, young infants can selectively attend to the face over some other pattern or object.

What about visual scenes with more than just two objects? How do infants select something to attend to then? To find out, researchers have studied infants' selective attention using versions of a *visual search* task. In this task, infants are shown an array of items, where there is one "target." For example, the target may be something the researchers think is interesting, like the human face in Figure 6.2.

Sometimes, researchers present infants with an array that has a *singleton*; that is, all the items in the array are the same except one, for example, an array that includes one bear and five sippy cups. When shown these kinds of arrays, 7- to 9-month-old infants in Malawi selectively attend to the unique object (Pyykkö et al., 2019). In other words, they looked first and more at the "odd" (singleton) item. When shown arrays like the one in Figure 6.2—where there are 6 different items, but one of them is a face, U.S. and British infants aged 6 months and older

FIGURE 6.2 ■ Visual Search Stimulus Array

will select the face; they look longer at the face, they are faster to look at the face, and their very first looks are more often directed toward the face than toward the other objects (Gliga et al., 2009; Kwon et al., 2016). Interestingly, even though U.S. infants younger than 6 months look *longer* at the face than at the other items, they do not look at the face *first* the way older infants do. Instead, their first looks seem to be drawn to the brightest item in the array, like the pink flower in Figure 6.2 (Kwon et al., 2016). In their first 6 months, infants develop the ability to select what to attend to based on their interest in social stimuli. Prior to that time, infants seem to be pulled toward items that are physically salient (bright and colorful) rather than social. Thus, although from birth infants have some selective attention abilities, there is development in the first 6 months in how infants select specific types of objects for attention. In other studies, infants from the United States and Great Britain selectively attended to faces and humans in natural scenes, such as photographs of people in a garden or office (Amso et al., 2014; Kelly et al., 2019), showing that infants likely can use selective attention even in their everyday lives.

Sometimes, we use selective attention to focus on one aspect of an event instead of one object in an array. For example, when viewing a woman brushing her hair, infants might selectively attend to her face or her action. Lorraine Bahrick and her colleagues (2002) have found that racially and ethnically diverse samples of 5- to 6-month-old infants in Florida attended to the action more than the face. When infants were habituated to a woman brushing her hair, for example, they noticed when that same woman changed her action (e.g., began brushing her teeth), but not when a new woman performed the familiar action (e.g., brushing her hair). Seven-month-old infants from this same population attended to both the face and the action.

Interestingly, one study comparing 2-year-old children from middle-class families in Illinois and 2-year-old children from middle-class families in Beijing suggests that this development might be a product of some aspect of U.S. culture. Specifically, as children watched a dynamic event (e.g., a girl petting a dog), U.S. children focused on the *objects* in events, whereas the Chinese children focused on the *actions* in the events (Waxman et al., 2016).

Maintaining Attention

Once infants have oriented to and selected a target of attention, effective processing of that target requires that infants maintain their attention to it. That is, they need to look (or attend) long enough to perceive it, remember it, and categorize it. This means that infants look for longer durations when they are taking more time to process the stimulus. In fact, when you show the same stimulus to younger and older infants, the younger infants look longer. This makes sense if the younger infants need more time to process the stimulus. Interestingly, this developmental trend is only true for the first 6 months or so, at least in the samples of Western middle-class families typically studied. Often, after 6 months, how long infants look at a stimulus depends on the characteristics of the stimulus (Courage et al., 2006).

You might think that because younger infants look longer than older infants at stimuli, the ability to maintain attention does not develop. However, most experiments are run in quiet lab rooms with few distractions, making it relatively easy for infants to maintain their attention. Often only one stimulus is presented at a time, so there is no competition for infants' attention as they look. These conditions might help infants maintain their attention, even when their attention maintenance is not well developed.

The situation is really different in infants' everyday lives, however. As mentioned earlier in this chapter, in order to continue attending to one thing, infants often have to ignore other stimuli. In the real world, infants often have to maintain attention when other interesting things are happening, such as an older sibling running into the room. Maintaining attention requires that infants ignore those other interesting stimuli. Studies that have examined how infants maintain their attention when there are distractions have shown that younger infants are more easily distracted by the competing stimuli than are older infants. For example, research with U.S. infants has shown that as they play with toys, 6-month-old infants were more likely than 10-month-old infants to turn away from a toy to look at a distracting stimulus (Oakes et al., 2002; Oakes & Tellinghuisen, 1994; Tellinghuisen & Oakes, 1997). Thus, not only are there changes in how long infants look, but there are also changes in how easily infants' attention can be interrupted and distracted.

Importantly, infants' developing ability to maintain attention seems to rely on aspects of their everyday experience. For example, Melissa Clearfield and Kelly Jedd (2013) found that differences associated with socioeconomic status (SES) were related to how infants in the United States maintain attention. Specifically, they measured attention in a group of 6- to 12-month-old infants as they played with toys. The infants were White or Hispanic and some were low SES (i.e., infants whose parents were less well educated and who had lower incomes) or higher SES (i.e., their parents had more education and higher incomes). When playing with multiple toys at once, the higher SES infants showed more attention to those toys than did infants who were lower SES. We don't know which aspects of the experience of infants in low and high SES households is responsible for this difference in attention, but studies like these—and the one by Siqueiros Sanchez and colleagues (2021) described earlier—show that the development of attention can vary with environmental factors.

Check Your Learning

1. Define attention, and explain the difference in orienting, selecting, and maintaining attention.

2. What is covert attention? How is it different from orienting, selecting, and maintaining attention?

3. Which infant behavior is often used to measure attention?

4. Is disengagement of attention most closely related to covert attention or orienting? Explain why.

5. What aspect of attention is the visual search task designed to measure?

6. How have infants from low versus high socioeconomic backgrounds been shown to differ in their attention?

THE DEVELOPMENT OF MEMORY

By the time children reach preschool age, they have excellent memories. One day while riding home from swim lessons, 4-year-old Carter asked his mom, "Remember when we were on that hill in that park eating peanut butter and jelly sandwiches. And there were boats?"

Carter's mom didn't remember any recent events like that. Then, she remembered that just after Carter's third birthday, about a year earlier, they had been in Central Park in New York City and they had a picnic with peanut butter and jelly sandwiches and they sailed boats in the pond. Carter recalled amazing detail of an event that had been notable and memorable from his perspective. But even as a 4-year-old, Carter did not tell stories or indicate that he remembered events before the New York City trip. Tesalia, on the other hand, remembers that at her second birthday party there was a toad in the baby pool, which likely made quite an impression! She also remembers that her parents forgot to bring a lighter and so they could not light the candles on her birthday cake. In contrast, at age 3, Charlie had trouble citing memories of specific events but could name all 50 United States—a skill that also requires memory, albeit a different kind.

The stories from Carter and Tesalia show that as toddlers and preschoolers, children do form memories, and when events are unusual and memorable, they remember them for months or years. These are examples of **episodic memories**, or memories of events that include information about what happened, where it happened, and the context of the event. They are also **autobiographical memories**, because they are memories about events that happened in their own lives. One interesting aspect of these memories is that people rarely remember events before the age of 3 or 4. If you think back to your earliest memory, it will probably be something that happened between the time you were 2 and 5. Likely it was something memorable, like moving, the birth of a sibling, a toad in the baby pool at the park, or one of your first birthday parties, like in the next photo. This inability to remember events from before the age of 2 or 3 has been

Photo of Twins Celebrating Their Birthday

iStock/kate_sept2004

called **infantile amnesia**. Although people from different cultures experience infantile amnesia, the early memories people report vary across cultures. North American adults report events like those described by Carter and Tesalia—specific events that were emotionally significant for them. Chinese adults, in contrast, are likely to report early memories that are more generic and more about relationships (Wang, 2003).

Until the 1980s, and even into the 1990s, psychologists believed that infantile amnesia was the result of infants being unable to form enduring memories. For a long time, scientists speculated that we experience infantile amnesia because as infants we didn't have the mental hardware to create those memories. Anyone who has interacted with a toddler or preschooler knows that young children do clearly form memories. Remember 20-month-old Charlie's answer to the question "what color is it" that we discussed in Chapter 4? At 20 months, Charlie clearly remembered that the answer to that question was "Ye-woah" (yellow). He also knew that Charlotte was the dog and Edwin was his big brother. He could count to 10 and recognize letters. All of this required memory. But this kind of memory—like his ability to remember all 50 states—is **semantic memory**, or memory for facts. This kind of memory involves different brain structures than episodic memory, so even though Charlie had rich semantic memories, it is possible that he did not yet have the brain structures to form robust episodic memories.

In this section we will discuss two issues related to infants' memory. First, we will discuss different methods used to measure infants' memory. Then we will discuss different kinds of memories and what evidence there is that infants possess those different kinds of memory.

Measuring Memory in Infancy

How do we measure memory in infants? As you've probably guessed by now, infants aren't so good at answering questions, especially about what they remember. In fact, when we ask infants and young children to tell us about what they remember, it appears that their memory is quite poor, especially before infants can talk. However, if we pay attention to what infants *do*, we can see that they form memories of some sort from very early on (Table 6.2). Like the study of infant attention, one way scientists have studied infants' memory is by measuring their looking behavior. Remember our discussion of habituation in Chapter 4? There we discussed how the duration of infants' looking decreases, or *habituates*, as a stimulus becomes familiar. The first time infants see an image, they look for a long time, but if they see that same image several times in a row, they lose interest and look for shorter and shorter amounts of time. At first, when the stimulus is new, infants look for a long time because they require time to process the information about the stimulus and form a memory of it. When the stimulus is shown again, infants can continue to learn about the stimulus and update that memory. But, once they have learned a stimulus, they rapidly recognize that it is the stimulus they remember, so they do not look at it as long. Thus, the fact that infants' looking time habituates has been taken as evidence that they form a memory of the visual stimulus.

Once a stimulus has become familiar, infants prefer to look at a novel stimulus. This might be observed in a habituation procedure, when infants show renewed interest in a novel stimulus following habituation. A variation of this procedure, often called the *visual paired-comparison* or

TABLE 6.2 ■ Ways of Measuring Memory		
Procedure	**Evidence of Memory**	**Findings**
Habituation	Decrease in response (typically looking) to a familiar stimulus, increase in response when a novel stimulus is presented	Infants show visual recognition memory for images, even after a delay
Visual paired-comparison/ Novelty preference	Following familiarization with one stimulus, infants prefer (look longer at) a novel stimulus over the familiar stimulus	Infants show visual recognition memory for images, even after a delay
Operant conditioning	Following training that a behavior (e.g., kicking) is associated with a rewarding event (e.g., a mobile moving overhead), infants will exhibit the behavior more even if it does not result in the reinforcing event	Infants remember the association between their behavior and the rewarding event even after a delay; changing the context disrupts the memory
Deferred imitation	Infants repeat an action modeled by an experimenter (e.g., turning a light on with their forehead)	Infants remember the action even after a delay; changing the context disrupts the memory

novelty preference procedure, is frequently used to study infant memory. Infants are presented with a stimulus for a period of time, and then they are shown the now-familiar stimulus paired with a novel stimulus. If infants look longer at the novel stimulus than at the familiar stimulus, it is concluded that they have a memory of the familiar stimulus. This behavior indicates that when infants look at the familiar stimulus they *recognize* that they already know that stimulus, so they direct their attention to something that is new. In other words, infants remember the familiar stimulus. For this reason, using infants' looking behavior in this way has often been referred to as testing infants' **visual recognition memory**. Importantly, although most studies in this domain have been conducted in Western countries, many of them were done with children of different racial and socioeconomic backgrounds (Fagan, 1970; Rose, 1981). Others have shown similar findings in infants tested in Peru (Colombo et al., 2014), Singapore (Singh et al., 2015), Mexico (Familiar et al., 2021), and in Inuit infants of Arctic Quebec (Jacobson et al., 2008).

Researchers have also used other behaviors or actions to study infant memory. Carolyn Rovee-Collier famously developed a memory procedure using *operant conditioning*. Operant conditioning procedures involve teaching the infant that when they perform a behavior, there is a rewarding outcome. As a graduate student working on her dissertation, Rovee-Collier was looking for some way to entertain her infant son. She took her belt and used it to fasten her young son's leg to a mobile that was hanging over his crib. Whenever her son kicked his leg, the mobile moved. Soon, this young infant had associated the movement of the mobile with his kicking, and he contentedly kicked away. Rovee-Collier had conditioned her son's kicking by rewarding it with the movement of the mobile. Through this mini home experiment, she not only discovered a way to keep her son entertained, but she also discovered a new and clever way to study infant memory.

In the lab, Rovee-Collier and her students conditioned infants' kicking by attaching their legs (using a ribbon rather than a belt) to a mobile, just like she did with her son (Rovee-Collier, 1999). But the key to using this procedure in the lab was that after infants' kicking was conditioned, Rovee-Collier and her students tested the infant's *memory* for this association by putting them back in the cribs with the mobile after some delay. Just one day after they were conditioned, even 2-month-old infants showed that they remembered the association: When they were placed under a mobile, they began to kick even before the ribbon was attached to their leg! Rovee-Collier and her students have shown this in several studies with mostly White infants from middle-class families. Emily Merz and her colleagues (Merz et al., 2017) found similar effects in a group of mostly Hispanic infants whose mothers were teenagers.

But, memory over longer delays develops slowly over the first year and a half. Although 2-month-old infants show memory after a 1-day delay, they did not show memory after a 1-week delay. And it wasn't until infants were 6 months old that they showed memory after a 2-week delay. Using a variation of this task, where the infant presses a lever to make a train go, Rovee-Collier and her colleagues showed that infants remembered the association (kicking and the mobile moving or pressing the lever and a train moving) for increasingly longer delays. By 12 months, infants remembered the action for 8 weeks and by 18 months, infants remembered it for almost 3 months.

Finally, researchers have used **imitation** to study memory. All around the world, infants and young children imitate, and imitation is considered to be an important way that children learn cultural-specific information (Legare, 2019). However, memory researchers use children's imitation to ask about memory development. In these experiments, infants are shown some novel action, such as taking a mitten off a puppet, or creating a rattle with two cups and a ball. When studying memory, it is important to use novel or unfamiliar actions. Because infants haven't seen the actions before, if they imitate, we know they have remembered the demonstration and are not simply performing previously learned actions with those objects. To make sure infants don't have existing knowledge of the actions, infants are first given the props before the actions are shown to them. Infants rarely perform the target actions: They don't spontaneously take the mitten off the puppet or make a rattle with two cups and a ball. Then an experimenter models the actions, and infants do perform the actions. When studying memory, researchers use **deferred imitation** tasks and only allow infants to imitate after a delay, which can range from several minutes to weeks or months.

Just as was found when using other procedures, studies using imitation showed that infants' memory develops over the first 2 years. Rachel Barr, Anne Dowden, and Harlene Hayne (1996) showed a group of New Zealand infants of European descent between 6 and 24 months actions performed on a puppet (e.g., putting a mitten on the puppet). Even 6-month-old infants imitated the action immediately, showing memory for the actions. But, infants 12 months and older showed deferred imitation, repeating the actions the next day when they were given the opportunity to perform them. Thus, at 12 months, infants showed they remembered the actions they saw the day before. Barr and her colleagues then gave 6-month-old infants more practice before testing them. They found that even these young infants showed deferred imitation after a 24-hour delay if they had more time to form the memory in the first place.

Andrew Meltzoff (1988) showed that it isn't until 14 months that infants can imitate an action after a relatively long (i.e., one week) delay. He brought U.S. infants into the lab and presented them with a series of novel, or weird actions—actions the infants are unlikely to do on their own. For example, the experimenter presented infants with a round light box on a table. But instead of turning it on with her hand or finger (like most people would do), she turned it on by touching it with her forehead. A week later, the infants were brought back to the lab. Instead of turning on the light box with their hands, they turned it on with their heads, just like they saw the wacky experimenter do a week earlier. Meltzoff (1995) found that 14- and 16-month-old infants would perform the novel actions, like leaning forward and touching a flat box with their head to make a light inside the box come on, even 2 or 4 months after they saw the experimenter perform it. Thus infants showed that they had formed memories of the actions and recalled them months later. This task has been used to demonstrate memory in toddlers all over the world, including German toddlers from middle-class families and Cameroonian Nso infants from farming families (Borchert et al., 2013).

Kinds of Memory

The research discussed in the previous section suggests that infants can form memories, and those memories can be enduring, at least for several months. Importantly, these tasks have shown memory in infants of different ethnic groups across the globe. So why then do we not remember our infancy? As suggested earlier, this might be a difference in the *kind* of memories infants can form (Table 6.3). When we recall the events of our lives, this is called autobiographical memory. Such memories are memories for events that have happened during one's life. Several skills and abilities are thought to be required for forming and recalling those memories. First, the memories have to be formed. As we have just learned, infants do form memories.

Second, the memories have to be accessible. It has been suggested that infants can form autobiographical memories, but we simply can't access those memories later in life. Some people believe that the ability to talk about events—as well as having conversations with parents about events—helps the memory of those events to be accessible later. For example, researchers found

TABLE 6.3 ■ Kinds of Memory

Type of Memory	Definition	Example
Autobiographical memory	Memory for the events of your life	Tesalia remembering her second birthday party
Short-term memory	Limited memory (i.e., only a few things can be stored there) that lasts only a few moments	Remembering a phone number you have been told, just long enough to make the phone call
Long-term memory	Unlimited memory that lasts (perhaps) indefinitely	Memories of facts and of events that have happened in our lives.
Episodic memory	Memories for events	Carter's memory of a picnic with boats
Semantic memory	Memory for facts	Charlie knowing state names

that talk between German mothers and Indian mothers and their 19-month-old children predicted those children's memory at age 3 (Schröder et al., 2012). Interestingly, there were cultural differences in what kind of talk predicted later memory. Specifically, German mothers' support of their 19-month-old infants' self-expression predicted their child's memory, and Indian 19-month-old infants' responses to their mothers' requests in these conversations predicted the children's memory (Schröder et al., 2012).

Third, it might be that autobiographical memories require that infants have developed a sense of self. As we will talk about in Chapter 9, infants don't seem to have a sense of self until about 18 months, which might be why children's autobiographical memory seems to start after that time in development. But, as we have shown in this chapter, infants do have memories. They can form memories and they can later recall those memories. What we have not shown in this chapter is whether the kinds of memories infants demonstrate, or the kinds of procedures we have described in this chapter, may not reflect the kind of memory involved in autobiographical memories.

Often, memory is described in terms of **short-term memory** and **long-term memory**. Short-term memory is a limited memory system. We can only store a few items in short-term memory and that information is rapidly forgotten (being replaced by newly encountered information). It is often referred to as a *working memory* because when information is in this memory store, it is being "worked" on. We maintain information in short-term or working memory long enough to remember a phone number to make a phone call, to keep in mind what we want to say in a conversation, or to recall why we walked into the kitchen (perhaps to get our keys).

It is easy to see how habituation and visual paired-comparison tasks might tap this kind of memory. Often infants are familiarized with a single image and then they are shown that image and a new image after a very short delay (usually less than 1 minute). Thus, infants need only keep in their memory one or two items, and they don't need to remember those items for very long before their memory is tested. However, infants show novelty preference in this task even when they are tested after delays from a few minutes to several hours. Clearly, their novelty preferences after this kind of delay does not reflect their short-term memory.

To know that infants actually have short-term memory, therefore, we need a task that measures what infants remember when they are shown something very briefly—1 second or less—and they only have to remember it for a short time. Researchers have used the kinds of sequences of stimuli shown in Figure 6.3 to test this kind of memory. Infants are shown the initial array of colored shapes for a very short time, the 1-second "sample array." Then there is a brief delay—the ½-second "retention interval" during which infants have to remember what they saw in the sample array. Then, they are shown the test array. In Figure 6.3, the circles in the test array are the same as in the sample array, except the circle that was originally red is now white. Studies conducted in the United States using this kind of procedure have found that infants between 5 and 10 months will look longer at the changed item, or the white circle in the test array of Figure 6.3 (Oakes et al., 2013; Ross-Sheehy & Eschman, 2019), showing that they can rapidly form a memory and keep it active for a short time.

But children have other kinds of memories too. At the start of this section, we described cases in which Carter and Tesalia showed episodic memory, or memories for events—they remembered a picnic with boats or a birthday party with a toad in the pool. Because they were

FIGURE 6.3 ■ **Stimuli Used by Oakes et al. (2013)**

A sequence of stimulus arrays in one trial testing infants' short-term memory.

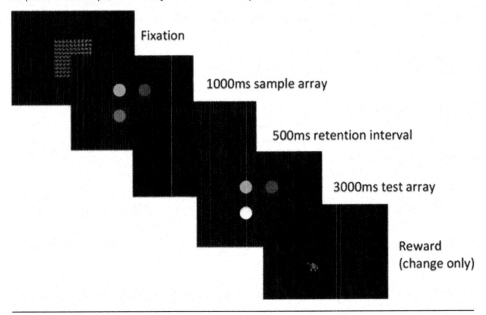

Fixation

1000ms sample array

500ms retention interval

3000ms test array

Reward
(change only)

Source: Ross-Sheehy & Eschman (2019).

memories about their lives, they were also autobiographical. Episodic memories usually involve temporal information about the order in which events occurred; they reflect the memory of one instance (e.g., a particular birthday party, not birthday parties in general) and include information about the context. Charlie's memory for the name of his dog and his brother, in contrast, were examples of semantic memory. Semantic memory is memory for facts or details. These memories do not include information about the context and probably were learned over many episodes or encounters with the information.

Both semantic and episodic memory are part of long-term memory. Unlike short-term memory, humans seem to be able to store an unlimited number of things in long-term memory, and that information can be stored forever (though we can't always retrieve information stored in long-term memory). As we have seen in this chapter, infants as young as 6 months show memory over a delay, although they forget that information as the delay gets longer. Thus, young infants do have some form of long-term memory. What we don't know is whether this long-term memory is *episodic* memory. How can we tell? It is complicated. The tasks we have described to measure infants' memory simply show that they remember the stimulus (e.g., the particular image or action). It isn't immediately clear how we would tell if that memory is episodic or semantic. Consider, for example, an infant who is shown a picture of a particular face, Betty. After that face is familiar, the infant is presented with that now-familiar face, Betty, along with a novel face, Tania. The infant shows memory for Betty's face by looking longer at Tania's novel face than at Betty's familiar face. We know that the infant has a memory. But what kind of memory is this? It might be a semantic memory for the face. In other words, when the infant looks at Tania's face, it may be more interesting because it does not trigger the memory of Betty's face. It could be episodic memory, however. The infant may remember the *episode* of seeing Betty's face moments, hours, or days before. That is, the infant may have formed a memory of the *event* in which Betty's face was previously presented, and the novelty preference reflects their memory for that event. Similarly, when the 14-month-old infant turns on a light with their forehead, as the experimenter previously did, it is impossible to know whether the infant remembered simply the box and the action or whether they remembered the encounter with the experimenter in which the action was performed.

So we need clever ways to reveal what kind of memories infants have formed. One way researchers have asked is whether infants include in their memory the *context*. That is, do infants not only remember that kicking makes a mobile move or that they've seen a particular face, but do they remember details about where they were when they learned that information? Carolyn Rovee-Collier and her students tested this by using distinctive liners, or blankets, on U.S. 6-month-old infants' cribs as they learned to kick to make a mobile move (Boller et al., 1996; Borovsky & Rovee-Collier, 1990). After the learning phase, infants showed memory for the kicking as long as the same liner was used. But, if a different liner was draped on the infants' crib, they didn't seem to remember that kicking made the mobile move. Thus, by 6 months, infants' memory for the association between their kicking and the mobile moving depended on the context. Emily Jones and her colleagues (Jones & Herbert, 2008; Jones et al., 2011) found similar effects of context on other memory tests. For example, 6-month-old infants showed better memory in a visual recognition memory task when the familiarization and test occurred in the same room; they did not show a preference for the novel image when the test was conducted in a different room from familiarization. Results like these suggest that even young infants' memory includes some information about the connection between when information was presented, where it was encountered, and what information was learned, suggesting that these memories might indeed be episodic.

Another feature of infants' episodic memories is that they are formed after only a single encounter. Eve Perris, Nancy Myers, and Rachel Keen Clifton (1990) assessed U.S. toddlers' memory for an event that happened 1 to 2 years earlier. When these children were infants, they participated in a study in which they reached for a rattle while in a dark experimental room. When the children revisited the lab 1 or 2 years later, they reached more for the rattle in the dark than did other children who had not participated in the infant study. In other words, these children showed memory for an experience that had happened only once 2 years earlier! Likewise, Patricia Bauer and Jacqueline Leventon (2013) showed that U.S. 16- and 20-month-old infants imitated actions after a 1-month delay, even when they had only been shown the modeling one time. Thus, infants can and do form memories for events that they experienced only one time.

But, it is also very clear that infants' episodic memory abilities are not mature. One feature of episodic memory is that it is a type of **explicit memory**. Explicit memories are those that you can consciously recall. Because infants can't tell us what they remember in words, it is very difficult to know whether their memories are explicit. Consider the case when infants perform actions with props or toys that they previously saw modeled by an experimenter. If the memory is explicit, infants consciously recall the experimenter performing those actions and are performing the actions themselves because of that memory. If the memory is **implicit,** or unconscious memories of the previous event, the presence of the toys or props primed infants' memory for the action without any conscious recall of the event. It seems unlikely that this reflects solely implicit memory, which is the kind of memory that allows us to form habits after repeatedly doing an action. But, we don't have good tests of whether an infant's memory is implicit or explicit.

Episodic memories not only involve contextual and temporal information, but they also involve the binding or combination of such information. In episodic memories, we don't simply recall facts; we remember where we learned those facts and who was there. This binding involves a brain region called the **hippocampus**, which develops from infancy into childhood. Thus, it is unlikely that infants have the ability to form mature episodic memories. When testing older children and adults, researchers can use fMRI to measure the activity in the hippocampus when a person is in an episodic memory task, such as recalling a particular event (e.g., their 10th birthday party) or where they learned specific information. How do we do this with infants? Lindsey Mooney and her colleagues (2021) used a clever procedure to test whether the hippocampus was related to episodic-like memory in toddlers. This study had several steps. First, they had 2-year-old children from northern California play games with puppets in the lab. Children played two games, each with a different puppet, while a different song played, and in a different room in the lab. Thus, children might form memories of the games that involved information about who (which puppet) played, where (which room), and the context (which song was played). Such memories would be episodic memories. Next, they tested children's memory for these games. They asked whether the toddlers recalled which puppet, room, and song went with each of the two games. Finally, they played the songs while the children slept, and used an MRI to measure the activity in the hippocampus as the song was played. How much episodic memory children appeared to have (as measured in the memory test) was related to how much the hippocampus was active when the song was played (as the children slept). Thus, Mooney and her colleagues showed that at least 2-year-old children seem to have some ability to form episodic memories that involve the hippocampus.

In general, however, researchers believe that at best, infants and very young children are capable of episodic-*like* memory. Clearly, research has shown that infants have memories with some of the features of episodic memory, but it is also clear that infants do not have the ability to develop mature episodic memories. This ability develops over many years throughout childhood.

BOX 6.2—INFANCY IN REAL LIFE: IS IT POSSIBLE TO REMEMBER BEING BORN?

Shortly before this book was published, one of our authors, Vanessa LoBue wrote a general audience article for various news outlets on infantile amnesia, reporting on much of the research we discuss here. To her surprise, within a week, she received over 100 emails from people describing their earliest memories, many of which were *before* the age of 2. In fact, several of these memories involved the experience of being born, or even of being inside their mothers' womb!

Can adults remember being born or even the time *before* they were born? The answer is no, and yes. It is no, because newborns don't have the tools to create autobiographical memories like the experience of being born. Further, as discussed in this chapter, the regions of the brain that are responsible for storing autobiographical memories are not yet fully developed, making it likely impossible for these memories to form in the prenatal or newborn period. What is more likely true is that memories we seem to recall before the age of 2 are constructed (at least partially) by someone else's retelling of an event. We often think about memories as photographs or video-like scenes that we store in a filing cabinet deep into our brains, and when we remember, we are simply looking at those photos or videos. However, our memories are usually incomplete records of what happens, and they are actually quite fluid—they can change over time. In fact, the very act of *remembering* can influence what is part of our memory for an event. On top of that, when we talk about an event with others, hearing those other people's perspectives on the same event or situation can change our memory of the event. In other words, memories aren't exact replicas of what actually happened to us, and they can be constructed and reconstructed based on a number of factors. And children are especially susceptible to suggestion in their remembering of events.

Stephen Ceci and his colleagues have looked at how reliable U.S. preschoolers' memories are. In one classic study, they told preschool-aged children about a guy named Sam Stone, who was clumsy and always getting himself into trouble. Soon after hearing about Sam Stone, an actual man named Sam Stone visited their classroom. But instead of behaving clumsily and causing a scene, he simply sat mishap-free and quietly in the corner of the classroom. After his visit, the children were asked about Sam's visit to the classroom and were asked to recall what he did. The researchers found that preschool-aged children were likely to provide tall tales of the silly things that Sam did when he visited the classroom, all of which matched what others told them about Sam Stone but none of which were true. Asking misleading questions exaggerated children's responses, as did simply repeating the same questions over and over again (Bruck & Ceci, 1999). The authors concluded that children's memories are quite malleable and susceptible to suggestion. On top of that, although younger children might be most susceptible to creating false memories, older children and adults do it too (Ghetti et al., 2002).

One important caveat is that just because memories can be false or elaborated by others, it doesn't mean those memories aren't real, or at least that the experience of these memories isn't real. They certainly *feel* real, and in fact, we as scientists can't tell them apart from real memories. So, while it is highly unlikely that we can remember our birth story or our experiences inside the womb, it is possible that others' retelling of these stories from our earliest moments can become implanted in our minds and feel like real memories. And over time, that's exactly what they become.

Check Your Learning

1. What is infantile amnesia? How have the earliest memories of adults from different cultures been shown to differ?

2. *Define* the methods to study memory in infants. What evidence is used in each method as an indicator of infant memory?

3. *Name* the different types of memory and provide an example of each.

4. *Define* the characteristics of explicit memory.

5. What is the hippocampus? What type of memory has been shown to be linked to activity in the hippocampus?

THE DEVELOPMENT OF CATEGORIZATION

We don't just store our knowledge about objects, events, and people in memory, we make connections between that knowledge, including information about how any individual object, event, or person is related to other objects, events, and people. We compare individuals and detect similarities and differences between them. It would be overwhelming—and impossible—to treat each new object, event, and person as unique. Instead, we form **categories** that allow us to treat collections of things in the same way. This has positive effects. For example, when you encounter a dog you have never seen before, you make inferences about how to treat it, what it eats, and under what conditions it might growl or even bite based on what you've learned about other dogs. Categorization is critical for learning about, labeling, and understanding objects such as cups, shoes, and trees. Forming categories also has a downside. If we depend too much on groups based on similarities between individuals, we are less likely to pay attention to the unique characteristics of individuals. As adults, this is something we should be aware of. As infants, categorization is critically important for the acquisition and organization of new knowledge.

How Do We Know That Infants Categorize?

The hallmark of categorization is treating members of a category as if they were the same. A toddler referring to all round objects as "ball" can be thought of as categorizing—those round objects all belong (from the toddler's perspective) to a category of objects that all can be called "ball." A young child at a petting zoo reaching out to pat each animal she encounters is categorizing those animals as belonging to the category of animals that can be patted. When 16-month-old Alison put all her dolls and stuffed animals to bed, she was categorizing them all as belonging to a category of things that go night-night. Importantly, categorization involves **generalization**, or extending your behavior to a new instance of a category. A toddler referring to a new round, bouncing, rolling object as "ball" is generalizing. They are using their category label in a new instance, demonstrating that they recognize that new object as a member of the category. Similarly, the children petting new animals at the zoo or Alison putting toys to bed were generalizing their categories to new instances.

Categorization refers to the process of grouping items that share some commonality. Sometimes the commonality has to do with what the items look like or their overall shape. Chairs, for example, usually have four legs, some sort of seat, and a back. Items like bean bags are often the topic of much debate about how well they fit in the category "chair," since bean bags don't have these distinct features. However, the *function* of the objects is also an important commonality for categorization. Chairs can be used for sitting, which can also be true of bean-bags. Likewise, balls can be thrown, kicked, rolled, and bounced. There are other instances where the commonality has more to do with abstract properties. Desserts, for example, are usually sweet and are eaten after a meal, but most desserts don't necessarily share specific shapes or functions. The point is that we easily recognize commonalities between items and group those items based on those commonalities. These groupings help us organize our memories, communicate to others, interact with new objects, and much more.

When do infants categorize? And what kinds of categories can they form and use? As with most areas in cognitive development, researchers have to come up with clever ways to determine whether infants can form categories. As we just learned, we know that infants can form memories from early in life, so many researchers have used the same methods they use to assess infants' memory to ask whether infants also *categorize* (Table 6.4). One of the most common ways to study infants' categorization is by using an adaptation of the habituation procedure. To test categorization, infants are presented with several images or stimuli during the habituation phase, an adaptation that has been called *multiple habituation*. In this variation of habituation, researchers ask if infants will habituate to, or decrease their interest in, a set of objects that are all from the same category. For example, does infants' looking time decrease when they are shown a series of different dogs, or different foods, or different pieces of furniture (Behl-Chadha, 1996; Quinn et al., 1993; Ross, 1980)? If so, infants have habituated to or learned something about what the items have in common.

For example, Paul Quinn and his colleagues asked whether a group of 3- and 4-month-old infants in the United States recognized the categories of *dog* and *cat*. They presented infants with a series of familiarization trials, each with pictures of two different dogs (e.g., a german shepherd and a beagle). After six trials, infants had looked at 12 different dogs. They familiarized another group of infants with pictures of cats. As when infants are familiarized or habituated to only one image, initially infants looked for a long time. But as they repeatedly saw dogs (or cats), their looking duration decreased, telling us that they recognized that the 12 dogs

TABLE 6.4 ■ Ways of Measuring Categorization in Infancy	
Procedure	**Evidence of Categorization**
Habituation/ familiarization	Decrease in response (typically looking) to a series of stimuli from the same category, increase in response when a novel stimulus from a new category is presented
Operant conditioning	Following training that a behavior (e.g., kicking) is associated with a series of rewarding events (e.g., several different mobiles moving overhead), infants will exhibit the behavior (generalize) when presented with a new mobile from the same category
Generalized imitation	Infants generalize an action modeled by an experimenter to a new instance within the category
Sequential touching	When presented with a collection of items (from two categories), infants touch in succession items from one category before touching items from the other category
EEG methods	Differences in brain waves to different categories of images

or 12 cats were similar in some way—the shape of their bodies or faces or ears (or all these features)— and became less interested in that kind of animal. This is one part of categorization: discovering the similarities between items within a category. But this doesn't tell us what category the infants recognized. As they looked at the 12 pictures of dogs (or cats), they might have recognized a category of any four-legged furry animal, instead of the category for "dog" or "cat." In this case, after seeing 12 dogs or 12 cats, these infants may generalize to any four-legged furry animal, including cats and dogs and cows and horses and tigers. Or infants might have recognized a narrower category, one that included *only* dogs or cats. As they viewed the 12 images, they may have noticed commonalities shared just by dogs or just by cats.

How can we tell what kind of category infants formed? After familiarization with items from one category, researchers test infants' generalization by recording how long they look at new items, some from within the learned category (e.g., a new dog) and some from a new category (e.g., a cat, a horse, a bird, or even a table). (See examples of images used to study categorization in Figure 6.4.) By observing which items infants treat as new, we can get a sense of which items they see as belonging together and which items they see as being different. Quinn and his colleagues (1993) found that 3- and 4-month-old infants who were familiarized with dogs looked longer at cats, and 3- and 4-month-old infants who were familiarized with cats looked longer at dogs, suggesting that these infants could form a specific category for each animal. In other words, during familiarization, they learned or recognized commonalities that were specific to dogs and not cats or vice versa.

But habituation is not the only way the infants' categorization has been studied. Rovee-Collier and her colleagues adapted the conditioning procedure described in the memory section to study infants' categorization. In this case, instead of training infants on only one mobile, they trained infants on several different mobiles that all had similar elements. Over 3 days of

---

FIGURE 6.4 ■ Cats and Dogs Used to Study Infants' Categorization

Source: Reprinted with permission from Kovack-Lesh, Horst, & Oakes (2008).

training, infants might see a mobile with red "A's" on day 1, a mobile with blue "A's" on day 2, and a mobile with yellow "A's" on day 3. All of the mobiles had "A's," but they varied in color. If infants learn the category (mobiles with "A's"), they should generalize their learning to a mobile with "A's" of a new color. Harlene Hayne, Carolyn Rovee-Collier, and Eve Parris (1987) trained 3-month-old U.S. infants to kick with either the same mobile on each of 3 days (e.g., a mobile with red "A's"), *or* three different mobiles with "A's" of different colors on each day. To test how infants generalized this training, Hayne and colleagues tested infants with a new mobile, for example, one with "A's" of yet another color. The two groups responded differently. Infants who saw the same mobile every day did not kick when presented with this novel mobile. These infants learned about the specific mobile, and a new mobile, even though it was from the same category, was not recognized as similar to the familiar mobile. But, infants who were trained on three different mobiles did kick when they saw the new mobile. Their learning generalized to a new mobile from the same category. This is evidence that infants detected the similarities across the training mobiles and saw the novel mobile as similar to the training set.

Jean Mandler and Laraine McDonough (1996) modified an imitation procedure to assess infants' categorization. As in any imitation procedure, infants were shown a model (an experimenter) who performed some action using props, and then the infants were given the opportunity to perform the action themselves. When testing categorization, however, researchers use *generalized imitation*. Instead of offering infants the same props used by the model, as is done to study memory, infants were given *different* props. The question is whether infants *generalize* their behavior to the new props. In this first study, a group of 14-month-old infants from the United States were shown a dog taking a drink from a cup. They were then given the cup and a cat toy and an airplane toy. Infants made the cat drink from the cup but not the airplane. In other words, they generalized the action to a new animal but not to a vehicle, showing that they recognized similarities between the dog and cat and that the vehicle was different.

Another way researchers have studied categorization in infancy is using a *sequential touching* task (Mandler et al., 1987, 1991). This task is similar to the sorting tasks commonly used to study categorization in older children and adults. That is, older subjects are given a collection of objects and they are asked to put them into two (or more) piles that correspond to categories. In the sequential touching task, toddlers are presented with collections of objects from two categories—for example, animals and vehicles—and they are simply given the opportunity to play with those objects. Mandler and her colleagues discovered that although you can't ask children between 12 and 30 months to *sort* the objects, they do have a tendency to *touch* several objects from one category in succession before touching any of the items from the other category. So, a child might touch a rabbit, then a horse, then a bird before touching any vehicles.

Finally, researchers have also used electroencephalogram, or EEG, measures to examine infants' categorization. In this case, infants' brain responses are recorded as they view images. Electrodes are placed on the infants' scalp, and these electrodes measure the amount of electrical activity that is produced by the activity of the brain as infants look at different kinds of images. One of the simplest of these studies was done by Vesna Marinović, Stefanie Hoel, and Sabina Pauen (2014). They recorded the EEG of German 4-month-old and 7-month-old infants as they looked at images of animals and people. Infants saw both animals and people, but one of the categories was presented more frequently than the other (Figure 6.5). It turns out that when we

FIGURE 6.5 ■ Stimuli From the EEG Categorization Task

Infants view some images more often than others. In panel A, for example, infants viewed more images of people than animals. In panel B, infants instead viewed more images of animals than people.

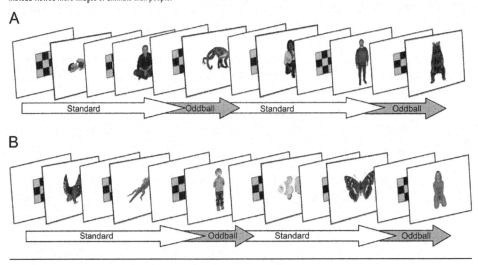

Source: Marinović, Hoel, & Pauen (2014).

see something that is infrequent, or an "oddball," our brain responds differently than when we see something that is frequent. Marinović and colleagues thought that if infants saw people and animals as different categories, they would respond to the oddball in this sequence; that is, their EEG would show evidence that the item from the infrequently presented category was different.

When shown sequences, 7-month-old infants' EEG revealed that they responded differently to the infrequent item. Their brain waves showed a pattern that indicated that they saw and categorized animals and people as different. The 4-month-old infants did not show this pattern, suggesting that for them, animals and people were not different.

Object Categories

Now that we know *how* to study categorization in infancy, we need to consider *what* categories infants notice and learn. The most common kinds of categories studied in infants are **object categories**. These are the categories for groups of objects, such as shoes, chairs, and dogs, that we commonly label with nouns, like the category of *animal*. There are several reasons why researchers have focused on these categories when studying infants. First, as we will discuss in Chapter 9, many of children's first words are nouns. Thus, when people first started to study infants' categorization they thought that learning categories might help children to learn their first words. Second, object categories are concrete and refer to objects that can be seen, heard, touched, and manipulated. Thus, object categories may be easier to learn than more abstract categories. Third, infants actually encounter these kinds of object categories frequently in their daily lives (Clerkin et al., 2017).

Many studies have shown that infants are quite sensitive to object categories. Studies using familiarization and habituation have shown that U.S. infants in the first year recognize categories of animals, such as dogs, cats, and horses (Eimas & Quinn, 1994; Kovack-Lesh & Oakes, 2007; Oakes & Ribar, 2005; Quinn et al., 1993). Other studies have shown that infants recognize categories such as bed and couch (Behl-Chadha, 1996), furniture and food (Ross, 1980), and land animals and sea animals (Oakes et al., 1997). Although this research has been conducted primarily with Western infants in North America and Europe, Kim Ferguson and Marianella Casasola (2015) found that 15-month-old U.S. infants and 15-month-old Malawian infants responded similarly to plastic replicas of animals and vehicles, apparently recognizing the similarities among the animals and generalizing to a new animal but not to a vehicle. In addition, Kosuke Tanigushi and colleagues (2020) found, in a sample of Japanese infants increased attention to this type of category across the first year. Thus, what little evidence we have suggests that infants in many parts of the world can categorize.

Studies using generalized imitation and sequential touching allow us to measure what kinds of categories toddlers spontaneously notice and what kinds of features infants think are characteristic of members of those categories. In general, studies using these procedures have shown that children are sensitive to categories such as animal, vehicle, horses, and telephones (Arterberry & Bornstein, 2012; Mandler et al., 1991; Mandler & McDonough, 1996), as well as categories such as "has wheels" versus "has legs" (Rakison & Butterworth, 1998) or is soft versus hard (Horst et al., 2009).

Clearly, therefore, infants and toddlers categorize. But how does categorization develop? Several general conclusions have been drawn about infants' categorization—at least categorization by the Western infants from middle-class families who are the subjects of most studies. First, the ability to categorize emerges early. Paul Quinn and his colleagues have conducted a number of studies showing categorization in 3- to 4-month-old infants (Eimas & Quinn, 1994; Quinn et al., 1993). These young infants respond to categories of dogs, cats, horses, and birds. They even found evidence that infants as young as 2 months recognize categories (Quinn & Johnson, 2000). It has been harder to show categorization in infants younger than 2 months. Chiara Turati, Francesca Simion, and Laura Zanon (2003) found that a group of Italian newborns responded to a category of open shapes (e.g., open square or open octagon) versus closed shapes (e.g., an X), suggesting that at birth, infants can recognize some similarities between different shapes. It is unknown, however, how much very young infants categorize. It is possible given their limited visual abilities that it is difficult for infants to detect the commonalities and differences between complex objects.

A second conclusion is that although infants from an early age are sensitive to *perceptual* categories, more abstract *conceptual* categories probably emerge later. Using habituation and familiarization procedures, researchers have shown that infants between 2 and 7 months of age respond to a wide variety of adult-defined categories, including cats versus dogs (Oakes & Ribar, 2005; Quinn et al., 1993), furniture versus mammals (Behl-Chadha, 1996; Quinn & Johnson, 2000), male versus female faces (Quinn et al., 2002; Rennels et al., 2016; Rennels & Kayl, 2017), and different emotional expressions (Kestenbaum & Nelson, 1990; Ruba et al., 2017). These categories seem to be based on perceptual features of the items. For example, sometimes 3- to 4-month-old infants separate animals into categories of dog or cat, for example, showing a novelty preference for cats after familiarization with dogs. Other times, infants of this age include dogs and cats into a single category, failing to show a novelty preference for cats after familiarization with dogs but showing a novelty preference for a vehicle (Oakes & Ribar, 2005; Quinn et al., 1993). Both kinds of categories make sense depending on what perceptual information you use. Cats and dogs have different shaped faces and ears, but they both are four-legged, furry, and have tails. If you categorize using perceptual information—or what the objects look like—you might respond to different categories in different situations. This is what 3- to 4-month-old infants do. Whether they respond to the more global category that includes both dogs and cats or two separate categories of just dogs and just cats depends on what pictures they are shown and other aspects of the procedure.

In contrast to perceptual categories, *conceptual* categories are based on information other than what the objects look like. When we have conceptual knowledge of categories, we know about abstract similarities, for example, how objects function or what kinds of internal organs people have. Mandler and her colleagues used sequential touching and showed that a sample of 20-month-old toddlers in the United States were sensitive to the difference between *kitchen things* (pan, spoon, plate) and *bathroom things* (toothbrush, comb, soap) (Mandler et al., 1987). Because the items within the category did not look alike, the children could not be categorizing them based on perceptual information. Instead, they could only categorize these items based on their knowledge of which items are found in the same context, which is more like conceptual information.

Using generalized imitation, Mandler and McDonough (1996) have shown that infants not only separate animals and vehicles into different categories, but by 14 months infants also have different expectations for the actions that can be performed by members of different categories. Remember the finding that 14-month-old infants who were shown a dog drinking from a cup will make a toy cat drink from a cup but won't make a toy airplane drink from a cup? It turns out that 14-month-old infants wouldn't make a vehicle drink, even if they were shown the experimenter making a vehicle drink. It seems that not only did infants generalize the property of "drinking" only to new items within a category, they also would not even imitate the property of drinking to inanimate vehicles.

But even if infants' and toddlers' information becomes more conceptual, they do not completely lose the ability to categorize based on perceptual features. David Rakison showed that infants and toddlers categorize in both sequential touching and generalized imitation using perceptual information (Rakison, 2007; Rakison & Butterworth, 1998). Thus, although infants' categorization develops and relies less on perceptual information, they continue to be able to recognize and use perceptual similarities when recognizing categories.

Other Kinds of Categories

Object categories are not the only kinds of categories infants can recognize. Infants also may recognize spatial categories (e.g., left vs. right or on vs. in) or categories of direction (e.g., into vs. around) or movement (e.g., jogging vs. hopping). Just like object categories, some attention to these kinds of categories seems to emerge very early. Lucia Gava, Eloisa Valenza, and

Chiara Turati (2009) found that a group of Italian newborn infants recognized a category of left (or right). They familiarized infants with a series of simple displays in which a square was to the left (or right) of a vertical line; in each display, the square was in a slightly different position, so what the displays had in common was whether the square was to the left or right of the vertical line. Infants then saw two new displays; one had the square on the same side of the line as in all the familiarization displays, and the other one had the square on the other side of the line. Newborn infants preferred to look at the display with the square in the unfamiliar location.

However, these categories are, in general, very abstract. Unlike categories such as "car" or "dog," you can't point to things that are "left" or "hopping." These categories require that children recognize relations between objects or how objects or people move through space over time, ignoring many of the features that are likely to draw their attention (e.g., the color or shape of the objects). In fact, a series of studies conducted by Paul Quinn and his colleagues in the United States showed that 3- to 4-month-old infants recognized categories of above and below (Quinn, 1994) and 6- to 7-month-old infants recognized spatial categories of between (Quinn et al., 2011) only when the displays included the same simple object on each trial. It was not until later in the first year that infants recognized these same categories when the objects were more complex or varied from trial to trial (Quinn et al., 2003).

Other spatial categories involve noticing the relation between objects. For example, researchers have been interested in when infants notice categories such as containment (i.e., one object *in* another), support (i.e., one object *on* another), and *behind*. When infants are habituated to different objects being placed *in* different containers, U.S. 6-month-old infants recognize the difference between in and on (Casasola et al., 2003). By 11 months, infants recognize the difference between in and behind (Rigney & Wang, 2015). However, their recognition of these categories is fragile and depends on a number of factors, such as the number of examples shown (Casasola, 2005). With development, infants become able to recognize these abstract categories under a wider range of situations.

Infants also notice categories of the direction (e.g., around) or manner (e.g., walking) in which a person moves. For example, 10- to 12-month-old English-learning infants in the United States recognized an animated starfish's path of motion, such as *over,* across different manners of motion (e.g., walking, jumping, spinning) (Konishi et al., 2016; Pruden et al., 2013). Infants of this age also can recognize the starfish's manner of motion (e.g., twirling) across different paths (back and forth, in a circle, across the screen) (Pruden et al., 2012). Similarly, English-learning U.S. 12-month-old infants recognize the path and manner of the movement of a human actor (Song et al., 2016). In addition, infants attend to the start and end points of action (Lakusta & Carey, 2015). The point is that infants recognize categories of movement, another arbitrary kind of category.

Check Your Learning

1. Provide a definition for *categorization*. What is a benefit for infants to form categories?

2. Describe each of the procedures to assess infants' categories.

3. Explain the distinction between perceptual categories and conceptual categories. Why does one emerge earlier in development than the other?

4. Describe categories other than objects that infants show evidence of forming.

SUMMARY

In this chapter, we started by discussing how infants' ability to orient, select, and maintain their attention allows them to process the information in their environment. Over their first year, infants become better able to disengage their attention from one stimulus to shift their attention to another. Infants are also forming memories, including episodic and semantic memories, of the information they encounter. But, their memory improves across development, and some forms of memory may emerge only after the period of infancy. Infants' increasing attention and memory are what allows infants to form categories, treating objects as equivalent members of a group, such as animals. They also form categories of types of motion or the type of spatial relations, such as containment and support.

KEY TERMS

attention

autobiographical memory

categories

categorizing

covert attention

deferred imitation

disengaging

episodic memory

explicit memory

generalization

hippocampus

imitation

implicit memory

infantile amnesia

long-term memory

maintaining attention

memory

object categories

orienting

selective attention

semantic memory

short-term memory

visual recognition memory

REVIEW QUESTIONS

1. Name the three types of attention, and provide an example of each.

2. How are infants in their first months different from those who are 6 months and older in their selection of attention?

3. List the different types of memory, and provide an example of each.

4. Describe the different methods to study infants' categorization.

CRITICAL THINKING QUESTIONS

1. If you wanted to test infants' orientation to one stimulus and disengagement from another stimulus, what sort of stimuli would you present and why?

2. Which procedure (or procedures) would be most appropriate for studying memory at each of the following ages? Two months vs. 6 months vs. 24 months. Explain your reasoning.

3. Describe the distinction between each pair of memory types:
    a. Short-term and long-term memory
    b. Explicit vs. implicit memory
    c. Episodic vs. semantic memory

4. You are asked to design a study of infant categorization of dogs. Do you select dogs that are similar to each other (e.g., a labrador retriever, a golden retriever, a pointer) or those that are less similar in appearance to each other (e.g., a chihuahua, a golden retriever, a poodle)? Explain your reasoning. How might your choice of stimuli differ if you were testing very young infants of 3 months versus older infants of 10 months?

5. Review the methods described for studying infant attention, memory, and categorization. Are there any methods that are used for studying all three of these processes in infants? If so, which ones? Why can the same methods be used to study different processes of infant development?

7 INFANTS' DEVELOPING UNDERSTANDING OF THE WORLD

One of Diego's favorite toys during his first year was a set of hollow cylinders that nested within each other. At 6 months, he could pull one cylinder off of another, but couldn't quite figure out how to nest them. With developing motor and cognitive skills, Diego's play with the cylinders changed as well. When he first became able to nest some of the cylinders within each other, he would put some of the smaller cylinders inside a larger cylinder, but he also mistakenly attempted to insert larger cylinders into smaller ones. Eventually, Diego became a master at this game, by learning that only a smaller cylinder could fit within a large one.

Diego's changing play with his toy cylinders reveals development in how he thought about and understood the physical world. His interactions with the cylinders show a changing understanding of *objects*, for example, recognizing that one object can fit into another object. It also shows his developing understanding of *space*, as he recognized that only smaller cylinders can fit into bigger cylinders. Children's understanding of space is also revealed in how they navigate the world. When Tesalia was about 18 months old, her favorite thing in the world was a splash pool with ducks at a local children's museum. Once when her family was about to leave the museum, Tesalia was suddenly nowhere to be found. After an extensive search (and lots of panic), Tesalia's parents found her back at the splash pool all the way on the other side of the museum. Somehow, at only 18 months, she had navigated the crowded and complex museum environment on her own, identifying the route that would lead her back to her happy place. Her great escape showed an increasing awareness of the spatial features of her environment.

Finally, children also develop an understanding of *number* in the first 2 years of life. When Charlie was a toddler, he liked to carefully arrange pencils, toy cars, or blocks in a long row based on their colors. After creating several long rows of objects on the coffee table, he would step back, survey the fruits of his hard work, and with great concentration, point to each of the items, saying "one, one, one, twee." Despite not being quite right, Charlie's pure enthusiasm for organizing objects into rows and then "counting" them shows his emerging sense of number, which he finally mastered by the time he turned 3 years old.

All of these changes in infants' understanding of objects, space, and number over the first year and into their second and third years are examples of developments in how infants *understand* the world. In the previous chapter, we discussed changes in basic cognitive processes and abilities. These changes are important for the development of cognition in infancy and early childhood. In this chapter, we will begin by describing major theories of cognitive development, many of which we will revisit in Chapter 8 when we discuss play and symbolic development. After describing the major theories of cognitive development, we will devote sections to what we know about how infants' understanding of objects, space, and number develop.

After reading this chapter, you will be able to:

1. *Describe* the major theories that explain infants' developing understanding of objects, space, and number.

2. *Outline* changes in infants' understanding of objects and the physical laws of how objects move.

3. *Explain* how infants' ability to represent the location of objects and navigate their environment changes across the first 3 years.

4. *Describe* the two systems of infants' number representation and how they develop.

THEORIES OF INFANT UNDERSTANDING

What do newborn infants understand about their world, and how does their knowledge change over time? All of the major theories reviewed in this chapter seek to answer these important questions. Each theory offers its own perspective on three central questions on the study of infants' understanding: What do infants know about the world at birth? What are the processes infants use to learn about the world? What is the trajectory of their growth in knowledge? Each of these theories was developed in a cultural context. Piaget's theory, the most famous theory of cognitive development, was developed based on his work with children in France and Switzerland, as well as his observations of his own three children. Vygotsky's theory was developed from his work in Russia. Both of these theories have been used to understand children from multiple cultures, but children from the European cultures where the theories originated are always the baseline by which children in other cultures are compared. The theories that have come after these classics were also mostly developed by researchers in the Western world (i.e., North America and Europe).

For example, research on infants' developing concepts of objects has been conducted almost exclusively in Western cultures, primarily with infants of European descent from middle-class families. This is important because some of the basic notions about object concepts are Western and come from Western philosophy. For example, comparisons of children raised in different cultures have suggested that constructs such as **object permanence** are not universally seen at the same ages (Rogoff et al., 2018). Thus, as we discuss what is known about infants' developing understanding of the world, it is important to remember that what we know derives from a subsample of infants around the globe. It is almost certainly the case that infants around the world learn about objects, space, and number, but we must be careful not to assume that the specific abilities that have been tested emerge at the same ages for all infants. So, as we discuss influential theories of cognitive development and the research they inspired, it is important to keep in mind the cultural biases that they may reflect.

There are several themes that each of the theories of cognitive development address (Table 7.1). First, these theories differ in terms of what they believe is innate, or present at birth. Some theories propose that newborn infants are born with concepts about objects, space, and number, and other theories contend that infants are born with strong learning mechanisms that they use to build understanding of the world from their experience. Theories also differ in whether the processes infants use to learn about their world are **domain general** (processes that can be used to learn across many domains) or **domain**

TABLE 7.1 ■ Characteristics of the Theories of Infants' Acquisition of Knowledge				
Theory	Key Points	Role of Innate Factors and Experience	Domain General vs. Domain Specific Processes	Development as Continuous or Discontinuous
Piaget	Development is a function of infants' active exploration of the physical environment and their adaptation of their schemes.	Both contribute but lean more toward experience and reflexes and senses as starting points.	Development proceeds using domain general mechanisms of accommodation and assimilation.	Development occurs in a series of discontinuous stages, each characterized by a qualitatively different way of thinking about and representing the world.
Vygotsky	Focus is on development resulting from social interactions.	Both contribute to infants' understanding, but the starting points are not strong at birth.	Development is the result of domain general processes of social interactions with a more advanced other.	Development is continuous and gradual
Information processing	Uses the analogy of a computer to specify what information infants encode and how they process that information.	Innate processes are very general, and infants' processing of information is influenced by their experience.	Processes are very general, such as recognizing the association between two things.	Development is continuous and gradual
Core knowledge	Infants are born with knowledge about objects, space, number, and agents.	Infants are born with innate core knowledge in some domains. They use this knowledge to learn from their experience.	The processes used for learning are domain specific.	There is continuity from infancy to later childhood and adulthood in these core domains.

(Continued)

			Domain	
			General	Development
		Role of Innate	vs. Domain	as
		Factors and	Specific	Continuous or
Theory	Key Points	Experience	Processes	Discontinuous
Systems and connectionist theories	Infants' development reflects the emergence of new abilities as a function of gradual continuous changes in many systems.	There is some variation across theories, but in general the emphasis is on very general biological factors interacting with experience.	The emphasis is on very general processes.	Apparent discontinuities in development emerge from continuous development.

TABLE 7.1 ■ Characteristics of the Theories of Infants' Acquisition of Knowledge (Continued)

specific (processes that are specialized for learning about a single domain). Although theories tend to focus on one or the other, it is likely that infants have both kinds of processes. These two aspects of cognitive developmental theories—what is innate and how much are processes domain specific—are not completely independent. Theories that posit domain general processes for learning also propose that infants can build their knowledge from these general processes and do not require innate concepts to acquire knowledge about the world. These ideas come from the empiricists, who argued that knowledge is acquired through experience using very general processes such as forming associations. Theories that include domain specific processes, in contrast, tend to argue infants are born with concepts, and those domain specific processes (and some knowledge) are innate. In psychology, this view has its origins in Chomsky's idea that children are born with an innate learning mechanism that can be used only for learning language (more about this in Chapter 9).

Finally, theories differ in whether they argue that infants' developing understanding of the world is *continuous*, building at a gradual and steady pace as infants' knowledge flourishes over the first years, or *discontinuous*, shifting in stages, with thinking and understanding at one stage being qualitatively different from thinking and understanding at other stages.

Piaget

One of the first and most famous theories of infant cognitive development is that of Jean Piaget. Based on his observations of his own three children, Piaget outlined a theory to explain how infants understand their world and how this understanding grows to be increasingly complex. His work on infancy was part of his broad theory of cognitive development across childhood, which was based not only on his observations of his own children but also on work with many children.

Piaget's View of Development

Piaget's theory was an *interactionist* theory, arguing that development is the result of both innate mechanisms and experience. He was particularly focused on the physical interactions children had with the world as they acted on the objects they encountered. In addition, he argued that those mechanisms were *domain general* and are broadly used to acquire a wide range of knowledge. Finally, Piaget's theory was a *discontinuous* stage theory, centered on the idea that infants, children, and adults are capable of *different* ways of thinking, and thus development progresses through a series of discontinuous stages.

For Piaget, the most basic element of infant thinking is the **scheme**. Roughly, a scheme is a unit of thought, or a mental representation. In infancy, the schemes are based on *actions* the infant performs. Whereas adults are capable of abstract, symbolic thought, Piaget argued that infants understand their world through their senses (what they can see, feel, taste, and hear) and their actions. For this reason, Piaget called the period of infancy (roughly age 0 to 2 years) the **sensorimotor stage**. The ability for symbolic thought emerges at the end of the sensorimotor stage and is how children's thought is qualitatively different in the preoperational stage, which begins at 18 to 24 months. In Chapter 8 we will talk about the transition from the sensorimotor stage to the preoperational stage. One important consequence of the sensorimotor nature of infants' thoughts is that because they cannot represent the world mentally, they operate in the here and now. For example, at 6 months, Carter would sit and look at all the baby books in the house. If his big sister Alison took some of the books away, he would happily look at the books that remained, without seeming to remember that those other books still existed.

According to Piaget, the development of the schemes is achieved by the use of two domain general processes: *assimilation* and *accommodation*. Each of these mechanisms involves the infant or child integrating new information into their existing scheme. When infants incorporate new information into an existing scheme, they do so through the process of **assimilation**. *Sucking* is one of the earliest schemes infants use, according to Piaget. From birth, infants suck on anything that is put in their mouth: a finger, a baby fist, a pacifier, or a nipple. Through their experience of feeding, infants learn how to suck effectively to get food. Because getting milk from the breast requires a different kind of sucking than getting milk from a bottle, infants who exclusively breast-feed have a different pattern of sucking when feeding than infants who are exclusively fed from a bottle (Moral et al., 2010). Infants who breastfeed use basically the same sucking scheme whether they nurse on one of their mother's breasts or the other. Similarly, infants who have been bottle fed use essentially the same sucking scheme when they are fed with the same kind of nipple on their bottle. These two examples illustrate *assimilation*. In both cases, the infant can use their existing sucking scheme to different nipples or breasts because that scheme is effective in each context.

However, if a breastfed infant is introduced to a bottle, or a bottle-fed infant is given a new kind of nipple, perhaps one that has a smaller hole than they are used to, their existing scheme will not work to get milk. In these cases, the infant needs to adjust or adapt their sucking, perhaps sucking harder or less frequently, to effectively get milk. These are examples of **accommodation** (see second photo). *Accommodation* occurs when infants encounter information in their environment that does not match their current scheme, and as a result, they have to change the scheme itself. It is the mismatch between the new information and the infant's existing scheme

BABY NURSING: Infants learn how to suck when nursing. They can use this same scheme whether feeding on the right or left breast, an example of assimilation.

iStock/PeopleImages

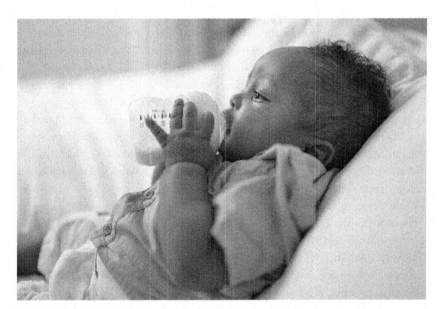

BABY WITH PLASTIC BOTTLE: When an infant who has breastfed is first given a bottle, they have to accommodate their sucking to feed. They learn to suck more slowly when drinking from a bottle. A bottle-fed infant can assimilate their scheme for feeding from a bottle if the nipple and bottle are not too different, but must accommodate when the flow of the new nipple is very different from the infant's familiar nipple.

iStock/LSOphoto

that causes infants to change their scheme. Infants again have to accommodate their scheme for drinking when they are first introduced to a sippy cup. Once they have accommodated their sucking scheme to this new type of container, infants use assimilation to drink from other sippy cups, assimilating these new sippy cups into their scheme.

Piaget's Sensorimotor Substages

Often we emphasize development between Piagetian stages, such as the difference between sensorimotor thought in infancy and preoperational thought in toddlers and preschoolers. These qualitative stages in how children can represent and think about the world are critically important for their cognitive abilities. However, Piaget also described development *during* a stage. In the sensorimotor stage, there are a series of substages that gradually move the infants' thinking closer to the kind of symbolic thinking characteristic of the preoperational stage. Piaget's six sensorimotor substages (Table 7.2) reflect changes in the nature of infants' schemes and therefore what they understand about the world. In the first substage, from birth to about the first month, often referred to as *reflexive schemes*, the newborn's schemes are based on their reflexes (see Chapter 5), such as sucking and grasping, and minimal learning happens. During this first stage, the newborn is mostly focused on eating and sleeping and practicing those reflexes.

The other stages reflect gradual changes in how infants can use their schemes. The second stage, *primary circular reactions*, is the stage when the infant begins to perform actions, such as grasping an object or sucking a finger. For Piaget, **circular reactions** are actions performed by the infant that are then repeated because of their effect. During the stage of primary circular reactions, infants repeat the actions because of the sensory experience that results: Infants suck on their fingers because it feels good on their fingers and mouth, and they stroke a blanket because the fabric feels good on their fingers. At this point, there is no external world for the infant.

During the next stage, *secondary circular reactions*, the infant begins to focus on the effect of their actions in the outside world. During this substage, infants repeat actions that are associated with an external interesting event, such as the sound a rattle makes when it is shaken. Although infants recognize a connection between their actions and the outcome, they do not yet understand that their actions on the object produced the sound. For example, an infant may find the sound of a rattle interesting and know that it is linked in some way to their own action, but the infant does not yet connect shaking the rattle with the rattle making the sound. Thus, the infant may try many actions (shaking, banging, kicking) to make the rattle sound again.

The fourth stage, *coordination of circular reactions*, is when infants can do two actions to produce an outcome. For example, if a toy is covered, the child can coordinate the actions of removing the object that is covering a toy and then reaching for that toy. The primary advances in this stage are in how infants use actions together to achieve a goal. Finally, at the stage of *tertiary circular reactions*, infants recognize that objects themselves have properties that can be explored. They begin to show trial-and-error behaviors in their actions. For example, an infant may bang a pot with a spoon, then turn the pot over and bang the inside, then bang the side of the pot, and so on. The child recognizes not only that their own actions produce effects, they now can explore new ways to act on the pot and discover its properties. At this point, children are on the verge of symbolic mental representations that will mark the end of infancy. The sixth substage, often referred to as *mental representations*, reflects a true transition from pure sensorimotor thought to mental

TABLE 7.2 ■ Piagetian Sensorimotor Stages				
Sensorimotor Stage	Approximate Age	Starting Point	What Changes	Example
Stage 1—Reflexive Schemes	Birth to 1 month	Action reflexes	Reflexes give way to more intentional actions	Sucking, grasping
Stage 2—Primary Circular Reactions	1 to 4 months	The first changes in actions	First adaptations in schemes	Sucking fingers, grasping an object
Stage 3—Secondary Circular Reactions	4 to 8 months	Infant applies schemes to objects and modifies schemes when needed	Infants learn to produce interesting effects	Shaking a rattle
Stage 4— Coordination of Secondary Circular Reactions	8 to 12 months	Infants begin to link together distinct schemes	Infant applies schemes to new situations	Using a lid and then a spoon to bang a pot
Stage 5—Tertiary Circular Reactions	12 to 18 months	Infants intentionally use schemes to act on their world and to explore	Infants actively experiment as they manipulate objects	Infants will experiment with how to fit objects through openings, such as placing shapes in a shape sorter
Stage 6—Mental Representation	18 to 24 months	Infant begins to form representations of objects or events	Infants can represent objects symbolically	Infants will pretend to put a doll to sleep

representations. Often it is difficult to see how thought in this stage is different from that in the preoperational stage, underscoring how although Piaget described development in terms of qualitatively different stages, the transitions from stage to stage are gradual and continuous. We will discuss the transition to preoperational thought in Chapter 8.

Vygotsky

About the time that Piaget was developing his theory, Lev Vygotsky (1980) was also formulating a theory of cognitive development. Like Piaget, Vygotsky viewed infants as curious and active in propelling their understanding of the world and thus emphasized infants' *experience* in development. However, whereas Piaget focused on the role of infants' *physical* interactions in their development (i.e., the actions infants perform), Vygotsky focused on the role of *social* interactions in infancy and beyond. For Vygotsky, social interactions were key to how children advanced their understanding. Specifically, Vygotsky argued that through social interactions with others, children undergo gradual, continuous change in how they think and understand the world.

According to Vygotsky, children learn when they engage with a more advanced social partner, what he called the **more knowledgeable other**. The more knowledgeable other could be a peer, sibling, parent, or any individual with more advanced skills than the child. Not just any social interaction will result in learning, however. The interactions that are most effective are when the more knowledgeable other allows children to engage in actions or activities that are just slightly beyond their ability. Think about helping a 2-year-old child solve a puzzle. It will be more effective to help the child to adjust how they hold a puzzle piece to insert it into one of six openings in a board puzzle, than to dump out a 100-piece jigsaw puzzle and hand the child the pieces. The first example is an activity that is in the child's **zone of proximal development** (ZPD), or the range of activities and tasks that are just beyond children's ability to do on their own. Children can succeed on activities and tasks in this zone with the help of another. The experience of doing a puzzle with the help of another person allows the child to gain experiences not possible alone and provides them with the opportunity to learn and internalize strategies shared by the more experienced social partner (see photo). Activities outside the ZPD, such as dumping a 100-piece jigsaw puzzle in front of a 2-year-old, will not promote development because the child can't succeed at those activities and tasks even with help. In this way, it is clear how Vygotsky emphasized social interactions in development.

Vygotsky's strong emphasis on the role of social interactions in how infants understand their world gave rise to the **sociocultural theory** of development. According to this perspective, development can be understood only by considering the individual's social and cultural contexts. This perspective contrasts with Piaget, who proposed that infants' understanding of the world followed a universal sequence with no attention given to the social contexts in which infants are embedded.

This discussion, as is often true with discussions of Vygotsky, seems to have little to do with cognitive development in infancy. It therefore may not be obvious how Vygotsky's thinking has shaped our understanding of cognitive development in infancy. However, the emphasis in this book on the development of the whole child reflects, in part, Vygotsky's influence. Because of Vygotsky's theories, researchers have considered development in context. For example, Barbara Rogoff and her colleagues have studied learning in early childhood in Mayan children in Guatemala and European heritage children in Utah (Chavajay & Rogoff, 1999, 2002; Correa-Chávez & Rogoff, 2009). In this work, Rogoff does not attempt to show that one group of children is superior in learning than the other, but rather she characterizes how the cultural context supports children's learning in different ways. As a result, children in different cultures have different strengths and different strategies for learning.

MOTHER SCAFFOLDING BABY'S PLAY. In his sociocultural theory, Vygotsky emphasized the importance of social interactions in the development of children's understanding of their world. Scaffolding by more expert social partners allows children to gain important skills that are just beyond their current skills, what Vygotsky called the zone of proximal development.

iStock/Zurijeta

Information Processing

The information processing theory of cognition represented a significant shift in how psychologists thought about the human mind and how knowledge is gained, stored, and represented. This approach compared the human mind to a computer, and emphasized memory systems and how information is taken in and processed to become stored in memory. For example, information can be stored in the **sensory register**, where visual and auditory information is first encoded and stored briefly; short-term memory, a limited capacity memory that maintains information for a short time; or long-term memory, an apparently limitless capacity memory where information is stored permanently. Imagine hearing someone speaking in the background as you are reading this chapter. Your sensory register would allow you to notice the voice but not to process what is being said. Understanding the words requires directing more of your attention to the voice and the words, a process that moves the information into your short-term memory. If the voice was providing a phone number, you would remember the phone number, or a few of the numbers, briefly. However, because only a few things can be stored in short-term memory at one time, to keep that information active in short-term memory, you need to rehearse it, or repeat it over and over again. If you don't do this, new information will be stored in short-term memory, replacing the phone number. If the phone number was important—for example, if it was your new love interest's number—processes might be engaged to store it in long-term memory.

Developmental psychologists adopted this approach to thinking about cognitive development. You probably recognized that this approach emphasizes the kind of abilities we described in Chapter 6 (attention, memory). Researchers who adopt the information processing perspective focus on domain general processes that can be used to understand objects, places, or people. These processes are innate and their development may be due to biological maturation. But, children's knowledge of the world comes from their experience using those processes as they encounter new information. For example, theorists in this tradition would argue that the ability to recognize the connection between two things (e.g., mom's voice and what her face looks like) or to see the similarities across different things (e.g., that dogs have four legs) are examples of the kinds of domain general learning mechanisms that are innate. From this perspective the *hardware* (e.g., the brain and how it is organized) and some *software* (e.g., how information is processed by the brain) may be the result of biological or innate forces, but what infants know is a function of their experience. As in the other theories we have discussed, information processing theories view infants as active in their own learning. But, rather than focusing on qualitative shifts in how information is represented or processed, the focus is on continuous, gradual changes in how much information can be processed and how quickly it can be processed.

The information processing approach has been important for the study of individual differences in cognitive abilities in infancy. At a general level, information processing approaches attribute uniformity to the specific processes that allow infants to construct their understanding, while still allowing for variations across how much or in what way a particular infant can process this information. Thus, all infants use the same processes, but there are differences in how those processes operate in an individual infant. For example, researchers like Susan Rose and colleagues (2005) and Marc Bornstein and colleagues (2013) have argued that we can measure individual differences in infants' information processing, and those individual differences are *stable* across time, predicting later abilities such as language or academic achievement.

Core Knowledge

Elizabeth Spelke developed a **core knowledge** theory of cognition in the late 1990s and early 2000s (Spelke, 2000; Spelke & Kinzler, 2007). This theory differs in several ways from the other theories we have described thus far. Central to this theory is that there are innate, domain specific processes for learning about the world. In addition, although children's understanding of the world develops, this development involves infants and young children using innate processes to interpret and understand people, objects, and places.

Not everything is innate, however. Spelke and her colleagues proposed that infants are born with knowledge and learning mechanisms relevant to the **core domains** of objects, number, geometry, and agents. Core knowledge theories solve the challenge of how infants can create abstract representations from their senses, actions, and social interactions by positing that infants have innate knowledge and mechanisms. The infant only needs to have some amount of input from their experiences, and their core knowledge will suffice to understand their world from that limited input.

These innate skills and knowledge are *domain specific*; that is, they are specific to each of the core domains. For example, infants use one set of processes to learn about objects and a different set of processes to learn about space. According to the core knowledge theory, these domains were selected by evolution to ensure the survival of the species. They are domains that are central to how we think about and interact with the world. In addition, the core domains are areas where nonhuman animals have been shown to be skillful, suggesting an evolutionary basis for the presence of these specific concepts. For example, both young children and rats search spaces (e.g., rooms) in similar ways (Hermer & Spelke, 1996). Other nonhuman animals are sensitive to differences in number (Gallistel & Gelman, 1992). And newborn chicks show a similar understanding of objects as do infants (Wood & Wood, 2016).

Because core knowledge is based on evolution, these researchers also argue that these skills and processes are universal and that infants should develop in the same way despite vastly distinct experiences (e.g., individuals of different ages or from different countries). However, very few studies have actually been conducted with individuals who are not from North America or western Europe. A few studies have been conducted comparing knowledge about geometry or number in children and adults from different cultures. For example, Véronique Izard and her colleagues found that children and adults in the United States, France, and the Mundurucu community—an indigenous people living in the Brazilian Amazon—had a similar understanding of geometric properties, such as lines, points, and surfaces. As a result, Izard and her colleagues argued that there is core knowledge about Euclidean geometry (Izard et al., 2011). This comparison was not done with infants, however.

Finally, even though core knowledge theories argue for innate domain specific intuitions and learning processes, they propose that this core knowledge undergoes further development throughout infancy and childhood. That is, core knowledge is a starting point and is not equivalent to adults' understanding of these concepts. Rather, core knowledge provides a foundational structure on which infants can build their understanding. But, this is not a series of discontinuous stages, as suggested by Piaget. Rather, this development involves continuity from the innate knowledge that guides how infants make sense of their world to the rich conceptual understanding of older children and adults.

Systems and Connectionist Theories of Cognitive Development

Throughout this book, we have talked about theories such as dynamic systems and developmental cascades. These are examples of a new kind of theory of development that emerged starting in the 1990s. The researchers who developed these theories were interested in understanding how several things develop together and how the emergence of any individual skill or ability (e.g., learning to walk, saying the first word) reflects the co-development of many things. So, rather than focusing on the development of a scheme, one memory system, or how a core knowledge system helps infants learn within a specific domain, these theories recognize that development is a product of how multiple things change over time and that no one thing develops completely on its own. These theories have also been used to understand cognitive development.

Because this is not just one theory, there is no single answer about what is innate or what the processes are. These modern theories do have several things in common, however. First, they focus on continuity in development. For these approaches, development might look discontinuous, but those discontinuities emerge from multiple continuous changes. Learning to walk, for example, may appear to be discontinuous. As we saw in Chapter 5, however, it is rare for a child to simply stand up and walk one day, moving from a pre-walking stage to a walking stage seemingly overnight. Rather, learning to walk is a gradual process. Walking emerges from making stepping movements, which infants do from birth, and develops across the first year or so as children develop the strength and coordination that allows them to walk independently.

These theories also focus on the *interaction* between what is innate and the experiences children have. That is, for connectionist and systems theories, it is less important precisely what is innate, and it is more important to understand how development reflects the interaction between what the child brings (either innate skills or things learned from past experience) and what is in the environment for them to learn. A related component of many of these theories is that development does not simply happen in one domain, but the dynamic systems theory makes this process explicit. As we discussed in Chapters 1 and 5, for this view, the development of any one ability (such as walking) actually reflects the development of multiple systems. Researchers who adopt this perspective focus on how abilities in one domain connect to development in another domain. We have seen examples of this when we talked about perceptual development in Chapter 4 and motor development in Chapter 5. For dynamic systems theories, the development of many systems allows new skills to emerge. So, seeing objects as three-dimensional develops not only because of changes in infants' visual abilities but also because of motor achievements, such as the ability to sit independently.

Likewise, a developmental cascades perspective focuses on how development in one domain, such as motor development, might cause changes in another domain, such as language. This perspective is similar to dynamic systems, but there is also an emphasis on understanding how some achievements set the stage for other developments. That is, dynamic systems theorists focus on how behaviors emerge from the development of multiple systems (e.g., action, perception, cognition, emotion). Developmental cascades are focused on understanding how some developmental changes *depend* on other developments. For example, independent sitting frees up the arms, which causes the infant to be able to explore objects in new ways. Those new ways of exploring objects—by picking them up, turning them around—can cause infants to learn new features about objects. The focus is on the chain or sequence of events that occur across development.

These theories tend to emphasize general purpose processes, rather than the very narrow and specific processes found in the core knowledge view. On top of that, these theories also focus on the *input* that is encountered, that is, the things infants see, hear, feel, and experience. According to connectionism, for example, development occurs as the child encounters input from the environment. When language is spoken by the people around them, the infant recognizes the regularities in that input and uses those regularities to learn that language. A key idea is that this input is not random, and there is enough information in the input to allow infants and young children to learn. To give another example, children can learn that objects fall when they are dropped because the only input they receive involves objects falling when they are dropped; they (almost) never see an object fly up when dropped. In this way, there are regularities in the input (objects being dropped and then falling) for infants and young children to learn about the world. As we will see in Chapter 9, this issue has been a source of debate in the study of language development, with some researchers arguing that the input really does not contain enough input and infants must have innate language learning mechanisms and connectionist theorists showing that even computer systems can learn about language from the language input that children hear.

The developmental cascades approach also emphasizes the input. In this case, however, the input not only is a function of the environment but also depends on the child's own development. Early in infancy when visual acuity is poor, infants will not learn the details of the faces around them because they cannot see those details. The details of faces are not part of the input. As their vision develops, however, the details of faces become part of the input infants receive, allowing infants to learn about them. The point is that in this view, infants learn from input or what they experience in the environment around them, but the input and what they experience depend on other aspects of development.

Check Your Learning

1. Describe the sensorimotor stages of Piaget's theory.

2. According to Vygotsky, how do infants acquire knowledge about their world?

3. List three processes that information processing theories claim are central to how infants take in, store, and represent information.

4. What features of the core knowledge theories are unique to this perspective?

5. Briefly describe the three more recent theories of infants' understanding: dynamic systems, connectionism, and developmental cascades.

6. Which theories ascribe domain specific processes to infants' learning and which outline domain general processes?

INFANTS' DEVELOPING UNDERSTANDING OF OBJECTS

When Alison was an infant, she loved to sit in the bath and use cups to scoop and pour water. She was discovering and exploring the properties of solid objects (the cup) and non-solid substances (the water). Likewise, as a toddler, Charlie's favorite outdoor toy was a water table, where he could practice submerging different objects in water and pouring water down chutes that spin and splash. How do infants learn about such properties of objects?

Theories of the Development of Object Knowledge

According to Piaget, infants learn through acting on objects. When Edwin was 7 months old, he went through a "throwing phase," throwing every new object he encountered to see if it would bounce like a ball. This experience may have shaped how Edwin learned about the objects around him and, specifically, what kinds of objects bounce and what kinds of objects don't bounce. Much of what we know about infants' developing understanding of objects has its origins in Piaget's observations for how his own children interacted with objects.

Elizabeth Spelke's core knowledge view has been a significant alternative to Piaget's perspective. According to Spelke, an understanding of objects and how objects can act in the physical world is one of the core knowledge domains. For core knowledge theorists, infants' object knowledge is either innate or develops early (without manual exploration). These researchers have conducted violation of expectation studies (see Box 7.1) to demonstrate infant object knowledge at a young age. These studies ask whether infants look longer when shown events that violate physical constraints on objects than when shown events that are consistent with physical constraints. For example, Elizabeth Spelke and her colleagues (Spelke et al., 1992) observed that infants looked longer at events in which one object appeared to *pass through* another solid object than at events in which the first object stopped when it encountered the second object. Other studies have shown that infants look longer when objects appear to be suspended in mid-air than when objects are supported by other objects (Hespos & Baillargeon, 2008; Needham & Baillargeon, 1993) and that infants seem to have different expectations for how liquid moves in a container than for how solid objects (don't) move in a container (Hespos & Rips, 2009). One of the goals of all of these studies is to show that an understanding of object properties is early emerging and that this understanding does not depend on infants' physical manipulation of objects.

Other views of object knowledge based on information processing, dynamic systems, or developmental cascades argue that infants learn about object properties gradually as they become able to attend to, process, and remember more information. Often this new information is gained through exploration, although the role of exploration is different in each of these theories. For example, many researchers adopting one of the more recent systems approaches to development have asked how object knowledge is related to infants' actions on objects. We saw this in Chapters 4 and 5, when discussing both perceptual and motor development. Some of these researchers have adopted a **perception-action** view that infants' perception and understanding of objects is related to, and probably develops from, their actions on objects. For example, infants who can sit can more actively explore objects with their hands, discovering new properties of objects, such as the fact that they are three-dimensional (Soska et al., 2010). The idea is that infants learn about object properties through exploration and interaction. So, infants who can sit have their arms and hands free to explore objects, and through that exploration they learn more about objects in general.

BOX 7.1—INFANCY RESEARCH: VIOLATION OF EXPECTATION

As we have seen throughout this book, research with infants has often involved habituation of infants' looking time. As we have also seen, habituation is a powerful tool using infants' looking behavior and interest in novelty for studying perceptual development and memory. Indeed, some researchers have used habituation to study infants' understanding and perception of objects. But researchers have also used a different type of looking time procedure, the violation of expectation procedure, to study infants' object knowledge and perception. Like habituation, the **violation of expectation** procedure also involves measuring how long infants look at different types of events and drawing inferences about their perception and knowledge of objects from their looking patterns. However, one test event is always *possible* and one is always *impossible*.

An example is given with stimuli from a classic study by Amy Needham and Renée Baillargeon (1993) on 4-month-old infants' perception and understanding of *support*. In these events, the possible event shows a typical support relation: One object is placed on top of a second object and remains where it was placed because it is fully and adequately supported. The impossible event shows a sequence of events that can't happen in the real world: The hand reaches out and places the box beyond the potential supporting box. But, instead of falling to the ground, it remains suspended in mid-air, as if it is supported.

As in a habituation study, infants' looking to these two "test" trials is recorded. Unlike a habituation study, there was no habituation event. Infants were simply shown these two events, and the question was whether they looked longer at the impossible event than at the possible one. The logic is that if infants have an understanding of how objects can interact in the world, their expectations should be violated in the impossible event and they should look longer at that event. In Needham and Baillargeon's study, 4.5-month-old infants looked longer at the impossible event than at the possible event. From this, they concluded that this impossible event violated infants' expectation that objects should fall if they are not supported.

In many ways, the violation of expectation and habituation procedures are quite similar. They both involve measuring infants' looking time to two types of events or scenes. They rely on infants' preference for some kinds of events or scenes over others. Even though the violation of expectation task does not *require* habituation, it is not uncommon for researchers to use a habituation or familiarization phase to get infants used to or familiar with some aspect of the experiment, so it will not be distracting during the test.

However, the violation of expectation task tests the assumptions that infants had *when they arrived at the lab*. So there is no need to habituate or teach infants anything before showing them the test events, because if they have the knowledge required, the impossible test event will violate their expectations and will be more surprising, interesting, or novel than the possible test event.

Infants' Knowledge of Object Properties

The first studies of infants' object understanding were focused on infants' developing object permanence. Specifically, based on his systematic observations of how his own three infants searched for hidden objects, Piaget described how infants come to be able to mentally represent objects that are out of view and have an understanding of objects as having a stable, permanent existence. We will discuss this in more detail in Chapter 8, but it is an important starting point for the research on infants' knowledge of objects. Some studies were conducted that raise questions about whether or not infants do represent objects that are out of sight. For example, although Piaget observed that infants won't search for a hidden object, other researchers found that infants saw an object and then the lights turned out, infants would reach in the dark for the previously seen object (e.g., Hood & Willatts, 1986). Other researchers observed that infants would follow with their eyes the movement of an object that went behind an occluder, apparently expecting it to appear on the other side (Bremner, 1985).

Although researchers have debated whether these behaviors reflect the kind of mental representation of objects that Piaget described, they did open the door for researchers to ask what else infants seem to know about objects.

In Spelke's core knowledge view, infants have an understanding that objects are continuous across space and time and are solid. In one study, Spelke and her colleagues (1992) used a violation of expectation procedure (see Box 7.1) to test this. They presented infants with events like those shown in Figure 7.1. In the *consistent* (or possible) event, the ball is dropped and when the occluder is removed to reveal the scene, the ball is *on* the platform, as it should be if the ball (and platform) are solid and continuous. In the *inconsistent* (or impossible) event, the ball is dropped and when the occluder is removed, the ball is *under* the platform, as if it passed right through the platform. They found that 4-month-old North American infants looked longer at the inconsistent event, as if they found it unexpected or more novel to see one solid object apparently pass through a second solid object. From results like these, Spelke and her colleagues argued that infants' core knowledge about objects includes the understanding that objects are solid and are continuous over space and time.

Researchers who adopt a perception-action perspective have a different view of how infants come to understand object properties such as solidity. In Chapter 5 we discussed how Kasey Soska, Karen Adolph, and Scott Johnson found that infants' ability to look at objects while manually exploring them seemed to be important for infants' learning that objects are solid and have a three-dimensional structure (Soska et al., 2010). Other researchers have shown that infants' manual exploration of objects and surfaces of different materials (e.g., squishy or solid) becomes more selective across infancy (Bourgeois et al., 2005). In general, this research suggests that infants can learn about objects through their manual exploration and that at least some aspects of infants' object perception and recognition are related to their developing exploration of objects.

Researchers adopting an information processing view look for gradual changes in how infants understand physical objects. We can see this in infants' developing **causal perception**, or their recognition that one action caused a particular effect (e.g., pushing a button caused a light to turn on, hitting an object caused it to move). Researchers have studied

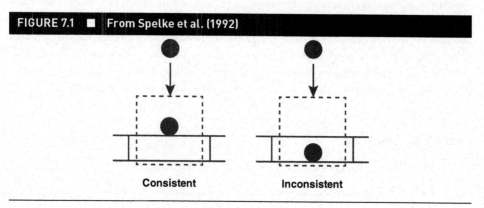

FIGURE 7.1 ■ From Spelke et al. (1992)

Consistent   Inconsistent

Source: Reprinted with permission from Spelke et al. (1992).

infants' causal perception by showing them simple events in which one ball rolls toward and hits a second ball, which then begins to move, much as in a game of pool or billiards. Seeing such an event as causal might mean that you recognize that one object can't pass through another object and that an object won't move unless there is a cause (e.g., being hit by the other, moving object).

Lisa Oakes and Les Cohen (Cohen & Oakes, 1993; Oakes & Cohen, 1990) studied infants' perception of this type of event and concluded that causal perception develops gradually as infants become able to process more information and do so more efficiently. In a series of studies with samples of infants in the United States, they used habituation and the kind of collision events just described. In the possible causal event, the first object hits the second object and the second object immediately begins to move; adults see this as the first object launching the second object into motion. For adults, the perception of the collision as causal can be disrupted either by not having the objects touch (e.g., the first object stops before hitting the second object, but the second object moves anyway) or by having a delay before the second object begins to move (e.g., after the first object hits the second object, both objects are stationary for a moment before the second object begins to apparently spontaneously begin to move).

Oakes and Cohen found that infants also respond differently to causal and non-causal collision events, suggesting that they perceive causality. However, this was not an all-or-none ability. Six- and 7-month-old U.S. infants perceived the causality of collisions only if the objects involved were simple, like colored spheres (Oakes, 1994). When the objects were more complex, such as toys, 10-month-old infants, but not 6-month-old infants, perceived the causality of collisions (Oakes & Cohen, 1990). And 10-month-old infants only perceived the causality of collisions with toys if the toys were the same on each habituation trial; when the toys changed from trial to trial (so infants saw many causal or many non-causal events), 10-month-old infants no longer seemed to perceive causality (Cohen & Oakes, 1993). From these kinds of results, Oakes and Cohen argued that infants must process each piece of the events—the kinds of objects, how the objects move, whether they touched, and so forth. When infants are younger, they can only perceive causality under simple conditions, when there are fewer pieces of the event to process.

This is only one way that researchers have interpreted infants' causal perception. Like other aspects of infants' object reasoning, some researchers have argued that infants' causal perception does not develop gradually (Leslie, 1982; Leslie & Keeble, 1987). In part, these differences reflect differences in how researchers ask their questions and what procedures they use. The main conclusion is that infants do develop some understanding of physical objects. But there is still significant debate about when sophisticated thinking emerges and how it develops.

Check Your Learning

1. Describe the different theories of infants' developing object knowledge.

2. Define causal perception, and describe its development in infants.

INFANTS' DEVELOPING UNDERSTANDING OF SPACE

As infants build their knowledge of objects, they also build their knowledge about the spatial features of their environment. Recall how Diego's play with his favorite toy, the wooden cylinders that nested smaller cylinders within larger, hollow ones, shifted over his first 2 years? Diego progressed from struggling to fit the cylinders within each other before he turned 1 year old, to becoming adept at predicting which cylinder nested within another as he approached his second birthday. Diego had gained an appreciation for the relation between the size of one cylinder and the opening of a larger cylinder. This shift in Diego's play with the nesting cylinders reflected advances in his spatial understanding. His spatial understanding fits with Piaget's view of infants' spatial skills. Piaget believed that infants' spatial understanding was constrained to their sensorimotor actions and, for this reason, were **egocentric**, or constrained to be understood only in relation to the infants' body.

There are many other experiences in infants' daily lives that use spatial knowledge. For example, when visiting a children's museum, Charlie would become engrossed in stacking large foam cubes to create a tower, demonstrating an awareness of how to arrange the cubes so that they would stack rather than topple, until he eventually delighted in knocking them down of course. Recall how 18-month-old Tesalia found her way back through a crowded children's museum to her favorite activity. Her success required that she attend to the spatial layout of the museum and the route taken through the other displays and crowds of people to get to that splash pad. Each of these examples reveals advances in spatial thinking, including the ability to track *where* an object is located, the spatial relation of objects, attending to the route objects take, as well as navigating the spatial layout of a room.

Spatial understanding includes small-scale information, such as the spatial configurations of objects (e.g., noting that the car keys are next to a coffee mug on the kitchen counter) and imagining the appearance of an object when viewed from a different angle (a skill known as mental rotation). It also includes large-scale spatial information, such as attending to the location of objects and the spatial layout of the environment. This large-scale information is also important for attending to the route that objects or people traverse and for tracking one's location in their environment to navigate a route to a desired location, which is useful for finding a favorite spot in a children's museum. All of these types of spatial understanding undergo substantial advances in the first 3 years (and, of course, continue to develop throughout childhood into adulthood).

There has been significant disagreement about infants' and young children's understanding of space. Piaget proposed that young infants lacked spatial concepts until toward the end of the sensorimotor stage, when they could form representations. In addition, he believed that infants were limited to acquiring spatial information that was egocentric, tied to their own bodies and their motor actions. In contrast, *geometry*, or an understanding of spatial relations, is one of the innate core domains for core knowledge theory. Other perspectives, such as information processing and dynamic systems, instead argue that the environment provides infants with the structure needed to quickly acquire their spatial understanding. According to these approaches, infants are equipped with strong domain-general learning mechanisms that they can use to learn about spatial relations and develop their spatial skills as they experience the position of objects and individuals in their world.

Small-Scale Spatial Information

Small-scale spatial information refers to the relations between the parts of an object, how an object is oriented in space, or relations between objects that are close together. This kind of information is important for learning the spatial relations between parts of an object, how two objects are arranged in space, and recognizing objects from different points of view. In one study with simple triangles, 7-month-old infants in Boston could recognize differences in spatial features of objects such as size, shape, and length (Dillon et al., 2020). In two other studies with infants in the United Kingdom and United States who were less than 4 months old, infants discriminated between a simple acute angle (an angle that is less than 90 degrees) and an obtuse angle (an angle that is greater than 90 degrees) (Cohen & Younger, 1984; Slater et al., 1991). These studies show that even young infants are sensitive to some small-scale spatial information.

Another kind of small-scale spatial information is how objects are arranged in space, for example, whether they are above or below one another, or to the left or right. Even newborns seem to be sensitive to these relations. In one study, a group of U.S. newborn infants were habituated to displays of a square *below* a triangle. These infants then looked longer at a display of a square *above* the triangle, indicating they recognized the change from below to above (Antell & Caron, 1985). In another study, Italian newborns noticed when an object appeared to the left of a line when they had previously seen the object presented to the right (Gava et al., 2009). But, infants' sensitivity to these kinds of spatial relations develops over time, and infants become sensitive to more abstract spatial relations as they get older. For example, Paul Quinn and his colleagues found that U.S. infants between 3 and 4 months could discriminate changes in the above-versus-below spatial relation for objects seen previously, but it was not until 6 to 7 months of age that infants could recognize a change in relation with new objects, or those not seen previously by infants during the task (Quinn et al., 1996, 2003). As noted in Chapter 6, the ability to generalize a spatial relation is critical for forming spatial categories and having more abstract representations of these spatial relations (Casasola, 2008).

Containment is another kind of small-scale spatial relation. As Diego played with his cylinders, he became increasingly aware of how one cylinder could be placed inside of another. Using a violation of expectation procedure, Susan Hespos and Renée Baillargeon (2001) showed U.S. 3 ½-month-old infants two events: (1) a possible containment event in which one object was inserted into a can with an open top, and (2) an impossible containment event in which the object was (apparently) inserted in a can with a lid, as if it had passed through the lid. The infants looked longer at the impossible event, suggesting to Hespos and Baillargeon that by 3 ½ months, long before they can insert one cylinder into another, infants have an understanding of containment.

Even when spatial understanding emerges early, it continues to develop as infants acquire new information. Interestingly, although English uses the word *in* to refer to any time one object is in (or contained by) another object and *on* to refer to any time one object is supported by another object (regardless of how the objects fit together), Korean uses the spatial term "tight fit" that refers to *either* containment *or* support relations where there is a tight fit between the two objects. Marianella Casasola and colleagues (Casasola & Ahn, 2018; Casasola & Cohen, 2002) asked how infants' understanding of containment changes when they have heard those words in each language. English-learning U.S. infants and Korean-learning U.S. and Korean infants were sensitive to the English concept of "in" by 10 months. By 18 months, infants in both groups could learn the concept of "tight fit," but Korean-learning infants were more attentive to the concept of "tight fit" than were the English-speaking infants. Thus, sensitivity to some spatial relations emerges in infancy regardless of language experience, but language experience shapes the *kinds* of spatial relations that children notice and attend to.

Finally, the ability to recognize objects in different orientations also emerges in infancy. This ability, **mental rotation**, involves rotating an image of an object in your mind to determine whether it matches another image or a memory of that object. Several researchers have used habituation to show that infants can match different views of the same object. In these studies, infants are habituated or familiarized with an object (like the ones shown in Figure 7.2) seen from one or more different views. Then they are tested with a new view of that familiar object or

FIGURE 7.2 ■ Mental Rotation Stimuli

Images used as stimuli in studies of mental rotation in infants.

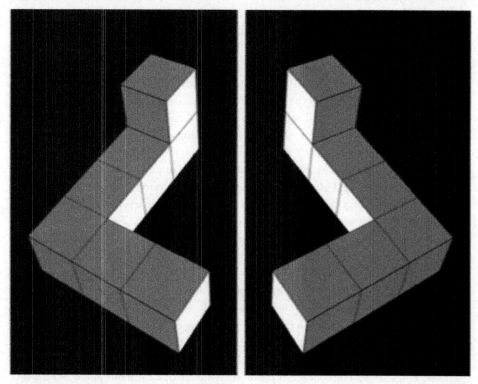

Source: Moore & Johnson (2008).

a completely new object. Using this procedure, David Moore and Scott Johnson (2008, 2020) found that U.S. 5-month-old infants looked longer at the view of the new object, apparently recognizing the new view of the familiar object as familiar. Interestingly, in these and other studies conducted in the United States (Quinn & Liben, 2008, 2014), infant boys often seem to be able to mentally rotate objects but infant girls do not, or boys succeed on mental rotation tasks at younger ages than do girls. This difference makes it seem like mental rotation is a biological ability that emerges through a process of maturation. However, differences between boys and girls are likely related both to hormonal and parenting differences (Constantinescu et al., 2018). These findings are consistent with a systems or cascades approach to mental rotation. Indeed, motor development and experience can shape the development of mental rotation (Frick & Möhring, 2013; Möhring & Frick, 2013). In addition, giving U.S. 4-month-old infants specific experience with reaching for and picking up objects seems to enhance their abilities to mentally rotate those objects (Slone et al., 2018).

Frames of Reference

Navigating across a room or from one room to another requires attending to spatial information. To track locations, infants can use one of two types of information, or frame of reference. When using an **egocentric frame of reference**, infants use their own perspective and note where a particular location is in relation to their own body. For example, an infant may encode that a teddy bear is to their own left. If the infant moves, however, they would need to update their egocentric representation of the object's location. When using an **allocentric frame of reference,** locations are encoded in relation to an external feature in the environment, such as a landmark. An infant using an allocentric frame of reference would note, for example, that their teddy bear is between the table and sofa in the living room (rather than encoding it egocentrically as to their left). If the infant moves, no change would be needed from the allocentric frame of reference, because the teddy bear is still between the table and the sofa.

Infants' use of frames of reference has been studied using an **object retrieval task** (Bremner, 1978). In this task (see the following photo), children observe a toy hidden in a particular location on a long table, either buried in sand or hidden in one of multiple containers. Then, the child's view of the table and hiding locations is changed, either by moving the child to the other side of the table or rotating the table 180 degrees. The question is: where do the children search? They will search in the wrong location if they use egocentric frames of reference; specifically, they will search where the object was in relation to their own body, even though they or the hiding locations have moved. In fact, 6- to 11-month-old infants in the United States and Great Britain make this error, searching in the location where the toy was hidden relative to their initial body position (e.g., on their left, if that is where the object was hidden, even though now the object is on their right) (Acredolo, 1978; Bremner, 1978).

It is tempting from this work to think that very young children are unable to use external or allocentric cues to find the object. However, infants in their first year can use a *beacon*, or a landmark, that is at or next to the location of the hidden object (Acredolo, 1978; Bremner, 1978; Lew et al., 2000). For example, if the object is hidden by a cloth or a pillow of a distinct color (e.g., a red pillow in a collection of green pillows), infants as young as 8 months will

RECTANGULAR HIDING TASK: A rectangular container in which a toy was hidden. Two landmarks (or external cues), the flags, are used to probe infants' and children's ability to code the location of a hidden object relative to the landmarks.

Simms & Gentner (2019).

find the object even when the table is rotated or the infant is moved (Lew et al., 2000, 2004, 2006). However, infants have more difficulty using landmarks if they are not right next to where the object is hidden. Specifically, landmarks that are next to the hiding location function as beacons, marking the exact location of the hidden objects. Landmarks that are some distance from the hiding location can't be used as beacons but instead can only help you find the hiding location if you have encoded that location by using the *distance* and *direction* from one or more landmarks (Newcombe et al., 1999; Vasilyeva & Lourenco, 2012). Whereas even 8-month-old infants (at least in the United States) can use *beacons*, using *landmarks* is much more difficult. For example, U.S. 9-month-old infants can use landmarks when they are tested in a familiar environment, such as their own home, but not when they are tested in an unfamiliar lab or office (Acredolo, 1979).

During infancy, infants' developing ability to use landmarks to search seems to be related to motor development and their ability to navigate environments on their own. Similarly, Melissa Clearfield (2004) found that locomotor experience—either crawling or walking—helped U.S. 8- to 14-month-old infants use landmarks to find a hidden object. Studies with children in the United States show that the ability to use landmarks continues to develop during the toddler and preschool years. At around 2 ½, children in the United States can not only use landmarks but also find objects hidden *between* two landmarks (Ankowski et al., 2012). Interestingly, at this age, English-learning children who understood the words *between* and *middle* were better at identifying the middle between two landmarks, suggesting that language and spatial development are related (Simms & Gentner, 2019).

Other studies have used non-search tasks to study infants' developing use of allocentric cues to "find" objects. Specifically, studies that have relied on where and how long infants look seem to show that infants can use allocentric cues. In one study, Jordy Kaufman and Amy Needham (2011) familiarized 4 ½-month-old infants to an interesting display (a rotating pig puppet) that was located at a particular place on a table. Then, the table was hidden from the infant's view and either the infant was moved (so the pig was in its original location but in a different location relative to the infant's body) or the object was moved (so the pig was in a new location). These young infants showed interest in both types of movement, suggesting they were able to form objective representations of space and did not simply rely on egocentric cues in this context. Similarly, Nora Newcombe and her colleagues (1999) recorded looking time in a group of U.S. 5-month-old infants as they watched a toy being hidden in a sandbox. After infants watched the toy being hidden in one location, they looked longer when the toy appeared 8 inches from where it had been hidden than when the toy appeared exactly where it had been hidden. These studies using infants *looking* rather than reaching suggest that infants can use allocentric cues to encode location, at least in some contexts.

Up to now, we have been talking about how infants develop the ability to use visual information as landmarks. What about visually impaired infants? Research shows that infants with visual impairments can also learn to use landmarks to navigate their environments using touch, or haptic information (Martolini et al., 2021). For example, Barbara Landau and her colleagues (1984) tested the use of landmarks by a 2-year-old toddler who had been blind since birth. An experimenter guided the child around the room—for example, from her mother to a chair or table, which the child touched, and then back to her mother. After the experimenter helped the child become familiar with the location of four landmarks in the room, Landau and her colleagues asked the child to move to one of the landmarks, such as the table, and then to another landmark. The child accurately moved from one landmark to another, demonstrating that she had formed a representation of the spatial layout of the room and the location of the landmarks in the room, showing that children can use inputs other than vision to form a mental map of their environment.

Reorientation

Humans can also use geometric cues to orient ourselves in space. Imagine yourself in a long, rectangular room. You can orient yourself by noticing where corners are and that some walls are long and others are short. We can also use landmarks, such as the color of a wall or the presence of a door, window, or object, to orient ourselves. Imagine yourself in a square room with two doors. You might remember that the door to the bathroom has a mirror next to it, whereas the door to the hallway is next to the TV. These landmarks help you position yourself in space and move toward the appropriate door.

Core knowledge theorists argue that the ability to use geometric cues is innate and that children from a young age prioritize this information over other types of external cues, or landmarks (Hermer & Spelke, 1996; Shusterman et al., 2011; Spelke & Kinzler, 2007). For example, Linda Hermer and Elizabeth Spelke (1994) had U.S. 18- to 24-month-old toddlers watch as a toy was hidden in the corner of a rectangular room. Then, the children were disoriented by closing their eyes and allowing the experimenter to turn them in circles. Finally, the child was allowed to search for the toy. Children used the geometry of the room (i.e., the length of the walls) to identify which corner to look for the toy, even ignoring a landmark such as one wall of the room being a different color. Results like this have been used by core knowledge theorists to argue that children have an innate sensitivity to this kind of geometric information.

However, other studies have shown that young children can use landmarks to reorient themselves. For example, Marko Nardini, Janette Atkinson, and Neil Burgess (2008) found that when the room was square, and geometric cues could not be used, 18- to 24-month-old children used the colors of the walls to reorient themselves. Likewise, Amy Learmonth, Nora Newcombe, and Janellen Huttenlocher (2001) found that toddlers used geometric cues in some contexts but landmarks in others. For example, when the rooms were small, U.S. 18- to 24-month-old children used geometric information to reorient, but when the rooms were bigger, they used landmarks to reorient. It is important to point out that this work was conducted in the United States or Great Britain, primarily with infants from middle-class families. It is therefore unknown how variations in experience as a result of culture, language, or SES contribute to this development or children's reliance on one kind of cue versus another. From the core knowledge perspective, the use of geometric information is universal. These theorists point to the fact that nonhuman animals, such as rats, as well as children and adults from both Western and non-Western cultures, use geometric cues to reorient (Cheng, 1986; Dehaene et al., 2006; Hermer & Spelke, 1996). But, there has been very little work conducted with young children from different cultures and contexts.

BOX 7.2—THE WHOLE INFANT: CRAWLING AND THE DEVELOPMENT OF SPATIAL SKILLS

You might remember the story from Chapter 1 (and other chapters) of Alison who crawled when she was about 6 months old, and when she first crawled she would bump her head into the coffee table. Clearly, Alison's crawling ability was ahead of her spatial skills. She had the motor skill and physical strength to move her body around, but she didn't have the spatial skills to recognize that she might bump her head or how to move her body in ways that would allow her to avoid that coffee table. We also talked about Joseph Campos's work on how infants' understanding of depth seems to develop with crawling experience (see Chapter 5). Both examples show how crawling experience seems to contribute to the development of infants' spatial skills. Indeed, many studies have shown that infants with more experience crawling demonstrate more advanced spatial skills than their less mobile or newly mobile peers.

For example, crawling may help infants orient themselves to a space (Acredolo et al., 1984; Campos et al., 2000; Kermoian & Campos, 1988). As infants crawl, they have experience observing changes in their environment as they move, perhaps providing them with input that shapes their developing orienting abilities. In one study, Melissa Clearfield (2004) recruited U.S. 8- and 11-month-old infants with varying levels of crawling experience. After watching an experimenter hide a toy, the infants were allowed to search for it. Infants with at least 6 weeks of crawling experience were more likely to find the toy than infants with less crawling experience. This suggests that infants who had more experience crawling seemed to be better able to orient themselves to a new space.

Crawling may also be related to other spatial skills. A number of studies suggests that crawling is related to the development of mental rotation skills (Frick & Möhring, 2013; Gerhard & Schwarzer, 2018; Schwarzer, Freitag, & Schum, 2013; Schwarzer, Freitag, Buckel, et al., 2013). Gudrun Schwarzer and her colleagues compared crawling and non-crawling German infants on their mental rotation ability, or how well they recognized an object when seen from a distinct viewing angle. Using a habituation procedure, they found that 9-month-old infants who had at least 9 weeks of crawling experience were more advanced in their mental rotation of images (similar to that in Figure 7.2) than were 9-month-old infants with less crawling experience (Gerhard-Samunda et al., 2021).

Why do these associations arise between crawling and advances in infants' spatial abilities? Theoretical perspectives like dynamic systems or developmental cascades emphasize that the ability to self-locomote by crawling provides infants with ample experience viewing objects and their environments from different visual perspectives. Thus, crawling influences the *input* infants have to represent objects in space. In addition, crawling requires infants to check their location in relation to their destination, which provides input into how to keep track of where they are in space. Kasey Soska, Scott Robinson, and Karen Adolph (2015) examined video recordings of infants crawling in their homes and in the laboratory. Infants were encouraged to crawl down a walkway to a parent, who enticed them to crawl in a straight path by holding a toy or food. Even so, infants did not crawl in a linear path. Instead, as they crawled, they would pause their crawling and shift to a sitting position, doing so as much as 6 times per minute!

Why do infants suddenly stop crawling to sit? The answer is not clear, but Soska and his colleagues think it is because sitting allows infants to view their environment more easily than from their crawling stance. When sitting, their head is upright and they can look around without craning their neck. When in a crawling position, infants have to awkwardly bend their neck to look around. However, sitting from a crawling position does not necessarily give the infant a view of what they were crawling toward. Instead, when sitting from crawling, infants often are facing a different direction than the direction they were facing when crawling, often as much as 180 degrees difference. To resume to their initial destination, infants must survey their environment and adjust their position to continue along their original path. This behavior—crawling, sitting, looking around, adjusting, and then crawling again—gives infants ample practice in noting their environment from different perspectives and then repositioning themselves to resume crawling in the direction they had initially intended. When this amount of practice is summed, it comes as no surprise that infants who crawl advance in several aspects of their object and spatial perception.

Check Your Learning

1. Explain the difference between using an egocentric versus allocentric frame of reference.

2. Why did Piaget believe infants only used one kind of frame of reference? Which frame of reference was this, and why did Piaget propose a reliance on this frame of reference?

3. Can infants less than 12 months of age use external cues in their environment to encode a location? What role does familiarity of the environment play?

4. Do infants use geometric cues for orientation over other types of cues?

INFANTS' DEVELOPING UNDERSTANDING OF NUMBER

At about 20 months, all of our six infants loved to count. Alison, for example, would glee-fully read a counting book with pictures of dogs, pointing to each animal and saying a num-ber. However, her points and labels were not coordinated—she would point to each of three dogs and say, "One, two, three, four, five," sometimes when her finger was on the page and sometimes when it was in mid-air. She understood that she was supposed to say the number names—she even knew the sequence—and that she was supposed to point to each object she was "counting." But she clearly did not understand how that pointing and saying the number names was related. Carter also enjoyed counting, but he also displayed a misunderstanding of counting and numbers. He would hold up his chubby hand and raise one finger and say, "One!" Then he would raise another finger and say "two" and then raise all five fingers and say, "three, four, 91, 92, 93, 96!"

These early counting errors are universal and suggest that learning about numbers is hard. In fact, the concept of "number" is very abstract. Consider different instances of a number: You can have four members of your family, four rules, or four cookies. Each of these sets may contain four items, but this is the only thing they have in common. It is not surprising, therefore, that children make mistakes when they are learning about number. However, number is one of the domains specified by the core knowledge theory to be innate and learned using innate domain specific skills. Thus researchers have been interested in whether or not infants are sensitive to number, despite the fact that toddlers and young preschoolers have difficulty counting.

How Do We Test Infants' Sensitivity to Number?

Given that number is such an abstract feature of sets, how can we test whether infants are sen-sitive to number, or whether they have some understanding of how many things are present? In the 1980s, researchers began to use habituation to ask whether infants are sensitive to dif-ferences in number. The idea was this: Would infants notice that a series of arrays were only alike in terms of the number of items presented? If so, infants' looking should habituate, or decrease over trials, and increase when they are subsequently shown an array that had a different number of items. In one of the first studies to take this approach, Prentice Starkey and Robert Cooper (1980) found that U.S. infants between 4 and 7 months discriminated between arrays with small numbers (two vs. three), but not arrays with larger numbers of items (four vs. six). Other researchers have used a **change detection task** as a way to measure infants' sensitivity to the number of items in a visual array. This task was based on the short-term memory task we described in Chapter 6. Infants are shown two stimulus streams, side by side. In each stream, an array of dots is presented briefly—sometimes for just ½ second—then it disappears for a fraction of a second and then the array reappears. This happens over and over again for many seconds. But, the array is not the same each time it reappears. Sometimes it has the same dots only arranged differently. Sometimes it has bigger or smaller dots. And sometimes the number of dots changes. Researchers ask if infants prefer to watch a stream in which the number of dots changes when compared to an array in which the number of dots stays the same but changes in the size of the dots or the arrangement of the dots. For example, using this procedure, Ariel Starr, Melissa Libertus, and Elizabeth Brannon (2013) found that U.S. 6-month-old infants discriminated one versus three dots and one versus two dots but not two versus three dots.

Other methods ask whether infants understand something more abstract about number. For example, people have probed whether infants recognize that two different kinds of stimuli, such as a series of sounds and an image of objects, have the same number. That is, do infants notice the *match* in number between two very different kinds of stimuli? This is called *cross-modal matching*. Prentice Starkey, Elizabeth Spelke, and Rochelle Gelman (1990) found that U.S. 7-month-old infants matched the number of drum beats they heard with the number of objects presented in an image. Infants heard a sequence of two or three drum beats and then saw two images side by side: One image had two objects, and the other had three objects. When infants heard two drum beats, they looked more at the image with two objects and when they heard three drum beats, they looked more at the image with three objects. Similarly, Kerry Jordan and Elizabeth Brannon (2006) found that U.S. 7-month-old infants also matched the number of voices they heard and the number of faces they saw. This cross-modal matching suggests that infants recognized something very abstract about the number of sounds and the number of objects seen. Thus, this research suggests that at least by 7 months, infants recognize the *match* between two sets that are the same only in terms of number.

What Underlies Infants' Sensitivity to Number?

At this point you might conclude that infants are obviously sensitive to number. After all, we have just described several studies using different procedures showing that infants discriminate between sets that differ in number, and they match stimuli in different modalities that are the same in number. Many researchers would agree with your conclusion. However, not all scientists agree that infants are actually responding to *number* per se and not some other feature of the stimuli.

Recall that number is one of the domains that core knowledge theorists believe is innate. Because rats and monkeys also can discriminate between different numbers, core knowledge theorists argue that some understanding of number is part of human's evolutionary history. Humans and other animals needed to keep track of number in order to survive. For researchers who have this perspective, infants are born with a mental mechanism that they can use to represent and reason about number (Wynn, 1998).

The core knowledge theorists argue that there are two different number systems. Studies using habituation and change detection procedures show that although infants are sensitive to precise differences between small sets (e.g., two vs. three), they have more difficulty discriminating between arrays with large numbers of items. It isn't the case that infants can *never* tell the difference between arrays that contain more than three items; it seems that when there are more items in the arrays, infants only discriminate between them if the larger array has at least twice as many items as the smaller array (Xu & Spelke, 2000). For example, U.S. 6-month-old infants can discriminate between arrays of 8 and 16 dots but don't seem to be able to tell the difference between arrays that have 8 and 12 dots. With large numbers, infants seem to *approximate* number and discriminate sets that are very different. Consider seeing two flocks of geese in the sky.

If there were many geese in both flocks and they only differed by a few geese, you might have difficulty determining which flock had more geese. But, if one flock had 30 geese and the other had 15, you probably could tell that they were different even if you didn't know precisely how many geese were in each flock. Thus, researchers have argued that infants (and adults) have *two* distinct number systems: one system for keeping track of the precise number of items in small arrays and a second system for approximating how many items are in large arrays (Feigenson et al., 2004). The point is that for these theorists, infants are actually responding to *number*.

Other theorists are more skeptical about whether infants' responding to these arrays reflects a sensitivity to number. Specifically, it is impossible for two sets to differ *only* in number. Consider two sequences of drum beats, one that has two drum beats and one that has three drum beats. If the drum beats are the same length and are spaced out in the same way, then the three–drum beat sequence will be longer in duration than the two–drum beat sequence. If we try to make the two sequences the same length, then the drum beats in the two sequences will not be the same—each drum beat in the three-beat sequence will be shorter or closer together (or both) than the drum beats in the two-beat sequence. The same is true for images. Consider two stimuli, one with two items and the other with three items. If the items are the same size, there will be less white space on the three-item display, more surface area will be taken up by the items, and there are (probably) more edges and corners. We can vary the sizes of the objects to try to equate these variables, but then the objects will be different sizes. We can spread apart and squish together the items, so the arrays don't vary in things like how much space there is between the items, but this means that larger and smaller sets will differ in some other way. The point is that sets of items that differ in number also always differ in other ways that infants might notice. Some researchers have argued that infants respond to these differences, and not number, when they discriminate between two sets that differ in number. In fact, perhaps noticing differences in area, edges, duration, and so on is what helps infants learn about number.

This question—whether infants are responding to number or other variables—has been one of the biggest questions about infants' number understanding. Melissa Clearfield and Kelly Mix (1999) showed that U.S. 6- to 8-month-old infants who were habituated to arrays of two or three squares responded when the contour length changed (i.e., the amount of edge around all the squares in the display) but not when number changed. Lisa Feigenson, Susan Carey, and Elizabeth Spelke (2002) found that U.S. 7-month-old infants who were habituated to one large or two small objects responded to a change in number but not changes in continuous variables, such as area. Others have also shown that infants respond to number and not area when the arrays are large (e.g., 8 vs. 16) (Brannon et al., 2004). In general, this question is still not answered. Different results are obtained depending on aspects of the procedure and the stimuli. What is clear is that by 6 or 7 months of age, infants are sensitive to some aspect of the quantitative differences—number of items, area, amount of edges—in these kinds of stimuli.

The Development of Numerical Reasoning Beyond the First Year

This section began with stories about our infants "counting" before their second birthdays. However, the research we have discussed up to now has focused on the emergence of numerical abilities before infants are even 1 year old. Given that Alison and Carter were not great at

GIRL COUNTING: A young child counting on her fingers.
iStock/MachineHeadz

counting at 20 months, it seems that despite any understanding of number that emerges in the first year, children's numerical understanding continues to develop beyond their first birthday. Indeed, even when children enter kindergarten their counting abilities are quite variable, and children's understanding of number develops well into childhood.

However, we know much less about children's developing understanding of number between infancy and the beginning of counting. Like Alison and Carter, children begin to "count" even before they are 3. Researchers have asked about the development of number ability during this age range by asking children to count, asking children to give an experimenter (or puppet) a certain number of objects, and to report how many objects are present. These tasks are very hard for young children. Karen Wynn (1990) found that when children around 2 years of age were asked to count, they performed like Alison and Carter—they repeated a list of number names and they pointed to objects as they counted. But it was not until sometime after the age of 3 that children seemed to understand the connection between counting and "how many" items are present. Younger children did not (necessarily) repeat the last number name in response to "how many," and they did not respond correctly when asked to give a specific number of items (e.g., Can you give me two?). Similarly, Barbara Sarnecka and Susan Carey (2008) found that U.S. children's performance in these tasks increased between the ages of 2 and 4. However, they also found that early in this age range, children begin to know some subsets of numbers; for example, they may know what two is or what three is. Only later do they understand that the last number said in counting is the number of items present. Thus, learning to count, and about number in general, during the toddler and preschool years is not simply learning how to say number names in order.

Children's learning to count is not universal, however, and depends on what language children learn when counting. Languages differ in how quantity is represented and in number names. One way languages differ is in how plurals are marked, or how you indicate that there is more than one of something. In English, we often (but not always) add an "s" sound at the end of nouns when we refer to more than one of something—one shoe, two shoes, one cookie, two cookies. This aspect of our language may help children learn that the number of items is important. Cynthia Lukyanenko and Cynthia Fisher (2016) found that 2- to 3-year-old English-speaking American children matched English phrases that either referenced a single object or multiple (e.g., apple vs. apples) with pictures depicting single or multiple objects. But other languages mark plurals in other ways. For example, Basque and Spanish mark plurals in different ways, and Spanish-speaking 2- to 3-year-old children showed evidence of better understanding of number than their Basque-speaking peers (Villarroel et al., 2011).

Languages also differ in how transparent their number names are. Mandarin number names, for example, are more transparent than English number names (e.g., the number "11" in Mandarin is "ten one" whereas in English it is "eleven"). This difference has led some to propose that children learning Mandarin should be better counters than children learning English. Indeed, when children are 4 or 5, Mandarin-speaking Chinese children can count higher than English-speaking American children (Miller et al., 1995). But, comparisons of Chinese 2- and 3-year-old children learning Mandarin and American 2- and 3-year-old children learning English showed that the American English-speaking children were slightly more advanced than their Chinese Mandarin-speaking counterparts (Le Corre et al., 2016). Thus, the advantage of Mandarin more transparently coding numbers might help children once they have the basic idea of counting, but it does not seem to give them an advantage when they are first beginning to count.

Even before children begin to count themselves, they develop the ability to *recognize* counting. For example, Virginia Slaughter, Shoji Itakura, Aya Kutsuki, and Michael Siegal (2011) presented children with videos in which a person pointed to fish on a display while saying number names. Sometimes they counted correctly (i.e., by saying a number whenever they touched a fish) and sometimes they counted incorrectly (i.e., by touching the fish at random times while saying the numbers). By 18 months, English-learning Australian infants and Japanese-learning Japanese infants preferred the correct counting if the counting words were in their "own" familiar language. That is, English-learning infants looked longer at correct counting in English than incorrect counting in English, and Japanese-learning infants looked longer at correct counting in Japanese than at incorrect counting in Japanese. They watched the correct and incorrect counting videos for the same amount of time if the counting was in an unfamiliar language (e.g., English learners hearing Japanese or Japanese learners hearing English) or if the number names were replaced with beeps. This suggests that when they heard counting in the familiar language they were learning, they could distinguish correct from incorrect counting, even though they were not yet able to count themselves. Younger 15-month-old English-learning Australian infants did not notice the difference between correct and incorrect counting, even in English. Thus, sometime in the second year, children begin to recognize counting when it is in a familiar language. In summary, number understanding develops throughout infancy and early childhood. Although there has been a significant focus on number abilities in infancy, there are considerable changes in children's numerical abilities between the ages of 1 and 3.

Check Your Learning

1. Describe the two tasks designed to assess infants' understanding of number.

2. Explain the difference in infants' ability to discriminate small sets (e.g., 1 vs. 2) versus larger sets of number (e.g., 12 vs. 20).

3. What is cross-modal matching? How has it been used in assessing infants' understanding of number?

4. What information besides number might infants be using to discriminate between sets of different sizes?

5. Provide one example of how children's understanding of number develops after their first birthday.

6. Describe how language may support children's understanding of number.

SUMMARY

An understanding of the physical world develops considerably over the first years of life. Although there are very different theoretical approaches explaining this development, there is little doubt that infants and toddlers come to understand objects, space, and number. These developmental changes are significant and allow infants to go from a newborn with rudimentary understanding of how the world works to a 3-year-old who will look for hidden objects, accurately count small numbers of objects, and understand how to put one object on another object. Understanding in each of these areas continues to develop after the third birthday, but this chapter has revealed both the amazing early abilities that allow infants to develop this sophisticated understanding. Finally, although these early abilities and developments may be universal to children around the world, the fact that most of this research has been conducted with Western, English-learning infants limits our understanding of any differences that may exist due to culture, parenting, or language.

KEY TERMS

accommodation

allocentric frame of reference

assimilation

causal perception

change detection task

circular reactions

core domains

core knowledge

domain general

domain specific

egocentric

egocentric frame of reference

mental rotation

more knowledgeable other

object permanence

object retrieval task

perception-action

scheme

sensorimotor stage

sensory register

sociocultural theory

violation of expectation

zone of proximal development

REVIEW QUESTIONS

1. Describe the major theories that explain infants' developing understanding of objects, space, and living things.

2. What does research tell us about how infants' understanding of objects change over the first 2 years?

3. What information do infants use to remember the location of objects and navigate their environment? How does this change across the first 3 years?

4. Compare how infants' understanding of number is distinct for small versus large sets of numbers.

CRITICAL THINKING QUESTIONS

1. What commonalities can you identify about the infants' learning about objects, space, and number?

2. What evidence is there that supports the core knowledge theory of the development in these domains?

3. Would you describe the difference between changes in 3-month-old and 12-month-old infants' understanding of the world as only a change in how much they know? Explain your reasoning.

4. Why does infants' performance on object permanence or spatial orientation tasks differ when infants are asked to reach versus look in tasks?

5. Consider infants with motor or visual impairments. How might their understanding of objects, space, or number differ from infants without these impairments? How might their understanding of these domains be the same?

8 THE DEVELOPMENT OF PLAY AND SYMBOLS

When Edwin was a toddler, he loved to play with his toy kitchen. He loved everything about it, and he especially loved playing with toy food. When he was between 12 and 18 months, every day, he would wake up, have breakfast, and arrange the food toys by color on the coffee table in the living room of his family's small suburban house. As he got older, his strategy for arranging the food toys progressed as his cognitive development progressed; now, he not only arranged them by color but by category as well, putting the fruits together, vegetables together, and meats together. By the age of 3 and 4, he had an elaborate organizational system that looked like a perfect rainbow of plastic delicacies that took up the entire living room floor. The problem was, by this time, Edwin also had a little brother—Charlie. And Charlie loved Edwin's food toys too. But as an infant, not only did he not understand Edwin's elaborate categorization system, but he also didn't understand that the food toys were just *toys*. More specifically, Edwin's food toys are replica toys—they are symbols for the real objects they represent. But instead of treating them like symbols, or toys, Charlie always tested out whether they were the real thing—by taking a bite. Soon, nearly all of Edwin's food toys were either missing a small bite-sized chunk, or they had teeth or gum marks commemorating the place where Charlie first tested out his developing symbolic understanding (see next photo).

The way in which infants play changes over the course of the first several years of life along with developments in their motor, cognitive, and social abilities. Their ability to understand symbols and to play symbolically also develops over the infancy period. Importantly, changes in infant play and developments in symbolic understanding open the door for further developments in children's cognitive and social skills, providing new opportunities to learn about objects and new ways to interact with social partners.

Here we will discuss how children play with objects, including symbolic objects, and how their play facilitates learning. Then we will talk about how infants develop symbolic understanding more generally, which affects development in many other domains, including play, language, and social interactions. More specifically, in this chapter you will learn:

1. *To define* play and describe how it contributes to infant development.

2. *To discuss* how infants develop dual representation and how it affects their symbolic understanding.

3. *To understand* how symbolic understanding affects infants' learning from various media, including pictures, books, and screens.

Edwin's Food Toys, After Charlie Got to Them

THE DEVELOPMENT OF PLAY

Play is a hallmark of infancy and early childhood. Indeed, the famous developmental psychologist Jean Piaget said, "play is the work of childhood," and Jerome Bruner suggests that "play has about it something of the quality of problem-solving, but in a most joyous fashion" (J. Bruner, 1983 p. 61). Human infants—as well as infants of other species—play when they feel happy and secure (Brown, 2009; Graham & Burghardt, 2010; Pellis & Pellis, 2013). As such, play is an indicator of healthy development, emerging when basic needs have been met and in the absence of stress. At the same time, play plays a crucial role in the development of healthy social skills, emotional skills, and advancing cognitive skills (Ginsburg et al., 2007). Through play, infants have the chance to bond with their playmates, practice regulating their emotions, and develop their motor, problem-solving, and communicative skills. In laboratory rats, play, particularly play with others, has been linked to greater connectivity in some brain areas (Burgdorf et al., 2010; M. C. Diamond et al., 1964; Vanderschuren et al., 2016). In fact, the American Academy of Pediatrics urges pediatricians to prescribe play as a necessary part of infants' daily activities (Yogman et al., 2018).

What Is Play?

The claim that play is important relies on the fact that we all know what play is. But it turns out that play is hard to define scientifically. Even without a single definition of play, researchers do agree that **play** is a spontaneous and voluntary activity, which is done for its own sake (rather than to achieve a goal) and is enjoyable (Graham & Burghardt, 2010; Pellegrini, 2009; Sutton-Smith, 2008). This is a very broad way of thinking about play and can include everything from an infant investigating their own hand and a child making up math problems to solve, to an adult playing a card game with a friend. In each case, the individual is engaged in something they find enjoyable, and they are engaged in the activity for the pleasure of doing it and not for the purpose of achieving a goal.

Infants' play changes as their motor skills, attention, memory, and categorization skills develop. For example, at 2 months, Diego loved the colorful ribbons that hung from the frame of the crossbars of a playmat that hung over his head, but he did not yet have the coordination and skill to reach out and grab them. His play behavior was limited to looking at the ribbons and smiling as they dangled overhead. At 4 months, once Diego's reaching and grasping abilities had developed, he was delighted when he could finally grasp the ribbons and was even more delighted if he could manage to lift his head up and place the ribbons in his mouth. Once he began to roll over onto his stomach at 5 months, Diego learned that if he pulled hard on the ribbons, they would jingle. At 6 months, when he could sit up, he could grasp the stuffed animals dangling from the bars above, and by 8 months Diego learned to make those animals squeak by squeezing them.

Clearly, Diego was playing. His actions with the ribbons and toy animals were voluntary, spontaneous, and, as shown by his sudden laughs, incredibly fun. But this play also helped him to learn about the world. His time spent playing allowed him to realize that objects were not simply interesting in their own right (or for their ease of mouthing) but also that objects have other properties or functions. Not only did Diego's play change with the development of other abilities, but his play also shaped his understanding of the world. Once he could pull on the ribbons to make the playpen jingle or squeeze the animals to make them squeak, Diego was able to gain important information that he could use to learn about the effect he had on the world. This almost certainly contributed to the developmental trajectory described by Piaget, which we discussed in Chapter 7, and the development of the self, which we will discuss in Chapter 10.

For researchers, infants' play serves as a window into their development. How infants engage in play reflects their motor, socioemotional, language, and cognitive skills. Researchers and clinicians can evaluate infant play to identify which children may be at risk for particular kinds of developmental delays (Campbell et al., 2018; Kaur et al., 2015; Molteno et al., 2010). But, as we just described, play is not just a reflection of children's development; it also *contributes* to their development. In fact, play has been used in interventions to promote the development of particular skills (Clearfield, 2019; Libertus et al., 2016; Needham, 2000; Needham et al., 2017; Schröder et al., 2020; Slone et al., 2018). Remember the "sticky mittens" procedure we described in Chapter 5? In that procedure, infants wear mittens with Velcro and they can pick up toys (also with Velcro) by swiping them with the mittens. Those studies showed how facilitating very young infants' play with objects influenced their perceptual development. Another study shows how play can have even more wide-ranging effects. In this study, mothers of 12-month-old infants in Brazil were encouraged to play with their infants. The infants of these mothers showed greater gains on measures of learning and motor skill than infants whose mothers had not participated in play (Eickmann et al., 2007). Results from such interventions highlight how play encourages and facilitates many aspects of development.

Importantly, play develops too, as we saw in the example of Diego's play with his play mat. Much of the research on play in infancy is about object exploration. This is probably not a surprise to anyone who has spent time with infants. During infancy and early childhood, infants engage with objects in many ways. And their play with objects changes over time as they develop new motor abilities and a new understanding of objects themselves. In addition, as infants become able to manipulate objects in new ways, it helps them explore new object properties and develop more sophisticated understanding of those properties (Bushnell & Boudreau, 1993).

But play changes in other ways as well, especially during the toddler years. Specifically, researchers have also been interested in the emergence of functional play and symbolic play. These types of play reflect the infant going beyond the physical properties of objects and beginning to understand and explore more abstract properties. Functional play involves relating objects to each other and recognizing their function. For example, infants and toddlers begin to stack blocks or stir spoons in pots. Symbolic play involves using one object to stand for another, as when a child holds a banana to their head and pretends to talk into it, using the banana to symbolize a phone.

Object Exploration

Although infants engage in play before they can consistently reach out and grab objects (e.g., by making sounds with their mouths, visually exploring their hands), once they develop the motor skills to reach and grasp, they begin to engage in object play. Infants engage their full senses with this type of play. They mouth, touch, and visually examine toys. Initially, as infants are just beginning to develop the motor skills to reach for objects, their exploration of objects is restricted to their grasping and mouthing (Rochat, 1989). However, as infants' fine motor skills develop, their exploration of objects shifts from predominantly placing objects in their mouths at 2 months to also spending more time looking at the objects they are holding at 4 months and older (although they also still love to put objects in their mouths). At 4 months, infants also begin to explore objects by fingering, or touching and scanning objects with their fingertips as they grasp the object in their other hand. Some aspects of infants' interest in objects appear to be universal, as they are observed not only in Western samples of infants but were also observed when evaluating the social play of a group of !Kung infants, a hunter-gatherer society, in the 1960s and 1970s (Bakeman et al., 1990).

Infants' ability to sit independently also influences their object exploration (see Chapter 6). Kasey Soska and Karen Adolph (2014) found that U.S. infants explored objects more when sitting than when on their backs or stomachs. In addition, infants who can achieve sufficient postural control to sit independently have both of their hands free to explore objects, transfer them between hands, and rotate the objects more than infants who have yet to achieve this postural milestone and must use one arm to stabilize their sitting posture (Soska et al., 2010). Thus, when infants become able to sit independently, their exploration of objects changes. As we saw in Chapter 5, however, there is large cultural variation for when infants achieve milestones such as sitting independently (Karasik et al., 2015). Thus, children growing up in different cultural contexts will have different opportunities to engage in object exploration and play.

Infants often explore and engage with objects during interactions with their mother or another caregiver. Indeed, the triadic interaction between mother (or other caregiver), infant, and object is thought to be important for many aspects of social, cognitive, and linguistic development (see Chapter 9 on joint attention and language). Studies of infants from Western, middle-class families have shown that mothers engage in object play with their infants, responding contingently to their infants' actions (de Barbaro et al., 2016; Tamis-LeMonda et al., 2013) and offering labels for those objects (Clerkin et al., 2017; Tamis-LeMonda et al., 2019). In addition, these interactions change how infants play across development. For example, Kaya de Barbaro

CARTER: Once infants can sit independently, both hands are free to explore and manipulate objects, like in this photo of Carter.

and her colleagues (de Barbaro et al., 2016) found that although U.S. 4-month-old infants mostly looked at objects held by their mothers during mother–infant toy play, by 6 to 8 months infants begin to divide their attention between objects they themselves are holding and objects being held by their mother. Thus, these U.S. mother–infant dyads showed how interactions around object exploration changed as infants' abilities changed. In particular, infants' ability to examine objects and share them with a caregiver shows their maturing ability to maintain, select, and shift attention.

Importantly, interactions between caregivers, infants, and objects also vary by culture. Rufan Luo and Catherine Tamis-LeMonda (2016) studied U.S. mother–infant dyads from African American, Dominican immigrant, or Mexican immigrant backgrounds. All three groups of mothers changed how they engaged in object play with their children between 14 to 36 months, providing different levels of instruction and assistance across age. But the mothers from different backgrounds also differed in their approach. Mexican mothers used more nonverbal strategies, such as gestures, whereas African American and Dominican mothers used more verbal strategies to help their toddlers. Even larger differences are observed when comparing mothers from even more diverse cultural backgrounds. One study examined face-to-face interactions between mothers from rural Gujarat, India; Nso mothers from rural Cameroon; and mothers from urban Athens, Greece, and their 9-month-old infants (Abels et al., 2017).

The Gujarati mothers engaged in less face-to-face interaction than the other mothers, likely reflecting the fact that they come from a cultural community in which these kinds of interactions between mothers and infants are discouraged and infants are more likely to play with someone other than their mother. This suggests that how infants and toddlers engage with their caregivers in object play is determined by multiple factors.

But do these opportunities to explore objects have any benefits to infants other than satisfying their curiosity or fulfilling that overpowering desire to put everything in their mouths? The answer to this question is a resounding yes. As we have seen throughout this book, the time Western infants spend holding and exploring objects—and, in particular, how much they look at objects as they explore them—is related to their attention to object appearance and their understanding of objects, such as recognizing the boundaries between two objects and appreciating that objects are often three-dimensional (Baumgartner & Oakes, 2013; Needham, 2000; Soska & Adolph, 2014).

In addition, infants' object play seems to be part of a cascade that determines other aspects of development. For example, in one study, 8-month-old infants in Germany were given experience every day for 2 weeks with one of two kinds of toys. Half of the infants got daily experience with blocks, and half of the infants got daily experience with book reading. The infants who were given experience with blocks were better at detecting differences in line drawings (Schröder et al., 2020). Thus, more time playing with objects facilitated aspects of infants' perceptual development.

Differences in infants' developing object exploration also seem to be associated with risks in other aspects of development. For example, Maninderjit Kaur and her colleagues (2015) found that U.S. infants who had an autistic older sibling (and thus the infant had higher likelihood of being autistic) engaged in object play differently than children of the same age who had no family history of autism. In particular, when and how much mouthing children used differed. During object exploration, 6-month-old infants with autistic siblings mouthed less than did infants without autistic siblings. However, at older ages, the infants with autistic siblings mouthed more than the infants without autistic siblings, who no longer mouthed objects as their predominant modality of exploring objects. Thus, differences in object exploration may be an early indicator of developmental differences that are related to a later diagnosis of autism.

Melissa Clearfield and her colleagues (2014) compared object exploration in children of higher and lower income households. A number of studies have shown that children from lower income households experience more stress and tend to be behind their peers from higher income families in language and cognitive abilities (Noble et al., 2012). Clearfield and her colleagues found that between 6 and 12 months, infants from low-income families in the United States showed a less dramatic increase in manual exploration of objects than did their peers from higher income homes. Infants from low SES homes did not finger, rotate, or transfer objects to each hand to the same degree as infants from the higher income homes. Likewise, another study showed that toddlers in India from low SES homes demonstrated less sophisticated play than toddlers from middle SES homes (Mohan & Bhat, 2022). Altogether, this work demonstrates that differences in how infants play with objects might be indicative of other developmental differences.

Functional Play

As they develop, infants' object exploration shifts from a focus on a single object (Bushnell & Boudreau, 1993), to exploring more than one object at a time and experimenting with how those objects relate to each other. We call this **functional play** (Belsky & Most, 1981; Bourgeois et al., 2005; Fenson et al., 1976). As a 7-month-old infant, Tesalia would often play with a set of nesting cups in the tub. She would hold one of the cups in her hands and study it as she rotated it and allowed water to splash over it, a classic example of object exploration. A couple of months later, her play with the cups began to include holding one cup in each hand and trying to fit one cup within the other, an example of functional play. Functional play allows infants to develop an appreciation for the *function* of everyday objects (i.e., how those objects can be used) and provides an important basis for using objects as tools (Lockman & Kahrs, 2017; Rachwani et al.,

DIEGO: Diego engaging in functional play by inserting one box into another.

2020). In U.S. infants, this kind of play emerges at about 8 to 9 months and continues to grow in complexity over the first year and beyond (Bakeman et al., 1990; Fenson et al., 1976; Lifter & Bloom, 1989).

The first instances of functional play involve the infant relating two objects, but not necessarily in the manner intended for the designed functions of the objects. Thus, early functional play is exploratory and does not necessarily mean that children know what objects are for or how they are used. For example, an infant might place the lid of a play pot on top of a toy plate. Later, functional play reflects more knowledge of what objects are used for. Any older child would demonstrate their knowledge of the intended relation between the lid and pot by placing the pot lid on top of the pot.

We can see children's functional play in their object constructions, such as building towers by stacking blocks or nesting one box in another larger box (see previous photo). Marianella Casasola and her colleagues (2017) found that when given a set of nesting cups, U.S. 8-month-old infants did not show any evidence of functional play. They tended to bang the cups on the table (with much gusto and glee), but they did not "nest" the cups or blocks. Twelve- and 18-month-old infants, in contrast, did show functional play, by inserting one object in another or by stacking the objects, and the oldest toddlers were even more successful than the 12-month-old infants. Judy DeLoache and her colleagues (1985) gave a group of U.S. children between 18 and 42 months an even harder task. Children were presented with a set of five cups to nest. Nesting all five5 cups required children to place cups within each other in the order of size. Eighteen-month-old toddlers could nest a few cups, but they were unable to solve the problem of how to nest all five cups. By 42 months, children were successful at nesting all five cups. Further, these older children not only could nest the set of five cups from smallest to largest, but they were also more sophisticated in how they corrected their mistakes. When younger children realized they made a mistake, they would often try to force (unsuccessfully) a larger cup into a smaller one. Older children were much more likely to identify where the cup fit within the series of cups and correct the error efficiently. Thus, children's problem-solving skills for this type of nesting task improves from infancy until children are 3 or 4 years old, as captured by their functional play.

Other aspects of functional play, such as fitting objects into openings, like when playing with a shape sorter or puzzle, also develops during late infancy and the toddler years. For example, Helena Örnkloo and Claes von Hofsten (2007) gave Swedish toddlers boxes with lids that had different shaped openings (circle, square, rectangle), along with blocks of the same shapes. Fourteen-month-old toddlers indiscriminately tried to fit an object through any opening, making no attempts to orient the object to align with its corresponding shape. But by 22 to 26 months, toddlers were pros at this task: They rotated the objects to match the orientation of the opening and they did so even *before* placing the objects into the opening. Thus, during their second year, children begin to adjust objects to align with openings, showing gains in their ability to recognize how the shape of objects relate to one another.

Importantly, the development of functional play in early childhood contributes to children's developing tool use. For example, over time toddlers' grasping and orienting of objects becomes specialized to the shape of an object (Jung et al., 2018). This means that as children approach their third birthday, they become better at grasping the functionally relevant portion of an object, like the handle of a spoon. Functional play also allows children to discover *novel* uses of objects. Karri Neldner and her collaborators (2020) observed that 2- to 5-year-old children from Australia and from the San Bushmen communities in South Africa invented uses for novel tools without ever seeing another person show them the tools' potential uses. These innovations are likely made possible by giving children time to play with objects, explore them, and experiment with how they can be used in relation to other objects.

Functional play in infancy and early childhood also seems to tell us something about differences in how children are developing. Aspects of functional play in infancy and early childhood predict functional play and other areas of development later on. For example, in a racially and ethnically diverse U.S. sample, Emily Marcinowski and her colleagues (2019) observed that the constructions children made when they were infants—by stacking or nesting cups, for example—predicted their ability to make more advanced constructions when they were older. In fact, they not only found that the quantity and quality of children's object constructions increased with age, but also that infants' object constructions at 10 months predicted their constructions at 24 months, showing continuity in how infants manipulate objects to create particular types of construction.

Symbolic Play

Symbolic play involves using objects, actions, and people to stand for something else (Lillard et al., 2013; McCune-Nicolich, 1981; Tamis-LeMonda et al., 1992; Weisberg, 2015). Indeed, a **symbol** is something that stands for something other than itself. We call that other "something" the symbol's **referent**. For example, a toddler may hold a banana to their ear, pretending to have a conversation as though the banana is a phone (see next photo). In this case the banana is the symbol and the phone is the referent.

Symbolic play develops through several stages over the course of infancy and early childhood, reflecting the child's increasing ability to consider multiple objects, actions, and perspectives at one time. The first step toward symbolic play is symbolic gestures, which emerge late in the first year or early in the second year (McCune-Nicolich, 1981; Orr & Geva, 2015). These first symbolic gestures are self-directed (e.g., pretending to feed oneself, pretending to talk on the phone) and often involve producing actions on familiar objects (e.g., pretending to eat with a spoon).

Symbolic play rapidly becomes more complex over time. In a longitudinal study of a group of Israeli infants, Edna Orr and Ronny Geva (2015) found that at 8 months, infants performed single actions on single objects (e.g., holding a block to the ear, like a telephone); by 10 months, infants performed several actions on a single object (e.g., pretending to drink from a bowl and putting on one's head like a hat); and by 12 months, infants engaged with multiple objects, sometimes performing a single action and other times performing multiple actions (e.g., placing several objects in a pot, stirring them, and putting the lid on).

When children use one object to stand for another object—such as the child in the next photo using a banana to stand for a phone—it is called **object substitution**. This kind of play requires that children keep in mind two representations of the same object, the pretend one (the phone) and the actual one (the banana). Although infants may perform appropriate gestures on

Child Using a Banana as a Phone
iStock/khalus

a realistic toy or object, this kind of object substitution emerges in the second year in U.S. children (McCune-Nicolich, 1981).

Across development, children's object substitution becomes less dependent on using objects that are very similar to the "real" objects. Very young children may pretend to talk on a toy telephone or drink from a cup, whereas slightly older children will use more varied objects as telephones or cups, sometimes substituting an object that is very different from the "real" object. Moreover, when children reach 3 years, they may even begin to pretend in the absence of objects, for example, talking about imaginary companions. When Alison was a preschooler, she had several imaginary friends (conveniently all named Julia) that she would push on the swings in the backyard.

Interestingly, children can engage in symbolic play before they recognize pretense in others. Infants begin to engage spontaneously in pretend play around 18 months, but at that age they do not necessarily recognize when others are engaging in pretend play, especially if the pretend play includes objects that are dissimilar from the objects they are meant to represent (Hopkins et al., 2016). Although they do not always recognize pretend play in others, infants will engage in pretend play if invited to participate in a pretend scenario by another person, for example, pretending to dry a doll that was "wet" or "eating" a bowl of imagined cereal (Bosco et al., 2006; Lillard et al., 2007; Nishida & Lillard, 2007).

As with other forms of play, there are differences in symbolic or pretend play that may be related to developmental outcomes. Some studies have shown that toddlers in Western societies who are later diagnosed as autistic engage in pretend play less frequently than do toddlers who are not later diagnosed as autistic (Baron-Cohen, 1987; Campbell et al., 2018). Thus, the lower levels of pretend play in these children may be an early indicator of differences in neurodevelopment that are related to autism. Engagement in symbolic play is also affected by early experiences. For a minute, let's recall the infants we discussed in Chapter 1 who were raised in Romanian orphanages under conditions of extreme social deprivation. That early social deprivation seemed to influence development leading to pretend play later: Children who were adopted as infants from Romanian orphanages into UK families engaged in less pretend play at 4 years than their peers who were adopted as infants from UK families into other UK families (Kreppner et al., 1999).

The development of symbolic play, or what we sometimes call pretend play, is determined, in part, by interactions with others. There is a high level of symbolic play between 1- to 2-year-old toddlers and their mothers who are Mexican American (Fletcher et al., 2020), U.S. South American Latino immigrants, U.S. Japanese immigrants, and European American heritage (Cote & Bornstein, 2009). Moreover, these interactions are dynamic. Marc Bornstein and colleagues (1999) found that both U.S. and Argentine 20-month-old toddlers adjusted their play based on their mothers' style. Infants whose mothers engaged in more exploratory play with toys did the same, while infants whose mother engaged in more symbolic play engaged more in this type of play.

However, parents from India, Turkey, Thailand, the United States, and Guatemala vary in how much they engage in symbolic play with their children and in their view of how pretend play may contribute to development (Callaghan et al., 2011; Roopnarine, 2011). For example, in Bornstein's study mothers and toddlers in the United States engaged in more exploratory play compared to the Argentine dyads. The Argentine mothers and toddlers spent more of their time engaging in symbolic play. Such differences reflect differences in parenting goals, with U.S. mothers encouraging independence and exploration and Argentine mothers emphasizing the development of interpersonal skills.

It is probably not surprising that symbolic play is also related to language development. After all, symbolic play involves using an object to represent something else, just like words represent things in the world (see Chapter 9). In the months before their first birthday, infants start to use symbolic gestures (e.g., pretending to drink from a cup). Children say their first words around their first birthday. At about 13 months, symbolic gestures and language are related in English-learning U.S. infants (Bates et al. 1980). In their Israeli sample, Orr and Geva (2015) found that when children first showed single object play predicted their language milestones.

The connection between gestures and language is so strong in infancy, that Linda Acredolo and Susan Goodwyn made popular "baby signs," or the gestures that infants and their parents use to communicate (Goodwyn et al., 2000). For example, by 12 months, Carter waved his hands back and forth to indicate "all done," Edwin and Charlie put their hands together to signal "more," and Diego used the American Sign Language sign for "help" to let his parents know he needed them to lend a hand.

This link between symbolic play and language is not limited to the emergence of language in infancy (Quinn et al., 2018). In fact, the amount of symbolic play is related to language in the preschool years (Kirkham et al., 2013). There are also other reasons why symbolic play and language development may develop together. Noëlie Creaghe and her colleagues (2021) found that Australian mothers and 18-month-old toddlers took more conversational turns and spent more time engaging with each other including looking at each other when given toys ideal for symbolic play (e.g., play pots) than when given toys ideal for functional play (e.g., hammer). Conversational turns and engagement are important for language development.

BOX 8.1—INFANCY IN REAL LIFE: DO "EDUCATIONAL TOYS" MATTER FOR INFANT LEARNING?

Choosing toys for infants can be overwhelming for parents, family members, and friends (especially friends who don't have kids themselves!). If you live in the United States and you've ever walked down the aisle of a children's toy store or even the toy section of your local department store, you'll find yourself surrounded by toys with flashing lights, toys that play music, and even some that will talk to you as you walk by. With so many choices, many parents and well-wishers flock to toys that boast educational value. Some of these "educational toys" are labeled with names like Mozart and Einstein, suggesting that they can make infants smarter or teach them something new. There are even subscription boxes you can buy that will send you toys each month that are optimally educational for your infant's specific age and stage of development.

Despite technological advancements that make toys these days look state of the art, the concept of educational toys is not new. In the early 19th century, Friedrich Fröbel developed "gifts" for children that were designed to actively engage and cater to development at specific ages. For example, the first gift, intended for infants, was a soft ball appropriately sized for a young child to squish, drop, and roll. The second gift, intended for toddlers, was a wooden sphere and a wooden cube that toddlers could actively explore to learn about shapes. Likewise, in the 1970s, Glenn Doman created "The Better Baby Institute," where he convinced thousands of parents that they could teach their infants and toddlers words, numbers, the alphabet, and even math using flash cards.

With advances in technology, the educational toys available for infants today literally have all the bells and whistles—they talk, they light up, and they spin around. For example, the brand "Baby Einstein" sells a play gym that is similar to the one Diego used as an infant but with 70 sounds and activities. Stacking ring toys now play music and light up. Shape sorters make sounds when the correct shape is inserted in an opening. These toys are marketed as having the ability to teach infants a number of new things—not only about shapes but also about letters, numbers, and colors.

But do these "educational" toys really make infants smarter? According to research, the answer is probably not. In fact, they might even *hinder* learning in several ways. For example, several studies suggest that parents talk less when using electronic toys than when using traditional toys. One study reported that when U.S. infants aged 10 to 16 months played with electronic toys like a baby cell phone, laptop, and talking farm, along with traditional toys like a shape sorter, wooden puzzle, and blocks, parents talked to their infants less and used lower quality language when playing with the electronic toys than with the traditional toys (Sosa, 2016). In another study, U.S. parents who played with an electronic shape-sorter with their 24-month-old toddlers used fewer unique words and fewer spatial words than parents who played with a traditional shape-sorter with their toddlers (Zosh et al., 2015). This is important, as how much parents talk to their infants—and how many unique words they use—predicts children's later word learning and literacy in school in samples collected in the United States (Hart & Risley, 1995). So even in today's high-tech world, sometimes less is more. And if toys talk, parents might think they don't have to, which isn't what's best for infants' learning.

Check Your Learning

1. List the characteristics that define play.

2. What are the three types of play described in the chapter? Define each and explain how they differ from each other.

3. Explain why functional play emerges after object play and why symbolic play emerges after functional play.

SYMBOLIC DEVELOPMENT

Symbolic play is only one aspect of infants' developing symbolic understanding. Indeed, symbolic development allows children to draw pictures, have a mental image, use a word, and read a map. Clearly these are not things that we observe during infancy, but we do see many of them emerge when children are toddlers and young preschoolers. In fact, Piaget, whose theory we discussed in Chapter 7, argued that developing the ability to represent the world symbolically was one of the most important achievements of the infancy period. And although infants are incapable of symbolic thought during the sensorimotor stage (at least according to Piaget), they gradually begin to develop this ability starting between 18 and 24 months of age.

Classic Theories of Symbolic Development

Some of the earliest theories of cognitive development in infancy were focused on how symbolic thought develops. Piaget's definition of the infancy period is that thought is sensorimotor in nature (also see Chapter 7). In other words, infants' thoughts are based only on their actions and sensations, and infants are unable to represent the world mentally. Over the course of the sensorimotor stage, through their interactions with the physical world, infants gradually develop the capacity for mental representations. Thus, for Piaget, infants are presymbolic. When children reach the preoperational stage at about 2 years of age, they have the ability to mentally represent the world, and as a result, they can use words, draw pictures, and engage in pretend play.

Vygotsky had a different view. Whereas Piaget believed that things like being able to use words and draw pictures came after children could represent the world mentally, Vygotsky argued that children's symbolic ability came from internalizing the "tools" of their culture—things like spoken language, writing, and numbers. First children learn to speak or count, for example, and by using those tools, words and numbers later become internalized, symbolic thought. Importantly, however, children can't learn just anything. As we learned in Chapter 7, for Vygotsky, children learn what is in their zone of proximal development. However, what is important to remember is that according to Vygotsky, the use of symbols, such as words and gestures, comes first and are the foundation of symbolic thought.

Object Permanence as a Step Toward Symbolic Thought

According to Piaget, one limitation of sensorimotor thought is that infants do not recognize that objects have a permanent, independent existence. This is in large part because infants do not have the ability to mentally represent the world. In fact, if you have interacted with young infants, you might have noticed their "out of sight, out of mind" reaction. To the relief of many parents, young infants' attention to an unwanted object can be diverted simply by putting the object where the infant can't see it.

Development during the sensorimotor stage represents a gradual shift from purely sensorimotor thought (all about the here and now) to mental representation and the ability to think about objects, people, and things that are not physically present. Although this is not precisely the same thing as symbolic thought, which involves using one thing to stand for another, it is an important aspect of symbolic thought, and for Piaget, it is a precursor to the child's ability to use symbols (e.g., speak words or engage in pretend play).

We can see this shift in children's object permanence, or their behavior toward objects that are hidden (Table 8.1). In the third sensorimotor substage, with secondary circular reactions, infants begin to connect their actions to outside events. However, they still do not understand that objects have independent existences. Piaget described how during this stage, his daughter Lucienne searched for an eraser she had begun to touch before it was fully hidden or for a favorite doll that was only partially hidden by a cloth.

In the fourth substage, beginning when the infants are about 10 months old, each of Piaget's children began searching for fully hidden objects, suggesting a more sophisticated understanding of the existence of objects they could no longer see. During this stage, Piaget argued that infants can now link the visual permanence of objects (where they can see them) with the tactile permanence of objects (where they can touch and manipulate them), but do not yet have complete object permanence. Piaget describes how at 10 ½ months, his daughter Jacqueline successfully found her toy parrot twice in a row when Piaget hid it under her mattress on her right, but when Piaget then hid the parrot on Jacqueline's left, she searched for it to her right. According to Piaget, this behavior, called the **A not B error**, reflects the fact that infants understand the object to be in the last place they found it, not where they had seen it hidden.

TABLE 8.1 ■ Object Permanence Behaviors in Each of Piaget's Six Sensorimotor Substages		
Sensorimotor Stage	**Behavior Toward Hidden Objects**	**Example**
Stages 1 & 2—Reflexive Schemes and Primary Circular Reactions	Infants make no search for hidden objects.	
Stage 3—Secondary Circular Reactions	Infants search for partially hidden, but not fully hidden, objects.	Lucienne searched for an eraser she had begun to touch when it was hidden.
Stage 4—Coordination of Secondary Circular Reactions	Infants search for fully hidden objects but make the A not B error.	Jacqueline successfully found her toy parrot twice in a row when Piaget hid it under her mattress on her right, but when Piaget then hid the toy parrot on Jacqueline's left, she searched for it to her right.
Stage 5—Tertiary Circular Reactions	Infants do not make the A not B error but are unable to follow invisible displacements.	Jacqueline could not find a potato after Piaget put it in a box, then put the box under a rug, and pulled the empty box out from under the rug (after dumping the potato under the rug).
Stage 6—Mental Representation	Infants can find objects even after invisible displacements.	Jacqueline looks for a coin under the rug, after not finding it in her father's hand (where she last saw it).

In the fifth stage, infants are no longer fooled by switching hiding locations, and they successfully find their toys in location B, even when they had previously found them in location A. Piaget thought this was because infants are starting to dissociate the object from their own actions on the object, an early form of mental representation. But, if the infant couldn't actually see the hiding, they fail. So, 18-month-old Jacqueline observed Piaget put a potato in a box, then put the box under a rug, and pull the box out empty (because he dumped the potato out when it was under the rug). Poor Jacqueline looked only in the box and couldn't figure out what happened to the potato.

Finally, in the sixth stage, infants can solve this invisible displacement problem. Piaget describes Jacqueline, Lucienne, and Laurent searching appropriately for coins and pencils that Piaget has surreptitiously deposited under a rug, a jacket, or a cushion. Although Piaget argues that the infant in this stage does not necessarily have a mental image of the object, he believed that at stage 6, the infant conceives of the object as an entity independent of their own perceptions or actions on it; this is a very important transition for having symbolic mental representations.

This developmental sequence has been observed by other researchers in laboratory tasks (Butterworth, 1977; Harris, 1973, 1975), demonstrating that it is highly reliable. In fact, researchers used children's development of object permanence to predict other aspects of symbolic development, such as language development (Corrigan, 1978). But are infants really unable to mentally represent objects until they are almost 2 years old? Many researchers have challenged Piaget's explanations and interpretations of infants' behavior in his tasks. It is possible, for example, that infants can mentally represent objects before the age of 2 but have difficulty planning their actions (which would be required for retrieving a hidden object). In the 1980s, Renée Baillargeon and her colleagues developed a test of infants' object permanence that did not rely on their ability to plan actions. Using a variation of habituation, Baillargeon and her colleagues developed a task that would become known as the violation of expectation procedure (see Box 7.1). The key question in this task is whether infants look longer—or prefer—events that violate their expectations of how the physical world works. In Baillargeon's case, her studies violated the expectation that objects continue to exist even when they are out of sight.

One of Baillargeon's (1987) studies is presented in Figure 8.1. Although this study used a violation of expectation procedure, as a first step infants were habituated to a part of the event that did not involve object permanence. Specifically, during habituation, infants saw a screen that rotated from lying flat in front of them all the way to lying flat the other way. This allowed them to learn how the screen moved back and forth. The violation of expectation came during the test. Baillargeon placed a solid box behind the screen. The logic was that if infants remembered that the object exists even when it is out of sight, they should look longer if the screen rotates as it did before, apparently rotating *through* the solid object hidden by the screen (left image, middle row, Figure 8.1), than if it stops when it should hit the box (left image, bottom row, Figure 8.1). This is precisely what young infants did. In these studies, which involved testing infants in the United States from primarily middle-class families, infants as young as 4 months looked longer at the *impossible* event, in which the screen apparently rotated through the hidden box, than at the *possible* event, in which the screen stopped when it hit the hidden box. Baillargeon reasoned that they looked longer at the impossible event because the outcome was unexpected; in other words, infants remembered that the box was hidden behind the screen (even though they could no longer see it) and expected that the screen would not be able to rotate through it. Baillargeon also used a control condition, in which infants watched the screen rotate without the box being hidden (right column of Figure 8.1). In this case, the infants looked equally at the two tests. Baillargeon reasoned that because no box was hidden behind the screen, infants' expectations about how the screen would rotate were not violated by the full 180-degree rotation. She concluded that by 4 months infants had object permanence, much earlier than Piaget's stage 4 when infants begin searching for hidden objects.

So, which is it? Do infants have object permanence only when they can uncover and find hidden objects, or do they have object permanence when they expect that a hidden object will interfere with the movement of another object? Other researchers have argued that object permanence is not an all-or-none phenomenon (Moore & Meltzoff, 2008). That is, infants do not simply recognize one day that hidden objects continue to exist, but rather, they learn this gradually, as they interact with objects and watch them appear and disappear in their everyday lives. This is why it seems like infants have object permanence in some tasks but not others. Younger infants may recognize that occluded objects should still exist even when they are out of sight, as suggested by Baillargeon's results, but they do not have a complete enough understanding of

FIGURE 8.1 ■ **Schematic Depiction of the Test and Experimental Conditions Used by Baillargeon (1987) to Study Object Permanence**

Object permanence in 3½- and 4½-month-old infants.

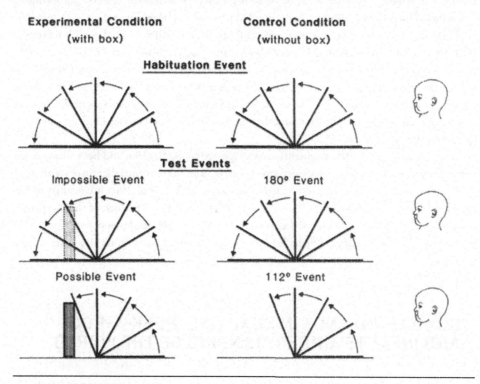

Experimental Condition
(with box)

Control Condition
(without box)

Habituation Event

Test Events

Impossible Event

180° Event

Possible Event

112° Event

Source: Baillargeon (1987).

object permanence to succeed at searching for hidden objects. In fact, Yuko Munakata and her colleagues provided support for this explanation (Munakata et al., 1997; Shinskey & Munakata, 2001). They showed that infants failed to search for a hidden object even when they could perform the actions required to find the hidden object. In a clever series of studies, Munakata and her colleagues presented U.S. 7- to 8-month-old infants with a blanket. Sometimes the infant could see that a toy was at the far end of the blanket. Sometimes the infant couldn't see that a toy was on the blanket, either because there was no toy or because the toy had been hidden by a screen. Infants pulled the blanket more when they could see the toy than when they could not see a toy, demonstrating the infants can produce the necessary action to retrieve a hidden object, but they only do so when the object is in plain sight. They didn't produce the action (pulling the blanket) when they couldn't see the object (either because it was not there or it was occluded by the screen), even at an age when Baillargeon's studies suggest they remember that a hidden object exists. If Baillargeon's results meant that infants represented the hidden object, then Munakata and her colleagues should have found that infants pulled the blanket to retrieve a hidden object. Thus, it does not seem that infants fail on object permanence tasks only because they can't perform the actions.

Other studies also suggest that infants' performance on different object permanence tasks reflects a developing understanding of or ability to represent hidden objects. For example, 7-month-old infants succeed more at finding hidden objects if they first are given training on how to bring a hidden object into view (O'Connor & Russell, 2015). In studies with infants in the United States, Adele Diamond (1985) showed that Piaget's A not B error does not simply appear, but rather it can be observed in infants of different ages by varying the time between the hiding and the finding portions of the task. Younger infants, around 8 months of age, showed the error almost immediately after the object was hidden. By 12 months, infants made the error only when there was more than 10 seconds between when they saw the object hidden and when they were allowed to search.

It is also possible that the original findings reported by Baillargeon and her colleagues do not actually show that infants represent hidden objects. Some have argued that there are alternative explanations for how infants responded in these tasks, for example, that infants may prefer events that have more movement (Rivera et al., 1999). Regardless of which of these explanations is correct, it is clear that infants' behavior toward hidden objects develops over the first 18 months and that these changes impact how they can interact with and think about the objects they encounter.

BOX 8.2—INFANCY IN REAL LIFE: PEEK-A-BOO AND INFANTS' UNDERSTANDING OF THE WORLD

If there is one game guaranteed to delight infants, it is peek-a-boo. Caregivers and infants from around the globe enjoy playing a version of this game in which one social partner hides and then reappears. Often, caregivers ask where the missing social partner has gone (e.g., "Where is Fátima?"), emphasizing their question with a rising tone (Fernald & O'Neill, 1993). The climax of the peekaboo game is the reappearance of the social partner, an event often marked with a gleeful exclamation, "There she is!" Although caregivers from different locales differ in exactly how they change their voice at the exciting moment when the hidden partner makes their grand reappearance, many cultures share this moment as a key point in the game, an event that typically elicits squeals of delight from the infant (Fernald & O'Neill, 1993).

Caregivers and infants usually repeat games of peekaboo for several rounds (J. S. Bruner et al., 1976). Infants' smiles and laughter during the game function as gratifying applause that are so enthusiastic that encores are clearly in order. Although caregivers and infants play peekaboo for enjoyment, this game has the bonus of fostering infants' understanding of the world. The modulating pitch in the caregiver's voice snaps infants to attention, ensuring that they follow the hiding and reappearance events in the game. Because caregivers repeat the same short phrases with the hiding and reappearance events, infants gain a foothold into deciphering the meaning of these phrases, with the social routine providing critical scaffolding for interpreting the meaning of the caregiver's words (J. S. Bruner et al., 1976;

A Mother and Infant Playing Peek-a-Boo.

iStock/kate_sept2004

Rohlfing et al., 2016; Snow, 1999). The highly structured nature of the game, paired with rounds of repetitions, can bolster infants' ability to anticipate the sequence of events and contributes to infants' ability to begin to form a representation of the structure of the game. The pauses in the game also offer an opportunity for the infant to join in a communicative exchange with their caregiver (J. S. Bruner et al., 1976; Fernald & O'Neill, 1993; Hsu et al., 2014). Peek-a-boo also inspires infants to babble in a more sophisticated manner. Hsu et al. (2014) found that U.S. 12-month-old infants produced more mature vocalizations during peek-a-boo than during an equally engaging but unstructured interaction, such as tickling.

How infants participate in peek-a-boo reveals their appreciation about the rules of the game. Young infants of 2 and 3 months are passive participants in the interaction, but over the course of their first year, infants become a more active partner in the game and even begin to initiate the game or to introduce variations (Miller & Commons, 2007; Stern et al., 1977). The change in how infants participate in peekaboo reveals their emerging understanding of their world. They learn that particular interactions follow a predictable structure and delight when they can anticipate the sequence of events in the game. By 4 and 6 months, infants smile more when peekaboo is played in its familiar sequence, but when the sequence is scrambled, infants smile less, showing that they are sensitive to the violation of the predictable sequence (Rochat et al., 1999). Infants' experiences with more structured versions of the game shape how easily they can participate. Polish mothers and their infants were filmed playing peekaboo when infants were 4 months and again, at 6 months. Mothers who took the time to signal to the infant that the game of peekaboo was about to begin, shaking the cloth in front of the infant prior to the hiding event, had infants who participated more actively in the game at both ages (Nomikou et al., 2017). As Vygotsky would argue, these mothers structured the social game to facilitate their infants' ability to anticipate the events and to contribute to the interaction.

The game of peek-a-boo also yields insights into an infant's **person permanence**, or their object permanence of an *individual* (Sherman et al., 2015). For example, U.S. 7-month-old infants smile less and raise their eyebrows more when the social partner who reappears is a different person than the person who had hidden (Parrott & Gleitman, 1989). This reaction shows that by 7 months, infants formed a representation of the original partner. Interestingly, infants with higher likelihood to be autistic do not differ in their engagement in peekaboo relative to typically developing infants with a lower likelihood to be autistic, perhaps because the game provides a level of predictability with its highly structured sequence (Macari et al., 2021).

Preoperational Thought

According to Piaget, infants move out of the sensorimotor stage and into the **preoperational stage**—which he hypothesized to encompass the ages of 2 to 7—once they are able to have mental representations of objects. However, this doesn't mean that young children are capable of full symbolic thought quite yet. In fact, according to Piaget's theory, the challenge for preoperational thinkers was to hold multiple mental representations in mind at once, or to update a mental representation without seeing any kind of change or transformation happen right in front of you. For example, let's say you were at a restaurant with a friend. While chatting, your friend spills water all over her blue shirt, and you give her a spare black sweater to put on in place of her now wet shirt. As she goes off to the bathroom to change, you can update your current representation of your friend—a woman wearing a blue shirt—and expect that she will be wearing a black sweater when she returns to the table, even though you don't actually see her change clothes. This is the kind of thing that would be difficult for children in Piaget's preoperational stage.

Patricia Ganea and colleagues tested this idea in U.S. 19- and 22-month-old infants (Ganea et al., 2007). During a session in the lab, a researcher played with the toddlers and two stuffed animals; one of the stuffed animals was named "Lucy," and the other one was referred to as Lucy's friend. After a while, the experimenter told the child that the animals were tired and placed them in a basket for a rest. Then the experimenter and the child left to play in an adjoining room. While they were reading a book in the adjoining room, a second experimenter entered with a bucket of water and walked into the room where the stuffed animals were resting to wash the table. After a few minutes, the second experimenter returned looking upset and announced that she accidentally spilled water all over Lucy and that now Lucy was all wet. At this point, the child and the experimenters went into the room where the stuffed animals were resting and the child saw three stuffed animals: a dry version of Lucy, an identical but wet version of Lucy, and a wet version of Lucy's friend. The child was then prompted to choose which stuffed animal was Lucy. The 22-month-old infants were able to correctly choose the wet version of Lucy, suggesting that they had updated their representation of Lucy in their minds after hearing that she had gotten wet. The 19-month-old infants, in contrast, were equally likely to choose the wet versus dry versions of Lucy (Ganea et al., 2007).

This suggests that by 22 months of age, infants can manipulate or change their mental representation of an object. This ability is important not just for updating current representations, but for other skills like theory of mind (which we will discuss in Chapter 11), and for infants' symbolic understanding. Indeed, you need to be able to hold and manipulate multiple representations at once in order to understand that what someone else is thinking or feeling (representation 1) might be different from what you are thinking and feeling (representation 2), or for understanding that a toy watermelon (representation 1) is only a symbol for a real watermelon (representation 2). As an infant, Charlie couldn't yet do this, and Edwin's food toys paid the price.

Dual Representation

When do infants gain full symbolic competence? According to Piaget, this ability develops at the end of the preoperational stage, around the age of 7. We now know that children begin to develop symbolic understanding slowly over the course of late infancy and early childhood, beginning at the ages of 2 ½ and 3. In the 1980s Judy DeLoache (1987) stumbled upon this accidentally when she was investigating the development of memory in 2 ½ and 3-year-old children from the United States. She designed a task that she thought would lead to easy memory recall for all children of this age. In the task, she introduced children to a small Snoopy doll and to Snoopy's "room," which was a small-scale model of a larger room (like a dollhouse). The model had a small couch, chair, table, and plant, which were just the right size for Little Snoopy, who was about the size of your pinky. After introducing the children to Little Snoopy's room and all of Little Snoopy's furniture, she then introduced Big Snoopy, who was a large stuffed animal that resembled Little Snoopy in every way except for its larger size. Of course, Big Snoopy had a room too. Big Snoopy's room was identical to Little Snoopy's room, except it was a full-sized room with full-sized furniture.

The child watched as the experimenter hid Little Snoopy somewhere in his little room (e.g., under the table, behind a pillow on the couch) and then explained that it was the child's job to go into the big room and find Big Snoopy, who was hiding in exactly the same place as Little Snoopy but in his big room. DeLoache thought for sure that children would have no problem with this task, using their memory of where Little Snoopy was hiding to find Big Snoopy. And as she expected, 3-year-old children had no problem with this task, easily retrieving Big Snoopy from his hiding place after watching where Little Snoopy was hidden in the scale model. However, 2 ½-year-old children failed this task entirely; even though they watched DeLoache hide Little Snoopy in his little house, they seemed utterly clueless as to where Big Snoopy could be hiding. Perhaps even more surprisingly, even though they couldn't find Big Snoopy in the big room, the younger children had no problem finding Little Snoopy in his small room. This suggests that the 2 ½-year-old children's failure to retrieve Big Snoopy had nothing to do with memory, as they could clearly remember where Little Snoopy was hidden. Instead, it seemed to have something to do with using the scale model to represent the larger room (DeLoache, 1987).

The results of this study led DeLoache to come up with a new hypothesis: She guessed that the reason why younger children had so much trouble with this task was that they could not simultaneously represent the scale model as an object in and of itself and as a symbol for the larger room. She called this the **dual representation theory**, which sounds a lot like children's difficulties in Piaget's preoperational stage. If Piaget were alive today, he'd likely agree with DeLoache and suggest that failure in her scale model task was because children of this age could not hold and manipulate multiple representations at the same time. Similarly, according to dual representation theory, 2 ½-year-old children could not represent the scale model in two ways at once (DeLoache, 1995).

But how to test this theory directly? DeLoache and her colleagues developed a procedure with an "incredible shrinking machine" to get children to believe that the small and big versions of objects were actually the same objects. In the first part of the experiment, 2 ½-year-old children met a troll doll called Terry, and they saw a shrinking machine (which was really just an old oscilloscope) that they were told could shrink Terry down to a miniature version of himself. The child and the experimenter turned the machine on, left the room, and listened as the machine "shrank" Terry (really a second experimenter played a cassette tape with some magical sounds, and swapped Terry the Troll with an identical but miniature version of himself). When they went back to the machine, children wholeheartedly believed that the machine worked and that little Terry was the same doll as the original Terry, just smaller. The experimenter and child then tested out the machine one more time and made Terry big again. The manipulation worked without a hitch, and the children easily believed that the machine could shrink Terry and make him big again.

In the next part of the experiment, children were shown how the machine could be used to shrink both Terry *and his room*. Terry's room was a lot like Big Snoopy's room from the last study: It was fully sized (kind of like a camping tent in this case) with several pieces of furniture. The child watched as the experimenter hid Terry and then listened as the shrinking machine shrank both Terry and his room. Once the room was shrunken down to a smaller version of itself (again just swapped with the big room by a sneaky experimenter), the child was asked to find Terry again. Unlike in the original experiment, because children believed that these were the same objects (only smaller because they had been shrunk), children did not have to reason about both the big room and its relation to the small room. Instead, the child only had to reason about one space, since the big room *was* the small room, just shrunken down. In other words, while DeLoache's original scale model study required dual representation (children had to represent the scale model as an object and a symbol for the bigger room), in the shrinking machine version of the study, children only needed to have a single representation of the room. This time, 2 ½-year-old children, the same age as the ones who failed the scale model task, found the object in the shrunken room with flying colors, providing strong support for DeLoache's dual representation theory (DeLoache et al., 1997).

Check Your Learning

1. What is the A not B error?

2. How does Renee Baillargeon's finding challenge Piaget's view of mental representations?

3. What is the difference between sensorimotor and preoperational thought?

4. What is the dual representation theory?

5. How do the results of the incredible shrinking room study support the dual representation theory?

LEARNING FROM SYMBOLIC MEDIA

The development of symbolic understanding is vitally important for how infants and young children reason about and interpret content from media, including photographs, books, and videos. Indeed, the images that we see every day through the media are all symbolic in nature, depicting images of objects and people who aren't right in front of us. As you can imagine, this suggests that it takes time for infants to understand how to interact with media and how to interpret what they see.

Grasping the Nature of Pictures

The most common symbols that infants encounter in their everyday lives are pictures (DeLoache & Ganea, 2009). What do infants see when they look at photographs? As we learned in Chapter 4, infants' vision improves significantly over the first year of life, so by the end of first year, infants should be able to see photographs quite clearly. The question is, what do they *perceive*? How do they interpret what they see in a photograph?

This is not an easy question, but researchers have come up with several clever ways to answer it. For example, studies by Theresa Gerhard and her colleagues showed that 7- to 9-month-old German infants prefer to look at real objects than at pictures of those objects (Gerhard et al., 2016), and that at 7 months of age, this preference for real objects was stronger for infants who engaged in more manual activity with objects (Gerhard et al., 2021). Although such studies can't tell us what infants understand about pictures, they do tell us that infants can *tell the difference* between real objects and pictures of those objects.

Infants' behaviors toward pictures reveals more about their understanding. Several researchers have provided infants with picture books and simply recorded what infants did when they saw the pictures. In the first study like this, DeLoache and colleagues (DeLoache et al., 1998) gave U.S. 9- and 19-month-old infants from mostly White, middle-class families books where each page depicted a photograph of a single object (e.g., bottle, toy) that could fit inside an infant's hand. Surprisingly, 9-month-old infants behaved as if the objects they saw in the book were the actual real objects; they tried to pick up the objects right off the page, rubbing them and scratching them along the way. Similarly, Christine Ziemer and colleagues (Ziemer et al., 2012) observed that a different group of mostly White U.S. 9-month-old infants grasped realistic images more than outlines of the objects or blobs. And Sarah Shuwairi and her colleagues (Shuwairi et al., 2010) found that yet another U.S. sample of infants tried to grasp images of structurally possible cubes but not images of structurally impossible cubes.

However, studies comparing how infants respond to depicted objects and real objects do reveal differences. Shuwairi (2019) found that although a racially diverse group of U.S. 9-month-old infants manually explored depicted objects, they treated depicted and real objects differently, exhibiting more grasping of real objects. The Ziemer et al. (2012) study described in the previous paragraph also compared infants' grasping at real objects and pictures placed behind a glass barrier and found that 9-month-old infants grasped at the real objects more than the pictures. Together these findings suggest that while young infants can differentiate between pictures and the real objects they depict, infants are still confused by the nature of realistic pictures and often try to interact with the objects in these pictures as if they were real.

By 19 months of age, infants have a clearer understanding of depicted objects. DeLoache et al (1998) found that at this age, infants rarely tried to grasp or pick up the depicted objects anymore; instead, they were more likely to point at the photos than to touch them. By 19 months,

U.S. Infants Grasping Photos of Objects From a Book

iStock/paintedlight

infants also labeled objects depicted in photos when pointing, suggesting that they understand the relation between the symbol (photo) and its referent (real object) (DeLoache et al., 1998).

Importantly, infants in the United States, even at 9 months, have likely had a great deal of experience looking at photos. How would infants in cultures where photos are less common react to these depictions? To study this question, DeLoache and colleagues (DeLoache et al., 1998) observed a group of Beng infants from a rural village in the Ivory Coast of Africa as they looked at depicted images in books. These infants had no previous experience with photographs. The Beng infants behaved in remarkably similar ways to the 9-month-old infants in the United States, exploring the photographs as if they were real objects. This suggests that in general, while infants can *see* the objects in photographs, they don't quite understand the nature of pictures early in development and that a full understanding of pictures might require experience exploring them.

Learning From Picture Books

If infants have difficulty understanding the nature of pictures at an early age, can they learn from pictures in a book? Research suggests that infants can start learning specific words from picture books shortly after their first birthdays. For example, one study showed that after hearing a new object label in a picture book, U.S. infants aged 15 to 18 months were able to transfer that new name to a real object and even to drawings of the object. However, infants had more difficulty transferring the name to a cartoon depiction of the object, suggesting that the similarity between the image in the book and the real-life object matters for whether infants can learn from the book (Ganea et al., 2008).

Besides learning new words from books, infants can also learn actions. In one study, researchers presented Western 13-, 15-, and 18-month-old infants with a series of photos of an adult eliciting a non-obvious property from an object (e.g., making a box light up by pressing a button on top). When the infants were later given the objects they saw in the book, they expected the objects to produce the non-obvious property the infants previously saw in the pictures (as evidenced by their repeated attempts to elicit the object's response) (Keates et al., 2014). In a similar study, researchers read 18- to 30-month-old infants a novel book that demonstrated how to put several objects together to make something new. After the storybook reading, the infants were able to successfully assemble several parts of a rattle and imitate specific movements, demonstrating that before the age of 2, infants can learn both words and actions from short and simple storybook interactions (Simcock & DeLoache, 2006).

Importantly, infants' ability to learn from picture books, at least at first, relies on experience, which differs by culture. In one study, researchers studied infants' ability to learn new words from picture books in a group of infants from 15 to 38 months of age from a rural village in Tanzania where infants had no prior experience with pictures or picture books. Infants were read a simple picture book where they saw novel objects and heard novel labels for those objects and were later tested on whether they learned those novel labels. In this sample, although even infants as young as 20 months could learn a new label when a real object was named, it wasn't until 27 months that infants learned a new label to an object they saw in a book. Thus, these infants did not have difficulty learning new labels in general, they just had difficulty learning

Joint Picture Book Reading
iStock/monkeybusinessimages

labels from photographs of those objects. This suggests that experience with books, and with photos specifically, might be necessary for infants' ability to learn from these books (Walker et al., 2013).

Altogether, this work suggests that infants can begin to learn from books by 15 to 18 months of age. However, this learning is culturally specific and depends on exposure to picture books. Not all cultures use picture books in infants' daily lives. In the United States, reading from picture books is so highly emphasized that the American Academy of Pediatrics suggests that parents should begin reading to infants as soon as possible to promote learning, particularly in terms of language (Council on Early Childhood et al., 2014). This is based on the U.S. assumption that reading to infants exposes them to more words. So far, research done in the United

States has supported this assumption: In one study, researchers examined 100 children's picture books and compared the words in those books to the words used by U.S. parents when they spoke to their children. The researchers found that the books contained more unique words than the speech that infants typically hear. This suggests that picture books can be an important source for vocabulary for infants, at least in the United States (Montag et al., 2015). But like infants' exposure to books, their exposure to language varies by culture as well, an issue we will talk more about in the next chapter.

Learning From Screens

Infants and toddlers don't only see objects depicted in picture books and photographs. Increasingly, infants and young children also interact with screens, viewing photographs, watching videos, and playing games. When Carter was 3 years old, his family traveled to London on an overnight plane. Carter was thrilled to have his own screen, and he watched the movie *Sky High* (not a movie for toddlers) at least 4 times on that trip. Nowadays, young children are given smartphones and tablets while they sit in the car or grocery cart, at least in Western, industrialized countries where screen media are widely available. YouTube channels have popped up that are aimed at infants, and there are dozens of television shows and movies meant for even the youngest viewers. But how do infants understand what they see on a television screen, computer, tablet, or phone? How do they interpret the symbolic nature of screens?

At first blush, research would suggest that infants from the United States (and in this study from the Midwest) treat images on screens and pictures in the same way, differentiating them from real objects (Ziemer & Snyder, 2016). Further, 9-month-old infants reach and grasp for the objects they see on a video, trying to pick them up off the screen, just as previous research has shown with pictures. And, like with pictures, older 15- to 19-month-old infants are much less likely to show this behavior and, instead, point at the objects on the screen, demonstrating some understanding that the objects in the video are just depictions of real-life objects (Pierroutsakos & Troseth, 2003).

This work suggests that infants might treat photographs and screen media similarly. But can infants learn from screens, like they can learn from picture books? Some of the first studies to ask this question, conducted by Andrew Meltzoff, were aimed at understanding whether infants would imitate an actor viewed on a television screen. As we discussed in Chapter 6, Meltzoff conducted several studies of infants' imitation, demonstrating developmental changes in infants' ability to remember and reproduce actions they had seen modeled. Meltzoff (1988) observed that both 14- and 24-month-old children would imitate a model they observed on a television screen. From these results, he concluded that toddlers could relate the two-dimensional representations on a TV screen to their own actions in three-dimensional space. However, despite this early evidence that children can learn from content presented on a screen, other research has shown that toddlers and preschoolers exhibit a **video deficit effect**, in that they learn less from video than from real-life experiences (Jing & Kirkorian, 2020). Importantly, the video deficit is not always seen, with infants and toddlers sometimes showing equivalent imitation of live and televised models (Strouse & Troseth, 2008). Moreover, during the period between 12 and 24 months, when the deficit can be most pronounced, it can be overcome by

Infant Watching Television
iStock/RichLegg

providing infants with extra exposure to the televised model (Barr et al., 2007) or presenting the televised information in a social context (Troseth et al., 2006).

Clearly, therefore, it is too simplistic to ask, "Can infants and young children learn from screens?" Infants and toddlers can map televised images onto their real-life counterparts, at least to some degree, and learn from those televised images. But their understanding of images presented on screens develops over the infancy and toddler period, as does their ability to *learn* from screens. The imitation work suggests that infants can learn actions from a televised model who is directing their actions at the infant, much as a person would in real-life interactions. However, screen media are more varied than simply showing infants novel actions performed by a model. Indeed, there is a large industry of television intended for young children, often with educational content. Can infants learn from these media?

To find out, Judy DeLoache and colleagues (DeLoache et al., 2010) gave parents of a group of 12- to 18-month-old U.S. infants a commercial DVD that was specifically designed to teach infants of this age group new words. Parents and their infants were randomly assigned to one of four groups: One group of parents was told to watch the video with their infant 5 times a week for 2 weeks; a second group of parents was told to let their infants watch the video alone 5 times a week for 2 weeks; a third group of parents weren't given the video at all and were instead given the list of words the video was designed to teach and were told to teach their infants the list of words over the course of 2 weeks; and one final group of parents received no intervention at all, no video and no word list. At the end of the 2-week period, the infants were tested on whether they recognized the new words presented in the video or by their parents. Surprisingly, infants who were given the video did not learn the new words—with or without their parents' presence while watching. In fact, the only infants who showed any evidence of learning were the infants whose parents were asked to teach their infants a list of words *without the video* (DeLoache et al., 2010).

Two additional studies with U.S. infants used a similar method and reported the same results. In one, 12– to 15-month-old infants watched *Baby Wordsworth* (a DVD that teaches infants 30 target words), and parents were told to have their infants watch the DVD 15 times over the course of 2 weeks (Robb et al., 2009). In the other, a group of infants from a wider age range (12 to 25 months) were shown a similar DVD for a similar amount of time (Fender et al., 2010). In both studies, there was no evidence that infants learned the target words, suggesting that unlike picture books, infants may not readily learn words from screen media.

Importantly, although infants might have difficulty learning from screen media, older children certainly don't. Research on U.S. children's learning from educational programming like *Sesame Street* and *Between the Lions* has shown that kids who watch these shows as preschoolers and kindergartners are less likely to fall behind in school (Kearney & Levine, 2015), and they have better word recognition, standardized reading scores, and phonemic awareness (letter–sound relations) compared to control groups of kids who didn't watch these shows (Linebarger et al., 2004). Children aged 2 to 6 can even learn social and emotional skills like empathy and emotion recognition by watching shows like *Daniel Tiger's Neighborhood*, which is designed to teach children prosocial skills (H. Wright et al., 2016). In fact, *Daniel Tiger's Neighborhood* has even been used effectively in teaching important prosocial skills to autistic children (Dotson et al., 2017).

One caveat is that these learning gains switch direction if children watch programming that isn't child-friendly or educational in nature. In fact, while children who watch child-audience educational programming show better performance in a variety of reading and number skills, children who watch general audience programs (or shows that are made for adults) show *poorer* performance on all of these skills (J. C. Wright et al., 2001). So the content of what kids are watching really matters. Another caveat is that television can be disruptive to infants' play if it's on in the background. In one study, researchers had 12-, 24-, and 36-month-old infants play for 1 hour. For 30 minutes of that hour, a game show was playing on a television in the background. The researchers found that when the TV was on, the quality of the infants' play, including the amount of focused attention and the length of play, was significantly reduced compared to when the television was off (Schmidt et al., 2008).

It is important to note that virtually all of this work was done on children's learning from TV shows where children watched passively, while sitting on their couches. Although DeLoache et al. did not find that parents watching with their infants helped the infants learn, other research on slightly older children's learning from more interactive media or learning from media with the help of an adult gives us cause to be more optimistic, especially in this time after the COVID-19 pandemic when people, including young children, are spending more time on screens. In fact, although research suggests that infants can't learn much from media, when they're using media to talk to a live person, like on FaceTime, they might understand or learn more than if just passively watching a regular TV show. For example, when the content is interactive, or when children are encouraged to respond to the characters on the screen in shows like in shows like *Blues Clues* or *Dora the Explorer*, there are learning benefits even for children as young as 2 ½ (Linebarger & Walker, 2005). Likewise, when children are engaging with a real

Infant Using FaceTime
iStock/Geber86

live person through a screen, like on FaceTime or Zoom, learning is also much improved, even for infants. In fact, one study suggests that infants as young as 12 to 25 months of age can learn new words if taught by a live person on video chat, but not if the same person is presented teaching the same words on a prerecorded video (Myers et al., 2016).

Altogether, this work suggests that while young infants don't readily learn from the passive viewing of screens, older children can learn from screen media, particularly if it's educational. And younger children's ability to learn from screens improves if the media are interactive, especially if there is a live person on the other side of the screen responding contingently to the infant. Further, it is important to note that nearly all of the studies we've discussed in this chapter were done on predominantly White, middle-class samples from the United States. Experience with symbolic media like photographs, books, and screens varies immensely based on experience, which varies immensely based on culture, so an individual's ability to learn from these media will vary as well. You might imagine that a realistic televised depiction of an event could be incredibly confusing to an individual who has never experienced this type of media before. Indeed, in one now classic study, researchers presented children with balloons on a television screen and asked them whether the balloons would fly out of the TV if you take the top off the screen (Flavell et al., 1990). Although 4-year-olds thought this was a silly question, children as old as 3 said yes, the balloons would fly out the top! The point is, learning to reason about symbols takes time to develop and requires experience with specific types of symbols to achieve full competence.

Check Your Learning

1. How does infants' behavior toward pictures change over the course of development?

2. How does infants' behavior toward screens change over the course of development?

3. Is there evidence that infants can learn from screen media? How do you know?

SUMMARY

As Jean Piaget once said, "play is the work of childhood." In this chapter, we learned about the various ways in which infants play and how the types of play they engage in change over the course of development. Importantly, we learned that play doesn't just serve to entertain but provides a context for infants to learn about the world around them, including how objects are related to each other and about their functional properties. We also learned how play can encourage development and social interactions, and how symbolic play, or pretend play, introduces infants to the world of symbols, which will later guide their development in other domains. Infants' ability to symbolically represent an object in their mind develops over the course of the first year of life, and their ability to manipulate those representations develops in the second and third years. Once children gain full symbolic competence, they can also gain the ability to take the perspective of others and even update their representation of a person or object that is out of sight. These abilities will all impact infants' other developing social and cognitive abilities, like language and theory of mind, which you will learn more about in the next few chapters.

KEY TERMS

A not B error

dual representation theory

functional play

object substitution

person permanence

play

preoperational stage

referent

symbol

symbolic play

video deficit effect

REVIEW QUESTIONS

1. What are the different types of play, and when does each develop in infancy?

2. What is dual representation, and how does it explain the development of infants' symbolic understanding?

3. How does infants' behavior toward photographs change over the course of infancy?

4. How does infants' behavior toward screens compare to their behavior toward pictures?

CRITICAL THINKING QUESTIONS

1. How are symbolic and play and language development related throughout development?

2. Why were the results of Renee Baillargeon's study problematic for Piaget's theory about the development of mental representations?

3. How are Judy DeLoache's dual representation theory and Piaget's theory of preoperational development similar?

4. How did the incredible shrinking machine study provide evidence to support dual representation theory?

5. How might cultural differences impact the way infants and young children understand media?

6. Do infants learn from screen media? Why or why not?

9 LANGUAGE DEVELOPMENT

When Carter was 12 months old, he pointed to the family cat and said "kkkkkk." For days, he would incessantly crawl after the poor kitty, stopping every few feet to point and say, "kkkkkkk." His parents were absolutely delighted, exclaiming, "Did you hear that? He said cat!" For Carter's parents, this was a clear signal that he was learning language. In fact, for them, that magical time had finally come when Carter became a full-fledged talking baby. The problem was, after only a few days of following the cat around the house, Carter lost interest and stopped using "kkkkk" altogether. It would be another month before he attempted to talk again. At that point, he started saying "Hi" when he saw new people, and from there, his language really took off.

Unlike Carter, Diego wasn't interested in speaking at 12 months because he communicated clearly with "baby signs" that he learned at daycare. He signed "more" when he wanted refills, "help" to request assistance, and "milk" when he was thirsty. At 14 months, Diego began to complement his baby signs with spoken words, such as "da" for daddy. Although most parents will boast about their infant's first word, Carter and Diego's first "words" show that language development is not always straightforward. Was Carter's first word cat or hi? Was Diego's first "word" the sign for "more" at 12 months or "da" at 14 months?

In this chapter, we describe the many steps infants take in learning language—a complicated process that recruits the perceptual and cognitive skills described in the previous chapters. For example, to understand language, infants must first tune to the sounds and rhythms of their language (or languages), parse words from a continuous stream of speech (or signs), and learn to link words to the objects, people, and events that they refer to. When learning to speak (or sign), infants also progress through many stages. Young infants initially coo, as Edwin did with his morning chats with Shelf (see Chapter 4). At about 6 months, those coos transform into babbles, and typically in the months around their first birthday, babbling blossoms into first words. As infants learn to say more words, they begin to combine them into short two- and three-word phrases. By toddlerhood, they can string these words into longer and more complex phrases, until they have finally acquired enough language to share stories, ask questions (oh, so many questions), tell jokes, and engage in lengthy conversations.

This progression holds for typically developing children around the world, regardless of which language or languages they are learning. Language acquisition includes both quantitative changes (e.g., from a first word to many words) and qualitative changes (e.g., from cooing to babbling). Infants' language development is social; it is embedded in social interactions. It also builds on the symbolic development we discussed in Chapter 8. It should come as no surprise then that infants' language development is linked to both their social skills (Chapter 10) and their motor skills (Chapter 5).

After reading this chapter, you will be able to:

1. *Explain* the difference between language and communication, *list* the components of language development, *describe* when a first language is most easily learned, and *explain* whether infants can learn more than one language.

2. *Compare* the theories of language development.

3. *Outline* one example that shows infants' biological preparedness to learn language and one example that shows how language experience can influence language learning.

4. *Define* speech perception, word segmentation, and receptive language, and *describe* their development.

5. *Describe the development of expressive language,* from coos to complete sentences.

LANGUAGE AND COMMUNICATION

Language is a formal system of **communication,** or a process by which we share information with others. Even newborns communicate, even though they do not realize that they are communicating. Newborns cry when they are uncomfortable, look at the faces of their caregivers when they are awake and alert, and make satisfied sounds when content and drowsy. These behaviors serve as signals to others about the infants' state, mood, and needs. But these are examples of *unintentional* communication. Across development, children's communication efforts can also be *intentional*; consider a toddler pointing to a snail to show interest (see next photo) or a young child waving to bid farewell. Whereas language is intentional, communication can be intentional or unintentional. Gradually, over the first year of life, some aspects of infants' communication becomes intentional as they gain **intersubjectivity**, or the understanding that they share thoughts and feelings with other people (Trevarthen, 2011).

Communicative Foundations of Language

Even before infants learn language, they engage in behaviors that support communication with others. For example, we learned in Chapter 4 that newborn infants look more at faces than at other stimuli and that they prefer to listen to human speech over other sounds. These preferences orient young infants to people and create opportunities not only for social interactions but also for receiving language input (Frank et al., 2009; Vouloumanos et al., 2010). Caregivers interpret a newborn's looking at faces as an invitation to interact. In fact, in the first few weeks of life, infants are more likely to gaze at a caregiver's face when they are awake and alert and are more open to external stimulation. Although this behavior may not be the newborn asking for interaction, it is behavior that communicates to others that the newborn is open to interaction. When newborn infants are overstimulated or their mood shifts, they

TODDLER POINTING AT A SNAIL: This toddler points to a snail to share their interest in it with a caregiver.

iStock/yaoinlove

look away, which should communicate to their social partner that the infant is no longer receptive to interaction.

These interactions between newborns and caregivers are just the start of face-to-face interaction. For example, in Western industrialized countries, caregivers and their young infants often communicate through face-to-face interactions that include vocal exchanges. When Charlie was 6 weeks old, he began to coo in response to his mother's questions and held her gaze as they chatted about such riveting topics as diaper changes and how to fit their many naps into a full schedule of feedings and walks. These back-and-forth interactions that parents share with their infants are called **proto-conversations**; they are an early form of social exchange that set the stage for later conversations, when infants have acquired their first words (Bateson, 1975). A caregiver smiles and speaks to an attentive infant, who vocalizes and smiles back at the caregiver. Infants coo when there is a pause in the caregiver's speech, demonstrating that they are already learning the important skill of turn-taking. In British samples, 8-month-old infants vocalized more during face-to-face interactions compared to interactions where an adult was not looking directly at the infant (Leong et al., 2017). These proto-conversations, seen in infant–parent dyads from diverse cultures, including German and Nso dyads (Demuth, 2013; Kärtner et al., 2010), provide practice with turn-taking and teach infants that communicative exchanges include a give-and-take between social partners.

However, mother–infant interactions are not limited to face-to-face interactions but can include interactions in other modalities, such as touch and body contact (Keller et al., 2009). In Chapter 12, you will read about different caregiving practices, which include the many ways caregivers interact with their infants. For example, some mothers in non-Western societies interact with their infants in ways that look different from the face-to-face interactions typical of mothers and infants in Western, industrialized populations (Cole & Moore, 2015; Halberstadt & Lozada, 2011; Kärtner et al., 2013; Keller et al., 1988). Mothers from the Cameroonian Nso farming community, for example, synchronize their communicative exchanges with their infants through touch and maintaining close body contact (Kärtner et al., 2010; Lavelli et al., 2019). Similarly, Ni-Vanuatu mothers—mothers from a rural, non-industrialized Melanesian community in the South Pacific—use touch in interacting with their infants much more than U.S. mothers, who instead use visual attention when interacting with their infants and a new object (Little et al., 2016). Even so, touch is not isolated to non-Western cultures; mothers in Western cultures also use touch in their interactions with their infants (Abu-Zhaya et al., 2017; Kärtner et al., 2010; Lavelli et al., 2019).

As they develop, infants begin to follow the gaze of their partner in interactions (Moore, 2008). By 6 to 9 months, infants in diverse cultures, including Germany, Bhutan, Sweden, Canada, and the United States, turn their heads to see where a caregiver is looking (Astor et al., 2022; D'Entremont, 2000; Gredebäck et al., 2018; Scaife & Bruner, 1975). Although **gaze following** itself may not be the infant communicating, it does show an increasing sensitivity to others' communication. Attending where others are looking facilitates infants' language learning. Infants around the world, including the United States, the Netherlands, and Japan, who spend more time attending to where others are looking have larger vocabularies as toddlers (Brooks & Meltzoff, 2008; Çetinçelik et al., 2020; Tenenbaum et al., 2015). Infants are more likely to track the direction of another's look when hearing infant-directed speech. For example, 6-month-old British and Ni-Vanuatu infants followed an adult's gaze only if the adult was

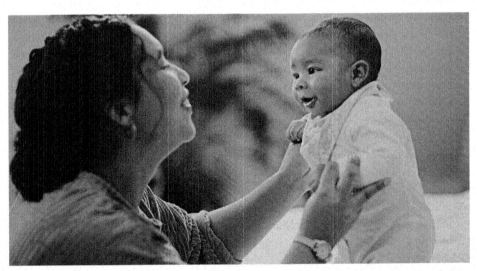

U.S. MOTHER AND INFANT: A U.S. mother engaging in a proto-conversation with her young infant in a face-to-face interaction.

iStock/Delmaine Donson

NI-VANUATU MOTHER AND INFANT: A Ni-Vanuatu mother and infant from Melanesian community of Tanna interacting through touch.

iStock/Laszlo Mates

using infant-directed speech (Hernik & Broesch, 2019; Senju & Csibra, 2008). Infant-directed speech is a type of speech adults (and children) use when addressing infants; although it varies with language community, it is generally simpler and more variable in its pitch than speech directed to adults (Fernald et al., 1989).

Toward the end of the first year, caregiver–infant interactions become object focused. At 9 months, infants in Western cultures begin to share the objects and events that capture their interests (Tomasello & Akhtar, 2000). For example, an infant may look at an object and then lift it toward a caregiver to share their interest in the object. This shared attention is related to children's language development. Studies with U.S. samples have shown that how much infants share attention to an object with caregivers when they are 9 months of age predicts the number of words they understand when they are 12 and 15 months (Yu et al., 2019). Other research has shown that spending more time sharing attention with a caregiver is related to more advanced language acquisition in U.S. children (Brooks & Meltzoff, 2008; Mundy et al., 2007) and children in Nigeria (Childers et al., 2007).

By the end of their first year, infants begin to point, marking the beginning of more forms of communication. Infants in many cultures point to share attention (Tomasello et al., 2007). Ulf Liszkowski, Penny Brown, and their colleagues compared the pointing of infants in Papua New Guinea, Indonesia, Japan, Peru, Canada, Tzeltal Maya, and Yucatec Maya. Despite vast differences in geographic, social, and economic characteristics among these groups of infants, there were no cultural differences in how often and when infants pointed (Liszkowski et al., 2012). These results indicate that pointing may be universal across infants and that it supports communication between infants and their caregivers.

Other studies have shown that infants point as a way of asking for information. Ágnes Kovács and her colleagues, for example, found that Hungarian-learning 12-month-old infants pointed more when an adult provided information about the target of their points, but they pointed less when the adult simply shared the object with the infants (Kovács et al., 2014). In addition, English-learning infants are more likely to learn the name of an object if they had pointed to it first (Begus et al., 2014; Lucca & Wilbourn, 2018, 2019). Just like sharing attention, pointing is linked to language development (Bates, 1979; Cameron-Faulkner et al., 2021; Colonnesi et al., 2010; Goldin-Meadow, 2007; Lieven & Stoll, 2013; Salo et al., 2019).

The point here (no pun intended) is that communication, although different from language, is an important part of language development, nudging infants toward practicing vocalizations and preparing them for acquiring speech. In one study, 18- to 30-month-old Korean infants who had some kind of language delay were most likely to catch up to their non-delayed peers if they attempted to communicate, for example, by using gestures (Hong & Kim, 2005). Thus, while many parents worry when their children show any kind of language delay, there is research suggesting that as long as they are attempting to *communicate* in other ways—by crying, pointing, or grunting—it's likely that they are on the right track.

Components of a Formal Language

What then is *language*? A **language** is a formal system of communication that is **generative**. The generative feature of language is why it is so powerful. With language, you can combine words in an infinite number of ways to express an equally infinite number of ideas. For example, even though you've never seen these words arranged in this particular order, the sentence is still understandable (at least we hope!). In addition, each of the more than 6,500 languages spoken today around the globe is a complex system with its own set of rules, whether the language is spoken, signed, or written.

All world languages have several components (Table 9.1). For example, each language has its own set of **phonemes**, or the most basic units that convey meaning. In spoken languages, phonemes are the individual sounds, and they vary in several ways, including when you open your lips and where your tongue is when you make the sound. For example, in English, the word "rake" has phonemes /r/, /a/, and /k/. In addition, "rake" and "lake" are distinct words because /r/ and /l/ are distinct phonemes. Signed languages also have phonemes, and they vary in features such as hand shape, location, movement, or palm orientation. Like the sounds of spoken language, signs that differ in these features differ in meaning (Cormier et al., 2018).

Although all spoken languages have phonemes, each spoken language uses a unique set of phonemes. Adult speakers of one language have difficulty hearing distinctions not used in their own native language. As one example, in contrast to English, which has distinct phonemes for the /r/ and /l/ speech sounds, Japanese combines /r/ and /l/ into a single phoneme. Adult speakers of Japanese cannot distinguish between words that differ only in their use of /r/ and /l/ (Best & Strange, 1992). As we saw in Chapter 4, infants initially can hear the

TABLE 9.1 ■ The Components of Language

Language Component	Definition	Examples From English
Phonemes	The smallest units of sounds of a language that are used to create meaning	"b" vs. "p" in English as in "bin" and "pin"
Morphemes	The smallest unit of meaning	"Dog," "-s" (as in dogs), "un-" (as in unkind), "-ing" (as in running)"
Syntax	The rules for combining and ordering categories of words into sentences, or grammar	"Anzila greeted Zara" vs. "Zara greeted Anzila."
Pragmatics	Rules about how and when to use language, including conversational norms and addressing individuals appropriately, given social norms	Irony, sarcasm, when it is appropriate to speak and how to engage in a conversation

distinction between phonemes of many different languages, but as they have experience with one (or more) language, their perception narrows. They become specialized and hear only the phonemes they will need to listen to and understand their "native" language, or the language they are learning.

Languages differ not only in the particular phonemes they use but also in the rules for how sounds can be combined. In English, for example, we commonly combine /t/ with /r/ to make the /tr/ sound in words such as "truck" or "trick." In contrast, English does not allow combining /t/ and /l/ to make /tl/. However, Nahuatl, a Uto-Aztecan language, allows this /tl/ combination, and it is commonly used in words in that language. As an undergraduate, one of the authors spent a semester in Mexico City and had to learn to pronounce the sites, streets, and metro stops that used the "t-l" sound combination, such as Tlatelolco, the archeological site of the pre-Colombian city-state, or Zapotitlán, a municipality south of Mexico City, near Puebla. The word "chocolate" came from Nahuatl (*choco-latl*) as did "avocado" (*ahuacatl*). Because Spanish, similar to English, does not use the /t/-/l/ sound combination, these words became "chocolate" and "aguacate" when adapted into the Spanish language.

Morphemes are another component of language and are the smallest unit of a word that denotes meaning. Morphemes can be individual words, such as "dog," "chair," and "walk." They can also be prefixes (i.e., the beginning of words) like the "un" in "undo," or suffixes (i.e., word endings) like adding "-s" to a count noun to indicate more than one dog or chair. These very small units of sound change the meaning of a word. For example, at some of their first pre-natal appointments, the authors of this book were delighted to hear the *heartbeat of their fetus* and relieved that it was not the *heartbeats* of their *fetuses*. (As amazing as twins are, the thought of having two newborns instead of just one can be intimidating to a new parent!)

Languages also have **syntax**, or the rules for how the categories of words, such as nouns and verbs, combine to create sentences. Recombining the same words into a different order not only changes the syntactic structure of a sentence but also its meaning. "Nizaiah hugged Maeve" evokes a different image than "Maeve hugged Nizaiah." Every language has a unique syntax, and children must learn the rules for combining words in their language. When Diego was first combining words to form short phrases, he would extend his arms, saying, "need you me" to request a cuddle; he had acquired (some of) the correct words to express his thoughts but not the correct syntax.

A final component of language is **pragmatics**, or knowing when and how to use language, as well as appreciating the intent of a speaker's words (Matthews et al., 2018; Papafragou, 2018). Pragmatic understanding requires a child to understand meaning within a social context; it includes "reading between the lines" to go beyond the literal meaning of words. A child with pragmatic intent understands that a parent who sighs "oh great" after the child flings spaghetti at the wall is not expressing pleasure at this action but rather the opposite sentiment. Irony and metaphors are examples of pragmatics. However, pragmatic understanding also includes knowing when it is appropriate to begin a conversation, how to respond appropriately to others in a social situation, and knowing how to address authority figures. In some languages, such as Spanish, speakers use a formal versus informal form of "you" depending on whom they are addressing (e.g., a professional colleague versus a close friend). Children who use each form of "you" appropriately show that they have acquired this aspect of pragmatic language.

When Can We Learn Language?

Our six infants all learned language on their own timelines. Tesalia produced her first words between 9 and 10 months, Alison and Carter both said their first words when they were between 11 and 12 months, Edwin and Charlie both said their first words right around their first birthdays, and Diego spoke his first word at about 14 months. They also varied in when they put words together. Not surprisingly, Tesalia was early at this as well, combining words as early as 14 months. Carter, on the other hand, didn't start to put words together until he was almost 2. However, despite this variation in timing, all of our children learned language during infancy.

Chapter 1 introduced the concept of *critical period*, a time during development that is especially sensitive to experience. Learning language, particularly a first language, has been argued to have a critical period. Specifically, learning a language is much easier at younger ages than older ages, and it may be impossible to learn a first language during adolescence or adulthood. How do we know this? It would not be ethical to test for critical periods in language acquisition by depriving children of language input. Instead, our understanding of critical periods in language has come, in part, from a few tragic cases of children raised without exposure to language. One famous case was Victor of Aveyron (the "Wild Child") who was found in France around 1800, living alone in the woods, where it seemed he had spent his entire childhood. When he was found, Victor was about 12 years old and did not speak at all. A young physician took him into his home and tried to teach him to speak, but Victor only made modest progress, never becoming able to really use spoken language.

More than a century and a half later, Genie, a 13-year-old girl, was rescued from an abusive household where she had been raised in social isolation. She had lived in a house in Southern California where her family kept her alone in a room, barely interacted with her, and did not speak to her at all. For several years after she was discovered, many therapists and researchers intensively tried to teach her spoken English and American Sign Language (ASL). Their efforts were more successful than were the efforts with Victor. Genie learned many more words than Victor had. However, like Victor, she did not become proficient at language. She never mastered syntax and grammar (Fromkin et al., 1974). Victor and Genie's struggles at learning language suggest that there may be a critical period for language development, and early exposure to language is required for language acquisition.

Although the examples of Victor and Genie are fascinating and suggest that language has a critical period, they are not ideal cases for drawing clear conclusions about critical periods in language development. These children suffered extreme abuse, and as a result, their difficulty with learning language might reflect the cognitive and emotional outcomes of their abuse rather than the ability to learn a first language as adolescents. In addition, although we assume that they would have learned language if given typical experience and exposure early in childhood, it is possible that each of these children had some disability or condition that would have prevented them from learning language even as infants.

There are other children who, like Victor and Genie, have little exposure to language, but unlike Victor and Genie, we know they are typically developing and have rich social interactions with their families. These are children who are born deaf. Ninety percent of deaf newborns are born to hearing families (Mitchell & Karchmer, 2004); these families usually do not know a formal sign language, so these children are left without language input until they enter a school for the Deaf, when they are 3 to 5 years of age. At that time, children are exposed to a formal sign language, such as American Sign Language (ASL). However, some individuals are unable to go to a school for the Deaf, and these late signers do not get exposed to a signed language until adolescence or even adulthood. Importantly, not only do these children begin to learn a first language at a much later age than is typical, but their language exposure also occurs outside of the home.

Comparing the language development of people who were exposed to sign language at different times can help us understand whether there are critical periods in language development. One way we can evaluate people's language is to present them with signed utterances and ask them if those utterances are grammatically correct. Rachel Mayberry did just this with people who learned ASL at different ages. She found that people who acquired ASL as infants (i.e., they had signing parents) were very accurate at making judgments about the grammaticality of signed utterances (Mayberry, 2010). People who acquired ASL later, and so were not exposed to language as infants, were not as good at judging whether the utterances were grammatically correct. Thus, it seems that being exposed to language earlier, at least for children learning ASL, is important for developing language skills. Together with findings from Victor and Genie, these results suggest that children more easily learn a first language at younger ages than at older ages.

BOX 9.1—INFANCY IN REAL LIFE: TIMING OF COCHLEAR IMPLANTS

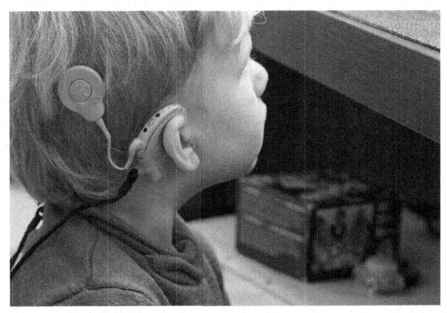

Young Child With a Cochlear Implant

iStock/icarmen13

You might have seen on social media a video of a deaf infant hearing their mother for the first time. The infant sits on a parent's lap and a cochlear implant that was surgically implanted a few weeks before is activated. The infant's mother or father calls the infant's name, and the infant breaks out in a big grin. The message is clear: The infant is happy to finally hear their parent's voice.

As we discussed in Chapter 3, approximately 1 or 2 infants in every 1,000 in the United States are born with profound hearing loss. If these infants are born into hearing families, as most are, they may not be exposed to language during infancy. Moreover, hearing parents may feel a desire for their deaf child to be exposed to sound and a spoken language. For many families, a cochlear implant provides a solution. Cochlear implants are electronic devices that help to transmit sound to the brain (Macherey & Carlyon, 2014). They are different from hearing aids, which amplify sound. Instead, a cochlear implant bypasses the cochlea and directly stimulates the auditory nerve via an array of surgically implanted electrodes.

There are several arguments for performing this surgery as early as possible. As we saw in Chapters 2 and 3, the development of the brain and perceptual systems depend on the input that is received. The brain regions and systems devoted to auditory perception—and the perception, detection, and processing of spoken language—won't get any stimulation if deaf infants do not have a cochlear implant (Gordon et al., 2011). Thus, just as surgically correcting cataracts as early as possible improves visual development (see Chapter 4), surgically correcting hearing loss with cochlear implants as early as possible improves auditory and speech development. Deaf children who will not be exposed to a signed language also can have access to spoken language during the critical period of language development if they have cochlear implants early. It might seem obvious that all children who are eligible should have cochlear implants as soon as they can. However, cochlear implants are quite controversial (Cooper, 2019). The Deaf community has a rich linguistic and cultural environment; they do not see deafness as something that needs to be fixed. Deaf individuals often attend schools for the Deaf and may live in Deaf communities. Some have argued that by "fixing" a child's deafness during infancy, parents are denying the child's opportunity to become fully integrated into the Deaf community.

Moreover, cochlear implants are not a "miracle cure." The YouTube videos make it appear that having these devices activated is a pleasant experience and that the brain immediately recognizes the stimulation from the device as sound. Neither thing is necessarily true. Many people find the stimulation from a cochlear implant unpleasant, and some people eventually have them deactivated. In addition, the brain does not immediately recognize the stimulation as sound. It takes months or years before cochlear implants can fully function. The brain receives the input from the implant, and only over time are those signals interpreted and recognized as speech. Indeed, although a recipient of a cochlear implant may have amazing abilities to hear and produce language, this is accomplished only with a significant amount of hard work, and an individual with a cochlear implant never processes sound in the same way that a hearing person does.

The controversy is driven by the fact that cochlear implants are most effective when they are implanted early, before a child can be involved in the decision of whether or not to use them. Parents—and more often than not, hearing parents—make the decision for their children. This decision is difficult because although for some aspects of development it is important to have the procedure early, by doing so early in infancy, parents are potentially making a decision that will isolate their child from the Deaf community without their explicit consent.

How Many Languages Can Infants Learn?

When Tesalia was a toddler, she was visiting her "abuela" (grandma in Spanish) and enjoying a breakfast of eggs and orange juice. When her juice cup was empty, she turned to her grandmother and requested, "more juice." But her pronunciation of the /j/ sounded a bit like /sh/, confusing her grandmother, who thought Tesalia was asking about her shoes. "You want your shoes?" "No," Tesalia replied, "more juice." "Something with your shoes?" her grandmother probed again, still not understanding. "NO!" cried Tesalia in exasperation. Taking a deep breath, she looked at her grandmother and said, "jugo," switching to Spanish in hopes of finally having her request understood and her thirst quenched.

Tesalia and Diego are among many U.S. children who are growing up bilingual, having regular exposure to two languages. About 23% of U.S. children fit this category, as reported by the Kids Count Data Center website, as of 2021. This percentage is much higher in some U.S. states, such as California, where 43% of children grow up bilingual. In many countries around the world, such as Singapore, learning two (or more) languages is the norm rather than the exception (Wu et al., 2020).

People often ask whether exposing infants to more than one language will confuse them and whether that confusion will slow their language development. However, infants exposed to two (or more) languages are not deficient in their language development (Fibla et al., 2022), provided they have sufficient exposure to their languages (Hoff et al., 2012; Höhle et al., 2020). Newborn infants from bilingual families discriminate between two languages that differ from each other in their rhythms (Byers-Heinlein et al., 2010), similar to newborn infants from monolingual families (Nazzi et al., 1998). Infants and young children who are regularly exposed to two languages acquire words in both of their languages. Both Diego and Tesalia learned "agua," the Spanish word for water, as one of their first words because they heard their mother use this word often at home. Because their father spoke English, they learned the English words "dog" and "ball" at about the same time. Bilingual children's language development can advance in a similar manner and on the same general timeline as children learning a single language (Höhle et al., 2020; Pearson et al., 1993), although the exact pace of each language may differ depending on exposure to the languages. For example, infants learning two languages say their first words around their first birthdays (Vihman et al., 2007). Infants acquire the languages that are meaningful in their interactions with others.

Research suggests that there are substantial *benefits* associated with growing up bilingual. For example, children who grow up bilingual are better at paying attention and switching between tasks (probably because of their ability to switch between languages) than children who only speak a single language (Bialystok, 2011; Kovács & Mehler, 2009). This attention-switching advantage is seen in infants between 6 to 10 months, suggesting that simply having exposure to bilingual environments benefits infants' processing of information (Arredondo et al., 2022; D'Souza et al., 2020; Kalashnikova et al., 2021; Kovács & Mehler, 2009; Singh, 2021). Infants regularly exposed to more than one language are also better at taking the perspective of others (Goetz, 2003) and show advantages in certain types of memory (Brito & Barr, 2012). Put into the context of critical periods for acquiring language, there are clear advantages for learning second languages in infancy and early childhood compared to waiting to do so at older ages.

Even though most children in the world are exposed to more than one language from infancy, most of what we know about language development has come from research on children learning only one language (Kidd & Garcia, 2022). Research on bilingual (and multilingual) infants' language development lags behind research on monolingual infants' language development, leaving many questions to be explored. Infants who hear two languages must learn two sets of phonemes, two vocabularies, and two grammars. How easily infants learn each of their languages depends on many factors, including how much they hear each language, whether the languages are spoken both in the home and outside of the home (e.g., daycare, school), and who is providing the language input (e.g., a native speaker or nonnative speaker of the language) (Floccia et al., 2018; Hoff, 2021). As discussed in the section on critical periods, infants must have exposure to a language to learn it. If an infant's exposure to one of their languages is limited, then they will learn that language more slowly than infants who have much more exposure to that language (Höhle et al., 2020). Despite variability in their exposure to two languages, infants will acquire two or more languages if their environment provides them with sufficient and regular experiences with those languages, as did Tesalia and Diego. There are over 12 million children in the United States and many more from around the world who provide clear evidence that children who are raised in bilingual or multilingual environments learn to speak these languages. Children are even aware of the fact they are doing this, as illustrated by Edwin's belief that "Acme" was the Spanish word for grocery store, because that's what his Spanish-speaking grandmother called it. (Acme was actually the name of a specific grocery store that his grandma often visited.)

Check Your Learning

1. Distinguish between language and communication. How are they the same and how are they different from each other?

2. Explain how proto-conversations, gaze following, and pointing are communicative.

3. List the components of a formal language, and give an example of each.

4. What is meant by a critical period for language development?

5. Can infants acquire more than one language? Explain why or why not.

THEORIES OF LANGUAGE DEVELOPMENT

How do children acquire such a complex system as language, and how do they manage it in such a relatively short time frame? There have been many theories of children's language acquisition that have sought to address this question. One of the most significant controversies is about the relative contributions of nature and nurture in language development. For example, the fact that language is a *human* achievement suggests that language is innate, or part of the human capacity to learn language (Lust et al., 2009; Pinker, 1984/2009). But there also seem to be a lot of environmental factors that influence language development. In addition, theorists have debated about whether infants and young children learn language using language-specific skills, or if language is learned using skills that are used to also learn other things. In the following sections we will discuss the major theories that have been proposed to explain language development (Table 9.2).

Behaviorist Views

In Chapter 1, we introduced philosopher John Locke's description of infants as "blank slates." Locke's emphasis on experience for learning deeply influenced the behaviorist movement in American psychology. According to this view, all behavior, including language, is learned from experiences, specifically through positive reinforcement of desirable behaviors and punishment of undesirable ones (Skinner, 1957). In fact, the behaviorists argued that the same mechanisms were used to learn language that are used to learn all behaviors. Thus, according to these views, the processes used to learn language are domain general, or broad and nonspecific. Certainly, some aspects of language are learned this way. For example, Carter's parents reinforced him for saying "kkkkk" when he saw the cat and later for saying "Hi" when he saw a person. However,

TABLE 9.2 ■ Theories of Language Acquisition			
Theoretical Perspective	**Main Points**	**Stance on Nature and Nurture**	**Specificity of Skills**
Nativist views	Children are born with grammatical knowledge, such as a language acquisition device that allows them to easily acquire language.	These views lean heavily on the nature side by positing innate representations of language structure.	Language learning is guided by skills specific to language.
Behaviorism	Language acquisition is explained by reinforcement of desirable behavior (correct speech, grammar).	These views embrace the environment's role in language acquisition. No mental representations are present at birth. Experience with language accounts for language acquisition.	General skills are recruited for language learning.
Interactionist views			
Connectionism	Language learning emerges from neural structures and language input. Often use computational models to show how language learning is possible with neural connections and powerful learning mechanisms that can detect patterns and structure in the input.	Interaction: Both biological capacities and experience with language input contribute to language acquisition.	General skills are recruited for language learning.
Statistical learning	Infants can extract the regularities in the language input.	Interaction: Both biological capacities and experience with language input account for language acquisition.	General skills are recruited for language learning.
Social interaction	Language is communicative and social. Children use social interactions to aid their language learning. Also, language learning builds on social skills.	Interaction: Both biological capacities and experience with language input contribute to language acquisition.	General skills, particularly those for social interaction, are recruited for language learning.

it does not take extensive observation of young children's language development to make it clear that this is not the only way, or even the primary way, language is learned. Despite all the reinforcement Carter got for saying "kkkkkk," he soon stopped producing it, moving on to other aspects of language development.

Even more problematic for the idea that language is learned solely from experience is the observation that children produce words or phrases not used by caretakers. For example, Alison would say, "My did it," when she meant to say, "I did it." Alison, like most children, would not be corrected. Her parents would correct her by saying, "No Alison, it's *I* did it" *every time* she produced this phrase, but she didn't change her behavior. Once, after such a correction, Alison even looked at her dad and said firmly, "My did it *too!*" It is also not the case that parents only respond to their child based on the grammaticality of their utterances; instead, they often respond based on whether their child said something that was understandable. For example, when he wanted to be picked up, Charlie would often tell his parents to "pick you up." Despite being grammatically incorrect, his parents knew what he was trying to say, always responding to his request by picking him up. Because of observations like these, it quickly became clear that the behaviorist view of language development could not explain all of children's language acquisition.

Nativist Views

Noam Chomsky proposed an alternative view with an extreme emphasis on nature. Chomsky argued that there is simply not enough information from the environment for children to learn language, which he called the **poverty of the stimulus**. According to this perspective, the stimulus, or input, for language development is insufficient for children to learn it just from what they hear. Therefore, Chomsky argued that infants must be born prepared to learn language. In fact, he proposed that infants have a **language acquisition device** (LAD) (Chomsky, 1959), or an instinctive mental capacity that allows them to acquire language even with minimal input. According to this view, language is learned using processes that are specialized for language learning only, and thus they are domain specific. Because all infants have the same LAD, Chomsky reasoned that all languages must have the same **universal grammar**, or a set of structures or rules that govern all languages, so that infants can learn any language from around the world. In proposing so much knowledge in an infant at birth, Chomsky's theory tipped the scale from one extreme of the theoretical spectrum to the other—from nurture to nature—giving a dominant role to innate knowledge where only minimal input from the environment is needed to acquire language.

According to Chomsky, because humans are born with a language acquisition device, language acquisition must be specific to humans. This view of language learning quickly gained influence over the behaviorist theory of language acquisition, as this view explained why children can rapidly acquire language and how they can produce language not heard in their environment, like Alison did when she said, "My did it" or when Charlie asked his parents to "Pick you up."

Interactionist Views

Modern theoretical accounts of language acquisition consider both the biological preparedness of a child to learn language *and* their experience with language in their environments.

Thus, these **interactionist views** recognize that human infants are prepared in some ways to learn language, but their language development is also shaped by their experiences. In addition, interactionist views recognize that infants use skills from other types of learning for language acquisition, such as the ability to track regularities or understand social interactions. In the following sections, we will briefly describe three kinds of interactionist views of language development.

Connectionism

In connectionist views of language development, the infant uses general-purpose learning mechanisms to quickly learn aspects of language from the input that they receive. These powerful learning mechanisms allow them to extract regularities, even if the input is impoverished, as Chomsky argued. In addition, the infant's brain is structured to quickly encode language input. As the brain encodes language input, connections in the brain architecture are strengthened (hence, the term **connectionism**). This is how the brain takes advantage of exposure to and experience with language to form structures to process language. Thus, according to connectionism, the infant is born with powerful learning mechanisms and a simple brain architecture; experience with language input allows the system to evolve to manage increasingly complex input.

Connectionist approaches emerged from information processing theories. In line with this theoretical tradition, one goal of researchers who adopted a connectionist view was to demonstrate how a computer model can learn from language input, mimicking the stages of infants' language development. Researchers would feed particular types of language input (e.g., actual sentences spoken to young children) into a computer model designed to mimic brain architectures and evaluate what the model learned. Using this approach, researchers showed that connectionist models could explain children's acquisition of the past tense (Rummelhart et al., 1986) and how infants learn to attend to the name of objects based on their shapes (Samuelson, 2002). In both cases, the computer model learned by adjusting connections in the architecture of the learning system (the computer model) in response to language inputs. Thus, these examples were powerful in documenting that an innate understanding of language was not required to learn at least some aspects of language. Rather, with the correct neural structures and language input, paired with strong learning processes, infants can acquire language.

Statistical Learning

Some theorists have argued that infants learn language through **statistical learning**. Unlike Chomsky, these theorists argue that there is structure in the language infants hear, and infants are sensitive to regularities in their environment that reflect that structure. In a remarkable and very important study, Jenny Saffran, Elissa Newport, and Dick Aslin found that English-learning 8-month-old infants in the United States could learn what sounds co-occur, just from listening to a new "language" for a few minutes. In this study, infants heard a stream of syllables strung together (e.g., bu-pa-ku); to adult speakers of English, this stream sounded like nonsense. However, it turned out that some syllables were always presented in sequence, and infants recognized those sequences of syllables just from hearing the stream for 2 minutes (Saffran et al., 1996).

Saffran and her colleagues argued that this may be how infants learn that syllables in natural language co-occur and how they identify words. For example, when English-learning infants hear the phrase "pretty baby," they may be able to identify the words because in their experience with English, they have learned that the sound "pre" is often followed by "ty," but that the sound "ty" is rarely followed by the sound "ba." Thus, infants can notice and chunk syllables without direct instruction and without feedback. Their ability to note the co-occurrence among syllables given only brief exposure (just 2 minutes) pointed to strong, domain-general learning mechanisms that support language acquisition. So, the proponents of the statistical learning view think that infants have a learning mechanism that helps them acquire language, just like Chomsky's view. However, unlike Chomsky's theory, this sensitivity to regularities in the input they hear is not specific to their processing of language.

Social Interaction

Several perspectives on language acquisition argue that children acquire language by building on the foundation of social skills and their communication abilities, skills such as gaze following, joint attention, and gestures. In contrast to Chomsky, who argued that the communicative function of language was not relevant to children's acquisition, Elizabeth Bates (1979) argued that the communication aspect of language is the very thing that *drives* language acquisition. Likewise, Jerome Bruner (1983) emphasized the importance of social games and routines in support of language learning. He believed that games such as peek-a-boo or patty-cake allow infants to learn about how to interact with others. These games are rich with social interaction; they also create rich contexts for providing exposure to language.

Related views emphasize that children's interactions with others play a key role in their acquisition of language (Tomasello, 2001; Tomasello & Akhtar, 2000). Some researchers, like Lois Bloom, believe that infants learn language so that they can express their needs and wants and share their thinking with other people (Bloom, 1993). This view not only embraces the perspective that children's desire to communicate motivates them to learn words (Bloom, 1993; Snow, 1999), but also that their social understanding aids in their language acquisition (Baldwin, 1993). Tomasello even argues that language acquisition is simply a by-product of infants' social interactions and their ability to interpret the intent of others' actions (Tomasello, 2001).

Check Your Learning

1. What is the language acquisition device, and what is universal grammar?

2. Which theories of language development emphasize innate grammar? Which ones instead emphasize experience with language?

3. What is meant by domain-specific versus domain-general learning? Which theories argue for domain-specific processes for language acquisition, and which argue for domain-specific processes in language acquisition?

WHAT SHAPES INFANTS' LANGUAGE DEVELOPMENT?

We have just described how theories of language development help us ask questions about nature and nurture in this process. Like most things, language development is the product of both nature *and* nurture. Although it may be tempting to think of nature and nurture as two parallel tracks unfolding side by side, it would be more accurate to think of them as two interwoven threads that intersect continually and mutually across infancy. Here, we will discuss some of the factors that contribute to language development.

Child's Characteristics

Nonhuman animals have difficulty learning language, even with extensive instruction. Human infants, in contrast, quickly pick up language, even though, as Chomsky asserted, the input seems insufficient. These factors have been the primary evidence that infants must be born to learn language and that there are biological factors that determine our language ability.

But this is not the only evidence that biology, or *nature*, influences language development. Look at the milestones in Table 9.3. You will see milestones in both infants' **receptive language**—or the skills related to *recognizing* and *understanding* language—and their **expressive language**—or their ability to produce words. It turns out that no matter what language, or languages, they are learning, children around the world follow the same general progression in their acquisition of language. If you look at the receptive side, you will see that infants first learn the speech sounds of their language and only later do they begin to understand their first words. On the expressive side, you see that infants produce one word at a time before they combine words into sentences. Finally, comparing the two columns, you will see that infants first recognize or comprehend words before they produce them. This universal progression, despite wide differences in which language or languages are learned, has been used as evidence that children are biologically prepared to learn language through a series of stages (Chomsky, 1986; Pinker, 1984/2009). However, as we discussed in Chapter 5 with respect to motor development, we must be careful about the conclusions we draw from observing an apparently universal sequence of developmental milestones. Just as we have seen in other areas of development, the universal sequences in language development may reflect the interaction of multiple systems and the cascading effect of early developmental achievements on later abilities. For example, infants' recognition of words may be a necessary step in their developing ability to produce those words, and the developmental sequence shows how language abilities build over development.

Other evidence of the role of nature comes from the fact that some aspects of language develop in infancy without any obvious experience with language. As we will discuss later when we talk about production of speech, both hearing and deaf infants go through the same early stages of vocalization development, exhibiting the same forms of vocal babbling at similar ages. Thus, vocal babbling appears to emerge without experience and therefore may be a biologically programmed behavior that contributes to language development. However, we will also see that the development of vocal babbling differs for deaf and hearing infants, demonstrating that this aspect of development is not completely determined by nature.

TABLE 9.3 ■ The Milestones of Infant Language Development		
Infant Age	**Receptive Language**	**Expressive Language**
0–3 months	Orients to speech	Cooing 6 ~ 8 weeks
3–7 months	Discriminates the speech sounds from all languages; at 6 months, first evidence of understanding highly frequent words	Simple babbling, such as "ba" or "mi," at 6 months
8–12 months	Speech perception narrows to those in infants' native language; receptive language continues to develop	Reduplicative babbling, such as "mamama" or "dadada," at 6–9 months
12–18 months	Receptive vocabulary continues to grow, understand simple questions and commands, can point to pictures or objects	First words Some toddlers may begin to combine two words (e.g., "More book").
18–24 months	Can understand more complex sentences	New words are added to expressive vocabularies at a faster rate than when they were first learning words. Two-word combinations or, for some toddlers, multiple word combinations are formed.
2–3 years	Can understand increasingly longer and complex sentences	Most toddlers will speak in two- and three-word phrases and say between 200 and 1,000 words. Multi-word combinations start to include plurals, verb forms (e.g., -ing), pronouns, and function words (e.g., "the" or "a").

Perhaps the strongest support for innate language ability comes from infants who are not exposed to a formal language, or whose exposure to language is not consistent—in particular, deaf children who are not exposed to ASL. We saw earlier how these children help us understand the role of critical periods in language development. But even more remarkable is that when infants are completely denied language, such as deaf infants being raised in a house where all language is spoken, they develop their own system of gestures to communicate, or what we call **home signs**. These are called home signs because they are not a formal signed language like ASL, but rather, they are a set of gestures that deaf infants and their hearing families create to communicate.

Susan Goldin-Meadow and her colleagues found that the signs are created by young deaf children, not their caregivers (Goldin-Meadow & Feldman, 1977). Nevertheless, these home signs are more than just communication. They have characteristics of language, as we defined it earlier. The young home signers used their signs in a much more systematic way than their hearing adult family members, suggesting that the signs have a different significance for the signers (who have no other language) and the hearing family members (Goldin-Meadow & Mylander, 1983). Even more remarkably, when home signers have the opportunity to interact

A Deaf Child Using Their Home Sign

iStock/tatyana_tomsickova

with each other, they share their home signs. In fact, in the 1970s when the first school for the Deaf opened in Nicaragua, children arrived without formal language but often with their own unique set of home signs. They shared their home signs with each other and eventually developed a formal language, which is the origin of Nicaraguan Sign Language (Senghas et al., 2004). The point is that there is strong evidence that infants who lack access to language *will create a language all on their own* if given the opportunity.

Environmental Influences on Language Development

As we saw with Genie and Victor, children who do not experience language don't learn it. However, infants don't just experience language; aspects of their environment actually facilitate and scaffold infants' language acquisition. One way adults and even older children change infants' experience with language is by using **infant-directed speech (IDS)** (Fernald et al., 1989). This type of speech has been described as "baby talk," "motherese," or "child-directed speech." It has been observed in many different cultures (Hilton et al., 2022; Kitamura et al., 2001) and is used by most parents, at least in the Western or urban populations that have most often been studied (Cristia, 2022; Fernald et al., 1989; Grieser & Kuhl, 1988; Soderstrom, 2007). It is even characteristic of lullabies that caregivers (mothers and fathers) from around the world sing to soothe their infants and lull them to sleep (Falk, 2009; Hilton et al., 2022; Trehub, 2001; Trehub & Trainor, 1998). If you need an example, all you have to do is picture yourself talking to a baby (or cat or puppy). How is it different from how you would speak to an adult? You might notice that compared to speech used with adults (adult-directed speech [ADS]), IDS is slower in tempo, spoken at a higher pitch, has large changes in pitch (i.e., from high to low), includes longer pauses between words, and exudes positive emotion (Saint-Georges et al., 2013). In addition, when using IDS, caregivers use simple words in short phrases or use words in isolation with lots of repetitions (Cristia et al., 2019; Soderstrom, 2007). A comparison of the acoustic properties of mother's speech to their infants in Fiji, Kenya, and North America suggests that some of these features are common across many diverse cultures and language communities (Broesch et al., 2016).

Why do caregivers use IDS with infants? One reason might be simply that infants like it. When given the choice, English-learning North American infants prefer to listen to IDS than to ADS (Byers-Heinlein et al., 2021; Werker & McLeod, 1989). This preference is particularly evident when the positive emotion of the speech is present (Singh et al., 2002). But the slow and variable tone of IDS might also help infants parse individual words more easily than they could from ADS, and hence, IDS could facilitate language learning. Indeed, Erik Thiessen and his colleagues found that English-learning U.S. infants more easily identified individual words in a continuous stream of speech spoken in IDS than in a continuous stream of speech spoken in ADS (Thiessen et al., 2005). In addition, training English-speaking U.S. parents to use more IDS with their 6-month-old infants leads to greater growth in infants' vocabulary by the time they are 18 months (Ferjan Ramírez et al., 2019). IDS is not universal, however, and infants learn language even in communities that do not use IDS. Nevertheless, in many cultures, one environmental influence on infants' language learning is the use of IDS by the adults who interact with them. And even when caregivers use IDS, there are differences between mothers and fathers in how often or when they do so, just as there are differences across cultures in the specific characteristics and frequency of IDS (Broesch & Bryant, 2018; Ferjan Ramírez, 2022; Fernald & Morikawa, 1993; Loukatou et al., 2021; Shapiro et al., 2021).

Caregiver sensitivity also impacts infants' language development (Tamis-LeMonda et al., 2014). In particular, responding *contingently* to the infants' actions may promote language development. Michael Goldstein and Jennifer Schwade showed how English-speaking U.S. caregivers' contingent responses can promote infants' vocal development (Goldstein & Schwade, 2008). They had mothers wear a wireless headset during interactions with their 9-month-old infants (so that the experimenters could tell them without the infant hearing when to smile, touch, and speak to their infant). Goldstein and Schwade had some mothers interact *contingently* with their infant; smiling at, touching, and speaking to their infant when their infant babbled. Other mothers interacted *noncontingently*; they were told to smile at, touch, and speak to their infant at times that were not related to their infants' vocalizations. Over time, infants whose mothers responded contingently babbled more, and they babbled *better* than before, producing sounds that more closely resembled the phonemes in their mother's spoken language (English). Infants whose mothers responded to them at random (not in response to babbling) did not change their babbling. And this phenomenon goes beyond babbling. Another study of English-speaking, middle-class families in the United States reported that infants whose parents who are particularly responsive to their vocalizations said their first words and combined words at younger ages than infants whose parents were less responsive (Tamis-LeMonda et al., 2001). Altogether, these results show how sensitive parents can help shape infants' language development.

Finally, the language children hear also influences their language development. It is no surprise that infants raised in an English-speaking environment learn to speak English, infants living in an Urdu-speaking environment learn Urdu, and infants living in a Mandarin-speaking environment learn Mandarin. What might be more surprising is that infants' language environment shapes not only *which* language they learn but also the trajectory of their language acquisition. English-learning infants in the United States who hear more language directed at them learn more words and build their vocabularies at a faster rate compared to infants in that community who hear less language (Hoff, 2003; Huttenlocher et al., 1991; Newman et al., 2016; Shneidman & Goldin-Meadow, 2012). Hearing more language also is related to faster processing of familiar words by infants, whether they are learning English (Fernald et al., 2006; Rowe, 2012; Weisleder & Fernald, 2013) or Spanish (Hurtado et al., 2008). But it's not just how much language children hear that matters. Regardless of whether they are learning one language or more than one language, English- and Spanish-learning children who hear high-*quality* language, for example, more unique words, more complex grammar, and decontextualized talk (e.g., beyond the here and now, such as talk about the past or future), have better vocabulary skills later in development (Anderson et al., 2021; Hoff, 2003; Potter et al., 2019; Rowe, 2012; Rowe & Snow, 2020; Weisleder & Fernald, 2013).

Differences in infants' language experience in their homes may be because of many factors, but one source of variability for infants in the United States is family income. On average, English-learning infants in the United States from middle- and high-income families hear more speech and a greater variety of speech directed to them than infants from low-income families (Dailey & Bergelson, 2022; Hart & Risley, 1995; Hoff, 2003; Rowe, 2012, 2018). Not only do English-learning children from low-income families hear less speech, but they also have fewer words in their vocabulary as toddlers and young children (Fernald et al., 2013; Hoff, 2003; Weisleder & Fernald, 2013). As a result of these observations, researchers and policy makers have created interventions to increase the amount of caregiver speech directed at infants, especially for families who are low income (Suskind et al., 2016) or those in cultures that do not typically address speech to infants (Weber et al., 2017). These interventions have been successful both at increasing the amount of speech that caregivers direct to their infants and the amount of language the children produce. Clearly, therefore, aspects of the environment can be shaped to affect children's language development.

The connection between socioeconomic status (SES), or family income, and children's language environment is controversial, however. When researchers measure the total amount of language in English-speaking homes (e.g., including language spoken between adults) rather than only the amount of language that is directed specifically to the child, the difference in infants' language experience across low- and middle-income homes is much smaller (Anderson et al., 2021; Dailey & Bergelson, 2022). In addition, there are large differences in infants' language experience within low, middle-, and higher-income homes. Some infants from low-income English-speaking homes hear more language directed to them than infants from some middle- or higher-income English-speaking homes (Rowe, 2018).

We also must be cautious in concluding that any one particular environmental influence is the only (or even the most important) way that caregivers can help their infants learn language. As we've noted repeatedly, most of the research described here has been done with infants from Western industrialized countries, and often those infants are mostly from White middle-class families. Studies of language learning have only sampled children's acquisition of a small percentage of the world's languages, with most studies biased toward Indo-European languages, leaving unexamined or understudied the vast majority of languages (Kidd & Garcia, 2022; Pye, 2021). But infants are excellent language learners and infants around the world acquire language under a wide range of learning environments. In some communities, such as the Kaluli in Papua New Guinea, infants are not considered communicative partners. As a result, infants typically face away from a caregiver when carried. In these communities, infants gain experience with language by observing conversations among those around them rather than from language directed to them (Ochs et al., 1984). The few studies that have been conducted in these communities show that these infants acquire language on the same developmental timeline as Western children, despite dramatically different methods of transmission (Casillas et al., 2020, 2021). And studies in the United States show that even children used to being addressed directly can still learn words that they overhear, when speech is directed to others (Akhtar et al., 2001; Gampe et al., 2012). Thus, there are multiple ways in which infants can get language input from others.

Check Your Learning

1. Explain how children contribute to their acquisition of language.

2. What are the characteristics of infant-directed speech?

3. Describe the environmental factors that can support language development.

RECEPTIVE LANGUAGE

Recall that receptive language abilities refer to the skills related to *recognizing* and *understanding* language. As we saw earlier, infants' receptive language abilities develop before their expressive language abilities. Before infants utter their first word, they must recognize the sounds (phonemes) and words that make up their language, learn how to segment words from the continuous stream of sounds, and identify words before they can begin to comprehend the *meaning* of a word.

Processing and Segmenting Speech

When Diego's mom was 7 months along in her pregnancy, she and Diego's dad traveled to Japan for a conference (one that brings together researchers who study infants). Diego's dad was so excited to travel to Japan that he spent months and months learning Japanese. However, even with months of practice, Diego's dad struggled to recognize the many words and phrases he had practiced hours to learn, demonstrating how hard it is to process language from fluent speech. Speech recognition—or parsing the speech stream into words and recognizing known words—involves several components. One is noting the **prosody**, or the rhythm and intonation, of a language. Differences in prosody give languages their unique sound, explaining why some languages sound distinct from each other (e.g., Turkish vs. Swedish) and how you might be able to tell what language a person is speaking even if you can't understand what they are saying. Speech recognition also involves speech perception, described in Chapter 4, or the ability to discriminate between the sounds of a language, or the phonemes. Recall from that chapter that as infants gain more and more experience with a particular language, their speech perception begins to change and becomes more specific to the language (or languages) they are most accustomed to hearing. This specialization to the phonemes of the language in an infant's environment also occurs in sign languages (Palmer et al., 2012). You can imagine how perceiving the sounds of a language would help with recognizing words. In fact, one study of monolingual English-learning infants found that infants who were more sensitive to differences in English speech sounds at 7 ½ months had larger vocabularies at age 2 ½ years. Interestingly, sensitivity to a difference in speech sounds used in Spanish, but not English, was not related to their later vocabulary, suggesting that specializing speech perception to be focused on the language in your environment is an important step in recognizing and learning words in that language (Zhao & Kuhl, 2022).

But recognizing the overall prosody and the speech sounds are not sufficient for speech recognition. Another important aspect of processing speech is **word segmentation**, the ability to parse words from a continuous stream of fluent speech. One reason Diego's dad struggled to comprehend Japanese once in Japan is because it was difficult for him to pick out a recognizable word when spoken by a native speaker in fluent speech. Fluent speakers of a language do not insert a pause between each word. Rather, speech is a continuous stream of sounds with no pauses. When listening to an unfamiliar language, it takes a lot of effort and careful attention to pick out individual words in the speech stream.

Imagine how challenging this task is for infants who have yet to understand words. Nevertheless, infants do segment words from fluent speech. Peter Jusczyk and Richard Aslin (1995) were the first to demonstrate this in a group of 7.5-month-old English-learning infants in the United States. They used a procedure in which infants first heard familiar English words (such as "cup" and "dog") one at a time. They made sure that infants were listening by teaching them that the words would repeat whenever they turned their heads to look at a light. After the infants heard the list of words, they heard sentences that contained the familiar words, for example, "His cup was filled with milk," and sentences that did not contain the familiar words, for example, "The girl rode her bike." Infants listened longer to the sentences that had the familiar words than to the sentences that did not. Thus, these 7.5-month-old English-learning infants learned the familiar words and then recognized sentences that contained those familiar words, demonstrating that they could segment familiar words from an ongoing stream of speech. Other studies have shown that like these English-learning infants, monolingual infants learning Dutch (Houston et al., 2000), German (Hohle & Weissenborn, 2003), Japanese (Kajikawa &

Masataka, 2003), and French (Nazzi et al., 2006; Polka et al., 2017) can segment familiar words from speech streams.

How do infants segment speech into words? One way is that they can recognize the statistical regularities of how the syllables in the speech are distributed to "find" words. An English-learning infant who hears, "Oooooh, what a lovely baby" one day and on another day, hears, "Let's see how this baby is feeling today" can notice that the syllable "by" follows the syllable "ba" regularly, but that "by" is followed by different things. Seven-month-old English-learning infants can rapidly learn those regularities, even in nonsense languages (Saffran et al., 1996). Between 7 and 9 months, infants learning only French or English can use the regularities in the language they hear around them to segment words from speech (Gonzalez-Gomez & Nazzi, 2013; Mattys & Jusczyk, 2001). Interestingly, infants who regularly hear two languages, but not infants who are exposed to only one language, can segment words from two new (nonsense) languages (Antovich & Graf Estes, 2018; Orena & Polka, 2019).

English-learning 7-month-old infants' ability to segment words is aided by seeing a speaker's face while hearing speech (Tan et al., 2022). Infants also use their knowledge of their language, including familiar words, to segment words. For example, German-learning 6.5-month-old infants more easily segmented words that sound similar to familiar words (Altvater-Mackensen & Mani, 2013), and English-learning U.S. 6-month-old infants segmented an unfamiliar word when it came after a highly familiar word, such as "mommy" (Bortfeld et al., 2005). Thus, infants use what they know of their native language to assist in segmenting words from the fluent speech they hear. How adults interact with infants also can aid infants' word segmentation. As one example, 7-month-old English-learning infants who heard sentences that included four nonsense words (dibo, kuda, lagoti, nifopa) were able to identify the "words" if they heard adults speak the sentences in IDS (infant-directed speech) but not if they heard adults speak the same sentences in ADS (adult-directed speech) (Thiessen et al., 2005). Adults can also aid English-learning infants' word segmentation by synchronizing a tactile cue (e.g., touching an infants' knee) with each occurrence of a particular word (Seidl et al., 2015).

One challenge infants must overcome in word segmentation is the variability in the surface form of words, such as changes in the affect of a word (positive vs. neutral tone) when it is spoken or changes in speaker. Lehrer Sigh and her colleagues (2004) found that English-learning infants in the United States had difficulty recognizing familiar words in fluent speech if the speaker changed the affect of how they said the word, such as switching from a positive to a neutral tone. Similarly, Katharine Graf Estes and Casey Lew-Williams (2015) found that English-learning U.S. 8-month-old infants did not recognize a word in fluent speech in an unfamiliar nonsense language when spoken by a new person. However, gaining experience with variations in the surface features of a word, such as the word said with many types of affect (Singh, 2008) or heard spoken by several different speakers (Graf Estes & Lew-Williams, 2015), aids infants in recognizing the words. These results highlight the importance of variability with the surface features of how words are articulated in fluent speech in facilitating infants' recognition of words in fluent speech. Infants' word segmentation continues to become more robust as infants gain more experience with their language and with exposure to a greater variety of speakers of their language.

Linking Words to Referents and Early Language Comprehension

One of the most exciting hallmarks of early language acquisition is when infants show that they recognize the meaning of the words they hear. In the previous section we showed that by the middle of the first year infants can "find" or parse words in fluent speech, even if they don't know what the words mean. What parents are most excited about is when infants show that they understand the *meaning* of the words they hear. As Diego approached his first birthday, he showed signs of understanding words he heard often. He would pick out a book when asked, "Do you want to read a book?" At 11 months, Alison would look at the Christmas tree when asked, "Where is the tree?" Edwin and Carter both understood when asked if they wanted more of their favorite food, even producing the sign for "more." Tesalia and Charlie would look for their older brothers when they heard their brothers' names.

These examples show how infants demonstrate that they understand some words, but we can't get a complete picture of the words infants understand from such examples. Researchers need tools to measure infants' language comprehension. One simple way to do this is to observe whether infants look toward the object or person that a word refers to. This is the idea behind the **looking-while-listening** procedure used to test infants' language comprehension. This task is a variation of the visual preference task we have talked about in previous chapters. Infants are shown two images side by side, and they hear a word or phrase spoken. One image is related to the word or phrase and the other is not; for example, the infant in the previous photo might hear "Where's the bottle?" If infants understand the word or phrase, they should look longer at the corresponding image than at the other image. Using this procedure, Elika Bergelson and Richard Aslin showed that when English-learning 6-month-old U.S. infants heard "mommy" and "daddy," they looked at the appropriate caregiver (Bergelson & Aslin, 2017). Other studies with English-learning infants showed that infants between 6 and 9 months of age looked longer at the appropriate object when they heard words like food items ("apple," "banana," "milk," "juice") or body parts ("nose," "feet," "face") (Bergelson & Swingley, 2012; Syrnyk & Meints, 2017; Tincoff & Jusczyk, 1999, 2012). Thus, in middle-class North American English-speaking homes, by 6 months, infants learn the meanings, or referents, of words they hear frequently.

Infants' ability to link words to their meanings continues to develop gradually over the first year. For example, studies with mostly White infants in Canada and the United States have shown that although 14-month-old English-learning infants can rapidly associate two new labels with two new objects (Werker et al., 1998), infants learning English only or English plus some other language can't do this if the two new words are very similar sounding (e.g., "bih" and "dih") until they are 17 to 20 months of age (Fennell et al., 2007; Werker et al., 2002). Note that in these studies infants *associate* novel words to novel objects. This is an important step in learning to link words with their referents, but it is not the same as understanding that a word is a symbol for an object. That is, forming these associations is an important step in the language development cascade that allows the emergence of words-as-symbols. For example, English-learning children's ability to form associations between words and objects at 17 to 20 months predicts their language skills 2 ½ years later (Bernhardt et al., 2007).

Infants also get help learning the meanings of words from the context in which they hear those words. For example, Carter heard "kitty" most often when the cat was present, and Diego most often heard "book" during reading time. The consistency of words in specific contexts, such as hearing the names of foods most often in the kitchen, may aid infants in learning how to link particular words with what the words refer to (Benitez & Smith, 2012; Custode & Tamis-LeMonda, 2020). But it is not simply the presence of the referent that matters. Aspects of the interactions between the person doing the naming and the toddler are also important. Parents' behaviors can help infants learn words by directing their attention to what is being named. For example, when asked to teach their infant the name of body parts, English-speaking U.S. parents synchronized touches to the infant's body when labeling the body part (Tincoff et al., 2018). In using touch and other attention-regulating behaviors, caregivers shape their child's attention during these interactions. These behaviors help children maintain their attention for longer to a referent that was named, touched, or to which a caregiver gestured (Mendive et al., 2013; Schatz et al., 2022).

These caregiver attention-regulating behaviors are associated with children's language development. One kind of caregiver attention-regulating behavior is **joint engagement** (Bakeman & Adamson, 1984), or coordinating attention so both the caregiver and child are attending to the same object at the same time. Dare Baldwin (1991) found that English-learning U.S. toddlers between 16 and 19 months learn novel object labels when the speaker and infant were both looking at the object being labeled, or when they were involved in joint engagement. When the speaker and infant were looking at different objects as the speaker utters a label, toddlers did not learn the label for the object. By 19 months, English-learning U.S. toddlers will follow the direction of a speaker's gaze to link a word to where the speaker is looking (Hollich et al., 2000), suggesting they recognize the importance of joint engagement during object labeling.

Parents seem to actively structure their interactions with their toddlers in ways that help language learning. For example, studies have shown that when Korean and U.S. mothers were more likely to follow their child's attention during interactions, labeling the objects that were the focus of their child's attention, their children had larger expressive vocabularies (Carpenter et al., 1998; Sung & Hsu, 2009). Chen Yu and Linda Smith have more systematically explored how parents structure their interactions with their toddlers in ways that help word learning. In samples of mostly White English-speaking families in the United States, Yu and Smith measure where the child and parent look during interactions by having them both wear cameras on their head (see next photo). The recordings of these interactions showed that parents didn't just name objects randomly; instead, they mostly named objects that the toddler was holding or had in front of them (Pereira et al., 2014; Yurovsky et al., 2013; Yu & Smith, 2012). What is more, the named objects were visually larger in the infants' view compared to other objects, facilitating infants' attention to the named object. In another study, Catalina Suarez-Rivera and her colleagues (2022) found that U.S. English-speaking mothers from middle-class families often named the objects their toddlers of 16 to 23 months were manipulating. Toddler-manipulated objects were more likely to be among the words that infants understood and spontaneously named compared to objects that toddlers did not handle. Thus, parents can structure their interactions with young children to help them learn the meanings of words.

THE VIEW OF AN OBJECT FROM A TODDLER'S HEAD-MOUNTED CAMERA: The view from a head-mounted camera worn by a toddler during a play task with novel objects that were labeled during the play session.

Pereira, Smith, & Yu (2014).

As children learn words, they develop expectations for the kinds of things words refer to. For example, in their second year, English-learning U.S. children assume that words refer to objects of the same *shape* rather than to objects that share a different feature, such as color or texture (Samuelson, 2002; Smith et al., 2002). When they learn a new word, young children also use it to refer to other objects with the same shape as the original object, what researchers have called a shape bias. This preference seems to reflect the fact that English-learning U.S. children hear (and learn) many more words that refer to categories of objects that share a common shape (e.g., ball, shoe). As they learn many of these category labels, they begin to expect that new labels also refer to things that have a common shape.

This bias, however, may depend on the language and culture the child is developing in. For example, Erin Hahn and Lisa Cantrell (2012) studied the shape bias in 2- to 3-year-old toddlers learning either English or Spanish. The children were taught a name for an unfamiliar object and then were asked which other objects had the same name. The English-speaking toddlers extended the name to an object based on shape, but the Spanish-speaking children did not. Even more remarkable, another study showed that 18- to 24-month-old toddlers learning *both* Spanish and English generalized a novel noun based on shape only when learning the word in English and not when learning the word in Spanish (Schonberg et al., 2020). Similarly, both child and adult speakers of Tsimané, a community in the Bolivian Amazon, did not extend a novel object based on shape to the same degree as English speakers in the United States (Jara-Ettinger et al., 2022). Further evidence about the differences comes from looking at children's vocabularies. English-learning 15- to 44-month-old children have many more words for objects than animals and Japanese-learning children of the same age have about the same number of words for both objects and animals (Yoshida & Smith, 2001). Thus, the shape bias for learning to name objects emerges in children learning English; children learning other languages develop different expectations that help them to learn new words based on how labels are used in their language.

EXPRESSIVE LANGUAGE

Although infants may learn the meaning of words by 6 or 7 months, across many different languages and cultures they don't say their first words until sometime around their first birthdays (Benedict, 1979; Casillas et al., 2020; Fenson et al., 1994; Huttenlocher & Smiley, 1987). And, just as infants' understanding of language builds on their speech perception, word segmentation, and word learning, infants' utterance of their first words builds on their first vocalizations.

Cooing and Babbling

The early development of vocalizations likely reflects infants' developing control over their tongue, mouth, and the ability to move air through their vocal track. Indeed, across many distinct language environments, the development of vocalization is the same. Even infants born deaf progress through the same early stages of vocalization development. At about 6 to 8 weeks, infants begin to produce coos, which sound like a single extended vowel sound. Over the next few weeks, infants begin to produce a greater variety of vowel sounds and combine vowel sounds as they approach 16 weeks of age.

Consonants first emerge in infants' vocalization at about 2 or 3 months of age, but they are limited to consonants produced in the back of the mouth, sounds such as the [k] or [g]. So, the idea that infants say "goo-goo gah-gah" likely originates from infants' reliance on these back-of-the-mouth consonants. It is not until 3 months later, when infants are 6 months of age that they produce consonants articulated in the front of the mouth, consonants such as [m], [p], [b], [d], [n] (Ingram, 1989; McCarthy, 1954). So, infants shift from producing only vowels in their first 2 months, to producing velar consonants (the [k] and [g]) in the back of the mouth, to producing consonants in the front of the mouth.

After the first months, two types of babbling emerge. Between 6 and 9 months, sequences of consonant–vowel sound combinations, such as "mamamama" or "dadadada," emerges (de Boysson-Bardies, 1996/1999). This type of babbling is described as **reduplicated babbling,** or canonical babbling, and is defined as having true syllables in the infants' vocal productions. Infants typically don't produce reduplicative babbling for communication, but rather they produce it as they are playing or moving about. It is as if they are simply practicing the speech sounds they can make. However, this type of babbling depends on hearing speech. For example, even though deaf infants produce the earlier types of babbling, they engage in much less canonical babbling, and it emerges much later (Oller & Eilers, 1988). Indeed, some deaf infants don't exhibit this type of babbling at all (Oller et al., 1985). Canonical or reduplicative babbling also varies among hearing infants, depending on their language and culture (Cychosz et al., 2020). By about 10 months, infants' reduplicative babbling begins to reflect the language they are hearing (Blake & de Boysson-Bardies, 1992; Whalen et al., 2007).

Non-reduplicated babbling, also known as variegated babbling, emerges a bit later than the reduplicated babbling. Whereas reduplicated babbling involves repeating the same sound ("baba"), non-reduplicated babbling includes two or more consonants. In this kind of babbling, infants produce sounds that combine different consonant–vowel combinations (e.g., "magu"). That is, infants shift from only producing a single consonant–vowel combination to incorporating distinct consonant–vowel combinations. Infants also use different intonations as they babble; that is, they add prosody. Thus, during this phase, infants sound as though they are producing words (until one listens carefully and realizes the infant is using entirely nonsense syllables). This milestone has been observed in infants learning different languages, including English (Oller et al., 2020), Catalan (Esteve-Gibert & Prieto, 2013), and Mandarin (Chen & Kent, 2009).

Although infants' babbling is adorable and fun, it is also important for their developing ability to articulate language. Specifically, by babbling, infants practice making sounds and develop the vocal repertoire for articulating their first words. For example, Seunghee Ha and her colleagues collected day-long recordings of Korean- and English-learning infants between 9 to 21 months (Ha et al., 2021) and found that although the two groups of infants had similar amounts of babbling, English-learning infants' babbling had sounds found in English, and Korean-learning infants' babbling had sounds found in Korean. In fact, infants' babbling is similar to the first words they speak (Keren-Portnoy et al., 2009; McCune & Vihman, 2001). Indeed, infants' production of speech sounds continues to develop even after they begin to produce their first word. When Alison was 16 months, she said "wah-wah," both for flower and for water because she was still developing the vocal motoric skills to articulate all of the sounds in the words "flower" and "water."

BOX 9.2—INFANCY RESEARCH: HOW DO WE STUDY EXPRESSIVE LANGUAGE DEVELOPMENT IN INFANCY?

Throughout this book we have discussed the challenges in studying infants. Conducting studies to give an accurate understanding of infants' developing expressive language is especially challenging. Often when in a laboratory setting, infants feel a little anxious and shy, so they don't talk as much as they do at home. In addition, it might take more than a short 10 or 15 minutes of interacting with an infant to get a good understanding of their expressive language abilities.

In fact, the first studies aimed at charting how infants learn language were conducted by parents who were researchers and who meticulously recorded every word and utterance their child said in a diary (Leopold, 1939), much like how Piaget described his own children's cognitive development (see Chapter 7). In the 1960s, Roger Brown launched a study of children's expressive language development using a fancy new technology at the time, audio recordings. Brown and his colleagues recorded the speech of three children, Adam, Eve, and Sarah (these were not their real names), starting when they were between 18 months and 2 years, every month during naturalistic interactions at home. These recordings were transcribed and became the first recordings included in a database of children's language called the Child Language Data Exchange System, or CHILDES. Brian MacWhinney and Catherine Snow created this database to provide researchers with access to as much data about language development as possible. Over the years, many researchers have added transcripts from recordings of other children across the world. CHILDES now has language development from over 130 children, including 32 different languages. This database is publicly available, and any researcher who has a question about language development can use it.

The advantage to the CHILDES database is that it has transcripts from recordings taken during the child's everyday life. Thus, it can provide an accurate sense of what language children produce. The CHILDES database has also been used to examine what language children actually hear (MacWhinney, 2000). Because many of the recordings involve children interacting with a parent or caregiver, the database also includes information about the language spoken to children during ordinary, everyday interactions. In addition, the efforts to collect data have been worldwide, so the CHILDES database contains transcripts of child language in languages ranging from English to Mandarin to Farsi to Danish. There are even transcripts for children learning more than one language.

But the CHILDES database has limitations, too. Many recordings, like the original ones of Adam, Eve, and Sarah, were short, so they only give a limited view of infants' expressive language. In 2004, Language ENvironment Analysis (LENA) system was developed. In this system, children wear a special recorder—usually tucked away in a pocket of a vest or t-shirt created just for this purpose—all day long, and all the language the child hears and produces is recorded. This system was originally created to help provide information about the quality and quantity of speech to young children and to support increasing the language input to young children. Researchers began to use it to get day-long recordings, often 2 or 3 days in a row. The LENA system has been especially important for understanding the language infants and young children hear (Bergelson et al., 2019; Bulgarelli & Bergelson, 2020; Gilkerson et al., 2017). Although these are rich datasets for understanding early language development, transcribing, coding, and analyzing multiple recordings that can be 12 or 13 hours long for multiple infants can be time consuming and expensive. Recently, some researchers have been developing computer programs to automatically code aspects of these recordings.

Perhaps the best source of information about infants' language development are parents or caregivers. In the 1990s, the MacArthur-Bates Communicative Development Inventories (MB-CDI) became available (Fenson et al., 1993). This is a checklist that researchers can give to parents or caregivers. It was developed by asking parents about their children's vocabularies, both the words they speak and understand. The result is a list of words and phrases that is several pages long. Parents and caregivers can check which of the listed words their infant understands or says. This checklist has been translated into many languages and can be used with infants and toddlers from 8 to 30 months. Researchers at Stanford University have created a word bank (http://wordbank.stanford.edu/) that has many responses from MB-CDIs around the world. This database allows researchers to examine trends in language development across data collected in many different labs and in different languages.

The MB-CDI is a great tool that allows researchers to get information about a child's language development from the people who know the infant best. It is not perfect, however.

When Alison was 14 months old, her mom filled out the checklist and indicated that Alison only understood four words and only said one word. This meant that Alison's language development was far behind other 14-month-old infants. However, Alison's mom, a developmental psychologist, had a pretty strict definition of what it meant for an infant to understand a word. Another parent might have reported that Alison had many more words. The point is when parents fill out the checklist they use their own ideas about what it means for infants to "understand" or "say" a word, so their responses reflect both their infants' language development and their own interpretation of their infants' behavior.

The other problem with checklists is that they can quickly get out-of-date. The MB-CDI was developed before *Dora the Explorer* came on TV. When Carter and Alison were toddlers, "backpack" was a word they both understood and said. However, because "backpack" was not on the checklist, the estimates of their vocabulary was short by at least one word.

What each of these examples shows is how researchers have overcome the challenges of studying the early development of expressive language. Although none of the solutions described here is perfect, each provides insight into how infants talk and what they hear during naturalistic, everyday interactions, and thus each is an important addition to laboratory observations.

First Words

Across many language environments studied, infants say their first words anywhere between 9 and 15 months (Bloom, 1993). Indeed, even in cultures where infants are not directly spoken to, they utter their first word during the same developmental period as infants in cultures where they are more often spoken to face-to-face. Most middle-class American parents recall their child's first words for many years after they are first uttered. Carter's parents still marvel at the fact that most of his first words were the sounds animals made, such as "woo-woo" for dogs. Not surprisingly, the first words expressed by Tesalia, who is very social, included names for each of her family members ("mama," "dada," and "Deedee" for Diego). Also reflecting her bilingual experience, one of Tesalia's first words was water in Spanish ("agua"). Diego focused his first words on those things he loved most: his parents (efficiently named by the same single-syllable word "Da" for each parent) and airplanes, which he pronounced as "aih-pee." Both Edwin and Charlie included their favorite toy (a ball) in the first words spoken. When Alison was 16 months, her parents would take her for walks around the neighborhood. She would yell "Ya-doh." Her parents had no idea what she was saying, but she kept saying it over and over again. Finally, they realized she was requesting "Old MacDonald," which they often sang as they pushed her in the stroller.

As these examples show, infants' first words refer to particular individuals, routines, or sound effects. This is true for infants learning different languages and raised in different cultures (Tardif et al., 2008). Mika Braginsky and colleagues examined parental reports of 32,000 children's word learning in 10 languages, Croatian, Danish, English (American), French (Quebec), Italian, Norwegian, Russian, Spanish (Mexican), Swedish, and Turkish (Braginsky et al., 2019). What they found was striking: Across all these languages, children learned first concrete nouns, or nouns that refer to objects, and highly frequent verbs, such as touch, kiss, and drink. Why do they learn these words first? These are the words that infuse infants' daily experiences and that can be linked easily to what is named (Laing & Bergelson, 2020).

Infants' first words may not have the same meaning as they do for an older speaker of a language. When naming, infants may extend a word too broadly. One example is the embarrassing incident of a young toddler's pointing to all adult males and pronouncing, "Daddy!" Such a naming error is known as **overextension**, or when a word is applied to a broader array than the meaning of the word. One of us knew a toddler who called the fish in the fish tank at the doctor's office "doggies" and "kitties." Charlie's answering every question about color with "yellow" (see Chapter 4) might be considered an overextension.

Sometimes children apply a word too narrowly, a phenomenon called **underextension**. In this case, a child uses a word for only very specific instances even though it would be appropriate to use it more broadly. Diego and Tesalia, for example, used the term "abuela" only to refer to their grandmother, believing it was her name. The same was true for one of the authors of this book, and in fact she referred to her Spanish-speaking grandmother as "Aba" (which is how she first learned to say "abuela" as an infant) for her entire life. Not until later did they learn that "abuela" is the Spanish term for grandmother and applies to all women with grandchildren.

Combining Words

By the time they approach their second birthday, children learning many different languages, including (American) English, Italian, Croatian, Estonian, and Finnish, have advanced from only saying only a few words around their first birthday to saying more than 200 words and have begun combining words (Caselli et al., 1999; Fenson et al., 1994; Hoff et al., 2018; Kuvač-Kraljević et al., 2021). Children shift from typically saying only one word (e.g., "up" or "more") to beginning to combine two words, producing short phrases (e.g., "more juice"). Infants' ability to combine words is related more to their increasing vocabulary than to their age (Caselli et al., 1999; Conboy & Thal, 2006; Devescovi et al., 2005; Hoff et al., 2018; Kuvač-Kraljević et al., 2021; Marchman et al., 2004). Young children rarely begin to combine words before they can say 50 words, and virtually all children combine words when they have vocabularies of between 50 and 200 words (Marchman et al., 2004). This relation between the number of words children say and their combining of words is seen in early talkers, late talkers, bilingual children, and children with Williams syndrome, who typically demonstrate language delays (Bates et al., 1997; Conboy & Thal, 2006; Thal et al., 1997). Just as with the timing of motor milestones (see Chapter 4), there is variability in when children achieve these different language milestones. In general, children who are slower to say their first words are often slower to begin to put words together. Both Carter and Diego did not really put words together until sometime around their second birthdays.

Children's early word combinations are often unique. Remember Charlie's utterance "pick you up"? When a babysitter wanted toddler Tesalia to get to bed, she refused, saying, "No. I busy. Book," pointing to her copy of *Goodnight Gorilla* to explain how her busy schedule simply did not allow for bedtime to occur any time soon. Of course, sometimes these early utterances are repetitions of what has been heard. At about 20 months, Alison dropped a shampoo bottle on the bathroom floor and said, "Oh sit!" mimicking something her mother had said (but leaving out an important letter). Even so, there are similarities in these early word combinations.

Typically, the first word combinations that young children produce are missing morphemes (e.g., such as, in English, the plural "s") and function words (e.g., in English "the," "a"). It is not until children begin stringing together three or more words together that they begin to add morphemes to words. Remember, morphemes are small units of speech that add meaning. So, when English-learning children are between 18 and 24 months, they start adding the morpheme ending "s" for plural (Brown, 1973; De Villiers & de Villiers, 1973) or "ing" for continuous verbs. They begin to talk about "reading" and "shoes," instead of just "read" and "shoe." Between the ages of 2 and 3 years, children begin to use pronouns, as in Charlie's "pick you up" and Diego's "need you me" and Alison's "my did it" described earlier in this chapter. Children begin to add more grammatical constructions during this time, although the emergence of some grammatical forms appear earlier in children's speech. For example, children across languages will use suffixes, such as the plural "s" in "dogs" in English, before using prefixes, such as the "un" in "unhappy" in English (Kuczaj, 1979). Children also begin to ask questions around their second birthdays (Vasilyeva et al., 2008). Wh-questions in simple sentences, such as "What doing?" branch out with age to a greater variety of questions embedded in more complex sentences, as in the thought-provoking query of "Which is bigger? A swimming pool or the ocean?"

Check Your Learning

1. Describe the stages of expressive language from cooing to combining words.

2. Define underextensions and overextensions. Give an example of each.

SUMMARY

This chapter provided an overview of language development in infancy during the first 2 years. The journey from producing only cries of distress to forming sentences unfolds to the pace of infants' biological readiness to attend to language, process it, and socially connect with others. The exact path of this journey varies with infants' language experiences, but the end point always converges at the same destination—infants' successful acquisition of language.

REVIEW QUESTIONS

1. Why is communication distinct from language? What are the components of language?

2. What are the theories outlined to account for infants' acquisition of language?

3. In what way do children contribute to their acquisition of language? In what ways might the environment (i.e., experience with language) contribute to their acquisition of language?

4. What is prosody, speech perception, word segmentation, and receptive language?

5. What are the stages of infants' expressive language development?

CRITICAL THINKING QUESTIONS

1. A friend tells you that their dog is so smart and understands many words. How might you ask your friend if their dog has truly acquired language?

2. One infant often points to objects to direct attention. Another infant does not try to communicate with their gaze or point. Which infant is more likely to begin to understand and say words earlier in development? Explain your answer.

3. Compare how infants learn to perceive and produce speech sounds.

4. Experience shapes language development in many ways. Describe one way that caregivers can shape their infants' language development in their interactions.

5. Which activity is better suited for helping infants learn new words, reading a book or playing with an electronic toy that plays a recording of the new word? Why?

6. Describe some of the ways that infants learn to link words to their referents.

7. Which toddler is more likely to be combining words into short sentences: the one who is 2 years old and says about 20 words or one who is about 20 months but says 60 words? Explain your reasoning.

KEY TERMS

communication
connectionism
expressive language
gaze following
generative
home signs
infant-directed speech (IDS)
interactionist views
intersubjectivity
joint engagement
language
language acquisition device
looking-while-listening
morphemes

non-reduplicated babbling
overextensions
phonemes
poverty of the stimulus
pragmatics
prosody
proto-conversation
receptive language
reduplicated babbling
statistical learning
syntax
underextensions
universal grammar
word segmentation

10 EMOTIONAL DEVELOPMENT

Any parent of multiple children (and perhaps even parents of one) will tell you that each child is born with their own individual personalities. These personalities are often evident right from birth and become more and more distinct over the course of the first year of life. When Alison was about 10 months old, her dad took her on a carousel ride for the very first time. She laughed with delight as she bounced up and down on the brightly painted horse while her dad held her tight around the waist. Alison showed instant happiness at this new and exciting experience. But when Alison's dad took her younger brother Carter on the same carousel ride when he was about the same age, his reaction couldn't have been more different. He sat very still on the horse, wearing a serious expression as the ride moved around and around. It wasn't until the carousel slowly made its final stop that Carter's serious expression morphed into a happy smirk. Like Alison and Carter, most infants have different emotional reactions to new and even exciting situations; and while some embrace these experiences with a fast smile, others need some time to warm up, while for others, the intensity of something so new can be overwhelming enough to bring a child to tears.

In this chapter, we will talk about how infants develop emotionally, and how their emotional reactions are dependent on concurrent changes in cognition, the social environment, and their own individual styles of responding to changes in the environment. After reading this chapter, you will be able to:

1. *Define* what an emotion is, and identify the ways in which we can measure emotions in infants.

2. *Explain* how affect and cognition interact to produce specific emotions and how changes in cognition affect the developmental trajectory of emotional expression.

3. *Describe* how children come to understand and identify the emotions of others.

4. *Explain* how temperament, or a child's individual style of responding emotionally to changes in the environment, shapes emotional behavior.

5. *Describe* developmental changes in infants' ability to regulate their emotional responses over time.

WHAT IS AN EMOTION?

In 1884, the famous American philosopher and psychologist William James wrote an essay that posed an important question: *What is an emotion?* At first blush, you might think you'd have an easy time coming up with an answer to his century-old musing. We've all experienced happiness when seeing a friend or family member for the first time in months, or when celebrating a promotion, getting a good grade, or finishing up a final exam. Likewise, many of us have experienced the sadness that comes with the loss of a loved one, or the anger that comes with not getting what we want or what we think we deserve. Indeed, emotions like fear, happiness, sadness, anger, and disgust are some of the few experiences that we likely all share at some point in our lives. But despite the commonality of these emotional experiences, emotions are notoriously hard to define scientifically and even harder to study in the lab, especially with infants.

Theories of Emotion

Researchers have argued with each other for hundreds of years about what an emotion is and how it is expressed. Unfortunately, we still haven't come to an agreement, and there is no widely accepted scientific definition for an emotion. Instead, there are two main kinds of theories of emotions, and each defines emotions in a different way. One theory is called the **discrete emotions theory**. According to this theory, emotions evolved as universal biological reactions to common challenges (Ekman & Cordaro, 2011; Izard, 2007; Panksepp, 2007). Scientists who endorse this theory believe that there is a set of "basic" emotions that typically include fear, happiness, anger, disgust, sadness, and surprise (Figure 10.1). Fear, for example, is an emotion that helps us respond quickly and efficiently to danger. If you were to come face to face with a snake while on a leisurely hike in the woods, the fear circuitry in your brain would be activated, causing a stereotyped set of responses, like faster heart rate and sweating. These responses prepare your body to act fast, and they are specific to fear; you would have different responses for other emotions like anger or sadness.

If you have seen the movie *Inside Out*, you are already familiar with this way of thinking about emotions. In the movie, each emotion has a distinct personality and lives in its own home inside the brain. This might make sense intuitively, but in reality, the distinction between different emotions isn't so clear. Think about a time when you've seen someone crying and you weren't sure if they were crying because they were angry, sad, or happy. You have probably also experienced a time when you weren't sure if your own emotional reactions were excitement or fear. Such examples suggest that emotions might not be as distinct and separate as this theory might suggest.

In response to some of these issues, a second kind of theory of emotions has been proposed, called an **emergent theory of emotion** (Coan, 2010). Although there are several different emergent theories, they have many features in common. Most importantly, according to emergent theories, emotions aren't individual characters in the brain. Instead, emotions are the outcome of a process that includes changes in the body and cognition about what's happening in the environment. Remember the example of encountering a

FIGURE 10.1 ■ CAFÉ Samples

Stereotypical depictions of six basic emotions and a neutral face, as posed by children: angry, happy, disgusted, fearful, neutral, sad, and surprised, with the children posing with their mouths open and closed. From the Child Affective Facial Expression Set.

Source: LoBue & Thrasher (2015). Licensed under Creative Commons Attribution License (CC BY), https://creat ivecommons.org/licenses/by/4.0/.

snake while walking in the woods? According to emergent perspectives, your fear reaction reflects several different steps. First, when you detect the snake, your brain prepares the body to act. Then, the prefrontal cortex, which is responsible for conscious thought, registers that what you're looking at is a snake. Your prefrontal cortex also might register that your heart is beating mighty fast. Your body is now ready to run if you need to. At this point, you might also be thinking about your previous experiences with snakes, what you have read and learned about snakes, and whether you think this particular snake is a threat to you. If you realize what you're looking at is a dangerous copperhead, you'd likely feel afraid and run. Instead, if what you're looking at is a harmless corn snake, you might relax your body and continue on your hike.

Although scientists still don't agree about which of these ways of thinking about emotions is right, in this book we will define emotions in a way that makes sense for studying infants. We will refer to an **emotion** as an internal, affective response that is about something specific or some change in the environment. By **affect,** or affective response, we mean a general feeling that is either positive or negative. Although these two are very closely related, they develop at different times (Table 10.1). The ability to experience positive and negative affect is present at or shortly after birth, whereas specific emotions (e.g., fear, sadness, and joy) emerge slowly over the course of development. For example, newborns can cry when they are uncomfortable or in pain, indicating that the newborns can experience negative affect, but the negative emotions of anger, sadness, and fear emerge later. These emotions develop with important changes in cognition. As you will see, cognition plays a large role in emotional expression, and the more thought or cognitive processing that an emotion requires, the later it will emerge in infancy.

Measuring Emotions

Besides not having a definition of emotions that we all agree on, another problem with studying emotions scientifically is that no two people express the same emotion in exactly the same way. For example, when some people are angry, they yell, scream, and may even physically lash out. Others smile, grit their teeth, and look quite calm. And there are some who get so overwhelmed by anger that they cry and look more stereotypically sad than angry. Tesalia, for example, furrowed her brow and made a stereotypically "angry" face when she was mad, whereas Alison cried as if she was sad. Carter in contrast, became very quiet, so much so that the people around him often didn't even know he was mad (let alone *why* he was mad). It can become even more complicated when we compare the emotional expressions of people from different cultures and backgrounds. For example, Antonia Muzard and colleagues observed

TABLE 10.1 ■ Affect vs. Emotion		
	Definition	Example
Emotion	Internal response about something specific or some change in the environment	Fear, sadness, joy
Affect	General feeling that is either positive or negative	Positive, negative

that 1-year-old infants in the United States were more intense in their expression of pleasure and discomfort than were 1-year-old infants in Chile (Muzard et al., 2017), suggesting that although infants in the United States don't necessarily *feel* more intense emotions than infants in Chile, infants in the two cultures have already learned something about how to express emotions from their interactions with others. Because of these stark differences in the way many of us express the very same emotion, the only real way to know if someone is experiencing an emotion is to ask them. Unfortunately, our job is to study infants, and infants aren't so good at answering questions.

One advantage of the fact that emotions are so complicated is that there are a lot of different ways to measure them. There are three major response systems that are all active during an emotional event, and we can measure all of them. The first is *subjective feelings* or thoughts, which can be measured by asking people how they feel or what they think. The second is *behavioral change*, like emotional facial expressions, vocalizations like crying, or approach and avoidance behaviors like running away or hiding. Finally, the third system involves *physiological change*, or changes in the brain or in the body, like faster heart rate and sweating (Table 10.2). Because infants can't talk, we can't measure their subjective feelings. But we can measure the other two response systems—behavioral (e.g., approach/avoidance, laughing/crying) and physiological (e.g., heart rate acceleration/deceleration, breathing faster/slower). However, any single behavior—take crying, for example—can mean a lot of different things if you're an infant (e.g., hungry, overwhelmed, wet, tired, etc.). So, it's pretty important to measure more than one thing if you can.

Check Your Learning

1. Compare discrete theories and emergent theories of emotion. What is the main difference between them?

2. Define affect and define emotion. How are they similar and how are they different?

3. Describe three different ways emotions can be measured in infants.

TABLE 10.2 ■ Ways to Assess Emotions

Emotion Response System	Possible Measures	Example
Subjective feelings or thoughts	Self-report	Asking someone how they feel about snakes
Behavioral changes	Facial expressions, vocalizations, approach and avoidance behaviors	Observing an infant's smiling and cooing in response to its mother
Physiological changes	Heart rate changes, sweating, brain responses	Measuring an infant's heart rate when approached by a stranger

EMOTIONAL EXPRESSION

In discussing the development of emotion, we next need to talk about the development of **emotional expression**, or the observable behavioral responses that are associated with emotions. Emotional expressions reflect both affect (either positive or negative) and cognitive evaluations of the situation. Here, we will focus on the expression of several emotions that are considered to be basic and universal, including happiness, anger, sadness, fear, and disgust (Table 10.3). According to the discrete emotions perspective, these emotions should be expressed in the same way in infants across the globe. Because of this assumption, much of the work on emotional development in infants has been done only in samples of infants from Western, industrialized countries. However, consistent with the emergent perspective, it is important to note that while people might experience these emotions all over the world, the way they are expressed varies greatly from culture to culture. Further, each culture has its own **display rules** for how and when to express emotions in particular social situations. And while children are only first learning about display rules in the infancy period, you'll see some differences in emotional expression across cultures even within the first year or two of life, suggesting that the social environment has a large role to play in the way we express ourselves emotionally.

Happiness

There are very few things that can brighten a room faster than a baby's smile. Lucky for us (and for parents in general), one of the first emotions that infants express is happiness or joy. Happiness is a positive affective response that usually involves smiling and laughter. Infants' very first smiles, or the **neonatal smile**, are typically seen soon after birth, although there is a lot of variability. Alison smiled on her first day, in her hospital bassinet. Charlie and Diego smiled on their second day, and Edwin and Tesalia on their third day. Carter took a bit longer. Unlike smiles that will occur later, these first smiles are not in response to something specific in the environment. Instead, they are thought to be the result of general arousal, and they occur most often during sleep (see next photo). Edwin's first smiles, for example, usually happened in his sleep, or after a satisfying poop.

TABLE 10.3 ■ Development of Emotional Expression		
Emotion	Age	Behavior
Happiness	1.5 to 2.5 months	Social smile
	2 to 5 months	Laughter
Anger	4 to 6 months	Negative affect when goal is blocked
Sadness	4 to 6 months	Negative affect when mother's attention is lost
Fear	8 to 12 months	Negative affect in response to a stranger
Disgust	3 to 12 years	Rejection of specific foods

Between 1 ½ and 2 months of age, the social smile emerges, at least in samples of infants from Western cultures. At this point, infants begin to smile in response to familiar people. In fact, to the delight of our authors, all of the infants we are following—Alison, Carter, Tesalia, Diego, Edwin, and Charlie—smiled at their moms first. In order for infants to express a social smile in response to someone specific, like their mothers, infants first have to learn who is familiar and who isn't. Thus, a social smile depends, in part, on *memory*. As we saw in Chapter 6, even newborn infants have some ability to remember, but many aspects of memory develop considerably during infancy. The emergence of the social smile also reflects the pattern of caregiver–infant interactions and can vary across cultures. For example, in a comparison of two cultures—one in which independence and autonomy is stressed (urban middle-class families from Münster, Germany) and a second in which interdependence among individuals is stressed (rural Nso families, Cameroon)—researchers observed that mothers and infants had more one-on-one interactions in the German sample, German mothers smiled more at their infants, and there was less social smiling by the infants in the Nso sample (Wörmann et al., 2014).

Laughter appears a bit later, between 2 and 5 months in Western samples and becomes more common at the end of the infancy period (24–36 months). When Alison was 5 months, she belly-laughed as her dad blew and popped bubbles with his gum. Edwin began laughing around the same time whenever his mother made raspberry sounds with her mouth. Charlie laughed early—by 3 months, he cackled every time he heard his favorite toy play music. Diego also began laughing at 3 months of age when playing a peek-a-boo game with his "abuelo"

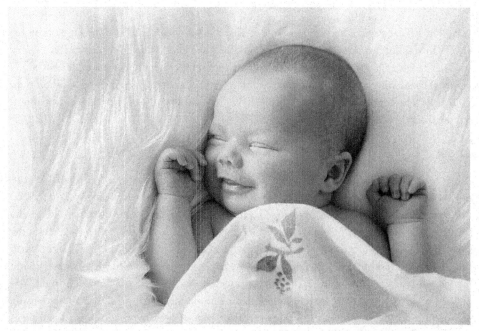

NEONATAL SMILE: Newborn's first smiles, called neonatal smiles, are not in response to anything specific in the environment, and they often occur during sleep.

iStock/NataliaDeriabina

SOCIAL SMILE: Social smiles, or smiles in response to another person, don't emerge until 1 or 2 months of age. Infant laughter emerges between 2 and 5 months of age.

iStock/PeopleImages

(grandpa). Tesalia was a very serious infant and did not laugh until she was 5 ½ months, always in response to something her 2-year-old brother Diego was doing. Importantly, like smiling, laughter is influenced by both culture and temperament. For example, one study reported that Chinese parents rate their infants as engaging in less smiling and laughter than do Spanish parents (Gartstein et al., 2006). We'll talk more about this issue—and infant temperament—in a later section.

Anger

Anger is a negative affective response to obstacles that stand in the way of a desired goal, object, or person. In infants, it can also happen when some kind of established contingency, or learned cause and effect relationship, is interrupted. Here's an example. Imagine 6-month-old Tesalia sitting in a highchair and playing with a spoon. She might discover that when she throws the spoon on the floor, it makes a fun banging sound, and an even more fun "SPLAT" sound when she fills it with food first. What do you suppose happens when mom inevitably steps in and takes the spoon away, interrupting the fun contingency that baby Tesalia has just learned? You guessed it—anger. Anger is generally identified using physical measures, like bodily tensing and/or an arched back, and measures of facial affect, like a furrowed brow and/or a squaring of the mouth. Tesalia was a very active infant and did not appreciate having to sit still; she arched her back in anger and frustration whenever forced to sit in a highchair at mealtime.

Diego's First Laugh (With His Grandpa)

Infants begin expressing anger shortly after they begin expressing happiness, sometime between 2 and 4 months of age in U.S. samples. In some of the earliest research on this topic, Michael Lewis and his colleagues (Lewis et al., 1990) presented U.S. infants between the ages of 2 and 8 months with a slideshow on a large screen. Half of the infants could pull a string to make the slideshow advance, while the other half had no control over when the photos changed. At some point in the experiment, the sneaky researchers switched the setup so that the string no longer made the slideshow go. Infants who initially had control over the slideshow demonstrated significantly more expressions of anger when compared to the group that never had control. These infants displayed more negative facial expressions and fussed or cried more than the other infants. In other words, the infants who learned that pulling the string made the slideshow advance weren't happy when the researchers interrupted their fun. Anger responses were especially strong in infants aged 4 months or older.

Like social smiling, the development of anger reflects, at least in part, cognitive development. Lewis and colleagues argued that the reason why infants don't express anger until around 4 months is because it requires a cognitive process called **means-ends reasoning**. Means-ends reasoning is the ability to understand the relation between your own body and an intended action or goal—a cognitive ability that takes several months to develop. Without it, infants likely can't make predictions about what effect their bodies have on the world, making it hard to plan actions and react negatively when those intended actions are blocked.

Sadness

Sadness is a negative affective response to losing something of value. There is a lot of overlap in infants' expressions of sadness and anger early in development, and these emotions tend to emerge around the same time. Researchers have suggested that the difference between the two lies in whether the emotion elicits approach behaviors, like in the case of anger (e.g., attempting to retrieve a removed toy), or withdrawal behaviors, like in the case of sadness (e.g., burying your head in your mom's lap) (Zeman et al., 2019). Researchers typically study sadness early in development by presenting infants with something positive and then removing that positive stimulus. For example, in the classic **still-face paradigm,** mothers are asked to smile and play with their infants, as they usually do. The infant is typically in an infant seat and the mom and infant interact face-to-face. At some point during the interaction, mothers are told to stop smiling and, instead, pose a neutral or "still" face, no longer responding to her infant. At first, infants keep smiling at their moms and try to re-engage her in play, but eventually they look away, sometimes demonstrating signs of negative affect by frowning or even crying after losing their mothers' attention (Lewis & Ramsay, 2005). Although there are differences in how mothers and infants in different cultures respond to the still-face procedure, research has shown that infants across the world, including infants in the United States, Argentina, China, and the Netherlands, are distressed when their mothers become nonresponsive (Handal et al., 2017; Li et al., 2019; Liu et al., 2020).

Losing something you like and having a goal blocked can sometimes involve similar, overlapping cognitive processes, so it isn't surprising that there is some overlap between the

A Mother Distracted by Her Phone

iStock/pixdeluxe

expression of anger and sadness early in life and likely over the course of development. Again, this is an example of how emotions are hard to identify and sometimes can even blend together depending on the context. I'm sure you can think of a time when you felt both a little sad and angry at the same time; it's possible that infants can feel that way too.

BOX 10.1—INFANCY IN REAL LIFE: CELL PHONES—A MODERN STILL-FACE PARADIGM

Many researchers still use the still-face paradigm to elicit negative affective responses from infants. But, posing a still face in the middle of playtime isn't really how mother–infant interactions take place in the real world. Researchers have begun to think about how infants and mothers actually interact every day to develop a new method for eliciting negative affect from infants in a way that more closely resembles real life. The solution that some researchers in the United States have recently come up with is using cell phones.

Indeed, nothing takes a parent's attention away from their children as effectively as a cell phone. In fact, according to Common Sense Media (2016), U.S. adults spend an average of 9 hours a day on screens, including cell phones, laptops, and tablets. That's a lot of screen time—and a lot of time when infants might be competing with screens for their parents' attention.

To study how infants respond when parents are interrupted by their cell phones, Sarah Myruski and her colleagues asked a group of U.S. mothers to interact with their infants, aged 7 to 24 months, in the lab with a bunch of toys. During playtime, the researchers interrupted the moms by prompting them on their cell phones to take a 2-minute survey. For those 2 minutes, mothers' attention was directed to their cell phones and away from their infants. Like infants' responses in the traditional still-face paradigm, infants in this study played less and tried to get their mothers' attention back while she was distracted by her phone. Even worse, when mothers finished the survey and turned their attention back to the infants, the infants didn't fully recover and played less than before their mothers were interrupted (Myruski et al., 2018).

Likewise, another study, by Jessa Reed, Kathy Hirsh-Pasek, and Roberta Golinkoff (Reed et al., 2017), suggests that being distracted by a cell phone not only interrupts playtime but can also have a negative impact on infants' learning. In this study, the researchers asked U.S. mothers to teach their 2-year-old infants two new words during a playful interaction. As the mothers were trying to teach their infants, the researchers interrupted half of them by calling their cell phones. The interruption was brief, and even with the interruption, mothers who were interrupted spent the same amount of time teaching their infants the words as the mothers who weren't interrupted. But there were still large differences in which infants learned. In fact, infants *only learned the new words* if their mothers weren't interrupted by their cell phones during the interaction.

These studies suggest that all that time parents spend on their cell phones might be affecting the way they interact with infants, at least for White middle-class families like those who were studied in this research. When mothers were interrupted by their phones, their infants learned less from the interaction. On top of that, they spent most of their time trying to get mothers' attention back and played less once they did. So, cell phones might indeed be a natural still-face experiment that happens in homes every day, and this natural loss of mom's attention might even make infants a little sad.

Fear

Fear is a negative affective response to imminent threat. It is thought to be one of our most basic and fundamental emotions because its function is to protect us from harm. However, fear requires a higher level of cognitive processing than sadness or anger. Deciding that something is threatening involves several processes. First, you have to recognize what's familiar and what's novel. If the threatening thing is familiar, you then have to recall your previous experience with it to decide if it has threatening properties (e.g., injections hurt, dogs bite). If the threat is unfamiliar (e.g., a stranger person or place), it might have unknown threatening properties. It's not surprising then that infants' first fear responses don't develop until they are between 8 and 12 months of age and tend to be responses to unfamiliar people, places, or objects.

The classic paradigm researchers have used since the 1960s and 1970s to measure infant fear is called the stranger approach paradigm. The procedure is simple: A novel adult (or stranger) approaches an infant slowly posing a neutral expression, and researchers observe the infants' reactions, which typically include whether the infants show negative affective expressions or whether they try to escape or cling to their moms. Early empirical studies with infants in the United States reported that stranger fear appeared in nearly every infant tested. In most of these early studies, fear first emerged around 8 or 9 months of age, peaked between 12 and 18 months, and then began to wane around the infants' second birthdays (Rheingold & Eckerman, 1973). Infants in these studies typically stopped what they were doing and wore a "sober" expression when the stranger approached, or their expression shifted from positive to neutral. Some infants avoided looking at the stranger altogether. Based on these very early reports of infants' responses to strangers, researchers concluded that stranger fear is innate and universal and should be observed in every infant.

As researchers studied infants in more contexts and used different procedures, however, they found that infants were much more variable in their responses to strangers. When U.S. infants are tested at home, for example, almost none of them show any evidence of stranger fear, even at 12 to 18 months of age when stranger fear is thought to be strong (Ricciuti, 1974; Smith, 1974). Likewise, when tested in a lab, U.S. infants show few negative responses to strangers if they are sitting on their mothers' laps, but more negative responses when they are seated on the floor or restrained in a highchair (Ricciuti, 1974; Smith, 1974). The behavior of the stranger seems to matter too, at least for infants tested in the United States in the 1970s. In one such study, infants showed few negative responses if the stranger stayed far away or if the stranger was a child instead of an adult (Brooks & Lewis, 1976). In other studies, infants showed more negative responses if the stranger was an adult male or if the stranger approached the infant quickly and tried to pick the infant up (Sroufe, 1977).

When you consider all of these results together, it is clear that fear is not a universal response to any stranger, but rather, fear is a specific response to perceived threat: When infants feel safe in the comfort of their own home or in their mother's arms, they don't really react negatively to the presence of a stranger. But when they feel more threatened—when they're in a new place, when they're away from their mothers, or when the stranger behaves in a more threatening way (e.g., is taller or tries to touch the infant)—infants are more likely to show fearful responses (see LoBue & Adolph, 2019, for a review of this literature). Cross-cultural studies have shown similar responses to strangers in infants tested outside of the United States, but there are significant differences in the number and intensity of fearful responses based on culture (e.g., Gartstein, Carranza, et al., 2016).

In other words, context matters; the more threatening the context, the more fear you'll likely observe. And even infants are beginning to learn how intensely fear is expressed in their culture. This isn't very different from the way adults express fear. Snakes can be pretty scary, but they aren't scary in every situation. As we discussed earlier, you might be afraid if you ran into a copperhead on a hiking trail, but you would be less afraid if you ran into a small corn snake. Likewise, if you're in a zoo and a snake is behind a glass wall, you might be fine approaching it. But if you're exploring the Amazon rainforest and a large snake drops down from a nearby tree, you might have a very different response. Of course, there are those of us who would be afraid in all of these situations. If that's you, you just might have a snake **phobia**, or a fear that doesn't depend on the actual threat relevance of the situation. But most infants' early fears, like most of yours, depend on context.

Disgust

Disgust is a unique affective response that typically generates feelings of nausea and avoidance behavior. For example, thinking about feces might make you feel a little woozy, and when you smell it (perhaps from a baby's diaper), you might turn around and walk the other way. Most people associate disgust responses with food, but people also tend to feel disgust toward other people, objects, and even situations or immoral behavior. Some researchers have long thought that disgust is one of the first developing emotions, as even newborns show negative affective responses to tasting something we would think of as disgusting, like something bitter (Rosenstein & Oster, 1988). But many researchers now distinguish between disgust, which involves some kind of cognitive evaluation, and distaste, which is a natural response to an unpleasant flavor. Even newborns can experience distaste, but disgust, at least in the way adults experience it, takes a long time to develop. Indeed, most parents will tell you that infants aren't disgusted very easily and have no problem eating food that has been dropped on the floor, putting things like playdough or dirt into their mouths, or even stomping around in their own poop. Disgusting.

Indeed, infants can do pretty disgusting things, and it's often because they don't experience disgust the same way we do. Fully-fledged disgust responses are mostly socialized or learned by both experience and observation of other people. A classic study by Paul Rozin and his colleagues (Rozin et al., 1985) showed that it isn't until about 6 to 8 years of age that U.S. children reject juice that has been stirred with a used comb or juice with a dead grasshopper visibly floating inside the glass. Younger children happily gulp down the juice, grasshopper and all.

This suggests that disgust develops pretty late in childhood and isn't something you're going to see much in infancy. This might seem counterintuitive, as disgust is often thought of as one of our most basic emotions, and one that protects us from potential harm. However, this is probably a good thing, as it allows infants the flexibility to learn what they think is disgusting and what's not by experiencing the world around them and by absorbing the norms of their own cultures. On a visit to the Audubon Insectarium once, Diego and Tesalia each *begged* for a scorpion lollipop. On the car ride home, while enjoying her lollipop, Tesalia proudly exclaimed, "I am crunching on the scorpion's head!" Indeed, while a grasshopper might be a pretty disgusting thing to eat if you're from the United States or Europe, grasshoppers are considered a delicacy in other parts of the world, like in Mexico, and even carry with them a surprising number of health benefits. (Grasshoppers are high in vitamins A, B, and C, and have lots of protein.) Yum.

Self-Conscious Emotions

There is a whole group of emotions that don't begin to develop until the second year, sometime after the child's first birthday. These are what researchers call the self-conscious emotions. These emotions, like guilt, empathy, shame, embarrassment, and pride, require infants to think about themselves as independent individuals that are distinct from others. Classically, researchers have called this ability a **sense of self**. It was originally measured using a task called the **rouge test** developed in the 1970s. It involves putting a red mark on an infant's face (e.g., lipstick or rouge smudge on their nose) and then presenting the infant with a mirror so that they can see their own rouge-covered reflections. This task was originally developed to see if animals could recognize their own image in a mirror. If they don't recognize their reflection, they'll likely touch the mirror; if they do recognize their reflection, they should touch their own face where the smudge is.

MIRROR RECOGNITION: INFANT. Before 18 months of age, there is little evidence that infants recognize themselves in the mirror. When gazing at their own reflection, try to touch the baby staring back at them.

iStock/nensuria

Before 18 months of age, human infants from Western cultures fail this test. They don't seem to recognize themselves in the mirror; they can certainly *see* themselves, but they behave as if it's some other cute baby looking back at them. Around a year and a half, their responses start to look a bit different, and instead of trying to touch the baby in the mirror, they touch their own face, specifically their rouge-covered noses, showing that they recognize their own reflection. However, this isn't the case for infants everywhere in the world. For example, a study that used a version of the rouge test with infants from Fiji, Saint Lucia, Grenada, Peru, the United States, and Canada revealed that few infants from countries outside the United States and Canada touched the mark on their face at all (Broesch et al., 2011). This calls into question whether mirror recognition is a valid predictor of the emergence of the self-conscious emotions, at least outside of the West. Indeed, it is likely that experience with a mirror might be important for mirror recognition.

But besides a sense of self, the self-conscious emotions also require infants to know something about the expectations of others. For example, to feel guilt or shame, an infant needs to understand that they have done something to hurt or upset someone else. Likewise, to feel pride, an infant needs to understand that they have done something that others value. The ability to reason about the thoughts of others is called theory of mind and is only beginning to develop between 18 to 24 months of age, which is another reason why the self-conscious emotions develop so late in infancy. We'll talk more about the development of theory of mind in the next chapter.

Factors That Influence Emotional Expression

The Role of Genetics

As we pointed out earlier, not everyone expresses emotions in exactly the same way. Remember how as infants, Alison, Carter, and Tesalia all expressed anger differently? One of the reasons people express emotions differently is because there are biological differences that contribute to the way emotions are expressed. As we will talk about later in this chapter, an infant's temperament, which is biologically based, plays a major role in their emotional expression. But there are other biological differences as well. For example, differences in chromosomes can create differences in emotional expression between infants. Consider two different developmental disorders that are caused by chromosomal abnormalities (see Chapter 3). Infants with fragile X syndrome, a developmental disorder caused by a genetic mutation on the X chromosome, typically express higher levels of social anxiety than other infants (Burris et al., 2019). In contrast, children with Down syndrome (DS), a disorder caused by an extra chromosome (three instead of the usual two) of the 21st chromosome, often demonstrate more positive affect and smiling when compared to other children. Other neurodevelopmental differences are associated with atypical emotional development. Autistic children often have difficulties identifying the emotions of others. Difficulties with processing emotional information also have been linked to both fragile X syndrome and Down syndrome. Some of these differences in emotional expression and emotion understanding lie in the underlying biology of the disorders themselves, particularly in the cognitive deficits that accompany them.

The Role of Parenting

Although there are clear differences, for example, in the emotional expressiveness of typically developing infants and infants with fragile X syndrome or Down syndrome, it is possible that these differences are not solely based on genetics. Instead, some of these differences could also result (at least in part) from the way that others respond to infants and young children with these disorders. For example, it could be that the added difficulties of parenting a child with a developmental disorder causes frustration and anxiety in parents, which in turn, affects the emotional signals they project to their infants.

Indeed, there is ample evidence that emotionality in parents affects the emotional development of their children. For example, children of parents with anxiety and depression are at increased risk of developing these same emotional problems themselves when they get older. This could be because of a genetic predisposition to experience anxiety and depression that gets passed down from parents to their infants. But it could also be that an anxious or depressed parent creates a specific emotional environment from which the developing infants learn. For example, anxious parents in the United States are less engaged and more withdrawn during interactions with their children when compared to non-anxious parents (Woodruff-Borden et al., 2002). Consider how this could lead to anxiety in the child. Children of anxious and depressed parents get less emotional information from their environments, and thus how children can learn and think about emotional information varies as a function of how anxious their parents are. Because the children of anxious parents are more likely to be anxious themselves, they may be particularly vulnerable to the quality of emotional information from the input.

There are also cultural differences in the emotional environment. As discussed in Chapter 1 and throughout this book, most of the studies reported here were done in the United States, on White, middle-class families. This is problematic, as cultural beliefs and norms can play a significant role in what infants learn about when and how it is acceptable to express emotions in front of others. In the United States and Western Europe, for example, parents tend to encourage infants and young children to express positive emotions as much as possible (Yang & Wang, 2019). Unfortunately, this comes at the expense of negative emotions, which are more likely to be minimized. Again, like in the movie *Inside Out*, while Joy is always embraced, Sadness is often ignored or pushed aside.

This is especially true for boys. Indeed, whereas girls in the United States are generally encouraged to talk about their negative emotions, boys are more likely to be discouraged from talking about emotions altogether, and emotions like sadness can be completely dismissed. Perhaps as a result, girls are generally better at controlling their emotions than boys are, starting before preschool age (more on this later) (Stifter & Augustine, 2019). In fact, in samples of mostly White, middle-class families in the United States, parents tend to use more emotion words when talking to their infant daughters than their sons, and there is even evidence that parents sing more to their infant girls than to their infant boys (Mascaro et al., 2017).

Furthermore, the expression of positive emotions isn't emphasized equally in all cultures. In Western cultures where independence and autonomy are highly valued, emotional expression is generally encouraged. In contrast, in East Asian countries, harmony within the group is valued more highly than independence. As a result, emotional expression can be viewed as something that might disrupt group harmony and is generally discouraged. Even within the United States, there is evidence of cultural variation in both emotional expressiveness and the developmental relation in emotional expressiveness between the mother and the infant (Rudy et al., 2021). Consistent with cultural norms, European American parents express more positive emotion toward their infants than do Chinese mothers. Likewise, both Asian and Asian American infants express fewer positive and negative emotions than do European American infants (Yang & Wang, 2019).

In some countries, however, infants aren't always raised in a household with just their parents, which is the most common model in the West. In many cultures, especially in countries within South America and Africa, infants are cared for by a system of caregivers that includes the mother and father, as well as other adults and older children. When infants are cared for by multiple people, they are likely impacted by the emotionality of not just their parents but also many of the caretakers around them (see Chapter 12). We can see these differences in a recent study conducted in Sweden and Bhutan. In the study, researchers observed the impact of mothers' postpartum depression (PPD) on infants' ability to follow her gaze. Not surprisingly, PPD negatively impacted Swedish infants' ability to gaze follow. Like most U.S. families, Swedish infants often live with just their parents as caregivers. In contrast, Bhutanese infants' gaze following was not affected by their mother's PPD. Unlike the Swedish infants, the Bhutanese infants are typically raised by many caregivers and are likely less dependent on their mothers' social signals for their own emotional development (Astor et al., 2022). Altogether, this suggests that infants' emotional behavior is determined both by biological, or internal factors driven by the infant, and external, or environmental factors related to the emotional input infants receive.

Check Your Learning

1. How are neonatal and social smiles different?

2. Explain why researchers believe that some emotions develop earlier in development than others.

3. Describe the development of anger, sadness, and fear, and discuss how they are different.

4. What are two cognitive prerequisites for the expression of the self-conscious emotions?

5. What are the ways that biology and the environment influence emotional expression?

EMOTION UNDERSTANDING

If it hasn't yet become clear, despite the fact that we all experience a myriad of emotions every day, an infant's emotional development is a long and complicated road. And although in the last section we only focused on the development of how infants come to *express* various emotions, emotional development also involves how infants learn to *recognize* and *respond to* the emotions of others. In this section, we will discuss how infants come to recognize and differentiate between emotions in other people, and when they begin to extract information about how to behave based on the emotions of others (Table 10.4).

TABLE 10.4 ■ Development of Emotion Understanding	
Developmental Milestone	**Age When Achieved**
Discrimination of different categories of stereotypical emotional facial expressions	3 to 6 months (varies as a function of whether visual information, auditory information, or both are available)
Preference or bias to look at fearful faces	7 months (at least for own race)
Matching voice and face of stereotypical emotion categories	5 to 7 months
Social referencing, or using the emotional expression of others to influence one's own behavior	12 months
Recognizing the emotional expression of others as a cause or consequence of their behavior	18 months

Emotion Perception

Imagine that you are a fetus, traveling down the birth canal and glimpsing the world outside the womb for the very first time. What do you see? First you might flinch at the brightness of the room (it's pretty dark in the womb), but then, you will likely see smiling faces, cooing and talking softly to you in a language you can't yet understand (although it probably seems familiar because you heard it while in the womb, see Chapters 3 and 8). The one face you'll likely see most often is the smiling face of your mother, as she gazes down at you. Not surprisingly, infants begin learning to recognize familiar and unfamiliar faces, and prefer faces to other objects, within hours of birth, which suggests that learning about faces begins almost immediately.

But infants need to do more than just tell the difference between familiar and new faces. They also need to recognize differences between emotional expressions and eventually learn what those differences mean. Within the first months after birth, infants can discriminate between photographs of adults posing different stereotypical emotional facial expressions, like a smiling face versus a droopy frown. For example, using a habituation paradigm like the one we discussed in several of our previous chapters, researchers found that by 3 months of age, U.S. infants discriminate between photographs of adults posing for stereotypically happy, sad, and surprised faces (Young-Browne et al., 1977). By 4 to 6 months, infants can differentiate between various negative affective expressions, like stereotypical photographs of adults posing for anger, fear, and surprise (Serrano et al., 1992). This developmental timing has been observed for infants of different racial and cultural groups, including infants in the United States and Sweden. However, infants from different cultures do use different strategies to discriminate between different emotions. For example, a comparison of infants from Japan and infants from the UK indicated that by 7 months, infants from different cultures use different strategies (e.g., looking at the eyes for Japanese infants vs. mouths for UK infants) to discriminate between emotional expressions (Geangu et al., 2016).

These results show that infants are sensitive to differences in facial expression, especially when those facial expressions reflect stereotypical emotional expressions. However, this does not necessarily mean that infants *understand* the emotional meaning behind those faces. That is, while young infants can see the difference between a smiling and frowning face, they probably don't understand that the smiling face is feeling happy and the frowning face is feeling sad. Instead, infants are likely picking up on physical differences between the faces that allows them to easily tell the faces apart. In other words, just because infants can tell that a smiling face and a droopy frown *look* different from each other, that doesn't mean they know that the frown suggests that the frowning person feels sad. As mentioned in Chapter 6, the first hint we have that infants are beginning to understand something about the meaning of some emotional expressions is when they begin to treat emotion categories differently. For example, at 7 months, infants in Sweden and the United States begin to look longer at photographs of adults posing fearful facial expressions over adults posing other facial expressions (e.g., Peltola et al., 2009). However, we don't know for sure that infants can understand the meaning of an emotional expression until they can use the emotions of others to guide action. We will talk about this more in the coming sections.

Multimodal Emotion Perception

Although many of us associate emotions with facial expressions, emotions are really a multimodal system. In other words, we express emotions in multiple modalities, including our faces, voices, and bodies. Likewise, we also perceive the emotions of others in multiple modalities. In fact, there is evidence that information from multiple modalities can help infants categorize emotional facial expressions sooner than if just given information from one. For example, Ross Flom and Lorraine Bahrick (Flom & Bahrick, 2007) used habituation to explore how a sample of mostly White U.S. infants used facial and vocal cues to discriminate between different emotions. They found that even 4-month-old infants could discriminate between happy, angry, and sad expressions if they were given both facial and auditory information (e.g., a happy face combined with a happy voice). By 5 months, infants could make this discrimination if they were given only auditory information (e.g., a happy voice). It was not until 7 months that infants could discriminate expressions if they were given only photos of posed facial expressions.

Additional work suggests that infants begin to combine emotional information from multiple modalities by 7 months of age, around the same time that they start to look longer at photos of fear faces over other posed facial expressions. Arlene Walker-Andrews (Walker, 1982; Walker-Andrews, 1986, 1997) studied this in samples of U.S. infants using a variation of the cross-modal preferential looking paradigm we discussed in Chapter 4. In this procedure, infants are presented with two photographs of adults posing stereotypical emotional facial expressions side by side on a large screen while a soundtrack is played that expresses one of the two emotions vocally. For example, infants might see a photograph of an adult posing a happy face next to a photograph of an adult posing an angry face and, at the same time, hear either a happy or angry voice. Walker-Andrews reasoned that if infants had formed multimodal categories of emotions, including both facial and vocal information, they should look longer at the photo of the posed face that matched the voice they heard in the background. At 5 to 7 months, the samples of U.S. infants Walker-Andrews studied consistently looked longer at the face that matched the voice they heard, regardless of the posed expression. This suggests that by the second half of the first year of life, infants (at least in Western cultures) are beginning to combine different kinds of emotional information to recognize the emotions of others.

Social Referencing

As mentioned earlier, it isn't clear that infants understand that different emotional expressions carry some underlying meaning until they can use emotional information to make predictions about how people will behave, or to guide their own behavior. One sign that infants are beginning to understand something about the meaning behind the emotional expressions of others is when they begin to engage in **social referencing** behavior, which emerges in typically developing infants in the United States between 10 to 12 months of age (Walden & Ogan, 1988). Social referencing is when infants look for information from others, usually a caregiver, when a situation is new or uncertain. In other words, when presented with a novel person, object, or situation, infants might look to their mothers' faces for information about what they should do. If mom smiles and nods, that tells the infant that it's safe to play. If, however, mom tenses up and shakes her head, that tells the infant that the situation is unsafe. Given that infants are faced with new and ambiguous situations all the time, social referencing is a great way for them to gather information and learn about which actions are appropriate and which actions are not.

Researchers have used infants' social referencing as a way of studying how infants understand the emotions of others. In these studies, researchers place infants in an ambiguous situation, for example, in a room with a new toy or unfamiliar person, and observe how the infants use an adult's facial expressions to adjust their own behavior. In some studies, the researchers will teach mothers to show fearfulness or happiness to see how the infants respond. In one study, U.S. 12-month-old infants avoided playing with a novel toy after watching an adult react to it with a negative versus positive or neutral facial expression (Mumme & Fernald, 2003). In another study, U.S. 12-month-old infants were more likely to avoid crossing the deep side of a visual cliff when their mothers stood on the other side posing a fearful expression than when she was posing a happy expression (Sorce et al., 1985).

Infants around the same age also infer the cause of an individual's behavior by looking at their emotional facial expressions. For example, Ashley Ruba, Andy Meltzoff, and Betty Repacholi found that U.S. 18-month-old infants looked longer when a researcher posed facial and vocal expressions that mismatched or were inconsistent with an event (i.e., showing disgust when trying to place three balls in a bowl and accidentally knocking one of the balls out of reach, or showing anger when pouring food into a bowl and taking a bite) than when the researcher's emotion matched or was consistent with the event (i.e., anger in response to the out-of-reach ball and disgust in response to the food), suggesting that the mismatch was unexpected (Ruba et al., 2019). This work and the work described in the previous paragraph suggest that between 12 and 18 months of age, infants (at least those tested in the United States) move beyond the ability to discriminate between different emotional expressions based purely on perceptual features and begin to link emotional information with their likely causes and consequences.

One limitation of our understanding of social referencing is that researchers have studied it only in North American and Western European samples. This makes it hard to know whether all children engage in this behavior, and if so, whether it develops in the same ways across cultures. What we do know is that the development of some of the basic aspects of social referencing, like gaze following and pointing behavior (which we will talk about more in the next chapter), develop universally along similar timelines, suggesting that social referencing might also be somewhat universal. But we also know that other aspects of the social environment, like how we communicate and how parents interact with their infants, varies widely from culture to culture, which might make the emotional information gleaned from social information vary as well (Fawcett & Liszkowski, 2015).

BOX 10.2—THE WHOLE INFANT: SOCIAL REFERENCING ON THE VISUAL CLIFF

When infants begin to crawl or walk independently, they can navigate the world on their own for the very first time, opening up significantly more possibilities to encounter unfamiliar objects and situations. This makes emotional signals from their caregivers about whether those new objects and situations are safe or risky even more important than ever before. As mentioned earlier, researchers have studied how mothers' emotional expressions help guide infants' behavior when presented with locomotor challenges, like the challenge of whether to cross the visual cliff. As a reminder, the visual cliff is an apparatus that contains a large piece of plexiglass covering a checkerboard cloth. The checkerboard cloth functions to make depth information visibly clear. On one side of the visual cliff (the shallow side), the checkerboard cloth is placed right below the plexiglass. On the other side (the deep side), the cloth is placed at some depth below the plexiglass, giving the appearance of a drop-off. However, the plexiglass top makes it so that an infant can crawl or walk across both sides of the apparatus completely safely (see Chapters 1 and 5).

To study the effect of social referencing on infants' behavior in this situation, Sorce and colleagues created an ambiguous version of the visual cliff. Instead of the big drop that is generally used, they used an ambiguous drop-off height (30 cm). This variation is important because infants would likely never crawl over the big drop-off that is typically used. But this 30-cm drop is more like a big step, so it might be safe for infants to step or crawl off. As mentioned earlier, in this situation, U.S. infants cross the deep side of the visual cliff if their mothers stand on the other side posing a happy face, but they refuse to cross if their mothers pose a fearful face.

But, the visual cliff is ambiguous or novel for infants in another way. It gives the appearance of a drop-off but is, in reality, perfectly safe because of the plexiglass top. The question is whether infants would really cross the visual cliff if there was no plexiglass. Lana Karasik and colleagues (2016) conducted just this study. They asked whether U.S. infants would cross a real cliff with no safety glass and whether the mother's emotional cues would have an effect on how infants behaved. They tested experienced 12-month-old crawlers, novice 12-month-old walkers, and experienced 18-month-old walkers from the United States. Instead of just presenting the infants with one ambiguous depth, the researchers presented them with different sized drop-offs, including safe ones (1 cm), dangerous ones (90 cm), and ambiguous ones (between 10 and 20 cm), where it wasn't exactly clear whether the drop-off was safe or too risky to descend. For safe 1-cm drop-offs, experienced 12-month-old crawlers and 18-month-old walkers crossed over the "cliff" (really a small step) regardless of their mother's emotional expression; it didn't matter to infants whether their mothers baited them to cross or warned them to stop. Experienced crawling and walking infants already knew that a 1-cm drop off is safe. As a result, they crossed regardless of their mothers' warnings. Infants also didn't use their mother's reactions for dangerous drop-offs. Infants with crawling and walking experience knew that a 90-cm drop-off could be potentially dangerous, and they refused to cross, even when their moms looked happy and motioned for them to come over. It was only when the infants were *uncertain* about the drop-off height—when it was an ambiguous drop-off (like a big step)—that they looked to mom for help. When they didn't know what to do, experienced crawling and walking infants generally crossed when mom said to cross, and they refused when mom told them to stay put. Novice 12-month-old walkers were inconsistent in whether they heeded their mothers' warnings, and usually only did so on the most dangerous drop-offs. This study suggests that emotional information from others can be important for guiding behavior, but by 12 to 18 months, infants have enough experience with the world to know when to use it wisely and when to rely on their own experience to get them over the edge.

Emotion Labeling

By the time they are 2 or 3 years old, young children begin understanding and producing emotion words, or labels. In addition, in the U.S. children learn to label photographs of posed stereotypical emotional facial expressions following the same developmental trajectory as their ability to differentiate between emotion categories and their ability to express them. First, children tested in the United States accurately label photographs of happy, angry, and sad posed expressions, and only later do they accurately label fear and disgust (Widen & Russell, 2003). Furthermore, when they make mistakes, they typically mix up the negative emotions that look similar to each other, like mistaking fear for sadness or anger, suggesting that they first develop broad categories for emotional expressions that range from positive to negative and later develop the ability to differentiate and label specific negative emotions, like anger, sadness, and fear (Widen, 2013; Widen & Russell, 2008).

Importantly, in most of the studies discussed in this chapter, when children are asked if they can tell the difference between and label the emotions of others, they are shown photographs of adults posing highly stereotyped emotional expressions. Although it's easy to recognize each of the expressions in this figure, it turns out that most people's natural, spontaneous emotional expressions don't quite look like these posed stereotypes.

Let's take the photo of Edwin. On this particular day, Edwin (aged 2 ½ years old) and his parents went to a local studio to coax him into posing for happy, smiling family photos in a photo shoot that lasted for more than an hour. Trying to get a 2 ½-year-old to sit still for enough time to take a single photo is hard enough, so you can imagine what it was like trying to get him to pose countless times in the scope of an hour. His parents did get a few smiling, happy family photos that day, but they also got the next photo. What emotion is Edwin expressing here? It's not quite a standard basic emotion. Instead, it looks like a blend of annoyance, incredulousness, and maybe even a touch of disgust at his parents' constant baiting for a smile. Further, you'll notice that while the photos of the posed, stereotyped expressions all look quite symmetrical, the left side of Edwin's face in the next photo is scrunched down, as if he's making a disgusted face, while the right side is pointed straight ahead, almost in anger.

EDWIN POSING A FACIAL EXPRESSION: Edwin, age 2 ½ years, depicting a natural, spontaneous emotional expression.
Venture Photography

The expression in this photo was produced spontaneously, and it reflects how emotions are often expressed in real life, as blends of many feelings all at once. A handful of studies using photographs of adults posing for emotional facial expressions of more varied intensities has shown that while children between the ages of 7 and 10 years are highly accurate at identifying high-intensity, stereotypical emotional expressions, there is a much longer developmental trajectory for accuracy in recognizing lower-intensity, more variable faces. Further, this trajectory differs for different categories of emotion (e.g., happy vs. disgusted), suggesting that emotional face recognition and the ability to label those emotions accurately may not reach maturity until we're adults (Gao & Maurer, 2010; L. A. Thomas et al., 2007). It also makes the fact that infants can use others' emotional expressions to guide action by 12 to 18 months of age quite remarkable.

Check Your Learning

1. How do researchers study infants' ability to differentiate between various emotional expressions, and what have they found?

2. What is multimodal emotion perception?

3. Describe social referencing and give an example.

4. When do children begin to use emotion labels?

TEMPERAMENT

At the beginning of this chapter, we told you a story about Alison and Carter's very first ride on a carousel. While Alison embraced the new experience right away, Carter took a little bit of time to warm up to it before deciding that he was having fun. These differences in Alison and Carter's emotional responses to a new experience can likely be attributed to differences in their **temperament**. As is probably clear to you by now, our six infants differ quite a bit in temperament. Temperament is a child's individual style of responding emotionally to changes in the environment. It is present from very early in life and is strongly tied to biology (but can be shaped by experience). This section will focus on the dimensions of temperament, how they lead to variability in infants' emotional responses, and how this variability changes over the course of development.

Origins of the Study of Temperament

Parents, physicians, and researchers have long observed that infants seem to have their own personalities right from birth. For example, Alison hardly cried in the first 24 hours after her birth. Carter seemed mad and uncomfortable as a newborn, but he didn't cry. Edwin would cry for hours on end. Beginning in the 1960s, scientists became interested in understanding why children are different from the start, and especially whether these early differences in infants' personalities were based on our biology. Alexander Thomas, Stella Chess, and Herbert Birch (A. Thomas et al., 1970) were some of the first researchers to investigate this question. Specifically, they wondered if there were categories of infant temperament types that they could identify very early in life. They reasoned that if they could classify infants by temperament shortly after birth, these temperament categories must be biologically based. Furthermore, if these differences are biologically based, they also should be stable across development.

To answer these questions, they carefully documented the behaviors of 141 U.S. infants and followed them until they were adults. During infancy, they used six dimensions, which can be found in Table 10.5, to classify the infants' behavior. These dimensions captured infants'

TABLE 10.5 ■ Dimensions of Temperament			
	Easy (40%)	Slow to Warm Up (15%)	Difficult (10%)
Activity Level	Varies	Low to moderate	Varies
Regularity	Regular	Varies	Irregular
Approach/Withdrawal	Positive approach	Partial withdrawal	Withdrawal
Adaptability	Very adaptable	Slowly adaptable	Slowly adaptable
Intensity	Low or mild	Mild	Intense
Mood	Positive	Slightly negative	Negative

Source: Based on A. Thomas, Chess, & Birch (1970).

emotionality and how they respond to changes in the environment. Importantly, these dimensions clustered, and the infants observed fell into one of three groups based on these clusters. The largest group of infants (40%) fit into a category that they called "easy." Easy infants are exactly what you would expect an easygoing infant to be: They are generally positive in mood, tend to approach new situations and new people happily, are adaptable to new situations, have laid-back or low-intensity responses to new things, and are fairly regular in their routines. Charlie was the perfect example of an easy infant. He was mostly positive all the time and embraced new situations and people with very little fear. Getting him to eat, sleep, and poop regularly was a piece of cake, and getting him to transition to new activities was painless. Alison was also a great example of an easy child; it took her no time to embrace her first carousel ride with a smile.

Another 10% of infants were categorized as "difficult," showing very different responses than the easy infants. Difficult infants are more likely to withdraw from new people and situations, do not quickly adapt to changes in the environment, are irregular in their routines, and are fairly negative in mood. These infants are most prone to tantrums and can be intense in their responses to arousing events, crying or laughing loudly when excited.

The final category, called "slow to warm up," made up 15% of infants. These infants fall somewhere in the middle between easy and difficult. In general, they approach new situations and people fairly negatively at first, but when given some time to adjust, they "warm up," and these initial negative responses become more positive, resembling those of an easy child. Carter fell into this category. Although he wasn't necessarily very negative, it usually took Carter a while to get accustomed to new situations and people. For example, when Carter and his mom regularly attended a "music together" class every Saturday morning, while the other infants were crawling around the room, Carter just sat on his mom's lap, holding a favorite toy. By the end of a 10-week session, Carter was comfortable and would more eagerly venture out, approaching the instruments offered by the teacher and interacting with the other children. But, at the start of each new session, or anytime there were new people in the class, Carter reverted back to his reserved demeanor.

Importantly, those of you who are observant or are just really good at math might have noticed that 40%, 10%, and 15% don't add up to 100%. In fact, 35% of Thomas, Chess, and Birch's sample did not fit neatly into any one of these three categories. Instead, this last 35% of children generally demonstrated behaviors that put them between two categories. Edwin is a good example of a child that straddled two temperament categories at once. Oftentimes, Edwin showed all signs of being an easy child. He was very positive most of the time and easily interacted with new people, regardless of age. However, sometimes he needed a little bit more time than most easy children to warm up to changes in his schedule, suggesting that he had some characteristics of a slow-to-warm-up child as well. Diego was a lot like Edwin: He was social, was outgoing with everyone, smiled easily, and was usually happy. But when faced with anything unfamiliar, he became hesitant, was mildly negative, and took time to adapt to the change. Tesalia, on the other hand, fit the pattern of an easy child, but her emotional reactions were intense, like a difficult child. When excited as an infant, she would flap her hands and kick her legs with excitement, and when upset, she was quick to let out piercing cries of anger or sadness. The point is that although Thomas and colleagues focused on their three temperament categories, their scheme did not fit all children. Since this pioneering work, many other researchers have developed theories of temperament introducing new dimensions or combining others, always with the goal of explaining as many of the differences between infants as possible.

Measurement of Temperament

The problem that Thomas, Chess, and Birch found that not every infant fit neatly into their distinct categories is common when measures are categorical, or measures of qualitative, discontinuous differences (see Chapter 1). Today, instead of identifying categories of children, the most commonly used temperament measures tend to be continuous, or measures of quantitative differences (again, see Chapter 1). In these measurements, infants fall on a spectrum ranging from difficult to easy, including every kind of variation in between. Mary Rothbart, for example, developed a series of questionnaires that parents can fill out to determine their child's temperament. In Rothbart's questionnaire, parents respond to questions such as "When introduced to an unfamiliar adult, how often did the baby cling to a parent?" Based on parents' responses to a large number of these questions, infants are given scores on dimensions such as activity and negativity. Although her measures include many of the same dimensions that Thomas, Chess, and Birch used, there is room for all infants, because she uses a continuous scale instead of a finite number of categories like easy, slow-to-warm-up, and difficult. Rothbart originally developed her scale with U.S. parents and infants, but research has shown that similar temperaments are revealed with this scale for infants in China, Japan, Poland, and Russia (Ahadi et al., 1993; Gartstein et al., 2005, 2010). Although there are some differences in the proportion of children who show specific types of temperament, the questionnaire seems to reveal the same dimensions in a wide range of cultures.

However, note that Rothbart's scales require *parents* to report on their own infants' behaviors. Although parent-report measures can be really useful in research, they can also be riddled with biases. Indeed, a mother might not be the most reliable judge of her own infant's behaviors. For example, all (or most) parents love their infants, bad behaviors and all, so parents might provide an overly positive assessment of their little ones' personalities. A parent's own personality might also color how they see and judge their own infant's behaviors. A parent who is highly reactive may rate their infant as harder to console or as crying more than a parent who is not as reactive. Parents may also have a smaller comparison group than a researcher; indeed, parents have likely only seen a handful of other infants, while researchers might have seen hundreds from working in a lab. Other parents might fully recognize that they gave birth to a tiny demon child but find it difficult, embarrassing, or guilt-inducing to admit their infants' difficult behaviors, or they might worry that their parenting style is being judged.

To deal with this issue, Mary Rothbart and Hill Goldsmith created a set of behavioral tasks designed to measure infant temperament by researchers in the lab. The result is a test called the **Lab-Tab**. This is a standardized *behavioral* assessment of early temperament in infants, toddlers, and preschool-aged children. Like the Rothbart questionnaires, this test is the same for all infants and allows for continuity in measurement; infants are not put into broad categories, but they are rated along a spectrum on a variety of dimensions. Like the classic work by Thomas,

Chess, and Birch, however, the ratings are based on behavioral observations rather than parental report, thus eliminating parental bias in the measure. For example, there is a stranger approach episode designed to elicit fear, a puppet show episode designed to elicit joy, and an episode in which an attractive toy is placed either behind a barrier or in a sealed container to elicit anger.

Much of the work on these scales were developed by U.S. scientists and tested with samples of infants in the United States. However, they have been adapted for and used for non-U.S. samples. Most of these studies report that non-U.S. infants demonstrate the same range of temperament behaviors when compared to infants in the United States, but the degree to which they express each can vary from country to country. For example, one study reported that infants from Spain showed stronger fear and distress reactions on the Lab-Tab than infants in the United States (Gartstein, Carranza, et al., 2016). Likewise, in a study comparing responses on Rothbart's questionnaires in U.S. infants and infants in Ethiopia, parents of infants in the United States reported more positive/affiliative behaviors and sadness, and parents of Ethiopian infants reported higher levels of fear and emotion regulation (Gartstein, Bogale, et al., 2016).

In both Thomas, Chess, and Birch's original work and in many studies using Rothbart's questionnaires, measures of temperament have been relatively stable across development. Thomas, Chess, and Birch for example, reported that the temperamental category infants were placed in at 2 and 6 months remained relatively the same when tested at ages 5 and 10 years. In fact, they found that 42 of the infants in their original sample later had behavioral problems that required clinical attention. A whopping 70% of these 42 individuals were originally classified

BABY WITH SANTA: Infants of different temperaments respond differently to strangers, including one of the most famous strangers. While many greet Santa with a smile, others don't quite have the same temperament.

iStock/eyesfoto

as "difficult" when Thomas and colleagues observed them as infants. Only 18% of the individuals who later had severe behavior problems were initially classified as "easy." A number of other studies (mostly done in the United States but some from across the globe) have shown that Rothbart's parent report measures are also stable over time (Rothbart et al., 2000).

The fact that temperament is stable has been interpreted by researchers to mean that temperament is biologically determined and does not change over development. However, temperament may be stable because the environment is stable, or because of the interaction between the environment and the child's biology. A parent whose child has a difficult temperament may provide that child with different opportunities than would a parent whose child has an easy temperament. In addition, it may be harder for other children to interact and play with a child with a difficult temperament. Such differences in experience, rather than differences in temperament, may be why there are different outcomes for children with difficult and easy temperaments. Indeed, a central idea of Thomas, Chess, and Birch's original work is goodness of fit, or the degree to which an infant's temperament is compatible with the infant's environment. For example, a difficult child might fare quite poorly in a high stress environment or with a parent who is prone to anxiety, but might fare rather well and become more comfortable with new situations with a parent who is sensitive to her infant's need for consistency. We will talk more about the fit between an infant's temperament and various parenting styles in the next chapter.

Shyness and Behavioral Inhibition

Studying temperament has helped researchers understand how infants develop the ability to engage in future social interactions, form attachments, and even make friends at school. Jerome Kagan, for example, was famous for studying the relationship between early infant temperament and the development of shyness in the preschool years (Kagan, 1997). Because he was specifically interested in one dimension of temperament—inhibition—he didn't examine 10 different dimensions of temperament. Instead, he measured a few simple behaviors. In his classic reactivity paradigm, 4-month-old U.S. infants were presented with different sized mobiles and their physical and facial responses were documented. He found that some infants had a **reactive temperament**; these infants became physically and emotionally stressed upon seeing the new mobile. They would thrash their arms and even cry, presumably because they got overwhelmed by the excitement of the new toy. Other infants had the opposite reaction; they were laid-back in the extreme, and with the exception of a faint smile, they barely even reacted to the mobile.

Importantly, and somewhat surprisingly, Kagan found that how these infants responded to the mobile at 4 months of age actually predicted their social behavior as toddlers. Specifically, children who were reactive as infants were the most likely to become shy and withdrawn in social situations once they entered preschool. This temperament type, which he called **behaviorally inhibited**, makes up about 10% to 15% of U.S. European-heritage middle-class infants. The infants that were laid-back in the extreme, in contrast, were the ones most likely to become quite talkative and social when they reached preschool age. Kagan thus dubbed them "uninhibited." Note that although there is continuity across development in infant temperament, infants' behaviors actually change. Kagan didn't identify infants who looked shy; he identified infants who got overstimulated or stressed by novelty. Early in infancy, they react to overstimulation by fussing and becoming agitated. When they are older, however, these same children react to overstimulation by becoming behaviorally inhibited—they reduce the stress caused by social situations by holding back or withdrawing from others, exhibiting what you would recognize as shyness.

While Kagan did most of his work in the United States, he did look at behavioral inhibition in cross-cultural samples as well. He found that overall, Chinese infants were less active and more irritable than American infants (Kagan et al., 1994). Similarly, Chinese and Korean infants are rated by their parents as more fearful of unfamiliar situations when compared to Australian and Italian infants. Finnish infants are rated as more positive than American infants, who are rated as more positive than Russian and Japanese infants (Yang & Wang, 2019).

What's most amazing about Kagan's research is that his team studied the same group of 4-month-old infants until they were teenagers or adults, some of whom eventually even had babies of their own. By tracking this same group of infants for so long, Kagan was able to look at how many of the reactive 4-month-old infants, who then became shy preschoolers, also became shy or socially anxious adults. He found that the infants who were distressed by the new toy at 4 months were still the most likely to be shy, even as adults. Even more striking is that in the United States behavioral inhibition is still the single best-known predictor of social anxiety, a chronic mental health condition in which social interactions elicit irrational amounts of anxiety. Nearly 40% of children who were classified as behaviorally inhibited as infants ended up with social anxiety later on (Kagan, 1997).

This doesn't mean that there's anything wrong with being a little shy, and *most* shy children do not grow up to have anxiety. The point we are trying to make here is that temperamental traits that are often identified in the first year of life are relatively stable over time and reliably predict how infants will respond emotionally to changes in environment. As we will see in the next section, how temperament in infancy shapes a person's ultimate personality is complexly determined by biological, inborn tendencies and environmental factors.

Determinants of Temperament

Biological Basis for Temperament

There is ample evidence that temperament has a biological basis. As we have seen in the previous sections, temperamental traits can be identified as early as 4 months of age and are relatively stable over time (Kagan, 1997). These are good indicators that there is a biological basis of temperament, but even stronger evidence comes from looking at infants' brains and physiology. Classic research by Richard Davidson and Nathan Fox showed that infants with different temperamental characteristics often showed different brain activity in the prefrontal cortex early in development. To study this, they use a technique called **electroencephalogram (EEG)** (see Chapter 1). In the EEG technique, researchers place a cap on the infants' head that contains a number of electrodes (see next photo). The electrodes in the cap measure the electrical activity on the scalp that is produced by the firing of neurons in the brain. By placing electrodes on different locations on the scalp, researchers can record the EEG produced by different brain regions. For example, electrodes placed just above the forehead will record activity from the prefrontal cortex. In general, Davidson and Fox found that when people are looking at something

Charlie, Age 8 Months, Wearing an EEG Cap

positive that they want to approach, the left side of the prefrontal cortex is more active. In contrast, the right side of the prefrontal cortex is more active when people are looking at something negative that they may want to avoid. This is true even for U.S. infants. For example, Fox and Davidson (1986) observed an increase in activation of electrodes over the left frontal brain region when something sweet was put on newborn infants' tongues. Likewise, 10-month-old infants have more left frontal activation when they are looking at a picture of an adult posing a happy face, and they have more right frontal activation when looking at a picture of an adult posing a sad face (Davidson & Fox, 1982).

These EEG patterns are different for U.S. children with different temperaments. For example, U.S. children with more reactive temperaments—those children that Kagan finds are more likely to become shy and socially anxious—tend to have more right frontal activation overall, even when looking at a relatively neutral image (Davidson & Fox, 1989; Fox & Davidson, 1987). Not only are these infants more reactive, as observed by Jerome Kagan, but their prefrontal cortex also seems to respond more negatively to a neutral stimulus than does the prefrontal cortex of less reactive infants. These differences between more and less reactive infants are also seen when we examine differences in their *physiological* responses, such as a startle, to new objects. Infants with more reactive temperaments startle more easily to a flash of light or loud noise than infants who have less reactive temperaments (Barker et al., 2014).

The Role of Attention

Despite the fact that temperament has a biological basis, it's important to remember that biology isn't destiny. Temperament is an infant's individual style of reacting emotionally to the environment. But **personality** is how an infant's temperament interacts with aspects of the environment over the course of development. Thus, like everything else, personality is based on both biological and environmental factors. This means that while temperament is relatively stable over time, there is room for change, and that change starts happening at birth—as soon as infants begin gaining experience from the environment.

One way that the environment can begin shaping temperament over time is through attention (see Chapter 6). Very young infants, who have little head control and can't navigate the world around them, may have little control over what they see. However, as infants grow, they develop better control over what they can do. As infants gain control of where they go—as they learn to crawl and walk—they also gain control of what they see. As discussed in Chapter 6, over time, attention becomes a filter for what information infants let in and what information gets ignored. In this way, attention to the environment can begin shaping temperament at a young age.

In fact, infants who have a behaviorally inhibited temperament might also have an early developing bias to pay more attention to negative social information. Behaviorally inhibited infants are especially prone to pay more attention to negative facial expressions than to positive ones and have difficulty looking away if they see a negative facial expression right in front of them. It turns out that U.S. infants who maintain this bias over time—the ones who keep paying attention to negative information—are the most likely ones to demonstrate anxiety symptoms later in life (Pérez-Edgar et al., 2010, 2011). In other words, infants who focus on the negative emotional information around them (instead of the positive) are the ones that are most likely to develop anxiety symptoms as teenagers. This suggests a developmental cascade in the U.S. infants that were tested: Infants who are behaviorally inhibited focus more on the negative emotional information around them. As a result, more of their experience is focused on negative (rather than positive) emotions. Because their experience has a stronger negative bias, it furthers their anxiety and contributes to the development of even more anxiety symptoms across development.

The Role of Parenting

Parenting can also play an important role in shaping infant temperament. Indeed, a central idea of Thomas, Chess, and Birch's original work is **goodness of fit**, or the degree to which an infant's temperament is compatible with the infant's environment. For example, a difficult child might fare quite poorly in a high stress environment, or with a parent who is prone to anxiety, but might fare rather well and become more comfortable with new situations with a parent who is sensitive to her infant's need for consistency. And even though Kagan found that behaviorally inhibited infants are the most likely infants to become shy preschoolers, this depended on parenting styles. Children were less likely to become shy later if they had parents who were particularly sensitive to their needs. In other words, although a behaviorally inhibited infant might face challenges in social situations, having a mom who responds to those challenges with patience and support can help the infant become more comfortable with social situations over time and create a buffer from the development of shyness and social anxiety (Penela et al., 2012).

Classic research from Stephen Suomi also suggests that behavior of the parent matters for the development of infant temperament, even for monkeys. Like humans, rhesus monkeys show temperamental differences at birth that are likely biologically based. And like humans, some monkeys start out with a reactive temperament. These monkeys are nervous in new situations and can often be seen clinging to their mothers, even in situations that are perfectly safe. Likewise, there are monkeys that have more laid-back personalities, who show little fear in new situations, playing freely and boldly with their monkey friends. To look at the effect of parenting on the development of monkey personality over time, Suomi and colleagues did an experiment that would be completely impossible (for ethical reasons) to do with human infants. They placed a group of reactive baby monkeys with "foster mothers" who were relaxed and laid-back. These mothers have different personalities from the anxious and overprotective mothers that typically give birth to highly reactive babies. The question Suomi and his colleagues asked was whether the reactive infants' temperament would change if they were raised by more relaxed mothers. That is, would infants learn the mother's relaxed nature, fostering the development of a less reactive, bolder infant monkey? In fact, reactive infant monkeys who grew up with relaxed mothers slowly became more comfortable exploring their environments without fear, like the infants born with more relaxed temperaments (Suomi, 1997), further showing how the environment shapes temperament.

Clearly, supportive parenting can decrease behavioral inhibition. However, the reverse is also true. Parents who are too overprotective, restricting their infant's exploration of a new environment, can also have infants who have prolonged behavioral inhibition over time. Indeed, North American inhibited toddlers who had overprotective parents were more stable in behavioral inhibition over development and were more likely to demonstrate anxious behaviors compared to behaviorally inhibited toddlers with less overprotective parents (Hastings et al., 2008; Rubin et al., 2002). The same seems to be true for intrusive parents. These parents tend to push their infants to engage with new environments forcefully before the infant is ready. Like infants of overprotective parents, infants of intrusive parents tend to show more stability in behavioral inhibition over time and are more likely to demonstrate anxious behaviors (Pérez-Edgar, 2019).

As we have described temperament, we have pointed out that infants in different cultures sometimes have been observed to have different temperaments. It is possible that biological factors (e.g., genetic differences between groups of people) are why children from different cultures differ in temperament. However, it is also possible that cultural norms and parents' expectations shape infants' temperament over time. Remember that a lot of temperament measures involve parents reporting *on their own perception* of their infants' behaviors, so it's possible that parents are simply evaluating their infants' behaviors as more or less positive or negative based on their own cultural values. Further, many of the reliable cross-cultural differences in temperament have to do with fearful behavior and self-control, which are highly shaped by context (as we saw in the stranger approach examples) and cultural expectations (e.g., as you'll see below with our example of the marshmallow study). The major point here is that culture and context begin shaping developmental trajectories right from birth, even for biologically based factors like temperament.

Altogether, research on infant temperament suggests that we are all born with our own emotional style of responding to changes in the environment. And although temperament is biologically based and relatively stable over time, the environment begins shaping the way we express our emotional responses almost immediately. A sensitive parent, for example, can help even the most behaviorally inhibited infant cope with the ever-changing environment and regulate their reactive responses so that strong emotional responses become more manageable. Exactly how infants begin to regulate their negative emotional responses, and how parents help them do it, is the focus of our next section.

Check Your Learning

1. What are Thomas, Chess, and Birch's three categories of infant temperament, and how do they differ from each other?

2. What are the different ways in which temperament is measured?

3. What is behavioral inhibition, and how does it relate to shyness?

4. List factors that can shape an infant's temperament over time.

5. What is the difference between temperament and personality?

EMOTION REGULATION

Have you ever had the experience of feeling like you wanted to cry while you're in a public place and had to struggle to fight back those potentially embarrassing tears? Maybe you were in a class and you just got back an exam with an extremely low grade written in red across the top. Or you were in a restaurant with friends, and one of them just criticized something you worked particularly hard on. Maybe you were staring lovingly at a boyfriend, girlfriend, or partner you cared deeply about, just as they were telling you that they wanted to see other people?

The hard work you put into holding back those feelings is what we call **emotion regulation**. Emotion regulation is the ability to respond with a wide variety of emotions to events in the environment in a socially acceptable way. Emotion regulation can be hard, and some of us are better at it than others. At first, infants can't regulate their emotional responses at all. Instead, they have to completely rely on their caregivers to do it for them. Unlike when you want to cry, infants don't have any strategies they can use to help them stop crying. Instead, they need their caregivers to soothe them in some way, by rocking, or singing, or touching them. Touch in particular can be a really important regulator for infants and, as it turns out, for adults too. As we saw in Chapter 3, touch is one of the earliest senses to develop. Information is learned from touch even before birth. Researchers have shown that touch from a caregiver can reduce stress hormones in an infant's body and lower their heart rate, effectively calming them down when they are upset (Feldman et al., 2014). The research on touch has had an influence on birth practices in the United States and other Western cultures. Pediatricians and nurses have increasingly acknowledged the importance of touch for infants and encourage what they call **skin-to-skin contact** between mother and infant right from birth. Nowadays, when an infant is born in a U.S. hospital, they are often placed directly on their mothers' chest so that skin-to-skin contact is one of the first experiences the infant has with the world outside the womb. As we saw in Chapter 3, there are many different practices in childbirth, and mothers around the world have skin-to-skin contact with their infants soon after birth.

On top of that, touch can be especially important for premature infants. Depending on how small they are and how early they are born, premature infants may not have fully developed lungs and need help breathing after birth. In developed countries, premature infants are routinely put on respirators in the neonatal intensive care unit (NICU) of a hospital to help them breathe. These infants don't get that important skin-to-skin contact with their mothers that infants born at term typically get right away. But Tiffany Field and colleagues came up with a clever way to provide skin-to-skin contact to premature babies. They had U.S. mothers and nurses provide "touch therapy" to these newborns, by sticking their hands through holes in the respirators to gently massage the infants. Premature infants who received touch therapy gained weight faster and were discharged from the hospital sooner than a control group of premature infants who didn't get touch therapy (Field et al., 1986).

The benefits of touch therapy on premature infants can be incredibly long lasting. Ruth Feldman and her colleagues asked a group of mothers in Israel to give their premature infants 2 weeks of skin-to-skin contact, while another group of premature infants simply remained in their respirators without any exposure to touch. The infants who got skin-to-skin contact with their mothers had healthier stress responses, better sleep patterns, and even higher cognitive abilities than babies who were given the standard respirator treatment (Feldman et al., 2014). Most importantly, these effects were still there when the researchers checked in on these children 10 years later! This goes to show that a little touch can go a long way in soothing an infant.

Given the importance of touch for emotion regulation, it is not surprising that across the world, parents and caregivers have developed strategies to increase how much time young infants are touched. For example, in many cultures, infants are carried nearly all day, either by necessity (e.g., newborns are strapped to their mothers who have to go back to work) or because of cultural tradition (Little et al., 2019). Babywearing has also increased in popularity in the United States and other Western industrialized countries. Organizations like La Leche League encourage new mothers in Western cultures to "wear" their infants in a sling or other baby carrier to help with breastfeeding. The popularity of this approach, however, likely also reflects the fact that when mothers or fathers wear their infants for long periods of time, this increases how much they can use touch to soothe a fussy baby.

To look at this question empirically, Emily Little and her colleagues experimentally assigned U.S. mothers to wear their infants for a set amount of time while they were in the lab. When mothers were wearing their infants, they touched their infants more and were more responsive to their infants' vocalizations than when they weren't wearing their infants (Little et al., 2019). On top of that, other research has shown that infants who are carried more by their mothers cry less than infants who aren't carried (Hunziker & Barr, 1986). Thus, wearing an infant, either in a sling or carrier, increases touching and may therefore have a calming effect. In many cultures, the advice you often get from your grandparents is that if you carry your infants too much, you might "spoil" them, and they eventually become fussy children who cling to their mothers. In fact, some of us heard this advice when our infants were newborns. It turns out that the opposite might be true. A study by Darcia Narvaez found that U.S. adults who were held and cuddled the most as infants were the most likely to be healthy and well-adjusted as adults. In fact, the more they were carried, the better they functioned emotionally (Narvaez et al., 2016).

Although parental touch is important for soothing throughout infancy, infants do develop some strategies to soothe themselves. Infants in the United States, who are often put in a crib to sleep on their own, learn some strategies by 4 to 6 months. For example, when they wake up at night, they might learn to pat themselves or stroke toys in their cribs to help them get back to sleep. Interestingly, many of these early strategies involve touch. Once they get a little older, they can develop more cognitive strategies to calm themselves down when they are upset. Edwin and Charlie's parents taught them to sing or count to 20 whenever they feel angry or sad to help them calm down. Similarly, Diego and Tesalia were taught to take deep breaths to achieve this same goal. Soon, infants will begin to learn about other people's expectations for when and how it's okay to express negative emotions—display rules—and importantly, what's not okay. But this understanding takes a long time to develop, alongside theory of mind, which we will talk more about in the next chapter.

Importantly, as we discussed earlier, infants' ability to feel and express a colorful array of emotional responses develops before the age of 2. Unfortunately for their parents, infants' ability to control these responses takes much (much, much, much) longer to develop. Have you ever heard of the "terrible 2's"? You've certainly witnessed them if you've seen a toddler melt down in a grocery store or a shopping mall. For example, 2-year-old Charlie had a complete and utter meltdown when he asked his mom for "orange," and she responded by giving him an orange crayon. Charlie was actually asking for orange *juice*, and he just did not have the skills to communicate that, but he did have the skills to express his disappointment. The reason why 2-year-old children are so "terrible" is that they are fully capable of expressing their emotions, but they are not fully capable of controlling them. On top of that, 2-year-old children don't yet have the language ability to articulate what they're feeling, which can add to the mounting frustration.

Although toddlers around the world are developing their ability to control and express their emotions, temper tantrums are not viewed as normative behavior around the world. Not all parents everywhere in the world expect their children to have emotional outbursts just because they're 2. One study showed the variability in children from different cultures by using a classic experiment typically used to measure emotion regulation in preschool-aged children. This study used a task developed by Walter Mischel called the "marshmallow task." In this task, young children are shown a snack—typically a marshmallow. Children are then told that the experimenter needs to leave the room, and if the child can wait until the experimenter comes back to eat the snack, they can have two sweet treats instead of one. If they can't wait, they can ring a bell and eat the single marshmallow instead of getting two. The children Mischel tested, who were children from Northern California living near Stanford University, had difficulty waiting.

But children's ability to wait depends on their culture. In a study using this task, only 30% of German preschool children were able to wait for the experimenter to come back to eat the marshmallow. The ones that were able to wait the longest relied on strategies to distract themselves, like fidgeting, singing, or talking to themselves. In stark contrast, preschool Nso children from Cameroon didn't have trouble with this task at all. In fact, 70% of these children were able to wait to get the marshmallow, and some of them even fell asleep while they were waiting patiently for the experimenter to return. Unlike the somewhat low bar we might set for children's ability to wait for something in Western countries, Nso children are expected to control their negative emotions at a very early age, and as a result, they learn how to regulate their emotional responses at a much younger age (Lamm et al., 2018).

Experience with the particular treat seems to matter too. A study using a similar task comparing 4- to 5-year-old children in Japan and the United States showed that Japanese children could wait patiently for food treats, while the U.S. children had difficulty waiting, replicating the studies described in the previous paragraph. However, the U.S. children were much more patient than the Japanese children when waiting to open a *wrapped gift* instead of a food treat (Yanaoka et al., 2022). It turns out that young Japanese children have lots of experience waiting to eat food that is in front of them but little experience waiting to open a wrapped gift, and young children in the United States have the opposite experience.

Luckily for parents everywhere, infants' ability to regulate their emotions does improve with age, but it is still developing in middle childhood and even into adolescence. Teenagers continue to struggle with a fully developed ability to feel a variety of mature emotional responses, while juggling an immature ability to keep those feelings under control. Even as they age out of childhood, Diego and Tesalia, for example, still require scaffolding when faced with an especially emotional situation. Reminding them to take a deep breath as well as getting a hug remain as effective as when they were toddlers. Indeed, many of us know some adults who still don't seem to know what kinds of emotional outbursts are appropriate and which ones aren't. At least we now know that a little hug can go a long way, which is true no matter how old you are.

Check Your Learning

1. What is emotion regulation?

2. How might touch help to regulate an infant's emotional responses?

SUMMARY

There are a few broad takeaway points from this chapter that are important to remember. First, infants' initial emotional responses start out as broad categories of positive and negative affect. These first affective responses aren't about anything specific in the environment and are usually general responses to discomfort or arousal. Specific, discrete emotional responses like anger, sadness, and fear develop as infants gain more experience interacting with the environment and, likewise, as their cognitive abilities grow. Biological differences based on temperament and genetic variation might cause individual infants' emotional responses to the environment to vary. And although some of these differences are biologically based, the environment also plays a role in shaping those emotional responses, starting from birth. Once children begin to learn about the expectations of others, they begin to express more complex emotions, like guilt, shame, pride, embarrassment, and empathy. They also learn to regulate their emotional responses based on those expectations. Importantly, cultural differences, gender, and parent beliefs and practices provide infants with information about how emotional responses should be expressed. These cultural expectations can encourage the expression of some emotions (e.g., happiness in Western countries) and the suppression of others (e.g., sadness in boys). In the end, the road to emotional development is long, and an infant's emotional expressiveness and understanding are still developing into adolescence and even adulthood.

KEY TERMS

affect

behavioral inhibition

discrete emotions theory

display rules

electroencephalogram (EEG)

emergent theories of emotion

emotion

emotion regulation

emotional expression

goodness of fit

Lab-Tab

means-ends reasoning

neonatal smile

personality

phobia

reactive temperament

rouge test

sense of self

skin-to-skin contact

social referencing

still-face paradigm

temperament

REVIEW QUESTIONS

1. What is an emotion, and how do we measure it in infants?

2. How do affect and cognition interact to produce happiness, anger, sadness, and fear?

3. How do we know that an infant can understand the meaning behind someone's emotional expression?

4. How does temperament shape an infant's emotional behavior?

5. How might parenting and the social environment affect infants' emotional behavior over the course of development?

6. What are different ways in which biology and the environment lead to different trajectories of emotional development?

CRITICAL THINKING QUESTIONS

1. Choose one emotion and describe the ways that biology and the environment influence its expression over time.

2. How do we know for sure when infants understand the meaning behind an emotional facial expression?

3. A new mom knows you just took an infant development class. You observe her newborn smile in their sleep. Your friend asks you, "Do you think the baby is happy?" What do you tell her?

4. Which of the following emotions develop last, and why: fear, sadness, or embarrassment?

5. What are some issues with Thomas, Chess, and Birch's measures of temperament, and how did Rothbart address them?

6. Why are 2-year-olds so prone to temper tantrums?

7. How is emotional expression and understanding shaped by culture?

8. How is temperament shaped by both biology and the environment?

9. What are different ways in which infants might regulate their emotional responses?

11 SOCIAL DEVELOPMENT

When Edwin was about 3 months old, he started talking. Not with real words of course, or any language that is understandable. As you learned in Chapter 9, infants don't say their first words until sometime around their first birthday. But around 3 months, when his mom talked to him, Edwin suddenly started responding by using babbles or raspberries or whatever sound he could muster. His mom would say good morning, and Edwin would smile and coo back at her. His mom would then ask how he slept, and Edwin would respond in kind. Even though it was all just baby babble, these proto-conversations (see Chapter 9) had the rhythm of a real-life conversation between a happy new mother and her 3-month-old son. Perhaps what was most noteworthy about Edwin's first conversations is that they weren't just directed at his mom. Many of them were also directed at other people and, in some cases, inanimate objects, like the wooden "Shelf" above his changing table (see Chapter 4) or even the stuffed sheep he had in his crib.

How did Edwin decide which people and objects were worth talking to and which ones likely wouldn't talk back? How do infants know who their social partners are, and how do they come to prefer some social partners (like their mothers) over others? In this chapter, we will explore the social world of the infant. We will begin by discussing infants' first social interactions with other people (and sometimes, objects). We will describe how infants know who to interact with, what those very first interactions look like, and what infants learn from them. Next, we will discuss what infants *know* about other people, how they reason about other people's thoughts and behaviors, and finally, how that reasoning gives rise to prosocial behaviors, like helping and sharing. After that, we'll talk about how and when infants form attachments to the people around them, especially their caregivers, and how those attachments provide a secure base for infants to explore the new people, places, and things they encounter in the world.

After reading this chapter, you will be able to:

1. *Discuss* how infants' early social interactions set the stage for the development of important social relationships and social learning.

2. *Describe* how infants' understanding of other people's intentions, thoughts, and desires promotes sociability.

3. *Define* attachment and explain why it is important for infants' social development.

INFANTS' EARLY SOCIAL INTERACTIONS

As we learned in Chapter 9, although infants don't start talking until about 12 months of age, they show signs of wanting to engage in communication with other people from the first months of life. On top of that, infants' early visual preferences set the stage for these initial social interactions, drawing attention to important social information in the environment.

Infants' Attentional References

From the first few days after birth, infants' have visual biases that cause them to focus on potential social partners. For example, newborns prefer to look at stimuli that resemble faces more than they like to look at most other things (see Chapter 4). In the few hours after birth, infants rapidly learn about the faces around them, and one study showed that Scottish 2-day-old infants could already tell the difference between their mother's (familiar) face and a stranger's (unfamiliar) face (Bushnell et al., 1989).

Although infants from birth seem to prefer to look at human faces over other stimuli, *how* infants look at faces changes with development. As they get older, infants' scanning of faces becomes more functional or concentrated around the areas of the face that produce the most useful information. Newborn infants spend most of their time looking at the area around the hairline of a face, probably because those areas of high contrast in color are what they can actually see (see Chapter 4). But only 1 month later, White infants in North America and Britain as

Couple and Newborn Infant Sharing a Mutual Gaze

iStock/monkeybusinessimages

well as Asian infants from China and Japan spend most of their time looking not at the hairline but, instead, at a face's eyes (Haensel et al., 2020; Maurer & Salapatek, 1976). This is important, as attention to a face's eyes draws attention not only to the face itself but also to where the face is *looking*.

Perhaps not surprisingly then, infants become highly attuned to other people's gaze very early in infancy. Indeed, one study showed that just days after birth, Italian infants shifted their gaze in the direction of where a caregiver was looking; this is a behavior known as gaze following (Farroni et al., 2004). And despite cultural variations in how acceptable or polite it is to look at someone else's eyes, sensitivity to where others are looking has been observed in infants from a wide range of cultures, including cultures of North America and Europe (e.g., Haensel et al., 2020; Maurer & Salapatek, 1976), Asia (e.g., Haensel et al., 2020; Maurer & Salapatek, 1976) and Chile (Peña et al., 2014), suggesting that this behavior might be universal. By 6 to 10 months of age, infants in Western cultures actively turn their heads to look in the same direction that a caregiver looks, allowing the infant to be included in the focus of their caregiver's attention (Farroni et al., 2004; Gredebäck et al., 2010). This behavior also allows infants to gather information and share a social connection. Importantly, however, research suggests that both Chinese and U.S. infants are more likely to follow the gaze of an adult who is of a familiar race and/or sex, suggesting that these effects might depend on whether the gazer is from a familiar or unfamiliar group (Pickron et al., 2017; Xiao et al., 2018).

Infants don't only prefer stimuli that *look* like people. Studies conducted in North America and Europe have shown that even as newborns, infants also prefer things that *move* like people—what researchers call **biological motion**—over things that move mechanically (Simion et al., 2008). Their preferences extend to living things in general. In one study, U.S. 4- to 12-month-old infants preferred to look at videos of animals over things like cars, boats, and helicopters, and they directed more emotional responses (almost all of them positive) to animals over toys, often smiling, laughing, or waving at them (DeLoache et al., 2011). Infants are also more likely to talk to animals than toys, demonstrating some evidence that they view animals (but not toys) as potential social partners (LoBue et al., 2013). These preferences mean that infants attend more to potential social partners in their environment. However, we don't know that very young infants look at faces and animals because they expect them to be social partners or they know that they will interact. Regardless of why infants show these biases, attending more to faces, biological movement, and animals early in infancy will have a cascading effect on their developing social interactions.

How Do Infants Know Who to Interact With?

These early attentional behaviors all set the stage for infants' first social interactions and lay the groundwork for building their most important social relationships. But how do infants know *whose* gaze to follow? How do they know who might return their bid for attention with a smile or a friendly coo? Edwin eventually learned that while his mother always talked back to him, Shelf and sleep sheep weren't exactly big on conversation. But why did he try to talk to them in the first place? What cues do infants use from the world around them to decide who is a potential social partner, and who (or more appropriately, *what*) is not?

Clearly infants' attention biases to look at faces and biological motion help them to focus on people over other things. But researchers have also asked what features of a person or object help infants decide whether something is a good social partner. Susan Johnson, Virginia Slaughter, and Susan Carey asked this question in a clever set of studies. They sat a group of U.S. 12-month-old infants on their caregivers' laps facing a brown furry object about the size of a small dog. Two novel toys were placed on either side of the room, between the infant and the brown fuzzy object. Johnson and her colleagues wanted to know whether the infants would follow the "gaze" of the brown furry object to look at one of the toys. They thought that infants might be more willing to follow the object if it had a face. So, they showed some infants a version of the toy without a face and other infants a version of the toy with two eyes, a black felt nose, and two rounded ears. Then Johnson and her colleagues simply observed what infants did when the brown fuzzy object turned in the direction of one of the two toys, as if it was "looking" at it. When the brown fuzzy object had a face, infants did indeed look in the same direction that the brown fuzzy object turned. But, when it didn't have a face, they did not follow its "gaze." This suggests that faces are a cue for whether an object can have goals or intentions, and whose gaze might be an important cue for where to look next (Johnson et al., 1998).

Further, Johnson and her colleagues also thought that infants might be more interested in following the object if it *interacted* with the infant. The researchers could make the object interact using a remote control to turn on and off a light and beeper inside the object. They tested two additional groups of infants; for one group the fuzzy brown object had a face and for the other group it did not. For these two new groups of infants, the brown fuzzy object interacted with the infant. Every time the infant babbled, the object responded with beeps, mimicking the tone and duration of the infants' speech. Both groups of infants who experienced the object "talking" to them shifted their gaze to look wherever the brown fuzzy object looked, even when it didn't have a face. Thus, not only do infants use a face to decide whether to follow an object's gaze, but they also use whether the object acts contingently to the infant's behavior. Other research has confirmed this conclusion, demonstrating that a group of U.S. 18-month-old infants followed the gaze of a social robot (Meltzoff et al., 2010) and that a group of 17-month-old Japanese infants followed the gaze of both a social human and a social robot (Manzi et al., 2020).

None of this research answers the question of why infants follow the gaze of people (and other objects with people-like features) in the first place. One reason may be that infants assume that people have *goals*. That is, people don't just act randomly, but their actions have a purpose. They turn their head to look because there is something interesting there to see. Amanda Woodward developed a procedure to determine whether infants see people, but not objects, as having intentions, or goals. She showed U.S. 5- to 9-month-old infants two toys, a ball and a bear, sitting on pedestals (Figure 11.1). As the infants watched, a person's hand reached in from the side, toward one of the two objects, touching it. As adults, we would conclude that the person's goal or intention was to touch or grasp the specific object (the ball or the bear).

Woodward showed infants the same action repeatedly, habituating the infants to the person reaching for the same object in the same location (e.g., seeing the person reach for the ball on the left pedestal many times in a row). Then she showed them two test events. In both test events, the ball and the bear switched locations. In one test event, the hand would reach for a

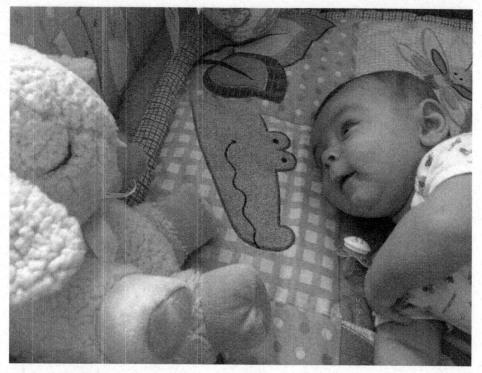

Edwin Talking to Sleep Sheep

different object in the same *location* (e.g., the left pedestal, which now had the bear); in the other test event the hand would reach for the same *object* in a different location (e.g., the ball, which was now on the right; see Figure 11.1). This way, Woodward could determine whether infants expected the hand to reach for the familiar location (regardless of which object was there) or the familiar object (regardless of where it was).

Infants in this study looked longer, or dishabituated, when they saw the person reach for the new object, even though the reach looked just the same as every reach in habituation. Infants did not dishabituate when the hand reached for the familiar object in a new location. Woodward interpreted this response as evidence that infants were paying the most attention to the reacher's intended *goal*, not the *location* of their reach. She tested another group of infants using an inanimate stick instead of a hand. In the events shown to these infants, a stick appeared from off screen and touched one of the objects, moving just as the hand did in the original study. However, in this version, infants did not seem to associate a goal with the stick, suggesting that infants recognize that people (but not objects) can have actions that are **goal directed**, or intentional (Woodward, 1998). This pattern has been observed with infants around the world, including in Japan (Kanakogi & Itakura, 2011) and Germany (Daum et al., 2008).

As egocentric as we'd like to be, people aren't the only ones that have goals. Indeed, our dogs, cats, and even pet birds can have goals too. And although having a face and respond-ing contingently both seem like good, reliable indicators of whether something can have

---

FIGURE 11.1 ■ Hand Reaching for Bear

Infants were habituated to one of the events on top, a hand reaching for either (A) the ball or (B) the bear. Infants saw the test events on the bottom, a hand reaching for (C) the same object in a new location or (D) a different object in the same location.

Source: Woodward (1998).

goals, not all animate, or goal-directed objects have faces, or even respond when we talk to them. Indeed, there are lots of living things that don't have either of these traits, like worms, snails, and jellyfish. How do infants know that these things are alive and can have goals as well? One thing that worms, snails, and jellyfish all have in common is that they move by themselves. This is what researchers called **self-propelled motion**, or the ability to move independently through space.

Szilvia Biro and Alan Leslie asked whether infants would attribute goals to inanimate objects that appeared to have self-propelled motion. They showed a group of 9- to 12-month-old infants events like those used by Woodward in her study, where a stick reached for and touched either the ball or the bear. However, some of the infants first saw the stick move by itself and attempted to pick up one of the objects. This time, infants behaved as if the stick was a person, and looked longer when the stick "reached" for the new object versus a new location (Biro & Leslie, 2007). This suggests that infants assume objects that move by themselves have goals, suggesting that they use self-propelled motion as another cue for what makes something a goal-directed agent.

So, infants use the presence of a face, contingent interactions, and self-propelled motion to decide whether an "actor" has goals. Importantly, none of these cues are privileged, or more important than the others. In the brown fuzzy object studies, infants followed the object's "gaze" in any condition where it had a face *or* responded to the infant contingently. On top of that, the infants assumed a self-propelled stick had goals if it moved by itself; the stick neither had a face nor did it respond contingently to the infant's vocalizations. This suggests that at least for infants from North America and Europe (the ones tested in most of these studies), there are several cues that can help determine whether something has intentions or goals.

What Do Infants Learn From Early Social Interactions?

Once infants can decide *who* to interact with, the next question is whether the social interactions they initiate are meaningful in some way. What do infants get from these early social interactions? And can these social interactions help infants learn about the world around them? **Social learning theory,** first proposed by Alfred Bandura (1977), emphasizes the importance of learning by observing, modeling, and imitating the behaviors of others. According to this theory, infants learn by first observing the behaviors of another person, or a **model**, and then by imitating the model's actions.

At first blush, you probably think that imitation is simply the act of copying what someone else does. Indeed, we've all had the experience of imitating another person, animal, or even an object. However, in terms of infancy, there are important distinctions between different kinds of imitation. The simplest form of imitation involves copying what you see right in front of you, or what researchers have called **mimicry**. True imitation involves copying not just another person's action, but also their intended *goal* (Tomasello, 1990). True imitation differs from mimicry because it involves understanding something about another person's thoughts and intentions. Finally, deferred imitation (which we talked about in Chapter 6) is true imitation that happens after some delay—several minutes, hours, or even days after observing an action. As you will see in this section, mimicry is something that infants can do quite early in development, even hours after birth. Imitation, however, is something that takes time to develop, and only occurs after infants can make inferences about the intentions of others. Deferred imitation is also something that takes time, as it requires infants to have a memory, or a mental representation of a past action, bringing it to mind when it's not right in front of them.

When Do Infants Imitate?

When do infants start imitating? Some researchers believe that even newborns can imitate what they see directly in front of them, or what we just described as mimicry. To demonstrate, Andrew Meltzoff and Keith Moore (1977) famously presented U.S. newborns who were only days old with three facial movements—mouth opening, tongue protrusions (i.e., sticking out your tongue), and lip pursing (i.e., kissy faces) and then observed whether the newborns mimicked what they saw. Surprisingly, the newborns did show evidence of mimicry: They were most likely to stick out their tongues after watching the experimenter stick out his tongue, and they were most likely to open their mouths after watching the experimenter open his mouth (Figure 11.2).

FIGURE 11.2 ■ Mouth Opening

Newborn imitating mom opening her mouth.

Source: iStock/Lisa5201

The authors concluded that infants show signs of imitation right from the first few weeks of life. For years, these findings led a lot of psychologists to believe that the ability to imitate was innate, or driven mostly by nature, since newborns couldn't have possibly learned to imitate other people only days or even hours after birth. However, other studies have attempted to replicate Meltzoff and Moore's findings and cast some doubt about whether newborns can really imitate. In one study, researchers tested a group of Australian newborns' ability to imitate mouth opening, tongue protrusions, and lip pursing along with several additional imitation tasks. They found that only about half the newborns they tested stuck out their tongues when they saw a model performing the same gesture. On top of that, the newborns just as frequently stuck out their tongues in response to seeing a model perform mouth openings, or a happy or a sad face (Oostenbroek et al., 2016). Altogether, this study found no evidence that newborns can imitate. The results of this and other studies have made the original findings by Meltzoff and Moore quite controversial.

There is less controversy about when more complicated forms of imitation, like deferred imitation, develops. Researchers tend to agree that this kind of imitation develops more slowly over the first 2 years of life and depends on several factors. For example, infants' ability to imitate actions after a delay changes with infants' other cognitive abilities like memory (see Chapter 6). Further, the types of things infants imitate also change over time, which we will discuss in the following sections.

What Do Infants Imitate?

Remember that true imitation involves copying the model's *goal*. This requires that infants recognize others' goals and intentions. To test infants' ability to imitate a person's *intended* action, instead of their actual action, Andrew Meltzoff (Meltzoff, 1995) presented U.S. 18-month-old infants with a variety of objects that you could perform a specific act on, for example, a dumbbell that you could pull apart (Figure 11.3). Half of the infants watched as an experimenter completed the intended action, in this case, pulling the dumbbells apart. The other half of the infants watched the experimenter try but fail to complete the intended action. In this condition, the experimenter repeatedly tried to pull the dumbbells apart, but as he pulled, his hand slipped off. After watching these displays, the infants were given the opportunity to imitate what they saw with the dumbbells. In both conditions, infants imitated the *intended* action; in other words, after watching an experimenter try but fail to pull the dumbbells apart, the infants didn't imitate what they saw; instead, they imitated the experimenter's intended goal and pulled the dumbbells apart even though they never saw the experimenter actually succeed at completing this action.

Once infants can make inferences about other people's intentions, they don't imitate nonintentional or accidental actions. Malinda Carpenter and her colleagues demonstrated this by presenting U.S. 14- to 18-month-old infants with objects that could do two things. They wondered if the infants would imitate the action a model intended to do and not the action the model did accidentally (Carpenter et al., 1998). In the study, an experimenter interacted in various ways with a small wooden box. For example, when she spun a spinner on the box, a light turned on. When she lifted a handle on the same box, a toy popped out of an opening. Children observed the experimenter complete one action (e.g., spinning a spinner to turn a light on) and say, "There!" suggesting that she intended to complete the target action. They also saw the experimenter complete the other action (e.g., lifting a hinge to make a toy pop out of an opening) and say, "Whoops!" indicating that she had done so accidentally. Infants of both ages were much more likely to imitate the experimenter's intentional actions (the one followed by "There!") than the accidental ones (the one followed by "Whoops!"), suggesting they used their inferences about the experimenter's intentions to decide which action to imitate.

FIGURE 11.3 ■ Dumbbell Experiment

Top row, an experimenter failing to pull dumbbells apart. Bottom row, pincers failing to pull dumbbells apart.

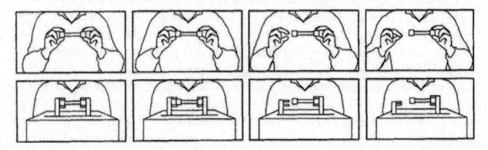

Source: Meltzoff (1995).

Infants are also more likely to imitate actions that are rational. In Chapter 6, we discussed a study by Meltzoff in which 14-month-old infants imitated an experimenter turning on a light-box with her forehead. In this study, infants watched as an experimenter bent over and touched a light with her forehead, apparently causing it to turn on. When given the opportunity, the infants performed the same action to turn on the light (Meltzoff, 1988b). Gyorgy Gergely, Harold Bekkering, and Ildiko Kiraly (2002) tested European 14-month-old infants in a variation of this study. In one condition, the infants watched as an experimenter turned on a light box with her head (just like in Meltzoff's study). But in a second condition, the experimenter appeared to be cold, with a blanket wrapped around her arms when she turned the light on with her head. If infants assumed that the experimenter meant to turn the light on with her head, they should touch their heads to the light both when the experimenter was not wrapped up in a blanket and when she was wrapped up in a blanket. However, when the experimenter was wrapped up in the blanket, infants might assume that she was only turning the light on with her head because her hands were otherwise occupied (in this case because of the blanket). If this is the case, they might imitate the more rational action and just turn it on with their hands. That is exactly what the researchers found: In the no blanket condition, infants turned the light on with their heads, whereas in the blanket condition, infants turned the light box on with their hands. Thus, by 14 to 18 months, at least in Western cultures, when infants watch others perform an action, they can make an inference about what the person's goal is and use that inference to guide their own imitative actions.

Who Do Infants Imitate?

Infants are also selective about *who* they imitate. This probably isn't surprising given the research we discussed earlier showing that infants seem to be more likely to attribute goals and intentions to human or apparently living entities. It turns out that infants are also more likely to imitate entities that are human-like. Remember the study we discussed earlier where Meltzoff (1995) found that 18-month-old infants imitated the intended action after seeing a person pulling (or trying to pull) dumbbells apart? In that study, Meltzoff also found that when a robotic set of pincers appeared to try and fail to pull the dumbbells apart (see Figure 11.3, bottom), infants were far less likely to imitate the target action. In fact, they were six times more likely to pull the dumbbells apart after watching a human try and fail than after watching the pincers try and fail.

Children also seem to be more likely to imitate a live actor (i.e., someone who they are interacting with) than a televised actor, although this finding is not universal. In one of the earliest studies to compare infants' imitation of live and televised actors, Meltzoff showed that 14- and 24-month-old U.S. infants can imitate simple actions (like pulling apart the dumbbell) that were presented to the infants by a model on television (instead of live), even after a 24-hour delay (Meltzoff, 1988a). However, other work suggests that imitating a televised model can be difficult. Rachel Barr and Harlene Hayne (1999) presented a group of 12-, 15-, and 18-month-old infants in New Zealand with either a live model or a model on television performing both simple and multistep actions. Infants' imitation of the actions was tested both immediately after the demonstration and again a day later. When the actions were performed by a live model, infants imitated the actions, even after a 24-hour delay. However, when the actions were presented by a televised model, infants only imitated when tested immediately after the action was modeled and only if the action was easy to reproduce. In fact, in another study, these researchers found that even at 24 and 30 months, infants were better at imitating events that they watch live versus on television (Hayne et al., 2003). This effect, which has now been replicated several times in the United States and New Zealand, has been called the video deficit effect, and lasts until children are around age 3 (also see Chapter 10). Thus, infants can imitate a televised model, but it is more difficult for them to do so.

Finally, infants are more likely to imitate some kinds of people than others. Specifically, infants are more likely to imitate people who seem familiar and are like the people in their lives. For example, infants are more likely to imitate models who share the same native language. In one study, 14-month-old German infants were told a story by two experimenters; one experimenter told the story in the infants' native language (German), and the other experimenter told the story in a foreign language (Russian). The infants then watched the experimenters turn on a light box with their foreheads, just like in the studies we talked about earlier. Infants were more likely to imitate the intended action (i.e., turning the light box on with your head) if it was demonstrated by the experimenter who told the story in German (familiar language) than if it was demonstrated by the experimenter who told the story in Russian (unfamiliar language) (Buttelmann et al., 2013).

But, like most things we've discussed in this book, preferences for some people, including a preference based on the language a person speaks, varies with experience. Specifically, infants' preferences for people who speak a familiar language seems to depend on their previous experience with people who speak other languages. Lauren Howard, Cristina Carazza, and Amanda Woodward (2014) found that U.S. infants of English-speaking parents imitated English-speaking adults, as expected from the study we just described. But whether infants of English-speaking parents imitated a Spanish-speaking adult depended on how much experience these infants had with Spanish-speaking individuals in their daily lives. In this study, infants of English-speaking parents were more likely to imitate a Spanish-speaking adult if they had more experience with Spanish-speaking individuals in their neighborhoods.

Is the Development of Imitation Universal?

Although most of the studies we discussed in this section so far were done with small samples of infants from mostly White, middle-class families in the United States, western Europe, or New Zealand, social learning happens in every country around the world. Cross-cultural studies have shown similarities in the development of infants' ability to imitate across very diverse cultural contexts. For example, in one study both German, White infants and Nso infants from northwestern Cameroon showed deferred imitation between 6 and 9 months (Graf et al., 2014). However, although social learning may be universal, there is a lot of variation between cultures with respect to how social learning takes place. Cultures differ in how caregivers talk to their infants, respond to their emotions, and transmit social information (e.g., physically, visually, or vocally) (Legare, 2017). For example, although much of the research on imitation has relied on visual information (i.e., infants watch models, infants assume goals and intention, in part, based on gaze information),

Toddler Imitating Mom

iStock/NataliaDeriabina

in cultures where mothers spend a lot of time carrying their infants on their backs, vocal cues might be more important in transmitting social information than gaze. Vocal cues are also more important for transmitting social information to blind infants (Akhtar & Gernsbacher, 2008). Further, in Western industrialized countries like the United States, caregivers often engage in direct instruction, explicitly teaching their infants how to behave, or they scaffold specific behaviors, modeling them for infants during face-to-face interactions. In contrast, in other countries, like Fiji for example, direct instruction is rare, and infants are expected to learn by watching others (Legare, 2017). On top of that, although the ability to imitate develops in all typically developing infants, *what* infants learn to imitate varies by what infants see in the world around them, which differs from family to family and from culture to culture. In fact, imitation is considered a powerful tool for cultural learning, whereby infants can learn societal rules and traditions.

Check Your Learning

1. Name some of the cues infants use to determine whether an object is likely to have goals or intentions.

2. What are the different kinds of imitation, and how do they differ?

3. What kinds of actions are infants most likely to imitate?

4. What kinds of models are infants most likely to imitate?

SOCIAL COGNITION

Children's understanding of social partners and the assumptions and thoughts they have about others undergoes developmental change in the first few years. You likely know other adults who seem unable to consider the thoughts and feelings of others. During infancy and toddlerhood, children are just beginning to show an understanding of the fact that others have thoughts and feelings. At 2 ½, Alison met her newborn brother, Carter, for the first time. She came to the hospital just hours after he was born and was introduced to him as he slept in his mother's arms. To her mother's alarm, Alison practically jumped on the bed, reached for the newborn, declaring "He wants me to hold him!" Her actions and statements revealed that her cognitions about others were still developing. She earnestly believed that newborn Carter could "want" her to hold him, projecting her own wants onto him. She also failed to read the cues of those around her that were signaling alarm at the movement of a clumsy 2 ½-year-old toward a fragile newborn.

Likewise, at age 3, Charlie was becoming more and more independent. He could climb onto and off of furniture on his own, brush his own teeth, and even put on his own shoes. He really liked this newfound independence and was excited to do things on his own, without the help of his doting mother. But unfortunately for her, when 3-year-old Charlie decided that he wanted to do something on his own, he would tell his mom, "I don't need you." Of course, he didn't literally mean that he didn't need her; he just meant that he didn't need her help with *this particular task*. As a developmental psychologist and infancy expert, Charlie's mom knew this, and she knew that he still needed her for many things, but it still stung every time those words left his mouth. How could Charlie say something so callous to his mom? The answer is that at age 3, Charlie didn't realize that his words would hurt her feelings, as he didn't yet have a strong ability to reason from his mother's, or anyone else's, perspective.

In this section, we will talk about social cognition, or how infants come to process and apply information about other people and social situations. Social cognition involves understanding other people's mental states, so that you can make predictions about what they might do, want, and feel, and appropriately navigate social situations and establish relationships with the people around you. For you, this type of reasoning might be second nature; indeed, we are making inferences about what other people are thinking and feeling all the time, perhaps even unconsciously. But this is a skill that develops slowly over the course of development, even into the teenage years, and is only first beginning to take shape in infancy.

Theory of Mind

Perhaps the most fundamental aspect of social cognition is what researchers call **theory of mind**. Theory of mind refers to our understanding of other people's mental states, or the ability to reason about the thoughts, beliefs, desires, intentions, and goals of others. It's how we differentiate between our own thoughts and feelings and another person's thoughts and feelings, coupled with the understanding that other people have thoughts and feelings that might be different from our own and from reality. Alison was clearly showing a lack of theory of mind when she attributed her own beliefs and desires to her newborn baby brother.

Theory of mind is crucial for navigating social interactions and for creating and maintaining social relationships. Let's go back to the example we just talked about with Charlie. Sure, when a 3-year-old says, "I don't need you," you might take it with a grain of salt, especially because you know that he doesn't quite understand how his words will be construed. But what if an adult said something like that to you? What if it was your colleague at work, a classmate, or a friend? Not only would the comment sting (like it does when Charlie said it), but it's also likely that you wouldn't brush it off as easily as Charlie's mom did. In fact, it might be hard to maintain a friendship or any kind of relationship with someone who says that they don't need you. Theory of mind is required for you to realize that saying something like that to a friend might hurt your friend's feelings. As a result, you probably wouldn't say, "I don't need you," if you wanted to do something yourself; instead, you'd anticipate how your words might affect your friend and choose different ones, like "Let me give this a try by myself." Without a theory of mind, you wouldn't be able to anticipate how your words might affect another person, you wouldn't be able to think about other people's emotional states at all (unless, of course, they were always the same as yours), and you wouldn't be able to make predictions about what people might do at any given time. This makes theory of mind incredibly important for social development.

Theory of mind has been measured in infants and young children in several ways. The most classic theory of mind task in psychological research is called the Sally and Anne task and is used to test theory of mind in preschoolers—3- to 5-year-old children (Figure 11.4). In the task, researchers present children with two dolls, one named Sally and one named Anne. Next, the children watch as the Sally doll plays with a marble, puts the marble in a basket, and then leaves the room. While Sally is gone, the Anne doll takes the marble from the basket and moves it to a box. The critical question that researchers ask children is where Sally will look for the marble when she comes back. The obvious answer is that she'll look in the basket (because that's where she saw it placed). But what do children need to do to get the answer right? They must be able to reason from Sally's perspective and understand that Sally believes the marble is in the basket, even though the child knows it's in the box.

You can imagine how 2 ½-year-old Alison might have answered this question—she likely would have said that Sally would look in the box, showing a difficulty in separating her own knowledge from that of another. In fact, preschool children's performance on this task varies, and they don't reliably get the answer right in this and similar tasks until the age of 4 or 5. Nevertheless, researchers have wondered if infants have some understanding of theory of mind, and they have developed simpler measures, like anticipatory looking to test infants' rudimentary understanding of theory of mind.

Victoria Southgate and her colleagues (2007) asked whether they could uncover infants' understanding of scenarios like the Sally and Anne task by measuring where toddlers look as the story unfolds. They tested 25-month-old British toddlers. First, toddlers were familiarized with scenes in which an experimenter sat between two boxes in front of the infant. The experimenter watched as a puppet entered the scene, placed a ball in one of the boxes and then left; the experimenter then looked at the box containing the ball and reached for it. On the critical test trials, after the puppet placed the ball in one of the two boxes, it seemed to change its mind and removed the ball from the first box and moved it to the second box, much like Anne moves the marble from the basket to the box in the Sally and Anne task. Sometimes the experimenter

FIGURE 11.4 ■ Sally and Anne

Source: Baron-Cohen et al. (1985).

was clearly watching the puppet moving the ball and sometimes the experimenter did not see the puppet moving the ball from one box to the other. When it was time for the experimenter to reach for one of the two boxes, the infants looked at the box where the experimenter *thought the ball should be*—in the second box in the condition in which the experimenter saw the puppet move the ball and in the first box in the condition in which she did not see the puppet move it (Southgate et al., 2007).

So, by measuring where infants looked, Southgate and her colleagues provided a suggestion that by the age of 2, toddlers have some developing understanding that another person can hold a **false belief**, or that a person can have a belief about that world that is different from reality. Other researchers have even suggested that false belief emerges as early as 15 months in U.S. samples (Onishi & Baillargeon, 2005). However, false belief understanding is just one aspect of theory of mind. Henry Wellman and David Liu (2004) developed a scale to measure several of the components of theory of mind, including false belief understanding, but also the ability to understand that two people can have different desires and beliefs about the same object, how a person might feel if they find out that they were mistaken about something, and whether people can express one emotion but feel something different. Wellman and Liu found that these components of theory of mind develop slowly over time, and research with children in Australia, North America, and Europe suggest that children in these Western, industrialized countries tend to move through them in the same sequence. There is a similar pattern in children from China and Iran, although children from these countries seem to reliably master a few of the tasks in a slightly different order when compared to Western children (Slaughter, 2015). False belief performance in general has been shown to develop at similar time points across various countries, including Canada, India, Peru, Samoa, and Thailand (Callaghan et al., 2005).

As we discussed earlier in this chapter, over the first 2 years of life, infants follow other peoples' gaze, they demonstrate some understanding that people (and not objects) have intentions, and they begin to imitate only intended and rational actions. These behaviors can be thought of as early theory of mind behaviors. Moreover, some researchers have shown that infants' responding on looking time false belief tasks is related to their later theory of mind. For example, one study showed that the more 18-month-old German infants look to where a searcher will look for an object in a looking time version of the Sally and Anne task, the more their verbal responses in the more standard false belief task at 28 months reflected recognition of false belief (Thoermer et al., 2012). Another group of researchers reported that 18-month-old Japanese infants' behavior in a looking time false belief task predicted their pretend play at ages 4 and 5 (Moriguchi et al., 2018). Results like these suggest that how infants perform on the infant looking time tasks is related to how they will perform later on other more complicated tasks. However, others have argued that the kinds of looking time false belief tasks tested in infancy tap into different cognitive processes than the theory of mind tasks used with older children (Oktay-Gür et al., 2018). Either way, it does appear that the precursors to a full-blown theory of mind begin to develop in infancy and guide infants' first social interactions with the people around them.

Prosocial Behavior

As we discussed in the previous section, theory of mind helps children navigate social situations and make predictions about other people's behavior. It also paves the way for infants to begin to develop **prosocial behaviors** like helping and sharing, or behaviors that are intended to benefit others. Think about it: Why would you help someone else or share your favorite cookies with them? Maybe you think they would appreciate the help, maybe you feel bad for them, or maybe you just think it's the right thing to do. But without a theory of mind, you wouldn't know any of these things. To understand that someone even needs help, you need to be able to reason about their intentions.

After infants show evidence of beginning to make inferences about the intentions of others, there is also some evidence that infants begin to prefer actions that are prosocial to actions that are antisocial. In a now famous study, Kiley Hamlin, Karen Wynn, and Paul Bloom (2007) familiarized a group of 10-month-old U.S. (mostly White, from middle-class families) infants to a live display of a character (the circle in Figure 11.5) who tried to climb up a hill. When the character was nearly at the top, it was either helped up the hill by a second character (i.e., the helper, the triangle in Figure 11.5) or pushed back down the hill by a third character (i.e., the hinderer, the square in Figure 11.5). The question was whether these 10-month-old infants learned something about the helper and hinderer that would influence how they perceived them in other events. To test this, Hamlin and her colleagues showed infants new events in which the climber just approached either the helper or the hinderer. Infants looked longer when the climber approached the hinderer than when the climber approached the helper. Hamlin et al. argued that because the helper acted prosocially, infants expected the climber to approach the helper. But, because the hinderer acted antisocially, seeing the climber approach this character violated their expectations. In addition to measuring how long infants looked, the researchers also offered the actual helper and the hinderer characters to the infants and recorded

FIGURE 11.5 ■ Helper and Hinderer

Helping and hindering habituation events from Hamlin, Wynn, and Bloom (2007). On each trial, the climber (circle) attempts to climb the hill, falling back to the bottom of the hill. In the test events, the climber is either bumped up the hill by the helper (left) or bumped down the hill by the hinderer (right).

Source: Hamlin, Wynn, & Bloom (2007).

which one infants reached for and touched first. They found that infants were also more likely to reach for the helper, providing additional support that they preferred this prosocial character.

Although infants may be sensitive to whether others act prosocially, they do not begin to engage in prosocial behaviors themselves until several months later. A series of studies with groups of German 12- and 18-month-old infants demonstrated this. In each of these studies, infants played in a room with an adult experimenter. In one study, there were several objects on the floor and after playing with one object, the experimenter dropped it on the floor and appeared confused, looking around for it (Liszkowski et al., 2006). In other studies, infants watched as an experimenter tried and failed to achieve a goal, like dropping a marker on the floor and then reaching for it repeatedly (Warneken et al., 2006; Warneken & Tomasello, 2007). In each of these studies, the question was simple: Do the infants understand the intention (or mental state) of the researcher, and if so, do they help the poor researcher achieve his goal? Infants as young as 12 to 14 months did indeed seem to understand the researcher's intention and responded by helpfully pointing at the lost object or picking up the marker and handing it to the researcher. This suggests that even infants as young as 12 months of age not only infer another person's intention but also behave prosocially and help when someone needs it. Prosocial behaviors such as helping first develop around 12 months of age, and they are generally observed in most cultures. However, as children get older, both their cultural experiences (e.g., parents' expectations, social norms) and children's motivations for helping (because it's fun, because of social affiliation, or because it leads to some reward) get increasingly more complex and differentiated (Hammond & Brownell, 2018; Kärtner et al., 2020).

Some researchers have argued that these initial prosocial behaviors and preference for prosociality are the beginnings of morality in infants. However, morality and moral behavior are cognitively and emotionally complex, and despite the fact that the foundations for these behaviors that we've discussed in this chapter—gaze following, imitation, and false belief understanding—seem to develop universally around the same time, moral behavior, including sharing, lying, and altruism, will all depend on the rules and customs of the infant's individual culture, which will all likely develop through social learning mechanisms like modeling, observation, and imitation.

How Does Social Cognition Develop?

To summarize what we've learned so far, social cognition, and theory of mind specifically, develops slowly over the course of infancy and early childhood. Infants are only starting to develop the very first signs of theory of mind by following others' gaze, inferring other people's intentions, and finally using that inference to help other people achieve their goals. More complex theory of mind reasoning like the reasoning required for understanding false belief tasks—and for correctly recognizing that your newborn brother does not want you to hold him—mostly develops after the infancy period, in preschool and beyond.

How does theory of mind understanding develop, and what are the causal mechanisms that underlie its development? We don't know for sure. But because of the early emergence of some of the precursors to theory of mind, some psychologists think that its foundations are innate. For example, the fact that behaviors like imitation and false belief understanding seem to develop in the same way across many different cultures and groups, following a relatively consistent order, suggests that there may be a biological basis for its development. Indeed, it is likely that maturation of several systems in the brain allow for theory of mind reasoning to unfold.

Further, theory of mind abilities sometimes show different developmental patterns in neurodivergent individuals, such as autistic children. Autism has been associated with challenges in meeting the expectations of social functioning by neurotypical individuals, and autistic individuals have difficulty with tasks that tap theory of mind. In general, autistic individuals perform significantly lower on theory of mind tests, including false belief tests, and tests that require participants to infer the emotions of others when compared with individuals without an autism diagnosis (Kimhi, 2014). Of course, an individual's ability to succeed on theory of mind tasks depends heavily on several factors, like IQ and language, which can also vary greatly in autistic individuals. But in the eye-tracking version of the Sally and Anne task described earlier (Southgate et al., 2007), autistic children and autistic adults do not show the same pattern as neurotypical toddlers. Specifically, researchers measured where subjects looked while an experimenter watched a series of actions on a ball; sometimes the actions resulted in the ball being where the experimenter had seen it placed, and other times the actions resulted in the ball being in a different location (e.g., it was moved when the experimenter was not looking). Whereas 25-month-old neurotypical infants look in anticipation of where an experimenter *thought* the ball should be, 6- to 8-year-old autistic children and autistic adults did not reliably look toward where the experimenter thought the ball should be. Results like these suggest that the challenges autistic children have with theory of mind tasks are not simply due to the effects of language difficulties on task performance (Slaughter, 2015).

This study compared how autistic children and adults performed with neurotypical toddlers. However, differences emerge even before autistic children can be tested on standard theory of mind tasks. Infants who are at a higher likelihood for a later autism diagnosis (i.e., because they have an autistic older sibling) show different patterns of behavior on tasks that could be considered precursors to theory of mind. For example, as mentioned in Chapter 4, many autistic individuals have difficulty making eye contact during interactions with others, and they may be unable to interpret social signals from others. At 2 months, most infants look at the eyes of a face for similar amounts of time, but by 6 months, infants who are later diagnosed as autistic look at the eyes less than infants who don't receive an autism diagnosis (Jones & Klin, 2013). This suggests that although there are no initial differences between children who are and are not later diagnosed as autistic, face processing develops differently in children who will go on to receive an autism diagnosis (Wagner et al., 2016, 2020). Thus, it is possible that very early differences in how infants process or attend to social information might later cascade into differences in how autistic and neurotypical individuals interpret social cues. As scientists have developed ways of identifying autistic children at younger ages, interventions have been developed that have been successful at influencing this cascade, and many autistic children who receive early interventions have an easier time functioning with neurotypical people, especially in terms of social interactions.

The effect of early interventions on the social functioning of autistic children suggests that social cognition isn't all innate. Instead, experience and learning play a role in shaping social cognition over time. In fact, there are lots of individual differences in social cognition, theory of mind, and related prosocial behaviors, and children express these behaviors at different times and in different ways. For example, although research suggests that infants from Western cultures start engaging in prosocial behaviors by 12 to 18 months, not all of them behave prosocially. And while we'd like to think that all infants are lovely, upstanding (albeit tiny) individuals, there are some that are more prone to helping and sharing than others. Even in the studies we discussed in which toddlers helped an adult who dropped a marker, many of the infants observed didn't help the experimenter on some of the tasks. This difference could be because there is a biological predisposition for some people to be more helpful than others. However, there are also lots of ways the infants' environment may influence this development.

One possible factor is that children who learn to consider other people's feelings will be more helpful. One way children may learn about other people's feelings is through interacting with other children. In this case, children with siblings should have an advantage over children without siblings. In fact, children with siblings seem to develop theory of mind a little earlier than children who don't have siblings. This difference is likely because siblings are an everyday source of information about other people's thoughts and beliefs (Slaughter, 2015).

Another possible factor on children's developing prosocial behavior is how much they talk about emotions and mental states (e.g., what someone is thinking) with other people. Parents who talk more about emotions and use more mental state terms with their children seem to help build their children's prosocial skills. For example, in one study, researchers counted how much emotion-related and mental state language a group of U.S. parents used as they read storybooks to their 18- to 30-month-old children. They also observed the children as they played with an experimenter and during a helping task similar to the one we discussed earlier, where children were cued to help an experimenter retrieve an out-of-reach toy (Brownell et al., 2013). They found that the more parents encouraged their children to talk about emotions while reading storybooks, the more the children shared toys with the experimenter during play and the more they helped the experimenter when she expressed some need for help. Altogether, this suggests that while some of the precursors to theory of mind might develop in every infant around the same time, there is still quite a lot of room for learning, especially if we want infants to someday use their theory of mind knowledge to behave prosocially.

BOX 11.1—INFANCY IN REAL LIFE: THE DARK SIDE OF SOCIAL LEARNING

As we've read in the chapter so far, imitation and theory of mind are important parts of infants' social development. These skills allow for social learning, for infants to make predictions about others, and for the development of prosocial behaviors. However, social learning also has a dark side. Indeed, if infants can imitate positive behaviors that lead to cultural transmission, they can also imitate negative or undesirable behaviors as well. When Alison was just under 2, she dropped a shampoo bottle and said, "Oh sit!" clearly repeating a foul phrase that she had heard from someone else. When they were small, Diego and Tesalia lived in student housing and the whole family regularly ate in the dining hall. Although their parents tried their best to get the kids to eat healthy foods, Diego and Tesalia once watched a few undergraduates eating sugary cereal for dinner. This resulted in them insisting that they also could have sugary cereal for dinner. And perhaps the darkest side of social learning is when children see aggressive behaviors, like hitting or biting, and then repeat them on their siblings or parents.

We already know from more than 50 years of research that watching others behave aggressively can cause children to behave more aggressively themselves. In one of the classic and most famous studies on the topic, Alfred Bandura, who we mentioned earlier in this chapter, randomly assigned some groups of preschoolers to watch an adult behave aggressively with an inflatable doll, hitting the doll with a mallet, punching the doll in the nose, and kicking it repeatedly. Another group of children were assigned to a control condition where they did not watch any aggressive behavior. Next, the children were placed in a playroom with the same inflatable doll and a bunch of other toys. Not surprisingly, the children who watched the adult behaving aggressively imitated what they saw, hitting the doll with a mallet, punching the doll, and kicking it. On top of that, they found new and creative ways to beat up the doll, and they played more aggressively with the other toys in the room as well. In other words, the study doesn't just show that children imitate the aggressive behaviors that they see, it also suggests that watching aggressive behaviors causes children to behave more aggressively *in general* (Bandura et al., 1963).

But this study was done in older children. Do infants also show evidence of aggressive behavior? In one study, 80% of Canadian infants began to engage in behaviors like biting, kicking, hitting, and pushing between 12 and 17 months of age (Tremblay et al., 1999). Such aggressive behaviors in infants are usually related to frustration (Calkins & Johnson, 1998), which can be particularly difficult for infants to cope with, given that they don't have the language ability needed to fully express their emotions (see Chapter 9) or the regulatory abilities to cope with them (see Chapter 10).

So, a big challenge that most parents face is how to discourage their infants from engaging in these aggressive behaviors, while at the same time, being sensitive to their infants' emotional needs. Another challenge for parents is deciding whether to *model* aggressive behaviors themselves. Spanking, for example, has been viewed as a form of aggressive behavior, and it is a common one. In fact, international data suggest that most kids have been spanked—close to 300 million worldwide (UNICEF, 2017). Spanking has been defined as open-handed hitting that does not injure a child, and it is typically done with the intention of modifying the child's bad behavior (Gershoff et al., 2016). In 1998, the American Academy of Pediatrics (AAP) wrote a statement for the first time discouraging parents from spanking their children as a method of punishment. They did this because research suggests that spanking isn't effective in stopping children from engaging in disruptive behaviors (Gershoff, 2013). Perhaps most importantly, many studies have also linked spanking with aggressive behaviors in children (Gershoff et al., 2016). These studies are correlational, so one could argue that spanking doesn't necessarily lead to aggression and, instead, that aggressive kids are just more likely to be spanked. However, one long-term study of over 12,000 children across the United States reported that children who were spanked at age 5 were more likely to act aggressively at ages 6 and 8. This study suggests that spanking comes *before* aggressive behavior in children. Further, these researchers controlled for the number of behavioral problems children had, meaning that the link between spanking and aggression was independent of whether or not the kids were particularly difficult or defiant (Gershoff et al., 2018). Why does spanking lead to more aggressive behavior? The answer is simple: By watching parents hit, children are likely learning that hitting is an acceptable behavior and a permissible form of punishment; in essence, they are engaging in social learning, imitating what they see.

Check Your Learning

1. What is theory of mind, and why is it so important for social development?

2. Describe the Sally and Ann task, and explain what ability it is designed to measure.

3. Outline the evidence that documents prosocial understanding in infants and prosocial behavior in toddlers.

4. What aspects of prosocial behavior are shaped by experience? Which aspects of prosocial behavior reflect differences in individuals' nature?

ATTACHMENT

Right from birth, Charlie was an incredibly laid-back baby. This early laid-back attitude turned into fearlessness when he became a toddler: He loved to dive off the couch, the bed, the stairs, and pounce on pretty much every new obstacle he was presented with. In fact, his mom (who studies the development of fear and anxiety) marveled at Charlie's behavior when she brought him into her lab at 12 months to assess his emotionality. As part of the assessment, her team presented Charlie with several emotion-inducing situations, one of which included the scariest stimulus they could find. It was a simple remote-control car that was covered by a brown box; but the brown box was designed to hide the car from view and to prop up a giant toy spider that was mounted on top. When the remote-control car moved forward, it looked like the giant spider was barreling toward you. As you can imagine, the spider is quite effective at inducing fear and usually sends infants (and sometimes their moms) running out of the room. But not Charlie. He ran right up to it, smiled, and started playing with its long furry legs. When it moved toward him, he simply kicked it to see if it would move again.

It seemed like nothing could get this kid down. That is, until about 18 months, when Charlie's parents put him in daycare over the summer. He was with a nanny or his mom for most of the time before that, so he had never experienced daycare before. For 3 full months, he cried and grasped for his mom every single time she dropped him off. Even for laid-back, fearless Charlie, having to cope with new situations without his mom was just too much.

Charlie's response is not at all uncommon; all six of our babies had similar reactions to being separated from their loved ones. Diego and Alison started daycare at 3 or 4 months, when they were too young to realize their moms were gone. However, 4-month-old Alison cried if anyone except her mom tried to hold her; it was so stressful that at one point her mom was convinced that Alison was going to get kicked out of daycare (she didn't). And as he became attached to his caregivers at daycare, Diego got upset whenever he had to switch classrooms or teachers. Edwin cried every day of his first week at preschool and, after that, had to repeat "Mommy always comes back" to himself at every drop-off (and multiple times during the day). At 14 months, Tesalia cried almost every time her mom left her at daycare even though she adored her teachers, and she would insist on nursing for comfort every time her mom picked her up at the end of the day.

At 12 months, Carter, who started daycare at 6 months, was so attached to one of his teachers that he would cry whenever she left the room. She had to carry him around with her as she did things at school.

Loving your mother, your father, your sister, your brother, your teachers, your friends, or your partner feels like the most natural thing in the world to some of us. In fact, when our loved ones are gone, we sometimes even cling to the things they left behind—a photograph, a blanket, or a locket—to remind us of them. But how do we come to love the most important people in our lives? And how do these relationships shape social development? In this section, we will talk about **attachment**. Attachment has many definitions, but for this chapter, we define attachment as the emotional bond between an infant and their caregiver. Most infants form an attachment with their primary caregiver in the first year of life, and there are several different kinds of attachment relationships and attachment styles. In developmental research, attachment relationships are most typically studied in infants and their mothers, since mothers are the ones who most commonly visit the lab. As a result, we will talk mostly about infants and their mothers. However, infants can form attachment relationships with anyone who spends time with them; they can have several different attachment relationships and those relationships can differ from each other. We will talk about this more in the next chapter. Regardless of which attachment figure we are talking about, you will see that strong attachments can provide a safe and secure base for infants to explore new things.

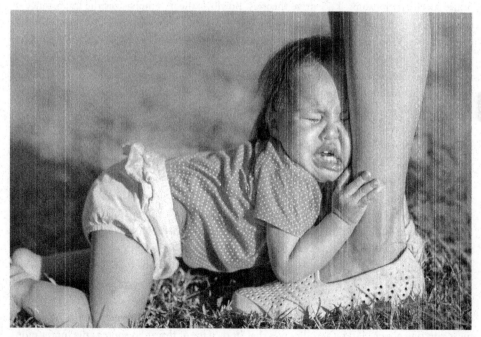

Infant Clinging to Mom
iStock/globalmoments

Theories of Attachment

How do infants first form attachments? For a century, many researchers have asked this question and have come up with different theories to explain how we come to love our caregivers. Early theories are what we call **drive reduction theories**. The idea behind these theories is that infants have basic needs that need to be filled. When the need for something, like food, is high, it drives the infant to change their behavior (e.g., cry). Once that need is met, the drive is reduced and the infant returns to a state of relaxation, or homeostasis. In the case of attachment, the predominant view in the 1950s was that the infant learns to associate the mother, who nurses the infant, with satisfying the infant's hunger drive. This association provides the basis for the initial attachment bond. In other words, you love the one that feeds you.

That is, until famous psychologist John Bowlby (1969) came along and proposed something new. He had been studying institutionalized children and the effects of deprivation and not having a primary caregiver. He proposed that infants have innate behaviors, like crying, cooing, and smiling, that naturally elicit care from their mother. By 7 or 8 months of age, infants of caregivers who are typically responsive to their infants have learned that they can rely on their mothers to comfort them in challenging situations. Some caregivers are inconsistent, responding sometimes but not always, and some are unresponsive, responding to few of their infants' behaviors. Infants of these caregivers do not learn to rely on their caregivers for help. According to Bowlby's theory, over time, infants form a mental representation of their primary caregiver—what he called an **internal working model**—that forms the basis for the development of their future social relationships. Like drive theories, Bowlby's theory emphasizes the importance of the mother for infants' healthy social development. Unlike drive theories, Bowlby deemphasized the role of feeding, turning his attention instead to the mother's role in providing infants with comfort and a secure base of support. However, Bowlby's view was controversial, and there were no strong experimental data that could support his hypothesis, since you can't ethically separate infants from their mothers to study how different kinds of maternal behaviors affect infants' developing attachment relationships.

This is when psychologist Harry Harlow (1958) entered the scene. Although it is not possible to test Bowlby's claims with human infants, Harlow could test some of these hypotheses with rhesus monkeys. He specifically asked whether food or physical comfort was most important to infant monkeys' developing attachment relationships with their mothers. To do this, he separated infant rhesus monkeys from their mothers at birth and paired them with two surrogate mothers. One of the surrogate mothers was a monkey doll made of wire with a bottle attached to it, and the other was a monkey doll made of cloth. Importantly, only the wire mother was equipped with a bottle to feed the baby monkeys, but only the cloth mother was comforting to touch. Harlow measured how much time the baby monkeys spent with each mother. He found that the infant monkeys spent almost all their time on the cloth mother and only went to the wire mother to eat. And when presented with new and potentially threatening objects and situations, they clung only to the cloth mother for comfort and support. What was most amazing about Harlow's studies was that in the face of threat, as soon as the infant monkeys received some comfort from their cloth mothers, they were able to gather up the courage to explore new environments.

Harlow concluded that Bowlby was right, and perhaps food isn't the most important element of infants' attachment to their mothers. Instead, physical comfort seemed to be what was most important to forming this initial bond.

Styles of Attachment

Recall that Bowlby thought that the infants' internal working model—and their attachment—would be influenced by how responsive their caregiver was. In Harlow's work, infant monkeys developed an attachment to a constantly available cloth mother, so we don't know whether they would have different attachments if they had mothers who were more or less responsive. In addition, because his work was on infant monkeys, it wasn't completely clear whether his results would be true of human infants, and of course it wouldn't be ethical to do those studies with human infants (and some people argued that it wasn't even ethical to do them with monkeys!).

Mary Ainsworth, inspired by the work of both Bowlby and Harlow, devised an ethical way to study attachment in infants called the **strange situation**. Using this new paradigm, Ainsworth tested the quality of infants' attachments by inviting mothers to bring their 12-month-old infants to a lab to play. She observed the infant and mother during several episodes, which involved both the mother and a novel experimenter entering and leaving the room at different times. Ainsworth was interested in how the infant reacted to mildly stressful situations and how the child's relationship with their mother helped them cope. Although Ainsworth studied only mothers, the strange situation can be used with any caregiver, and infants can become attached to anyone who cares for them (e.g., mothers, fathers, grandparents, daycare providers).

Table 11.1 lists the episodes. First, the mother and infant played alone for a period of time. At some point during play, an experimenter that the infant had never seen before entered the room. After a few minutes, the infant's mother exited the room, leaving the infant alone with the experimenter. Finally, the mother returned to the room and was reunited with her infant. Each episode was 3 minutes, but if the infant was very distressed when their mom was not present, the mom could end the episode if she wanted the infant to be comforted. Ainsworth

TABLE 11.1 ■ Strange Situation		
Episode	People Present	Events
1	Caregiver, infant	Caregiver and infant play together
2	Caregiver, infant, stranger	Stranger enters and plays with infant
3	Infant, stranger	Parent leaves the room
4	Caregiver, infant	Parent returns, stranger leaves the room
5	Infant	Parent leaves the infant alone in the room
6	Infant, stranger	Stranger returns to the room
7	Caregiver, infant	Parent returns, stranger leaves the room

Source: Based on Ainsworth & Wittig (1969).

was particularly interested in what the infants would do when the stranger came in, what they would do when their mothers left, and, most importantly, what they would do when their mothers returned.

According to Ainsworth, there are two characteristics of a "healthy" attachment. The first is what she called **proximity seeking**. This is any behavior by the infant, including looking, crawling, reaching out, and touching, that has the goal of the infant being close to or in physical contact with their mother. She argued that from an evolutionary perspective, being close to one's mothers would have been beneficial for survival, so that the mother could protect the infant from danger. The second characteristic was **exploration**. It might seem counterintuitive, but according to Ainsworth, while staying close to mom would be important for survival, so would exploring your surroundings. So, in theory, being somewhat close to mom should function to make the infant feel safe enough to explore the world around them (Ainsworth et al., 1970). Again, Charlie behaved fearlessly when his mom was around, but as soon as she left him at daycare, he was afraid to explore, and instead, would cry, and cling to the teacher (so much for "I don't need you").

Ainsworth used these behaviors in the strange situation to classify infants into different attachment styles. Ainsworth (1979) identified the first three. In her original U.S. sample, most infants (65%) were **securely attached**. Securely attached infants played happily when their mothers were in the room, were distressed when their mothers left, and were comforted when their mothers came back. Studies have shown that infants in North America and western Europe who are classified as securely attached later are more independent, better able to regulate their emotions, less likely to demonstrate problem behaviors and emotional problems, and more likely to maintain close relationships with their peers (Cassidy & Shaver, 1999).

Insecure/avoidant infants also played happily when their mothers were in the room but didn't seem to notice when she left or when she came back. In fact, they seemed completely indifferent to her presence. About 10% to 15% of infants in the United States are characterized this way. Another 5% to 10% of infants in U.S. samples are **anxious/resistant**. These infants did not play happily in the lab; they clung to their mothers from the minute they entered the lab, and they were incredibly upset when she left. Interestingly, they couldn't be comforted when she came back, and some of them even seemed angry with her for leaving in the first place. Later, researchers recognized a fourth group, **disorganized/disoriented** (Main & Solomon, 1986). These infants didn't fit into any of the other categories, showing a mix of approach and avoidance responses to their mothers and the experimenter. Generally, only a very small proportion of U.S. samples are classified as disorganized/disoriented.

Remember that Bowlby's research was on institutionalized children who did not have a consistent primary caregiver. It is not surprising, therefore, that he believed that not having a warm and stable relationship with a primary caregiver would result in significant and irreversible mental health consequences. Consistent with this view, securely attached infants from Western cultures tend to develop positive expectations about social interactions, and they tend to have positive social interactions and build positive social relationships over time. In contrast, according to a large analysis of 42 different studies that were mostly from Western countries that varied widely in socioeconomic status, insecure and disorganized attachments are predictive of both internalizing behaviors like anxiety and sadness and externalizing behaviors like aggression (Groh et al., 2012). However, these effects are pretty small and don't show that insecure attachments always result in significant mental health consequences. Indeed, attachment relationships can change over time, and infants can form attachment relationships with many different people, in fact, anyone that they have consistent contact with.

Regardless, a lot of parents in the United States worry about their infants forming a secure attachment, so much so that there are entire parenting philosophies (e.g., "attachment parenting") devoted to teaching parents strategies that promote secure attachment relationships. In general, research shows that secure attachments form between infants and *sensitive* caregivers, that is, caregivers who are consistent and responsive to their infants' needs. The idea is that infants of caregivers who respond to their infants learn that when they are upset, their caregivers will reliably be there to comfort them. In this way, caregivers become a secure home base: Their presence makes infants feel safe so that they can experiment with the world around them. With a dependable caregiver nearby, infants learn that they will get the help they need if something goes wrong, but they also feel free to explore and discover the world on their own. This is likely why Ainsworth used the term *secure attachment*: Securely attached infants feel confident when their caregivers are there, which gives them the freedom to explore new situations. When their caregivers are not there, they feel less confident, but the caregivers' return immediately restores them so they can continue to explore the world.

It is important to point out that these notions of sensitive parenting and security are *Western* ideas and perhaps even more true of the values and beliefs of North Americans than of some Europeans. However, attachment theory is based on the notion that attachment to one's caregiver is adaptive. According to Bowlby and Ainsworth, attachment helps to ensure the infants' survival. Thus, for attachment theory, aspects of attachment are likely innate in typical environments, and attachment styles are somewhat universal. Indeed, Mary Ainsworth's ideas were based on her observations of both mothers and infants in Uganda (Ainsworth, 1967) and mothers and infants in the United States (Ainsworth & Wittig, 1969). Despite these origins, it is important to remember that the strange situation was designed by someone from the United States and was thus based on Western customs and ideals, which has been a consistent criticism of Ainsworth's theory.

It turns out that the "universality" of attachment is complicated. In general, in every study conducted with children from North America, Europe, Asia, or Africa, secure attachment is the most common. In fact, in a review of various cross-cultural studies, researchers have reported fairly universal attachment behaviors in different regions of Africa, including in areas where infants are raised by several adults instead of a single primary caregiver, as is typical in North American and European cultures (van IJzendoorn & Sagi-Schwartz, 2008). What often differs from group to group is the proportions of the insecurely and disorganized attachment classifications. For example, one study in a South African settlement reported rates of securely attached infants similar to those found in the United States and Uganda but higher rates of disorganized attachment and lower rates of avoidant attachment (Tomlinson et al., 2005). A meta-analysis of studies using the strange situation across eight different countries revealed that anxious-avoidant classifications were most common in western European countries, anxious-resistant classifications were most common in Israel and Japan, and the United States fell in the middle. In fact, the differences in different regions of a single country were often larger than differences across countries, particularly in the United States (van IJzendoorn & Kroonenberg, 1988).

Part of the issue here is that secure attachment is thought to be a function of how *sensitive* the caregiver is to an infant's needs. But there are vast cultural differences regarding what constitutes sensitive, responsive parenting (Mesman et al., 2016). For example, in the United States, sensitive parenting is typically viewed as a response to an infant's displays of distress—to help comfort an infant once it has demonstrated that it is unable to calm itself. And ultimately the goal is for the infant to be able to soothe itself and regulate its own emotions, which is part of being successful in a culture that values independence. In contrast, in Japanese culture, sensitive parenting involves anticipating situations that might cause distress and eliminating or avoiding them preemptively. Because Japanese culture values relying on others for emotional support, sensitive parents intervene before children experience distress. For Japanese parents, observing a U.S. parent watch her infant to see if he will self-soothe seems to reflect insensitive parenting. Likewise, focusing only on the Western view of sensitivity might lead to Japanese infants being labeled as insecurely attached (Rothbaum et al., 2000).

What Is the Function of Attachment?

Why do we attach? And what function does attachment serve? Going back to drive reduction theories, researchers initially hypothesized that infants have a need—in this case, hunger—that mothers respond to and reduce. However, Harlow and Ainsworth's work suggests that food isn't necessarily what endears you to an infant. Instead, providing support and comfort seems to be what infants really need, and gives them the confidence to explore their environments freely and without fear.

More recent work using advanced techniques suggests that caregiving may be important for the developing brain in ways that help the individual deal with fear and stress. Again, this is hard to study in humans, but we have a hint from work with rats. Adult rats can be conditioned to associate the smell of peppermint with a mild electric shock; after conditioning, the rats avoid locations that smell of peppermint (Moriceau & Sullivan, 2006). As adult rats learn this association, the amygdala—the part of the brain that is most active during fear conditioning or avoidance learning—is active. They learn the fear response because the conditioning causes the amygdala to become engaged.

However, this system does not seem to operate in the same way for newborn rat pups. If newborn pups are near their mother when they are conditioned to associate the smell of peppermint with an electric shock, they actually develop a *preference* for peppermint! They don't learn to avoid the peppermint at all; instead, they learn to approach it. Once the pups become mobile and wander away from the nest for the first time, newly mobile rats who are conditioned to associate the smell of peppermint with an electric shock show the adult response and avoid peppermint.

Why do rats' approach/avoidance behaviors develop in this way? One possibility is that independent mobility activates the amygdala for the first time so that rat pups can learn to avoid things that threaten them. The amygdala in the newborn pups doesn't activate because they are not yet mobile. However, recall that newborn pups, who can't yet independently move, spend most of their time sleeping in proximity to their mother. It turns out that when pups are in close proximity to their mothers, they show the strange pattern we described in the previous paragraph: They learn to approach stimuli associated with a mild shock. But, if pups are separated from their moms, they instead show the adult pattern of behavior and learn to *avoid* stimuli associated with a shock. Ordinarily, rat pups learn those responses when they are developed enough to wander outside of the nests on their own, not because independent locomotion causes the amygdala to start responding but because being close to their mom keeps rats from learning to be afraid of new things and instead elicits approach, or exploratory behaviors (Moriceau & Sullivan, 2006).

We don't yet know whether a caregiver's presence serves as a similar buffer over amygdala activation in human infants, but there is some evidence that a similar process may be at play in studies with older children. For example, when children (aged 4–10 years) are presented with something scary, their amygdalas are less active when their mothers are in the room than when they are not. Importantly, this is not the case for adolescents, whose amygdalas are equally active with and without their mothers present, likely because they are close to adulthood and no longer need their mothers to help them in the face of threat (Gee et al., 2014). Further, the amygdala is activated more readily in children who grow up in foster care, typically without a primary caregiver (Gee et al., 2013). This work suggests that like in rats, a caregiver's presence serves a regulatory function for human infants, acting as a buffer from activating the part of the brain most associated with fear, giving infants the freedom to explore new things confidently in the comfort of their mother's presence.

This work implies that a secure attachment might also serve as a buffer from stress in new situations. A group of researchers tested this theory by studying U.S. infants' attachment security when they were 15 months of age and using it to predict how these infants would fare when starting daycare for the first time 5 months later. They found that infants who were securely attached had lower levels of a stress hormone called cortisol in their systems when adapting to daycare when compared to infants who were insecurely attached (Ahnert et al., 2004). These findings are consistent with the idea that secure attachment could serve to protect infants from stress.

What Determines Attachment Style?

Ainsworth's theory was that attachment style reflected the kind of sensitive parenting infants had experienced. She not only characterized infants' behavior during the strange situation, but she also provided descriptions of mothering styles that led to each of those attachment classifications (Ainsworth, 1979). Research has supported her conclusions, at least in Western cultures. Secure attachment is associated with sensitive parenting, insecure-avoidant attachment has been associated with intrusive or over-involved parenting, and insecure-resistant attachment is associated with inconsistent or unresponsive parenting. For example, infants and preschoolers of mothers in the United States and the United Kingdom who are chronically depressed are more likely to develop an insecure attachment when compared to children of non-depressed mothers (Martins & Gaffan, 2000; Teti et al., 1995). Similarly, having an insecure or disorganized attachment is related to childhood instances of maltreatment and neglect by parents (Baer & Martinez, 2006).

The presence of an attachment figure early in life also seems to be important. For example, various studies have suggested that adopted children are at risk for the development of an insecure attachment relationship. Indeed, adopted children not only lack a consistent primary attachment figure early in life but also are at greater risk of experiencing maltreatment and neglect. According to a meta-analysis of 39 studies of adopted children and 11 studies of foster children, when children were adopted before their first birthday, they were just as likely to form a secure attachment with their caregiver when compared to same-aged infants who were not put up for adoption. In contrast, infants adopted after 12 months were more likely to develop an insecure attachment (van den Dries et al., 2009).

Further research has shown that the absence of a primary attachment figure for prolonged periods of time can have detrimental effects on development more broadly. Remember the Bucharest Early Intervention Project (BEIP) that we talked about way back in Chapter 1? To remind you, the goal of BEIP is to study the long-term effects of early deprivation in Romanian orphanages and how children raised in these orphanages might benefit from being placed in foster care. The study started with 136 children between the ages of 6 and 31 months living in orphanages, and half were randomly assigned to move to high-quality foster care, while the other half remained institutionalized. High-quality foster care meant being placed in a family and having a stable caregiver. The children who remained in the orphanages did not have a stable caregiver. The researchers have now been studying these children for over 10 years to document the long-term differences between the group that remained institutionalized and the group that was moved to high-quality foster care. One of their main questions was how the lack of a primary attachment figure affects social and emotional development over time and whether placing these children in homes with the opportunity to form attachments with their new caregivers for the first time might improve that development.

They found that children growing up without an attachment figure or a primary caregiver (i.e., those who were institutionalized as infants and young children) tended to show a behavior called indiscriminate friendliness, where they treat everyone the same way. This might sound great at first; indeed, everyone wants to see a world with equality and have children who are nice to everyone. But these children are also willing to walk away with a stranger, get in anyone's car, or hold anyone's hand, regardless of how familiar or unfamiliar the person might be (Gleason et al., 2014). They treat loved ones and strangers in the same way, which is actually quite a disturbing behavior if you've ever seen it firsthand.

But importantly, children who were placed in foster care as infants were much more likely to have secure attachments between the ages of 3 and 4 years than were children who remained in institutionalized care (Smyke et al., 2010). Further, the attachment relationships infants formed in foster care played an important role in children's long-term social development. Infants in the foster care group who formed secure attachments to their new caregivers were the least likely to later develop emotional problems like anxiety and depression compared to both the children who were never in foster care or those children in foster care who didn't develop a secure attachment relationship (McGoron et al., 2012; McLaughlin et al., 2012). The point is that the effects of a lack of sensitive parenting early in development can be overcome if children can develop a secure attachment as toddlers. This is even true for infants who develop in typical households in the United States; if infants with insecure attachments then receive highly responsive parenting, they show improvements in social and emotional development (Belsky & Fearon, 2002).

Although we tend to think secure attachment as positive and insecure or disorganized attachment as negative, insecure attachments can be considered adaptive in some circumstances. Indeed, from an evolutionary perspective (and from a practical one), it makes sense to learn not to rely on caregivers who are inconsistent and unreliable (Belsky et al., 1991). Given that certain unfamiliar objects and people can threaten an individual's survival, an infant or child who has unreliable parents who don't generally comfort or protect them from threat *should* be more vigilant and thus have a bigger stress response when facing uncertainty when compared to infants who have learned that they can rely on their caregivers to protect them. If attachment is indeed an adaptive system, then how it develops depends heavily on context and characteristics of the infant's environment.

BOX 11.2—INFANCY IN REAL LIFE: HOW MOTHERS' BRAINS HELP PROMOTE A SECURE ATTACHMENT

As you already know from Chapter 3, when a woman gets pregnant, her body undergoes a series of changes that prepare her for pregnancy. What you may not know is that a woman's brain also undergoes a series of changes with pregnancy that might help prepare her for parenthood. Importantly, the regions where the most change is observed serve specific functions that might help the infant develop a secure attachment.

A group of researchers collected brain scans using fMRI from Spanish mothers before and after they gave birth to see if their brains changed in any noticeable way before and after having children. The structure of mothers' brains did in fact undergo significant changes that were long lasting, remaining for at least 2 years after the women gave birth. Importantly, the parts of their brains that changed most were the ones that were active when the mothers were looking at pictures of their own infants. The researchers think that these changes might help women to be extra attentive to the emotional needs of their newborns (Hoekzema et al., 2017).

Similar changes seem to take place in fathers' brains as well. Another group of researchers found that becoming a parent for the first time activates what they call a "parental caregiving network" in the brain, engaging areas most responsible for emotional processing, social understanding, and empathy. This network becomes active in both mothers and fathers after having children. Although just giving birth (and not the amount of caregiving provided) determined this activity for mothers, for fathers the amount of direct caregiving experience they had with their infants was related to how active their parental caregiving network was (Abraham et al., 2014).

Further, there is evidence that changes in mothers' brains following childbirth function not only to increase sensitivity to infants' needs but also to prepare the body to spring into action if something goes wrong. A recent study of over 700 mothers and their infants across 11 different countries (Argentina, Belgium, Brazil, Cameroon, France, Kenya, Israel, Italy, Japan, South Korea, and the United States) showed that universally, mothers respond quickly to hearing their babies' cry, moving closer to them and talking to them to soothe their distress. Additional brain data collected in three of these countries—the United States, China, and Italy—demonstrated that regions of the mothers' brains that prepare the body for action were activated immediately upon hearing their infants' cry, for both brand new mothers and mothers who had more experience hearing infants' cries (Bornstein et al., 2017).

So, while becoming a parent can turn new moms into sappy, emotional wrecks, these emotional changes might be a good thing, helping new parents become extra sensitive and quick to respond to their infants' needs. And as we just learned, parental sensitivity and responsiveness are some of the main factors that predict a secure attachment relationship as the infant gets older, so these early changes in parents' brains could help establish a foundation for the child's healthy social relationships.

Check Your Learning

1. What is the difference between drive reduction theories and Bowlby's theory of attachment?

2. What are the most common behaviors of a securely attached infant?

3. Name the different attachment styles.

4. What is the function of attachment from a physiological perspective?

5. What are the main predictors of an insecure attachment?

SUMMARY

Infants begin to engage with the social world right from birth. Some early preferences for faces and human motion orient infants to social information so that they can begin to distinguish who and what would make a good social partner. In the first year of life, they begin to show some understanding that others are alive and have thoughts and intentions, first by following the gaze of others and then by engaging in joint attention. They use this information to decide what to imitate and when, which sets the stage for social learning. As they begin to interact more with the social world, they also learn about the thoughts and intentions of others, a skill called theory of mind. And while a sophisticated theory of mind does not develop until after the infancy period, the foundation for theory of mind is developed in these early years, allowing for the initial development of prosocial behaviors like helping and sharing. Perhaps the most important social relationship infants develop is with their primary caregiver, to whom they form an attachment relationship. Infants of sensitive, responsive caregivers tend to form secure attachments, which allow them to explore new places and objects with the confidence that their caregivers will be there to lend a helping hand if needed. This important relationship provides a model for other relationships infants have throughout their lives, helping the infant develop into a socially competent adult.

KEY TERMS

anxious/resistant
attachment
biological motion
disorganized/disoriented
drive reduction theories
exploration
false belief
goal directed
insecure/avoidant
internal working model

mimicry
model
prosocial behaviors
proximity seeking
securely attached
self-propelled motion
social learning theory
strange situation
theory of mind

REVIEW QUESTIONS

1. Name the three features that inspire infants to follow gaze or interact socially.

2. Define each type of imitation and the order in which they emerge in development.

3. Define *theory of mind* and *false belief.* Explain how the Sally and Ann task measures false belief.

4. What evidence points to infants' understanding of prosocial behavior?

5. Define an internal working model.

6. Name the different attachment styles and describe their characteristics.

7. List the order of the episodes in the strange situation.

CRITICAL THINKING QUESTIONS

1. A friend is expecting a baby and you would like to select a "stuffie" that the infant will enjoy looking at and bonding with. Do you select the stuffie that is a very soft and colorful ball or the stuffie that has eyes, a mouth, and ears? Explain your choice.

2. What aspects of imitation seem to be universal, and what aspects differ based on infants' experience?

3. Explain why each of the three types of imitation emerge at different points in development.

4. How are social cognitive skills related to infants' prosocial behaviors like helping and sharing?

5. What is the evidence that aspects of social cognition are driven by nature? What is the evidence that aspects of social cognition are driven by nurture?

6. Is forming attachments to a caregiver universal? Provide an example of when an infant may not have the opportunity to form a secure attachment to a caregiver.

12

THE CONTEXT OF INFANT DEVELOPMENT—PARENTING, PEERS, AND COMMUNITY

As you've read through the chapters in this book, you've learned a lot about infant development across various domains, including both cognitive and social. And in the first chapter, we pointed out that while researchers tend to talk about domains separately, these systems continually interact over the course of development, and development is happening in the *whole child*, not just in a single isolated system. In this last chapter, we return to the important issue of understanding that development does not happen in a vacuum. Our six children developed in their first few years in a rich environment. They had parents who cared for them and spent time with them. They each had siblings—Carter, Charlie, and Tesalia had siblings throughout infancy, and Alison, Diego, and Edwin became older siblings sometime between the ages of 2 and 3. They had playgroups and music classes and attended daycare from an early age. They were raised in North America in two-parent homes. They all had European heritage, and four of them also had Latine heritage. They all heard English, and Charlie, Diego, Edwin, and Tesalia heard Spanish to some extent. Some of them went to church, and all of them went to the grocery store and played in local parks. Although children around the world have different early experiences, all children's development during infancy happens in a context that includes family, peers, and a rich environment.

Way back in Chapter 1, we discussed Urie Bronfenbrenner's (1979) ecological systems theory. The theory is used to help us understand how different aspects of the child's context influences their development. This is particularly useful when thinking about how parenting can influence the infant's development on a number of levels. Flip back and take a look at Figure 1.3 again. You will see that within the innermost rings lies the infant's parents, along with their siblings and their peers. This is where the family, their behaviors, and the structure of where they live—in a house, an apartment, or even in a hut—can have a direct influence on the infant's development. As your eyes move toward the outer rings, you'll see that politics, neighborhood, and cultural attitudes and practices can also affect the infants' development, oftentimes indirectly, through the parents. In this chapter, we will discuss in more detail how these aspects of infants' daily lives shape their development.

Throughout this book, we have talked about influences at different levels. We have touched on differences in cultures, or how cultural values and practices shape development; in these examples, we were referring to the outermost ring. We have also touched on the innermost rings within domains, for example, when referring to parental input to language development or infant temperament inducing different types of parenting. In this final chapter, we take a closer look at the influences of family and community factors on infant development.

By the end of this chapter, you will be able to:

1. *Describe* the four different categories of infant caregiving behaviors.

2. *Explain* how siblings or peers can shape learning and social development.

3. *Describe* the distinct ways infants are cared for in different places around the world.

PARENTING

Parenting is clearly important: Everything a parent does can impact infant development, and nearly all of infant development is impacted by parenting. First, the parents' own genetic material is inherited by the fetus at conception. As the fetus develops during the prenatal period, everything the mother does can affect the fetal environment, from diet and mental health to movement and stimulation (see Chapter 3). Parents' behaviors then start shaping infants' attention, language, and other types of learning as well as their social world from birth. How much parents talk to their infants (see Chapter 9), how they structure the infant's environment, and even their beliefs about the world can all have an impact on the infant in more subtle ways.

But parenting is highly culturally determined. This is clear when we consider *who* the infant's parent is. In many cultures, parents are the two individuals who brought the child into their family, through reproduction or adoption, and who take care of the child's needs. In these cultures, parents are often thought of as a mother and father who are married and live together and who both live

Large Family in Sudan
iStock/Claudiad

with the infant. However, even when this is the common definition of parent in a culture, there are increasingly more one-parent families, families with two mothers or two fathers, or families that include two parents who never live together as a family. But who is considered a parent varies widely when we consider parenting around the globe. For many infants, older siblings, grandparents, or unrelated adults in their community act as caregivers, and are in effect "parents" to the infants.

In this section, we will report on what is known about parenting, but the research has primarily been conducted with mothers in middle-class Western cultures. The cross-cultural work that does exist often compares differences in parenting by mothers, with less attention paid to others who "parent" an infant. These "others" clearly impact the infants' world as well; we just know a lot less about that impact.

Parenting Behaviors

Humans are not the only species that engage in parenting of their offspring. When you look at parenting across species, you'll see a set of common behaviors. Indeed, most parents across a wide range of species engage in taking care of their infants' biological needs, like feeding, grooming, as well as protecting them from harm. In humans, however, as is true of so many things, parenting behavior is a bit more complicated. Humans don't just make sure their infants are fed, groomed, and safe; among many other things, human parents also support the child's emotional development, teach them expectations and values for social interactions, and create a context through which children can learn language. Of course, other species also engage in some of these aspects of parenting, but for no other species does parenting involve as many different areas as it does for humans.

In fact, researchers have identified four different categories of parenting behaviors exhibited by human parents (Table 12.1). The first is **nurturant caregiving**, which encompasses behaviors that meet the infants' basic biological needs, centering on keeping the infant healthy and safe. These are activities such as feeding the infant and making sure they are warm when it is cold out. **Social caregiving** involves helping the infant build social relationships and helping

TABLE 12.1 ■ The Four Types of Caregiving Behaviors		
Type of Caregiving	**Definition**	**Example**
Nurturant	Behaviors that meet child's biological, physical, and health needs	Feeding and clothing an infant, keeping an infant safe from physical harm
Social	Behaviors that foster social connection with an infant and allow an infant to manage emotions and social interactions	Smiling, touching, or soothing an infant
Didactic	Behaviors that stimulate, engage, or promote infant learning	Naming objects or actions or reading to the infant
Material	Behaviors that organize or arrange the infant's physical world	Providing toys or books to have in the home or in other environments in which the infant spends time

the infant regulate their emotions. This type of caregiving involves engaging infants in inter-personal exchanges (e.g., turn-taking, peek-a-boo) and expressions of affection. **Didactic caregiving** involves engaging infants in the world around them, by focusing their attention and providing the infant with opportunities to learn. This type of caregiving involves labeling and pointing and drawing infants' attention to objects and events around them. Finally, **material caregiving** involves organizing the infants' physical space, including the objects around the infant and providing limits to the infants' physical freedom (Bornstein, 2019). Researchers have also described physical caregiving, or promoting the infants' motor development, and language caregiving, which involves verbal communication (Bornstein et al., 2022). These categories aren't mutually exclusive, meaning that parents often use combinations of them at the same time. In addition, what each of these types of caregiving looks like will depend on the time in history, cultural expectations, parental personality, and much more.

Consider something as simple as how to feed a newborn infant. In the United States, there have been significant debates about whether to use formula in feeding newborns, whereas in several small hunter-gatherer communities, formula would not be considered an option. Mothers in the United States pay attention to infants' schedules and even if they "feed on demand," they make sure newborn infants are fed every 2 to 4 hours, even waking up a sleeping infant for feeding if too much time has passed. Contrast this with mothers in Namibia who breastfeed their infants exclusively, feeding their newborns small amounts continuously throughout the day. These are all examples of nurturant caregiving, and infants in each of these contexts will grow and thrive, but the particular way in which parents approach nurturant caregiving varies.

Other important characteristics of parenting infants are the frequency, timing, and regularity of those caregiving behaviors. In general, there is agreement across cultures about what makes a "good" mother. For example, Judi Mesman and her colleagues (Mesman et al., 2016) found that mothers from 15 countries, including Chile, China, the United States, and Zambia, agreed that ideal mothers show affection toward their children, seek physical contact with their children, keep their children safe, and respond appropriately to their children's sadness. Researchers have often called this and similar clusters of behaviors "sensitive" parenting. Across cultures, people agree that sensitive parents are responsive to their infants' bids for attention (Emmen et al., 2012). On top of that, those responses are prompt and reliable over time. In other words, sensitive parents recognize infants' needs and respond to them quickly and appropriately. Some basic needs are universal and elicit universal responses from caregivers. For example, new mothers in countries such as Argentina, Kenya, Israel, and the United States responded to their infants' distress vocalizations by picking them up and holding them (Bornstein et al., 2017).

Although accepted by many cultures, this view of sensitive parenting may not be universal, and there are cross-cultural differences in parenting (Keller et al., 2018), and what constitutes a sensitive parent varies widely from culture to culture. For example, in foraging cultures, such as the Yahgan of Tierra del Fuego and the Garo from Bengal, mothers engage in a lot of face-to-face interaction, and may show behaviors that would be classified as sensitive. In farming cultures, such as Ngandu of Central Africa, mothers engage in more distal parenting and have fewer face-to-face interactions with their young children compared to other cultures in Central Africa (Lancy, 2007). These mothers would presumably appear to be less sensitive to mothers who prefer more face-to-face interactions. However, in these farming cultures where face-to-face interactions are less common, breastfeeding on demand is more common, which means that while these infants receive less face-to-face interaction with their mothers, they receive more physical interaction, which could also provide the infant with comfort and support (Mesman et al., 2018).

Importantly, parents' quick, sensitive responding does appear to be important in Western cultural contexts, and in those cultural groups, this kind of parenting is associated with more positive outcomes, such as more regulated behaviors in infants. For example, Sylvia Bell and Mary Ainsworth (1972) conducted a now-classic study with a group of White, American mothers from middle-class families and their infants. They found that mothers who were consistently prompt at responding to their infants' crying had infants who tended to cry less over time. Likewise, infants of mothers who are most responsive are, in turn, most responsive to their mothers (Symons & Moran, 1987), demonstrating that maternal responsiveness has cascading effects on the mother–infant relationship more broadly. This is how secure attachment relationships develop (see Chapter 11) and how infants learn that they can rely on their caregivers for help.

Sensitive parenting has positive effects on infant development in other groups as well. For example, one characteristic of parenting in some Latine communities is *respeto*, or respect. Respeto overlaps with other aspects of parental sensitivity as defined in European-heritage North American families, but it also involves calm parental authority and child affiliative obedience (Tamis-LeMonda et al., 2020). In one study of Mexican-heritage low-income families in Dallas, Texas, respeto in parenting with 2.5-year-old toddlers was linked to positive child behaviors (Tamis-LeMonda et al., 2020). Further, an intervention study with young (adolescent) first-time mothers in El Salvador demonstrated that training mothers to be sensitive to their infants' needs—by talking to their infants and engaging them in play—resulted in infants who were better able to regulate their emotions at 6 months (Valades et al., 2021). In another study, Chinese and Dutch infants whose mothers responded more quickly and appropriately during play at 4 months had better memory and control at 14 months (Li et al., 2021).

Sensitive parenting also shapes infants' language development (see Chapter 9). Consider an intervention study with Brazilian mothers from low-income homes. One group of mothers was taught to respond contingently to their infants' behaviors and a control group of mothers received no training. Mothers in the intervention group were more responsive to their infants, using their speech and touch to respond to their infants' behavior. Their infants, in turn, had more communicative behaviors than infants in the control group (Alvarenga et al., 2021). This study shows how maternal sensitivity can shape the communicative interactions between infants and their mothers.

In addition to responding promptly to their infants' current needs, sensitive parents also flexibly adapt their behaviors to the infants' *changing* needs over time. However, those needs will vary depending on the broader culture. For example, in North American culture, how much freedom and autonomy that a parent gives an infant to navigate the home environment should change as the infant gets older and as the infant becomes a more competent walker. That is, in this culture, in which independence and self-sufficiency is valued, parenting practices encourage independent exploration when it is safe and when the child has sufficient skills. But in a culture where there are more potential dangers, infants may be given less freedom to protect them from those dangers. The point is that there is no correct amount of freedom and autonomy that a child should be given at any given age, and recognizing when it is and is not appropriate to grant that autonomy is part of being a sensitive parent.

Parents also need to be responsive to individual differences in their infant as they adjust their expectations and their parenting strategies. Although parents in North America may generally value the infants' opportunities to learn autonomy, infants' freedom to navigate the social world might depend on their temperament. Parents may have to intervene more often with fearless infants than with infants who are more cautious. As an infant, Carter would sit for hours playing with toys and looking at books, never venturing to dangerous spots like the top of the stairs or the bathroom. In contrast, Charlie's favorite activities seemed to always be the *most* dangerous ones; he absolutely loved navigating the stairs or jumping off every piece of furniture he could manage to climb on. As a result, Carter was likely given more autonomy than Charlie, regardless of their age. Even within the same culture, parents will hold different beliefs about how to respond to their infants' changing needs. In the United States, beliefs about how much freedom an infant should have varies from parent to parent, and although some parents can seem overprotective, allowing infants little autonomy in navigating the environment, others believe in "free range" parenting, allocating more individual freedom to the infant at a young age (Skenazy, 2009).

Parent Cognitions

Parents' beliefs, not only about how much freedom infants should have, but also all of their ideas, knowledge, values, goals, and attitudes about the world, can affect the developing infant. Even something as simple as sensitivity and responsiveness can vary based on parents' ideas about parenting and about the world around them and whether parents typically respond to their infants verbally or with touch. Indeed, several cross-cultural studies have indicated that overall rates of caregivers' responses to infants are similar across cultures, but the types of contingent behavior differ based on cultural norms. For example, although both French and American mothers value stimulating and responding to infants, French mothers put more value on stimulating while American mothers put more value on responding (Suizzo, 2004). German mothers tend to respond to infants visually more often than rural Nso mothers, whereas Nso mothers tend to respond more with touch (Kärtner et al., 2010). Mothers in these different cultures are sensitive and responsive, but they use different behaviors or use the same behaviors in different ways.

One example that illustrates the role of cognitions on parenting is how parents think about gender and, as a result, how they parent their children. It might seem surprising to talk about gender in infancy, given that (as we discussed in Chapter 3) gender is a social category that relates to how a person thinks about themselves. But the development of gender begins in infancy and is typically tied to a person's sex assigned at birth (which is what we are referring to here when we use the terms *boys* and *girls*). Although there aren't a whole lot of differences in behavior between infant boys and girls at birth, over the first few years some differences do emerge. In U.S. samples, boys are more aggressive, more active (even in the womb!), and less fearful than girls. Girls are more emotional, more verbal (they speak and read sooner), and generally more compliant than boys (Ruble et al., 2006). Other, stereotypical differences, such as differences in spatial and math ability, do not appear consistently until later in development. All of these differences reflect both biological differences and differences in how infants are socialized by the people around them, especially by their caregivers. In fact, differences in gendered behavior vary considerably across cultures. Boys outperform girls in math in some countries, but not in others, and there are even countries where girls outperform boys in math (Miller & Halpern, 2014). In this way, parents' (and society's) expectations play a large role in shaping gendered behavior.

Research has shown, for example, that even before their infants are born, parents have expectations about their infants based solely on the infants' sex. In one study, expecting parents in the United States were asked to choose from a set of adjectives to describe their fetuses. These adjectives were pairs of opposites, like firm or soft, large or small, coordinated or awkward, and strong or weak. Parents chose gender-stereotyped adjectives like *strong, noisy, big*, and *hardy* to describe their unborn males and adjectives like *soft, small*, and *quiet* to describe their unborn females. Most importantly, they chose these adjectives based only on knowing the fetus's sex (Sweeney & Bradbard, 1988). These differences in expectations—and treatment—continue after birth. In another study, U.S. parents of 11-month-old crawling infants expected their boys to be able to descend steeper slopes than their girls (when in reality, their abilities are the same) (Mondschein et al., 2000). So even early in infancy, parents already have expectations about what their infants are going to be like, and they base these expectations on a variety of factors, including sex.

Boys and girls are treated differently right from birth. For example, U.S. mothers talk more to their infant girls than to their infant boys (Johnson et al., 2014). Further, both English-speaking (Adams et al., 1995) and Spanish-speaking mothers (Aznar & Tenenbaum, 2013) use more emotion words when they talk to girls than when they talk to boys, and so do fathers. In fact, fathers even *sing* to their infant girls more than they sing to their infant boys (Mascaro et al., 2017). It is important to note that in terms of broad parenting styles, there are little difference in how boys and girls are treated (Mesman & Groeneveld, 2018). Instead, the differences are more in specific parenting practices, such as modeling certain behaviors and the kind of feedback parents give to their young children for different behaviors. It is likely that parents aren't doing these things on purpose or even consciously, but even subtle differences in parents' beliefs can shape the way they interact with infants, which in turn, shapes what infants learn and how they interact with the world.

So far you might be thinking, so what? The reason this matters is because people's expectations can shape an individual's behavior over time. The most classic example of this is the Rosenthal effect. In the 1960s, undergraduate students were each given a rat to teach how to run through a maze. Half the undergraduates were told that their rats were "bright" and should learn to navigate the maze relatively quickly, and the other students were told that their rats were "dull" and may have more difficulty learning the maze. At the end of the study, the bright rats did learn more quickly and ran the maze faster than the dull rats. However, it turns out that the "bright" and "dull" rats weren't actually different at all; they were even matched for age and sex. The "bright" rats presumably ran the maze faster because the undergraduates who taught them had higher expectations for their behavior, which likely influenced how they treated the mice (Rosenthal & Fode, 2007).

The Rosenthal effect has also been observed with children. For example, in one study, elementary students in the United States were given an IQ test at the beginning of a school year. Based on this test, teachers were told that some of their students were "bloomers" and were expected to demonstrate high academic achievement over the course of the school year. As expected, the students identified as "bloomers" outperformed their classmates at the end of the year. But, just as with the rat studies, the "bloomers'" were chosen at random and didn't actually score any differently on the IQ tests at the beginning of the school from their classmates (Rosenthal & Jacobson, 1968). The "Rosenthal effect" is thus a powerful example of the sort of self-fulfilling prophecy that adults' expectations can have on children's behavior.

You might now see how parents' expectations about how boys and girls should behave could impact an infant's actual behavior over time. In fact, although gender differences in reading (favoring girls) and spatial abilities (favoring boys) can be found in many countries around the world, the magnitude of these differences varies based on the amount of gender inequality found within that culture. In countries with more gender inequality, the advantage for boys in spatial ability and math is much greater, presumably because boys are given more advantages in these areas by their parents and teachers (Miller & Halpern, 2014). This suggests that the way boys and girls are treated might have a large impact on the way they behave and what they learn.

BOX 12.1—INFANCY IN REAL LIFE: GENDER-NEUTRAL PARENTING OF INFANTS

In 1972, *Ms.* magazine published "X: A fabulous child's story," written by Lois Gould. This was the fictional story of a child called X, who was being raised with their gender unknown to everyone except their parents and the scientists conducting the experiment. The child's parents, Mr. and Mrs. Jones, gave X toys and clothes meant for both boys and girls. In 1972, this kind of parenting seemed far-fetched and impossible. Indeed, in the story, the writer described how parents of other children were afraid of the influence X would have on their

Infant in Gender-Neutral Clothing
iStock/LSOphoto

own kids and protested when X's peers began rejecting gender norms. It all worked out in the end with X being declared by scientists as perfectly normal.

However, in the 21st century, as some parents throw "gender reveal parties" to celebrate the sex of their unborn child, there are nonfictional stories of parents raising their infants as gender neutral or engaging in gender-creative parenting. This movement is motivated by the idea that it is best to wait until the *child* decides their gender before assigning them one, even one that matches their sex as assigned at birth. So, the parents use *they/them* pronouns with their child, allow their child to wear clothing meant for any gender, and let them engage in a variety of activities.

For example, in 2011, Toronto parents Kathy Witterick and David Stocker made public their intention to raise their child Storm as gender neutral, and they would not reveal Storm's sex. As a result, the Witterick-Stocker family were the focus of media scrutiny for years, and they received both comments of support and comments of concern from thousands of strangers. In 2020, *The New Yorker* published a brief documentary about another family who engaged in gender-creative parenting, called "Raising Baby Grey" (Long, 2020). This documentary described a Brooklyn couple's efforts to raise their child, Grey, as gender neutral. Like the Witterick-Stocker family, Grey's family used *they/them* pronouns to refer to Grey and dressed Grey in a variety of clothing. However, Grey's family generally received more positive support than the Witterick-Stocker family did.

Raising children using gender-creative parenting is challenging and requires that family, friends, and childcare providers are all on board with the gender-neutral approach. It is also challenging because, as seen by the reactions to the Witterick-Stocker family and Grey's family, strangers can be hurtful and judgmental. Nevertheless, this approach to childrearing is an option for parents who feel strongly about allowing their child to have the freedom to select their own gender at some point beyond infancy. In addition, gender-neutral or gender-creative parenting is becoming increasingly accepted in some areas of the United States. Six states—California, Colorado, Michigan, New Jersey, Oregon, and Washington—now allow parents to label their newborn baby's gender as "X" on their birth certificate. These policies contrast with laws that have been passed in other states that ban transgender children from using the bathroom corresponding to their gender and prohibiting gender-affirming medical treatment to minors. Clearly there is a wide range of opinions even within the United States about how much flexibility we should give children in determining their own gender identity.

But gender-neutral parenting doesn't always have to be this extreme. It may simply be exposing children to toys, clothes, and activities that cross gender lines. When Edwin was born, for example, his parents chose not to reveal his sex until close to his birth to avoid receiving any sort of gendered clothing or toys. However, they did give him a name that is typically male and did use the pronouns *he/him* after Edwin was born. Researchers argue that to truly focus early development on individual personality and traits rather than gender, gender-neutral parenting needs to begin as early as possible. Making choices of colors, clothing, and toys is a start. Referring to children by their names instead of "the girls" or "the boys" is another good strategy.

Parent Traditions and Culture

One of the most prominent sources of variation in how parents shape the infant's learning and social world is through their family traditions and cultural norms. In fact, there are so many examples in the psychological literature of parenting differences based on tradition and

Example of Proximal Parenting
iStock/Nikada

Example of Distal Parenting
iStock/praetorianphoto

culture that it would take volumes to discuss them all. One very general example is the difference between **proximal parenting,** which involves maintaining close physical proximity to the infant with a lot of physical contact, and **distal parenting**, which emphasizes more face-to-face interactions and interactions with objects (Table 12.2). Whether parents adopt more proximal or distal styles varies based on a number of factors, including cultural norms, parents' views and individual needs, and the presence of potential dangers. For example, proximal parenting is more common in cultures that emphasize social connections over autonomy. Distal parenting is more common in North America and Europe and in cultures that emphasize the importance of independence (Keller et al., 2009). But whether or not parenting is more proximal or distal is also related to the challenges different environments pose to infants. For example, two groups of people who live in central Africa—the Aka, who are hunter-gatherers, and the Ngandu, who are farmers—differ in their parenting approaches. The Aka engage in more physical contact and less looking to communicate with their infants compared to the Ngandu (Hewlett et al., 1998; Lancy, 2007). This difference has implications for the other aspects of parenting we have discussed, in particular for *how* parents respond to their infants. Because Ngandu parents hold their infants less than Aka parents, they verbalize more when their infant cries or fusses, a distal parenting response. But parents can be sensitive and responsive regardless of whether they adopt more proximal or distal parenting styles.

And although socialization and learning take place between parents and children in all cultures, the mechanisms of transmission, or exactly how parents confer information onto their infants also varies based on cultural beliefs and practices. In Western, industrialized countries, parents are often viewed as teachers, whereas in less industrialized countries, parents are viewed more primarily as providers and protectors, and children learn through observation rather than from direct instruction (Lancy, 2010). In the United States, for example, caregivers often engage in a lot of direct instruction, explicitly teaching infants names for objects or how to behave, scaffolding specific behaviors, or modeling behaviors for infants during face-to-face interactions. In contrast, in other countries, for example, Fiji, direct instruction is rare, and infants are expected to learn by watching the adults around them (Legare, 2017).

There is even a wide array of cultural differences in how parents typically interact with their infants within the United States. For example, one study reported that compared to European American mothers, African American mothers spend more time with their infants and demonstrate more nurturing behaviors. The same study found that low-income families were more

TABLE 12.2 ■ Proximal vs. Distal Parenting		
Parenting Style	**Description**	**Examples**
Distal	Face-to-face interactions when an infant is physically separated from a caregiver Includes interactions with object	Caregiver shows the infant an object as a way of interacting
Proximal	Close bodily contact, keeping infant physically close	Infant is held by mother or physically attached to caregiver during the day or sleeps with caregiver

likely to have extended family members living with them in their households and taking on a caregiving role when compared to infants from middle-income families (Fouts et al., 2012). Latine families in the United States tend to emphasize the importance of the family more than European American families and thus have been shown to have larger social networks, with more close connections and active contact with extended family members. Latine parents also place more emphasis on instrumental independence and encourage infants to do more on their own, like achieving motor milestones, self-feeding, and dressing themselves at earlier ages (Harwood et al., 2002).

Beyond Mothers

So far, much of the research we have discussed has focused on mothers as primary caregivers. And for good reason: A large cross-cultural study, including Fiji, Vanuatu, Bolivia, Peru, and the Central African Republic, reported that children younger than age 5 spend most of their time with one female adult. In fact, until they were about 7 years old, children in this study spent most of their time within 2 feet of a single female adult (Broesch et al., 2021). Given that the majority of infants in the world spend a lot of their early days with a female adult caregiver, it makes sense to spend a lot of time talking about moms (and moms also happen to be the ones who typically show up when families are invited to labs to do research).

But this isn't the only model, and moms aren't the only ones who are important for infants' development. Dads are important too. Research suggests that both mothers and fathers are sensitive to their infants' needs and that there is a relation between attachment security to one parent and attachment security to the other. In other words, if infants have a secure attachment to their mothers, they are likely to have the same attachment style to their fathers (Fox et al., 1991). But infants don't always have the same attachment style to both parents. Some studies have shown that children who are securely attached to *either* the mother or father have the same outcomes, suggesting that attachment to the father is as important as attachment to the mother (Dagan & Sagi-Schwartz, 2018) In addition, two studies conducted in the United Kingdom showed that higher involvement of fathers in infancy predicted better cognitive abilities at age 2 (Sethna et al., 2017) and healthier socioemotional behaviors at age 3 (McMunn et al., 2017). The point is that both mothers and fathers are important for child development.

However, fathers can take on different roles when compared to mothers within family units. Attachment security in North American fathers from middle-class families and their infants is related both to play and involvement in caregiving (Brown et al., 2018). But the level of fathers' involvement in caretaking can vary from family to family and from culture to culture. In some countries, fathers play a very small or nonexistent role in caregiving and are mostly seen as the provider. In other cultures, fathers can take on an equal role in caregiving with the mother, or act as the primary caregiver, as in the case of the Aka (Hewlett, 1993). Even in Western countries such as the United States and Europe, where fathers are seen as taking a relatively large role in parenting, mothers are often observed to be more sensitive (Hallers-Haalboom et al., 2017) and more supportive of autonomy (Hughes et al., 2018). To be clear, these differences are small, and fathers can be sensitive and supportive parents of

Dad and Baby
iStock/monkeybusinessimages

infants. Indeed, in same sex-couples, in which infants can have two fathers and no mother or two mothers and no father, the division of caretaking labor is more likely to vary, based on specific family circumstances and not the identity of one parent as "mother" and the other as "father." Studies on same-sex families have shown that the fact that this division of labor is between two individuals identifying as the same gender (as opposed to a male and a female parent) has little impact on development: A large longitudinal study of children adopted by same-sex and opposite-sex parents found that children in both groups appear to be equally well-adjusted. In fact, for both kinds of parent families, the biggest predictor of developmental problem behaviors late in development was parenting stress, which is consistent with what we've known about opposite-sex parent families for decades (Farr, 2017).

On top of that, while two-parent households are the norm in the West, they are by no means the only model. According to the 2020 census, approximately 70% of children in the United States live in two-parent households, 21% live just with their mothers, and just under 5% live just with their fathers. In these single-parent households, infants might be raised by a single mother or father, who takes on 100% of the caretaking responsibilities. Even when infants live with both parents, they may also live with extended family members, like grandparents, who share the infant's caretaking responsibilities. Likewise, it is common in some cultures for older siblings to take a large role in taking care of younger, infant siblings. Indeed, in the study we described earlier that looked at families in Fiji, Vanuatu, Bolivia, Peru, and the Central African Republic, there was a marked shift in caretaking patterns in some of these countries by the time children turned 5, when children started spending significantly more time with other children

(Broesch et al., 2021). Several researchers have even suggested that the most advantageous way to raise infants is by surrounding them with a *system* of caregivers to provide for the infant—not just the mother and father, but other adults (and older children) who provide care. This type of system is called **alloparenting**, and it involves situations where several people care for an infant besides the infant's parents (Hrdy, 2011). Indeed, research suggests that the higher the number of close and caring relationships one has, the better the person's health and well-being will be throughout life (e.g., Feeney & Collins, 2014). So, in some places, parenting literally takes a village. We will talk more about other members of this village, including siblings, peers, grandparents, and community members, in the coming sections.

Infant Factors

Parents and caregivers clearly can shape how infants develop in a number of ways. But it's important to point out that this relationship is bidirectional, and while parents shape infants' behavior, infants' behavior also shapes parenting. In Chapter 3 we described how having an anxious mother can even affect the developing infant prenatally. Now imagine an anxious mother who has an infant with colic, which (as we also learned in Chapter 3) can involve long periods of inconsolable crying. That anxious mother might become more anxious as a result of the crying, which will further affect how she interacts with her infant. This is a good example of Thomas, Chess, and Birch's concept of goodness of fit from Chapter 10, or the degree to which an infant's temperament is compatible with the infant's environment. An infant that is difficult or prone to crying might fare quite poorly with a parent who is prone to anxiety, and likewise, a highly anxious parent might fare just as poorly with a difficult infant.

As a result, the efficacy of parenting behaviors and strategies may vary based on an individual infant's needs and temperament. One of the most well-known examples comes from research by Grazyna Kochanska. She asked how temperament in U.S. toddlers aged 2 to 3 was related to the child's willingness to commit a transgression (to break a rule stated by the experimenter) when they were 4 or 5. In particular, she was interested in whether some kinds of parenting styles would be a better fit for some temperaments, and as a result children who experienced that good fit would be less likely to break the rule. She found that for toddlers who were identified as particularly fearful, gentle discipline from parents is what led to the development of a strong conscience, or an unwillingness to break the rule, at later time points (Kochanska, 1997). The fearful children whose parents used gentle discipline were less likely to break a rule than the fearful children whose parents were firmer with them. She explains that this is because fearful children are likely to feel anxious about transgressions on their own and don't need much discipline from parents to correct potentially bad behavior.

In contrast, a different kind of parenting was effective with fearless children. These children didn't feel incredibly anxious at the thought of a transgression. As a result, gentle discipline wasn't effective. These children needed alternative parenting strategies for the development of a strong conscience, with firmer discipline and clear, consistent consequences. Although this specific example involved families from a particular cultural context—namely, families with European heritage from a midwestern U.S. community—the general conclusion is that sensitive parenting is not one single thing. In some cases, it means being responsive to an infant, but it also means being flexible and adapting parenting behavior so that it fits with an individual infant's personality and needs, which can change dynamically as the infant develops over time.

BOX 12.2—INFANCY IN REAL LIFE: DIFFERENT STROKES FOR DIFFERENT FOLKS

Edwin and Charlie may be siblings, but they couldn't be more different, from the time that they were born throughout their entire infancy. Edwin was a bit of a sensitive baby; he had colic for 2 months, crying uncontrollably for hours and hours during the day and generally approaching new situations with watchful concern. Charlie was as easy as a baby could be. He adapted easily to new situations, immediately adjusted to routines set in place for him by his parents and approached all new people and events with enthusiasm. Based on the temperament styles we learned about in Chapter 10, Charlie was a textbook easy baby, and Edwin was a bit slow to warm up.

But "easy" doesn't always mean *easy*, especially for parents. Charlie may have embraced new situations happily as an infant, but when he started walking, this new motor skill also meant happily approaching new situations that might be potentially dangerous. For example, while Edwin was cautious the first time he approached a swimming pool by himself, Charlie literally walked right in. When Edwin saw a new dog, he approached slowly and offered his hand. Charlie would run at full speed and wrap his stocky body around the dog's neck, regardless of the dog's size. These very different children need very different kinds of parents, even though they happen to share the same pair.

Infants like Edwin who are slow to warm up, or are more sensitive to environmental changes, need time to adjust to new situations; pushing them before they are ready could intensify any fear they might have. While this tendency requires parents to be a bit patient with their infants, it also means caring for an infant who applies caution to new situations on their own. As implied by Kochanska's (1997) work discussed earlier in the chapter, fearful infants only require gentle discipline from their parents to correct problem behavior, since they are likely to internalize or feel anxious about transgressions. As such, Edwin didn't often break rules, and when he did, even getting gently reprimanded usually brought him to tears, so he didn't need to be told twice not to engage in a specific problem behavior.

Infants like Charlie who were easy and even fearless in new situations are happy, sociable babies that sleep through the night and are flexible with new foods. These features made Charlie a dream baby in a lot of ways. But in other ways, Charlie was an absolute terror for a parent. While he approached new situations quite readily, he was very difficult to discipline, since he didn't feel anxious about breaking the rules and wasn't easily discouraged by gentle punishments. As such, Charlie usually received several time-outs a day, and his parents often have to resort to taking away his favorite toy or dessert to keep him from engaging in problem behaviors repeatedly.

As these children get older, the differences between them will likely grow, and their parents will have to modify their parenting strategies and the freedoms that they allow as the children get older and their individual needs change. This is all part of sensitive parenting: Being responsive to children's needs, *and* being flexible not only to their changing needs but also to their differences. No one tells you when you become a parent that you might have to vary your parenting strategies to fit your individual children's needs, but children are different, and their needs change, so parents have to change as well.

Check Your Learning

1. Define the four types of parenting behaviors, and provide an example of each.

2. What are some of the behaviors of sensitive parents? Give one example of how these behaviors can vary across cultures.

3. What are parent cognitions? What is one way that parents' cognitions could drive infant behavior?

4. Explain the difference between proximal and distal parenting.

5. What is alloparenting?

6. How might infants themselves play a role in shaping parenting behaviors?

SIBLINGS AND PEERS

Infants' development is shaped not only by their parents and other caregivers but also by the other children they encounter. Infants may have older siblings, or they may have interactions with peers in playgroups or daycare. How do these experiences with other children, whether a sibling or peer, impact infants' development? In this section we show how siblings and peers can shape infants' learning and social world.

Siblings

Older siblings can have an important impact on an infant. When Carter was 18 months old, he would sit with Alison and play with her Polly Pockets—and by "play," we mean that he would sit and hold Alison's toys quietly while she played a complex, pretend game around him. Tesalia copied everything her big brother Diego did; her eyes followed him wherever he went, and she imitated his every move. "Diego" was one of Tesalia's first words, and "Edwin" was one of Charlie's. And to this day, Edwin is Charlie's favorite person in the entire world. For Carter, Tesalia, and Charlie, having their big brothers and sisters—Alison, Diego, and Edwin (respectively)—in their lives changed their world dramatically. Alison, Diego, and Edwin spent the first few years of their lives with just their parents and no other children living in their homes. They had their parents' undivided attention and resources. Although Carter, Tesalia, and Charlie were born into a world with divided attention and resources from their parents, they had their siblings to make up for it.

Having older siblings has an impact on infants' learning and social functioning. For example, research conducted in Western contexts has revealed that having siblings, especially older ones, is related to the development of theory of mind (Devine & Hughes, 2018; Ruffman et al., 1998) and prosocial emotions like empathy and sympathy (Harper, Padilla-Walker, & Jensen, 2016). Older siblings, particularly sisters, help younger siblings develop better language skills (Havron et al., 2019). Infants with an older sibling hear language directed to that sibling and benefit from this language input in the home (Oshima-Takane et al., 1996). Infants imitate their older siblings,

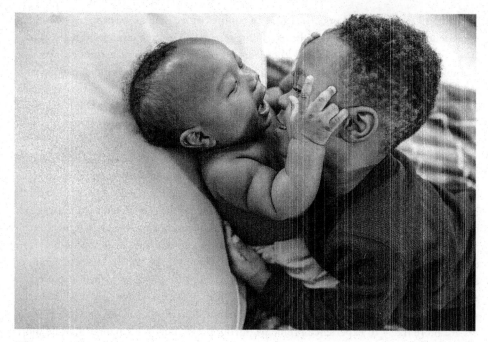

Siblings

iStock/kate_sept2004

expanding their repertoire of behaviors from observing their siblings (Barr & Hayne, 2003), and having an older sibling shapes infants' exposure to media (Siibak & Nevski, 2019).

These findings were all from children in Western societies. But around the world, including in subcultures in North America, older siblings play an important role in infant care and development and, in some cases, are one of an infant's primary caregivers. For example, it is common in sub-Saharan Africa for siblings to be charged with the care of infants once they begin to walk (Mweru, 2017). These sibling interactions are different from those often observed in Western societies and involve more caregiving. Indeed, infants form attachments to their older siblings who care for them. For example, in one study, Haatembo Mooya and colleagues (2016) observed infants in Lusaka, Zambia, interacting with their mother and, on a separate occasion, with a sibling who participated in caretaking on a regular basis. When assessed on their attachment to each caretaker (mother and sibling), infants had an attachment to their older sibling that was unique to that sibling (and not necessarily the same type of attachment as to the infant's mother).

Siblings also shape infants' learning and their social interactions. As familiar members of their household, young children can learn better from their siblings than from peers (Azmitia & Hesser, 1993). In fact, older siblings in Western contexts adapt their behavior to be appropriate so that their young siblings can learn (Dunn & Kendrick, 1982). Infants often build their repertoire of behaviors by imitating the actions of their older siblings (Barr & Hayne, 2003). In some families and in some cultures, such as communities in Indonesia, Mexico, and Kenya, toddlers spend more time playing with older siblings than with their mothers (C. P. Edwards &

Whiting, 1993; Farver & Wimbarti, 1995). In cultures where siblings are caregivers, teaching may occur through play. In these cultures, sibling caregivers are often responsible for transmitting important customs and cultural knowledge to young children, often through play. For example, Ashley Maynard observed Mayan children, who were 3 to 11 years old, playing with their 2-year-old sibling (Maynard, 2002). The older children taught their younger siblings to do daily household tasks, such as cleaning and cooking, while playing together. Similarly, in the Wolof of Senegal, cultural transmission to younger children occurs through caregiving from older siblings (Rabain-Jamin et al., 2003).

For infants, having an older sibling, rather than a same-aged sibling (i.e., twins), seems to be beneficial. Infant or toddler twins don't necessarily even engage much with their same-age sibling, preferring instead to engage with a more competent social partner, such as their mother (Aldrich et al., 2015). Being an older sibling may offer some benefits, although the findings in this literature are mixed. However, the most consistent finding across studies is that in Western societies children who are born first tend to do better in school than children who are born later (Hotz & Pantano, 2015). In contrast, younger siblings tend to be more rebellious (Paulhus et al., 1999) and open to new experiences (Healey & Ellis, 2007). There are several possible explanations for this. For example, mothers are older when they have their second (third, fourth, etc.) child, and older mothers are more likely to experience problems during pregnancy (see Chapter 3). The more widely accepted explanation is that parents have more one-on-one attention to give to their first-born children than children who are born later. Second, third, and even later-born children have parents who have fewer financial resources and less attention to give, both academically and socially. Likewise, as the result of getting more attention from their parents, it could be that first-born children are more motivated to meet their parents' expectations, while younger siblings are less conforming and more rebellious (Sulloway, 2001). Again, these findings are mixed and likely depend on a number of factors, including how many siblings there are, how far apart they are in age, their genders, and their cultural and family traditions. Regardless of the precise effects of birth order, however, *any* birth order effects that are consistent between studies suggests that having one or more siblings changes an infant's environment in various ways, subsequently impacting the infant's social world.

Peers

Starting when Alison was about 2 months old, her mom gathered once a month with a group of other new moms, each with infants between 2 and 5 months of age. These moms met to spend time together, share stories and advice, and support each other through the challenges of parenting an infant. This playgroup met monthly for 4 years, and during that time the *infants* also interacted. In the early months, the infants simply spent time in their own car seats or in their mother's arms, but as they developed, they attended more to each other and interacted. They watched each other, learned how to say the other children's names, and played with the same toys. Their interactions were typical for North American children. They interacted regularly—but not daily—and as soon as they were old enough, they engaged in structured activities, such as decorating cupcakes, going to a children's museum, or having pizza.

Infant Peer Interactions
iStock/FatCamera

Infants' experiences with peers vary across families, communities, and cultures. The families in Alison's playgroup were all isolated from their extended families. They lived in a college town in the Midwest and none of them lived near grandparents, aunts and uncles, or cousins. This group of six families was their primary social network, and (except for daycare) this was the peer group that these children interacted with most. Other U.S. families have even more extensive social networks that allow infants to interact regularly with others, including infant peers. And in other countries and cultures, starting from infancy, children spend a significant amount of time with other children. In Jakarta, Indonesia, for example, young toddlers spend more of their time with mixed-aged peer groups compared to toddlers in the United States (Farver & Howes, 1988).

Even within the United States, there can be huge variability in how much exposure infants have to same-aged or mixed-aged peers. Children in childcare, for example, are in frequent contact with other children; the amount of contact children who are not in childcare have with other children is more variable. Further, events like the COVID-19 pandemic that began in March 2020 limited many children's experiences with peers. It is yet unknown how the lack of contact with others during the pandemic will affect development, but we do know that as a result of the isolation and social distancing measures taken during that time, young children around the world developed without the kind of social interaction that was typical prior to the pandemic. Although peer interactions can be an important part of early social development— providing children with the opportunity to share and take turns—those skills develop over many years, and children who have little social interaction as infants and toddlers will likely acquire those skills during peer interactions later in development.

Whether they spend time with peers regularly, on occasion, or rarely, infants are fascinated by other infants. In one study, 6- to 9-month-old infants preferred to look at images or video of same-age peers than to images and videos of older or younger infants (Sanefuji et al., 2006). During face-to-face interactions, infants engage peers by looking, smiling, or touching them, and often infant peers reciprocate by also smiling, looking, or touching their same-aged play-mate (Eckerman & Peterman, 2001; Vandell et al., 1980). Infants and toddlers also imitate their peers as a way to connect during their social exchanges (Eckerman & Didow, 1996).

However, interactions between same-age (infant or toddler) peers are quite different from interactions between a child and a caregiver. Adults and older children adapt their interactions to the infant. Recall the box in Chapter 8 that described how caregivers play peek-a-boo with their young infants? The caregiver often takes the lead in this sequence of hiding and reappearing. Caregivers are able to "read" their infants' social responses and adjust the game of peek-a-boo to match how their infants are responding. But infants do not yet have the skills to adapt their responses to their same-age social partners.

It is probably not surprising then that peer interactions start off simple and short. As infants, Alison and her peers would play separately, each focusing on their own toys in their own space. When they did interact, their interactions were short. Infants will respond to the social bid of a peer, but then the interaction fizzles. This is because infants do not yet know how to build on their initial social interactions. In one study, Deborah Vandell and her colleagues observed a group of infants during peer interactions (Vandell et al., 1980). Even at 6 months, infants engaged in socially directed behavior, such as vocalizing at another infant or responding to the vocalization of another infant. However, the time infants spent in social acts increased from 6 to 12 months. The fact that infants' interactions are brief and that they increase over the first year is not surprising; at this age infants do not yet have the skills to coordinate their actions with a peer (Brownell & Brown, 1992; Eckerman et al., 1989; Eckerman & Whatley, 1977; Hay & Ross, 1982; Howes et al., 1988).

Peer interactions begin to change after the first birthday, when toddlers improve in coordinating their social interactions. As a result, social exchanges between peers become longer, with several rounds of one toddler looking at or touching a peer and the peer responding in turn (Eckerman & Whatley, 1977; Vandell et al., 1980). These changes in how infants and young toddlers interact have been observed not only in U.S. children but also in toddlers in Papua New Guinea (Eckerman & Whitehead, 1999), suggesting there are at least some commonalities across a wide range of infants in how peer interactions develop.

These simple behaviors set the foundation for later, more complex peer interactions, like pretend play and cooperative games. Infants' and toddlers' coordination and interaction help them practice the skills they need to become competent social partners. But even young children vary in how skilled they are as social partners. Moreover, these individual differences in social competence emerge in infancy and seem to remain stable into early childhood (Hay et al., 2004). One study found that toddlers who smiled more at peers, initiated play with them, or who responded to a peer initiating play were more open to peers 6 months later (S. T. Williams et al., 2007). Other studies have shown that differences in infants' social interaction abilities are stable into the preschool years (Howes et al., 1988) and early school-age (Hay et al., 2021).

Peers Playing
iStock/FatCamera

Why are some children better at social interactions, even starting in infancy? It is likely that some of this is due to temperament. Children who are more fearful and inhibited, for example, probably have more difficulty initiating interactions with peers. But infants' experiences with peers also plays a role. Infants who have more (and more positive) interactions with other children are likely more comfortable interacting with peers, and this may contribute to how skilled they are in peer interactions.

Check Your Learning

1. How might an older sibling change the social environment for a developing infant?

2. What are some of the benefits of having an older sibling?

3. How do young infants interact with same-aged peers?

4. Explain how peer interactions change with infant age.

COMMUNITY

Throughout this book we have talked about differences in children's experiences and how those differences contribute to development. When possible, we have described research from multiple cultures or multiple racial and ethnic groups. Our goal was to provide an understanding of what is—and what is not—universal in infant development. In this section, we discuss how aspects of the community influence infant development. As we will see in the final section of this chapter, these influences are not independent of the other influences we have discussed, but it is important to understand how the community children live in, and the values and resources of that community, contribute to their development.

For example, Alison, Carter, Charlie, Diego, Edwin, and Tesalia were all born at a time when in the United States, infants—especially those of educated parents from middle-class families—were put to sleep on their backs, breastfed exclusively until 6 months, and had special equipment like car seats and strollers that kept them safe. Their parents could purchase lots of special clothes and toys and could create a very baby-centered household where they were free to explore some spaces. This is not always the way U.S. infants experience infancy. It was not that long ago that in the United States infants were mostly fed formula, they were put to sleep on their stomach, and there were no car seats (or even seatbelts!). These differences certainly influenced aspects of the health and development of infants at different historical times in the United States. But there are many other kinds of cultural and societal differences that influence infants' daily lives and their development. In this section we will talk about two aspects of the community that influence infant development: (1) childcare and (2) neighborhood and socioeconomic factors.

Who Cares for Infants?

Infants are born relatively helpless and need around-the-clock care. How do human societies solve this problem? In "traditional" middle-class families in countries like the United States, the mother stays home and takes care of the children. Indeed, around the globe mothers have carried the primary responsibility for infant care, although there are differences in the roles of fathers, older siblings, other female relatives, and community members. In many countries, such as the United States, mothers have returned to the workforce either by necessity or by choice, which means there has been an increased demand for childcare over the past several decades.

Importantly, the demand for alternative childcare is cultural. In many countries and cultural groups, infant care is not solely left to the child's biological parents. As mentioned earlier, traditional hunter-gatherer groups engage in alloparenting, or the care of children by people other than the parents. For example, in the Hadza of Tanzania and the !Kung of Botswana, mothers return to foraging and hunting when infants are weaned, leaving their toddlers with older children. Alloparenting is also found in agricultural cultures, and women collaborate with each other in their agricultural and childcare responsibilities.

In other countries, especially in industrialized countries, this type of parenting is less common, and families must find alternatives when nonparental care is needed. In some countries, including Ireland, China, and Turkey, grandparents or other family members often provide such care. However, such arrangements are not common in the United States (less than 20% of children), although the rates of grandparents caring for children are on the rise. Thus, parents who need nonparental care search for other options, including nannies or au pairs in their own home, childcare in someone else's home, or formal childcare centers. All of these options are expensive. In 2020, the cost of childcare in the United States was on average around $10,000 per child per year, but it can range from $8,000 all the way up to $20,000 and varies depending on location and type of care.

Perhaps even more important is the cost and availability of *high-quality* childcare. Indeed, research has shown that the effect of nonparental care on infant development depends on the quality of that care. Overall, infants who are in childcare are still securely attached to their parents at rates that mimic those of infants not in childcare, and infants are more likely to be securely attached to their mother or father than to their childcare provider (Ahnert et al., 2006). But attachment seems to be related to the quality of the childcare setting. A large study in Israel found that poor childcare quality and high infant–caregiver ratio was associated with higher infant–mother insecure attachments (Love et al., 2003).

Research suggests that attending high-quality childcare might help bolster children's academic performance later in kindergarten, but this might not be the case for other, lower quality childcare centers. But what does it mean for childcare to be "high-quality"? One feature of high-quality childcare is that each teacher doesn't have many children to care for (i.e., there is a small teacher-to-child ratio at the center), so each child gets more one-on-one attention. Another feature is that the teachers have some kind of specialized training in early childcare. Finally, high-quality childcare centers typically have a professionally developed curriculum that they follow. Research suggests that children who attend childcare centers with these features are happier than other kids, perform better on language and other academic tests, and have better social skills (Vandell, 2004). These benefits are especially strong for children growing up in low-income households.

Access to affordable, quality childcare varies considerably across the world. UNICEF released a report about how the richest countries in the world are doing with respect to childcare. They considered four factors: the *cost* of childcare, the *availability* of childcare, the *quality* of childcare, and *parental leave policies*. Why consider parental leave policies when evaluating childcare? In countries such as the United States with poor parental leave policies, parents (usually mothers) must choose between staying home with their infant or keeping their jobs. Thus, good parental leave policies are an important aspect of childcare: They allow parents to stay home with their young infant, if they choose, without risking their future employment. Since the 1970s, maternal leave policies in rich countries have increased from about 4 months to close to a year, except in the United States, which is the only rich country without a national parental leave policy. Although leave policies for a father or second parent are not as generous, many countries also have policies allowing a second parent to take leave.

Unfortunately, when countries fail to implement family leave policies, women suffer the most, as women usually take on most of the burden of childcare. Even for heterosexual couples that are generally pretty egalitarian in their gender roles, the birth of a child often leads to a switch to a more gender-stereotyped division of labor, with the woman taking on most of the childcare responsibilities (Rehel, 2014). The same is true even when both the father and the mother have similar jobs and workloads—after having children, women begin to shoulder more of the burden at home (Yavorsky et al., 2015). This shouldn't be surprising for countries like the United States, where most family leave policies (when they exist) offer time off only for the mother. Policies that give parental leave only to mothers enable the traditional idea that women are the ones that should be caring for the children, and fathers should be the ones working. In fact, research has shown that when fathers take extended leave after the birth of a child (i.e., more than 3 weeks), men become more comfortable caring for the infant, which subsequently leads to their greater involvement in sharing the parenting responsibilities (Rehel, 2014). Importantly, in a recent study of ethnically and racially diverse infants in the United States, researchers reported that infants of mothers with and without paid leave had different EEG (or brain-related) profiles, with infants of mothers with paid leave demonstrating more mature patterns of brain activity (Brito et al., 2021). In other words, paid leave seems to benefit both mothers *and* their infants.

Altogether, this work suggests that *who* takes care of our infants varies widely based on both community and cultural factors. And no matter who is taking care of infants or where they are cared for, the most important factors in determining whether infants have positive experiences with that care seems to be whether it is of good quality and whether it is made widely available to the caregivers who need it.

Neighborhood and Socioeconomic Factors

Infant development is not just influenced by the people who are around them and the people who care for them. Both neighborhood and socioeconomic factors that impact the family also influence infant development. Differences between neighborhoods and families are often described using **socioeconomic status**, or SES. SES refers to the social standing or class of an individual, and it includes income, education level, and type of occupation. Psychologists measure SES in a number of ways. One of the most common ways SES is measured is by quantifying a family's income, or their income as a function of how many individuals live in their household, what is referred to as **income-to-needs ratio**. Individuals who have an income-to-needs ratio under a certain threshold lack the resources they need for everyday life, including enough food, clean water, shelter, and clothing, a condition that is commonly referred to as **poverty**. Because the cost of such expenses changes from year to year, the exact amount of income-to-needs that defines poverty in the United States shifts yearly; in 2021, it was $12,880 for a single person and $26,500 for a family of four.

SES is more complex than simply how much money a family has, however. It refers *both* to the family's economic and social background and relates to wealth, status, and prestige. Thus, a family with a low income but highly educated parents and a high-status job has a different SES than a family with the same low income but with parents who are not educated and who have working-class jobs. Thus, other ways that SES is measured is by parents' education or a combination of income and education (Clearfield & Niman, 2012; Noble et al., 2012; Norcross et al., 2020). Researchers most commonly use income and education because they are easy to quantify; it is more difficult to categorize occupations by the skills they require and the prestige they carry (Muscatell, 2018). More recently, researchers have also been using both subjective and objective measures of a family's neighborhood as an index of SES. Subjective measures can include a family's own perception of their social status and the characteristics of their neighborhood. Objective measures often include statistics about a family's neighborhood based on their home address, a process called **geocoding**. This usually involves collecting census data based on a family's zip code on factors like the highest educational attainment of the general population in the area, the school dropout rate, employment status, poverty status, as well as general crime statistics.

Importantly, differences in SES are associated with differences in various cognitive and emotional factors throughout development, at least in Western countries like the United States, the United Kingdom, and Australia. Infants from lower SES backgrounds, for example, tend to be behind their peers in language and cognitive development (Golinkoff et al., 2019), particularly when SES is measured by maternal education (Hoff, 2003). Poverty is also stressful. Mothers who live in poverty have limited resources. The stress that results from limited resources may be one reason why mothers from low-income backgrounds speak less and use less complex language to their infants compared to mothers from higher SES backgrounds (Fernald et al., 2013; Hoff, 2003). Thus, this effect may not be an effect of SES *in general*, but rather may be an effect of one aspect of SES. Poverty has different effects. Infants whose families live below the poverty level or who have poor income-to-needs ratios have poorer regulation and executive function abilities (Hackman et al., 2015; Lawson et al., 2018) and show stronger stress responses (Clearfield et al., 2014).

But family SES is not the only factor that contributes to infant and child development. Characteristics of the neighborhood, or the immediate geographical area where the family lives, also play a role. Neighborhoods vary in many ways, for example, the SES levels of the people who live there, the availability of public and private resources, the languages spoken by the residents, the national origins of the residents, availability of open spaces, libraries, grocery stores, and much more. You may recall from Chapter 9 studies that reported that infants from low-SES households hear fewer words spoken by their parents when compared to infants in mid- to high-SES households, which might contribute to why infants from low-SES households lag behind their peers in language and cognitive development (Hart & Risley, 1995) However, also recall that low-income families are more likely to have extended family members living with them in their households (Fouts et al., 2012). In fact, another study examining five different neighborhoods in the United States reported that the difference between spoken language to low-SES versus higher-SES infants disappears when the researchers considered language spoken by those other than the primary caregiver, including siblings, grandparents, and other people in the neighborhood. In some cases, low-SES households showed an *advantage* over higher SES households in exposure to spoken language when including these additional members of the household (Sperry et al., 2019). This work suggests that SES alone is not always representative of what the infant experiences.

Neighborhoods are so important for child development and well-being that the U.S. government and researchers have conducted projects like Moving to Opportunity (Chetty et al., 2016), a program that examined the effects of moving families with children from some of the most disadvantaged neighborhoods in the United States to less distressed neighborhoods. In this project, families were *randomly assigned* to the kind of opportunity they were given—to move within public housing, to move to a less distressed neighborhood, or to stay in their current situation. Overall, this project revealed that when young children moved to less distressed neighborhoods, their income was higher when they were adults, they were more likely to attend college, and they were less likely to become a single parent. Because this study involved random assignment, we know that these outcomes were caused by changing neighborhoods and not some other difference between the individuals.

But how can a neighborhood influence child development? First, neighborhood factors can have **direct effects** on an infant's development (Table 12.3). These can include factors like food insecurity, exposure to pollution, less access to resources like toys or school supplies, higher noise levels in the environment, or poorer quality childcare. For example, one reason children in poor neighborhoods fall behind their peers from more affluent neighborhoods in language and cognitive development is that the childcare available in poor neighborhoods is lower in quality (Dupere et al., 2010).

One fairly recent example you might have heard about is the water crisis in Flint, Michigan, that occurred between 2014 and 2019. Nearly 40% of families in Flint live in poverty, and the city itself has suffered several financial crises. In 2014, during one such financial crisis, the leaders of Flint changed the source of their drinking water. For about 18 months, instead of drinking treated water from Detroit, Flint residents drank water from the Flint River. Because officials did not treat the water with corrosion inhibitors, lead from old pipes leached into the water. Once it was discovered that the water had high lead levels, the city switched back to Detroit water, but it was too late. About 100,000 residents, many of whom were young children, drank water with elevated lead levels during that 18-month period. Exposure to high levels of lead in early childhood can have permanent effects on the child's brain and nervous system, causing intellectual disabilities. This shows how aspects of a neighborhood can have direct effects on development. The young children in Flint experienced the negative effects of lead exposure simply because of where they lived. The issue was so serious that not only did the city change its water source, but it also began replacing all their lead pipes in 2016. And in the summer of 2020, a lawsuit was settled that paid over $600 million to the affected children.

Besides direct effects, SES and neighborhood can also have **indirect effects** on an infant's development. Indirect effects are those things that influence the people around the infant, which then changes how those people interact with and treat the infant. For example, the number of

TABLE 12.3 ■ Direct and Indirect Effects of SES		
SES Effect	**Definition**	**Examples**
Direct	Any environmental circumstance that directly affects the infant	Food insecurity, exposure to pollution, poorer access to resources like toys or school supplies, high noise levels in the environment, or poorer quality childcare
Indirect	Any environmental circumstance that directly affects the infants' caregivers and has an impact on the way the caregiver interacts with their infants	Living in a neighborhood with a lot of crime might be stressful for the mother, which could in turn affect how responsive she is to her infant's needs. Indeed, poverty is also associated with living in neighborhoods with more violence and crime; direct, less outdoor time, fewer parks; indirect, stress on family.

broken windows in a neighborhood is associated with poor health in general, likely because more deteriorated neighborhoods have more broken windows, and those neighborhoods are associated with less outdoor physical activity (Cohen et al., 2003). That is, the broken windows themselves—or even the deterioration of the neighborhood—don't directly affect health, but it creates a context where people don't engage in as much activity, which does directly affect their health. At least in Western Industrial societies, including North America, Western Europe, and Australia, physical aspects of the neighborhood, especially the availability of outdoor space, has an effect on young children's health and social competence (Christian et al., 2015). One study in Australia reported that neighborhood cleanliness was positively related to preschool children's prosocial behavior (B. Edwards & Bromfield, 2009). The availability of outdoor spaces is an indirect effect because it creates opportunities for particular types of activities, and it creates a particular type of atmosphere that may affect people's moods and behaviors.

Similarly, the level of *social cohesion* in neighborhoods, or the amount of mutual trust and support among neighbors, can affect child development (Maguire-Jack & Showalter, 2016). In particular, when parents feel comfortable asking their neighbors for help, they appear to be more likely to meet their child's basic needs, such as providing them with adequate food, not leaving them unattended, and taking them to the doctor. Characteristics of neighborhoods can also influence a person's mental health, which then affects parenting. Living in a neighborhood with a lot of crime might be stressful for the mother, which could in turn affect how responsive she is to her infant's needs. In Australia, parents' perception of a neighborhood as unsafe was related to how many behavior problems a child has (B. Edwards & Bromfield, 2009). In fact, in the Moving to Opportunity study, moving to neighborhoods with less poverty had a positive effect on the caregiver's mental health (Kling et al., 2007).

Most research has focused on the negative effects of neighborhood characteristics on child development. It is clear from our example of the water in Flint that being exposed to pollution in the water or air can have a negative impact on infant development. But some research has examined how neighborhood characteristics can have a positive effect on development. For example, some neighborhoods are **ethnic enclaves**, or neighborhoods where most people come from the same ethnic or cultural background. These neighborhoods often have a high proportion of immigrants. Some studies have shown that mothers and infants have better outcomes in these enclaves. For example, one study showed that mothers from India who lived in an ethnic enclave in New Jersey were less likely to smoke and more likely to get prenatal care than mothers from India who lived in more diverse neighborhoods. Similar positive effects on pregnancy for mothers living in ethnic enclaves in the United States have been found for Hispanic mothers (Noah et al., 2015) and Asian and Pacific Islander mothers (A. D. Williams et al., 2020). Ethnic enclaves are not always positive, however. Some studies have found that living in ethnic enclaves are associated with worse outcomes for U.S.-born Mexican-origin mothers compared to Mexican-born mothers (Osypuk et al., 2010).

Interacting Factors

So far, we've been talking about how individual factors in an infant's environment or community might directly or indirectly affect their development. This is often how we study development in the lab: We isolate a single independent variable to see how it relates to or affects an outcome, or a dependent variable. But in reality, development doesn't happen in a vacuum, and most of the factors we study are constantly interacting with other, related factors to determine infant outcomes.

SES, for example, impacts infant development on a number of levels—it affects parenting practices, parenting attitudes, the way infants and parents interact with each other, and how infants and parents interact with the greater community. In fact, in a large longitudinal study of infants from birth to adulthood, Arnold Sameroff and his colleagues tried to pinpoint various environmental factors that tend to co-occur with income that might be risk factors for poor emotional and cognitive functioning in development. They found that a number of factors that are indeed predictive of poor child outcomes tend to co-occur with being from low-income backgrounds, including a history of parental mental illness, maternal anxiety, low maternal education, the head of the household holding a job that involves unskilled labor, disadvantaged minority status, single parenthood, stressful life events, and a large family size (Sameroff, 1998). Importantly, they found that infants who only had one or two of these risk factors fared pretty well over time; it was the infants who had several risk factors that experienced the poorest developmental outcomes. Furthermore, Sameroff argued that as the number of risk factors increased, it became more difficult to determine the unique effects of each one; instead, it was the co-occurrence or interaction of these risks over time that was most problematic for development.

Importantly, the impact of these risks starts at the earliest possible points in development. Indeed, as we discussed in Chapter 3, the prenatal environment sets the stage for development from conception, and everything that the mother does can potentially impact the developing fetus based on the timing and frequency of exposure. Maternal anxiety, a poor diet, or poor access to prenatal care, and maternal stress can all affect the prenatal environment in negative ways. This environment tends to continue after the fetus is born. Thus, the effects of these risk factors can begin impacting the infant prenatally, with cascading effects into the infancy and early childhood periods.

Although here we are using a cascades model to discuss how various risk factors can accumulate over time to create adverse outcomes for infants, throughout this book we have also used developmental cascades as a more general model for typical infant development. In other words, it isn't only risk factors that cascade over time to determine developmental trajectories, but various infant behaviors or changes to the environment constantly interact throughout the child's lifetime to predict outcomes across various domains. Indeed, infants are constantly changing and adapting to changes in their environments. In fact, sometimes changes to the environment include changes to the infant's own body. Over the first year of life, infants grow, they get stronger, they gain more control over their bodies, and they experience a variety of transitions, from sitting, to crawling, to walking. Each of these transitions creates a new context for learning. Take the example of sitting. When infants can sit on their own for the first time, they can see the entire room in front of them, giving them a different visual perspective of the world around them. Further, their arms are suddenly free to reach for and manipulate objects without fighting gravity like when they are lying on their backs. Not surprisingly, these changes in posture have been shown to have cascading effects on infant perception. As we saw in Chapter 5, sitting ability allows infants to hold and manipulate more objects, which in turn leads to better three-dimensional (3D) object completion. In other words, the more experience infants have with sitting, the more they explore objects, and the more likely they are to visualize objects in three dimensions (Soska et al., 2010).

While changes to the infant's environment can give rise to developmental changes in the infant, changes to the infant can likewise induce changes in the physical and social environment. Continuing with our example in motor development, once an infant becomes mobile, several changes to the physical environment—what U.S. parents often call "baby proofing"—are required in order to keep the infant safe so that they don't tumble down a flight of stairs or get hold of something sharp. Infant mobility also introduces changes to the social environment. As mentioned in Chapter 10, researchers have long hypothesized that with the onset of walking comes rules and regulations on what the infant can and can't do for the very first time and may even increase the amount of negative emotion that parents express around their infants (Campos et al., 2000).

Another example comes from research by Lana Karasik and colleagues where they video-recorded 50 infants in their homes when they were 11 months and then again when they were 13 months of age. They observed infants' motor behavior and how infants handled objects with their caregivers. They found that when infants started to walk, they handled objects differently than when they were crawling. With their hands now free to move while carrying objects, infants now traveled longer distances to obtain objects and carried them to their mothers in a bid to engage in play. Further, infants who managed to bring objects to their caregivers as 11-month-old crawlers were more likely to walk at 13 months, suggesting that the act of carrying and sharing objects might promote further motor developments (Karasik et al., 2011). On top of that, when infants walked over to their mothers to share objects, their mothers were more likely to respond verbally to their infants with action directives, altogether suggesting that the onset of infant walking results in infants carrying more objects to their mothers, which in turn leads to changes in mothers' language toward their infants (Karasik et al., 2014).

Altogether, the major point here is that different kinds of environmental characteristics—including risks as well as more typical changes to infants' bodies and environment—interact with other concurrent developmental changes that can cascade into long-lasting effects for the infant. And although we tend to measure independent variables in development, including risks, one at a time, and while we tend to study domains of development, like motor skills and perception, separately, it's important to remember that all of these factors are interacting to drive child outcomes over the lifespan, demonstrating both the complexity and richness that is the whole baby.

Check Your Learning

1. List some of the features of high-quality childcare.

2. Define socioeconomic status (SES), income-to-needs ratio, and poverty.

3. Provide an example of a direct effect of SES on infants and an example of an indirect effect of SES on infants.

4. Describe how the number of social risk factors for a child relates to their mental health.

5. Explain the significance of infants' transition to walking as one example of interactions that can lead to long-term effects.

SUMMARY

As we pointed out in the beginning of this chapter, although infants from around the world have different early experiences, development during infancy always happens in a context that includes family, peers, and a rich environment. First, we talked about parents, and how everything a parent does—their behavior, their cognitions, their cultural beliefs and attitudes—can impact infant development. While parents can often include a mother and a father, there are many different types of parents and parenting styles, all of which are culturally determined. And infants have relationships with other people besides their parents; infants' siblings, peers, and other caretakers also impact their environments and, as a result, their development. Finally, infants interact with the various people in their lives in their neighborhood and broader community, both of which shape the context of infant development. Community and neighborhood factors can shape development by having a direct impact on the infants' behavior, or indirectly, through their caregivers. Together, all of these factors are constantly interacting to shape the development of the whole baby.

KEY TERMS

alloparenting

didactic caregiving

direct effects

distal parenting

ethnic enclaves

geocoding

income-to-needs ratio

indirect effects

material caregiving

nurturant caregiving

poverty

proximal parenting

social caregiving

socioeconomic status

REVIEW QUESTIONS

1. What are the different kinds of caregiving, and why is each important?

2. What are some of the benefits of older siblings or same-aged peers on infants?

3. What is family leave policy, and how might it influence who cares for infants?

4. Explain the relation among socioeconomic status (SES), income-to-needs ratio, and poverty.

5. Outline how infants can shape parenting behaviors but also how infants' community or neighborhood can have a direct or indirect effect on infants.

CRITICAL THINKING QUESTIONS

1. How do the four types of caregiving behaviors relate to proximal versus distal parenting?

2. How might culture shape the four types of caregiving behaviors or parent cognition? Give an example.

3. Your friend is about to have her second child. What would you tell her about how having an older sibling might influence her new baby's development?

4. Outline how a direct effect and an indirect effect of SES shape infants' development. How might these effects differ as the number of social risk factors increases?

5. What is the distinction between subjective and objective measures of SES, and how is each measured? Explain if one may matter more than the other in an infant's development.

GLOSSARY

A not B error: an error in which infants search for an object in the last location where they found it and not in the last location where they saw it hidden

accommodation: according to Piaget's theory, the process by which infants change their scheme when they encounter information in their environment that does not match their current scheme

affect: a general feeling that is either positive or negative

affordance: the relation between an infant's real abilities and the properties of the environment

age-held-constant design: a design to study development in which all children tested are the same age, but they vary in some other way

alleles: different forms of a gene

allocentric frame of reference: encoding locations in relation to an external feature in the environment, such as a landmark

alloparenting: situations where several people care for an infant besides the infant's parents

amniotic sac: thinned walled sac filled with liquid (called amniotic fluid) that will hold the fetus and protect it

from getting injured during pregnancy

amodal information: information that is the same in different sensory modalities, such as rhythm or tempo

anxious/resistant: attachment style in which infants do not play happily in the strange situation task; instead, they cling to their mothers from the minute they enter the lab, and they are incredibly upset when she leaves

assimilation: according to Piaget's theory, the process by which infants integrate new information into an existing scheme

attachment: the emotional bond between an infant and their caregiver

attention: the process of selecting some subset of those things to focus on, while putting other less important things out of focus

auditory perception: the interpretation of auditory information

autobiographical memory: memories about events that happened in one's own life

Babinski reflex: a reflex that is elicited when you stroke the bottom of an infant's foot, and the infant's big toe turns upward while the other toes fan out

behavioral genetics: the study of how an individual's genetic makeup and environment determine behavior

behavioral inhibition: temperament style characterized by shy and withdrawn behavior in social situations

binocular depth cues: information about depth that is available by combining the information from both eyes

biological motion: motion type that characterizes living things or things that move like people

breastfeeding: feeding an infant with milk from the breast

categories: a division of people or things that share the same characteristics, allowing us to treat collections of things in the same way

categorizing: forming groups of objects, events, and people that reflect the similarities among them

causal perception: recognition that one action produced a particular effect (e.g., pushing a button caused a light to turn on, hitting an object caused it to move)

cephalocaudal direction: from head to foot

change detection task: a short-term memory task that assesses the viewer's ability to see differences in rapidly presented stimuli

chromosomes: the threadlike structures in a cell's nucleus that contain DNA

circular reactions: actions performed by the infant and then are repeated because of their effect

cohort-sequential design: a design for the study of development in which all children are evaluated at multiple time points, but different groups of children, or cohorts, are tested, each of which starts the study at different ages

colic: inconsolable crying for more than 3 hours a day

communication: the process by which we share information with others

cones: a type of photoreceptor in the retina of the eye; they allow us to see color

connectionism: a theory of cognitive development that proposes that children use general-purpose learning mechanisms to quickly learn all aspects of cognition and language from the input that they receive

constructivism: a theory of perceptual and cognitive development in which children actively build or create their understanding of the world from their experiences

core domains: domains in which young children use innate processes to interpret and understand, which include objects, number, geometry, and agents

core knowledge: the idea that there are innate, domain

specific processes for learning about the world

correlational design: a design in which two or more features or characteristics, or variables, of a group of people are measured and the relation or association between those variables is evaluated

covert attention: attending to something without looking at it

critical periods: windows of time when development is most vulnerable or susceptible to variations in experience or conditions

cross-cultural approach: an approach that focuses on differences between samples from different cultural, economic, or regional contexts

cross-sectional design: a design for studying development in which different children are tested at each age

deferred imitation: a task in which children's imitation is tested after a delay

developmental cascades: a view in which achievements that occur at one point in development have effects at a later point, even in a different area of development

didactic caregiving: engaging infants in the world around them, by focusing their attention and providing the infant with opportunities to learn

dilation: opening up of the cervix during labor

direct effects: factors that can influence an infant directly

discrete emotions theory: theory that emotions evolved as universal biological reactions to common challenges

disengaging: removing attention from the current focus

disorganized/disoriented: attachment style characterized by behaviors that do not fit into any of the other categories in the strange situation, and usually involves infants showing a mix of approach and avoidance responses to their mothers and the experimenter

display rules: cultural norms for the way emotions are expressed

distal parenting: parenting style that emphasizes more face-to-face interactions and interactions with objects

DNA: deoxyribonucleic acid (DNA) molecule that makes up our chromosomes

domain general: refers to general and broad processes that support learning in different domains

domain specific: refers to processes that are specialized for learning in a single domain, such as language

dominant: a gene that is expressed when two different alleles of a gene are inherited

drive reduction theories: the theory that infants have basic needs that need to be filled, and once those needs are met, the drive is reduced and the infant returns to a state of relaxation, or homeostasis

dual representation theory: the theory that symbols require two representations—one representation of the object and a second representation of what the object stands for

dynamic systems theory: according to this perspective, behaviors emerge (or disappear) as the result of multiple, independent systems, each of which develops on its own time course

ecological systems theory: Bronfenbrenner's theory in which development is a complex system of relationships affected by multiple levels of the environment, including immediate family and school, to broad cultural values, laws, and customs

effacement: thinning of the cervix during labor

egocentric: constrained to be understood only in relation to the infant's body

egocentric frame of reference: when infants use their own perspective and note where a particular location is in relation to their own body

electroencephalogram (EEG): technique in psychological research in which researchers place electrodes on the subject's head to record the electrical activity on the scalp

embryonic stage: state of prenatal development that lasts from about 2 to 8 weeks following conception

emergent theories of emotion: theories of emotions in which emotions are the outcome of a process that includes changes in the body and cognitions about what's happening in the environment

emotion: an internal, affective response that is about something specific or some change in the environment

emotional expression: the observable behavioral responses that are associated with emotions

emotion regulation: the ability to respond with a wide variety of emotions to events in the environment in a socially acceptable way

epigenetics: reversible changes in how genes are expressed due to behaviors and the environment that do not involve changes in the DNA itself

episodic memory: memories of events that include information about what happened, where it happened, and the context of the event

ethnic enclaves: neighborhoods where most people come from the same ethnic or cultural background

experience-dependent plasticity: how brain development adapts to idiosyncratic experiences

experience-expectant plasticity: plasticity that reflects the brain adapting to experiences that are common to virtually all members of a species

experimental design: a design in which study participants are randomly assigned to different groups, treatments, or conditions to evaluate how those groups, treatments, or conditions cause differences in a measured variable

explicit memory: memory that is available to conscious recall

exploration: in the context of infant–caregiver attachment, venturing away from one's caregiver to investigate the environment

expressive language: the ability to produce words in a language

failure to thrive: when an infant's increases in height, weight, and/or head circumference do not follow standard growth charts

fallopian tube: tube that connects the ovaries to the woman's uterus

false belief: understanding that a person can have a belief about the world that is different from reality

fetal stage: stage of prenatal development that lasts from about 8 to 38 weeks after conception, or from about the 10th week of pregnancy until birth

fovea: a region of the retina that is densely packed with cones and is the part of the retina that has the sharpest, clearest vision

functional play: exploring more than one object at a time and experimenting with how those objects relate to each other

gahvora cradle: a crib commonly used in Tajikistan where infants are wrapped tightly in swaddles, with their entire bodies restricted so that they can"t move their arms and legs or move their heads from side to side

gaze following: the ability to align one's gaze with another person's

gene–environment correlations: when genetically influenced traits elicit or evoke environmental responses from others so that genes and the environment are similar

gene–environment interactions: how the pattern of genes can make one more or less sensitive to environmental factors

generalization: extending behavior to a new instance of a category

generative: the feature of language that makes it possible to combine words in an infinite number of ways to express an equally infinite number of ideas

genes: segments of DNA (deoxyribonucleic acid) that are the basic unit of heredity

genotype: the unique genetic makeup of an individual (i.e., an individual's collection of genes)

geocoding: objective measure of neighborhood characteristics that involves collecting census data, based on a family's zip code, on factors like the highest educational attainment of the general population in the area, the school dropout rate, employment status, poverty status, as well as general crime statistics

glia: also known as gliocytes, are non-neuronal cells in the nervous system that support the functioning of neurons

goal directed: a characteristic of actions indicating that the actions are intentional or performed as a way of attaining some goal or completing some task

goodness of fit: the degree to which an infant's temperament is compatible with the infant's environment

grasping reflex: newborn reflex where the infant's palm is touched or stroked, and the infant closes its fingers tightly and grasps

growth charts: norms or averages for healthy infants receiving an appropriate amount of nutrition over time on a number of measurements, including weight, height, and head circumference

haptic perception: the interpretation of touch information

heredity: the transmission of genetic information across generations and how that genetic information translates to differences in physical characteristics and behavior

heterozygous: when each parent contributes a different allele for a particular gene

hippocampus: a brain region involved in memory representation, including the binding of facts and context

home signs: system of gestures that deaf children develop to communicate when exposed to only spoken language

homozygous: when both parents contribute the same allele of a particular gene

imitation: intentionally repeating an action performed by another

implicit memory: memory that is not available to conscious recall, or unconscious memory

income-to-needs ratio: quantification of income as a function of how many individuals live in a household

indirect effects: factors that influence the people around the infant, which then change how those people interact with and treat the infant

infancy: the period of development beginning at birth until 2 or 3 years of age

infant-directed speech (IDS): a type of speech used to address infants that is simpler and more variable in its pitch than speech directed to adults

infantile amnesia: the inability to remember events from before the age of 2 or 3

innate: present at birth; also can mean characteristics that are inborn, genetically determined, or biological

insecure/avoidant: attachment style characterized by infants who play happily in the strange situation when their mothers are in the room but don't seem to notice when she leaves or when she comes back

interactionist views: theories that recognize that development reflects both biological and innate influences as well as experience

intermodal or multimodal perception: the recognition that sensory information in two (or more) modalities corresponds in some way and can be linked

internal working model: a mental representation of a primary caregiver that forms the basis for the development of future social relationships

intersensory redundancy: a phrase that refers to when the same amodal information is specified in more than one sensory modality

intersubjectivity: the understanding that thoughts and feelings are shared with other people

joint engagement: coordinating attention so both the caregiver and child are attending to the same object at the same time

kinematic depth perception: using movement information to perceive how things are arranged in depth

Lab-Tab: a standardized behavioral assessment of early temperament in infants, toddlers, and preschool-aged children

language: a formal system of communication, or a process by which we share information with others, that is structured and comprises grammar and vocabulary

language acquisition device: an instinctive mental capacity that is argued to allow for the acquisition of language with minimal input

lens: part of the eyeball that helps to make sure that light is focused on the retina

longitudinal design: a design for studying development in which the same children are tested at multiple ages

long-term memory: a memory store in which an unlimited number of things can be stored forever

looking-while-listening: a procedure used to test infants' language comprehension that uses infants' looking at images on a screen while hearing speech

maintaining attention: keeping attention on the information of interest, resisting the pull of other information that might be present and distracting

malnutrition: lack of proper nutrition

material caregiving: organizing the infant's physical space, including the objects around the infant, and providing limits to the infant's physical freedom

maturational states: developmental milestones that are governed by the development of the central nervous system

means-ends reasoning: the ability to understand the relation between your own body and an intended action or goal

memory: a process by which the brain stores and retrieves information

mental rotation: the ability to imagine different (rotated) views of an object

microgenetic design: a design to study development in which children are tested frequently, separated by short time periods such as days or weeks

migration: the movement of newly formed neurons from the ventricular or subventricular zone to their final location

mimicry: copying what you see right in front of you

model: a person whose actions are imitated

monocular depth cues: cues to depth that are available even with just one eye

more knowledgeable other: according to Vygotsky's theory, a social partner who is more advanced than a child and promotes their learning through their engagement

moro/startle reflex: a reflex where if an infant experiences a sudden movement or sound, the infant might throw its head back, extend its arms out and quickly pull them back in, almost as if trying to find a place to grab onto for support

morphemes: the smallest unit of a word that denotes meaning

motor milestones: physical achievements that the infant is expected to reach in the first year and a half, starting with pushing up and rolling over, and ending with the ultimate feat of walking

moving room: a large, human-sized box with three walls and a ceiling, where the back wall moves forward and backward

myelination: the formation of the fatty sheaths (called myelin) on the axons of neurons during neural development

nature: a characteristic that is inherent in the individual

neonatal smile: infants' first smiles, which usually occur during sleep

neural plate: three-layered structure that makes up the spinal cord and brain in prenatal development

neural tube: structure that forms the spinal cord in prenatal development

neuron: a type of cell that is the basic unit of the nervous system

newborn reflexes: automatic behavioral responses to a

stimulus that are present at birth

non-reduplicated babbling: also known as variegated babbling, a type of babbling that includes a combination of two or more consonant-vowel combinations (e.g., "mabu")

nurturant caregiving: behaviors that meet the infant's basic biological needs, centering around keeping the infant healthy and safe

nurture: the environment, treatment, or experience

object categories: groupings of objects that are commonly labeled with nouns

object permanence: the understanding that an object continues to exist when it cannot be seen or heard

object retrieval task: a task where children observe a toy being hidden in a particular location; then the child's view of the table and hiding locations is changed, and the child is allowed to search for the object

object substitution: when children use one object to stand for another object

optic flow: perception of the movement that is created while traveling around a room

optic nerve: the nerve that carries messages from the retina to the brain

orienting: directing attention to specific objects or locations

ovaries: a pair of female glands where eggs form and hormones like estrogen and progesterone are made

overextensions: a type of error children produce when they apply words to a broader array of referents than the meaning of the word (e.g., using the word *dog* to refer to horses)

papillae: protrusions on the tongue where our taste buds are located

perception: the interpretation of sensory information

perception-action: a theory of infants' perception and understanding of the world as a function of their ability to act on objects

perceptual narrowing: developmental phenomenon in which perception is initially relatively broad and, with experience, becomes more narrow and specialized

personality: how an infant's temperament interacts with aspects of the environment over the course of development

person permanence: object permanence of an individual, or the understanding that a person continues to exist even when they cannot be seen

phenotype: the observable characteristics, or traits, of an individual, from physical (e.g., freckles, dimples, height) to psychological (e.g., personality, intelligence)

phobia: fear that does not depend on the actual threat relevance of the situation

phonemes: the most basic units of a language that convey meaning; in spoken languages, phonemes are the individual sounds

photoreceptors: neurons in the retina that absorb light and send information via the optic nerve to the brain

placenta: a small organ that filters the exchange of materials between the mother and the fetus, allowing some things (like food and antibodies) in and carrying other things (like waste) out

plasticity: the adaptive ability of the brain to change or adjust in response to variations in the environment and experience

play: a spontaneous and voluntary activity that is enjoyable and done for its own sake (rather than to achieve a goal)

poverty: a condition where the income-to-needs ratio lacks necessary resources, including enough food, clean water, shelter, and clothing

poverty of the stimulus: Chomsky's argument that the language children hear is insufficient for learning

pragmatics: understanding when and how to use language, as well as appreciating the intent of a speaker's words

preoperational stage: the second stage of cognitive development in Piaget's theory, from the ages of 2 to 7, marked by children's ability to have mental representations of objects

proprioception: perceptual information gleaned from the position and movement of your body

prosocial behaviors: behaviors that are intended to benefit others

prosody: the rhythm and intonation of a language

proto-conversation: an early form of social exchange characterized by vocalizations by infants and speech by a caregiver

proximal parenting: maintaining close physical proximity to the infant with a lot of physical contact

proximity seeking: any behavior by the infant, including looking, crawling, reaching out, and touching, that has the goal of the infant being close to or in physical contact with their mother

pruning: the elimination of synapses during neural development

psychological construct: a concept or process we wish to measure

qualitative change: discontinuous change or changes in kind

quantitative change: continuous change or changes in amount

quasi-experimental design: a design in which participants' group assignment is not randomly assigned but depend on characteristics of the individual, for example, age or hometown; also called a natural experiment

reactive temperament: infants that become physically and emotionally stressed upon seeing a new stimulus

receptive language: recognizing and understanding language

recessive: the non-expressed allele when a child inherits two different alleles from each parent

reduplicated babbling: also known as canonical babbling, a type of babbling that includes true syllables in the infants' vocal productions; a single consonant–vowel combination is repeated in this type of babbling (e.g., "mamamama" or "gagagaga")

referent: the object or thing that a symbols stands for

REM sleep: rapid eye movement sleep, a deep cycle of sleep where the brain is very active

rods: photoreceptors that function in low light and are not sensitive to color

rooting reflex: reflex that is elicited when you stroke the infant's cheek or the corner of the infant's mouth, and the infant will turn its head toward you and open its mouth

rouge test: procedure where you place a red mark on an infant's face (e.g., lipstick or rouge smudge on their nose) and then present the infant with a mirror so that they can see their own rouge-covered reflections

scheme: according to Piaget's theory, the most basic element of infant thinking

secular trend: any trend that occurs globally over a long period of time

securely attached: attachment style where infants play happily in the strange situation when their mothers are in the room, are distressed when their mothers leave, and are comforted when their mothers come back

selective attention: the filtering of available information in order to focus on just some of it

self-propelled motion: the ability to move independently through space

semantic memory: memory for facts

sense of self: the ability to think about oneself as an independent individual that is distinct from others

sensorimotor stage: according to Piaget's theory, the first stage of cognitive development, from age 0 to 2 years, in which infants understand their world through their senses (what they can see, feel, taste, and hear) and their actions

sensory register: a memory store in which visual and auditory information is stored very briefly

short-term memory: a limited memory system in which only a few items can be stored, and that information is rapidly forgotten

skin-to-skin contact: direct physical contact between infants and their caregivers

social caregiving: involves helping the infant build social relationships and regulate their emotions

social learning theory: the theory that infants learn by first observing the behaviors of another person, or a model, and then by imitating the model's actions

social referencing: when infants look for information from others, usually a caregiver, when a situation is new or uncertain

sociocultural theory: a theoretical perspective that proposes that development can only be understood by considering the individual's social and cultural context

socioeconomic status: the social standing or class of an individual, household, or family; includes income, education level, and type of occupation

speech perception: the ability of listeners to discriminate the sounds in a language

statistical learning: a theory that proposes that infants are sensitive to regularities in their environment that reflect that structure and that they use this information to acquire language

stepping reflex: reflex that is elicited when you place the infant's feet on a solid surface (while the infant is in a standing position), and the infant moves its legs back and forth, mimicking the motion of walking

stereopsis: the difference between the two images seen by the two eyes to see the three-dimensional structure and depth

still-face paradigm: paradigm where mothers are asked to smile and play with their infants and, at some point during the interaction, mothers are told to stop smiling and, instead, pose a neutral or "still" face, no longer responding to her infant

strange situation: test of the quality of infants' attachments by observing the infant and mother during several episodes, which involve both the mother and a novel experimenter entering and leaving the room at different times

sucking reflex: reflex that is elicited when you touch the roof of an infant's mouth, and the infant sucks

swaddling: wrapping an infant tightly in some type of cloth

symbol: something that stands for something other than itself

symbolic play: a type of play where children use objects, actions, and people to stand for something else (e.g., a banana as a telephone)

synapse: the space between two neurons and through which neural signals are transmitted

synaptogenesis: the creation of synapses during neuronal development

syntax: the rules for how the categories of words, such as nouns and verbs, combine to create sentences

taste buds: gustatory receptors that detect different chemicals in our food

temperament: an infant's own style of responding emotionally to changes in the environment

teratogen: any factor that causes malformation in prenatal development

theory of mind: understanding of other people's mental states, or the ability to reason about the thoughts, beliefs, desires, intentions, and goals of others

tonic neck reflex: reflex elicited anytime an infant turns its head to one side, and the infant''s arm on the same side stretches out, while the opposite arm bends at the elbow

trichromatic: perceiving color by comparing how the three types of cones in the retina respond to light

umbilical cord: cord that connects the fetus to the placenta

underextensions: an expressive language error in which children apply a word too narrowly

universal grammar: a set of structures or rules that govern all world languages

valid measure: a measure that accurately reflects the process or construct of interest

video deficit effect: a phenomenon where infants learn less from video than from real-life experiences

violation of expectation: a procedure in which infants' looking to events that are possible or plausible is compared to their looking at events that are impossible or implausible

visual acuity: the amount of detail you can see

visual cortex: the part of the brain that processes, represents, and interprets information transmitted from the retinas, by way of the optic nerve

visual evoked potentials (VEPs): the electrical activity generated by the brain as the infant looks at a visual stimulus, as recorded from electrodes placed on the infant's scalp

visual habituation: a procedure in which infants are repeatedly shown a visual stimulus and their looking time decreases as the stimulus becomes familiar

visual paired-comparison: a procedure in which infants are first familiarized with a visual stimulus and then they are shown that stimulus paired with a novel stimulus

visual perception: the interpretation of visual sensory information

visual preference: a procedure in which infants are shown two images side by side and their looking at each is recorded

visual recognition memory: infants' memory for a familiar visual stimulus

whole child: a focus on all the systems of the child together rather than focusing on a single isolated system

word segmentation: the ability to parse words from a continuous stream of fluent speech

zone of proximal development: from Vygotsky's theory, the range of activities and tasks that are just beyond children's ability to do on their own

zygotic stage: the period of prenatal development from conception to implantation, about 2 weeks

REFERENCES

CHAPTER 1

Associated Press. (1999, May). Night lights linked to vision problem. *The New York Times.* https://www.nytimes.com/1999/05/13/us/night-lights-linked-to-vision-problem.html

Bell, M. A., & Fox, N. A. (1992). The relations between frontal brain electrical activity and cognitive development during infancy. *Child Development, 63*(5), 1142–1163.

Brito, N., & Barr, R. (2012). Influence of bilingualism on memory generalization during infancy. *Developmental Science, 15*(6), 812–816.

Bronfenbrenner, U. (1979). *The ecology of human development.* Harvard University Press.

Campbell, D. G. (1997). *The Mozart effect: Tapping the power of music to heal the body, strengthen the mind, and unlock the creative spirit.* Avon Books.

Campos, J. J., Bertenthal, B. I., & Kermoian, R. (1992). Early experience and emotional development: The emergence of wariness of heights. *Psychological Science, 3*(1), 61–64.

Chan, S. (2019). Daoist nature or Confucian nurture: Moral development in the Yucong 語 叢 (Thicket of Sayings). In S. Chan (Ed.), *Dao companion to the excavated Guodian bamboo manuscripts* (pp. 259–283). Springer.

DeStefano, F., & Shimabukuro, T. T. (2019). The MMR vaccine and autism. *Annual Review of Virology, 6*(1), 585–600.

Fantz, R. L. (1963). Pattern vision in newborn infants. *Science, 140*(3564), 296–297.

Flaherty, D. K. (2011). The vaccine-autism connection: A public health crisis caused by unethical medical practices and fraudulent science. *Annals of Pharmacotherapy, 45*(10), 1302–1304.

Ghera, M. M., Marshall, P. J., Fox, N. A., Zeanah, C. H., Nelson, C. A., Smyke, A. T., & Gutherie, D. (2009). The effects of foster care intervention on socially deprived institutionalized children's attention and positive affect: Results from the BEIP study. *Journal of Child Psychology and Psychiatry, 50*(3), 246–253.

Goren, C. C., Sarty, M., & Wu, P. Y. K. (1975). Visual following and pattern discrimination of face-like stimuli by newborn infants. *Pediatrics, 56*(4), 544–549.

Harper, J. M., Padilla-Walker, L. M., & Jensen, A. C. (2016). Do siblings matter independent of both parents and friends? Sympathy as a mediator between sibling relationship quality and adolescent outcomes. *Journal of Research on Adolescence, 26*(1), 101–114. https://doi.org/10.1111/jora.12174

Karasik, L. B., Tamis-LeMonda, C. S., & Adolph, K. E. (2014). Crawling and walking infants elicit different verbal responses from mothers. *Developmental Science, 17*(3), 388–395.

Lavelli, M., & Fogel, A. (2013). Interdyad differences in early mother–infant face-to-face communication: Real-time dynamics and developmental pathways. *Developmental Psychology, 49*(12), 2257–2271.

LoBue, V., Reider, L. B., Kim, E., Burris, J. L., Oleas, D. S., Buss, K. A., Pérez-Edgar, K., & Field, A. P. (2020). The importance of using multiple outcome measures in infant research. *Infancy, 25*(4), 420–437.

Matheny, A. P., Riese, M. L., & Wilson, R. S. (1985). Rudiments of infant temperament: Newborn to 9 months. *Developmental Psychology, 21*(3), 486–494.

Maugh, T. H., II. (1999, May 13). Night lights linked to babies' nearsightedness. Los Angeles Times. https://www.latimes.com/archives/la-xpm-1999-may-13-mn-36731-story.html

Nelson, C. A., Furtado, E. A., Fox, N. A., & Zeanah, C. H. (2009). The deprived human brain: Developmental deficits among institutionalized Romanian children—and later improvements—strengthen the case for individualized care. *American Scientist*, *97*(3), 222–229.

Oakes, L. M., & Rakison, D. H. (2019). *Developmental cascades: Building the infant mind.* Oxford University Press.

Quinn, G. E., Shin, C. H., Maguire, M. G., & Stone, R. A. (1999). Myopia and ambient lighting at night. *Nature*, *399*(6732), 113–114.

Rauscher, F. H., Shaw, G. L., & Ky, K. N. (1993). Music and spatial task performance. *Nature*, *365*(6447), 611.

Rothbaum, F., Weisz, J., Pott, M., Miyake, K., & Morelli, G. (2000). Attachment and culture security in the United States and Japan. *The American Psychologist*, *55*(10), 1093–1104.

Sack, K. (1998, January). Georgia's governor seeks musical start for babies. The New York Times. https://www.nytimes.com/1998/01/15/us/georgia-s-governor-seeks-musical-start-for-babies.html

Thelen, E., & Smith, L. B. (1994). *A dynamic systems approach to the development of cognition and action.* The MIT Press.

Thelen, E., & Ulrich, B. D. (1991). Hidden skills: A dynamic systems analysis of treadmill stepping during the first year. *Monographs of the Society for Research in Child Development*, *56*(1), 1–98; discussion 99–104.

Watson, J. B. (1924). *Behaviorism.* The People's Institute.

Zadnik, K., Jones, L. A., Irvin, B. C., Kleinstein, R. N., Manny, R. E., Shin, J. A., & Mutti, D. O. (2000). Myopia and ambient night-time lighting. CLEERE study group. Collaborative longitudinal evaluation of ethnicity and refractive error. *Nature*, *404*(6774), 143–144.

Zeanah, C. H., Fox, N. A., & Nelson, C. A. (2012). The Bucharest early intervention project: Case study in the ethics of mental health research. *Journal of Nervous and Mental Disease*, *200*(3), 243–247.

CHAPTER 2

Alegría-Torres, J. A., Baccarelli, A., & Bollati, V. (2011). Epigenetics and lifestyle. *Epigenomics*, *3*(3), 267–277.

Balas, B. J., & Saville, A. (2015). N170 face specificity and face memory depend on hometown size. *Neuropsychologia*, *69*, 211–217.

Betancourt, L. M., Avants, B., Farah, M. J., Brodsky, N. L., Wu, J., Ashtari, M., & Hurt, H. (2016). Effect of socioeconomic status (SES) disparity on neural development in female African-American infants at age 1 month. *Developmental Science*, *19*(6), 947–956.

Bick, J., Zhu, T., Stamoulis, C., Fox, N. A., Zeanah, C., & Nelson, C. A. (2015). Effect of early institutionalization and foster care on long-term white matter development: A randomized clinical trial. *JAMA Pediatrics*, *169*(3), 211–219.

Brito, N. H., Piccolo, L. R., Noble, K. G., & Pediatric Imaging, Neurocognition, and Genetics Study. (2017). Associations between cortical thickness and neurocognitive skills during childhood vary by family socioeconomic factors. *Brain and Cognition*, *116*, 54–62.

Carhart-Harris, R. L., & Nutt, D. J. (2017). Serotonin and brain function: A tale of two receptors. *Journal of Psychopharmacology*, *31*(9), 1091–1120.

Caspi, A., Sugden, K., Moffitt, T. E., Taylor, A., Craig, I. W., Harrington, H., McClay, J., Mill, J., Martin, J., Braithwaite, A., & Poulton, R. (2003). Influence of life stress on depression: Moderation by a polymorphism in the 5-HTT gene. *Science*, *301*(5631), 386–389.

Chugani, H. T., Behen, M. E., Muzik, O., Juhász, C., Nagy, F., & Chugani, D. C. (2001). Local brain functional activity following early deprivation: A study of postinstitutionalized Romanian orphans. *NeuroImage*, *14*(6), 1290–1301.

Cioffi, C. C., Leve, L. D., Natsuaki, M. N., Shaw, D. S., Reiss, D., & Neiderhiser, J. M. (2020). Does maternal warmth moderate longitudinal associations between infant attention control and children's inhibitory control? *Infant and Child Development*, *29*(1). https://doi.org/10.1002/icd.2147

Clearfield, M. W., & Niman, L. C. (2012). SES affects infant cognitive flexibility. *Infant Behavior & Development*, *35*(1), 29–35.

Cohen Kadosh, K., & Johnson, M. H. (2007). Developing a cortex specialized for face perception. *Trends in Cognitive Sciences*, *11*(9), 367–369.

Constantino, J. N., Kennon-McGill, S., Weichselbaum, C., Marrus, N., Haider, A.,

Glowinski, A. L., Gillespie, S., Klaiman, C., Klin, A., & Jones, W. (2017). Infant viewing of social scenes is under genetic control and is atypical in autism. *Nature, 547*(7663), 340–344.

Dehaene-Lambertz, G., Dehaene, S., & Hertz-Pannier, L. (2002). Functional neuroimaging of speech perception in infants. *Science, 298*(5600), 2013–2015.

DiLalla, L. F. (2002). Behavior genetics of aggression in children: Review and future directions. *Developmental Review: DR, 22*(4), 593–622.

Dominus, S. (2015, July 9). The mixed-up brothers of Bogotá. *The New York Times*. https://www.nytimes.com/2015/07/12/magazine/the-mixed-up-brothers-of-bogota.html

Dubois, L., Ohm Kyvik, K., Girard, M., Tatone-Tokuda, F., Pérusse, D., Hjelmborg, J., Skytthe, A., Rasmussen, F., Wright, M. J., Lichtenstein, P., & Martin, N. G. (2012). Genetic and environmental contributions to weight, height, and BMI from birth to 19 years of age: An international study of over 12,000 twin pairs. *PLOS ONE, 7*(2), e30153.

Fernald, A., Marchman, V. A., & Weisleder, A. (2013). SES differences in language processing skill and vocabulary are evident at 18 months. *Developmental Science, 16*(2), 234–248.

Gottschling, J., Hahn, E., Beam, C. R., Spinath, F. M., Carroll, S., & Turkheimer, E. (2019). Socioeconomic status amplifies genetic effects in middle childhood in a large

German twin sample. *Intelligence, 72*, 20–27.

Greenough, W. T., Black, J. E., & Wallace, C. S. (1987). Experience and brain development. *Child Development, 58*(3), 539–559.

Hackman, D. A., & Farah, M. J. (2009). Socioeconomic status and the developing brain. *Trends in Cognitive Sciences, 13*(2), 65–73.

Hackman, D. A., Farah, M. J., & Meaney, M. J. (2010). Socioeconomic status and the brain: Mechanistic insights from human and animal research. *Nature Reviews. Neuroscience, 11*(9), 651–659.

Hur, Y.-M., Kaprio, J., Iacono, W. G., Boomsma, D. I., McGue, M., Silventoinen, K., Martin, N. G., Luciano, M., Visscher, P. M., Rose, R. J., He, M., Ando, J., Ooki, S., Nonaka, K., Lin, C. C. H., Lajunen, H. R., Cornes, B. K., Bartels, M., van Beijsterveldt, C. E. M., . . . Mitchell, K. (2008). Genetic influences on the difference in variability of height, weight and body mass index between Caucasian and East Asian adolescent twins. *International Journal of Obesity, 32*(10), 1455–1467.

Jaffee, S. R., & Price, T. S. (2008). Genotype-environment correlations: Implications for determining the relationship between environmental exposures and psychiatric illness. *Psychiatry, 7*(12), 496–499.

Jelenkovic, A., Sund, R., Hur, Y.-M., Yokoyama, Y., Hjelmborg, J. V. B., Möller, S., Honda, C., Magnusson, P. K. E., Pedersen, N. L., Ooki, S., Aaltonen, S., Stazi, M. A., Fagnani,

C., D'Ippolito, C., Freitas, D. L., Maia, J. A., Ji, F., Ning, F., Pang, Z., . . . Silventoinen, K. (2016). Genetic and environmental influences on height from infancy to early adulthood: An individual-based pooled analysis of 45 twin cohorts. *Scientific Reports, 6*, 28496.

John, R. M., & Rougeulle, C. (2018). Developmental epigenetics: Phenotype and the flexible epigenome. *Frontiers in Cell and Developmental Biology, 6*, 130.

Johnson, M. H. (2011). Interactive specialization: A domain-general framework for human functional brain development? *Developmental Cognitive Neuroscience, 1*(1), 7–21.

Kochanska, G., Kim, S., Barry, R. A., & Philibert, R. A. (2011). Children's genotypes interact with maternal responsive care in predicting children's competence: Diathesis-stress or differential susceptibility? *Development and Psychopathology, 23*(2), 605–616.

Kolb, B. (1989). Brain development, plasticity, and behavior. *The American Psychologist, 44*(9), 1203–1212.

Lemery-Chalfant, K., Kao, K., Swann, G., & Goldsmith, H. H. (2013). Childhood temperament: Passive gene-environment correlation, gene-environment interaction, and the hidden importance of the family environment. *Development and Psychopathology, 25*(1), 51–63.

Lionetti, F., Aron, A., Aron, E. N., Burns, G. L., Jagiellowicz, J., & Pluess, M. (2018). Dandelions, tulips and orchids: Evidence for the existence of low-sensitive, medium-sensitive and high-sensitive individuals. *Translational Psychiatry, 8*(1), 24.

Lionetti, F., Aron, E. N., Aron, A., Klein, D. N., & Pluess, M. (2019). Observer-rated environmental sensitivity moderates children's response to parenting quality in early childhood. *Developmental Psychology, 55*(11), 2389–2402.

Macgregor, S., Cornes, B. K., Martin, N. G., & Visscher, P. M. (2006). Bias, precision and heritability of self-reported and clinically measured height in Australian twins. *Human Genetics, 120*(4), 571–580.

Martínez, R. M., Chen, C.-Y., Liao, T.-T., Cheng, Y., Fan, Y.-T., Chou, S.-H., & Chen, C. (2020). The multifaceted effects of serotonin transporter polymorphism (5-HTTLPR) on anxiety, implicit moral attitudes, and harmful behaviors. *Frontiers in Psychology, 11,* 1521.

May, L., Byers-Heinlein, K., Gervain, J., & Werker, J. F. (2011). Language and the newborn brain: Does prenatal language experience shape the neonate neural response to speech? In *Frontiers in Psychology, 2.* https://doi.org/10.3389/fpsyg.2011.00222

Montirosso, R., Provenzi, L., Fumagalli, M., Sirgiovanni, I., Giorda, R., Pozzoli, U., Beri, S., Menozzi, G., Tronick, E., Morandi, F., Mosca, F., & Borgatti, R. (2016). Serotonin transporter gene (SLC6A4) methylation associates with neonatal intensive care unit stay and 3-month-old temperament in preterm infants.

Child Development, 87(1), 38–48.

Nelson, C. A., Furtado, E. A., Fox, N. A., & Zeanah, C. H. (2009). The deprived human brain: Developmental deficits among institutionalized Romanian children—and later improvements—strengthen the case for individualized care. *American Scientist, 97*(3), 222–229.

Nisbett, R. E., Aronson, J., Blair, C., Dickens, W., Flynn, J., Halpern, D. F., & Turkheimer, E. (2012). Intelligence: New findings and theoretical developments. *The American Psychologist, 67*(2), 130–159.

Noble, K. G., Engelhardt, L. E., Brito, N. H., Mack, L. J., Nail, E. J., Angal, J., Barr, R., Fifer, W. P., Elliott, A. J., & PASS, Network. (2015). Socioeconomic disparities in neurocognitive development in the first two years of life. *Developmental Psychobiology, 57*(5), 535–551.

Nystrom, M., & Mutanen, M. (2009). Diet and epigenetics in colon cancer. *World Journal of Gastroenterology: WJG, 15*(3), 257–263.

Perola, M., Sammalisto, S., Hiekkalinna, T., Martin, N. G., Visscher, P. M., Montgomery, G. W., Benyamin, B., Harris, J. R., Boomsma, D., Willemsen, G., Hottenga, J.-J., Christensen, K., Kyvik, K. O., Sørensen, T. I. A., Pedersen, N. L., Magnusson, P. K. E., Spector, T. D., Widen, E., Silventoinen, K., . . . GenomEUtwin Project. (2007). Combined genome scans for body stature in 6,602 European twins: Evidence for common Caucasian loci. *PLOS Genetics, 3*(6), e97.

Plomin, R., DeFries, J. C., Knopik, V. S., & Neiderhiser, J. M. (2016). Top 10 replicated findings from behavioral genetics. *Perspectives on Psychological Science: A Journal of the Association for Psychological Science, 11*(1), 3–23.

Provenzi, L., Fumagalli, M., Giorda, R., Morandi, F., Sirgiovanni, I., Pozzoli, U., Mosca, F., Borgatti, R., & Montirosso, R. (2017). Maternal sensitivity buffers the association between SLC6A4 methylation and socio-emotional stress response in 3-month-old full term, but not very preterm infants. *Frontiers in Psychiatry / Frontiers Research Foundation, 8,* 171.

Provenzi, L., Fumagalli, M., Scotto di Minico, G., Giorda, R., Morandi, F., Sirgiovanni, I., Schiavolin, P., Mosca, F., Borgatti, R., & Montirosso, R. (2020). Pain-related increase in serotonin transporter gene methylation associates with emotional regulation in 4.5-year-old preterm-born children. *Acta Paediatrica, 109*(6), 1166–1174.

Provenzi, L., Fumagalli, M., Sirgiovanni, I., Giorda, R., Pozzoli, U., Morandi, F., Beri, S., Menozzi, G., Mosca, F., Borgatti, R., & Montirosso, R. (2015). Pain-related stress during the neonatal intensive care unit stay and SLC6A4 methylation in very preterm infants. *Frontiers in Behavioral Neuroscience, 9,* 99.

Rowe, M. L. (2008). Child-directed speech: Relation to socioeconomic status, knowledge of child development and child vocabulary skill. *Journal of Child Language, 35*(1), 185–205.

Rowe, M. L. (2012). A longitudinal investigation of the role of quantity and quality of child-directed speech in vocabulary development. *Child Development*, *83*(5), 1762–1774.

Scarr-Salapatek, S. (1971). Race, social class, and IQ. *Science*, *174*(4016), 1285–1295.

Tomalski, P., Moore, D. G., Ribeiro, H., Axelsson, E. L., Murphy, E., Karmiloff-Smith, A., Johnson, M. H., & Kushnerenko, E. (2013). Socioeconomic status and functional brain development—Associations in early infancy. *Developmental Science*, *16*(5), 676–687.

Turkheimer, E., Haley, A., Waldron, M., D'Onofrio, B., & Gottesman, I. I. (2003). Socioeconomic status modifies heritability of IQ in young children. *Psychological Science*, *14*(6), 623–628.

Veenendaal, M. V. E., Painter, R. C., de Rooij, S. R., Bossuyt, P. M. M., van der Post, J. A. M., Gluckman, P. D., Hanson, M. A., & Roseboom, T. J. (2013). Transgenerational effects of prenatal exposure to the 1944-45 Dutch famine. *BJOG: An International Journal of Obstetrics and Gynaecology*, *120*(5), 548–553.

CHAPTER 3

Akman, I., Kuşçu, K., Ozdemir, N., Yurdakul, Z., Solakoglu, M., Orhan, L., Karabekiroglu, A., & Ozek, E. (2006). Mothers' postpartum psychological adjustment and infantile colic. *Archives of Disease in Childhood*, *91*(5), 417–419.

Barr, R. G., Trent, R. B., & Cross, J. (2006). Age-related incidence curve of hospitalized shaken baby syndrome cases: Convergent evidence for crying as a trigger to shaking. *Child Abuse & Neglect*, *30*(1), 7–16. https://doi.org/10.1016/j.chiabu.2005.06.009

Barre, N., Morgan, A., Doyle, L. W., & Anderson, P. J. (2011). Language abilities in children who were very preterm and/or very low birth weight: A meta-analysis. *Journal of Pediatrics*, *158*(5), 766–774.e1.

Best, K., Bogossian, F., & New, K. (2018). Language exposure of preterm infants in the neonatal unit: A systematic review. *Neonatology*, *114*(3), 261–276.

Birch, L. L., & Fisher, J. O. (1998). Development of eating behaviors among children and adolescents. *Pediatrics*, *101*(3 Pt 2), 539–549.

Black, R. A., & Hill, D. A. (2003). Over-the-counter medications in pregnancy. *American Family Physician*, *67*(12), 2517–2524.

Boismier, J. D. (1977). Visual stimulation and wake-sleep behavior in human neonates. *Developmental Psychobiology*, *10*(3), 219–227.

Bradley, R. M., & Stern, I. B. (1967). The development of the human taste bud during the foetal period. *Journal of Anatomy*, *101*(Pt 4), 743–752.

Chik, Y.-M., Ip, W.-Y., & Choi, K.-C. (2017). The effect of upper limb massage on infants' venipuncture pain. *Pain Management Nursing*, *18*(1), 50–57. https://doi.org/10.1016/j.pmn.2016.10.001

Coles, C. D., Brown, R. T., Smith, I. E., Platzman, K. A., Erickson, S., & Falek, A. (1991). Effects of prenatal alcohol exposure at school age. I. Physical and cognitive development. *Neurotoxicology and Teratology*, *13*(4), 357–367.

Cowart, B. J. (1981). Development of taste perception in humans: Sensitivity and preference throughout the life span. *Psychological Bulletin*, *90*(1), 43–73.

Das, S., Seepana, R., & Bakshi, S. S. (2020). Perspectives of newborn hearing screening in resource constrained settings. *Journal of Otology*, *15*(4), 174–177.

DeCasper, A. J., & Spence, M. J. (1986). Prenatal maternal speech influences newborns' perception of speech sounds. *Infant Behavior & Development*, *9*(2), 133–150.

Dominguez-Bello, M. G., Costello, E. K., Contreras, M., Magris, M., Hidalgo, G., Fierer, N., & Knight, R. (2010). Delivery mode shapes the acquisition and structure of the initial microbiota across multiple body habitats in newborns. *Proceedings of the National Academy of Sciences of the United States of America*, *107*(26), 11971–11975.

Doty, R. L. (1986). Ontogeny of human olfactory function. In W. Breipohl & R. Apfelbach (Eds.), *Ontogeny of olfaction: Principles of olfactory maturation in vertebrates* (pp. 3–17). Springer.

Field, T., Diego, M., Dieter, J., Hernandez-Reif, M., Schanberg, S., Kuhn, C., Yando, R., & Bendell, D. (2004). Prenatal depression effects on the fetus and the newborn. *Infant Behavior and Development, 27*(2), 216–229. https://doi.org/10.10 16/j.infbeh.2003.09.010

Franks, M. E., Macpherson, G. R., & Figg, W. D. (2004). Thalidomide. *The Lancet, 363*(9423), 1802–1811.

Gerrish, C. J., & Mennella, J. A. (2001). Flavor variety enhances food acceptance in formula-fed infants. *American Journal of Clinical Nutrition, 73*(6), 1080–1085.

Graven, S. N., & Browne, J. (2008). *Auditory development in the fetus and infant. 8*(4), 187–193.

Hafstad, G. S., Abebe, D. S., Torgersen, L., & von Soest, T. (2013). Picky eating in preschool children: the predictive role of the child's temperament and mother's negative affectivity. *Eating Behaviors, 14*(3), 274–277.

Hall, J. W., III. (2000). Development of the ear and hearing. *Journal of Perinatology: Official Journal of the California Perinatal Association, 20*(1), S12–S20.

Hamilton, B. E., Martin, J. A., & Ventura, S. J. (2013). Births: Preliminary data for 2012. *National Vital Statistics Reports, 62*(3), 1–20.

Hendrickson, A. (1992). A morphological comparison of foveal development in man and monkey. *Eye, 6*(2), 136–144.

Hernandez-Reif, M., & Bahrick, L. E. (2001). The development of visual-tactual perception of objects: Amodal relations provide the basis for learning arbitrary relations. *Infancy: The Official Journal of the International Society on Infant Studies, 2*(1), 51–72.

Hernandez-Reif, M., Field, T., Diego, M., & Largie, S. (2003). Haptic habituation to temperature is slower in newborns of depressed mothers. *Infancy, 4*(1), 47–63. https://doi.org/10. 1207/S15327078IN0401_3

Honda, A., Choijookhuu, N., Izu, H., Kawano, Y., Inokuchi, M., Honsho, K., Lee, A.-R., Nabekura, H., Ohta, H., Tsukiyama, T., Ohinata, Y., Kuroiwa, A., Hishikawa, Y., Saitou, M., Jogahara, T., & Koshimoto, C. (2017). Flexible adaptation of male germ cells from female iPSCs of endangered Tokudaia osimensis. *Science Advances, 3*(5), e1602179.

Huh, S. Y., Rifas-Shiman, S. L., Zera, C. A., Rich Edwards, J. W., Oken, E., Weiss, S. T., & Gillman, M. W. (2012). Delivery by cesarean section and risk of obesity in preschool age children. *Obstetrical & Gynecological Survey, 67*(11), 673–674. http s://doi.org/10.1097/ogx.0b013 e31827412c5

Jensen, M. P., Allen, C. D., Eguchi, T., Bell, I. P., LaCasella, E. L., Hilton, W. A., Hof, C. A. M., & Dutton, P. H. (2018). Environmental warming and feminization of one of the largest sea turtle populations in the world. *Current Biology: CB, 28*(1), 154–159.e4.

Jones, N. A., Field, T., Lundy, B., & Davalos, M. (1996). One-month-old infants of depressed mothers and right frontal asymmetry. *Infant Behavior & Development, 19, Suppl 1)*, 529.

Kaplan, L. A., Evans, L., & Monk, C. (2008). Effects of mothers' prenatal psychiatric status and postnatal caregiving on infant biobehavioral regulation: Can prenatal programming be modified? *Early Human Development, 84*(4), 249–256.

Kisilevsky, B. S., Hains, S. M. J., Brown, C. A., Lee, C. T., Cowperthwaite, B., Stutzman, S. S., Swansburg, M. L., Lee, K., Xie, X., Huang, H., Ye, H.-H., Zhang, K., & Wang, Z. (2009). Fetal sensitivity to properties of maternal speech and language. *Infant Behavior & Development, 32*(1), 59–71.

Lee, G. Y., & Kisilevsky, B. S. (2014). Fetuses respond to father's voice but prefer mother's voice after birth. *Developmental Psychobiology, 56*(1), 1–11.

Li, Z., van der Horst, K., Edelson-Fries, L. R., Yu, K., You, L., Zhang, Y., Vinyes-Pares, G., Wang, P., Ma, D., Yang, X., Qin, L., & Wang, J. (2017). Perceptions of food intake and weight status among parents of picky eating infants and toddlers in China: A cross-sectional study. *Appetite, 108*, 456–463.

Magoon, E. H., & Robb, R. M. (1981). Development of myelin in human optic nerve and tract. A light and electron microscopic study. *Archives of Ophthalmology, 99*(4), 655–659. https://doi.org/10.1001/archop ht.1981.03930010655011

Maier, A., Chabanet, C., Schaal, B., Leathwood, P., & Issanchou, S. (2007). Food-related sensory experience from birth through weaning: contrasted patterns in two nearby European regions. *Appetite, 49*(2), 429–440.

Maier-Nöth, A., Schaal, B., Leathwood, P., & Issanchou, S. (2016). The Lasting Influences of Early Food-Related Variety

Experience: A Longitudinal Study of Vegetable Acceptance from 5 Months to 6 Years in Two Populations. *PloS One*, *11*(3), e0151356.

May, L., Byers-Heinlein, K., Gervain, J., & Werker, J. F. (2011). Language and the newborn brain: Does prenatal language experience shape the neonate neural response to speech? *Frontiers in Psychology*, *2*, 222.

May, L., Gervain, J., Carreiras, M., & Werker, J. F. (2018). The specificity of the neural response to speech at birth. *Developmental Science*, *21*(3), e12564.

Mennella, J. A., Forestell, C. A., Morgan, L. K., & Beauchamp, G. K. (2009). Early milk feeding influences taste acceptance and liking during infancy. *The American Journal of Clinical Nutrition*, *90*(3), 780S–788S.

Mennella, J. A., Jagnow, C. P., & Beauchamp, G. K. (2001). Prenatal and postnatal flavor learning by human infants. *Pediatrics*, *107*(6), e88–e88.

Mennella, J. A., Lukasewycz, L. D., Castor, S. M., & Beauchamp, G. K. (2011). The timing and duration of a sensitive period in human flavor learn a randomized trial. *The American Journal of Clinical Nutrition*, *93*(5), 1019–1024.

Neu, J., & Rushing, J. (2011). Cesarean versus vaginal delivery: Long-term infant outcomes and the hygiene hypothesis. *Clinics in Perinatology*, *38*(2), 321–331.

Nowlis, G. H., & Kessen, W. (1976). Response: Differentiation of differing concentrations of sucrose and glucose by human newborns. *Science*, *193*(4259), 1267. https://doi.org/10.1126/science.193.4259.1267-b

O'Connor, T. G., Heron, J., & Glover, V. (2002). Antenatal anxiety predicts child behavioral/emotional problems independently of postnatal depression. *Journal of the American Academy of Child and Adolescent Psychiatry*, *41*(12), 1470–1477.

Olson, K. R., Key, A. C., & Eaton, N. R. (2015). Gender cognition in transgender children. *Psychological Science*, *26*(4), 467–474.

Pak-Gorstein, S., Haq, A., & Graham, E. A. (2009). Cultural influences on infant feeding practices. *Pediatrics in Review / American Academy of Pediatrics*, *30*(3), e11–e21.

Pandi-Perumal, S. R., Seils, L. K., Kayumov, L., Ralph, M. R., Lowe, A., Moller, H., & Swaab, D. F. (2002). Senescence, sleep, and circadian rhythms. *Ageing Research Reviews*, *1*(3), 559–604.

Partanen, E., Kujala, T., Näätänen, R., Liitola, A., Sambeth, A., & Huotilainen, M. (2013). Learning-induced neural plasticity of speech processing before birth. *Proceedings of the National Academy of Sciences of the United States of America*, *110*(37), 15145–15150.

Patel, M. D., Donovan, S. M., & Lee, S.-Y. (2020). Considering Nature and Nurture in the Etiology and Prevention of Picky Eating: A Narrative Review. *Nutrients*, *12*(11). https://doi.org/10.3390/nu12113409

Pineda., R., Durant, P., Mathur, A., Inder, T., Wallendorf, M., & Schlaggar, B. L. (2017). Auditory exposure in the neonatal intensive care unit: Room type and other predictors. *Journal of Pediatrics*, *183*, 56–66.e3.

Renz-Polster, H., David, M. R., Buist, A. S., Vollmer, W. M., O'Connor, E. A., Frazier, E. A., & Wall, M. A. (2005). Caesarean section delivery and the risk of allergic disorders in childhood. *Clinical and Experimental Allergy: Journal of the British Society for Allergy and Clinical Immunology*, *35*(11), 1466–1472.

Rosenstein, D., & Oster, H. (1988). Differential facial responses to four basic tastes in newborns. *Child Development*, *59*(6), 1555–1568.

Sato, H., Hirabayashi, Y., Tsubokura, H., Kanai, M., Ashida, T., Konishi, I., Uchida-Ota, M., Konishi, Y., & Maki, A. (2012). Cerebral hemodynamics in newborn infants exposed to speech sounds: a whole-head optical topography study: Whole-head NIRS in neonates. *Human Brain Mapping*, *33*(9), 2092–2103.

Schaal, B., Marlier, L., & Soussignan, R. (2000). Human foetuses learn odours from their pregnant mother's diet. *Chemical Senses*, *25*(6), 729–737.

Shim, J. E., Kim, J., Mathai, R. A., & STRONG, Kids Research Team. (2011). Associations of infant feeding practices and picky eating behaviors of preschool children. *Journal of the American Dietetic Association*, *111*(9), 1363–1368.

Sorcinelli, A., Ference, J., Curtin, S., & Vouloumanos, A. (2019). Preference for speech in infancy differentially predicts language skills and autism-like behaviors. *Journal of Experimental Child Psychology*, *178*(5), 295–316.

Taffel, S. M., Placek, P. J., & Liss, T. (1987). Trends in the United States cesarean section rate and reasons for the 1980-85 rise. *American Journal of Public Health*, *77*(8), 955–959.

Taylor, C. M., Wernimont, S. M., Northstone, K., & Emmett, P. M. (2015). Picky/fussy eating in children: Review of definitions, assessment, prevalence and dietary intakes. *Appetite*, *95*, 349–359.

Thackray, H., & Tifft, C. (2001). Fetal alcohol syndrome. *Pediatrics in Review / American Academy of Pediatrics*, *22*(2), 47–55.

Thomason, M. E., Hect, J. L., Waller, R., & Curtin, P. (2021). Interactive relations between maternal prenatal stress, fetal brain connectivity, and gestational age at delivery. *Neuropsychopharmacology: Official Publication of the American College of Neuropsychopharmacology*, *46*(10), 1839–1847.

Van den Bergh, B. R. H., Marcoen, A., & Lagae, L. (2004). Maternal anxiety during pregnancy on self-regulatory behavior in child and adolescent. In *PsycEXTRA Dataset*. https://doi.org/10.1037/e524332011-084

Van den Bergh, B. R. H., van den Heuvel, M. I., Lahti, M., Braeken, M., de Rooij, S. R., Entringer, S., Hoyer, D., Roseboom, T., Räikkönen, K., King, S., & Schwab, M. (2020). Prenatal developmental origins of behavior and mental health: The influence of maternal

stress in pregnancy. *Neuroscience and Biobehavioral Reviews*, *117*, 26–64.

Ventura, A. K., & Worobey, J. (2013). Early influences on the development of food preferences. *Current Biology*, *23*(9), R401–R408.

Vouloumanos, A., Hauser, M. D., & Werker, J. F. (2010). The tuning of human neonates' preference for speech. *The Child*, *81*(2), 517–527. https://srcd.onlinelibrary.wiley.com/doi/abs/10.1111/j.1467-8624.2009.01412.x

Witt, M., & Reutter, K. (1996). Embryonic and early fetal development of human taste buds: A transmission electron microscopical study. *The Anatomical Record*, *246*(4), 507–523.

World Health Organization. (2021, June 16). *Caesarean section rates continue to rise, amid growing inequalities in access*. https://www.who.int/news/item/16-06-2021-caesarean-section-rates-continue-to-rise-amid-growing-inequalities-in-access

Yoon, P. W., Freeman, S. B., Sherman, S. L., Taft, L. F., Gu, Y., Pettay, D., Flanders, W. D., Khoury, M. J., & Hassold, T. J. (1996). Advanced maternal age and the risk of Down syndrome characterized by the meiotic stage of chromosomal error: A population-based study. *American Journal of Human Genetics*, *58*(3), 628–633.

Zielinski, R., Ackerson, K., & Kane Low, L. (2015). Planned home birth: benefits, risks, and opportunities. *International Journal of Women's Health*, *7*, 361–377.

CHAPTER 4

Albareda-Castellot, B., Pons, F., & Sebastián-Gallés, N. (2011). The acquisition of phonetic categories in bilingual infants: New data from an anticipatory eye movement paradigm. *Developmental Science*, *14*(2), 395–401.

Alegria, J., & Noirot, E. (1978). Neonate orientation behaviour towards human voice. *International Journal of Behavioral Development*, *1*(4), 291–312.

Allen, D., Banks, M. S., & Norcia, A. M. (1993). Does chromatic sensitivity develop more slowly than luminance sensitivity? *Vision Research*, *33*(17), 2553–2562.

Anzures, G., Wheeler, A., Quinn, P. C., Pascalis, O., Slater, A. M., Heron-Delaney, M., Tanaka, J. W., & Lee, K. (2012). Brief daily exposures to Asian females reverses perceptual narrowing for Asian faces in Caucasian infants. *Journal of Experimental Child Psychology*, *112*(4), 484–495.

Bahrick, L. E., & Lickliter, R. (2000). Intersensory redundancy guides attentional selectivity and perceptual learning in infancy. *Developmental Psychology*, *36*(2), 190–201.

Bahrick, L. E., Lickliter, R., & Flom, R. (2004). Intersensory redundancy guides the development of selective attention, perception, and cognition in infancy. *Current Directions in Psychological Science*, *13*(3), 99–102.

Bahrick, L. E., McNew, M. E., Pruden, S. M., & Castellanos, I. (2019). Intersensory redundancy promotes infant detection of prosody in infant-directed speech. *Journal of Experimental Child Psychology, 183*, 295–309.

Bar-Haim, Y., Ziv, T., Lamy, D., & Hodes, R. M. (2006). Nature and nurture in own-race face processing. *Psychological Science, 17*(2), 159–163.

Berg, K. M., & Boswell, A. E. (2000). Noise increment detection in children 1 to 3 years of age. *Perception & Psychophysics, 62*(4), 868–873.

Bornstein, M. H. (1976). Infants are trichromats. *Journal of Experimental Child Psychology, 21*(3), 425–445.

Bornstein, M. H., Kessen, W., & Weiskopf, S. (1976). Color vision and hue categorization in young infants. *Journal of Experimental Psychology. Human Perception and Performance, 2*, 115–129.

Bourgeois, K. S., Khawar, A. W., Neal, S. A., & Lockman, J. J. (2005). Infant manual exploration of objects, surfaces, and their interrelations. *Infancy: The Official Journal of the International Society on Infant Studies, 8*(3), 233–252.

Bushnell, I. W. R., Sai, F., & Mullin, J. T. (1989). Neonatal recognition of the mother's face. *British Journal of Developmental Psychology, 7*(1), 3–15.

Chládková, K., & Paillereau, N. (2020). The what and when of universal perception: A review of early speech sound acquisition. *Language Learning, 70*(4), 1136–1182.

Clearfield, M. W., Bailey, L. S., Jenne, H. K., Stanger, S. B., & Tacke, N. (2014). Socioeconomic status affects oral and manual exploration across the first year. *Infant Mental Health Journal, 35*(1), 63–69.

Dobson, V., Teller, D. Y., & Belgum, J. (1978). Visual acuity in human infants assessed with stationary stripes and phase-alternated checkerboards. *Vision Research, 18*(9), 1233–1238.

Dorn, K., Weinert, S., & Falck-Ytter, T. (2018). Watch and listen—A cross-cultural study of audio-visual-matching behavior in 4.5-month-old infants in German and Swedish talking faces. *Infant Behavior & Development, 52*, 121–129.

Eimas, P. D., Siqueland, E. R., Jusczyk, P., & Vigorito, J. (1971). Speech perception in infants. *Science, 171*(3968), 303–306.

Elfenbein, J. L., Small, A. M., & Davis, J. M. (1993). Developmental patterns of duration discrimination. *Journal of Speech and Hearing Research, 36*(4), 842–849.

Ellis, A. E., Xiao, N. G., Lee, K., & Oakes, L. M. (2017). Scanning of own-versus other-race faces in infants from racially diverse or homogenous communities. *Developmental Psychobiology, 59*(5), 613–627.

Fantz, R. L. (1958). Pattern vision in young infants. *The Psychological Record, 8*, 43–47.

Field, J., Muir, D., Pilon, R., Sinclair, M., & Dodwell, P. (1980). Infants' orientation to lateral sounds from birth to three months. *Child Development, 51*(1), 295–298.

Gibson, E. J., & Walk, R. D. (1960). The" visual cliff.". *Scientific American, 202*(4), 64–71.

Gottfried, A. W., Rose, S. A., & Bridger, W. H. (1977). Cross-modal transfer in human infants. *Child Development, 48*(1), 118–123.

Hannon, E. E., Soley, G., & Levine, R. S. (2011). Constraints on infants' musical rhythm perception: Effects of interval ratio complexity and enculturation. *Developmental Science, 14*(4), 865–872.

Hartmann, E. E., Lynn, M. J., Lambert, S. R., & Infant Aphakia Treatment Study Group, . (2014). Baseline characteristics of the infant aphakia treatment study population: Predicting recognition acuity at 4.5 years of age. *Investigative Ophthalmology & Visual Science, 56*(1), 388–395.

He, C., Hotson, L., & Trainor, L. J. (2009). Development of infant mismatch responses to auditory pattern changes between 2 and 4 months old. *European Journal of Neuroscience, 29*(4), 861–867.

Hernandez-Reif, M., & Bahrick, L. E. (2001). The development of visual-tactual perception of objects: Amodal relations provide the basis for learning arbitrary relations. *Infancy: The Official Journal of the International Society on Infant Studies, 2*(1), 51–72.

James, W. (1890). *The principles of psychology* (Vol. 2). Dover.

Johnson, M. H., Dziurawiec, S., Ellis, H., & Morton, J. (1991). Newborns' preferential tracking of face-like stimuli and its subsequent decline. *Cognition, 40*(1–2), 1–19.

Jones, W., & Klin, A. (2013). Attention to eyes is present but in decline in 2–6-month-old infants later diagnosed with autism. *Nature, 504*(7480), 427–431.

Kellman, P. J., & Spelke, E. S. (1983). Perception of partly occluded objects in infancy. *Cognitive Psychology, 15*(4), 483–524.

Kelly, D. J., Liu, S., Ge, L., Quinn, P. C., Slater, A. M., Lee, K., Liu, Q., & Pascalis, O. (2007). Cross-race preferences for same-race faces extend beyond the African versus Caucasian contrast in 3-month-old infants. *Infancy: The Official Journal of the International Society on Infant Studies, 11*(1), 87–95.

Kelly, D. J., Liu, S., Lee, K., Quinn, P. C., Pascalis, O., Slater, A. M., & Ge, L. (2009). Development of the other-race effect during infancy: Evidence toward universality? *Journal of Experimental Child Psychology, 104*(1), 105–114.

Kelly, D. J., Quinn, P. C., Slater, A. M., Lee, K., Ge, L., & Pascalis, O. (2007). The other-race effect develops during infancy: Evidence of perceptual narrowing. *Psychological Science, 18*(12), 1084–1089.

Kelly, D. J., Quinn, P. C., Slater, A. M., Lee, K., Gibson, A., Smith, M., Ge, L., & Pascalis, O. (2005). Three-month-olds, but not newborns, prefer own-race faces. *Developmental Science, 8*(6), F31–F36.

Kuhl, P. K., & Meltzoff, A. N. (1984). The intermodal representation of speech in infants. *Infant Behavior & Development, 7*(3), 361–381.

Kühnle, S., Ludwig, A. A., Meuret, S., Küttner, C., Witte, C., Scholbach, J., Fuchs, M., & Rübsamen, R. (2013). Development of auditory localization accuracy and auditory spatial discrimination in children and adolescents. In *Audiology and Neurotology, 18*(1), 48–62. https://doi.org/10.1159/000342904

Kushnerenko, E., Ceponiene, R., Fellman, V., Huotilainen, M., & Winkler, I. (2001). Event-related potential correlates of sound duration: similar pattern from birth to adulthood. *Neuroreport, 12*(17), 3777–3781.

Laeng, B., Brennen, T., Elden, A., Gaare Paulsen, H., Banerjee, A., & Lipton, R. (2007). Latitude-of-birth and season-of-birth effects on human color vision in the Arctic. *Vision Research, 47*(12), 1595–1607.

Liu, S., Xiao, W. S., Xiao, N. G., Quinn, P. C., Zhang, Y., Chen, H., Ge, L., Pascalis, O., & Lee, K. (2015). Development of visual preference for own- versus other-race faces in infancy. *Developmental Psychology, 51*(4), 500–511.

Macchi Cassia, V., Turati, C., & Simion, F. (2004). Can a non-specific bias toward top-heavy patterns explain newborns' face preference? *Psychological Science, 15*(6), 379–383.

Maurer, D., & Lewis, T. L. (2018). Visual systems. In R. Gibb & B. Kolb (Eds.), *The neurobiology of brain and behavioral development* (pp. 213–233). Academic Press.

Maurer, D., & Salapatek, P. (1976). Developmental changes in the scanning of faces by young infants. *Child Development, 47*(2), 523–527.

Meltzoff, A. N., & Borton, R. W. (1979). Intermodal matching by human neonates. *Nature, 282*(5737), 403–404.

Mugitani, R., Kobayashi, T., & Hiraki, K. (2008). Audiovisual matching of lips and non-canonical sounds in 8-month-old infants. *Infant Behavior & Development, 31*(2), 307–310.

Náñez, J. E., & Yonas, A. (1994). Effects of luminance and texture motion on infant defensive reactions to optical collision. *Infant Behavior & Development, 17*(2), 165–174.

Nava, E., Grassi, M., Brenna, V., Croci, E., & Turati, C. (2017). Multisensory motion perception in 3–4 month-old infants. *Frontiers in Psychology, 8*, 1994.

Needham, A. (1998). Infants' use of featural information in the segregation of stationary objects. *Infant Behavior & Development, 21*(1), 47–76.

Oakes, L. M., DeBolt, M. C., Beckner, A. G., Voss, A. T., & Cantrell, L. M. (2021). Infant eye gaze while viewing dynamic faces. *Brain Sciences, 11*(2), 231.

Oakes, L. M., & Ellis, A. E. (2013). An eye-tracking investigation of developmental changes in infants' exploration of upright and inverted human faces. *Infancy: The Official Journal of the International Society on Infant Studies, 18*(1), 134–148.

Özgen, E. (2003). Language, learning, and color perception. *Current Directions in Psychological Science, 13*, 95–98.

Palmer, C. F. (1989). The discriminating nature of infants' exploratory actions.

Developmental Psychology, *25*(6), 885–893.

Pascalis, O., de Haan, M., & Nelson, C. A. (2002). First year of life? Is face processing species-specific during the. *Science*, *296*(5571), 1321–1323.

Patterson, M. L., & Werker, J. F. (2003). Two-month-old infants match phonetic information in lips and voice. *Developmental Science*, *6*(2), 191–196.

Pelphrey, K. A., Sasson, N. J., Reznick, J. S., Paul, G., Goldman, B. D., & Piven, J. (2002). Visual scanning of faces in autism. *Journal of Autism and Developmental Disorders*, *32*(4), 249–261.

Piaget, J. (1952). *Origins of intelligence in children.* (M. Cook, Ed.), , International Universities Press.

Pons, F., Bosch, L., & Lewkowicz, D. J. (2015). Bilingualism modulates infants' selective attention to the mouth of a talking face. *Psychological Science*, *26*(4), 490–498.

Rochat, P. (1989). Object manipulation and exploration in 2- to 5-month-old infants. *Developmental Psychology*, *25*(6), 871–884.

Rosa Salva, O., Farroni, T., Regolin, L., Vallortigara, G., & Johnson, M. H. (2011). The evolution of social orienting: Evidence from chicks (*Gallus gallus*) and human newborns. *PLOS ONE*, *6*(4), e18802.

Rose, S. A., Gottfried, A. W., & Bridger, W. H. (1981). Cross-modal transfer and information processing by the sense of touch in infancy. *Developmental Psychology*, *17*(1), 90–98.

Ruff, H. A. (1984). Infants' manipulative exploration of objects: Effects of age and object characteristics. *Developmental Psychology*, *20*(1), 9–20.

Simonsz, H. J., Kolling, G. H., & Unnebrink, K. (2005). Final report of the early vs. late infantile strabismus surgery study (ELISSS), a controlled, prospective, multicenter study. *Strabismus*, *13*(4), 169–199. https://doi.org/10.1080/09273970500416594

Singarajah, A., Chanley, J., Gutierrez, Y., Cordon, Y., Nguyen, B., Burakowski, L., & Johnson, S. P. (2017). Infant attention to same-and other-race faces. *Cognition*, *159*, 76–84.

Sinnott, J. M., Pisoni, D. B., & Aslin, R. N. (1983). A comparison of pure tone auditory thresholds in human infants and adults. *Infant Behavior & Development*, *6*(1), 3–17.

Skelton, A. E., Maule, J., & Franklin, A. (2022). Infant color perception: Insight into perceptual development. *Child Development Perspectives*, *16*(2), 90–95.

Soska, K. C., & Adolph, K. E. (2014). Postural position constrains multimodal object exploration in infants. *Infancy: The Official Journal of the International Society on Infant Studies*, *19*(2), 138–161.

Soska, K. C., & Johnson, S. P. (2008). Development of three-dimensional object completion in infancy. *Child Development*, *79*(5), 1230–1236.

Spelke, E. S. (1979). Perceiving bimodally specified events in infancy. *Developmental Psychology*, *15*(6), 626–636.

Streri, A. (1987). Tactile discrimination of shape and intermodal transfer in 2- to 3-month-old infants. *The British Journal of Developmental Psychology*, *5*(3), 213–220.

Streri, A., Lhote, M., & Dutilleul, S. (2000). Haptic perception in newborns. *Developmental Science*, *3*(3), 319–327.

Striano, T., & Bushnell, E. W. (2005). Haptic perception of material properties by 3-month-old infants. *Infant Behavior & Development*, *28*(3), 266–289.

Sugden, N. A., Mohamed-Ali, M. I., & Moulson, M. C. (2014). I spy with my little eye: Typical, daily exposure to faces documented from a first-person infant perspective. *Developmental Psychobiology*, *56*(2), 249–261.

Sugita, Y. (2004). Experience in early infancy is indispensable for color perception. *Current Biology: CB*, *14*(14), 1267–1271.

Sugita, Y. (2008). Face perception in monkeys reared with no exposure to faces. *Proceedings of the National Academy of Sciences of the United States of America*, *105*(1), 394–398.

Tacke, N. F., Bailey, L. S., & Clearfield, M. W. (2015). Socioeconomic status (SES) affects infants' selective exploration: SES and selectivity. *Infant and Child Development*, *24*(6), 571–586.

Tarquinio, N., Zelazo, P. R., & Weiss, M. J. (1990). Recovery of neonatal head turning to decreased sound pressure level. *Developmental Psychology*, *26*(5), 752–758.

Teller, D. Y. (1979). The forced-choice preferential looking procedure: A psychophysical technique for use with human infants. *Infant Behavior & Development*, *2*(2), 135–153.

Teller, D. Y., Morse, R., Borton, R., & Regal, D. (1974). Visual acuity for vertical and diagonal gratings in human infants. *Vision Research*, *14*(12), 1433–1439.

Trehub, S. E., & Hannon, E. E. (2006). Infant music perception: domain-general or domain-specific mechanisms? *Cognition*, *100*(1), 73–99.

Trinder, J., Newman, N. M., Le Grande, M., Whitworth, F., Kay, A., Pirkis, J., & Jordan, K. (1990). Behavioural and EEG responses to auditory stimuli during sleep in newborn infants and in infants aged 3 months. *Biological Psychology*, *31*(3), 213–227.

Volbrecht, V. J., & Werner, J. S. (1987). Isolation of short-wavelength-sensitive cone photoreceptors in 4-6-week-old human infants. *Vision Research*, *27*(3), 469–478.

Wagner, J. B., Keehn, B., Tager-Flusberg, H., & Nelson, C. A. (2020). Attentional bias to fearful faces in infants at high risk for autism spectrum disorder. *Emotion*, *20*(6), 980–992.

Wagner, J. B., Luyster, R. J., Tager-Flusberg, H., & Nelson, C. A. (2016). Greater pupil size in response to emotional faces as an early marker of social-communicative difficulties in infants at high risk for autism. *Infancy: The Official Journal*

of the International Society on Infant Studies, *21*(5), 560–581.

Werker, J. F. (1989). Becoming a native listener. *American Scientist*, *77*(1), 54–59.

Werker, J. F., & Tees, R. C. (1984). Cross-language speech perception: Evidence for perceptual reorganization during the first year of life. *Infant Behavior & Development*, *7*(1), 49–63.

Werker, J. F., Gilbert, J. H., Humphrey, K., & Tees, R. C. (1981). Developmental aspects of cross-language speech perception. *Child Development*, *52*(1), 349–355.

Yonas, A., Elieff, C. A., & Arterberry, M. E. (2002). Emergence of sensitivity to pictorial depth cues: Charting development in individual infants. *Infant Behavior & Development*, *25*(4), 495–514.

CHAPTER 5

Adolph, K. E. (1997). Learning in the development of infant locomotion. *Monographs of the Society for Research in Child Development*, *62*(3), I–1–VI.158.

Adolph, K. E., Cole, W. G., Komati, M., Garciaguirre, J. S., Badaly, D., Lingeman, J. M., Chan, G. L. Y., & Sotsky, R. B. (2012). How do you learn to walk? Thousands of steps and dozens of falls per day. *Psychological Science*, *23*(11), 1387–1394.

Adolph, K. E., Kretch, K. S., & LoBue, V. (2014). Fear of heights in infants? *Current Directions in Psychological Science*, *23*(1), 60–66.

Adolph, K. E., Rachwani, J., & Hoch, J. E. (2016). Motor and physical development: Locomotion. In J. Stein, D. Bennett, C. Coen, R. Dunbar, G. Goodwin, M. Husain, E. Mann, J. Morris, E. Rolls, J. S. H. Taylor & V. Walsh (Eds.), *The curated reference collection in neuroscience and biobehavioral psychology*, (pp. 359–373). Elsevier Science.

Adolph, K. E., & Robinson, S. R. (2013). The road to walking. In P. D. Zelazo (Ed.), *The Oxford handbook of developmental psychology: (Vol. 1). Body and mind*. Oxford University Press.

Adolph, K. E., Robinson, S. R., Young, J. W., & Gill-Alvarez, F. (2008). What is the shape of developmental change? *Psychological Review*, *115*(3), 527–543.

Bass, J. L., Gartley, T., & Kleinman, R. (2019). World Health Organization baby-friendly hospital initiative guideline and 2018 implementation guidance. *JAMA Pediatrics*, *173*(1), 93–94.

Bell, M. A., & Fox, N. A. (1996). Crawling experience is related to changes in cortical organization during infancy: Evidence from EEG coherence. *Developmental Psychobiology*, *29*(7), 551–561.

Bertenthal, B. I., & Bai, D. L. (1989). Infants' sensitivity to optical flow for controlling posture. *Developmental Psychology*, *25*(6), 936–945.

Campos, J. J. ., Anderson, D. I., Barbu-Roth, M. A., Hubbard, E. M., Hertenstein, M. J., & Witherington, D. (2000). Travel broadens the mind. *Infancy*, *1*(2), 149–219.

Campos, J. J., Bertenthal, B. I., & Kermoian, R. (1992). Early experience and emotional development: The emergence of wariness of heights. *Psychological Science, 3*(1), 61–64.

Cashon, C. H., Ha, O. R., Allen, C. L., & Barna, A. C. (2013). A U-shaped relation between sitting ability and upright face processing in infants. *Child Development, 84*(3), 802–809.

Czerwinski, S. A., Lee, M., Choh, A. C., Wurzbacher, K., Demerath, E. W., Towne, B., & Siervogel, R. M. (2007). Genetic factors in physical growth and development and their relationship to subsequent health outcomes. *American Journal of Human Biology: The Official Journal of the Human Biology Council, 19*(5), 684–691.

DeLoache, J. S., LoBue, V., Vanderborght, M., & Chiong, C. (2013). On the validity and robustness of the scale error phenomenon in early childhood. *Infant Behavior & Development, 36*(1), 63–70. https://doi.org/10.1016/j.infbeh.2012.10.007

DeLoache, J. S., Uttal, D. H., & Rosengren, K. S. (2004). Scale errors offer evidence for a perception-action dissociation early in life. *Science, 304*(5673), 1027–1029.

Doucleff, M. (2017, June 26). *Secrets of breast-feeding from global moms in the know.* National Public Radio.

Dubois, L., Ohm Kyvik, K., Girard, M., Tatone-Tokuda, F., Pérusse, D., Hjelmborg, J., Skytthe, A., Rasmussen, F., Wright, M. J., Lichtenstein, P., & Martin, N. G. (2012). Genetic and environmental

contributions to weight, height, and BMI from birth to 19 years of age: An international study of over 12,000 twin pairs. *PLOS ONE, 7*(2), e30153.

Embleton, N. E., Pang, N., & Cooke, R. J. (2001). Postnatal malnutrition and growth retardation: An inevitable consequence of current recommendations in preterm infants? *Pediatrics, 107*(2), 270–273.

Franchak, J. M. (2019). Changing opportunities for learning in everyday life: Infant body position over the first year. *Infancy: The Official Journal of the International Society on Infant Studies, 24*(2), 187–209.

Franchak, J. M., & Adolph, K. E. (2012). What infants know and what they do: Perceiving possibilities for walking through openings. *Developmental Psychology, 48*(5), 1254–1261.

Gesell, A. (1946). The ontogenesis of infant behavior. In L. Carmichael (Ed.), *Manual of child psychology* (pp. 295–331). John Wiley & Sons. https://doi.org/10.1037/10756-006

Guerrant, R. L., Oriá, R. B., Moore, S. R., Oriá, M. O. B., & Lima, A. A. M. (2008). Malnutrition as an enteric infectious disease with long-term effects on child development. *Nutrition Reviews, 66*(9), 487–505.

Herbert, J., Gross, J., & Hayne, H. (2007). Crawling is associated with more flexible memory retrieval by 9-month-old infants. *Developmental Science, 10*(2), 183–189.

Hewitt, L., Kerr, E., Stanley, R. M., & Okely, A. D. (2020). Tummy time and infant health

outcomes: A systematic review. *Pediatrics, 145*(6). https://doi.org/10.1542/peds.2019-2168

Higgins, C. I., Campos, J. J., & Kermoian, R. (1996). Effect of self-produced locomotion on infant postural compensation to optic flow. *Developmental Psychology, 32*(5), 836–841.

Hoddinott, P., Craig, L. C. A., Britten, J., & McInnes, R. M. (2012). A serial qualitative interview study of infant feeding experiences: Idealism meets realism. *BMJ Open, 2*(2), e000504.

Hopkins, B., & Westra, T. (1988). Maternal handling and motor development: An intracultural study. *Genetic, Social, and General Psychology Monographs, 114*(3), 377–408.

Karasik, L. B., Adolph, K. E., Fernandes, S. N., Robinson, S. R., & Tamis-LeMonda, C. S. (2023). Gahvora cradling in Tajikistan: Cultural practices and associations with motor development. *Child Development, 94*(4), 803–1086.

Karasik, L. B., Tamis-Lemonda, C. S., & Adolph, K. E. (2011). Transition from crawling to walking and infants' actions with objects and people. *Child Development, 82*(4), 1199–1209.

Karasik, L. B., Tamis-Lemonda, C. S., & Adolph, K. E. (2014). *Crawling and walking infants elicit different verbal responses from mothers.* 17(3), 388–395.

Karasik, L. B., Tamis-LeMonda, C. S., Adolph, K. E., & Bornstein, M. H. (2015). Places and postures: A cross-cultural comparison of sitting in 5-month-olds. *Journal of Cross-Cultural Psychology*, *46*(8), 1023–1038.

Karasik, L. B., Tamis-LeMonda, C. S., Ossmy, O., & Adolph, K. E. (2018). The ties that bind: Cradling in Tajikistan. *PLOS ONE*, *13*(10), e0204428.

Kretch, K. S., & Adolph, K. E. (2013). Cliff or step? Posture-specific learning at the edge of a drop-off. *Child Development*, *84*(1), 226–240.

Lampl, M. (1993). Evidence of saltatory growth in infancy. *American Journal of Human Biology: The Official Journal of the Human Biology Council*, *5*(6), 641–652.

Lampl, M. (2020). Infant physical growth. In J. B. Benson (Ed.), *Encyclopedia of infant and early childhood development* (2nd ed., pp. 170–182). Elsevier.

Lobo, M. A., & Galloway, J. C. (2012). Enhanced handling and positioning in early infancy advances development throughout the first year. *Child Development*, *83*(4), 1290–1302. https://doi.org/10.1111/j.1467-8624.2012.01772.x

LoBue, V., & Adolph, K. E. (2019). Fear in infancy: Lessons from snakes, spiders, heights, and strangers. *Developmental Psychology*, *55*, 1889–1907.

McGraw, M. B. (1935). *Growth: A study of Johnny and Jimmy.* (Preface by F. Tilney; Introduction by J. Dewey). https://psycnet.apa.org/fulltext/1935-06046-000.pdf

Merali, Z. (2009). Blasts from the past. *Scientific American*, *301*(1), 16–17, 20.

Mlakar, J., Korva, M., Tul, N., Popović, M., Poljšak-Prijatelj, M., Mraz, J., Kolenc, M., Resman Rus, K., Vesnaver, T. V., Fabjan. Vodušek, V., Vizjak, A., Pižem, J., Petrovec, M., & Avšič Županc, T. (2016). Zika virus associated with microcephaly. *New England Journal of Medicine*, *374*(10), 951–958.

Munn, A. C., Newman, S. D., Mueller, M., Phillips, S. M., & Taylor, S. N. (2016). The impact in the United States of the baby-friendly hospital initiative on early infant health and breastfeeding outcomes. *Breastfeeding Medicine: The Official Journal of the Academy of Breastfeeding Medicine*, *11*(5), 222–230.

Needham, A. W., Barrett, T. M., & Peterman, K. (2002). A pick me up for infants' exploratory skills: Early simulated experiences reaching for objects using "sticky" mittens enhances young infants' object exploration skills. *Infant Behavior & Development*, *25*(3), 279–295.

Oakes, L. M. (2017). Plasticity may change inputs as well as processes, structures, and responses. *Cognitive Development*, *42*, 4–14.

Rakison, D. H., & Krogh, L. (2012). Does causal action facilitate causal perception in infants younger than 6 months of age? *Developmental Science*, *15*(1), 43–53.

Ross-Sheehy, S., Perone, S., Vecera, S. P., & Oakes, L. M. (2016). The relationship between sitting and the use of symmetry as a cue to figure-ground assignment in 6.5-month-old infants.

Frontiers in Psychology, *7*(May), 1–10.

Section on Breastfeeding. (2012). Breastfeeding and the use of human milk. *Pediatrics*, *129*(3), e827–e841.

Shankar, K., Pivik, R. T., Johnson, S. L., van Ommen, B., Demmer, E., & Murray, R. (2018). Environmental forces that shape early development: What we know and still need to know. *Current Developments in Nutrition*, *2*(8), nzx002.

Slone, L. K., Moore, D. S., & Johnson, S. P. (2018). Object exploration facilitates 4-month-olds' mental rotation performance. *PLOS ONE*, *13*(8), e0200468.

Soska, K. C., & Johnson, S. P. (2008). Development of three-dimensional object completion in infancy. *Child Development*, *79*(5), 1230–1236.

Soska, K. C., Adolph, K. E., & Johnson, S. P. (2010). Systems in development: Motor skill acquisition facilitates 3D object completion. *Developmental Psychology*, *46*(1), 129–138.

Taylor, J. S., Risica, P. M., Geller, L., Kirtania, U., & Cabral, H. J. (2006). Duration of breastfeeding among first-time mothers in the United States: Results of a national survey. *Acta Paediatrica*, *95*(8), 980–984.

Thelen, E. (1996). The improvising infant: Learning about learning to move. In M. R. Merrens & G. G. Brannigan (Eds.), *The developmental psychologists: Research adventures across the life span* (pp. 21–35).

UNICEF. (2018). *Breastfeeding: A mother's gift, for every child.*

https://data.unicef.org/resources/breastfeeding-a-mothers-gift-for-every-child/

Wagner, E. A., Chantry, C. J., Dewey, K. G., & Nommsen-Rivers, L. A. (2013). Breast-feeding concerns at 3 and 7 days postpartum and feeding status at 2 months. *Pediatrics*, *132*(4), e865–e875. https://doi.org/10.1542/peds.2013-0724

Walle, E. A. (2016). Infant social development across the transition from crawling to walking. *Frontiers in Psychology*, *7*, 960.

Walle, E. A., & Campos, J. J. (2014). Infant language development is related to the acquisition of walking. *Developmental Psychology*, *50*(2), 336–348. https://doi.org/10.1037/a0033238

Zelazo, P. R., Zelazo, N. A., & Kolb, S. (1972). "Walking" in the newborn. *Science*. https://science.sciencemag.org/content/176/4032/314.abstract?casa_token=JAZEgxDSrk0AAAAA:qZiimVgpr6K_HY2LRDjJGLRQXwxUBcTtrU6O2y2Pxojchhb0lrkcq2a08hF-Gwg7TBPjthtb6EvzTFk

CHAPTER 6

Amso, D., Haas, S., & Markant, J. (2014). An eye tracking investigation of developmental change in bottom-up attention orienting to faces in cluttered natural scenes. *PLOS ONE*, *9*(1), e85701.

Arterberry, M. E., & Bornstein, M. H. (2012). Categorization of real and replica objects by 14- and 18-month-old infants.

Infant Behavior & Development, *35*(3), 606–612.

Bahrick, L. E., Gogate, L. J., & Ruiz, I. (2002). Attention and memory for faces and actions in infancy: The salience of actions over faces in dynamic events. *Child Development*, *73*(6), 1629–1643.

Barr, R., Dowden, A., & Hayne, H. (1996). Developmental changes in deferred imitation by 6- to 24-month-old infants. *Infant Behavior & Development*, *19*(2), 159–170.

Bauer, P. J., & Leventon, J. S. (2013). Memory for one-time experiences in the second year of life: Implications for the status of episodic memory. *Infancy: The Official Journal of the International Society on Infant Studies*, *18*(5), 755–781.

Behl-Chadha, G. (1996). Basic-level and superordinate-like categorical representations in early infancy. *Cognition*, *60*(2), 105–141. https://doi.org/10.1016/0010-0277(96)00706-8

Boller, K., Rovee-Collier, C., Gulya, M., & Prete, K. (1996). Infants' memory for context: Timing effects of postevent information. *Journal of Experimental Child Psychology*, *63*(3), 583–602.

Borchert, S., Lamm, B., Graf, F., & Knopf, M. (2013). Deferred imitation in 18-month-olds from two cultural contexts: The case of Cameroonian Nso farmer and German-middle class infants. *Infant Behavior & Development*, *36*(4), 717–727.

Borovsky, D., & Rovee-Collier, C. (1990). Contextual constraints on memory retrieval

at six months. *Child Development*, *61*(5), 1569–1583.

Brennan, W. M., Ames, E. W., & Moore, R. W. (1966). Age differences in infants' attention to patterns of different complexities. *Science*, *49*(3708), 354–356.

Bruck, M., & Ceci, S. J. (1999). The suggestibility of children's memory. *Annual Review of Psychology*, *50*(1), 419–439. https://doi.org/10.1146/annurev.psych.50.1.419

Casasola, M. (2005). When less is more: How infants learn to form an abstract categorical representation of support. *Child Development*, *76*(1), 279–290.

Casasola, M., Cohen, L. B., & Chiarello, E. (2003). Six-month-old infants' categorization of containment spatial relations. *Child Development*, *74*(3), 679–693.

Clearfield, M. W., & Jedd, K. E. (2013). The effects of socioeconomic status on infant attention. *Infant and Child Development*, *22*(1), 53–67.

Clerkin, E. M., Hart, E., Rehg, J. M., Yu, C., & Smith, L. B. (2017). Real-world visual statistics and infants' first-learned object names. *Philosophical Transactions of the Royal Society of London Series B, Biological Sciences*, *372*(1711). https://doi.org/10.1098/rstb.2016.0055,

Cohen, L. B. (1972). Attention-getting and attention-holding processes of infant visual preferences. *Child Development*, *43*(3), 869–879.

Cohn, J. F., Matias, R., Tronick, E. Z., Connell, D., & Lyons-Ruth, K. (1986). Face-to-face interactions of depressed mothers and their infants. *New Directions for Child and Adolescent Development*, 1986(34), 31–45. https://doi.org/10.1002/cd.23219863405

Colombo, J., Zavaleta, N., Kannass, K. N., Lazarte, F., Albornoz, C., Kapa, L. L., & Caulfield, L. E. (2014). Zinc supplementation sustained normative neurodevelopment in a randomized, controlled trial of Peruvian infants aged 6–18 months. *Journal of Nutrition*, 144(8), 1298–1305.

Courage, M. L., Reynolds, G. D., & Richards, J. E. (2006). Infants' attention to patterned stimuli: Developmental change from 3 to 12 months of age. *Child Development*, 77(3), 680–695.

Cousijn, J., Hessels, R. S., Van der Stigchel, S., & Kemner, C. (2017). Evaluation of the psychometric properties of the gap-overlap task in 10-month-old infants. *Infancy: The Official Journal of the International Society on Infant Studies*, 22(4), 1–9.

de Haan, M., Belsky, J., Reid, V., Volein, A., & Johnson, M. H. (2004). Maternal personality and infants' neural and visual responsivity to facial expressions of emotion. *Journal of Child Psychology and Psychiatry, and Allied Disciplines*, 45(7), 1209–1218.

DeNicola, C. A., Holt, N. A., Lambert, A. J., & Cashon, C. H. (2013). Attention-orienting and attention-holding effects of faces on 4- to 8-month-old infants. *International Journal of Behavioral Development*, 37(2), 143–147.

Eimas, P. D., & Quinn, P. C. (1994). Studies on the formation of perceptually based basic-level categories in young infants. *Child Development*, 65(3), 903–917.

Fagan, J. F. (1970). Memory in the infant. *Journal of Experimental Child Psychology*, 9(2), 217–226.

Familiar, I., Boivin, M., Magen, J., Azcorra, J. A., Phippen, C., Barrett, E. A., Miller, S., & Ruisenor-Escudero, H. (2021). Neurodevelopment outcomes in infants born to women with Zika virus infection during pregnancy in Mexico. *Child: Care, Health and Development*, 47(3), 311–318.

Ferguson, K. T., & Casasola, M. (2015). Are you an animal too? US and Malawian infants' categorization of plastic and wooden animal replicas. *Infancy: The Official Journal of the International Society on Infant Studies*, 20(2), 189–207.

Field, T. (1992). Infants of depressed mothers. *Development and Psychopathology*, 4(1), 49–66.

Gava, L., Valenza, E., & Turati, C. (2009). Newborns' perception of left-right spatial relations. *Child Development*, 80(6), 1797–1810.

Ghetti, S., Qin, J., & Goodman, G. S. (2002). False memories in children and adults: Age, distinctiveness, and subjective experience. *Developmental Psychology*, 38(5), 705–718. https://doi.org/10.1037/0012-1649.38.5.705

Gliga, T., Elsabbagh, M., Andravizou, A., & Johnson, M. (2009). Faces attract infants' attention in complex displays.

Infancy: The Official Journal of the International Society on Infant Studies. https://doi.org/10.1080/15250000903144199

Hayne, H., Rovee-Collier, C., & Perris, E. E. (1987). Categorization and memory retrieval by three-month-olds. *Memory*, 58(3), 750–767.

Hood, B. M., & Atkinson, J. (1993). Disengaging visual attention in the infant and adult. *Infant Behavior & Development*, 16(4), 405–422.

Horst, J. S., Ellis, A. E., Samuelson, L. K., Trejo, E., Worzalla, S. L., Peltan, J. R., & Oakes, L. M. (2009). Toddlers can adaptively change how they categorize: Same objects, same session, two different categorical distinctions. *Developmental Science*, 12(1), 96–105.

Jacobson, J. L., Jacobson, S. W., Muckle, G., Kaplan-Estrin, M., Ayotte, P., & Dewailly, E. (2008). Beneficial effects of a polyunsaturated fatty acid on infant development: Evidence from the Inuit of Arctic Quebec. *Journal of Pediatrics*, 152(3), 356–364.e1.

James, W. (1890). The perception of reality. In *Principles of psychology* (Vol. 2, pp. 283–324). Holt.

Jones, E. J. H., & Herbert, J. S. (2008). The effect of learning experiences and context on infant imitation and generalization. *Infancy: The Official Journal of the International Society on Infant Studies*, 13(6), 596–619.

Jones, E. J. H., Pascalis, O., Eacott, M. J., & Herbert, J. S. (2011). Visual recognition memory across contexts.

Developmental Science, 14(1), 136–147.

Kelly, D. J., Duarte, S., Meary, D., Bindemann, M., & Pascalis, O. (2019). Infants rapidly detect human faces in complex naturalistic visual scenes. *Developmental Science, 22*(6), e12829.

Kestenbaum, R., & Nelson, C. A. (1990). The recognition and categorization of upright and inverted emotional expressions by 7-month-old infants. *Infant Behavior & Development, 13*(4), 497–511.

Konishi, H., Pruden, S. M., Golinkoff, R. M., & Hirsh-Pasek, K. (2016). Categorization of dynamic realistic motion events: Infants form categories of path before manner. *Journal of Experimental Child Psychology, 152*, 54–70.

Kovack-Lesh, K. A., Horst, J. S., & Oakes, L. M. (2008). The cat is out of the bag: The joint influence of previous experience and looking behavior on infant categorization. *Infancy: The Official Journal of the International Society on Infant Studies, 13*(4), 285–307.

Kovack-Lesh, K. A., & Oakes, L. M. (2007). Hold your horses: How exposure to different items influences infant categorization. *Journal of Experimental Child Psychology, 98*(2), 69–93. https://doi.org/10.1016/j.jecp.2007.05.001,

Kwon, M.-K., Setoodehnia, M., Baek, J., Luck, S. J., & Oakes, L. M. (2016). The development of visual search in infancy: Attention to faces versus salience. *Developmental Psychology, 52*(4), 537–555.

Lakusta, L., & Carey, S. (2015). Twelve-month-old infants' encoding of goal and source paths in agentive and non-agentive motion events. *Language Learning and Development: The Official Journal of the Society for Language Development, 11*(2), 152–157.

Legare, C. H. (2019). The development of cumulative cultural learning. *Annual Review of Developmental Psychology, 1*(1), 119–147.

Leppänen, J. M., Moulson, M. C., Vogel-Farley, V. K., & Nelson, C. A. (2007). An ERP study of emotional face processing in the adult and infant brain. *Child Development, 78*(1), 232–245.

LoBue, V., Buss, K. A., Taber-Thomas, B. C., & Perez-Edgar, K. (2017). Developmental differences in infants' Attention to social and nonsocial threats. *Infancy: The Official Journal of the International Society on Infant Studies, 22*(3), 403–415.

LoBue, V., & DeLoache, J. S. (2010). Superior detection of threat-relevant stimuli in infancy. *Developmental Science, 13*(1), 221–228.

Mandler, J. M., Bauer, P. J., & McDonough, L. (1991). Separating the sheep from the goats: Differentiating global categories. *Cognitive Psychology, 23*(2), 263–298.

Mandler, J. M., Fivush, R., & Reznick, J. S. (1987). The development of contextual categories. *Cognitive Development, 2*(4), 339–354.

Mandler, J. M., & McDonough, L. (1996). Drinking and driving don't mix: Inductive generalization in infancy. *Cognition, 59*(3), 307–335.

Marinović, V., Hoehl, S., & Pauen, S. (2014). Neural correlates of human-animal distinction: An ERP-study on early categorical differentiation with 4- and 7-month-old infants and adults. *Neuropsychologia, 60*(1), 60–76.

Meltzoff, A. N. (1988). Infant imitation after a 1-week delay: Long-term memory for novel acts and multiple stimuli. *Developmental Psychology, 24*(4), 470–476.

Meltzoff, A. N. (1995). What infant memory tells us about infantile amnesia: Long-term recall and deferred imitation. *Journal of Experimental Child Psychology, 59*(3), 497–515.

Merz, E. C., McDonough, L., Huang, Y. L., Foss, S., Werner, E., & Monk, C. (2017). The mobile conjugate reinforcement paradigm in a lab setting. *Developmental Psychobiology, 59*(5), 668–672.

Mooney, L. N., Johnson, E. G., Prabhakar, J., & Ghetti, S. (2021). Memory-related hippocampal activation during sleep and temporal memory in toddlers. *Developmental Cognitive Neuroscience, 47*, 100908.

Muir, D., & Field, J. (1979). Newborn infants orient to sounds. *Child Development, 50*(2), 431–436.

Nakagawa, A., & Sukigara, M. (2019). Early development of attentional disengagement and phasic alertness. *Infant Behavior & Development, 55*, 38–45.

Nelson, C. A., & De Haan, M. (1996). Neural correlates of infants' visual responsiveness to facial expressions of emotion. *Developmental Psychobiology, 29*(7), 577–595.

Oakes, L. M., Baumgartner, H. A., Barrett, F. S., Messenger, I. M., & Luck, S. J. (2013). Developmental changes in visual short-term memory in infancy: Evidence from eye-tracking. *Frontiers in Psychology, 4*(October). https://doi.org/10.3389/fpsyg.2013.00697

Oakes, L. M., Coppage, D. J., & Dingel, A. (1997). By land or by sea: The role of perceptual similarity in infants' categorization of animals. *Developmental Psychology, 33*(3), 396–407. https://doi.org/10.1037/0012-1649.33.3.396

Oakes, L. M., Kannass, K. N., & Shaddy, D. J. (2002). Developmental changes in endogenous control of attention: The role of target familiarity on infants' distraction latency. *Child Development, 73*(6), 1644–1655.

Oakes, L. M., & Ribar, R. J. (2005). A comparison of infants' categorization in paired and successive presentation familiarization tasks. *Infancy: The Official Journal of the International Society on Infant Studies, 7*(1), 85–98.

Oakes, L. M., & Tellinghuisen, D. J. (1994). Examining in infancy: Does it reflect active processing? *Developmental Psychology, 30*(5), 748–756. https://doi.org/10.1037/0012-1649.30.5.748

Peltola, M. J., Leppänen, J. M., Mäki, S., & Hietanen, J. K. (2009). Emergence of enhanced attention to fearful faces between 5 and 7 months of age. *Social Cognitive and Affective Neuroscience, 4*(2), 134–142. https://doi.org/10.1093/scan/nsn046

Peltola, M. J., Leppänen, J. M., Palokangas, T., & Hietanen, J. K. (2008). Fearful faces modulate looking duration and attention disengagement in 7-month-old infants. *Developmental Science, 11*(1), 60–68. https://doi.org/10.1111/j.1467-7687.2007.00659.x

Peltola, M. J., Leppänen, J. M., Vogel-Farley, V. K., Hietanen, J. K., & Nelson, C. A. (2009). Fearful faces but not fearful eyes alone delay attention disengagement in 7-month-old infants. *Emotion, 9*(4), 560–565.

Perris, E. E., Myers, N. A., & Clifton, R. K. (1990). Long-term memory for a single infancy experience. *Child Development, 61*(6), 1796–1807.

Pruden, S. M., Göksun, T., Roseberry, S., Hirsh-Pasek, K., & Golinkoff, R. M. (2012). Find your manners: How do infants detect the invariant manner of motion in dynamic events? *Child Development, 83*(3), 977–991.

Pruden, S. M., Roseberry, S., Göksun, T., Hirsh-Pasek, K., & Golinkoff, R. M. (2013). Infant categorization of path relations during dynamic events. *Child Development, 84*(1), 331–345.

Pyykkö, J., Forssman, L., Maleta, K., Ashorn, P., Ashorn, U., & Leppänen, J. M. (2019). Early development of visual attention in infants in rural Malawi. *Developmental Science, 22*(5), e12761.

Quinn, P. C. (1994). The categorization of above and below spatial relations by young infants. *Child Development, 65*(1), 58–69.

Quinn, P. C., Adams, A., Kennedy, E., Shettler, L., & Wasnik, A. (2003). Development of an abstract category representation for the spatial relation between in 6- to 10-month-old infants. *Developmental Psychology, 39*(1), 151–163.

Quinn, P. C., Doran, M. M., & Papafragou, A. (2011). Does changing the reference frame affect infant categorization of the spatial relation BETWEEN? *Journal of Experimental Child Psychology, 109*(1), 109–122.

Quinn, P. C., Eimas, P. D., & Rosenkrantz, S. L. (1993). Evidence for representations of perceptually similar natural categories by 3 and 4 month old infants. *Perception, 22*(4), 463–475.

Quinn, P. C., & Johnson, M. H. (2000). Global-before-basic object categorization in connectionist networks and 2-month-old infants. *Infancy: The Official Journal of the International Society on Infant Studies, 1*(1), 31–46.

Quinn, P. C., Yahr, J., Kuhn, A., Slater, A. M., & Pascalis, O. (2002). Representation of the gender of human faces by infants: A preference for female. *Perception, 31*(9), 1109–1121.

Rakison, D. H. (2007). Inductive categorization: A methodology to examine the basis for categorization and induction in infancy [Special issue]. *Cognitie Creier Comportament / The Development of Categorization, 11*(4), 773–790.

Rakison, D. H., & Butterworth, G. E. (1998). Infants' use of object parts in early categorization. *Developmental Psychology*, *34*(1), 49–62.

Rennels, J. L., & Kayl, A. J. (2017). How experience affects infants' facial categorization. In *Handbook of categorization in cognitive science* (Vol. 331, pp. 637–652). Elsevier.

Rennels, J. L., Kayl, A. J., Langlois, J. H., Davis, R. E., & Orlewicz, M. (2016). Asymmetries in infants' attention toward and categorization of male faces: The potential role of experience. *Journal of Experimental Child Psychology*, *142*, 137–157.

Rigney, J., & Wang, S.-H. (2015). Delineating the boundaries of infants' spatial categories: The case of containment. *Journal of Cognition and Development: Official Journal of the Cognitive Development Society*, *16*(3), 420–441.

Rose, S. A. (1981). Developmental changes in infants' retention of visual stimuli. *Child Development*, *52*(1), 227–233.

Ross, G. S. (1980). Categorization in 1- to 2-yr-olds. *Developmental Psychology*, *16*(5), 391–396.

Ross-Sheehy, S., & Eschman, B. (2019). Assessing visual STM in infants and adults: Eye movements and pupil dynamics reflect memory maintenance. *Visual Cognition*, *27*(1), 1–15.

Rovee-Collier, C. (1999). The development of infant memory. *Current Directions in Psychological Science*, *8*(3), 80–85.

Ruba, A. L., Johnson, K. M., Harris, L. T., & Wilbourn, M. P. (2017). Developmental changes in infants' categorization of anger and disgust facial expressions. *Developmental Psychology*, *53*(10), 1826–1832.

Schröder, L., Kärtner, J., Keller, H., & Chaudhary, N. (2012). Sticking out and fitting in: Culture-specific predictors of 3-year-olds' autobiographical memories during joint reminiscing. *Infant Behavior & Development*, *35*(4), 627–634.

Singh, L., Fu, C. S. L., Rahman, A. A., Hameed, W. B., Sanmugam, S., Agarwal, P., Jiang, B., Chong, Y. S., Meaney, M. J., Rifkin-Graboi, A., & GUSTO, Research Team. (2015). Back to basics: A bilingual advantage in infant visual habituation. *Child Development*, *86*(1), 294–302.

Siqueiros Sanchez, S. M., Ronald, A., Mason, L., Jones, E. J. H., Bölte, S., & Falck-Ytter, T. (2021). Visual disengagement in young infants in relation to age, sex, SES, developmental level and adaptive functioning. *Infant Behavior & Development*, *63*, 101555.

Song, L., Pruden, S. M., Golinkoff, R. M., & Hirsh-Pasek, K. (2016). Prelinguistic foundations of verb learning: Infants discriminate and categorize dynamic human actions. *Journal of Experimental Child Psychology*, *151*, 77–95.

Taniguchi, K., Tanabe-Ishibashi, A., & Itakura, S. (2020). The categorization of objects with uniform texture at superordinate and living/non-living levels in infants: An exploratory study. *Frontiers in Psychology*, *11*, 2009.

Tellinghuisen, D. J., & Oakes, L. M. (1997). Distractibility in infancy: The effects of distractor characteristics and type of attention. *Journal of Experimental Child Psychology*, *64*(2), 232–254.

Turati, C., Simion, F., & Zanon, L. (2003). Newborns' perceptual categorization for closed and open geometric forms. *Infancy: The Official Journal of the International Society on Infant Studies*, *4*(3), 309–325.

Turati, C., Valenza, E., Leo, I., & Simion, F. (2005). Three-month-olds' visual preference for faces and its underlying visual processing mechanisms. *Journal of Experimental Child Psychology*, *90*(3), 255–273.

Wang, Q. (2003). Infantile amnesia reconsidered: A cross-cultural analysis. *Memory*, *11*(1), 65–80.

Waxman, S. R., Fu, X., Ferguson, B., Geraghty, K., Leddon, E., Liang, J., & Zhao, M.-F. (2016). How early is infants' attention to objects and actions shaped by culture? New evidence from 24-month-olds raised in the US and China. *Frontiers in Psychology*, *7*, 97. https://doi.org/10.3389/fpsyg.2016.00097

CHAPTER 7

Acredolo, L. P. (1978). Development of spatial orientation in infancy. *Developmental Psychology*, *14*(3), 224–234.

Acredolo, L. P. (1979). Laboratory versus home: The effect of environment on the 9-month-old infant's choice of spatial reference system. *Developmental Psychology, 15*(6), 666–667.

Acredolo, L. P., Adams, A., & Goodwyn, S. W. (1984). The role of self-produced movement and visual tracking in infant spatial orientation. *Journal of Experimental Child Psychology, 38*(2), 312–327.

Ankowski, A. A., Thom, E. E., Sandhofer, C. M., & Blaisdell, A. P. (2012). Spatial language and children's spatial landmark use. In *Child Development Research, 2012,* 1–14. https://doi.org/10.1155/2012/427364,

Antell, S. E. G., & Caron, A. J. (1985). Neonatal perception of spatial relationships. *Infant Behavior & Development, 8*(1), 15–23.

Bornstein, M. H., Hahn, C.-S., & Suwalsky, J. T. D. (2013). Physically developed and exploratory young infants contribute to their own long-term academic achievement. *Psychological Science, 24*(10), 1906–1917.

Bourgeois, K. S., Khawar, A. W., Neal, S. A., & Lockman, J. J. (2005). Infant manual exploration of objects, surfaces, and their interrelations. *Infancy: The Official Journal of the International Society on Infant Studies, 8*(3), 233–252.

Brannon, E. M., Abbott, S., & Lutz, D. J. (2004). Number bias for the discrimination of large visual sets in infancy. *Cognitive Psychology, 93*(2), B59–B68.

Bremner, J. G. (1978). Egocentric versus allocentric spatial coding in nine-month-old infants: Factors influencing the choice of code.

Developmental Psychology, 14(4), 346–355.

Bremner, J. G. (1985). Object tracking and search in infancy: A review of data and a theoretical evaluation. *Developmental Review, 5*(4), 371–396.

Campos, J. J., Anderson, I. D., Barbu-Roth, M. A., Hubbard, E. M., Hertenstein, M. J., & Witherington, D. (2000). Travel broadens the mind. *Infancy: The Official Journal of the International Society on Infant Studies, 1*(2), 149–219.

Casasola, M. (2008). The development of infants' spatial categories. *Current Directions in Psychological Science, 17*(1), 21–25. https://doi,org/10.1111/j.1467-8721.2008.00541.x

Casasola, M., & Ahn, Y. A. (2018). What develops in infants' spatial categorization? Korean infants' categorization of containment and tight-fit relations. *Child Development, 89*(4), e382–e396. https://doi.org/10.1111/cdev.12903

Casasola, M., & Cohen, L. B. (2002). Infant categorization of containment, support and tight-fit spatial relationships. *Developmental Science, 5*(2), 247–264. https://doi.org/10.1111/1467-7687.00226

Chavajay, P., & Rogoff, B. (1999). Cultural variation in management of attention by children and their caregivers. *Developmental Psychology, 35*(4), 1079–1090.

Chavajay, P., & Rogoff, B. (2002). Schooling and traditional collaborative social organization of problem solving by Mayan mothers and children. *Developmental Psychology, 38*(1), 55–66.

Cheng, K. (1986). A purely geometric module in the rat's spatial representation. *Cognition, 23*(2), 149–178.

Clearfield, M. W. (2004). The role of crawling and walking experience in infant spatial memory. *Journal of Experimental Child Psychology, 89*(3), 214–241.

Clearfield, M. W., & Mix, K. S. (1999). Number versus contour length in infants' discrimination of small visual sets. *Psychological Science, 10*(5), 408–411.

Cohen, L. B., & Oakes, L. M. (1993). How infants perceive a simple causal event. *Developmental Psychology, 29*(3), 421–433.

Cohen, L. B., & Younger, B. A. (1984). Infant perception of angular relations. *Infant Behavior & Development, 7*(1), 37–47.

Constantinescu, M., Moore, D. S., Johnson, S. P., & Hines, M. (2018). Early contributions to infants' mental rotation abilities. *Developmental Science, 21*(4), e12613.

Correa-Chávez, M., & Rogoff, B. (2009). Children's attention to interactions directed to others: Guatemalan Mayan and European American patterns. *Developmental Psychology, 45*(3), 630–641.

Dehaene, S., Izard, V., Pica, P., & Spelke, E. (2006). Core knowledge of geometry in an Amazonian indigene group. *Science, 311*(5759), 381–384.

Dillon, M. R., Izard, V., & Spelke, E. S. (2020). Infants' sensitivity to shape changes in 2D visual forms. *Infancy: The Official Journal of the*

International Society on Infant Studies, 25(5), 618–639.

Feigenson, L., Carey, S., & Spelke, E. S. (2002). Infants' discrimination of number vs. continuous extent. *Cognitive Psychology, 44*(1), 33–66.

Feigenson, L., Dehaene, S., & Spelke, E. S. (2004). Core systems of number. *Trends in Cognitive Sciences, 8*(7), 307–314.

Frick, A., & Möhring, W. (2013). Mental object rotation and motor development in 8- and 10-month-old infants. *Journal of Experimental Child Psychology, 115*(4), 708–720.

Gallistel, C. R., & Gelman, R. (1992). Preverbal and verbal counting and computation. *Cognition, 44*(1–2), 43–74.

Gava, L., Valenza, E., & Turati, C. (2009). Newborns' perception of left-right spatial relations. *Child Development, 80*(6), 1797–1810.

Gerhard, T. M., & Schwarzer, G. (2018). Impact of rotation angle on crawling and non-crawling 9-month-old infants' mental rotation ability. *Journal of Experimental Child Psychology, 170*, 45–56.

Gerhard-Samunda, T. M., Jovanovic, B., & Schwarzer, G. (2021). Role of manually-generated visual cues in crawling and non-crawling 9-month-old infants' mental rotation. *Cognitive Development, 59*, 101053.

Hermer, L., & Spelke, E. S. (1994). A geometric process for spatial reorientation in young children. *Nature, 370*(6484), 57–59.

Hermer, L., & Spelke, E. (1996). Modularity and development:

The case of spatial reorientation. *Cognition, 61*(3), 195–232.

Hespos, S. J., & Baillargeon, R. (2001). Reasoning about containment events in very young infants. *Cognition, 78*(3), 207–245.

Hespos, S. J., & Baillargeon, R. (2008). Young infants' actions reveal their developing knowledge of support variables: Converging evidence for violation-of-expectation findings. *Cognitive Psychology, 107*(1), 304–316.

Hespos, S. J., & Rips, L. J. (2009). Five-month-old infants have different expectations for solids and liquids. *Psychological Science, 20*(5), 603–611.

Hood, B. M., & Willatts, P. (1986). Reaching in the dark to an object's remembered position: Evidence for object permanence in 5-month-old infants. *British Journal of Developmental Psychology, 4*(1), 57–65.

Izard, V., Pica, P., Spelke, E. S., & Dehaene, S. (2011). Flexible intuitions of Euclidean geometry in an Amazonian indigene group. *Proceedings of the National Academy of Sciences of the United States of America, 108*(24), 9782–9787.

Jordan, K. E., & Brannon, E. M. (2006). The multisensory representation of number in infancy. *Proceedings of the National Academy of Sciences of the United States of America, 103*(9), 3486–3489.

Kaufman, J., & Needham, A. W. (2011). Spatial expectations of young human infants, following passive movement. *Developmental Psychobiology, 53*(1), 23–36.

Kermoian, R., & Campos, J. J. (1988). Locomotor experience: A facilitator of spatial cognitive development. *Child Development, 59*(4), 908–917.

Landau, B., Spelke, E., & Gleitman, H. (1984). Spatial knowledge in a young blind child. *Cognition, 16*(3), 225–260.

Le Corre, M., Li, P., Huang, B. H., Jia, G., & Carey, S. (2016). Numerical morphology supports early number word learning: Evidence from a comparison of young Mandarin and English learners. *Cognitive Psychology, 88*, 162–186.

Learmonth, A. E., Newcombe, N. S., & Huttenlocher, J. (2001). Toddlers' use of metric information and landmarks to reorient. *Journal of Experimental Child Psychology, 80*(3), 225–244.

Leslie, A. M. (1982). The perception of causality in infants. *Perception, 11*(2), 173–186.

Leslie, A. M., & Keeble, S. (1987). Do six-month-old infants perceive causality? *Cognition, 25*(3), 265–288.

Lew, A. R., Bremner, J. G., & Lefkovitch, L. P. (2000). The development of relational landmark use in six- to twelve-month-old infants in a spatial orientation task. *Child Development, 71*(5), 1179–1190.

Lew, A. R., Foster, K. A., & Bremner, J. G. (2006). Disorientation inhibits landmark use in 12–18-month-old infants. *Infant Behavior & Development, 29*(3), 334–341.

Lew, A. R., Foster, K. A., Crowther, H. L., & Green, M. (2004). Indirect landmark use at 6 months of age in a spatial orientation task. *Infant*

Behavior & Development, 27(1), 81–90.

Lukyanenko, C., & Fisher, C. (2016). Where are the cookies? Two- and three-year-olds use number-marked verbs to anticipate upcoming nouns. *Cognition, 146,* 349–370.

Martolini, C., Cappagli, G., Saligari, E., Gori, M., & Signorini, S. (2021). Allocentric spatial perception through vision and touch in sighted and blind children. *Journal of Experimental Child Psychology, 210,* 105195.

Miller, K. F., Smith, C. M., Zhu, J., & Zhang, H. (1995). Preschool origins of cross-national differences in mathematical competence: The role of number-naming systems. *Psychological Science, 6*(1), 56–60.

Möhring, W., & Frick, A. (2013). Touching up mental rotation: Effects of manual experience on 6-month-old infants' mental object rotation. *Child Development, 84*(5), 1554–1565.

Moore, D. S., & Johnson, S. P. (2008). Mental rotation in human infants. *Psychological Science, 19*(1), 1063–1066. https://doi.org/10.1111/j.1467-9280.2008.02200.x

Moore, D. S., & Johnson, S. P. (2020). The development of mental rotation ability across the first year after birth. *Advances in Child Development and Behavior, 58,* 1–33.

Moral, A., Bolibar, I., Seguranyes, G., Ustrell, J. M., Sebastiá, G., Martínez-Barba, C., & Ríos, J. (2010). Mechanics of sucking: Comparison between bottle feeding and breastfeeding. *BMC Pediatrics, 10*(1), 6.

Nardini, M., Atkinson, J., & Burgess, N. (2008). Children reorient using the left/right sense of coloured landmarks at 18–24 months. *Cognition, 106*(1), 519–527.

Needham, A., & Baillargeon, R. (1993). Intuitions about support in 4.5-month-old infants. *Cognition, 47*(2), 121–148.

Newcombe, N., Huttenlocher, J., & Learmonth, A. (1999). Infants' coding of location in continuous space. *Infant Behavior & Development, 22*(4), 483–510.

Oakes, L. M. (1994). Development of infants' use of continuity cues in their perception of causality. *Developmental Psychology, 30*(6), 869–879.

Oakes, L. M., & Cohen, L. B. (1990). Infant perception of a causal event. *Cognitive Development, 5*(2), 193–207.

Quinn, P. C., Adams, A., Kenned., E., Shettler, L., & Wasnik, A. (2003). Development of an abstract category representation for the spatial relation between in 6- to 10-month-old infants. *Developmental Psychology, 39*(1), 151–163. https://doi.org/10.1037/0012-1649.39.1.151

Quinn, P. C., Cummins, M., Kase, J., Martin, E., & Weissman, S. (1996). Development of categorical representations for above and below spatial relations in 3- to 7-month-old infants. *Developmental Psychology, 32*(5), 942–950. https://doi.org/10.1037/0012-1649.32.5.942

Quinn, P. C., & Liben, L. S. (2008). A sex difference in mental rotation in young infants. *Psychological Science, 19*(11), 1067–1070. https://doi.org/10.1111/j.1467-9280.2008.02201.x

Quinn, P. C., & Liben, L. S. (2014). A sex difference in mental rotation in infants: Convergent evidence. *Infancy: The Official Journal of the International Society on Infant Studies, 19*(1), 103–116.

Rogoff, B., Dahl, A., & Callanan, M. (2018). The importance of understanding children's lived experience. *Developmental Review, 50,* 5–15.

Rose, S. A., Feldman, J. F., Jankowski, J. J., & Van Rossem, R. (2005). Pathways from prematurity and infant abilities to later cognition. *Child Development, 76*(6), 1172–1184.

Sarnecka, B. W., & Carey, S. (2008). How counting represents number: What children must learn and when they learn it. *Cognition, 108*(3), 662–674.

Schwarzer, G., Freitag, C., & Schum, N. (2013). How crawling and manual object exploration are related to the mental rotation abilities of 9-month-old infants. *Frontiers in Psychology, 4,* 97.

Schwarzer, G., Freitag, C., Buckel, R., & Lofruthe, A. (2013). Crawling is associated with mental rotation ability by 9-month-old infants. *Infancy: The Official Journal of the International Society on Infant Studies, 18*(3), 432–441.

Shusterman, A., Lee, S. A., & Spelke, E. S. (2011). Cognitive effects of language on human navigation. *Cognition, 120*(2), 186–201.

Simms, N. K., & Gentner, D. (2019). Finding the middle: Spatial language and spatial reasoning. *Cognitive Development, 50*, 177–194.

Slater, A., Mattock, A., Brown, E., & Bremner, J. G. (1991). Form perception at birth: Revisited. *Journal of Experimental Child Psychology, 51*(3), 395–406.

Slaughter, V., Itakura, S., Kutsuki, A., & Siegal, M. (2011). Learning to count begins in infancy: Evidence from 18 month olds' visual preferences. *Proceedings of the Royal Society, Biological Sciences, 278*, 1720(278), 2979–2984.

Slone, L. K., Moore, D. S., & Johnson, S. P. (2018). Object exploration facilitates 4-month-olds' mental rotation performance. *PLOS ONE, 13*(8), e0200468.

Soska, K. C., Adolph, K. E., & Johnson, S. P. (2010). Systems in development: Motor skill acquisition facilitates three-dimensional object completion. *Developmental Psychology, 46*(1), 129–138.

Soska, K. C., Robinson, S. R., & Adolph, K. E. (2015). A new twist on old ideas: How sitting reorients crawlers. *Developmental Science, 18*(2), 206–218.

Spelke, E. S. (2000). Core knowledge. *The American Psychologist, 55*(11), 1233–1243.

Spelke, E. S., Breinlinger, K., Macomber, J., & Jacobson, K. (1992). Origins of knowledge. *Psychological Review, 99*(4), 605–632.

Spelke, E. S., & Kinzler, K. D. (2007). Core knowledge. *Developmental Science, 10*(1), 89–96.

Starkey, P., & Cooper, R. G. (1980). Perception of numbers by human infants. *Science, 210*(4473), 1033–1035.

Starkey, P., Spelke, E. S., & Gelman, R. (1990). Numerical abstraction by human infants. *Cognitive Psychology, 36*(2), 97–127.

Vasilyeva, M., & Lourenco, S. F. (2012). Development of spatial cognition. *Wiley Interdisciplinary Reviews. Cognitive Science, 3*(3), 349–362.

Villarroel, J. D., Miñón, M., & Nuño, T. (2011). The origin of counting: A study of the early meaning of "one," "two" and "three" among Basque- and Spanish-speaking children. *Educational Studies in Mathematics, 76*(3), 345–361.

Vygotsky, L. S. (1980). *Mind in society: The development of higher psychological processes.* Harvard University Press.

Wood, J. N., & Wood, S. M. W. (2016). The development of newborn object recognition in fast and slow visual worlds. *Proceedings of the Royal Society, Biological Sciences, 283*(1829), https://doi.org/10.1098/rspb.2016.0166,

Wynn, K. (1998). Psychological foundations of number: Numerical competence in human infants. *Trends in Cognitive Sciences, 2*(8), 296–303.

Xu, F., & Spelke, E. S. (2000). Large number discrimination in 6-month-old infants. *Cognitive Psychology, 74*(1), B1–B11.

CHAPTER 8

Abels, M., Papaligoura, Z., Lamm, B., & Yovsi, R. D. (2017). How usual is "play as you usually would"? A comparison of naturalistic mother-infant interactions with video-recorded play sessions in three cultural communities. *Child Development Research, 2017*(5), 1–8. https://doi.org/10.1155/2017/7842030

Baillargeon, R. (1987). Young infants' reasoning about the physical and spatial properties of a hidden object. *Cognitive Development, 2*(3), 179–200.

Bakeman, R., Adamson, L. B., Konner, M., & Barr, R. G. (1990). Kung infancy: The social context of object exploration. *Child Development, 61*(3), 794–809.

Baron-Cohen, S. (1987). Autism and symbolic play. *British Journal of Developmental Psychology, 5*(2), 139–148.

Barr, R., Muentener, P., Garcia, A., Fujimoto, M., & Chávez, V. (2007). The effect of repetition on imitation from television during infancy. *Developmental Psychobiology, 49*(2), 196–207.

Baumgartner, H. A., & Oakes, L. M. (2013). Investigating the relation between infants' manual activity with objects and their perception of dynamic events. *Infancy: The Official Journal of the International Society on Infant Studies, 18*(6), 983–1006.

Belsky, J., & Most, R. K. (1981). From exploration to play: A cross-sectional study of infant free play behavior. *Developmental Psychology, 17*(5), 630–639.

Bornstein, M. H., Haynes, O. M., Pascual, L., Painter, K. M., & Galperín, C. (1999). Play in two societies: Pervasiveness of process, specificity of structure. *Child Development, 70*(2), 317–331.

Bosco, F. M., Friedman, O., & Leslie, A. M. (2006). Recognition of pretend and real actions in play by 1- and 2-year-olds: Early success and why they fail. *Cognitive Development, 21*(1), 3–10.

Bourgeois, K. S., Khawar, A. W., Neal, S. A., & Lockman, J. J. (2005). Infant manual exploration of objects, surfaces, and their interrelations. *Infancy: The Official Journal of the International Society on Infant Studies, 8*(3), 233–252.

Brown, S. L. (2009). *Play: How it shapes the brain, opens the imagination, and invigorates the soul.* Penguin.

Bruner, J. (1983). Play, thought, and language. *Peabody Journal of Education, 60*(3), 60–69.

Bruner, J. S., Sherwood, V., Jolly, A., & Sylva, K. (1976). Early rule structure: The case of peekaboo. In *Readings on the Development of Children* (pp. 71–75).

Burgdorf, J., Kroes, R. A., Beinfeld, M. C., Panksepp, J., & Moskal, J. R. (2010). Uncovering the molecular basis of positive affect using rough-and-tumble play in rats: A role for insulin-like growth factor I. *Neuroscience, 168*(3), 769–777.

Bushnell, E. W., & Boudreau, J. P. (1993). Motor development and the mind: the potential role of motor abilities as a determinant of aspects of

perceptual development. *Child Development, 64*(4), 1005–1021.

Butterworth, G. (1977). Object disappearance and error in Piaget's stage IV task. *Journal of Experimental Child Psychology, 23*(3), 391–401.

Callaghan, T., Moll, H., Rakoczy, H., Warneken, F., Liszkowski, U., Behne, T., & Tomasello, M. (2011). Early social cognition in three cultural contexts. *Monographs of the Society for Research in Child Development, 76*(2), vii-1–viii.142.

Campbell, S. B., Mahoney, A. S., Northrup, J., Moore, E. L., Leezenbaum, N. B., & Brownell, C. A. (2018). Developmental changes in pretend play from 22- to 34-months in younger siblings of children with autism spectrum disorder. *Journal of Abnormal Child Psychology, 46*(3), 639–654.

Casasola, M., Bhagwat, J., Doan, S. N., & Love, H. (2017). Getting some space: Infants' and caregivers' containment and support spatial constructions during play. *Journal of Experimental Child Psychology, 159*, 110–128. https://www.sciencedirect.com/science/article/pii/S0022096517300553

Clearfield, M. W. (2019). Play for success: An intervention to boost object exploration in infants from low-income households. *Infant Behavior & Development, 55*, 112–122.

Clearfield, M. W., Bailey, L. S., Jenne, H. K., Stanger, S. B., & Tacke, N. (2014). Socioeconomic status affects oral and manual exploration across the first year. *Infant Mental Health Journal, 35*(1), 63–69.

Clerkin, E. M., Hart, E., Rehg, J. M., Yu, C., & Smith, L. B. (2017). Real-world visual statistics and infants' first-learned object names. *Philosophical Transactions of the Royal Society of London. Series B, Biological Sciences, 372*(1711), https://doi.org/10.1098/rstb.2016.0055,

Corrigan, R. (1978). Language development as related to stage 6 object permanence development. *Journal of Child Language, 5*(2), 173–189.

Cote, L. R., & Bornstein, M. H. (2009). Child and mother play in three U.S. cultural groups: Comparisons and associations. *Journal of Family Psychology: JFP:. Journal of the Division of Family Psychology of the American Psychological Association, 23*(3), 355–363.

Council on Early, Childhood., High, P. C., & Klass, P. (2014). Literacy promotion: An essential component of primary care pediatric practice. *Pediatrics, 134*(2), 404–409.

Creaghe, N., Quinn, S., & Kidd, E. (2021). Symbolic play provides a fertile context for language development. *Infancy: The Official Journal of the International Society on Infant Studies*, 1–31.

de Barbaro, K., Johnson, C. M., Forster, D., & Deák, G. O. (2016). Sensorimotor decoupling contributes to triadic attention: A longitudinal investigation of mother-infant-object interactions. *Child Development, 87*(2), 494–512.

DeLoache, J. S. (1987). Rapid change in the symbolic functioning of very young children. *Science, 238*(4833), 1556–1557.

DeLoache, J. S. (1995). Early understanding and use of symbols: The model model. *Current Directions in Psychological Science*, 4(4), 109–113.

DeLoache, J. S., Chiong, C., Sherman, K., Islam, N., Vanderborght, M., Troseth, G. L., Strouse, G. A., & O'Doherty, K. (2010). Do babies learn from baby media? *Psychological Science*, 21(11), 1570–1574.

DeLoache, J. S., & Ganea, P. A. (2009). Symbol-based learning in infancy. In A. Woodward & A. Needham (Eds.), *Learning and the infant mind* (pp. 263–285). Oxford University Press.

DeLoache, J. S., Miller, K. F., & Rosengren, K. S. (1997). The credible shrinking room: Very young children's performance with symbolic and nonsymbolic relations. *Psychological Science*, 8(4), 308–313.

DeLoache, J. S., Pierroutsakos, S. L., Uttal, D. H., Rosengren, K. S., & Gottlieb, A. (1998). Grasping the nature of pictures. *Psychological Science*, 9(3), 205–210.

DeLoache, J. S., Sugarman, S., & Brown, A. L. (1985). The development of error correction strategies in young children's manipulative play. *Child Development*, 56(4), 928–939.

Diamond, A. (1985). Development of the ability to use recall to guide action, as indicated by infants' performance on AB̄. *Child Development*, 56(4), 868–883.

Diamond, M. C., Krech, D., & Rosenzweig, M. R. (1964). The effects of an enriched environment on the histology of the rat cerebral cortex. *Journal of Comparative Neurology*, 23(1),

111–19. https://doi.org/10.1002/cne.901230110

Dotson, W. H., Rasmussen, E. E., Shafer, A., Colwell, M., Densley, R. L., Brewer, A. T., Alonzo, M. C., & Martinez, L. A. (2017). Evaluating the ability of the PBS children's show *Daniel Tiger's Neighborhood* to teach skills to two young children with autism spectrum disorder. *Behavior Analysis in Practice*, 10(1), 67–71.

Eickmann, S. H., Lima, A. C. V., Guerra, M. Q., Lima, M. C. I. P., Huttly, S. R. A., & Worth, A. A. (2007). Improved cognitive and motor development in a community-based intervention of psychosocial stimulation in northeast Brazil. *Developmental Medicine and Child Neurology*, 45(8), 536–541.

Fender, J. G., Richert, R. A., Robb, M. B., & Wartella, E. (2010). Parent teaching focus and toddlers' learning from an infant DVD. *Infant and Child Development*, 19(6), 613–627. https://doi.org/10.1002/icd.713

Fenson, L., Kagan, J., Kearsley, R. B., & Zelazo, P. R. (1976). The developmental progression of manipulative play in the first two years. *Child Development*, 47(1), 232–236.

Fernald, A., & O'Neill, D. K. (1993). Peekaboo across cultures: How mothers and infants play with voices, faces, and expectations. In *Parent-child play: Descriptions and implications* (pp. 259–285).

Flavell, J. H., Flavell, E. R., Green, F. L., & Korfmacher, J. E. (1990). Do young children think of television images as pictures or real objects? *Journal of Broadcasting & Electronic*

Media, 34(4), 399–419. https://doi.org/10.1080/08838159009386752

Ganea, P. A., Pickard, M. B., & DeLoache, J. S. (2008). Transfer between picture books and the real world by very young children. *Journal of Cognition and Development: Official Journal of the Cognitive Development Society*, 9(1), 46–66.

Ganea, P. A., Shutts, K., Spelke, E. S., & DeLoache, J. S. (2007). Thinking of things unseen: Infants' use of language to update mental representations. *Psychological Science*, 18(8), 734–739.

Gerhard, T. M., Culham, J. C., & Schwarzer, G. (2016). Distinct visual processing of real objects and pictures of those objects in 7- to 9-month-old infants. *Frontiers in Psychology*, 7, 827.

Gerhard, T. M., Culham, J. C., & Schwarzer, G. (2021). Manual exploration of objects is related to 7-month-old infants' visual preference for real objects. *Infant Behavior & Development*, 62, 101512.

Ginsburg, K. R. (2007). American Academy of Pediatrics Committee on Communications, & American Academy of Pediatrics Committee on Psychosocial Aspects of Child and Family Health. The importance of play in promoting healthy child development and maintaining strong parent-child bonds. *Pediatrics*, 119(1), 182–191.

Goodwyn, S. W., Acredolo, L. P., & Brown, C. A. (2000). Impact of symbolic gesturing on early language development. *Journal of Nonverbal Behavior*, 24(2), 81–103.

Graham, K. L., & Burghardt, G. M. (2010). Current perspectives on the biological study of play: Signs of progress. *Quarterly Review of Biology, 85*(4), 393–418.

Harris, P. L. (1973). Perseverative errors in search by young infants. *Child Development, 44*(1), 28–33.

Harris, P. L. (1975). Development of search and object permanence during infancy. *Psychological Bulletin, 82*(3), 332–344.

Hart, B., & Risley, T. R. (1995). *Meaningful differences in the everyday experience of young American children.* Brookes.

Hopkins, E. J., Smith, E. D., Weisberg, D. S., & Lillard, A. S. (2016). The development of substitute object pretense: The differential importance of form and function. *Journal of Cognition and Development: Official Journal of the Cognitive Development Society, 17*(2), 197–220.

Hsu, H.-C., Iyer, S. N., & Fogel, A. (2014). Effects of social games on infant vocalizations. *Journal of Child Language, 41*(1), 132–154.

Jing, M., & Kirkorian, H. (2020). Video deficit in children's early learning. In J. Van den Bulck, D. R. Ewoldsen, M.-L. Mares, & E. Scharrer (Eds.), *The international encyclopedia of media.* Wiley. https://www.researchgate.net/profile/Mengguo-Jing/publication/345435187_Video_Deficit_in_Children's_Early_Learning/links/6070da7392851c8a7bb708bb/Video-Deficit-in-Childrens-Early-Learning.pdf

Jung, W. P., Kahrs, B. A., & Lockman, J. J. (2018). Fitting handled objects into apertures by 17- to 36-month-old children: The dynamics of spatial coordination. *Developmental Psychology, 54*(2), 228–239.

Karasik, L. B., Tamis-LeMonda, C. S., Adolph, K. E., & Bornstein, M. H. (2015). Places and postures. *Journal of Cross-Cultural Psychology, 46*(8), 1023–1038.

Kaur, M., Srinivasan, S. M., & Bhat, A. N. (2015). A typical object exploration in infants at-risk for autism during the first year of life. *Frontiers in Psychology, 6,* 798.

Kearney, M. S., & Levine, P. B. (2015). *Early childhood education by MOOC: Lessons from Sesame Street,* (No. 21229). National Bureau of Economic Research, https://doi.org/10.3386/w21229

Keates, J., Graham, S. A., & Ganea, P. A. (2014). Infants transfer nonobvious properties from pictures to real-world objects. *Journal of Experimental Child Psychology, 125,* 35–47.

Kirkham, J., Stewart, A., & Kidd, E. (2013). Concurrent and longitudinal relationships between development in graphic, language and symbolic play domains from the fourth to the fifth year. *Infant and Child Development, 22*(3), 297–319.

Kreppner, J. M., O'Connor, T. G., Dunn, J., & Andersen-Wood, L., & English and Romanian Adoptees (ERA) Study Team (1999). The pretend and social role play of children exposed to early severe

deprivation. *British Journal of Developmental Psychology, 17*(3), 319–332.

Libertus, K., Joh, A. S., & Needham, A. W. (2016). Motor training at 3 months affects object exploration 12 months later. *Developmental Science, 19*(6), 1058–1066.

Lifter, K., & Bloom, L. (1989). Object knowledge and the emergence of language. *Infant Behavior & Development, 12*(4), 395–423.

Lillard, A. S., Lerner, M. D., Hopkins, E. J., Dore, R. A., Smith, E. D., & Palmquist, C. M. (2013). The impact of pretend play on children's development: A review of the evidence. *Psychological Bulletin, 139*(1), 1–34.

Lillard, A. S., Nishida, T., Massaro, D., Vaish, A., Ma, L., & McRoberts, G. (2007). Signs of pretense across age and scenario. *Infancy: The Official Journal of the International Society on Infant Studies, 11*(1), 1–30.

Linebarger, D. L., & Walker, D. (2005). Infants' and toddlers' television viewing and language outcomes. *American Behavioral Scientist, 48*(5), 624–645.

Linebarger, D. L., Kosanic, A. Z., Greenwood, C. R., & Doku, N. S. (2004). Effects of viewing the television program between the lions on the emergent literacy skills of young children. *Journal of Educational Psychology, 96*(2), 297–308. https://doi.org/10.1037/0022-0663.96.2.297

Lockman, J. J., & Kahrs, B. A. (2017). New insights into the development of human tool use. *Current Directions in*

Psychological Science, 26(4), 330–334.

Luo, R., & Tamis-LeMonda, C. S. (2016). Mothers' verbal and nonverbal strategies in relation to infants' object-directed actions in real time and across the first three years in ethnically diverse families. *Infancy: The Official Journal of the International Society on Infant Studies, 21*(1), 65–89.

Macari, S., Milgramm, A., Reed, J., Shic, F., Powell, K. K., Macris, D., & Chawarska, K. (2021). Context-specific dyadic attention vulnerabilities during the first year in infants later developing autism spectrum disorder. *Journal of the American Academy of Child and Adolescent Psychiatry, 60*(1), 166–175.

Marcinowski, E. C., Nelson, E., Campbell, J. M., & Michel, G. F. (2019). The development of object construction from infancy through toddlerhood. *Infancy: The Official Journal of the International Society on Infant Studies, 24*(3), 368–391.

McCune-Nicolich, L. (1981). Toward symbolic functioning: Structure of early pretend games and potential parallels with language. *Child Development, 52*(3), 785–797.

Miller, P. M., & Commons, M. L. (2007). Stages of infant development, as illustrated by responses to the peek-a-boo game. *Behavioral Development Bulletin, 13*(1), 18–23.

Mohan, M., & Bhat, J. S. (2022). Influence of socio-economic status on play development in toddlers – a mother child dyadic interaction based study. *Neuropsychiatrie de l'Enfance et de l'Adolescence,*

70(2), 68–74. https://doi.org/10 .1016/j.neurenf.2021.11.005

Molteno, C. D., Jacobson, J. L., Carter, R. C., & Jacobson, S. W. (2010). Infant symbolic play as an early indicator of fetal alcohol-related deficit. *Infancy: The Official Journal of the International Society on Infant Studies, 15*(6), 586–607.

Montag, J. L., Jones, M. N., & Smith, L. B. (2015). The words children hear: Picture books and the statistics for language learning. *Psychological Science, 26*(9), 1489–1496.

Moore, M. K., & Meltzoff, A. N. (2008). Factors affecting infants' manual search for occluded objects and the genesis of object permanence. *Infant Behavior & Development, 31*(2), 168–180.

Munakata, Y., McClelland, J. L., Johnson, M. H., & Siegler, R. S. (1997). Rethinking infant knowledge: Toward an adaptive process account of successes and failures in object permanence tasks. *Psychological Review, 104*(4), 686–713.

Myers, L. J., LeWitt, R. B., Gallo, R. E., & Maselli, N. M. (2016). Baby FaceTime: Can toddlers learn from online video chat? *Developmental Science.* http://doi.wiley.com/10.1 111/desc.12430

Needham, A. W. (2000). Improvements in object exploration skills may facilitate the development of object segregation in early infancy. *Journal of Cognition and Development: Official Journal of the Cognitive Development Society, 1*(2), 131–156.

Needham, A. W., Wiesen, S. E., Hejazi, J. N., Libertus,

K., & Christopher, C. (2017). Characteristics of brief sticky mittens training that lead to increases in object exploration. *Journal of Experimental Child Psychology, 164*, 209–224.

Neldner, K., Reindl, E., Tennie, C., Grant, J., Tomaselli, K., & Nielsen, M. (2020). A cross-cultural investigation of young children's spontaneous invention of tool use behaviours. *Royal Society Open Science, 7*(5), 192240.

Nishida, T. K., & Lillard, A. S. (2007). The informative value of emotional expressions: "social referencing" in mother-child pretense. *Developmental Science, 10*(2), 205–212.

Noble, K. G., Houston, S. M., Kan, E., & Sowell, E. R. (2012). Neural correlates of socioeconomic status in the developing human brain. *Developmental Science, 15*(4), 516–527.

Nomikou, I., Leonardi, G., Radkowska, A., Rączaszek-Leonardi, J., & Rohlfing, K. J. (2017). Taking up an active role: Emerging participation in early mother–infant interaction during peekaboo routines. *Frontiers in Psychology, 8*, 1656.

O'Connor, R. J., & Russell, J. (2015). Understanding the effects of one's actions upon hidden objects and the development of search behaviour in 7-month-old infants. *Developmental Science, 18*(5), 824–831.

Ornkloo, H., & von Hofsten, C. (2007). Fitting objects into holes: On the development of spatial cognition skills. *Developmental Psychology, 43*(2), 404–416.

Orr, E., & Geva, R. (2015). Symbolic play and language development. *Infant Behavior & Development*, *38*, 147–161.

Parrott, W. G., & Gleitman, H. (1989). Infants' expectations in play: The joy of peek-a-boo. *Cognition and Emotion*, *3*(4), 291–311.

Pellegrini, A. D. (2009). Research and policy on children's play. *Child Development Perspectives*, *3*(2), 131–136.

Pellis, S., & Pellis, V. (2013). *The playful brain: Venturing to the limits of neuroscience.* Simon & Schuster.

Pierroutsakos, S. L., & Troseth, G. L. (2003). Video verité: Infants' manual investigation of objects on video. *Infant Behavior and Development*, *26*(2), 183–199. https://doi.org/10.1016/s0163-6383(03)00016-x

Quinn, S., Donnelly, S., & Kidd, E. (2018). The relationship between symbolic play and language acquisition: A meta-analytic review. *Developmental Review*, *49*, 121–135.

Rachwani, J., Tamis-LeMonda, C. S., Lockman, J. J., Karasik, L. B., & Adolph, K. E. (2020). Learning the designed actions of everyday objects. *Journal of Experimental Psychology. General*, *149*(1), 67–78.

Rivera, S. M., Wakeley, A., & Langer, J. (1999). The drawbridge phenomenon: Representational reasoning or perceptual preference? *Developmental Psychology*, *35*(2), 427–435.

Robb, M. B., Richert, R. A., & Wartella, E. A. (2009). Just a talking book? Word learning from watching baby videos.

British Journal of Developmental Psychology, *27*(1), 27–45. https://doi.org/10.1348/026151008x320156

Rochat, P. (1989). Object manipulation and exploration in 2- to 5-month-old infants. *Developmental Psychology*, *25*(6), 871–884.

Rochat, P., Querido, J. G., & Striano, T. (1999). Emerging sensitivity to the timing and structure of protoconversation in early infancy. *Developmental Psychology*, *35*(4), 950–957.

Rohlfing, K. J., Wrede, B., Vollmer, A.-L., & Oudeyer, P.-Y. (2016). An alternative to mapping a word onto a concept in language acquisition: Pragmatic frames. *Frontiers in Psychology*, *7*, 470.

Roopnarine, J. L. (2011). Cultural variations in beliefs about play, parent-child play, and children's play: Meaning for childhood development. *The Oxford Handbook of the Development of Play*, *377*, 19–37.

Schmidt, M. E., Pempek, T. A., Kirkorian, H. L., Lund, A. F., & Anderson, D. R. (2008). The effects of background television on the toy play behavior of very young children. *Child Development*, *79*(4), 1137–1151.

Schröder, E., Gredebäck, G., Gunnarsson, J., & Lindskog, M. (2020). Play enhances visual form perception in infancy–an active training study. *Developmental Science*, *23*(3), 591.

Sherman, L. J., Rice, K., & Cassidy, J. (2015). Infant capacities related to building internal working models of attachment figures: A theoretical and empirical review.

Developmental Review, *37*, 109–141.

Shinskey, J. L., & Munakata, Y. (2001). Detecting transparent barriers: Clear evidence against the means-end deficit account of search failures. *Infancy: The Official Journal of the International Society on Infant Studies*, *2*, 395–404.

Shuwairi, S. M. (2019). Haptic exploration of depicted and real objects by 9-month-old infants. *Infant and Child Development*, *28*(2), e2125.

Shuwairi, S. M., Tran, A., DeLoache, J. S., & Johnson, S. P. (2010). Infants' response to pictures of impossible objects. *Infancy: The Official Journal of the International Society on Infant Studies*, *15*(6), 636–649.

Simcock, G., & DeLoache, J. S. (2006). Get the picture? The effects of iconicity on toddlers' reenactment from picture books. *Developmental Psychology*, *42*(6), 1352–1357.

Slone, L. K., Moore, D. S., & Johnson, S. P. (2018). Object exploration facilitates 4-month-olds' mental rotation performance. *PLOS ONE*, *13*(8), e0200468.

Snow, C. E. (1999). Social perspectives on the emergence of language. In B. MacWhinney (Ed.), *The emergence of language* (pp. 257–276). Erlbaum.

Sosa, A. V. (2016). Association of the type of toy used during play with the quantity and quality of parent-infant communication. *JAMA Pediatrics*, *170*(2), 132–137.

Soska, K. C., & Adolph, K. E. (2014). Postural position constrains multimodal object exploration in infants. *Infancy:*

The Official Journal of the International Society on Infant Studies, 19(2), 138–161.

Stern, D. N., Stern, D., & Others. (1977). *The first relationship: Mother and infant.* Harvard University Press.

Strouse, G. A., & Troseth, G. L. (2008). "Don't try this at home": Toddlers' imitation of new skills from people on video. *Journal of Experimental Child Psychology, 101*(4), 262–280.

Sutton-Smith, B. (2008). Play theory: A personal journey and new thoughts. *American Journal of Play, 1*(1), 80–123.

Tamis-LeMonda, C. S., Bornstein, M. H., Cyphers, L., Toda, S., & Ogino, M. (1992). Language and play at one year: A comparison of toddlers and mothers in the United States and Japan. *International Journal of Behavioral Development, 15*(1), 19–42.

Tamis-LeMonda, C. S., Kuchirko, Y. A., Escobar, K., & Bornstein, M. H. (2019). Language and play in parent–child interactions. In M. H. Bornstein (Ed.), *Handbook of parenting: The practice of parenting* (pp. 189–213). Routledge. https://psycnet.apa.org/record/2019-10604-007

Tamis-LeMonda, C. S., Kuchirko, Y., & Tafuro, L. (2013). From action to interaction: Infant object exploration and mothers' contingent responsiveness. *IEEE Transactions on Autonomous Mental Development, 5*(3), 202–209.

Troseth, G. L., Saylor, M. M., & Archer, A. H. (2006). Young children's use of video as a source of socially relevant information. *Child Development, 77*(3), 786–799.

Vanderschuren, L. J. M. J., Achterberg, E. J. M., & Trezza, V. (2016). The neurobiology of social play and its rewarding value in rats. *Neuroscience and Biobehavioral Reviews, 70,* 86–105.

Walker, C. M., Walker, L. B., & Ganea, P. A. (2013). The role of symbol-based experience in early learning and transfer from pictures: Evidence from Tanzania. *Developmental Psychology, 49*(7), 1315–1324.

Weisberg, D. S. (2015). Pretend play. *Wiley Interdisciplinary Reviews. Cognitive Science, 6*(3), 249–261.

Wright, H., Densley, R. L., White, S., Rasmussen, E. E., Shafer, A., Colwell, M. J., & Punyanunt-Carter, N. (2016). Relation between active mediation, exposure to Daniel Tiger's neighborhood, and US preschoolers' social and emotional development. *Journal of Children and Media, 10*(4), 443–461.

Wright, J. C., Huston, A. C., Murphy, K. C., St. Peters, M., -on, M. P., Scantlin, R., & Kotler, J. (2001). The relations of early television viewing to school readiness and vocabulary of children from low-income families: The early window project. *Child Development, 72*(5), 1347–1366. https://doi.org/10.1111/1467-8624.t01-1-00352

Yogman, M., Garner, A., Hutchinson, J., Hirsh-Pasek, K., & Golinkoff, R. M., Committee on Psychosocial Aspects of Child and Family Health, & Council on Communications and Media. (2018). The power of play: A pediatric role in enhancing development in young children. *Pediatrics, 142*(3). https://doi.org/10.1542/peds.2018-2058

Ziemer, C. J., Plumert, J. M., & Pick, A. D. (2012). To grasp or not to grasp: Infants' actions toward objects and pictures. *Infancy, 17*(5), 479–497. https://doi.org/10.1111/j.1532-7078.2011.00100.x

Ziemer, C. J., & Snyder, M. (2016). A picture you can handle: Infants treat touch-screen images more like photographs than objects. *Frontiers in Psychology, 7,* 1253.

Zosh, J. M., Verdine, B. N., Filipowicz, A., Golinkoff, R. M., Hirsh-Pasek, K., & Newcombe, N. S. (2015). Talking shape: Parental language with electronic versus traditional shape sorters. *Mind, Brain and Education: The Official Journal of the International Mind, Brain, and Education Society, 9*(3), 136–144.

CHAPTER 9

Abu-Zhaya, R., Seidl, A., & Cristia, A. (2017). Multimodal infant-directed communication: How caregivers combine tactile and linguistic cues. *Journal of Child Language, 44*(5), 1088–1116.

Akhtar, N., Jipson, J., & Callanan, M. A. (2001). Learning words through overhearing. *Child Development, 72*(2), 416–430.

Altvater-Mackensen, N., & Mani, N. (2013). Word-form familiarity bootstraps infant speech segmentation.

Developmental Science, 16(6), 980–990.

Anderson, N. J., Graham, S. A., Prime, H., Jenkins, J. M., & Madigan, S. (2021). Linking quality and quantity of parental linguistic input to child language skills: A meta-analysis. *Child Development, 92*(2), 484–501. https://doi.org/10.11 11/cdev.13508

Antovich, D. M., & Graf Estes, K. (2018). Learning across languages: Bilingual experience supports dual language statistical word segmentation. *Developmental Science, 21*(2), e12548. https://doi.org/10.1111 /desc.12548

Arredondo, M. M., Aslin, R. N., Zhang, M., & Werker, J. F. (2022). Attentional orienting abilities in bilinguals: Evidence from a large infant sample. *Infant Behavior & Development, 66*, 101683.

Astor, K., Lindskog, M., Juvrud, J., Wangchuk, Namgyel, S. C., Wangmo, T., Tshering, K., & Gredebäck, G. (2022). Maternal postpartum depression impacts infants' joint attention differentially across cultures. *Developmental Psychology, 58*(12), 2230–2238. h ttps://doi.org/10.1037/dev00 01413

Bakeman, R., & Adamson, L. B. (1984). Coordinating attention to people and objects in mother-infant and peer-infant interaction. *Child Development, 55*(4), 1278–1289.

Baldwin, D. A. (1991). Infants' contribution to the achievement of joint reference. *Child Development, 62*(5), 875–890.

Baldwin, D. A. (1993). Infants' ability to consult the speaker

for clues to word reference. *Journal of Child Language, 20*(2), 395–418.

Bates, E. (1979). Cognition and communication from 9 to 13 months: Correlational findings. In E. Bates (Ed.), *The Emergence of Symbols: Cognition and communication in infancy*. Academic Press. h ttps://ci.nii.ac.jp/naid/100101 64605/

Bates, E., Thal, D., Trauner, D., Fenson, J., Aram, D., Eisele, J., & Nass, R. (1997). From first words to grammar in children with focal brain injury. *Developmental Neuropsychology, 13*(3), 275–343.

Bateson, M. C. (1975). Mother-infant exchanges: The epigenesis of conversational interaction. *Annals of the New York Academy of Sciences, 263*(1), 101–113.

Begus, K., Gliga, T., & Southgate, V. (2014). Infants learn what they want to learn: Responding to infant pointing leads to superior learning. *PLOS ONE, 9*(10), e108817.

Benedict, H. (1979). Early lexical development: Comprehension and production. *Journal of Child Language, 6*(2), 183–200.

Benitez, V. L., & Smith, L. B. (2012). Predictable locations aid early object name learning. *Cognition, 125*(3), 339–352.

Bergelson, E., & Aslin, R. N. (2017). Nature and origins of the lexicon in 6-mo-olds. *Proceedings of the National Academy of Sciences, 114*(49), 12916–12921. https://www.p nas.org/content/114/49/1291 6.short

Bergelson, E., Casillas, M., Soderstrom, M., Seidl, A.,

Warlaumont, A. S., & Amatuni, A. (2019). What do North American babies hear? A large-scale cross-corpus analysis. *Developmental Science, 22*(1), e12724.

Bergelson, E., & Swingley, D. (2012). At 6–9 months, human infants know the meanings of many common nouns. *Proceedings of the National Academy of Sciences, 109*(9), 3253–3258.

Bernhardt, B. M., Kemp, N., & Werker, J. F. (2007). Early word-object associations and later language development. *First Language, 27*(4), 315–328.

Best, C. T., & Strange, W. (1992). Effects of phonological and phonetic factors on cross-language perception of approximants. *Journal of Phonetics, 20*(3), 305–330.

Bialystok, E. (2011). Reshaping the mind: the benefits of bilingualism. *Canadian Journal of Experimental Psychology = Revue Canadienne de Psychologie Experimentale, 65*(4), 229–235.

Blake, J., & de Boysson-Bardies, B. (1992). Patterns in babbling: A cross-linguistic study. *Journal of Child Language, 19*(1), 51–74.

Bloom, L. (1993). *The transition from infancy to language: Acquiring the power of expression*. Cambridge University Press.

Bortfeld, H., Morgan, J. L., Golinkoff, R. M., & Rathbun, K. (2005). Mommy and me: Familiar names help launch babies into speech-stream segmentation. *Psychological Science, 16*(4), 298–304.

Braginsky, M., Yurovsky, D., Marchman, V. A., & Frank, M. C. (2019). Consistency and variability in children's word learning across languages. *Open Mind: Discoveries in Cognitive Science, 3*(3), 52–67.

Brito, N., & Barr, R. (2012). Influence of bilingualism on memory generalization during infancy. *Developmental Science, 15*(6), 812–816.

Broesch, T., & Bryant, G. A. (2018). Fathers' infant-directed speech in a small-scale society. *Child Development, 89*(2), e29–e41.

Broesch, T., Rochat, P., Olah, K., Broesch, J., & Henrich, J. (2016). Similarities and differences in maternal responsiveness in three societies: Evidence from Fiji, Kenya, and the United States. *Child Development, 87*(3), 700–711.

Brooks, R., & Meltzoff, A. N. (2008). Infant gaze following and pointing predict accelerated vocabulary growth through two years of age: A longitudinal, growth curve modeling study. *Journal of Child Language, 35*(1), 207–220.

Bruner, J. S. (1983). *Child's talk: Learning to use language*. Oxford University Press.

Bulgarelli, F., & Bergelson, E. (2020). Look who's talking: A comparison of automated and human-generated speaker tags in naturalistic day-long recordings. *Behavior Research Methods, 52*(2), 641–653.

Byers-Heinlein, K., Burns, T. C., & Werker, J. F. (2010). The roots of bilingualism in newborns. *Psychological Science, 21*(3), 343–348.

Byers-Heinlein, K., Tsui, A. S. M., Bergmann, C., Black, A. K., Brown, A., Carbajal, M. J., Durrant, S., Fennell, C. T., Fiévet, A.-C., Frank, M. C., Gampe, A., Gervain, J., Gonzalez-Gomez, N., Hamlin, J. K., Havron, N., Hernik, M., Kerr, S., Killam, H., Klassen, K., . . . Wermelinger, S. (2021). A multilab study of bilingual infants: Exploring the preference for infant-directed speech. *Advances in Methods and Practices in Psychological Science, 4*(1), 2515245920974622.

Cameron-Faulkner, T., Malik, N., Steele, C., Coretta, S., Serratrice, L., & Lieven, E. (2021). A cross-cultural analysis of early prelinguistic gesture development and its relationship to language development. *Child Development, 92*(1), 273–290.

Carpenter, M., Nagell, K., & Tomasello, M. (1998). Social cognition, joint attention, and communicative competence from 9 to 15 months of age. *Monographs of the Society for Research in Child Development, 63*(4), i–vi, 1–143.

Caselli, C., Casadio, P., & Bates, E. (1999). A comparison of the transition from first words to grammar in English and Italian. *Journal of Child Language, 26*(1), 69–111.

Casillas, M., Brown, P., & Levinson, S. C. (2020). Early language experience in a Tseltal Mayan village. *Child Development, 91*(5), 1819–1835. https://doi.org/10.1111/cdev.13349

Casillas, M., Brown, P., & Levinson, S. C. (2021). Early language experience in a Papuan community. *Journal of Child Language, 48*(4), 792–814.

Çetinçelik, M., Rowland, C. F., & Snijders, T. M. (2020). Do the eyes have it? A systematic review on the role of eye gaze in infant language development. *Frontiers in Psychology, 11*, 589096.

Chen, L.-M., & Kent, R. D. (2009). Development of prosodic patterns in Mandarin-learning infants. *Journal of Child Language, 36*(1), 73–84.

Childers, J. B., Vaughan, J., & Burquest, D. A. (2007). Joint attention and word learning in Ngas-speaking toddlers in Nigeria. *Journal of Child Language, 34*(2), 199–225.

Chomsky, N. (1959). A review of B. F. Skinner's verbal behavior. *Language, 35*(1), 26–58.

Chomsky, N. (1986). *Knowledge of language: Its nature, origin, and use*. Greenwood.

Cole, P. M., & Moore, G. A. (2015). About face! Infant facial expression of emotion. *Emotion Review: Journal of the International Society for Research on Emotion, 7*(2), 116–120.

Colonnesi, C., Stams, G. J. J. M., Koster, I., & Noom, M. J. (2010). The relation between pointing and language development: A meta-analysis. *Developmental Review, 30*(4), 352–366.

Conboy, B. T., & Thal, D. J. (2006). Ties between the lexicon and grammar: Cross-sectional and longitudinal studies of bilingual toddlers. *Child Development, 77*(3), 712–735. https://doi.org/10.1111/j.1467-8624.2006.00899.x

Cooper, A. (2019). Hear me out: Hearing each other for the first time: The implications of cochlear implant activation.

Missouri Medicine, 116(6), 469–471.

Cormier, K. A., Brentari, D., & Fenlon, J. (2018). *Sign language phonology.* Oxford University Press.

Cristia, A. (2022). A systematic review suggests marked differences in the prevalence of infant-directed vocalization across groups of populations. *Developmental Science, 26*(10), e13265.

Cristia, A., Dupoux, E., Ratner, N. B., & Soderstrom, M. (2019). Segmentability differences between child-directed and adult-directed speech: A systematic test with an ecologically valid corpus. *Open Mind: Discoveries in Cognitive Science, 3*, 13–22.

Custode, S. A., & Tamis-LeMonda, C. (2020). Cracking the code: Social and contextual cues to language input in the home environment. *Infancy: The Official Journal of the International Society on Infant Studies, 25*(6), 809–826. https://doi.org/10.1111/infa.12361

Cychosz, M., Cristia, A., Bergelson, E., Casillas, M., Baudet, G., Warlaumont, A. S., & Seidl, A. (2020). Canonical babble development in a large-scale crosslinguistic corpus. *PsyArXiv.* Retrieved March 14, 2020

D'Entremont, B. (2000). A perceptual-attentional explanation of gaze following in 3- and 6-month-olds. *Developmental Science, 3*(3), 302–311.

D'Souza, D., Brady, D., Haensel, J. X., & D'Souza, H. (2020). Is mere exposure enough? The effects of bilingual environments on infant

cognitive development. *Royal Society Open Science, 7*(2), 180191.

Dailey, S., & Bergelson, E. (2022). Language input to infants of different socioeconomic statuses: A quantitative meta-analysis. *Developmental Science, 25*(3), e13192.

de Boysson-Bardies, B. (1999). *How language comes to children. From birth to two years* (M. DeBevoise, Trans.). MIT Press. (Original work published 1996)

Demuth, C. (2013). Protoconversation and protosong as infant's socialization environment. In T. M. S. Tchombe, A. B. Nsamenange, H. Keller, & M. Fülöp (Eds.), *Cross-cultural psychology: An Africentric perspective* (pp. 232–256). DESIGN House.

Devescovi, A., Caselli, M. C., Marchione, D., Pasqualetti, P., Reilly, J., & Bates, E. (2005). A crosslinguistic study of the relationship between grammar and lexical development. *Journal of Child Language, 32*(4), 759–786.

Esteve-Gibert, N., & Prieto, P. (2013). Prosody signals the emergence of intentional communication in the first year of life: Evidence from Catalan-babbling infants. *Journal of Child Language, 40*(5), 919–944.

Falk, D. (2009). *Finding our tongues: Mothers, infants, and the origins of language.* Basic Books.

Fennell, C. T., Byers-Heinlein, K., & Werker, J. F. (2007). Using speech sounds to guide word learning: The case of bilingual infants. *Child Development, 78*(5), 1510–1525.

Fenson, L., Dale, P. S., Reznick, J. S., Bates, E., Thal, D. J., & Pethick, S. J. (1994). Variability in early communicative development. *Monographs of the Society for Research in Child Development, 59*(5), 1–173; discussion 174–185.

Fenson, L., Dale, P., Reznick, J. S., Thal, D., Bates, E., Hartung, J., & Pethick, S. R. (1993). *The MacArthur communicative development inventories: User's guide and technical manual.* Singular Pub Group.

Ferjan Ramírez, N. (2022). Fathers' infant-directed speech and its effects on child language development. *Language and Linguistics Compass, 16*(1), e12448. https://doi.org/10.1111/lnc3.12448

Ferjan Ramírez, N., Lytle, S. R., Fish, M., & Kuhl, P. K. (2019). Parent coaching at 6 and 10 months improves language outcomes at 14 months: A randomized controlled trial. *Developmental Science, 22*(3), e12762.

Fernald, A., Marchman, V. A., & Weisleder, A. (2013). SES differences in language processing skill and vocabulary are evident at 18 months. *Developmental Science, 16*(2), 234–248.

Fernald, A., & Morikawa, H. (1993). Common themes and cultural variations in Japanese and American mothers' speech to infants. *Child Development, 64*(3), 637–656.

Fernald, A., Perfors, A., & Marchman, V. A. (2006). Picking up speed in understanding: Speech processing efficiency and vocabulary growth across the 2nd year. *Developmental Psychology, 42*(1), 98–116.

Fernald, A., Taeschner, T., Dunn, J., Papousek, M., de Boysson-Bardies, B., & Fukui, I. (1989). A cross-language study of prosodic modifications in mothers' and fathers' speech to preverbal infants. *Journal of Child Language, 16*(3), 477–501. https://doi.org/10.1017/s0305000900010679

Fibla, L., Kosie, J., Kircher, R., Lew-Williams, C., & Byers-Heinlein, K. (2022). Bilingual language development in infancy: What can we do to support bilingual families? *Policy Insights from the Behavioral and Brain Sciences, 9*(1), 35–43. https://doi-org.proxy.library.cornell.edu/10.1177/23727322211069

Floccia, C., Sambrook, T. D., Delle Luche, C., Kwok, R., Goslin, J., White, L., Cattani, A., Sullivan, E., Abbot-Smith, K., Krott, A., Mills, D., Rowland, C., Gervain, J., & Plunkett, K. (2018). I: Introduction. *Monographs of the Society for Research in Child Development, 83*(1), 7–29.

Frank, M. C., Vul, E., & Johnson, S. P. (2009). Development of infants' attention to faces during the first year. *Cognition, 110*(2), 160–170.

Fromkin, V., Krashen, S., Curtiss, S., Rigler, D., & Rigler, M. (1974). The development of language in genie: A case of language acquisition beyond the "critical period." *Brain and Language, 1*(1), 81–107.

Gampe, A., Liebal, K., & Tomasello, M. (2012). Eighteen-month-olds learn novel words through overhearing. *First Language, 32*(3), 385–397.

Gilkerson, J., Richards, J. A., Warren, S. F., Montgomery, J. K., Greenwood, C. R., Kimbrough Oller, D., Hansen, J. H. L., & Paul, T. D. (2017). Mapping the early language environment using all-day recordings and automated analysis. *American Journal of Speech-Language Pathology, 26*(2), 248–265.

Goetz, P. J. (2003). The effects of bilingualism on theory of mind development. *Bilingualism: Language and Cognition, 6*(1), 1–15.

Goldin-Meadow, S. (2007). Pointing sets the stage for learning language—and creating language. *Child Development, 78*(3), 741–745.

Goldin-Meadow, S., & Feldman, H. (1977). The development of language-like communication without a language model. *Science, 197*(4301), 401–403.

Goldin-Meadow, S., & Mylander, C. (1983). Gestural communication in deaf children: Noneffect of parental input on language development. *Science, 221*(4608), 372–374.

Goldstein, M. H., & Schwade, J. A. (2008). Social feedback to infants' babbling facilitates rapid phonological learning. *Psychological Science, 19*(5), 515–523.

Gonzalez-Gomez, N., & Nazzi, T. (2013). Effects of prior phonotactic knowledge on infant word segmentation: the case of nonadjacent dependencies. *Journal of Speech, Language, and Hearing Research, 56*(3), 840–849.

Gordon, K. A., Jiwani, S., & Papsin, B. C. (2011). What is the optimal timing for bilateral cochlear implantation in children? *Cochlear Implants International, 12*(Suppl 2), S8–S14.

Graf Estes, K., & Lew-Williams, C. (2015). Listening through voices: Infant statistical word segmentation across multiple speakers. *Developmental Psychology, 51*(11), 1517–1528.

Gredebäck, G., Astor, K., & Fawcett, C. (2018). Gaze following is not dependent on ostensive cues: A critical test of natural pedagogy. *Child Development, 89*(6), 2091–2098.

Grieser, D. L., & Kuhl, P. K. (1988). Maternal speech to infants in a tonal language: Support for universal prosodic features in motherese. *Developmental Psychology, 24*(1), 14–20.

Ha, S., Johnson, C. J., Oller, K. D., & Yoo, H. (2021). Cross-linguistic comparison of utterance shapes in Korean- and English-learning children: An ambient language effect. *Infant Behavior & Development, 62*, 101528.

Hahn, E. R., & Cantrell, L. (2012). The shape-bias in Spanish-speaking children and its relationship to vocabulary. *Journal of Child Language, 39*(2), 443–455.

Halberstadt, A. G., & Lozada, F. T. (2011). Emotion development in infancy through the lens of culture. *Emotion Review: Journal of the International Society for Research on Emotion, 3*(2), 158–168.

Hart, B., & Risley, T. R. (1995). *Meaningful differences in the everyday experience of young American children*. Brookes.

Hernik, M., & Broesch, T. (2019). Infant gaze following depends on communicative signals: An eye-tracking study of 5- to 7-month-olds in Vanuatu. *Developmental Science, 22*(4), e12779.

Hilton, C. B., Moser, C. J., Bertolo, M., Lee-Rubin, H., Amir, D., Bainbridge, C. M., Simson, J., Knox, D., Glowacki, L., Alemu, E., Galbarczyk, A., Jasienska, G., Ross, C. T., Neff, M. B., Martin, A., Cirelli, L. K., Trehub, S. E., Song, J., Kim, M., . . . Mehr, S. A. (2022). Acoustic regularities in infant-directed speech and song across cultures. *Nature Human Behaviour, 6*, 1545–1556.

Hoff, E. (2003). The specificity of environmental influence: Socioeconomic status affects early vocabulary development via maternal speech. *Child Development, 74*(5), 1368–1378.

Hoff, E. (2021). Why bilingual development is not easy. *Advances in Child Development and Behavior, 61*, 129–167.

Hoff, E., Core, C., Place, S., Rumiche, R., Señor, M., & Parra, M. (2012). Dual language exposure and early bilingual development. *Journal of Child Language, 39*(1), 1–27. https://doi.org/10.1017/s0305 000910000759

Hoff, E., Quinn, J. M., & Giguere, D. (2018). What explains the correlation between growth in vocabulary and grammar? New evidence from latent change score analyses of simultaneous bilingual development. *Developmental*

Science, 21(2), e12536. https://doi.org/10.1111/desc.12536

Höhle, B., Bijeljac-Babic, R., & Nazzi, T. (2020). Variability and stability in early language acquisition: Comparing monolingual and bilingual infants' speech perception and word recognition. *Bilingualism: Language and Cognition, 23*(1), 56–71.

Höhle, B., & Weissenborn, J. (2003). German-learning infants' ability to detect unstressed closed-class elements in continuous speech. *Developmental Science, 6*(2), 122–127. https://doi.org/10.111 1/1467-7687.00261

Hollich, G. J., Hirsh-Pasek, K., Golinkoff, R. M., Brand, R. J., Brown, E., Chung, H. L., Hennon, E., & Rocroi, C. (2000). Breaking the language barrier: An emergentist coalition model for the origins of word learning. *Monographs of the Society for Research in Child Development, 65*(3), i–vi, 1 – 123.

Hong, G. H., & Kim, Y. T. (2005). A longitudinal study of predictors for expressive vocabulary development of late-talkers. *Communication Sciences & Disorders, 10*(1), 1–24.

Houston, D. M., Jusczyk, P. W., Kuijpers, C., Coolen, R., & Cutler, A. (2000). Cross-language word segmentation by 9-month-olds. *Psychonomic Bulletin & Review, 7*(3), 504–509.

Hurtado, N., Marchman, V. A., & Fernald, A. (2008). Does input influence uptake? Links between maternal talk, processing speed and vocabulary size in Spanish-learning

children. *Developmental Science, 11*(6), F31–F39.

Huttenlocher, J., Haight, W., Bryk, A., Seltzer, M., & Lyons, T. (1991). Early vocabulary growth: Relation to language input and gender. *Developmental Psychology, 27*(2), 236–248.

Huttenlocher, J., & Smiley, P. (1987). Early word meanings: The case of object names. *Cognitive Psychology, 19*(1), 63–89. https://doi.org/10.1016/0010-0 285(87)90004-1

Ingram, D. (1989). *Phonological disability in children*. Wiley.

Jara-Ettinger, J., Levy, R., Sakel, J., Huanca, T., & Gibson, E. (2022). The origins of the shape bias: Evidence from the Tsimane'. *Journal of Experimental Psychology. General, 151*(10), 2437–2447.

Jusczyk, P. W., & Aslin, R. N. (1995). Infants' detection of the sound patterns of words in fluent speech. *Cognitive Psychology, 29*(1), 1–23.

Kajikawa, S., & Masataka, N. (2003). Recognition of sound pattern of words extracted from spoken sentences by preverbal infants. *Japanese Journal of Psychology, 74*(3), 244–252. https://doi.org/10.49 92/jjpsy.74.244

Kalashnikova, M., Pejovic, J., & Carreiras, M. (2021). The effects of bilingualism on attentional processes in the first year of life. *Developmental Science, 24*(2), e13011.

Kärtner, J., Holodynski, M., & Wörmann, V. (2013). Parental ethnotheories, social practice and the culture-specific development of social smiling in infants. *Mind, Culture, and Activity, 20*(1), 79–95.

Kärtner, J., Keller, H., & Yovsi, R. D. (2010). Mother-infant interaction during the first 3 months: The emergence of culture-specific contingency patterns. *Child Development*, *81*(2), 540–554.

Keller, H., Borke, J., Staufenbiel, T., Yovsi, R. D., Abels, M., Papaligoura, Z., Jensen, H., Lohaus, A., Chaudhary, N., Lo, W., & Su, Y. (2009). Distal and proximal parenting as alternative parenting strategies during infants' early months of life: A cross-cultural study. *International Journal of Behavioral Development*, *33*(5), 412–420.

Keller, H., Scholmerich, A., & Eibl-Eibesfeldt, I. (1988). Communication patterns in adult-infant interactions in western and non-western cultures. *Journal of Cross-Cultural Psychology*, *19*(4), 427–445.

Keren-Portnoy, T., Majorano, M., & Vihman, M. M. (2009). From phonetics to phonology: The emergence of first words in Italian. *Journal of Child Language*, *36*(2), 235–267.

Kidd, E., & Garcia, R. (2022). How diverse is child language acquisition research? *First Language*, *42*(6), 703–735.

Kitamura, C., Thanavishuth, C., Burnham, D., & Luksaneeyanawin, S. (2001). Universality and specificity in infant-directed speech: Pitch modifications as a function of infant age and sex in a tonal and non-tonal language. *Infant Behavior and Development*, *24*(4), 372–392. https://doi.or g/10.1016/s0163-6383(02)00 086-3

Kovács, Á. M., & Mehler, J. (2009). Flexible learning of multiple speech structures in bilingual infants. *Science*, *325*(5940), 611–612.

Kovács, Á. M., Tauzin, T., Téglás, E., Gergely, G., & Csibra, G. (2014). Pointing as epistemic request: 12-month-olds point to receive new information. *Infancy: The Official Journal of the International Society on Infant Studies*, *19*(6), 543–557.

Kuczaj, S. A. (1979). Evidence for a language learning strategy: On the relative ease of acquisition of prefixes and suffixes. *Child Development*, *50*(1), 1–13.

Kuvač-Kraljević, J., Blaži, A., Schults, A., Tulviste, T., & Stolt, S. (2021). Influence of internal and external factors on early language skills: A cross-linguistic study. *Infant Behavior & Development*, *63*, 101552.

Laing, C., & Bergelson, E. (2020). From babble to words: Infants' early productions match words and objects in their environment. *Cognitive Psychology*, *122*, 101308.

Lavelli, M., Carra, C., Rossi, G., & Keller, H. (2019). Culture-specific development of early mother-infant emotional co-regulation: Italian, Cameroonian, and West African immigrant dyads. *Developmental Psychology*, *55*(9), 1850–1867.

Leong, V., Byrne, E., Clackson, K., Georgieva, S., Lam, S., & Wass, S. (2017). Speaker gaze increases information coupling between infant and adult brains. *Proceedings of the National Academy of Sciences of the United States of America*, *114*(50), 13290–13295.

Leopold, W. F. (1939). *Speech development of a bilingual child: A linguist's record*. Northwestern University.

Lieven, E., & Stoll, S. (2013). Early communicative development in two cultures: A comparison of the communicative environments of children from two cultures. *Human Development*, *56*(3), 178–206.

Liszkowski, U., Brown, P., Callaghan, T., Takada, A., & de Vos, C. (2012). A prelinguistic gestural universal of human communication. *Cognitive Science*, *36*(4), 698–713.

Little, E. E., Carver, L. J., & Legare, C. H. (2016). Cultural variation in triadic infant-care-giver object exploration. *Child Development*, *87*(4), 1130–1145.

Loukatou, G., Scaff, C., Demuth, K., Cristia, A., & Havron, N. (2021). Child-directed and overheard input from different speakers in two distinct cultures. *Journal of Child Language*, 1–20.

Lucca, K., & Wilbourn, M. P. (2018). Communicating to learn: Infants' pointing gestures result in optimal learning. *Child Development*, *89*(3), 941–960.

Lucca, K., & Wilbourn, M. P. (2019). The what and the how: Information-seeking pointing gestures facilitate learning labels and functions. *Journal of Experimental Child Psychology*, *178*, 417–436.

Lust, B. C., Foley, C., & Dye, C. D. (2009). The first language acquisition of complex sentences. In E. L. Bavin (Ed.), *The Cambridge handbook of child language* (pp. 237–258). https:/

/doi.org/10.1017/cbo97805115 76164.014

Macherey, O., & Carlyon, R. P. (2014). Cochlear implants. *Current Biology*, *24*(18), R878–R884.

MacWhinney, B. (2000). *The CHILDES project: Tools for analyzing talk. Transcription format and programs*. Psychology Press.

Marchman, V. A., Martínez-Sussmann, C., & Dale, P. S. (2004). The language-specific nature of grammatical development: Evidence from bilingual language learners. *Developmental Science*, *7*(2), 212–224.

Matthews, D., Biney, H., & Abbot-Smith, K. (2018). Individual differences in children's pragmatic ability: A review of associations with formal language, social cognition, and executive functions. *Language Learning and Development*, *14*(3), 186–223.

Mattys, S. L., & Jusczyk, P. W. (2001). Phonotactic cues for segmentation of fluent speech by infants. *Cognition*, *78*(2), 91–121.

Mayberry, R. I. (2010). Early language acquisition and adult language ability: What sign language reveals about the critical. In M. Marschark & P. E. Spencer (Eds.), *The Oxford handbook of deaf studies, language, and education* (Vol. 2, pp. 281–291). Oxford University Press.

McCarthy, D. (1954). Language disorders and parent-child relationships. *Journal of Speech and Hearing Disorders*, *19*(4), 514–523.

McCune, L., & Vihman, M. M. (2001). Early phonetic and lexical development. *Journal of Speech Language and Hearing Research*, *44*(3), 670–684. http s://doi.org/10.1044/1092-4388 (2001/054)

Mendive, S., Bornstein, M. H., & Sebastián, C. (2013). The role of maternal attention-directing strategies in 9-month-old infants attaining joint engagement. *Infant Behavior & Development*, *36*(1), 115–123.

Mitchell, R. E., & Karchmer, M. A. (2004). Chasing the mythical ten percent: Parental hearing status of deaf and hard of hearing students in the United States. *Sign Language Studies*, *4*(2), 138–163.

Moore, C. (2008). The development of gaze following. *Child Development Perspectives*, *2*(2), 66–70.

Mundy, P., Block, J., Delgado, C., Pomares, Y., Van Hecke, A. V., & Parlade, M. V. (2007). Individual differences and the development of joint attention in infancy. *Child Development*, *78*(3), 938–954.

Nazzi, T., Bertoncini, J., & Mehler, J. (1998). Language discrimination by newborns: Toward an understanding of the role of rhythm. *Journal of Experimental Psychology. Human Perception and Performance*, *24*(3), 756–766.

Nazzi, T., Iakimova, G., Bertoncini, J., Frédonie, S., & Alcantara, C. (2006). Early segmentation of fluent speech by infants acquiring French: Emerging evidence for cross-linguistic differences. *Journal of Memory and Language*, *54*(3), 283–299.

Newman, R. S., Rowe, M. L., & Bernstein Ratner, N. (2016). Input and uptake at 7 months predicts toddler vocabulary: the role of child-directed speech and infant processing skills in language development. *Journal of Child Language*, *43*(5), 1158–1173.

Ochs, E., Schieffelin, B., & Others. (1984). Language acquisition and socialization. In *Culture theory: Essays on mind, self, and emotion* (pp. 276–320). Cambridge University Press.

Oller, D. K., & Eilers, R. E. (1988). The role of audition in infant babbling. *Child Development*, *59*(2), 441–449.

Oller, D. K., Eilers, R. E., Bull, D. H., & Carney, A. E. (1985). Prespeech vocalizations of a deaf infant: A comparison with normal metaphonological development. *Journal of Speech and Hearing Research*, *28*(1), 47–63.

Oller, D. K., Griebel, U., Bowman, D. D., Bene, E., Long, H. L., Yoo, H., & Ramsay, G. (2020). Infant boys are more vocal than infant girls. *Current Biology*, *30*(10), R426–R427.

Orena, A. J., & Polka, L. (2019). Monolingual and bilingual infants' word segmentation abilities in an inter-mixed dual-language task. *Infancy: The Official Journal of the International Society on Infant Studies*, *24*(5), 718–737.

Palmer, S. B., Fais, L., Golinkoff, R. M., & Werker, J. F. (2012). Perceptual narrowing of linguistic sign occurs in the 1st year of life. *Child Development*, *83*(2), 543–553.

Papafragou, A. (2018). Pragmatic development. *Language*

Learning and Development, 14(3), 167–169.

Pearson, B. Z., Fernández, S. C., & Oller, D. K. (1993). Lexical development in bilingual infants and toddlers: Comparison to monolingual norms. *Language Learning, 43*(1), 93–120.

Pereira, A. F., Smith, L. B., & Yu, C. (2014). A bottom-up view of toddler word learning. *Psychonomic Bulletin & Review, 21*(1), 178–185.

Pinker, S. (2009). *Language learnability and language development.* Harvard University Press. (Original work published 1984)

Polka, L., Orena, A. J., Sundara, M., & Worrall, J. (2017). Segmenting words from fluent speech during infancy - challenges and opportunities in a bilingual context. *Developmental Science, 20*(1), e12419. https://doi.org/10.1111/desc.12419

Potter, C. E., Fourakis, E., Morin-Lessard, E., Byers-Heinlein, K., & Lew-Williams, C. (2019). Bilingual toddlers' comprehension of mixed sentences is asymmetrical across their two languages. *Developmental Science, 22*(4), e12794.

Pye, C. (2021). Documenting the acquisition of indigenous languages. *Journal of Child Language, 48*(3), 454–479.

Rowe, M. L. (2012). A longitudinal investigation of the role of quantity and quality of child-directed speech in vocabulary development. *Child Development, 83*(5), 1762–1774.

Rowe, M. L. (2018). Understanding socioeconomic differences in parents' speech

to children. *Child Development Perspectives, 12*(2), 122–127. https://srcd.onlinelibrary.wiley.com/doi/abs/10.1111/cdep.12271

Rowe, M. L., & Snow, C. E. (2020). Analyzing input quality along three dimensions: Interactive, linguistic, and conceptual. *Journal of Child Language, 47*(1), 5–21.

Rummelhart, D. E., McClelland, J. L., Group, P. R., & Others. (1986). *Parallel distributed processing.* MIT Press.

Saffran, J. R., Aslin, R. N., & Newport, E. L. (1996). Statistical learning by 8-month-old infants. *Science, 274*(5294), 1926–1928.

Saint-Georges, C., Chetouani, M., Cassel, R., Apicella, F., Mahdhaoui, A., Muratori, F., Laznik, M.-C., & Cohen, D. (2013). Motherese in interaction: At the cross-road of emotion and cognition? (A systematic review). *PLOS ONE, 8*(10), e78103.

Salo, V. C., Reeb-Sutherland, B., Frenkel, T. I., Bowman, L. C., & Rowe, M. L. (2019). Does intention matter? Relations between parent pointing, infant pointing, and developing language ability. *Journal of Cognition and Development, 20*(5), 635–655.

Samuelson, L. K. (2002). Statistical regularities in vocabulary guide language acquisition in connectionist models and 15-20-month-olds. *Developmental Psychology, 38*(6), 1016–1037.

Scaife, M., & Bruner, J. S. (1975). The capacity for joint visual attention in the infant. *Nature, 253*(5489), 265–266.

Schatz, J. L., Suarez-Rivera, C., Kaplan, B. E., & Tamis-LeMonda, C. S. (2022). Infants' object interactions are long and complex during everyday joint engagement. *Developmental Science, 25*(4), e13239.

Schonberg, C. C., Russell, E. E., & Luna, M. L. (2020). Effects of past language experience and present language context on the shape bias in Spanish-English bilingual children. *Developmental Science, 23*(2), e12879.

Seidl, A., Tincoff, R., Baker, C., & Cristia, A. (2015). Why the body comes first: Effects of experimenter touch on infants' word finding. *Developmental Science, 18*(1), 155–164.

Senghas, A., Kita, S., & Ozyürek, A. (2004). Children creating core properties of language: Evidence from an emerging sign language in Nicaragua. *Science, 305*(5691), 1779–1782.

Senju, A., & Csibra, G. (2008). Gaze following in human infants depends on communicative signals. *Current Biology, 18*(9), 668–671.

Shapiro, N. T., Hippe, D. S., & Ramírez, N. F. (2021). How chatty are daddies? An exploratory study of infants' language environments. *Journal of Speech, Language, and Hearing Research, 64*(8), 3242–3252.

Shneidman, L. A., & Goldin-Meadow, S. (2012). Language input and acquisition in a Mayan village: How important is directed speech? *Developmental Science, 15*(5), 659–673.

Singh, L. (2008). Influences of high and low variability on

infant word recognition. *Cognition*, *106*(2), 833–870.

Singh, L. (2021). Evidence for an early novelty orientation in bilingual learners. *Child Development Perspectives*, *15*(2), 110–116.

Singh, L., Morgan, J. L., & Best, C. T. (2002). Infants' listening preferences: Baby talk or happy talk? *Infancy: The Official Journal of the International Society on Infant Studies*, *3*(3), 365–394.

Singh, L., Morgan, J. L., & White, K. S. (2004). Preference and processing: The role of speech affect in early spoken word recognition. *Journal of Memory and Language*, *51*(2), 173–189.

Skinner, B. F. (1957). *Verbal behavior*. Appleton-Century-Crofts.

Smith, L. B., Jones, S. S., Landau, B., Gershkoff-Stowe, L., & Samuelson, L. (2002). Object name learning provides on-the-job training for attention. *Psychological Science*, *13*(1), 13–19.

Snow, C. E. (1999). Social perspectives on the emergence of language. In B. MacWhinney (Ed.), *The emergence of language* (pp. 257–276). Erlbaum.

Soderstrom, M. (2007). Beyond babytalk: Re-evaluating the nature and content of speech input to preverbal infants. *Developmental Review*, *27*(4), 501–532.

Suarez-Rivera, C., Linn, E., & Tamis-LeMonda, C. S. (2022). From play to language: Infants' actions on objects cascade to word learning. *Language Learning*, *72*(4), 1092–1127.

Sung, J., & Hsu, H.-C. (2009). Korean mothers' attention regulation and referential speech: Associations with language and play in 1-year-olds. *International Journal of Behavioral Development*, *33*(5), 430–439.

Suskind, D. L., Leffel, K. R., Graf, E., Hernandez, M. W., Gunderson, E. A., Sapolich, S. G., Suskind, E., Leininger, L., Goldin-Meadow, S., & Levine, S. C. (2016). A parent-directed language intervention for children of low socioeconomic status: a randomized controlled pilot study. *Journal of Child Language*, *43*(2), 366–406.

Syrnyk, C., & Meints, K. (2017). Bye-bye mummy—Word comprehension in 9-month-old infants. *British Journal of Developmental Psychology*, *35*(2), 202–217.

Tamis-LeMonda, C. S., Bornstein, M. H., & Baumwell, L. (2001). Maternal responsiveness predicts children's early language achievement. In *PsycEXTRA Dataset*. https://doi.org/10.1037/e325342004-008

Tamis-LeMonda, C. S., Kuchirko, Y., & Song, L. (2014). Why is infant language learning facilitated by parental responsiveness? *Current Directions in Psychological Science*, *23*(2), 121–126.

Tan, S. H. J., Kalashnikova, M., & Burnham, D. (2022). Seeing a talking face matters: Infants' segmentation of continuous auditory-visual speech. *Infancy: The Official Journal of the International Society on Infant Studies*. https://doi.org/10.1111/infa.12509

Tardif, T., Fletcher, P., Liang, W., Zhang, Z., Kaciroti, N., & Marchman, V. A. (2008). Baby's first 10 words. *Developmental Psychology*, *44*(4), 929–938.

Tenenbaum, E. J., Sobel, D. M., Sheinkopf, S. J., Shah, R. J., Malle, B. F., & Morgan, J. L. (2015). Attention to the mouth and gaze following in infancy predict language development. *Journal of Child Language*, *42*(6), 1173–1190.

Thal, D. J., Bates, E., Goodman, J., & Jahn-Samilo, J. (1997). Continuity of language abilities: An exploratory study of late-and early-talking toddlers. *Developmental Neuropsychology*, *13*(3), 239–273.

Thiessen, E. D., Hill, E. A., & Saffran, J. R. (2005). Infant-directed speech facilitates word segmentation. *Infancy: The Official Journal of the International Society on Infant Studies*, *7*(1), 53–71.

Tincoff, R., & Jusczyk, P. W. (1999). Some beginnings of word comprehension in 6-month-olds. *Psychological Science*, *10*(2), 172–175.

Tincoff, R., & Jusczyk, P. W. (2012). Six-month-Olds comprehend words that refer to parts of the body: Six-month-olds comprehend words. *Infancy: The Official Journal of the International Society on Infant Studies*, *17*(4), 432–444.

Tincoff, R., Seidl, A., Buckley, L., Wojcik, C., & Cristia, A. (2018). Feeling the way to words: Parents' speech and touch cues highlight word-to-world mappings of body parts. *Language Learning and Development*, *15*(2), 1–23.

Tomasello, M. (2001). Perceiving intentions and learning words in the second year of life. *Language Acquisition and Conceptual Development, 3*, 132–158.

Tomasello, M., & Akhtar, N. (2000). The social nature of words and word learning. In R. M. Golinkoff & K. Hirsh-Pasek (Eds.), *Becoming a word learner. A debate on lexical acquisition* (pp. 115–135). Oxford University Press. https://doi.org/10.1093/acprof:oso/9780195130324.003.005

Tomasello, M., Carpenter, M., & Liszkowski, U. (2007). A new look at infant pointing. *Child Development, 78*(3), 705–722.

Trehub, S. E. (2001). Musical predispositions in infancy. *Annals of the New York Academy of Sciences, 930*, 1–16.

Trehub, S. E., & Trainor, L. (1998). Singing to infants: Lullabies and play songs. *Advances in Infancy Research, 12*, 43–78.

Trevarthen, C. (2011). What is it like to be a person who knows nothing? Defining the active intersubjective mind of a newborn human being. *Infant and Child Development, 20*(1), 119–135.

Vasilyeva, M., Waterfall, H., & Huttenlocher, J. (2008). Emergence of syntax: Commonalities and differences across children. *Developmental Science, 11*(1), 84–97.

Vihman, M. M., Thierry, G., Lum, J., Keren-Portnoy, T., & Martin, P. (2007). Onset of word form recognition in English, Welsh, and English–Welsh bilingual infants. *Applied Psycholinguistics, 28*(3), 475–493.

Vouloumanos, A., Hauser, M. D., Werker, J. F., & Martin, A. (2010). The tuning of human neonates' preference for speech. *Child Development, 81*(2), 517–527. https://srcdonlinelibrary.wiley.com/doi/abs/10.1111/j.1467-8624.2009.01412.x

Weber, A., Fernald, A., & Diop, Y. (2017). When cultural norms discourage talking to babies: Effectiveness of a parenting program in rural Senegal. *Child Development, 88*(5), 1513–1526.

Weisleder, A., & Fernald, A. (2013). Talking to children matters: Early language experience strengthens processing and builds vocabulary. *Psychological Science, 24*(11), 2143–2152.

Werker, J. F., Cohen, L. B., Lloyd, V. L., Casasola, M., & Stager, C. L. (1998). Acquisition of word–object associations by 14-month-old infants. *Developmental Psychology, 34*, 1289–1309.

Werker, J. F., Fennell, C. T., Corcoran, K. M., & Stager, C. L. (2002). Infants' ability to learn phonetically similar words: Effects of age and vocabulary size. *Infancy: The Official Journal of the International Society on Infant Studies, 3*(1), 1–30.

Werker, J. F., & McLeod, P. J. (1989). Infant preference for both male and female infant-directed talk: A developmental study of attentional and affective responsiveness. *Canadian Journal of Psychology, 43*(2), 230–246.

Whalen, D. H., Levitt, A. G., & Goldstein, L. M. (2007). VOT in the babbling of French- and English-learning infants. *Journal of Phonetics, 35*(3), 341–352.

Wu, C. Y., O'Brien, B. A., Styles, S. J., & Chen, S. H. A. (2020). *Transforming teaching and learning in higher education.* Springer.

Yoshida, H., & Smith, L. B. (2001). Early noun lexicons in English and Japanese. *Cognition, 82*(2), B63–B74.

Yu, C., & Smith, L. B. (2012). Embodied attention and word learning by toddlers. *Cognition, 125*(2), 244–262.

Yu, C., Suanda, S. H., & Smith, L. B. (2019). Infant sustained attention but not joint attention to objects at 9 months predicts vocabulary at 12 and 15 months. *Developmental Science, 22*(1), e12735.

Yurovsky, D., Smith, L. B., & Yu, C. (2013). Statistical word learning at scale: The baby's view is better. *Developmental Science, 16*(6), 959–966.

Zhao, T. C., & Kuhl, P. K. (2022). Development of infants' neural speech processing and its relation to later language skills: A MEG study. *NeuroImage, 256*, 119242.

CHAPTER 10

Ahadi, S. A., Rothbart, M. K., & Ye, R. (1993). Children's temperament in the US and China: Similarities and differences. *European Journal of Personality, 7*(5), 359–378.

Astor, K., Lindskog, M., Juvrud, J., Wangchuk, Namgyel, S. C., Wangmo, T., Tshering, K., & Gredebäck, G. (2022). Maternal postpartum depression impacts infants' joint attention differentially across cultures. *Developmental Psychology, 58*(12), 2230–2238. https://doi.org/10.1037/dev0001413

Barker, T. V., Reeb-Sutherland, B. C., & Fox, N. A. (2014). Individual differences in fear potentiated startle in behaviorally inhibited children. *Developmental Psychobiology, 56*(1), 133–141. https://doi.org/10.1002/dev.21096

Broesch, T., Callaghan, T., Henrich, J., Murphy, C., & Rochat, P. (2011). Cultural variations in children's mirror self-recognition. *Journal of Cross-Cultural Psychology, 42*(6), 1018–1029.

Brooks, J., & Lewis, M. (1976). Infants' responses to strangers: Midget, adult, and child. *Educational Testing Service, 47*(323–332), 1–11.

Burris, J. L., Chernenok, M., Bussey, T. R., & Rivera, S. M. (2019). Emotional development in the context of developmental disorders. In V. LoBue, K. Pérez-Edgar, & K. A. Buss (Eds.), *Handbook of emotional development* (pp. 749–766). Springer.

Coan, J. A. (2010). Emergent ghosts of the emotion machine. *Emotion Review, 2*(3), 274–285.

Common Sense Media. (2016, December 6). *The Common Sense Census: Plugged-in parents of tweens and teens, 2016.* https://www.commonsensemedia.org/research/the-common-sense-census-plugged-in-parents-of-tweens-and-teens-2016

Davidson, R. J., & Fox, N. A. (1982). Asymmetrical brain activity discriminates between positive and negative affective stimuli in human infants. *Science, 218*(4578), 1235–1237.

Davidson, R. J., & Fox, N. A. (1989). Frontal brain asymmetry predicts infants' response to maternal separation. *Journal of Abnormal Psychology, 98*(2), 127–131.

Ekman, P., & Cordaro, D. (2011). What is meant by calling emotions basic. *Emotion Review, 3*(4), 364–370.

Fawcett, C., & Liszkowski, U. (2015). Social referencing during infancy and early childhood across cultures. In J. D. Wright (Ed.), *International encyclopedia of the social & behavioral sciences* (pp. 556–562). Elsevier.

Feldman, R., Rosenthal, Z., & Eidelman, A. I. (2014). Maternal-preterm skin-to-skin contact enhances child physiologic organization and cognitive control across the first 10 years of life. *Biological Psychiatry, 75*(1), 56–64.

Field, T. M., Schanberg, S. M., Scafidi, F., Bauer, C. R., Vega-Lahr, N., Garcia, R., Nystrom, J., & Kuhn, C. M. (1986). Tactile/kinesthetic stimulation effects on preterm neonates. *Pediatrics, 77*(5), 654–658.

Flom, R., & Bahrick, L. E. (2007). The development of infant discrimination of affect in multimodal and unimodal stimulation: The role of intersensory redundancy. *Developmental Psychology, 43*(1), 238–252.

Fox, N. A., & Davidson, R. J. (1986). Taste-elicited changes in facial signs of emotion and the asymmetry of brain electrical activity in human newborns. *Neuropsychologia, 24*(3), 417–422.

Fox, N. A., & Davidson, R. J. (1987). Electroencephalogram asymmetry in response to the approach of a stranger and maternal separation in 10-month-old infants. *Developmental Psychology, 23*(2), 233–240.

Gao, X., & Maurer, D. (2010). A happy story: Developmental changes in children's sensitivity to facial expressions of varying intensities. *Journal of Experimental Child Psychology, 107*(2), 67–86.

Gartstein, M. A., Bogale, W., & Meehan, C. L. (2016). Adaptation of the Infant Behavior Questionnaire-Revised for use in Ethiopia: Expanding cross-cultural investigation of temperament development. *Infant Behavior & Development, 45*(Pt A), 51–63.

Gartstein, M. A., Carranza, J. A., González-Salinas, C., Ato, E., Galián, M. D., Erickson, N. L., & Potapova, N. (2016). Cross-cultural comparisons of infant fear: A multi-method study in Spain and the United States. *Journal of Cross-Cultural Psychology, 47*(9), 1178–1193.

Gartstein, M. A., Gonzalez, C., Carranza, J. A., Ahadi, S. A., Ye, R., Rothbart, M. K., & Yang, S. W. (2006). Studying cross-cultural differences in the development of infant temperament: People's Republic of China, the United States of America, and Spain. *Child*

Psychiatry and Human Development, *37*(2), 145–161.

Gartstein, M. A., Knyazev, G. G., & Slobodskaya, H. R. (2005). Cross-cultural differences in the structure of infant temperament: United States of America (U.S.) and Russia. *Infant Behavior and Development*, *28*(1), 54–61. https://doi.org/10.1016/j.infbeh.2004.09.003

Gartstein, M. A., Slobodskaya, H. R., Zylicz, P. O., Gosztyla, D., & Nakagawa, A. (2010). A cross-cultural evaluation of temperament: Japan, USA, Poland, and Russia. *International Journal of Psychology and Psychological Therapy*, *10*(1), 55–75. https://www.redalyc.org/pdf/560/56017066004.pdf

Geangu, E., Ichikawa, H., Lao, J., Kanazawa, S., Yamaguchi, M. K., Caldara, R., & Turati, C. (2016). Culture shapes 7-month-olds' perceptual strategies in discriminating facial expressions of emotion. *Current Biology*, *26*(14), R663–R664.

Handal, A. J., Saavedra, L. G., Schrader, R., Aragón, C. L., Páez, M., & Lowe, J. R. (2017). Assessment of maternal-infant interaction: Application of the still face paradigm in a rural population of working women in Ecuador. *Maternal and Child Health Journal*, *21*(3), 458–466.

Hastings, P. D., Sullivan, C., McShane, K. E., Coplan, R. J., Utendale, W. T., & Vyncke, J. D. (2008). Parental socialization, vagal regulation, and preschoolers' anxious difficulties: Direct mothers and moderated fathers. *Child Development*, *79*(1), 45–64.

Hunziker, U., & Barr, B. (1986). Increased carrying reduces infant crying. *Pediatrics*, *77*(5), 641–648.

Izard, C. E. (2007). Basic emotions, natural kinds, emotion schemas, and a new paradigm. *Perspectives on Psychological Science*, *2*(3), 260–280.

Kagan, J. (1997). Temperament and the reactions to unfamiliarity. *Child Development*, *68*(1), 139–143.

Kagan, J., Arcus, D., Snidman, N., Feng, W. Y., Hendler, J., & Greene, S. (1994). Reactivity in infants: A cross-national comparison. *Developmental Psychology*, *30*(3), 342–345.

Karasik, L. B., Tamis-LeMonda, C. S., & Adolph, K. E. (2016). Decisions at the brink: Locomotor experience affects infants' use of social information on an adjustable drop-off. *Frontiers in Psychology*, *7*, 797.

Lamm, B., Keller, H., Teiser, J., Gudi, H., Yovsi, R. D., Freitag, C., Poloczek, S., Fassbender, I., Suhrke, J., Teubert, M., Vöhringer, I., Knopf, M., Schwarzer, G., & Lohaus, A. (2018). Waiting for the second treat: Developing culture-specific modes of self-regulation. *Child Development*, *89*(3), e261–e277.

Lewis, M., Alessandri, S. M., & Sullivan, M. W. (1990). Violation of expectancy, loss of control, and anger expressions in young infants. *Developmental Psychology*, *26*(5), 745–751.

Lewis, M., & Ramsay, D. (2005). Infant emotional and cortisol responses to goal blockage. *Child Development*, *76*(2), 518–530. https://doi.org/10.1111/j.1467-8624.2005.00860.x

Li, W., Woudstra, M. J., Branger, M. C. E., Wang, L., Alink, L. R. A., Mesman, J., & Emmen, R. A. G. (2019). The effect of the still-face paradigm on infant behavior: A cross-cultural comparison between mothers and fathers. *Infancy: The Official Journal of the International Society on Infant Studies*, *24*(6), 893–910.

Little, E. E., Legare, C. H., & Carver, L. J. (2019). Culture, carrying, and communication: Beliefs and behavior associated with babywearing. *Infant Behavior & Development*, *57*, 101320.

Liu, C. H., Zhang, E., Snidman, N., & Tronick, E. (2020). Infant affect response in the face-to-face still face among Chinese- and European American mother-infant dyads. *Infant Behavior & Development*, *60*, 101469.

LoBue, V., & Adolph, K. E. (2019). Fear in infancy: Lessons from strangers, heights, snakes, spiders, and other scary stuff. *Developmental Psychology*, *55*(9), 1889–1907.

Mascaro, J. S., Rentscher, K. E., Hackett, P. D., Mehl, M. R., & Rilling, J. K. (2017). Child gender influences paternal behavior, language, and brain function. *Behavioral Neuroscience*, *131*(3), 262–273.

Mumme, D. L., & Fernald, A. (2003). Is visual reference necessary? Contributions of facial versus vocal cues in 12-month-olds' social referencing behavior. *Child Development*, 1–17.

Muzard, A., Kwon, A. Y., Espinosa, N., Vallotton, C. D., & Farkas, C. (2017). Infants' emotional expression: Differences in the expression of pleasure and discomfort between infants from Chile and the United States. *Infant and Child Development*, *26*(6), e2033.

Myruski, S., Gulyayeva, O., Birk, S., Perez-Edgar, K., Buss, K. A., & Deniis-Tiwary, T. (2018). Digital disruption? Maternal mobile device use is related to infant social-emotional functioning. *Developmental Psychology*, *21*(4), e12610.

Narvaez, D., Wang, L., & Cheng, Y. (2016). The evolved developmental niche in childhood: Relation to adult psychopathology and morality. *Applied Developmental Science*, *20*(4), 294–309.

Panksepp, J. (2007). Neurologizing the psychology of affects: How appraisal-based constructivism and basic emotion theory can coexist. *Perspectives on Psychological Science*, *2*(3), 281–296.

Peltola, M. J., Leppänen, J. M., Mäki, S., & Hietanen, J. K. (2009). Emergence of enhanced attention to fearful faces between 5 and 7 months of age. *Social Cognitive and Affective Neuroscience*, *4*(2), 134–142. https://doi.org/10.1093/scan/nsn046

Penela, E. C., Henderson, H. A., Hane, A. A., Ghera, M. M., & Fox, N. A. (2012). Maternal caregiving moderates the relation between temperamental fear and social behavior with peers. *Infancy*, *17*(6),

715–730. https://doi.org/10.1111/j.1532-7078.2012.00114.x

Pérez-Edgar, K. (2019). Through the looking glass: Temperament and emotion as separate and interwoven constructs. In V. LoBue, K. Pérez-Edgar, & K. A. Buss (Eds.), *Handbook of emotional development* (pp. 139–168). Springer.

Pérez-Edgar, K., Bar-Haim, Y., Mcdermott, J. M., Chronis-Tuscano, A., Pine, D. S., & Fox, N. A. (2010). Attention biases to threat and behavioral inhibition in early childhood shape adolescent social withdrawal. *Emotion*, *10*(3), 349–357.

Pérez-Edgar, K., Reeb-Sutherland, B. C., Mcdermott, J. M., White, L. K., Henderson, H. A., Degnan, K. A., Hane, A. A., Pine, D. S., & Fox, N. A. (2011). Attention biases to threat link behavioral inhibition to social withdrawal over time in very young children. *Journal of Abnormal Child Psychology*, *39*(6), 885–895.

Reed, J., Hirsh-Pasek, K., & Golinkoff, R. M. (2017). Learning on hold: Cell phones sidetrack parent-child interactions. *Developmental Psychology*, *53*(8), 1428–1436.

Rheingold, H. L., & Eckerman, C. O. (1973). Fear of the stranger: A critical examination. *Advances in Child Development and Behavior*, *8*, 185–222.

Ricciuti, H. N. (1974). Fear and the development of social attachments in the first year of life. *The Origins of Fear*, *2*, 73–106.

Rosenstein, D., & Oster, H. (1988). Differential facial responses to four basic tastes

in newborns. *Child Development*, *59*(6), 1555–1568.

Rothbart, M. K., Derryberry, D., & Hershey, K. (2000). Stability of temperament in childhood: Laboratory infant assessment to parent report at seven years. In V. J. Molfese, D. L. Molfese, & R. R. McCrae (Eds.), *Temperament and personality development across the life span* (pp. 85–119). Erlbaum.

Rozin, P., Fallon, A., & Augustoni-Ziskind, M. L. (1985). The child's conception of food: The development of contamination sensitivity to. *Developmental Psychology*, *21*(6), 1075–1079.

Ruba, A. L., Meltzoff, A. N., & Repacholi, B. M. (2019). How do you feel? Preverbal infants match negative emotions to events. *Developmental Psychology*, *55*(6), 1138–1149.

Rubin, K. H., Burgess, K. B., & Hastings, P. D. (2002). Stability and social-behavioral consequences of toddlers' inhibited temperament and parenting behaviors. *Child Development*, *73*(2), 483–495.

Rudy, D., Ispa, J. M., Fine, M. A., & James, A. G. (2021). Ethnic variations in mothers' and children's positive and negative emotional expressions toward each other. *Social Development*, *30*(2), 515–535. https://doi.org/10.1111/sode.12495

Serrano, J. M., Iglesias, J., & Loeches, A. (1992). Visual discrimination and recognition of facial expressions of anger, fear, and surprise in 4- to 6-month-old infants. *Developmental Psychobiology*, *25*(6), 411–425. https://doi.org/10.1002/dev.420250603

Smith, P. K. (1974). Social and situational determinants of fear in the playgroup. *The Origins of Fear*, 107–129.

Sorce, J., Emde, R., Campos, J., & Klinnert, M. (1985). Maternal emotional signaling: Its effect on the visual cliff behavior of 1-year-olds. *Developmental Psychology*, *21*(1), 195–200.

Sroufe, L. (1977). Wariness of strangers and the study of infant development. *Child Development*, *48*(3), 731–746.

Stifter, C., & Augustine, M. (2019). Emotion regulation. In V. LoBue, K. Pérez-Edgar, & K. A. Buss (Eds.), *Handbook of emotional development* (pp. 405–430). Springer.

Suomi, S. J. (1997). Early determinants of behaviour: Evidence from primate studies. *British Medical Bulletin*, *53*(1), 170–184.

Thomas, A., Chess, S., & Birch, H. G. (1970). The origin of personality. *Scientific American*, *223*(2), 102–109.

Thomas, L. A., De Bellis, M. D., Graham, R., & LaBar, K. S. (2007). Development of emotional facial recognition in late childhood and adolescence. *Developmental Science*, *10*(5), 547–558.

Walden, T. A., & Ogan, T. A. (1988). The development of social referencing. *Child Development*, *59*(5), 1230–1240.

Walker, A. S. (1982). Intermodal perception of expressive behaviors by human infants. *Journal of Experimental Child Psychology*, *33*(3), 514–535.

Walker-Andrews, A. S. (1986). Intermodal perception of expressive behaviors. Relation of eye and voice? *Developmental Psychology*, *22*(3), 373–377.

Walker-Andrews, A. S. (1997). Infants' perception of expressive behaviors: Differentiation of multimodal information. *Psychological Bulletin*, *121*(3), 437–456.

Widen, S. C. (2013). Children's interpretation of facial expressions: The long path from valence-based to specific discrete categories. *Emotion Review*, *5*(1), 72–77.

Widen, S. C., & Russell, J. A. (2003). A closer look at preschoolers' freely produced labels for facial expressions. *Developmental Psychology*, *39*(1), 114–128.

Widen, S. C., & Russell, J. A. (2008). Children acquire emotion categories gradually. *Cognitive Development*, *23*(2), 291–312.

Woodruff-Borden, J., Morrow, C., Bourland, S., & Cambron, S. (2002). The behavior of anxious parents: examining mechanisms of transmission of anxiety from parent to child. *Journal of Clinical Child and Adolescent Psychology*, *31*(3), 364–374.

Wörmann, V., Holodynski, M., Kärtner, J., & Keller, H. (2014). The emergence of social smiling: The interplay of maternal and infant imitation during the first three months in cross-cultural comparison. *Journal of Cross-Cultural Psychology*, *45*(3), 339–361.

Yanaoka, K., Michaelson, L. E., Guild, R. M., Dostart, G., Yonehiro, J., Saito, S., & Munakata, Y. (2022). Cultures crossing: The power of habit in delaying gratification. *Psychological Science*, *33*(7), 1172–1181.

Yang, Y., & Wang, Q. (2019). Culture in emotional development. In V. LoBue, K. Pérez-Edgar, & K. A. Buss (Eds.), *Handbook of emotional development* (pp. 569–593). Springer.

Young-Browne, G., Rosenfeld, H. M., & Horowitz, F. D. (1977). Infant discrimination of facial expressions. *Child Development*, *48*(2), 555–562.

Zeman, J., Cameron, M., & Price, N. (2019). Sadness in youth: Socialization, regulation, and adjustment. In V. LoBue, K. Pérez-Edgar, & K. A. Buss (Eds.), *Handbook of emotional development* (pp. 227–256). Springer.

CHAPTER 11

Abraham, E., Hendler, T., Shapira-Lichter, I., Kanat-Maymon, Y., Zagoory-Sharon, O., & Feldman, R. (2014). Father's brain is sensitive to childcare experiences. *Proceedings of the National Academy of Sciences*, *111*(27), 9792–9797.

Ahnert, L., Gunnar, M. R., Lamb, M. E., & Barthel, M. (2004). Transition to child care: Associations with infant-mother attachment, infant negative emotion, and cortisol elevations. *Child Development*, *75*(3), 639–650.

Ainsworth, M. D. (1967). *Infancy in Uganda: Infant care and the growth of love*. https://psycnet.apa.org/fulltext/1967-35025-000.pdf

Ainsworth, M. S. (1979). Infant–mother attachment. *American Psychologist*, *34*(10),

932–937. https://doi.org/10.10 37/0003-066X.34.10.932

Ainsworth, M. D., Salter, M. D., & Bell, S. M. (1970). Attachment, exploration, and separation: Illustrated by the behavior of one-year-olds in a strange situation. *Child Development, 41*(1), 49–67.

Ainsworth, M. D., & Wittig, B. A. (1969). Attachment and exploratory behaviour of one-year-olds in a strange situation. In B. M. Foss (Ed.), *Determinants of infant behaviour* (Vol. 4, pp. 113–136). Methuen.

Akhtar, N., & Gernsbacher, M. A. (2008). On privileging the role of gaze in infant social cognition. *Child Development Perspectives, 2*(2), 59–65.

Baer, J. C., & Martinez, C. D. (2006). Child maltreatment and insecure attachment: A meta-analysis. *Journal of Reproductive and Infant Psychology, 24*(3), 187–197. https://doi.org/10.1080/0264683060 0821231

Bandura, A. (1977). *Social learning theory.* Prentice Hall.

Bandura, A., Ross, D., & Ross, S. A. (1963). Imitation of film-mediated aggressive models. *Journal of Abnormal and Social Psychology, 66*(1), 3.

Baron-Cohen, S., Leslie, A. M., & Frith, U. (1985). Does the autistic child have a "theory of mind"? *Cognition, 21*(1), 37–46.

Barr, R., & Hayne, H. (1999). Developmental changes in imitation from television during infancy. *Child Development, 70*(5), 1067–1081.

Belsky, J., & Fearon, P. R. M. (2002). Early attachment security, subsequent maternal sensitivity, and later child development: Does continuity in development depend upon continuity of caregiving? *Attachment & Human Development, 4*(3), 361–387. https://doi.org/10.1080/14616730210 167267

Belsky, J., Steinberg, L., & Draper, P. (1991). Childhood experience, interpersonal development, and reproductive strategy: An evolutionary theory of socialization. *Child Development, 62*(4), 647–670.

Biro, S., & Leslie, A. M. (2007). Infants' perception of goal-directed actions: development through cue-based bootstrapping. *Developmental Science, 10*(3), 379–398. https://doi.org/10.1111/j.1467-7687.2006.0 0544.x

Bornstein, M. H., Putnick, D. L., Rigo, P., Esposito, G., Swain, J. E., Suwalsky, J. T. D., Su, X., Du, X., Zhang, K., Cote, L. R., De Pisapia, N., & Venuti, P. (2017). Neurobiology of culturally common maternal responses to infant cry. *Proceedings of the National Academy of Sciences of the United States of America, 114*(45), E9465–E9473.

Bowlby, J. (1969). *Attachment and loss: Attachment.* Basic Books.

Brownell, C. A., Svetlova, M., Anderson, R., Nichols, S. R., & Drummond, J. (2013). Socialization of early prosocial behavior: Parents' talk about emotions is associated with sharing and helping in toddlers. *Infancy: The Official Journal of the International Society on Infant Studies, 18*(1), 91–119.

Bushnell, I. W. R., Sai, F., & Mullin, J. T. (1989). Neonatal recognition of the mother's face. *British Journal of Developmental Psychology, 7*(1), 3–15.

Buttelmann, D., Zmyj, N., Daum, M., & Carpenter, M. (2013). Selective imitation of in-group over out-group members in 14-month-old infants. *Child Development, 84*(2), 422–428. https://doi.org/10.1111/j.1 467-8624.2012.01860.x

Calkins, S. D., & Johnson, M. C. (1998). Toddler regulation of distress to frustrating events: temperamental and maternal correlates. *Infant Behavior & Development, 21*(3), 379–395.

Callaghan, T., Rochat, P., Lillard, A., Claux, M. L., Odden, H., Itakura, S., Tapanya, S., & Singh, S. (2005). Synchrony in the onset of mental-state reasoning: evidence from five cultures. *Psychological Science, 16*(5), 378–384.

Carpenter, M., Akhtar, N., & Tomasello, M. (1998). Fourteen- through 18-month-old infants differentially imitate intentional and accidental actions. *Infant Behavior & Development, 21*(2), 315–330.

Cassidy, J., & Shaver, P. R. (1999). *Handbook of attachment: Theory, research, and clinical applications.* Rough Guides.

Daum, M. M., Prinz, W., & Aschersleben, G. (2008). Encoding the goal of an object-directed but uncompleted reaching action in 6- and 9-month-old infants. *Developmental Science, 11*(4), 607–619.

DeLoache, J. S., Pickard, M. B., & LoBue, V. (2011). How very young children think about animals. In P. McCardie, S. McCune, J. A. Griffin, & V. Maholmes (Eds.), *How animals affect us: Examining the influences of human–animal interaction on child development and human health* (pp. 85–99). American Psychological Association. https://doi.org/10.1037/12301-004

Farroni, T., Massaccesi, S., Pividori, D., & Johnson, M. H. (2004). Gaze following in newborns. *Infancy, 5*(1), 39–60. https://doi.org/10.1207/s15327078in0501_2

Gee, D. G., Gabard-Durham, L. J., Flannery, J., Goff, B., Humphreys, K. L., & Telzer, E. H. (2013). Early developmental emergence of human amygdala—prefrontal connectivity after maternal deprivation. *Proceedings of the National Academy of Sciences of the United States of America, 110*(39), 15638–15643.

Gee, D. G., Gabard-Durham, L., Telzer, E. H., Humphreys, K. L., Goff, B., Shapiro, M., Flannery, J., Lumian, D. S., Fareri, D. S., Caldera, C., & Tottenham, N. (2014). Maternal buffering of human amygdala-prefrontal circuitry during childhood but not during adolescence. *Psychological Science, 25*(11), 2067–2078.

Gergely, G., Bekkering, H., & Király, I. (2002). Rational imitation in preverbal infants. *Nature, 415*(6873), 755.

Gershoff, E. T. (2013). Spanking and child development: We know enough now to stop hitting our children. *Child Development Perspectives, 7*(3), 133–137.

Gershoff, E. T., & Grogan-Kaylor, A. (2016). Spanking and child outcomes: Old controversies and new meta-analyses. *Journal of Family Psychology, 30*(4), 453–469.

Gershoff, E. T., Sattler, K. M. P., & Ansari, A. (2018). Strengthening causal estimates for links between spanking and children's externalizing behavior problems. *Psychological Science, 29*(1), 110–120.

Gleason, M. M., Fox, N. A., Drury, S. S., Smyke, A. T., Nelson, C. A., & Zeanah, C. H. (2014). Indiscriminate behaviors in previously institutionalized young children. *Pediatrics, 133*(3), e657–e665. https://doi.org/10.1542/peds.2013-0212

Graf, F., Borchert, S., Lamm, B., Goertz, C., Kolling, T., Fassbender, I., Teubert, M., Vierhaus, M., Freitag, C., Spangler, S., Keller, H., Lohaus, A., Schwarzer, G., & Knopf, M. (2014). Imitative learning of Nso and German infants at 6 and 9 months of age: Evidence for a cross-cultural learning tool. *Journal of Cross-Cultural Psychology, 45*(1), 47–61.

Gredebäck, G., Fikke, L., & Melinder, A. (2010). The development of joint visual attention: A longitudinal study of gaze following during interactions with mothers and strangers. *Developmental Science, 13*(6), 839–848.

Groh, A. M., Roisman, G. I., van IJzendoorn, M. H., Bakermans-Kranenburg, M. J., & Pasco Fearon, R. (2012). The significance of insecure and disorganized attachment for children's internalizing symptoms: A meta-analytic study. *Child Development, 83*(2),

591–610. https://doi.org/10.1111/j.1467-8624.2011.01711.x

Haensel, J. X., Ishikawa, M., Itakura, S., Smith, T. J., & Senju, A. (2020). Cultural influences on face scanning are consistent across infancy and adulthood. *Infant Behavior & Development, 61*, 101503.

Hamlin, J. K., Wynn, K., & Bloom, P. (2007). Social evaluation by preverbal infants. *Nature, 450*(7169), 557–559.

Hammond, S. I., & Brownell, C. A. (2018). Happily unhelpful: Infants' everyday helping and its connections to early prosocial development. *Frontiers in Psychology, 9*. https://doi.org/10.3389/fpsyg.2018.01770,

Harlow, H. F. (1958). The nature of love. *American Psychologist, 13*(12), 673–685.

Hayne, H., Herbert, J., & Simcock, G. (2003). Imitation from television by 24- and 30-month-olds. *Developmental Science, 6*(3), 254–261. https://doi.org/10.1111/1467-7687.00281

Hoekzema, E., Barba-Müller, E., Pozzobon, C., Picado, M., Lucco, F., García-García, D., Soliva, J. C., Tobeña, A., Desco, M., Crone, E. A., Ballesteros, A., Carmona, S., & Vilarroya, O. (2017). Pregnancy leads to long-lasting changes in human brain structure. *Nature Neuroscience, 20*(2), 287–296.

Howard, L. H., Carrazza, C., & Woodward, A. L. (2014). Neighborhood linguistic diversity predicts infants' social learning. *Cognition, 133*(2), 474–479. https://doi.org/10.1016/j.cognition.2014.08.002

Johnson, S., Slaughter, V., & Carey, S. (1998). Whose

gaze will infants follow? The elicitation of gaze following in 12-month-olds. *Developmental Science, 1*(2), 233–238.

Jones, W., & Klin, A. (2013). Attention to eyes is present but in decline in 2–6-month-old infants later diagnosed with autism. *Nature, 504*(7480), 427–431.

Kanakogi, Y., & Itakura, S. (2011). Developmental correspondence between action prediction and motor ability in early infancy. *Nature Communications, 2*, 341.

Kärtner, J., Schuhmacher, N., & Giner Torréns, M. (2020). Culture and early social-cognitive development. *Progress in Brain Research, 254*, 225–246.

Kimhi, Y. (2014). Theory of mind abilities and deficits in autism spectrum disorders. *Topics in Language Disorders, 34*(4), 329.

Legare, C. H. (2017). Cumulative cultural learning: Development and diversity. *Proceedings of the National Academy of Sciences of the United States of America, 114*(30), 7877–7883.

Liszkowski, U., Carpenter, M., Striano, T., & Tomasello, M. (2006). 12- and 18-month-olds point to provide information for others. *Journal of Cognition and Development, 7*(2), 173–187. https://doi.org/10.12 07/s15327647jcd0702_2

LoBue, V., Bloom Pickard, M., Sherman, K., Axford, C., & DeLoache, J. S. (2013). Young children's interest in live animals. *British Journal of Developmental Psychology, 31*(Pt 1), 57–69.

Main, M., & Solomon, J. (1986). Discovery of an insecure-disorganized/disoriented attachment pattern. In T. B. Brazelton (Ed.), *Affective development in infancy* (Vol. 161, pp. 95–124). Ablex.

Manzi, F., Ishikawa, M., Di Dio, C., Itakura, S., Kanda, T., Ishiguro, H., Massaro, D., & Marchetti, A. (2020). Publisher Correction: The understanding of congruent and incongruent referential gaze in 17-month-old infants: An eye-tracking study comparing human and robot. *Scientific Reports, 10*(1), 21599.

Martins, C., & Gaffan, E. A. (2000). Effects of early maternal depression on patterns of infant-mother attachment: A meta-analytic investigation. *Journal of Child Psychology and Psychiatry, and Allied Disciplines, 41*(6), 737–746.

Maurer, D., & Salapatek, P. (1976). Developmental changes in the scanning of faces by young infants. *Child Development, 47*(2), 523–527.

McGoron, L., Gleason, M. M., Smyke, A. T., Drury, S. S., Nelson, C. A., Gregas, M. C., Fox, N. A., & Zeanah, C. H. (2012). Recovering from early deprivation: attachment mediates effects of caregiving on psychopathology. *Journal of the American Academy of Child & Adolescent Psychiatry, 51*(7), 683–693. https://doi.org/10.10 16/j.jaac.2012.05.004

McLaughlin, K. A., Zeanah, C. H., Fox, N. A., & Nelson, C. A. (2012). Attachment security as a mechanism linking foster care placement to improved mental health outcomes in previously institutionalized

children. *Journal of Child Psychology and Psychiatry, and Allied Disciplines, 53*(1), 46–55.

Meltzoff, A. N. (1988a). Imitation of televised models by infants. *Child Development, 59*(5), 1221–1229.

Meltzoff, A. N. (1988b). Infant imitation after a 1-week delay: Long-term memory for novel acts and multiple stimuli. *Developmental Psychology, 24*(4), 470–476.

Meltzoff, A. N. (1995). Understanding the intentions of others: Re-enactment of intended acts by 18-month-old children. *Developmental Psychology, 31*(5), 838–850.

Meltzoff, A. N., & Moore, M. K. (1977). Imitation of facial and manual gestures by human neonates. *Science, 198*(4312), 75–78.

Mesman, J., van IJzendoorn, M., Behrens, K., Carbonell, O. A., Cárcamo, R., Cohen-Paraira, I., de la Harpe, C., Ekmekçi, H., Emmen, R., Heidar, J., Kondo-Ikemura, K., Mels, C., Mooya, H., Murtisari, S., Nóblega, M., Ortiz, J. A., Sagi-Schwartz, A., Sichimba, F., Soares, I., … Zreik, G. (2016). Is the ideal mother a sensitive mother? Beliefs about early childhood parenting in mothers across the globe. *International Journal of Behavioral Development, 40*(5), 385–397.

Moriceau, S., & Sullivan, R. M. (2006). Maternal presence serves as a switch between learning fear and attraction in infancy. *Nature Neuroscience, 9*(8), 1004–1006.

Moriguchi, Y., Ban, M., Osanai, H., & Uchiyama, I. (2018). Relationship between implicit false belief understanding and role play: Longitudinal study. *European Journal of Developmental Psychology, 15*(2), 172–183.

Oktay-Gür, N., Schulz, A., & Rakoczy, H. (2018). Children exhibit different performance patterns in explicit and implicit theory of mind tasks. *Cognition, 173*, 60–74.

Onishi, K. H., & Baillargeon, R. (2005). Do 15-month-old infants understand false beliefs? *Science, 308*(5719), 255–258.

Oostenbroek, J., Suddendorf, T., Nielsen, M., Redshaw, J., Kennedy-Costantini, S., Davis, J., Clark, S., & Slaughter, V. (2016). Comprehensive longitudinal study challenges the existence of neonatal imitation in humans. *Current Biology, 26*(10), 1334–1338.

Peña, M., Arias, D., & Dehaene-Lambertz, G. (2014). Gaze following is accelerated in healthy preterm infants. *Psychological Science, 25*(10), 1884–1892.

Pickron, C. B., Fava, E., & Scott, L. S. (2017). Follow my gaze: Face race and sex influence gaze-cued attention in infancy. *Infancy: The Official Journal of the International Society on Infant Studies, 22*(5), 626–644.

Rothbaum, F., Weisz, J., Pott, M., Miyake, K., & Morelli, G. (2000). Attachment and culture. Security in the United States and Japan. *American Psychologist, 55*(10), 1093–1104.

Simion, F., Regolin, L., & Bulf, H. (2008). A predisposition for biological motion in the newborn baby. *Proceedings of the National Academy of Sciences, 105*(2), 809–813. https://doi.org/10.1073/pnas.0707021105,

Slaughter, V. (2015). Theory of mind in infants and young children: A review. *Australian Psychologist, 50*(3), 169–172.

Smyke, A. T., Zeanah, C. H., Fox, N. A., Nelson, C. A., & Guthrie, D. (2010). Placement in foster care enhances quality of attachment among young institutionalized children. *Child Development, 81*(1), 212–223. https://doi.org/10.1111/j.1467-8624.2009.01390.x,

Southgate, V., Senju, A., & Csibra, G. (2007). Action anticipation through attribution of false belief by 2-year-olds. *Psychological Science, 18*(7), 587–592.

Teti, D. M., Gelfand, D. M., Messinger, D. S., & Isabella, R. (1995). Maternal depression and the quality of early attachment: An examination of infants, preschoolers, and their mothers. *Developmental Psychology, 31*(3), 364–376. https://doi.org/10.1037/0012-1649.31.3.364

Thoermer, C., Sodian, B., Vuori, M., Perst, H., & Kristen, S. (2012). Continuity from an implicit to an explicit understanding of false belief from infancy to preschool age. *British Journal of Developmental Psychology, 30*(Pt 1), 172–187.

Tomasello, M. (1990). Cultural transmission in the tool use and communicatory signaling of chimpanzees? In S. T. Parker & K. R. Gibson (Eds.), *"Language" and intelligence in monkeys and apes: Comparative developmental perspectives* (pp. 274–311). Cambridge University Press.

Tomlinson, M., Cooper, P., & Murray, L. (2005). The mother-infant relationship and infant attachment in a South African peri-urban settlement. *Child Development, 76*(5), 1044–1054.

Tremblay, R. E., Japel, C., Perusse, D., Mcduff, P., Boivin, M., Zoccolillo, M., & Montplaisir, J. (1999). The search for the age of "onset" of physical aggression: Rousseau and Bandura revisited. *Criminal Behaviour and Mental Health, 9*(1), 8–23.

van den Dries, L., Juffer, F., van IJzendoorn, M. H., & Bakermans-Kranenburg, M. J. (2009). Fostering security? A meta-analysis of attachment in adopted children. *Children and Youth Services Review, 31*(3), 410–421.

van IJzendoorn, M. H., & Kroonenberg, P. M. (1988). Cross-cultural patterns of attachment: A meta-analysis of the strange situation. *Child Development, 59*(1), 147–156.

van Ijzendoorn, M. H., & Sagi-Schwartz, A. (2008). Cross-cultural patterns of attachment: Universal and contextual dimensions. In J. Cassidy & P. R. Shaver (Eds.), *Handbook of attachment: Theory, research, and clinical applications* (2nd ed., pp. 880–905). Guilford Press.

Wagner, J. B., Keehn, B., Tager-Flusberg, H., & Nelson, C. A. (2020). Attentional bias to fearful faces in infants at high risk for autism spectrum disorder. *Emotion, 20*(6), 980–992.

Wagner, J. B., Luyster, R. J., Tager-Flusberg, H., & Nelson, C. A. (2016). Greater pupil size in response to emotional faces as an early marker of social-communicative difficulties in infants at high risk for autism. *Infancy: The Official Journal of the International Society on Infant Studies, 21*(5), 560–581.

Warneken, F., Chen, F., & Tomasello, M. (2006). Cooperative activities in young children and chimpanzees. *Child Development, 77*(3), 640–663. https://doi.org/10.1111/j.1467-8624.2006.00895.x

Warneken, F., & Tomasello, M. (2007). Helping and cooperation at 14 months of age. *Infancy: The Official Journal of the International Society on Infant Studies, 11*(3), 271–294.

Wellman, H. M., & Liu, D. (2004). Scaling of theory-of-mind tasks. *Child Development, 75*(2), 523–541. https://doi.org/10.1111/j.1467-8624.2004.00691.x

Woodward, A. L. (1998). Infants selectively encode the goal object of an actor's reach. *Cognition, 69*(1), 1–34.

Xiao, N. G., Wu, R., Quinn, P. C., Liu, S., Tummeltshammer, K. S., Kirkham, N. Z., Ge, L., Pascalis, O., & Lee, K. (2018). Infants rely more on gaze cues from own-race than other-race adults for learning under uncertainty. *Child Development, 89*(3), e229–e244. https://doi.org/10.1111/cdev.12798

CHAPTER 12

Adams, S., Kuebli, J., Boyle, P. A., & Fivush, R. (1995). Gender differences in parent-child conversations about past emotions: A longitudinal investigation. *Sex Roles,* 33(5–6), 309–323. https://doi.org/10.1007/bf01954572

Ahnert, L., Pinquart, M., & Lamb, M. E. (2006). Security of children's relationships with nonparental care providers: A meta-analysis. *Child Development, 77*(3), 664–679.

Aldrich, N. J., Brooks, P. J., Yuksel-Sokmen, P. O., Ragir, S., Flory, M. J., Lennon, E. M., Karmel, B. Z., & Gardner, J. M. (2015). Infant twins' social interactions with caregivers and same-age siblings. *Infant Behavior & Development, 41,* 127–141.

Alvarenga, P., Kuchirko, Y., Cerezo, M. Á., de Mendonça Filho, E. J., Bakeman, R., & Tamis-LeMonda, C. S. (2021). An intervention focused on maternal sensitivity enhanced mothers' verbal responsiveness to infants. *Journal of Applied Developmental Psychology, 76,* 101313.

Azmitia, M., & Hesser, J. (1993). Why siblings are important agents of cognitive development: A comparison of siblings and peers. *Child Development, 64*(2), 430–444.

Barr, R., & Hayne, H. (2003). It's not what you know, it's who you know: Older siblings facilitate imitation during infancy. *International Journal of Early Years Education, 11*(1), 7–21.

Bornstein, M. H. (2019). Parenting infants. In M. H. Bornstein (Ed.), *Handbook of parenting* (Vol. 1, pp. 3–55). Routledge.

Bornstein, M. H., Putnick, D. L., & Esposito, G. (2022). The nature and structure of mothers' parenting their infants.

Parenting, Science and Practice, 22(2), 83–127.

Bornstein, M. H., Putnick, D. L., Rigo, P., Esposito, G., Swain, J. E., Suwalsky, J. T. D., Su, X., Du, X., Zhang, K., Cote, L. R., De Pisapia, N., & Venuti, P. (2017). Neurobiology of culturally common maternal responses to infant cry. *Proceedings of the National Academy of Sciences of the United States of America, 114*(45), E9465–E9473.

Brito, N. H., Werchan, D., Brandes-Aitken, A., Yoshikawa, H., Greaves, A., & Zhang, M. (2021, August 20). *Paid maternal leave is associated with infant brain function at 3-months of age.* [Web preprint]. PsyArXiv. Webhttps://doi.org/10.31234/osf.io/t4zvn

Broesch, T., Carolan, P. L., Cebioğlu, S., von Rueden, C., Boyette, A., Moya, C., Hewlett, B., & Kline, M. A. (2021). Opportunities for interaction: Natural observations of children's social behavior in five societies. *Human Nature, 32,* 208–238. https://doi.org/10.1007/s12110-021-09393-w

Brown, G. L., Mangelsdorf, S. C., Shigeto, A., & Wong, M. S. (2018). Associations between father involvement and father-child attachment security: Variations based on timing and type of involvement. . *Journal of Family Psychology: JFP: Journal of the Division of Family Psychology of the American Psychological Association, 32*(8), 1015–1024.

Brownell, C. A., & Brown, E. (1992). Peers and Play in Infants and Toddlers. In V. B. Van Hasselt & M. Hersen (Eds.), *Handbook of social* development: A lifespan perspective (pp. 183–200). Springer.

Campos, J. J., Anderson, D. I., Barbu Roth, M. A., Hubbard, E. M., Hertenstein, M. J., & Witherington, D. (2000). Travel broadens the mind. *Infancy: The Official Journal of the International Society on Infant Studies*, *1*(2), 149–219.

Chetty, R., Hendren, N., & Katz, L. F. (2016). The effects of exposure to better neighborhoods on children: New evidence from the moving to opportunity experiment. *American Economic Review*, *106*(4), 855–902.

Christian, H., Zubrick, S. R., Foster, S., Giles-Corti, B., Bull, F., Wood, L., Knuiman, M., Brinkman, S., Houghton, S., & Boruff, B. (2015). The influence of the neighborhood physical environment on early child health and development: A review and call for research. *Health & Place*, *33*, 25–36.

Clearfield, M. W., Carter-Rodriguez, A., Merali, A.-R., & Shober, R. (2014). The effects of SES on infant and maternal diurnal salivary cortisol output. *Infant Behavior & Development*, *37*(3), 298–304.

Clearfield, M. W., & Niman, L. C. (2012). SES affects infant cognitive flexibility. *Infant Behavior & Development*, *35*(1), 29–35.

Cohen, D. A., Farley, T. A., & Mason, K. (2003). Why is poverty unhealthy? Social and physical mediators. *Social Science & Medicine*, *57*(9), 1631–1641.

Dagan, O., & Sagi-Schwartz, A. (2018). Early attachment

network with mother and father: An unsettled issue. *Child Development Perspectives*, *12*(2), 115–121.

Devine, R. T., & Hughes, C. (2018). Family correlates of false belief understanding in early childhood: A meta-analysis. *Child Development*, *89*(3), 971–987.

Dunn, J., & Kendrick, C. (1982). Siblings and their mothers: Developing relationships within the family. In M. E. Lamb & B. Sutton-Smith (Eds.), *Sibling relationships: Their nature and significance across the lifespan* (pp. 39–60). Psychology Press.

Dupere, V., Leventhal, T., Crosnoe, R., & Dion, E. (2010). Understanding the positive role of neighborhood socioeconomic advantage in achievement: The contribution of the home, child care, and school environments. *Developmental Psychology*, *46*(5), 1227–1244.

Eckerman, C. O., Davis, C. C., & Didow, S. M. (1989). Toddlers' emerging ways of achieving social coordinations with a peer. *Child Development*, *60*(2), 440–453.

Eckerman, C. O., & Didow, S. M. (1996). Nonverbal imitation and toddlers' mastery of verbal means of achieving coordinated action. *Developmental Psychology*, *32*(1), 141–152.

Eckerman, C. O., & Peterman, K. (2001). Peers and infant social/communicative development. In G. Bremner & A. Fogel (Eds.), *Blackwell handbook of infant development*, (pp. 326–350). Blackwell, https://psycnet.apa.org/record/2002-02376-012

Eckerman, C. O., & Whatley, J. L. (1977). Toys and social interaction between infant peers. *Child Development*, *48*(4), 1645–1656.

Eckerman, C. O., & Whitehead, H. (1999). How toddler peers generate coordinated action: A cross-cultural exploration. *Early Education and Development*, *10*(3), 241–266.

Edwards, B., & Bromfield, L. M. (2009). Neighborhood influences on young children's conduct problems and prosocial behavior: Evidence from an Australian national sample. *Children and Youth Services Review*, *31*(3), 317–324.

Edwards, C. P., & Whiting, B. B. (1993). "Mother, older sibling, and me": The overlapping roles of caregivers and companions in the social world of two- to three-year-olds in Ngeca, Kenya. In K. B. MacDonald (Ed.), *Parent–child play: Descriptions and implications* (pp. 305–329). State University of New York Press.

Emmen, R. A. G., Malda, M., Mesman, J., Ekmekci, H., & van IJzendoorn, M. H. (2012). Sensitive parenting as a cross-cultural ideal: sensitivity beliefs of Dutch, Moroccan, and Turkish mothers in the Netherlands. *Attachment & Human Development*, *14*(6), 601–619.

Farr, R. H. (2017). Does parental sexual orientation matter? A longitudinal follow-up of adoptive families with school-age children. *Developmental Psychology*, *53*(2), 252–264.

Farver, J. A. M., & Howes, C. (1988). Cross-cultural differences in social interaction: A comparison of American and

Indonesian children. *Journal of Cross-Cultural Psychology*, *19*(2), 203–215. https://doi.org/10.1177/0022022188192006

Farver, J. A. M., & Wimbarti, S. (1995). Indonesian children's play with their mothers and older siblings. *Child Development*, *66*(5), 1493–1503. https://doi.org/10.1111/j.1467-8624.1995.tb00947.x

Feeney, B. C., & Collins, N. L. (2014). A theoretical perspective on the importance of social connections for thriving. In M. Mikulincer & P. R. Shaver (Eds.), *Mechanisms of social connection: From brain to group* (pp. 291–314). American Psychological Association. https://doi.org/10.1037/14250-017

Fernald, A., Marchman, V. A., & Weisleder, A. (2013). SES differences in language processing skill and vocabulary are evident at 18 months. *Developmental Science*, *16*(2), 234–248.

Fouts, H. N., Roopnarine, J. L., Lamb, M. E., & Evans, M. (2012). Infant social interactions with multiple caregivers: The importance of ethnicity and socioeconomic status. *Journal of Cross-Cultural Psychology*, *43*(2), 328–348.

Fox, N. A., Kimmerly, N. L., & Schafer, W. D. (1991). Attachment to mother/attachment to father: A meta-analysis. *Child Development*, *62*(1), 210. https://doi.org/10.2307/1130716

Golinkoff, R. M., Hoff, E., Rowe, M. L., Tamis-LeMonda, C. S., & Hirsh-Pasek, K. (2019). Language matters: Denying the existence of the 30-million-word gap has serious

consequences. *Child Development*, *90*(3), 985–992.

Hackman, D. A., Gallop, R., Evans, G. W., & Farah, M. J. (2015). Socioeconomic status and executive function: Developmental trajectories and mediation. *Developmental Science*, *18*(5), 686–702.

Hallers-Haalboom, E. T., Groeneveld, M. G., van Berkel, S. R., Endendijk, J. J., van der Pol, L. D., Linting, M., Bakermans-Kranenburg, M. J., & Mesman, J. (2017). Mothers' and fathers' sensitivity with their two children: A longitudinal study from infancy to early childhood. *Developmental Psychology*, *53*(5), 860–872.

Hart, B., & Risley, T. R. (1995). *Meaningful differences in the everyday experience of young American children*. Brookes.

Harwood, R., Leyendecker, B., Carlson, V., Asencio, M., & Miller, A. (2002). Parenting among Latino families in the U.S. In M. H. Bornstein (Ed.), *Handbook of parenting: Social conditions and applied parenting* (Vol. 4, pp. 21–46). Routledge.

Hay, D. F., Paine, A. L., Perra, O., Cook, K. V., Hashmi, S., Robinson, C., Kairis, V., & Slade, R. (2021). Prosocial and aggressive behavior: A longitudinal study. *Monographs of the Society for Research in Child Development*, *86*(2), 7–103.

Hay, D. F., Payne, A., & Chadwick, A. (2004). Peer relations in childhood. *Journal of Child Psychology and Psychiatry, and Allied Disciplines*, *45*(1), 84–108.

Hay, D. F., & Ross, H. S. (1982). The social nature of early

conflict. *Child Development*, *53*(1), 105–113.

Healey, M. D., & Ellis, B. J. (2007). Birth order, conscientiousness, and openness to experience. Tests of the family-niche model of personality using a within-family methodology. *Evolution and Human Behavior*, *28*(1), 55–59.

Hewlett, B. S. (1993). *Intimate fathers: The nature and context of Aka pygmy paternal infant care*. University of Michigan Press.

Hewlett, B. S., Lamb, M. E., Shannon, D., Leyendecker, B., & Schölmerich, A. (1998). Culture and early infancy among central African foragers and farmers. *Developmental Psychology*, *34*(4), 653–661.

Hoff, E. (2003). The specificity of environmental influence: Socioeconomic status affects early vocabulary development via maternal speech. *Child Development*, *74*(5), 1368–1378.

Hotz, V. J., & Pantano, J. (2015). Strategic parenting, birth order, and school performance. *Journal of Population Economics*, *28*(4), 911–936.

Howes, C., Rubin, K. H., Ross, H. S., & French, D. C. (1988). Peer interaction of young children. *Monographs of the Society for Research in Child Development*, *53*(1), i – 92.

Hrdy, S. B. (2011). *Mothers and others*. Harvard University Press.

Hughes, C., Lindberg, A., & Devine, R. T. (2018). Autonomy support in toddlerhood: Similarities and contrasts between mothers and fathers. *Journal of Family Psychology*, *32*(7), 915–925.

Johnson, K., Caskey, M., Rand, K., Tucker, R., & Vohr, B. (2014). Gender differences in adult-infant communication in the first months of life. *Pediatrics, 134*(6), e1603–e1610.

Karasik, L. B., Tamis-LeMonda, C. S., & Adolph, K. E. (2011). Transition from crawling to walking and infants' actions with objects and people. *Child Development, 82*(4), 1199–1209.

Karasik, L. B., Tamis-LeMonda, C. S., & Adolph, K. E. (2014). Crawling and walking infants elicit different verbal responses from mothers. *Developmental Science, 17*(3), 388–395.

Kärtner, J., Keller, H., & Yovsi, R. D. (2010). Mother-infant interaction during the first 3 months: The emergence of culture-specific contingency patterns. *Child Development, 81*(2), 540–554.

Keller, H., Bard, K., Morelli, G., Chaudhary, N., Vicedo, M., Rosabal-Coto, M., Scheidecker, G., Murray, M., & Gottlieb, A. (2018). The myth of universal sensitive responsiveness: Comment on Mesman et al. (2017) [Review of *The Myth of Universal Sensitive Responsiveness: Comment on Mesman et al. (2017)*]. *Child Development, 89*(5), 1921–1928.

Keller, H., Borke, J., Staufenbiel, T., Yovsi, R. D., Abels, M., Papaligoura, Z., Jensen, H., Lohaus, A., Chaudhary, N., Lo, W., & Su, Y. (2009). Distal and proximal parenting as alternative parenting strategies during infants' early months of life: A cross-cultural study. *International Journal of Behavioral Development, 33*(5), 412–420.

Kling, J. R., Liebman, J. B., & Katz, L. F. (2007). Experimental analysis of neighborhood effects. *Econometrica: Journal of the Econometric Society, 75*(1), 83–119.

Kochanska, G. (1997). Multiple pathways to conscience for children with different temperaments: From toddlerhood to age 5. *Developmental Psychology, 33*(2), 228–240.

Lancy, D. F. (2007). Accounting for variability in mother? Child play. *American Anthropologist, 109*(2), 273–284.

Lancy, D. F. (2010). Learning "from nobody": The limited role of teaching in folk models of children's development. *Childhood in the Past, 3*(1), 79–106.

Lawson, G. M., Hook, C. J., & Farah, M. J. (2018). A meta-analysis of the relationship between socioeconomic status and executive function performance among children. *Developmental Science, 21*(2), 12529. https://doi.org/10.1111/desc.12529

Legare, C. H. (2017). Cumulative cultural learning: Development and diversity. *Proceedings of the National Academy of Sciences of the United States of America, 114*(30), 7877–7883.

Li, W., Devine, R. T., Ribner, A., Emmen, R. A. G., Woudstra, M.-L. J., Branger, M. C. E., Wang, L., van Ginkel, J., Alink, L. R. A., & Mesman, J. (2021). The role of infant attention and parental sensitivity in infant cognitive development in the Netherlands and China. *Journal of Experimental Child Psychology, 215*, 105324.

Long, C. (2020, June 24). "Raising baby grey" explores the world of gender-neutral parenting. *The New Yorker*. https://www.newyorker.com/culture/the-new-yorker-documentary/raising-baby-grey-explores-the-world-of-gender-neutral-parenting

Love, J. M., Harrison, L., Sagi-Schwartz, A., van IJzendoorn, M. H., Ross, C., Ungerer, J. A., Raikes, H., Brady-Smith, C., Boller, K., Brooks-Gunn, J., Constantine, J., Kisker, E. E., Paulsell, D., & Chazan-Cohen, R. (2003). Child care quality matters: How conclusions may vary with context. *Child Development, 74*(4), 1021–1033.

Maguire-Jack, K., & Showalter, K. (2016). The protective effect of neighborhood social cohesion in child abuse and neglect. *Child Abuse & Neglect, 52*, 29–37.

Mascaro, J. S., Rentscher, K. E., Hackett, P. D., Mehl, M. R., & Rilling, J. K. (2017). Child gender influences paternal behavior, language, and brain function. *Behavioral Neuroscience, 131*(3), 262–273.

Maynard, A. E. (2002). Cultural teaching: the development of teaching skills in Maya sibling interactions. *Child Development, 73*(3), 969–982.

McMunn, A., Martin, P., Kelly, Y., & Sacker, A. (2017). Fathers' involvement: Correlates and consequences for child socioemotional behavior in the United Kingdom. *Journal of Family Issues, 38*(8), 1109–1131.

Mesman, J., & Groeneveld, M. G. (2018). Gendered parenting

in early childhood: Subtle but unmistakable if you know where to look. *Child Development Perspectives*, *12*(1), 22–27.

Mesman, J., Minter, T., Angnged, A., Cissé, I. A. H., Salali, G. D., & Migliano, A. B. (2018). Universality without uniformity: A culturally inclusive approach to sensitive responsiveness in infant caregiving. *Child Development*, *89*(3), 837–850.

Mesman, J., van IJzendoorn, M., Behrens, K., Carbonell, O. A., Cárcamo, R., Cohen-Paraira, I., de la Harpe, C., Ekmekçi, H., Emmen, R., Heidar, J., Kondo-Ikemura, K., Mels, C., Mooya, H., Murtisari, S., Nóblega, M., Ortiz, J. A., Sagi-Schwartz, A., Sichimba, F., Soares, I., . . . Zreik, G. (2016). Is the ideal mother a sensitive mother? Beliefs about early childhood parenting in mothers across the globe. *International Journal of Behavioral Development*, *40*(5), 385–397.

Miller, D. I., & Halpern, D. F. (2014). The new science of cognitive sex differences. *Trends in Cognitive Sciences*, *18*(1), 37–45.

Mondschein, E. R., Adolph, K. E., & Tamis-LeMonda, C. S. (2000). Gender bias in mothers' expectations about infant crawling. *Journal of Experimental Child Psychology*, *77*(4), 304–316.

Mooya, H., Sichimba, F., & Bakermans-Kranenburg, M. (2016). Infant-mother and infant-sibling attachment in Zambia. *Attachment & Human Development*, *18*(6), 618–635.

Muscatell, K. A. (2018). Socioeconomic influences on brain function: implications for

health. *Annals of the New York Academy of Sciences*, *1428*(1), 14–32.

Mweru, M. (2017). Sibling Caregiving and its implications in Sub-Saharan Africa. In A. Abubakar & F. J. R. van de Vijver (Eds.), *Handbook of applied developmental science in sub-Saharan Africa* (pp. 99–113). Springer.

Noah, A. J., Landale, N. S., & Sparks, C. S. (2015). How does the context of reception matter? The role of residential enclaves in maternal smoking during pregnancy among Mexican-origin mothers. *Maternal and Child Health Journal*, *19*(8), 1825–1833.

Noble, K. G., Houston, S. M., Kan, E., & Sowell, E. R. (2012). Neural correlates of socioeconomic status in the developing human brain. *Developmental Science*, *15*(4), 516–527.

Norcross, P. L., Bailes, L. G., & Leerkes, E. (2020). Effects of maternal depressive symptoms on sensitivity to infant distress and non-distress: Role of SES and race. *Infant Behavior & Development*, *61*, 101498.

Oshima-Takane, Y., Goodz, E., & Derevensky, J. L. (1996). Birth order effects on early language development: Do secondborn children learn from overheard speech? *Child Development*, *67*(2), 621–634.

Osypuk, T. L., Bates, L. M., & Acevedo-Garcia, D. (2010). Another Mexican birthweight paradox? The role of residential enclaves and neighborhood poverty in the birthweight of Mexican-origin infants. *Social Science & Medicine*, *70*(4), 550–560.

Paulhus, D. L., Trapnell, P. D., & Chen, D. (1999). Birth order effects on personality and achievement within families. *Psychological Science*, *10*(6), 482–488.

Rabain-Jamin, J., Maynard, A. E., & Greenfield, P. (2003). Implications of sibling caregiving for sibling relations and teaching interactions in two cultures. *Ethos*, *31*(2), 204–231.

Rehel, E. M. (2014). When dad stays home too: Paternity leave, gender, and parenting. *Gender & Society*, *28*(1), 110–132.

Rosenthal, R., & Fode, K. L. (2007). The effect of experimenter bias on the performance of the albino rat. *Systems Research*, *8*(3), 183–189.

Rosenthal, R., & Jacobson, L. (1968). Pygmalion in the classroom. *Urban Review*, *3*(1), 16–20.

Ruble, D. N., Martin, C. L., & Berenbaum, S. A. (2006). Gender development. In N. Eisenberg (Ed.), *Handbook of child psychology: Social, emotional, and personality development* (Vol. 3, pp. 858–932). Wiley..

Ruffman, T., Perner, J., Naito, M., Parkin, L., & Clements, W. A. (1998). Older (but not younger) siblings facilitate false belief understanding. *Developmental Psychology*, *34*(1), 161–174.

Sameroff, A. J. (1998). Environmental risk factors in infancy. *Pediatrics*, *102*(Suppl. E1), 1287–1292.

Sanefuji, W., Ohgami, H., & Hashiya, K. (2006). Preference for peers in infancy. *Infant*

Behavior & Development, 29(4), 584–593.

Sethna, V., Perry, E., Domoney, J., Iles, J., Psychogiou, L., Rowbotham, N. E. L., Stein, A., Murray, L., & Ramchandani, P. G. (2017). Father-child interactions at 3 months and 24 months: Contributions to children's cognitive development at 24 months. *Infant Mental Health Journal, 38*(3), 378–390.

Siibak, A., & Nevski, E. (2019). Older siblings as mediators of infants' and toddlers' (digital) media use. In O. Erstad, R. Flewitt, B. Kümmerling-Meibauer, & Í. S. Pereira (Eds.), *The Routledge handbook of digital literacies in early childhood* (pp. 123–133). Routledge.

Skenazy, L. (2009). *Free-range kids: Giving our children the freedom we had without going nuts with worry.* Wiley.

Soska, K. C., Adolph, K. E., & Johnson, S. P. (2010). Systems in development: Motor skill acquisition facilitates 3D object completion. *Developmental Psychology, 46*(1), 129–138.

Sperry, D. E., Sperry, L. L., & Miller, P. J. (2019). Reexamining the verbal environments of children from different socioeconomic backgrounds. *Child Development, 90*(4), 1303–1318.

Suizzo, M.-A. (2004). French and American mothers' child-drearing beliefs. *Journal of Cross-Cultural Psychology, 35*(5), 606–626.

Sulloway, F. J. (2001). *Birth order, sibling competition, and human behavior.* In H. R. Holcomb (Ed.), Conceptual challenges in evolutionary psychology (Vol. 27, p. chap. 2). Springer.

Sweeney, J., & Bradbard, M. R. (1988). Mothers' and fathers' changing perceptions of their male and female infants over the course of pregnancy. *Journal of Genetic Psychology, 149*(3), 393–404.

Symons, D. K., & Moran, G. (1987). The behavioral dynamics of mutual responsiveness in early face-to-face mother-infant interactions. *Child Development, 58*(6), 1488–1495.

Tamis-LeMonda, C. S., Caughy, M. O., Rojas, R., Bakeman, R., Adamson, L. B., Pacheco, D., Owen, M. T., Suma, K., & Pace, A. (2020). Culture, parenting, and language: Respeto in Latine mother-child interactions. *Social Development, 29*(3), 689–712.

Valades, J., Murray, L., Bozicevic, L., De Pascalis, L., Barindelli, F., Meglioli, A., & Cooper, P. (2021). The impact of a mother-infant intervention on parenting and infant response to challenge: A pilot randomized controlled trial with adolescent mothers in El Salvador. *Infant Mental Health Journal, 42*(3), 400–412.

Vandell, D. L., Wilson, K. S., & Buchanan, N. R. (1980). Peer interaction in the first year of life: An examination of its structure, content, and sensitivity to toys. *Child Development, 51*(2), 481–488.

Williams, A. D., Messer, L. C., Kanner, J., Ha, S., Grantz, K. L., & Mendola, P. (2020). Ethnic enclaves and pregnancy and behavior outcomes among Asian/Pacific Islanders in the USA. *Journal of Racial and Ethnic Health Disparities, 7*(2), 224–233.

Williams, S. T., Ontai, L. L., & Mastergeorge, A. M. (2007). Reformulating infant and toddler social competence with peers. *Infant Behavior & Development, 30*(2), 353–365.

Yavorsky, J. E., Dush, C. M. K., & Schoppe-Sullivan, S. J. (2015). The production of inequality: The gender division of labor across the transition to parenthood. *Journal of Marriage and the Family, 77*(3), 662–679.

INDEX